Retail Management

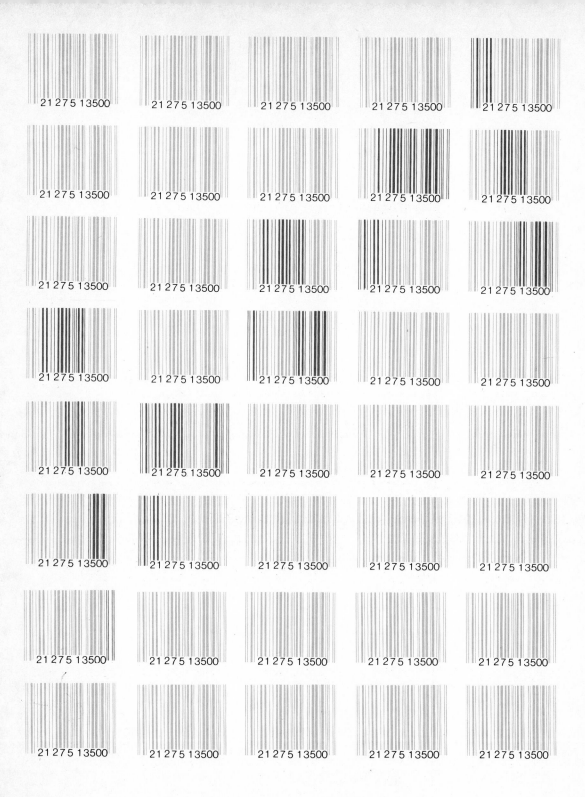

Retail Management

Satisfaction of Consumer Needs
Third Edition

Raymond A. Marquardt University of Wyoming

James C. Makens Wake Forest University

Robert G. Roe University of Wyoming

The Dryden Press

Chicago   New York   Philadelphia   San Francisco   Montreal   Toronto
London   Sydney   Tokyo   Mexico City   Rio de Janeiro   Madrid

Acquisitions Editor: Karen Emilson
Project Editor: Ruta Graff
Managing Editor: Jane Perkins
Design Director: Alan Wendt
Production Manager: Mary Jarvis

Text and cover design by Bernard Arendt
Copy editing by Marlene Targ Brill
Indexing by Ann Spohr
Composition by Bi-Comp. Inc.
Text type: 10/12 Melior

Address orders to:
383 Madison Avenue
New York, New York 10017

Address editorial correspondence to:
One Salt Creek Lane
Hinsdale, Illinois 60521

Library of Congress Catalog Card Number: 82-72311
ISBN 0-03-062608-0
Printed in the United States of America
6789-016-9876543

CBS College Publishing
The Dryden Press
Holt, Rinehart and Winston
Saunders College Publishing

The Dryden Press Series in Marketing
Stephen W. Brown, Consulting Editor

PRINCIPLES OF MARKETING

Boone and Kurtz
Contemporary Marketing,
Fourth Edition

Kurtz and Boone
Marketing

Rice and Smith
The Marketing Experience

Talarzyk
Cases for Analysis in Marketing,
Second Edition

Talarzyk
Contemporary Cases in Marketing,
Third Edition

ADVERTISING

Dunn and Barban
Advertising: Its Role in Modern
Marketing, Fifth Edition

CONSUMER BEHAVIOR

Blackwell, Engel, and Talarzyk
Contemporary Cases in Consumer
Behavior

Block and Roering
Essentials of Consumer Behavior,
Second Edition

Engel and Blackwell
Consumer Behavior,
Fourth Edition

RETAILING

Marquardt, Makens, and Roe
Retail Management: Satisfaction
of Consumer Needs, Third Edition

Rogers and Gamans
Fashion: A Marketing Approach

SALESMANSHIP

Hise
Effective Salesmanship

Young and Mondy
Personal Selling: Function,
Theory, and Practice,
Second Edition

SALES MANAGEMENT

Futrell
Contemporary Cases in Sales
Management

Futrell
Sales Management: Behavior,
Practice, Cases

MARKETING RESEARCH

Churchill
Marketing Research: Meth-
odological Foundations,
Third Edition

Zikmund
Exploring Marketing Research

Sciglimpaglia
Applied Marketing Research

**Zikmund, Lundstrom, and
Sciglimpaglia**
Cases in Marketing Research

**ADVANCED MARKETING
RESEARCH**

Green
Analyzing Multivariate Data

CHANNELS

Rosenbloom
Marketing Channels: A Management View, Second Edition

INTERNATIONAL MARKETING

Terpstra
International Marketing,
Third Edition

INDUSTRIAL MARKETING

Hutt and Speh
Industrial Marketing Management

Preface

Approach

Retailing, as interpreted in this book, refers to all business activities concerned with selling goods and services directly to ultimate consumers. The definition includes all forms of direct selling: direct-to-consumer sales made through store outlets, house-to-house canvass, mail order, and sale of services as well as goods. This last inclusion broadens the definition of retailing in an important sense, as annual growth in consumer demand for services is expanding faster than demand for many merchandise items.

A retailer cannot be limited by a narrow definition of a business. The firm's very existence depends upon its ability to satisfy consumer wants. This cannot always be accomplished if a retailer retains the traditional product-service offering. Rising levels of competition offered by other retailers, decreasing discretionary personal income, increased consumer mobility, and the psychological need of consumers for individualized, personal service make it imperative that retailers truly satisfy consumers' needs even to remain in the retailing business.

Clearly, the retailer must first determine what the consumer wants. Then, the firm can incorporate all elements in the marketing mix (such as price, promotion, service, merchandise selection, and location) to satisfy these consumer needs. This is not an easy task. Retailers must use a great deal of ingenuity and creativity to determine and to meet the ever-changing needs of consumers.

Any change in merchandise selection, price, promotion, location, or service involves consideration of many alternatives. To further complicate matters, a change in any one element may affect all other elements the retailer uses to sell merchandise. For example, changing from a high-price policy to a low-price policy will also affect the quality of merchandise carried, the merchandise assortment offered, the level of service provided, and the type of promotion implemented. Although a retailer may not be able to investigate every interrelationship in detail, he or she must be able to determine which interactions are significant and then analyze the consequences of these interactions.

This book discusses the continual process of choice in retailing. It provides the reader with more than a descriptive view of retailing by using marketing analysis to obtain the *why* and *how,* in addition to the *what,* of retailing. The retail manager is the decision maker who determines goals and objectives, defines problems needing attention, and then generates and evaluates alternative courses of action. This view of the retailer should provide the reader with a broad, sound understanding of the retailing process.

Retailing is influenced by many external factors besides consumer preferences. Our legal system prevents the retailer from having complete control over most elements of the marketing mix. Increased government regulation over pricing, advertising, and mergers illustrates a trend toward restrictions on retailers. This book examines some of the important current legislation that influences retailing, since in some areas restrictions may become so involved that firms spend most of their time and effort in complying with the law. The area of business law may well become a functional, as well as theoretical, part of the firm's activities.

Audience

This book is written for several types of prospective readers. The person who investigates retailing because of vocational interest will find a comprehensive treatment of fundamental retailing principles. The more casual reader looking at the book to see what goes on in a retail store will find a discussion of the actions that take place in the entire retailing system. Such readers will find that economic, social, and legal environments affect retailing greatly.

Some of the newer retail concepts derived from the fields of marketing, finance, economics, statistics, and the behavioral sciences have been integrated with the retailing basics. This has been done so that the reader benefits by the exposure to new ideas. Thus, the book contains material that will be useful to persons presently engaged in retailing and to those who later will begin retailing careers.

Organization

This book proceeds from the general to the specific. Part 1 presents an overview of the retail environment, including current retailing trends and some of the alternatives available to would-be retailers. Part 2 consists of two chapters which discuss how one can develop a marketing strategy that can be used successfully to guide a retail firm. Specific contributions to retailing from the fields of consumer behavior, management, and marketing are discussed in Chapters 2 and 3.

Part 3 consists of 12 chapters that identify retailing opportunities available through the application of proper procedures
in planning a retail mix. Product planning (Chapters 4 and 5),
store location (Chapters 6 and 7), and store layout (Chapter 8) are
discussed first. These three procedures require careful planning
before the outlet is opened because they involve fairly long-term
commitments. The merchandise assortment is probably determined first because it is usually dependent upon specialized
managerial skills or particular market demands. After this decision is made, the retailer must choose an optimal location for the
firm and create an attractive shopping experience.

Operation policies, practices, and controls are discussed in the
next four chapters. Merchandise buying and handling, physical
distribution, and management decisions are presented in Chapters 9, 10, and 11. Pricing is the subject of Chapter 12. The topic
included in this section is a discussion of sales stimulation policies, such as promotion strategy (Chapter 13), promotion (Chapter 14), and personal selling and customer services (Chapter 15).
Standard operating policies and procedures are required in these
areas so that the manager does not become so occupied with routine operating details that major decisions are given insufficient
consideration. Poor management, especially in the planning
area, is the prime cause of business failure. Part 3 consists of
three chapters on operations management. Chapter 16 is a discussion of organization design; Chapter 17 is a presentation of
management of human resources; and Chapter 18 examines
financial control. Successful store operation requires that a large
number of tasks be performed by the store's personnel, who use
their skills and the firm's equipment and labor-saving techniques
to reach the business's goals. Financial control conserves expensive capital resources which increases profitability. It involves
seeing that the firm's performance conforms to company plans,
establishing desired standards of financial performance, providing for periodic information on whether the plan is being carried
out, and taking appropriate action to bring ineffective activities
back in line with the plan.

Part 4 is devoted to special retail situations and future considerations. One chapter, Chapter 19, presents some of the peculiarities that retail service firms incur in their effort to serve customer needs at a profit.

The concluding two chapters are concerned with planning for
the future and evaluating the effectiveness of the retailer's current activities. Chapter 20 contains a discussion of the planning,
research efforts, and management information systems needed to
prepare for changes that seem likely to occur in the future. Chapter 21 integrates all the previous concepts together in the form of
a retailing audit. This chapter considers the retailing audit as

something separate from and more comprehensive than other control efforts. This chapter provides an opportunity to review the major concepts in effective contemporary retailing.

Each chapter begins with several learning goals and a list of key terms and concepts, and each chapter concludes with a summary and a short case. The cases are designed to illustrate the principles developed in the chapter. A glossary of the more important retailing terms is presented at the end of the book.

A great deal of change has occurred in the past few years, and we have attempted to reflect these changes in this third edition. Thus, coverage in all of the chapters and organization of the book have been altered somewhat since the second edition to incorporate recent changes in the industry.

Acknowledgments

It is impossible to enumerate all the persons who contributed to the preparation of this book. Especially helpful criticisms and comments were made by Professor W. Daniel Rountree of Appalachian State University; Professor Charlotte M. Raphaelson of Syracuse University; Professor Mary C. Gilly of Southern Methodist University; Professor John B. Gifford of Miami University of Ohio; Mr. William V. Roberti, Senior Vice-President of Maas Brothers; Ms. Helen Galland, President of Bonwit Teller; Mr. George P. Kelly, Chairman of Marshall Field and Company; Mr. Earle L. Ingalls, President of Porteus; Mr. Charles E. Griffin, President of Sanger Harris; Mr. Tom Roach, Chairman and Chief Executive Officer, The Denver; Mr. Fred Ross, Manager of Executive Recruitment, Carter, Hawley, Hale; Ms. Norine Holthe, Director of Executive Placement and Training, Emporium-Capwell; Ms. Lizette Weiss, Public Information Manager, Mervyn's; Mr. Stephen J. Lourie, Divisional Vice-President, Famous-Barr; Mr. Rick Duval, Project Supervisor of the Public Relations Department, Pay 'N Save Corporation.

We are also very much indebted for the exceptional typing and organizational assistance of Suzanne Roe, Debra and Alberta Marquardt, and Georgia Mitchell.

Finally, we take pleasure in thanking our wives—Alberta, Kay, and Suzanne—for patience and assistance under sometimes chaotic conditions.

To all these people we are deeply grateful. Responsibility for any errors or omissions is certainly ours, but the book would not have been possible without the help of these people.

Raymond A. Marquardt
James C. Makens
Robert G. Roe

Contents

Part Two

Developing a Retailing Mix

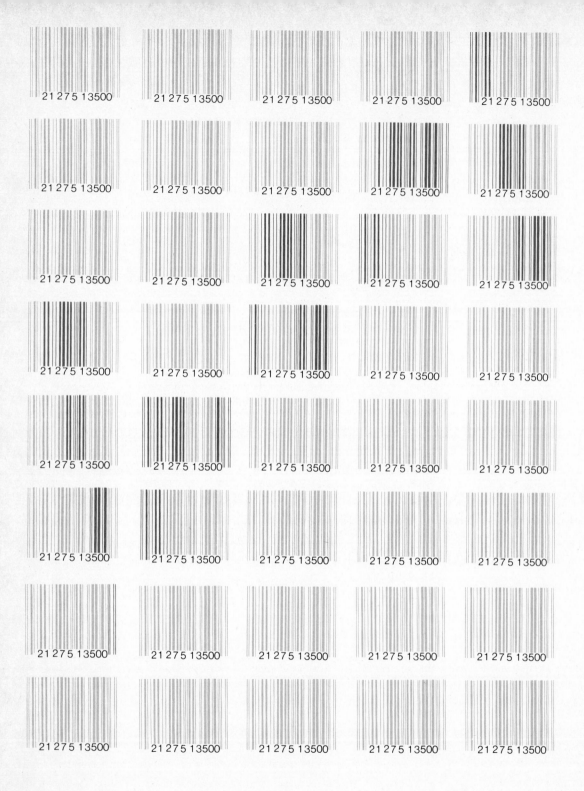

Part One | Developing a Marketing Strategy

Comments from the CEO

George P. Kelly
*Chairman Chicago
Division Marshall Field
& Company*

What kind of store *are* you now? What kind of store do you *want* to be? What kind of store *can* you be? These are questions that must be answered in detail and with real objectivity for most multistore retailers to guide their organizations through the 1980s and into the 1990s successfully. Those who are based in the Southeast, Southwest, and California are in the enviable position of being able to capitalize on dramatic population growth and so concentrate primarily on new store location opportunities. For the remaining retailers, however, the ground rules have changed as growth rates have slowed dramatically or, in some cases, reversed due to a net outflow of people from older communities.

Most important for continued volume and profit is growth in market share within existing trading areas. This is a new challenge for most retailers who have prospered during the last twenty to twenty-five years primarily from adding more and more branches. To increase market share retailers must develop their businesses on a location-by-location basis. To know how to do this, we must have clear answers—answers that may indicate the need for a radical shift in emphasis from the current direction of some existing stores.

As a result, more and more retailers will initiate formal market research programs in order to fully understand the demographic and psychographic characteristics of each specific trading area within their store locations. Communities change in population make-up over time, and a realistic, objective understanding of each separate community is necessary prior to making price, merchandise, service, and sales promotion mix decisions for any single location. For Marshall Field's, the mix for the Water Tower store in Chicago is dramatically different than the mix used for outlying branches. Increase in *total* market share and, as a result, sales volume, will equal the sum of share increases in each of the *separate* trading areas within the Chicago and Milwaukee standard metropolitan statistical areas. No longer can any major retailer in a no-growth market look at business as simply an aggregate.

To be successful in achieving the goal of increasing sales volume as a result of increasing market share, senior management must have more broad-based skills than was the case in the past.

The entrepreneurial spirit is still a necessity, but this spirit must be mixed with well-developed planning skills and an underlying intellectual curiosity. For Marshall Field's this means finding and hiring people who have varied backgrounds and interests and who can look beyond today and perceive the reality of what is both continuing and changing in our society. Field's needs people *not* just with business backgrounds, but also with a knowledge of social sciences and the resulting understanding of the world outside the store. It will be a difficult but exciting period for anyone who chooses retailing as a career; but for those who are successful, it is a career which promises real financial and ego rewards.

Chapter 1	# Overview of the Retail Environment

Learning Goals

1. To be aware of the size and significant characteristics of our nation's population.
2. To learn what functions retailing plays in an economic system.
3. To know how population demographics can be used to define a market and how retailers use the data to identify retail opportunities.
4. To understand the present state of retailing.
5. To discuss how projected trends will affect specific segments of the retail industry.

Key Terms and Concepts

retailing
demographic characteristics
life cycle
marketing functions

marketing specialists
SMSA
SCSA

Chapter 1 presents a broad picture of an environment in which retailers attempt to make a profit while providing customer satisfaction. Specifically, the chapter offers a brief outline of the vital role retailing plays in our society, a definition of retailing, the structure of retailing in the nation's economy, consumer demographic characteristics, and future retailing trends. The chapter concludes with a detailed examination of some familiar retail institutions as they position themselves to prosper in the 80s.

Fundamental Considerations

Retailing in our interdependent society determines daily survival. Each person has certain daily minimum requirements for food, shelter, and clothing. Additionally, other "necessities" must be provided if that person is to be productive. These fundamental facts are vividly brought to light during a natural or economic disaster. The importance of retailing was also emphasized during the last decade when many individuals took action to decrease their dependence on "the system" by returning to a rural setting to become more self-sufficient. However, their experience has shown that individuals are incapable of complete self-sufficiency and, therefore, must partly depend on others for certain goods and services.

Extraction or growth of raw materials and commodities, orderly transformation of these commodities, and distribution of these need-satisfying elements to individuals must be accomplished in any society. Our society has delegated the final link in the distribution process to the retail industry and rewards those retail firms which are efficient and effective with profits and survival. Retailers who forget that their fundamental reason for existence is to serve the public, both individually and collectively, risk governmental regulation or ultimate extinction in the marketplace.

Wide Range of Challenges

As we begin discussion of the retail process three important qualifications must be established. First, we feel that the most effective way to present the material is to assume that the reader is starting a new retailing firm. Thus, the choice of topics and sequence of their presentation conforms with decisions which a new retailer might experience in the real world as he or she sets about establishing the new business. As retail alumni we realize that, unfortunately, the decision-making challenges in the ongoing retailing world do not occur in the neatly packaged sequence of events we are about to discuss. In reality, most retailers find themselves dealing with an irate customer one moment and revising an advertising schedule the next. Therefore, the reader should be prepared to cope with a wide range of challenges each day while progressing toward the ultimate goal of providing customer goods and services at a profit.

Secondly, we realize that the retail industry has many and varied participant firms. Alphabetically they range from accounting firms to zoos and all kinds of products and services in between. Due to space limitations it is impossible to consider all types of retail firms, so if you fail to find your particular product or service discussed do not feel that we do not think it is worthy of consideration. We have consciously attempted to include both traditional and modern retailing examples which illustrate various principles and practices, realizing full well that we are only touching on a few selected retail situations.

Lastly, successful retailing requires significant amounts of personal interest, enthusiasm, and courage. The retail industry is in a constant state of dynamic growth and change. One year big cars are "in" and the next year customers decide to concentrate their transportation purchases on small imported automobiles. Since our "crystal ball" for anticipating future retail developments is a bit clouded, we will focus on fundamental retailing issues and practices which will be relevant regardless of current economic conditions. We have shaped our presentation so that readers will develop a set of tools which will help them cope effectively with the ever changing challenges of successful retailing. With these caveats in mind we turn to the discussion of satisfying consumer needs through retailing management.

Definition of Retailing

Retailing may be defined as all of those activities performed by merchants in order to offer goods and services for sale to the ultimate consumer. In contrast, any goods purchased for incorporation into other goods and services or to be consumed by governmental agencies are considered wholesale sales. For example, if Ford Motor Company purchases Motorola car radios to be installed in vehicles as factory options, the price of that radio is included in the final retail price charged by the local Ford dealership. The original purchase would be considered by Motorola as a wholesale transaction with the Ford Motor Company. Conversely, if the local Ford dealership sells the same type of radio over the parts counter to an ultimate consumer, the transaction would be a retail sale.

Structure of Retailing in the U.S. Economy

The structure of retailing can be analyzed from several points of view, but space limitations confine our discussion to the classification systems used to describe retail stores.

Classification of Retail Stores

Four **retail classification systems** will be used to describe retailing from various viewpoints: the type of merchandise or service offered, the number of outlets owned or controlled by a single firm, the relative emphasis on prices, and the number and nature of surrounding stores.

   Merchandise offered This classification groups retail establishments according to the types of merchandise offered for sale. Several classification systems are commonly used. The Bureau of Census considers the predominant type of merchandise offered by a store as its criterion, such as building materials, hardware, farm equipment dealers, general merchandise group stores (which include department stores, discount department stores, and variety stores), food stores, apparel and accessory stores, gasoline service stations, and nonstore retailers.[1] Trade associations recognize specific merchandise classifications such as the National Automobile Dealers Association.

Alternately one might construct a continuum ranging from general store on one end to specialty store on the other end. A store with a wide offering of different types of products to meet a wide range of consumer needs would be classed as a general store. Many large-scale mass merchandisers, such as K mart, offer "one-stop shopping" that is reminiscent of the earlier general store. Admittedly, the variety of goods has been significantly expanded, but so have consumer needs. The largest single example of this strategy called the hypermarket (which combines a large supermarket and a discount store) is Meijers Thrifty Acres in Detroit or Oshawa in Canada.[2]

On the other end of the spectrum are specialty stores that have a narrow range of merchandise which appeals to a specific segment of the market. Thom McAn shoe store and Mrs. Stevens' candy shops exhibit a narrow line or assortment of merchandise and service. Their competitive advantage lies in their depth of assortment. They usually operate under the motto, "If we don't have it, or can't get it, you don't need it."

The nation has experienced a significant increase in the number of specialty stores such as the furniture warehouse, the home improvement center, and the catalog showroom. Department stores are retrenching in certain merchandise areas and no longer can be considered as full line, but are not quite specialized. In fact, they seem to be searching for a profitable identity somewhere in the clothing fashions. The consuming public seems to be in a state of change in its shopping habits and currently enjoys a large variety of stores and a wide selection of merchandise. Customers seem to be shopping for the lowest price on items which meet everyday needs and expressing their desire for individuality by buying quality goods at higher prices in specialty stores. Consumers are willing to spend a larger proportion of their discretionary income on services than in past decades.

Service offered The quality and quantity of services that a retail firm offers may determine its survival. Accordingly, the product offered for sale today tends to be a product-service mixture.

In economy grocery stores the consumer expects little or no service.[3] Conversely, in specialty stores such as a ski shop, potential customers expect to be greeted and professionally assisted in their purchase decisions. Thus the breadth of merchandise is generally inversely related to the amount of service provided. Department stores, having made a point of recognizing specific needs of particular consumer groups, provide a wide assortment of fashion products ranging from custom eyeglass frames to fashion footwear. Therefore, the store helps the customer validate his or her self-concept as being a member of the "in" group through purchase and use of trendy items.

Number of outlets under common ownership Another method of classifying retail activity is by the number of outlets owned by a retail organization. The term **chain store** is often used to designate a group of stores under common ownership. For present purposes the term will refer to geographically dispersed, commonly owned units that number four or more. Common examples would be Safeway, Skaggs Drug, and K mart. Such stores have grown because of economies of scale that can be effected through more efficient advertising exposure and centralized buying of goods. All units within the chain generally exhibit uniform architectural motif, pricing, and availability of credit. Such firms as J. C. Penney and Montgomery Ward attempt to centralize all their purchasing and credit operations so that consistent prices and credit policies are presented to customers everywhere in the nation. Regional grocery chains, such as Ralph's in Los Angeles, will often attempt to accomplish similar objectives with regard to price, product assortment, and store decor.

Another aspect of classification by number of outlets is the branch or catalog store. In both cases, firms attempt to establish a presence in a suburban or rural community. They rely on central warehouse or main store stocks and expeditious merchandise interchange and delivery to meet customer needs. This practice makes it unnecessary for each store to carry duplicate or complete assortments of merchandise, and it limits the amount of fixed overhead required in numerous buildings. Recent renewed consumer interest in catalog sales, if not discouraged by costly and ineffective delivery systems, may reduce the need for numerous outlets while still producing additional sales revenues.

Relative emphasis on price A close relationship exists between classifying a store according to merchandise diversity and according to relative emphasis on price. There are no free services. Every activity performed by a retailer costs money that must be recouped either by charging directly for it or by distributing the cost over the entire merchandise line and raising prices to higher levels. Retail establishments that emphasize relatively lower prices either perform fewer customer services than competitors or use a variable markup strategy to achieve higher than normal markups on noncomparable or luxury items. The point is that retailers tend to differentiate themselves on the basis of initial markup on the merchandise they offer. Suffice it to say, retail organizations generally can be categorized by their relative emphasis on markups, which results in varying price lines and price images in the mind of the consumer.

Nature of neighborhood Lastly, it is possible to group retail establishments according to the number and nature of neighboring stores. Historically, retailers have gathered together at convenient points of travel. Early settlements were usually placed at the convergence of rivers, land trails, or transportation intersections. Today this same tendency can be observed in (a) central business districts, (b) regional shopping centers, (c) community shopping centers, (d) neighborhood shopping centers, and (e) free-standing units. The specific characteristics of each retailing cluster will be presented in Chapter 6.

Certain types of retail stores require more "aggregate convenience" than others to prosper and grow.[4] Here again the assortment of offered goods becomes important when viewed in the light of consumer shopping habits. For example, when consumers want to do comparative shopping for apparel, they may frequent a regional shopping center because the central business district, containing the "main" stores, no longer has complete assortments or depth of stock. Many small retailers prosper in close proximity to large "anchor" department or chain stores that serve as focal points for regional shopping malls. These shops attempt to intercept customers as they shop for unique, personalized apparel.

Similarly, it is quite common for neighborhood shopping center clusters to contain supermarkets, drug centers, hardware stores, and service stations because they complement each other's merchandise assortments and are convenient for customers. If properly located, merchandised, and managed, these complementary stores should succeed as a collective unit.

Consumer Demographic Characteristics

In order to gain some appreciation and understanding of the enormous daily challenge of the retailing industry, it is necessary to examine the total United States retail market. Population data stating how many persons of a certain age, sex, or race live in a given place are referred to as **demographic characteristics**. Additionally, such personal attributes as marital and employment status are included to give an aggregate view of the nation's human resources.

In the next few pages the text will sketch the general portrait of the American population. Keep in mind that as each demographic characteristic is presented an additional piece of information is available to define the market. The process will be similar to an artist creating a mosaic tile mural. If one stands very close to the wall, only bits of colored tile and mortar seams will be seen. The image is unclear; the picture is incomplete. However, if one steps back across the room, the entire mural comes into focus and the little colored chips blend into a complete segment of the greater design. Viewed individually the following data may present an incomplete picture, but by the end of the discussion the retail market picture will become clearer.

Population

The 1980 census counted 226.5 million persons who were considered U.S. residents. This represents an increase of 11.4 percent in the population during the last ten years. The average 1.1 percent annual increase continues the downward trend of the 1950s of 1.7 percent and the 1960s rate of 1.3 percent.[5] Depending on assumptions accepted from demographers, the population is projected to increase and reach a level of 248 to 283 million by the year 2000. Regardless of the exact population by the year 2000, one can be assured that the needs of this expanding population will represent a continuing challenge for the retail industry during the intervening decades.[6]

National Migration Patterns

Regional Population

The nation has experienced major shifts in population distribution during the last ten years. During the 1970s significant numbers of individuals and families moved from the Northeastern and Midwestern states to the Southeastern and Southwestern states. Also, many persons began to discover new appealing lifestyles and job opportunities in the Rocky Mountain states. These generalizations are supported by regional census data. Approximately 33 percent of the nation's population lives in the South. About 26 percent of the people live in the North Central states, while 22 percent reside in the Northeast. In addition, 19 percent of the nation's residents live in the West, including 23.7 million people who reside in the most populous state of California.[7] Comparing 1980 census figures with those of 1970, one finds that Nevada has experienced the largest percentage growth (63.5%) followed by Florida (43.4%), Wyoming (41.6%), and Alaska (32.4%). Those areas actually losing population include the District of Columbia (−15.6%), New York (−3.6%) and Rhode Island (−0.03%).[8]

While these figures may seem insignificant, one must realize that such shifts in population are accompanied by shifts in retail buying power. One national chain, J. C. Penney Company, recognized the importance of these national migration trends and moved one of their regional offices to Atlanta, Georgia so that the firm's regional merchandisers could better meet the needs of that growing Southeastern market. Such strategic decisions are necessary if national firms are to remain competitive in today's fast paced changing world.

Changing Age of the Population

According to 1980 census data the median age of the population increased from 28 to 30 years during the 1970s. This general trend should continue due to the fact that the number of children under 15 years of age declined from 58 million to 51 million and the number of persons over 65 increased by 28 percent to 25.5 million. The home-formation group, ranging from 24–40 years of age, grew by 25 percent during the 1970s, and the 35–44 age group is expected to grow by approximately 42 percent during the 1980s. This segment is rapidly maturing into the **full nest** stage of the family life cycle where purchases of homes and home furnishings are at their peak.

Median Age

Major median age differences between racial groups will have a significant effect on retailers appealing to different market segments. Whites have a median age of 31.3 years as contrasted with 24.9 for blacks and 23.3 for Hispanics. Regional differences in median age groups will play a role in the merchandising policies of most retailers. Florida, with its large retirement communities, has the highest median age, 34.7 years, compared with Utah's 24.2, which is the lowest among the states.

Maturity Market

Another significant age group for retailers is the "gray market" or "maturity market," composed of persons 55 and older who are being recognized as one of the most underdeveloped retail markets in our nation. This group accounts for 20.5 percent of the population and represents $400 billion in annual personal income and approximately one-fourth of all consumer expenditures in the country.[9] Contrary to popular belief this consumer force of 45 million is considered by many to be the "growth market" of the 1980s.

Lifestyle Changes

The population's lifestyle seems to be in transition as noted in Table 1.1. By 1980, 63 percent of all women in the 24–40 age bracket were in the labor force. With active enforcement of the Civil Rights Act during the 1970s and changing social values, women have begun to see viable alternatives to the traditional careers of wife and mother. During the last decade an increasing number of women elected to remain single and pursue careers outside the home.

Working Women

Another lifestyle trend which is emerging is that people are

Table 1.1   Lifestyle Trends and Marketing Implications for the 1980s

Specific Trends	Implied Growth Areas

1. *At-Home Lifestyle*
   a. Control of home environment
   b. New experiences brought into the home
	1. Housing "after–market" (do–it–yourself)
	Protection and security
	Home computers and electronic gadgetry
	Home communications systems

2. *Working Women*
   a. Role overlap in household
   b. Time–money and time–gratification tradeoffs
	2. Apparel ⎫
	Jewelry ⎬ Quality
	Services ⎭
	   Child care
	   Restaurants/sports/entertainment
	   Medical care for the elderly
	   Financial and counseling services
	   Adult education and self-improvement
	Easy maintainence, carefree goods
	Products that stress efficient use of time

3. *Time Efficiency and Convenience Recreation*	**3.** Recording/sound equipment Microwave ovens Catalog (and cable TV) shopping and expanded store hours Individual and small group forms of exercise close to home Home electronic toys

4. *"Get Away" and the Spread of Cosmopolitan Tastes*
   a. Back to nature
   b. Interest in world cultures
   c. Escape to home environment
	4. Travel
	Photography (small families also a plus)
	Hotels/better restaurants and clubs
	Portable, adaptable, convenient equipment

5. *Investment Orientation*	**5.** Housing but more factory–built homes and components Financial and educational services Quality products
6. *Urban Movement*	**6.** City-based forms of entertainment/recreation Urban renewal/remodeling/refurbishing of existing structures Security and crime protection Mass transit Rental and K/D furniture Multifamily construction Space efficient products

General Trends	Implied Growth Areas
1. *Sophisticated Consumers and Segmented Markets*	**1.** Market research/information services Advertising Segmented distribution networks
2. *Emphasis on Quality and Awareness of Price/Quality Tradeoffs*	**2.** All product areas gain general improvement in profit margins

Source: Carol Brock Kenney and Leslie J. Moran, "Consumer Capsule" (New York, N.Y.: Shearson/American Express, Inc., Vol. VII, No. 3, 1981): 26.

reducing the size of their household. This trend is illustrated by the census data which show that the number of households has grown from 63.4 million to 80.4 million or about 27 percent during the last ten years. In contrast the number of persons living in a household increased by only 12 percent, giving a net decline from 3.11 persons in 1970 to 2.75 persons in 1980. This downward trend may level off and even reverse for a short period as a significant number of childless women approach the end of child bearing age and elect to interrupt their careers to have children. Also economic conditions may require some independent, single persons to return home or group together to share the rising cost of housing, thus increasing the size of households.

Housing

The cost of home ownership has more than doubled during the 1970s to an average of $88,900 on a new one-family home in June of 1981. If housing costs continue to rise as anticipated, both new apartments and houses will tend to shrink in average square footage which will put a premium on personal privacy and perhaps create a whole new retail market for small television/entertainment equipment and privacy related items. Homes of the late 1980s will not contain the fixed interior walls but instead will have lighting, movable room dividers, dual purpose furniture, and mobile fixtures to achieve higher utilization from a smaller space (e.g., many kitchens of the future will be converted into family rooms during certain times of the day.)

Energy Costs

The energy crisis will continue to increase utility bills and cause further inflationary pressure on consumers. This will accelerate the do-it-yourself trend. In 1981, Americans spent about $19 billion on tools and supplies used for home improvement projects. If the do-it-yourself concept continues to grow at its current rate, the market will increase to more than $24 billion by 1989. It will provide opportunities for retailers who sell the "right" tools, hardware, paint, fabrics, lighting, and building materials to meet the needs of this market.

The energy crunch has increased demand for warm bedding, heaters and insulation. Despite higher energy costs, sales of labor saving household appliances are projected to increase. The effect increased gasoline prices will have upon automobile driving is likely to be minimal as automobile companies are projected to continue to improve their miles per gallon obtained during the 1980s. Shoppers are expected to stay closer to home

Home Entertainment

during the 1980s and use the latest television games, computers, and cable television for work, recreation, and educational purposes. This trend will benefit small retailers, who, if they keep abreast of changes in consumer demand, will capture a higher percentage of the consumer dollar.

Flight to the Suburbs

The decade of the 1970s was marked by a major migration of people to the suburbs. New larger homes, the promise of better schools, accessibility of modern shopping centers and availability of relatively cheap transportation lured many families to the suburbs.

Small town and rural populations grew by 15 percent between the 1970 and 1980 census. In contrast the metropolitan areas grew by 10 percent. This movement from the core city was further evident after examining the 1980 Standard Metropolitan Statistical Areas (SMSA) data. To qualify as an SMSA, the area must contain at least one city encompassing 50,000 persons. Prior to 1980, 284 areas were considered as SMSAs. After reviewing 1980 census data the Office of Management and Budget (OMB) approved 35 new SMSAs and dropped one, for a new total of 318. These 318 SMSAs contain 75 percent of the population. Major metropolitan areas such as New York, Newark, and Jersey City which incorporate more than two SMSAs are considered Standard Consolidated Statistical Areas (SCSA). Over 30 percent of the nation's population now reside in these 14 SCSAs. Perhaps a more telling statistic is that while the 429 central cities in the nation increased 0.1 percent during the decade, the suburban communities increased 18 percent.

SMSA/SCSA

Suburban Migration

This mass movement to the suburbs included all racial and ethnic groups. In the 38 largest metropolitan areas the black population increased from 2.3 million in 1970 to 3.7 million in 1980. In communities of 500,000 to 1 million the number of black persons declined from 5.3 to 3.1 percent of the population. Further examination of the data suggests that generally a significant portion of the white population has been moving further out into new growth and prosperity areas while some of the black population has been moving into economically declining suburbs. Thus, it appears that the urban blight of the 1960s and 1970s threatens to become the suburban blight of the 1980s.

Urban Revitalization

With passage of time, certain critical events and changing personal perceptions have begun to slow this movement and in some cases have actually led some to move back into the central city. With the help of the federal government such cities as Boston, Detroit, and Minneapolis have revitalized their downtown areas so that people who have become disenchanted with suburban home ownership, long commuting times, and increasing crime are choosing to live in these cities in newly constructed high-rise apartments and condominiums. Whether this trend will continue remains to be seen; but in the meantime some retailers are cautiously renovating their downtown stores while new merchants are moving in to serve this new highly affluent group of consumers.

Retailing Trends in the '80s

The most significant short-term trends in the retail industry focus on the challenges of coping with high levels of inflation, recession, restrictive monetary policies by the Federal Reserve Board, increased minimum wage levels, and declining productivity in a labor intensive industry. Despite these concerns the retail industry was expected to generate over $1 trillion in sales and provide employment for 14.5 percent of the labor force. This level is quite extraordinary in light of the fact that over 40 percent of all retail sales are made with assistance of some sort of credit which costs the purchaser 16–21 percent interest. Retailers everywhere are contributing to this effort in a variety of ways as they search for keys to their survival.

Inventory Control

Inventory Concerns

Retailers who survived the 1974–1975 recession vividly recall the problems generated by overstocked situations. They have monitored their current inventory conditions carefully and have made both quantitative and qualitative changes in merchandise policies. Relatively less amounts of merchandise are being creatively displayed to give the impression of full assortments. Slow moving or low markup items are being replaced by fast moving, high markup goods. The appropriate implementation of this strategy generates more sales per square foot and improves return on invested capital. This trend is evident in specialty shops and department stores.

Leased Departments

New Leased Departments

Another significant trend in retailing is for firms with large stores to "downsize" or reduce their total floor space per unit. This is in keeping with their attempt to reduce merchandise offerings. Many department stores and some national chains are turning to leasing space to independent merchants who provide expanded products and services without the added cost of inventory and staffing. The host store provides store maintenance and the cost of sales systems while the leasees provide well-trained, knowledgeable, motivated sales specialists who are needed to effectively sell such products as sewing machines, shoes, watches, and fine jewelry. In addition, many labor intensive retail services such as travel agencies, auto repair, shoe repair, and photo studios generate additional customer traffic and a share of the profits for the leasing store. Currently 6 percent of the total department store sales and 10 percent of the specialty store sales originate in leased departments. These figures are sure to increase as more retail firms include professional services such as dentistry, fashion eyeware, legal and accounting services as leasee tenants.

Technological Changes

POS

Computer applications continue to dominate the technological evolution in retailing. As competition increases, particularly among small and medium size retailers, and the high costs of carrying inventory continue, more and more retailers are installing computerized point-of-sale (POS) transaction centers to manage their inventories, track results of promotional campaigns, and implement credit transactions. This trend has been encouraged by declining computer costs per transaction and the increasing acceptance of universal product codes and marketing systems. According to the National Retail Merchants Association (NRMA) over 300 general merchandise firms now have adopted the Optical Character Reader (OCR-A) system, and over 90,000 system wands are currently in use. This number is expected to increase to over 200,000 by 1983. Adoption of this technology combined with other forms, including Electronic Funds Transfer Systems (EFTS) and automated distribution center systems, should make significant contributions to improving the level of productivity in the retail industry.

Third Party Credit and Debit Cards

With increasing employment of EFTS systems, more and more retail firms are accepting third party payment cards from VISA, Mastercard, American Express, and Diners Club. Montgomery Ward and J. C. Penney now accept third party credit cards of VISA and Mastercard in addition to their own credit cards. This strategic decision was made, in part, because previously profitable credit operations have become unprofitable due to the high cost of money and increasing bad debt losses. By accepting bank credit cards firms reduce their credit operation costs and free badly needed capital to apply in alternative merchandising enterprises (e.g., Sears and Roebuck Company's move into insurance and financial services). In turn, banks have begun to deemphasize credit cards and are promoting debit cards which permit them to immediately deduct the purchase from the customer's account instead of extending credit and increasing their operation costs. With deregulation of the financial system, retailers may wish to consider accepting other debit cards which may be offered by savings and loan institutions and brokerage houses. Such actions will only be possible if the acceptance of EFTS by the consuming public and the retail industry continues to expand.

Generic and Private Labels

Generic Labels

Consumers, pressed by inflation and fear of recession, are searching the marketplace for "value" more than ever. They seem to be reevaluating purchase priorities. This trend is manifested in the widespread acceptance of generic food products and private labeled goods. Food and other products ranging from generic beef to generic motor oil now command a major share of their respective markets as buyers place less emphasis on implied brand benefits. Such actions lower their costs of living so that additional discretionary income may be freed for investing in homes, cars, entertainment equipment, higher quality clothing, or just making ends meet. As consumers reduce their brand loyalties in search of the best value, retail store image and price will become more important in consumers' purchase decisions.

In the near future, "retailing without stores" will be made possible by the introduction and widespread adoption of Videotex.[10] Consumers can sit in their living rooms and shop for goods by using a computer terminal connected to their cable-wired television set (Figure 1.1).[11] When they wish to purchase a displayed item they simply key the item number, quantity desired, bank credit card number, and their address into the termi-

Figure 1.1   Changing Concepts of Retail Distribution

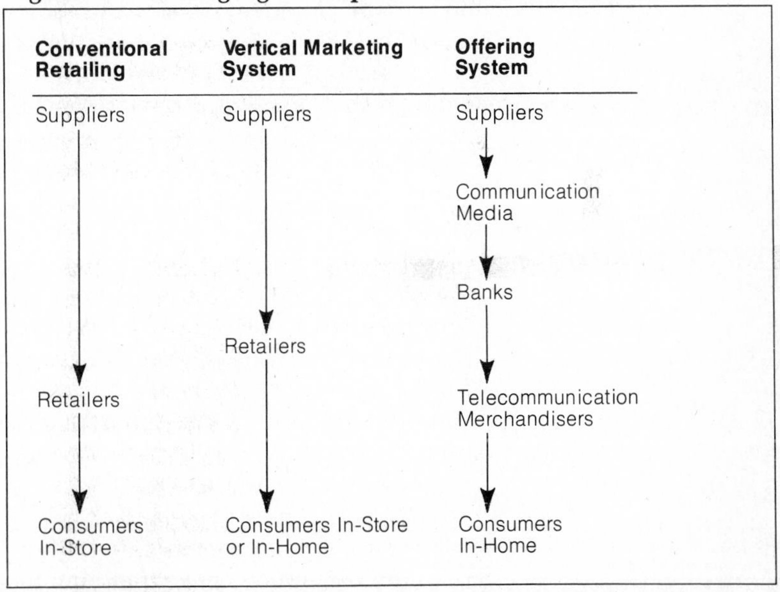

Conventional Retailing	Vertical Marketing System	Offering System
Suppliers	Suppliers	Suppliers
		↓
		Communication Media
		↓
		Banks
	Retailers	↓
Retailers		Telecommunication Merchandisers
↓	↓	↓
Consumers In-Store	Consumers In-Store or In-Home	Consumers In-Home

Source: Reprinted by permission of the *Harvard Business Review*. Exhibit from "Retailing Without Stores" by Larry J. Rosenberg and Elizabeth C. Hirschman (July/August 1980): 107. Copyright © 1980 by the President and Fellows of Harvard College; all rights reserved.

nal. The goods will be delivered to their door, saving the consumer time and transportation costs.

Industry Trends

Uncertain Economic Times

The retailing industry will face significant challenges in the 1980s. Even though retail sales volume is expected to rise due to a 20 million increase in population, the rate of retail sales expansion will not match the last decade. Fueled by rising employment, a larger disposable income, increased use of available inexpensive consumer credit, and greater utilization of second mortgages on real estate, consumers went on an unmatched consumption binge in the 1970s. Now in the 1980s credit charges are coming due, inflation continues to erode consumer purchasing power, rising unemployment and the fear of unemployment cause consumers to reconsider liberal use of expensive consumer credit. Despite this rather gloomy assessment there is still reason to expect unexcelled opportunities in selected segments of the industry.

Department Stores

Department stores can reasonably project that they will experience increased patronage during the 1980s. All across the nation department stores are developing new strategies to capitalize on the demand for quality merchandise, particularly in apparel and cosmetics. Most stores recognize that in order to succeed they must appeal to a more highly educated selective group of customers who demand a wide variety of merchandise which will suit their individual needs. Those firms which effectively communicate their commitment to offering good values, fashion leadership, and a modern, progressive, and innovative store image will succeed.

General Merchandise Chain

General merchandise chains such as Montgomery Ward, J. C. Penney, and Sears, Roebuck will experience modest growth during the decade as they establish new smaller stores in overlooked locations and expand their efforts into nonstore activities. In a bid for more business both Penney's and Montgomery Ward's have begun to deemphasize or drop some house brands and substitute national labels which have wider consumer recognition.

All firms will be attempting to upscale their merchandise offerings and raise their price points. Those firms with established mail order operations are expanding them to take advantage of renewed interest in catalog shopping by working women. With installation of on-line computer facilities the consumer can phone in the order and find out if the goods are in stock for immediate delivery. Such operations can offer a wider assortment of goods, in greater quantities and at lower costs, than conventional stores which have higher overhead expenses. Without doubt the retail mail order business should experience major growth in the '80s.

Departmentalized Discount Stores

Established departmentalized discount stores, which feature self-service to sell apparel, health and beauty aids, hard goods, and general merchandise, will continue to cut into traditional department store sales. These stores, which numbered over 7,200 with an annual sales volume of $55 billion in 1979, will continue to be the leaders in merchandising housewares, toys, sporting goods, and children's wear.[12] Discount retailers will continue to downsize their units to achieve savings in initial construction and interest costs as well as realize lower future operating costs.

The industry represented by such firms as Target, Venture, and Gold Circle is expected to increase its number of stores by 16 percent while experiencing a 36 percent growth in sales by 1985.[13] Some of the anticipated increase in sales may be attributed to adoption of certain trade-up policies, particularly in fashion merchandise. Other increases will come from the spread of "off-price" apparel chains such as J. Brannam and T. J. Maxx.

Off-price Chains

Additional sales will come from newly established factory outlets and discount malls. New factory discount centers, featuring a wide line of both soft and hard goods and constructed on the perimeters of large cities, will join the current 10 malls now in operation. The main attraction of these manufacturer outlets, which range in size from 2,000 to over 10,000 square feet, is women's apparel offered at substantial savings over similar merchandise offered by regular priced retailers. As inflation continues, more and more consumers are expected to patronize these stores in search of better bargains.

Catalog Showrooms

Catalog showrooms, once the fastest rising sector in the discount retailing industry, are expected to continue to grow in the '80s but not at the meteoric rates of the '70s. With $9.4 billion in sales in 1982, the industry expects to continue to expand in Florida and California, having effectively saturated the Atlantic coast and the Midwest. Continuing sales volume increases may become increasingly difficult to achieve if the industry does not successfully expand sales beyond its current money makers of jewelry, housewares, electronics, watches, and personal care products. Many of these product lines are highly dependent on substantial amounts of discretionary income which may not be readily available during the decade. Hence, sales may decline substantially.

Drug Store Chain

Drug store chains are expected to continue their ten year growth trend right on through the 1980s. Currently these chains account for about 70 percent of all drug store sales. Control of the industry rests with some 25 firms which control 90 percent of the industry's sales.[14] Much of the past success can be attributed to chain expansion into nondrug merchandise competing directly with supermarkets and discount retailers. As the industry continues to upgrade its professional image, some firms plan to introduce optic and dental departments as well as concentrating on other health care products such as surgical supplies and convalescent aids.

Combination Stores

Perhaps the greatest industry growth will come from the combination drug/food stores such as Family Center, Osco, and Sav-on. Much of the new business will come from mergers of drug and supermarket chains such as the Skaggs combination with the American Stores firm. Such mergers may be an attempt by grocery chains to acquire a share of the fast-growing prescription business. As Americans age, this part of the industry's business is expected to grow faster than any segment in the retail sector, and with proper management, it may become one of the most profitable.

International Retailing

American businesspeople have been traditionally somewhat egocentric and reluctant to adopt new ideas which originate on foreign shores. Overseas markets generate billions of dollars worth of imports which are sold each year in the American consumer market in the form of fashion, electronics, photographic and automotive products. Yet, foreign distribution ideas such as the French supermarket/discount merchandise concept, called a "hypermarket," fail to gain acceptance. Conversely, the American fast food franchise model has been adopted world-wide.

Hypermarket

The 1980s will see significant increases of international participation in America's retail distribution system. Increased foreign investment such as the British firm's bid to gain control of Marshall Field and Company will become commonplace. Joint ventures between European, Japanese and American firms in the department store, discount, and franchising industries will bring new management concepts into the retail system while significantly increasing the level of competition. Any retailer who continues to assume a "business as usual" posture will be swiftly eliminated from the marketplace as retailing becomes an international enterprise.

Era of Consolidation and Adaptation

The retail landscape will change markedly in the 1980s. Economic conditions will take their toll on both large and small firms, but the biggest loser will be small independent retailers. Pressed by a rising cost structure, high interest rates on all forms of borrowed funds, shrinking value of limited equity capital, rising consumer prices, increased unemployment, and increased financial rewards for saving, the small marginal retailer will be forced out of business at considerable personal loss. Special situations will be created by innovative entrepreneurs. But as they succeed and require more costly capital to expand, they will be bought up by larger retail firms who have survived and will be seeking new investment and merchandising opportunities which have been proven in the marketplace. Thus, the 1980s will be the era of retailing consolidation and adaptation.

Summary

In this chapter we have attempted to identify the significant retail institutions and to examine the future of the retail industry. We found that the general trend of retail growth is healthy, while significant changes are taking place among various retail institutions. Large, multi-unit organizations are growing at the most rapid rate. Catalog stores, discount stores, furniture warehouse retailers, supermarkets, drug store chains, franchises, and carefully managed specialty stores are expanding their sales volume. However, the number of small, independent retailers continues to decline.

These changes have resulted from environmental influences (such as increased incomes, population increases, movement to the suburbs, increased mobility, and technological changes) and the resulting managerial responses to these changes.

Products and services must continue to reach the consumer in the form and at the time and place that he or she desires. The retailing industry plays an important role in this process, but individual retailers will continue to be successful only if they are the most efficient means by which manufacturers and producers can reach the ultimate consumer.

Questions

1. What role does retailing play in our society? What function(s) does retailing serve in meeting individual needs?
2. What are demographic characteristics? Why should a retailer be interested in them?
3. What are the retail implications of the population migration to the South, Southeast, Southwest, and the West Coast? Explain.
4. What actions might consumers take to cope with inflation? Should retail organizations play any part in such efforts? Explain.
5. What are four methods of classifying retail institutions? What are the advantages and disadvantages of using each method?
6. What would be the impact on the retail community if gasoline reached a price of $3.00 per gallon in 1985? Would all retailers be affected equally?
7. How would you characterize the future for retailing during the next twenty years? Explain.

Footnotes

1. U.S. Department of Commerce, Bureau of the Census, *1972 Census of Retail Trade, Area Statistics, United States, RC–72–A–52* (Washington, D.C.: Government Printing Office, 1975), p. 38.

2. Albert D. Bates, "Ahead—The Retrenchment Era," *Journal of Retailing* 53 (Fall 1977): 34.

3. Walter H. Heller, "Economy Store Census," *Progressive Grocer* 60 (May 1981): 89.

4. Reavis Cox, "Consumer Convenience—Retail Structure of Cities," *Journal of Marketing* 23 (April 1959): 355–362.

5. Philip M. Hauser, "The Census of 1980," *Scientific American* (November 1981): 56.

6. Ibid., p. 59.

7. *1980 Census of Population and Housing: Advance Reports* (Washington, D.C.: U.S. Department of Commerce, Bureau of the Census, 1981), p. 4.

8. Ibid.

9. Carole B. Allan, "Over 55: Growth Market of the '80s," *Nations Business* 69 (April 1981): 26–32.

10. Larry J. Rosenberg and Elizabeth C. Hirschman, "Retailing Without Stores," *Harvard Business Review* 58 (July–August 1980): 103–112.

11. Ibid., p. 107.

12. Rudy Macher, "Retailing: Department, Discount, Specialty Drug Stores," *Standard and Poor's Industry Surveys* (New York: Standard and Poor's, 1980), Section 2, pp. R 111–146.

13. Ibid.

14. Ibid.

Chapter 2 | Developing Market Strategy for Retailing

Chapter 1 demonstrated that retailing is the most important institution in the process of distributing goods and services throughout the American economy. In this chapter we will demonstrate how retailers can apply the process of strategic market planning to accomplish their dual mission of achieving long term profitability and providing greater consumer satisfaction. Although the retail process has succeeded in assembling vast assortments of merchandise to meet client needs, it has not yet totally implemented a true marketing concept. The retail process, as practiced by a significant sector of the economy, is a relic of a past emphasis on production that is in need of innovation and change.

Creating the Retail Firm's Master Plan for Success

Historically, retailers have plied their trade by serving small local markets and making decisions based on careful observation, hunch, and intuition. These bases were supplemented by personal experience which was often gained by apprenticeships in successful retail operations. With widespread adoption and implementation of the marketing concept after World War II, major changes were effected in the retail marketplace. For the first time a modern firm's performance of business activities which directed the flow of goods and services from producer to consumer or user was used to satisfy customer needs and accomplish the firm's objectives. Such innovations as discounting, franchising, consumer credit, and such environmental changes as population growth and migration, changing values and lifestyles have had an impact on retail markets and significantly altered traditional retail practices.

Visceral decision making is now no match for the large retail chain's systematic long-range planning strategies. Current retailers must adopt and adapt the tools of modern management if they have any hope of succeeding in today's complex dynamic markets. Obviously an in-depth discussion of these techniques is beyond the scope of this text. However, basic ideas and their retail applications are outlined so that the reader may sketch his or her own grand design for success in retailing.

Retail Organization Mission

Every retail firm in our nation must daily justify its reason for existence in the marketplace. Each firm must create a mission statement which clearly and concisely states why the firm exists and what unique contribution the business can make to the society which it serves. Peter Drucker has noted that "To know what a business is we have to start with its **purpose**. Its purpose must lie outside of the business itself. In part, it must lie in society since business enterprise is an organ of society. There is only one valid definition: **to create a customer**."[1] Drucker goes on to note that ". . . any serious attempt to state 'what our business is' must start with the customer, his realities, his situation, his behavior, his expectations and his values."[2] Successful retailers long ago realized that the customers' perceptions were more important than objective facts. "The customer is always right even when he is wrong."[3]

Today, a retailer's mission is to meet the needs of a selected segment of consumers by "having the right goods, at the right price, in the right place, at the right time, in the right assortment, and in the right quantities" and provide this service at a profit. But in modern inflationary periods retailers are hard pressed to generate sufficient profits to assure future survival. Rising labor and inventory costs must be passed on to customers who are reluctant to buy because of high interest rates. Even if the retailer is successful and adjusts financial data to reflect true inflationary costs there is no assurance that the operation is adequately profitable to survive in the long run.

For example, real estate brokers all across the nation are going bankrupt because their management did not charge enough commission, adequately control costs, and generate an adequate surplus to carry them over this difficult economic period. According to Drucker, ". . . the cost of capital is always the lowest cost of staying in business."[4] Using this rule of thumb, brokers should have been charging 15 to 17 percent commission instead of 4 to 6 percent of the selling price of the property. Ten years ago, who would have forecast that cost of capital would have zoomed upward as it did?

Each retail firm must anticipate future events which will generate changes in the social, economic, competitive and technological environments. Any firm which can accurately forecast the future has the opportunity to devise and implement appropriate strategies which may lead to the ultimate mission: survival.

Building a Successful Retail Business through Goal Accomplishment

The concept of goals is a powerful managerial tool. If an individual can identify some future state to attain, that person can focus his or her behavior to accomplish that desired goal. Note that goals imply that there is a significant gap between the individual's present state and some future desired state or condition. The same concept applies to retail organizations. Managerial decision makers can analyze their organization's present situation and then determine where the firm ought to be in five or ten years. This future state then becomes an objective or focal point for all organizational activities.

A retail firm might set out in 1983 to capture 35 percent of the market and increase the firm's return on its investment by 10 percent by 1986. These future quantifiable objectives permit all organizational members to know what the firm wants to achieve during the next three years. In order to achieve these objectives the retail decision makers must devise a strategic plan of action which will systematically link all elements of the firm into a goal achieving entity. Simply put, **strategic planning** is the process of positioning an organization so it can prosper and survive in the future.

Strategic Planning Process

The strategic planning process has been the subject of many articles and books describing different perceptions of this critical activity. After considerable research one can distill the essence of the process without becoming burdened by excessive vocabulary and minute detail. The process begins with a current assessment of organizational objectives, organizational performance,

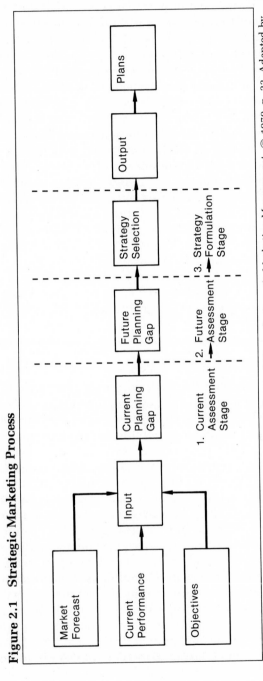

Figure 2.1   Strategic Marketing Process

Source: David J. Luck/O. C. Ferrell, *Marketing Strategy and Plans: Systematic Marketing Management*, © 1979, p. 23. Adapted by permission of Prentice-Hall, Inc., Englewood Cliffs, N.J.

and the retail firm's market position.[5] Both retail objectives and performance can be measured in terms of gross sales, sales per square foot, share of the market, return on investment, etc. Any significant differences between current performance and current objectives represent a current planning gap.[6]

Following this assessment, the retail planner must make a future assessment by forecasting future retail market potentials and critical environmental changes such as major changes in national or local economies, the nature and extent of retail competition, technological innovations which will impact on either the merchandising or operations policies, anticipated consumer behavior changes, etc. In light of these prognostications retail decision makers must set future objectives with intermediate goals to assure the retail firm's future survival through appropriate adaptation. The difference between the current situation and the future desired situation is known as the **future planning gap.**[7] This future planning gap is usually spanned by creating strategic growth based on the retail firm's internal marketing capabilities, perceived differential advantages, and available repertoire of strategic alternatives.[8]

Specific Strategic Growth Strategies

There are three basic corporate growth strategies which retailers may elect to adopt and implement. The first strategy, **retail concentration,** prescribes that the retailer should continue to concentrate on those activities which have led to past successes. For example, thousands of loyal customers have asked the L. L. Bean Company, the Maine outdoor outfitter, to establish retail stores in selected cities throughout the nation in addition to maintaining their highly successful retail mail order business. Considerable competitive pressure was exerted when one of the firm's major competitors, Eddie Bauer, opened retail stores in selected cities in the 1970s. However the company held to its original mail order concept and expanded its offerings all the while stressing value and service. Year after year the firm's sales have grown as well as their profitability. In fact the firm is doing so well that it is a constant target of takeover propositions from larger diversified organizations. Another outstanding example of the effective implementation of this type of growth strategy is the McDonald fast-food retailer who continues to lead all competition in the field.

Retail diversification, the second strategic growth strategy, can be accomplished by adopting different merchandising modes or by expanding into different product lines. Perhaps the most successful example of such action is Kresge's strategic move into discounting with their now famous K mart stores. The new K mart operation soon eclipsed the parent variety stores in sales performance and profitability. Now it is the accepted leader in retail discounting. It remains to be seen what new strategic decisions will be made by the firm as they exhaust profitable new locations near newly built suburban subdivisions. What will they do to match their meteoric performance of the past?

A third strategic growth strategy is based on **conglomeration.** The classic acquisition of the Dayton Department Store by the J. L. Hudson Company brought together the marketing and financial resources of two successful organizations which later permitted the new conglomerate, Dayton-Hudson Company, to launch their very successful Target and B. Dalton Book Store operations. Such conglomerate growth strategies will become the rule rather than the exception in the future as successful smaller retailers develop very attractive consumer offerings but lack access to adequate sources of capital to permit profitable growth. Each growth strategy may be appropriate, depending on the firm's identified objectives and the forecasted environmental situation.

Critical Elements in a Strategic Plan

Every successful strategic plan must include an accurate definition of a customer need, which requires satisfaction and a deliverable product or service which will satisfy that need (both will be discussed in detail later in the chapter).[9] However, in order to have deliverable goods and services, the retail firm must acquire the appropriate combination of financial resources, physical facilities, technology, equipment, time, talent, and market position. Once these elements are in place, the retailer must consider leverages.[10] **Leverages** or **strategic advantages** are specific incentives offered to the firm's customers to entice them to buy a given product or service from the firm instead of patronizing the competitors. Specifically, strategic advantages might include location, carrying an exclusive line of merchandise, epitomizing a particular popular lifestyle, or creation of a consistent customer perception as offering "value" at a popular price. Usually these strategic advantages are unique strengths which the firm deliberately cultivates over time.

Strategic Market Planning in Action

The classic retail example of strategic market planning was the confrontation of Sears Roebuck and Company and the Montgomery Ward Company. In 1945 retailers were aware of the fact that there was a 17-year demand for consumer goods waiting to be satisfied. This pent up demand had resulted, in part, from the consuming public's inability to afford goods during the Depression. After the Depression, all productive capacity which could be spared was devoted to making war material. All during the war, civilians were working long hours and saving their money because there were few nonrationed consumer goods available. The ideal combination of consumer need and the ability to buy came together after the war ceased.

Sears, under the leadership of Robert Woods, analyzed their position and forecast that the production transition from making war related goods to peacetime consumer products would be relatively brief and consumer goods would be available within a matter of months. In order to position themselves to take advantage of the anticipated situation, Sears borrowed every cent they could put their collective hands on and leased land, built new stores and expanded their merchandise offering as the goods became available. In contrast Montgomery Ward, under the leadership of Sewell Avery, assessed their situation and projected a major depression immediately after the war because they felt the national production facilities would not be able to adjust quickly to consumer goods production. Following this forecast, Avery converted every asset he could muster into cash so that Wards would be able to weather the forecasted depression and be able to come out of it with liquid assets to then build the organization. Subsequent historical events have vindicated Woods' forecast and choice of strategy. Even today while Sears positions itself to become America's retail financial institution of the 1990s, Montgomery Ward, now a subsidiary of Mobil Oil, continues to search for a competitive retail strategy which will assure their survival.

Another example is provided by the J. C. Penney Company's decision to establish their own credit system. James Cash Penney had built his retail empire of over 1700 stores based on the policy of "cash and carry." He strongly believed that extending credit to customers was doing them a disservice. In the late 1950s when Mr. Penney began to take a less active role in the firm, the professional executive team realized that the J. C. Penney Company had become the "King of the Softgoods." If the firm was to have any hope of growth in the future the company would have to expand its merchandise offerings to include appliances and automotive service and supply. Additionally, the management realized that Penney's was not only competing with Sears and Roebuck and Montgomery Ward, but in reality was in direct competition for the consumer's discretionary buying dollars with all retailers of goods and services. Once consumers had met basic needs for food, clothing, and shelter, they were free to purchase automobiles, boats, travel accommodations, stereos, etc. Thus, Penney's set out to create a strategy to increase its share of this pool of consumer buying power.

Early in their current assessment stage they realized that successful merchandising of hardgoods required extensive use of credit. One could not expect the prospective consumer to save for these large dollar purchases and pay cash or put them on "layaway." A viable credit program would also help with the firm's planned merchandise strategy of "upscaling" the quality of fashion merchandise which would bear higher prices and higher profit margins than had been found previously in the company's stores. No longer would Penney customer's buying power be limited to the cash in his or her pocket or handbag.

In 1958 the firm introduced its credit program in three test markets around the country. Every sale was concluded with the phrase, "May I have your Penney's Charge Card please?" If the answer was "I don't have one," the sales associate was supposed to give the customer a short sales presentation and a credit application. With this point of purchase effort and supportive advertising campaign the credit program was successfully launched. After two years of experimentation and system adjustment, credit was offered nationwide and the rest is history. While merchandising results from addition of hardlines have been mixed, the entire strategic move would not have been possible without first establishing a viable customer credit system so that the customer could implement his or her purchase decision.

Today exciting strategic positioning decisions are being made in all areas of retailing. Major department stores throughout the nation are searching for new strategies which will position them to take advantage of the changing lifestyles and purchase behavior of 1980s consumers. Firms are painfully aware that their downtown "flagship" stores cannot be expanded economically, yet their profitability needs continual improvement. After considerable analysis of each store's marketing capabilities, differential advantages, and changing consumer lifestyles, some firms have made the strategic decision to abandon their "Budget Basements." Such department stores as Maas Brothers in Tampa, Denver Dry Goods in Denver, Frederick & Nelson in Seattle and Stix, Baer & Fuller in St. Louis have converted their basements and left behind their "budget image."[11] According to Charles Moxley, senior vice president for sales promotion for Maas Brothers, "The proliferation of so many mass merchandisers killed the market for us, especially since budget was not our real strength. We were getting better return on investment with our main floor merchandise. We have moved with the times, and customers' desires, into designer name goods."[12]

Echoing the same sentiment, Robert Snyder, divisional merchandise manager for Denver Dry Goods, noted, "We are after fashion and quality, and the budget department is not in keeping with the image of the store."[13] As a result of this strategic decision, Denver Dry Goods has leased 15,000 square feet to Gart Brothers Sporting Goods Company and remodeled the other half of the vacated area into boutique shops which include stationery, books, luggage, a florist, post office, and Datatix, a ticket distributor.[14]

Other major department stores see the future differently. The May Company in Los Angeles, Dayton's in Saint Paul, Gimbels in Milwaukee, and J. L. Hudson in Detroit are actively pursuing profits in basement areas selling budget merchandise. Dennis Jurcak, vice president and general merchandise manager for May of California, reported they are "Bullish on Budget." He continued, "It does a lot of volume—high volume—and it's very profitable. Furthermore, we're the only budget department store in L.A."[15] Les Dietzman, vice president and general merchandise manager for J. L. Hudson, said, "We are a broad-based department store appealing to a broad segment of customers who shop upstairs and downstairs. But the bottom line is it produces a profit for the company."[16] These are just a few examples of different strategic plans of various companies attempting to position themselves in different markets to take advantage of future consumer markets.

Strategic Fundamentalism

Even detailed self-examination by retailers may not be enough to meet the challenges ahead.[17] Such fine tuning as incorporation of home improvement centers or diversification into catalog showrooms are, at best, short-term remedies. What is needed is a fundamental reconsideration of the target market to be served by retail firms. How can this be done profitably in light of shorter retail life cycles with less investment in construction, fixturing, and merchandise inventory, and with fewer employees? Perhaps warehouse retailing is a partial answer. Physically, facilities can be built quickly, at low cost, usually with exposed beam rafters rather than ceilings, bare cinder block walls, rough wood interiors that suggest a degree of temporariness. A true warehouse outlet is characterized by:

1. Large, low-cost physical facilities—a store size that is several times that of conventional outlets and built economically
2. Warehouse operations—the use of low-cost warehouse operating techniques

3. Warehouse merchandising—displaying merchandise in a vertical rather than horizontal format, and utilizing warehouse fixturing

4. Large, narrow inventory—maintaining a rather substantial inventory to satisfy large sales volume levels, but carrying only the leading items

5. Service reduction—a total elimination of every nonessential customer service

6. Price appeal—a reliance on price as a major consumer variable[18]

The most popular example of this type of operation is the food warehouse. Goods are stacked on the floor in original cases, prices marked by customers using an ordinary grease pencil, and purchases sacked by individual customers in self-provided boxes and reused cloth or paper bags. Usually these outlets are located in recycled buildings near shopping centers and trade lower prices for lack of convenience.

An alternative to warehouse retailing is the wider adoption of "rationalized retailing."[19] Simply stated, this approach relies on highly centralized management control and strict operating procedures that leave no detail to chance. Perhaps the most familiar example is Tandy's Radio Shack operation. Every store carries exactly the same assortment displayed on identical racks or wall fixtures in the same general location in each store. Such standardization permitted the firm to remain profitable under adverse conditions.

Retailers' Traditionalism

Established retail institutions sometimes resist any change that might better meet the needs of the consumer if the changes also threaten a loss of patronage to their establishments. One might call such retailers "protectionists" or "micro-oriented merchandisers." Philosophically, the average retailer takes the present retail system as a given and attempts to fine-tune the system by maximizing internal efficiencies. However, such preoccupation with detail encourages nonretailers to innovate and carve out new structural niches for themselves. For example, why did the low-price restaurants not recognize and respond to the need for fast-service, limited-menu outlets? They were too busy serving food and competing with each other. Such conservative traditionalism serves as an invitation for the development of new forms of institutional competition by nontraditional retail-oriented enterprises.

Environmental Factors

Much speculation has been advanced as to why and how retail institutions either fail or adapt and survive. The concept of **natural selection,** or survival of the fittest, maintains that the retail institution that most effectively adapts to its environment is the one most likely to survive and grow. A firm must be able to adjust to changes in technology, competition, consumer demographics, economic conditions, and social and cultural attitudes on relatively short notice if it is going to survive in the competitive business world. Retail organizations must be flexible enough to make needed responses quickly.

The **wheel of retailing,** or life cycle, concept explains the evolution of retail institutions. The basic premise, developed by Professor Malcolm P. McNair, is that a new retail institution first appears with low-margin, low-price, and minimum-service offerings. As time passes, these establishments add more service and upgrade their facilities and offerings. These changes require higher margins and higher prices. The process continues until these firms eventually become high-cost, high-price retailers that are therefore vulnerable to the next innovator.

An **accordion theory** is frequently used by retailers to explain fluctuations in merchandise assortments. This theory describes the tendency for retail business to become dominated (in an alternating pattern) first by general stores, then by specialty stores, and again by general stores. This concept suggests that merchandise balance is yet another element that influences retail institutional change. A new institution would probably begin as a specialty store because of limited capital and managerial knowledge. Gradually, as it became more successful, it would tend to expand offerings until it eventually became a general store.

A common thread runs through these three explanations—inappropriate cost management. In each case, a new institution is launched with a limited selection that is deliberately chosen for a specific customer group that purchases on the basis of price. It is located in a simple facility, which results in lower overhead costs. Combined, all these factors permit the new retailer to offer relatively low-price products and services. If the firm is successful, it is emulated by other competitors, each trying to win a share of the relevant market segment.

If one assumes that for all practical purposes prices cannot be significantly lowered, then the emulators practice one-upmanship by adding "free services," broader assortments, credit, and even trading stamps to hold or increase their share of the market. As the services become institutionalized by this steady, incremental, spiral process, the affected retail institutions become "fat," traditional, and generally locked into a higher cost level of operation due to consumer expectations. In the mean-

Table 2.1 Management Activities in the Life Cycle

Subject of Concern	Stage of Life Cycle Development			
	1. Innovation	2. Accelerated Development	3. Maturity	4. Decline
Market Characteristics				
Number of competitors	Very few	Moderate	Many direct competitors Moderate indirect competition	Moderate direct competition Many indirect competitors
Rate of sales growth	Very rapid	Rapid	Moderate to slow	Slow or negative
Level of profitability	Low to moderate	High	Moderate	Very low
Duration of new innovations	3 to 5 years	5 to 6 years	Indefinite	Indefinite
Appropriate Retailer Actions				
Investment/growth/risk decisions	Investment minimization— high risks accepted	High levels of investment to sustain growth	Tightly controlled growth in untapped markets	Minimal capital expenditures and only when essential
Central management concerns	Concept refinement through adjustment and experimentation	Establishing a preemptive market position	Excess capacity and "overstoring" Prolonging maturity and revising the retail concept	Engaging in a "run-out" strategy
Use of management control techniques	Minimal	Moderate	Extensive	Moderate
Most successful management style	Entrepreneurial	Centralized	"Professional"	Caretaker
Appropriate Supplier Actions				
Channel strategy	Develop a preemptive market position	Hold market position	Maintain profitable sales	Avoid excessive costs
Channel problems	Possible antagonism of other accounts	Possible antagonism of other accounts	Dealing with more scientific retailers	Servicing accounts at a profit
Channel research	Identification of key innovations	Identification of other retailers adopting the innovation	Initial screening of new innovation opportunities	Active search for new innovation opportunities
Trade incentives	Direct financial support	Price concessions	New price incentives	None

Source: Reprinted by permission of the *Harvard Business Review*. Exhibit from "The Retail Life Cycle" by William R. Davidson, Albert D. Bates and Stephen J. Bass (November/December 1976): 92. Copyright © 1976 by the President and Fellows of Harvard College; all rights reserved.

time, prices have been gradually and selectively raised—and are usually publicly justified on the basis of increased manufacturing costs—until the very thing that gave the institution its start, low price, has been lost.

Astute marketers detect periodic consumer dissatisfaction with relatively high prices, particularly during periods of significant recession or inflation. They rush in with the original low-price concept, and the cycle repeats itself.

Some retailers justify adding frills by saying that as their target market's income is increased, they must trade up or lose the market, because the consumers want to shed their "poor" image and buy products and services that carry more status. This may be an appropriate strategy for some merchandise, but it has been overused.

The **retail life cycle** theory represents an attempt to apply the product life cycle concept to the evolutionary changes that retail firms seem to exhibit.[20] The classic terms **innovation, accelerated development, maturity,** and **decline** are applied to identify specific unique stages that retail firms usually encounter. The most useful application of this concept is found in Table 2.1, where the terms suggest appropriate management activities for each stage of life cycle development. As the text explores these managerial concerns in more detail in later chapters, one should refer back to this set of recommendations for further information and validation.

The life cycle of certain retail institutions provides evidence that retail institution life cycles are becoming significantly shorter. Thus, there should be considerable managerial attention devoted to staying flexible, to analyzing risks and profits, particularly the idea of utilizing second-use space for new retail ventures, to extending the maturity stage by attracting new market segments while retaining existing customers, and to emphasizing ongoing research.[21] Even though the future retail environment may become more turbulent, adoption of these suggestions may mean the difference between survival and failure.

The Marketing Concept's Contribution to Retail Marketing Strategy

A brief review of economic history reveals that prior to the late 1950s the nation was operating on a limited production base which caused a scarcity of consumer goods; that is, not enough goods and services were produced at low enough prices for mass consumption and mass consumer satisfaction. Particularly during the depression years of the 1930s, when there were few jobs and little money to buy available goods, people were concerned with meeting their basic needs for food, clothing, and shelter. Some economic historians claim this was a period of surplus, but to the family without work it was a time of scarcity and economic hardship.

The period from 1946 to 1948 was marked by national emergency labor disputes and a transition from a wartime economy to a peacetime consumer oriented production effort. As consumer goods began to flow into the marketplace, liquid assets of the nation became available, and prices for scarce goods were bid higher. Just as supply began to catch up with pent-up demand, the Korean conflict again thrust the nation into a partial war effort, and consumer goods again became scarce. However, by the late 1950s the nation's manufacturing and distribution system satisfied consumer demand, and a subtle but profound change occurred in the nation's economic system. Manufacturers and marketers alike needed a new method of tapping the relative affluence of the consumers. A new, more appropriate concern for individual consumers was required to encourage consumption. The **marketing concept** was formulated to meet this challenge.

The essence of this change in thinking is expressed in the definition of **marketing** as "the performance of business activities which direct the flow of goods and services from producer to consumer or user in order to satisfy customers and accomplish the company's objectives.[22] Instead of centering all the firm's efforts on inventing, producing, and selling a generalized product, the emphasis shifted to determining consumer needs and wants. Using these findings, the firm can then attempt to develop, produce, and make available the best product or service to meet perceived consumer needs.

When a firm adopts this philosophy, "the consumer is king." All company efforts are focused on having the right product at the right place, at the right time, at the right price, and in the right quantity to capture the consumer's dollars—profitably.

How does the marketing concept facilitate formation of a retailer's marketing strategy? Implementation of the marketing concept is based on three major concerns: genuine consumer orientation, an integrated marketing approach, and generation of customer satisfaction.[23]

Consumer orientation is implemented by the retail firm's (1) adopting a definition of the basic needs that it intends to serve, (2) identifying the target group(s) of customers it wants to serve, and (3) meeting the varying needs of its target group(s) by using a differentiated product/service offering.

Each person is unique. Each human being expresses his or her individuality through decisions ranging from clothing to cars and houses to hair style. This desire for personal uniqueness is moderated by the social desire to be liked and accepted by peers. Teenagers are particularly conscious of the conflicting need to be independent yet also conforming to peer group values and behavior. This sorting process continues throughout one's lifetime in the form of education, job choice, and evolving lifestyle decisions.

As individuals choose to be like others they form groups with specific aggregate needs which are identifiable through application of appropriate market research techniques. The critical question is, "Which groups exhibiting what needs does the retail firm want to attempt to satisfy?" Typically, specific socioeconomic groups of a certain age range, earning a given amount, living in a particular geographical location are singled out for study to determine their needs and current levels of satisfaction. Any significant gap between need and satisfaction levels presents a potential retail opportunity.

Once consumer analysis has identified specific retail opportunities, the firm, as noted earlier, must examine its relative comparative advantage over other retail competitors to determine which specific set of consumer need opportunities present the most potentially rewarding challenge. What special attributes of knowledge, skill, experience, resources, and technology can the firm bring to bear in these situations which will result in greater consumer satisfaction and an acceptable profit level for the retail firm? In a proprietorship these qualities may be embodied in one person directing others; or it may be a large corporate retail giant such as K mart with multiple divisions and departments combining and coordinating thousands of employees across the nation to give their customers the best value for their money. Regardless of size, each retail employee must realize that their actions will affect the company's ability to attract and retain customers. In practicing **integrated marketing** the retail organization's entire effort must be coordinated to build a strong, positive, consistent image of consumer satisfaction in the minds of its customers.

An alternate method of identifying potential retail opportunities is to do a macroeconomic analysis (Figure 2.2). The analysis might begin with an investigation of the projected Gross National Product, which is published by the government and includes all products, goods, and services produced in the nation.

Secondly, an industry analysis, in this case the retail industry, might be undertaken to determine the size of the market and the extent and quality of services offered by industries competing for

Figure 2.2   Assessing a Marketing Opportunity

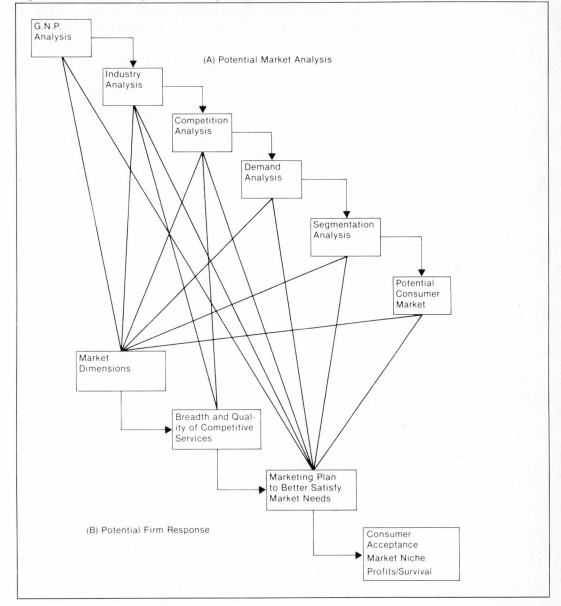

the consumer's discretionary income and to identify marketing opportunities for unmet consumer needs. Additional information can be gained by executing a competition and demand analysis. If additional information from these research efforts validates the previously identified market opportunity, the retail firm must conduct a segmentation analysis to determine whether the group is large enough to make it profitable to develop and implement a retail offering. (A detailed discussion of these analytical processes will be found in later chapters.)

The third major concern of the marketing concept involves recognition that the firm's long-run welfare is dependent upon the amount of customer satisfaction it is able to provide. A firm's sales force can periodically report relevant customer comments on the performance of the firm and its product/service offerings. Sales personnel are helpful in supplementing research efforts to analyze consumer repeat purchase patterns, attitudes toward merchandise selection, store image, and other measures of customer satisfaction.

The firm can also conduct in-depth studies to analyze consumer repeat purchase patterns and to obtain other measures of consumer satisfaction. The spirit of appropriate customer concern seems to be captured by the following:

The Customers

A Customer is the most important person in any business.

A Customer is not dependent on us. We are dependent on him.

A Customer is a part of our business—not an outsider.

A Customer is not just a statistic. He is a flesh-and-blood human being with feelings and emotions, like ourselves.

A Customer does us a favor when he comes in. We are not doing him a favor by serving him.

A Customer is deserving of the most courteous and attentive treatment we can give him.

A Customer is the life-blood of this and every other business. Without him we would have to close our doors. Don't ever forget it.[24]

Developing a Retail Marketing Strategy

Once the retail firm accepts the need for a marketing orientation, the next step is to consider development of a competitive retail marketing strategy.[25] Formation of a retail strategy consists of (1) identification of target markets and their needs and (2) formulation of a retailing mix that satisfies the needs of the target market.[26]

**Target Market:
Appropriate
Consumer with
Buying Power**

A retailer's most fundamental task is to identify and satisfy a profitable **target market** (group of consumers that the retailer is trying to satisfy). The effective retailer concentrates on satisfying a profitable set of needs held in common by a certain group of consumers within reasonable geographic proximity and does not try to be "all things to all people." For a hardware store this usually means that its relevant market lies within a circle with a radius that represents fifteen minutes driving time to the store. The distance will vary with the type of merchandise carried by the store, other competition, and other factors.

Consumers with unmet needs do not automatically become a profitable target market. For many years retailers have concentrated on that segment of the consuming public which has been young, affluent, status-conscious, and who purchased the most goods and services in the economy. Vast segments of the consuming public have been overlooked, such as black consumers, "gray" consumers, and the single parent consumer. Each of these segments has needs which have been only marginally met. Travel agents have discovered that the "gray" consumer market is a profitable market when courted with special travel packages during off-season periods.

Success lies in being more perceptive about what consumers want than the competition, and then providing those goods and services at the right time, at the right place, at the right price, in the right assortment, in an attractive, pleasing environment so that consumers will become profitable customers. The wants and needs of any chosen target market will be constantly changing, and the retailers who correctly anticipate these changes will be successful in the short run and survive in the long run. Therefore, the retailer should concentrate on identifying consumers who have similar needs as well as the economic ability (money and credit) to purchase need—satisfying goods or services. Thus, the retailer's target market is defined as a specific group of qualified buyers with inadequately satisfied needs.

**Market
Segmentation:
Characteristics of
Qualified Buyers**

Market segmentation is the practice of dividing the population into subgroups or segments on the basis of demographic characteristics of sex, age, marital status, gross income, geographical location, or some combination of these variables. Stanley J. Goodman, the National Retail Merchants Association's 1981 Gold Medal Award winner and retired head of The May Department Stores Company, has noted, ". . . Marketing segmentation is the key strategy of the future. I see an acceleration of the shakeout of merchants who lack precision. The merchant who has the clearest picture of his customer has the best chance of growing in the future."[27] As a consultant, Goodman advocates what he calls "people merchandising," which is the concept of analyzing changing customer demographics, lifestyle, and profiles and stresses the need of increasing segmentation into more specific narrower and smaller groups with specialized interests. Howard Eilenberg, senior vice-president for research, Frederick Atkins, agrees, noting that ". . . subsegmentation will become increasingly refined. The New York buying office is developing ethnic-oriented market research to refine and better meet the specific needs of some of our customers."[28]

Subsegmentation might be applied to the gray market as a potential new client group for travel experiences. Rather than use a generalized approach to classify senior citizen travel needs, a specific travel agency in Chicago might design a particular travel package to appeal to "romantic" couples who might like to take the "second honeymoon" trip which they previously did not have the time or money to enjoy.

By zeroing in on a specific target market (gray market) and segmenting the population into ethnic groups, one is able to offer a special package of need-satisfying experiences by providing an attractive way to relive treasured memories of earlier times. This same approach to retail market segmentation can be applied in any retailing situation to more precisely define characteristics of consumers the firm plans to appropriately service.

Product Differentiation: A Unique Total Offering

Product differentiation is an image-creation process whereby a product or service that is similar to other products or services is emphasized in the consumer's mind. Often retailers lose sight of the fact that products alone do not yield customer satisfaction, and that products or services are means to an end. The consumer's mere possession of a product does not accomplish any goal in and of itself. The perceived usefulness that the product or service will provide in the hands of the owner is the reason the customer wants to acquire it. The retail firm must remember that its ultimate goal is customer need satisfaction, not just the sale of goods or services.

Such need satisfaction may be achieved in three ways. First, the product or service may, in the act of being consumed, serve some physical need, such as hot coffee on a cold day. Second, the possession or use of a product or service may serve to meet psychological needs—for example, a visit to a beauty salon may result in a new fashion hair style for that "special" occasion.

Last, a combination of physical and psychological needs may

be met by the acquisition and use of products or services—
perhaps a Honda Accord LX for a couple in suburban Chicago. In
each case the retailer sold a physical product/service, but in reality also sold human need satisfaction.

Consumer satisfaction is affected by the concept of relative
value derived over time. A consumer who has made a sizeable
investment will be especially sensitive to any indications that
the investment will or will not prove satisfying over a long period of time. The product may perform perfectly and reliably but
yet not be perceived by the purchaser as meeting his or her
needs. As a result, postpurchase dissatisfaction will be felt. For
example, it is quite common for automobile purchasers to search
for postpurchase support for their decision to buy a certain car.
Often the complaints that are made during the immediate warranty period (ninety days) include "rattles in the dash," "poor
mileage," and other general nonspecific dissatisfactions which
may reflect psychological dissatisfaction. The quality of followup service received during this postpurchase period is critical to
long term, repeat business, word-of-mouth advertising, and ultimately to the firm's survival.

Branding may play a large part in a product's success and
hence affect the retailer's degree of success. Branding becomes
particularly important to retailers when national producers develop consumer confidence in their branded product to the point
that a significant segment of the population will not accept a
substitute. Such customer loyalty is often associated with products that are distributed through exclusive dealerships. For many
years, the California Packing Company built and maintained
such a strong reputation for quality that the retailer was able to
charge premium prices for Del Monte foods. More recently, Cal-
vin Klein has been successful in associating his label with quality merchandise. Any apparel store is assured of added prestige
and profitable sales from customers who recognize and appreciate quality merchandise. Thus, whenever consumers cannot
determine value/price/quality comparisons readily by inspection,
branding may become a valuable part of product satisfaction for
them.

In addition to the physical aspects of products, the retailer can
differentiate the firm's product assortment for the chosen target
market by varying the amount, kind, and quality of supporting
services provided. Such services may include installation of
major appliances, education in the use of certain products (such
as microwave ovens), repair of products, delivery of goods
(either free or for a minimum charge), gift wrapping, clothing
alterations, return of merchandise privileges, and credit. Each of
these services may enhance the attractiveness of a product or the

patronage of an establishment because the combined product package provides better customer need satisfaction. Every added service cost must be covered by higher gross margins, be recoverable in increased volume at normal markups on the products, or as a last resort, be paid by direct charge. Accurate retailer perception of the target market's needs will determine the composition of the total product the firm can attempt to provide profitably.

Product differentiation may be achieved by artfully blending the four marketing variables of product, place, price, and promotion into a **retail marketing mix.** Each of these variables can be combined in an almost infinite number of sets to generate a wide range of consumer need-satisfying products and services. The question for the retailer is how to combine these variables into a unique dynamic package to meet the needs of the chosen target market better than any other current and potential competitor.

Product/Service Offering: A Means to Consumer Satisfaction

The selection of product/service assortments to offer the consumer represents the toughest and least-well-performed function in retailing. Retailers generally identify a target market, then search out the various goods being produced and purchase items that they feel will appeal to their customers. Generalizations are always dangerous, but frequently small retailers go to merchandise shows or markets semiannually and make buying decisions based solely on past personal experience and some vague rough summary of sales records.

Through a combination of economies of scale, large concentrations of capital, and intensive and extensive consumer research through advertising agencies, producers or manufacturers more or less dictate what products will be available in the retail marketplace. Retailing—the very institution that deals most directly with the consumer—has generally performed the preproduction consumer information-gathering and product-shaping functions very poorly. With some marked exceptions, many retailers view their role in product management as determining the location and arrangement of goods that are demanded by their patrons who have been presold by mass media techniques.

What product variables can be used to tailor products to a target market's need satisfaction? The physical product can vary in quality or workmanship, type and quality of materials used, or design and manufacture.

The concept of multiple usage seems to be assuming more importance in the products sold in retail markets today, particularly appliances. More and more radios, stereos, and television sets are being produced that use conventional alternating current or that may be powered by batteries. Small imported cars made by Toyota, Datsun, and Volkswagen Jetta are being purchased for multiple uses such as commuting and as general-purpose runabouts.

Similarly, products are being produced that have broad product adaptability to individual requirements. Such items as pocket calculators perform mathematical functions, calculate biorhythms, and provide the user with day, date, and time. Thus, a single product (calculators), based on micro-chip circuitry, serves a range of consumer needs.

Another aspect of product determination that may often be overlooked is the package in which a product is presented to the customer. With heavy emphasis on preselling merchandise by mass media and with self-service facilities, the package becomes the point-of-purchase sales agent. Some years ago a major manufacturer of breakfast food introduced individual servings in a liquid-tight container. All the user had to do was cut along the perforated lines and add milk for an instant breakfast. Kodak has attempted to increase its film sales by attaching rack hanging cards to its standard film boxes and distributing the film in every convenience, grocery, and discount store across the country. Long ago cosmetic manufacturers discovered the power of packaging in their merchandising efforts.

A package may enhance or encourage appropriate use of a product. For example, birth control pill prescriptions were delayed until a suitable package was perfected that would assist in maintaining daily usage of the product. A whole range of products has been introduced into mass markets since the widespread adoption of "plastic bubble" packaging. Such packaging not only protects merchandise but also permits the potential user to see the product without opening or destroying the package.

Another aspect of packaging is providing the appropriate quantity for convenience of purchase and consumption. For example, Coors Brewing Company spent considerable sums of money on research to determine the average beer consumption by women at one sitting. The results indicated that women prefer smaller quantities at one sitting than men. Coors developed a 7-ounce aluminum can for the female market, and subsequently has enjoyed great success in tapping that market.

Similar decisions made by manufacturers of hundreds of items have allowed retailers to better satisfy consumer preferences. As a result, more pressure is placed on stores to offer a greater assortment of different quantities of goods. If the retailers agree, they encounter shelf-space limitations that may force them to reduce their merchandise assortment or ultimately move to a larger facility. This is just one example of the interrelatedness of variables in the marketing mix. Just one small change in a basic decision has its effect throughout the operation.

Proper Product Placement: Location

The one market variable that cannot be duplicated is place. Only one store can occupy a prescribed space at a given time. Department and chain stores such as the Jane Jefferson division of Montgomery Ward and Company have found that previously occupied locations in established shopping centers provide a cheaper and quicker way to enter a new market than building from the ground up in new shopping center locations. While there are physical limitations, these vacant store sites can be acquired at lower lease costs and remodeled for less than paying current new construction costs. Some firms who have been unsuccessful as retailers in certain locations have found that their lease on that location is a valuable asset that can be sold for a tidy profit to another retailer who can make better use of the property. One should not be led to think that the location variable is *the* most important market variable, but its value should not be overlooked.

For all practical purposes, the place variable can be thought of as yielding convenience satisfaction for the customer. Degree of convenience is closely related to the type of product(s) currently needed by the customer to meet perceived wants. Entire retail businesses, such as the 7–11 Stores, have been based on merchandising a limited assortment of convenience merchandise in high-population densities and operating from 7 a.m. to 11 p.m. daily. The specific location of a retail establishment has been the subject of considerable research, and will be discussed at length in Chapters 6 and 7.

Store location is doubly important now, when greater consumer attention is being directed toward rising transportation costs and the constant threat of petroleum shortages. Some futurists predict a complete change of the American lifestyle, which until now has been based on a high degree of mobility. At the moment, however, despite repeated efforts to lure the population to use mass transit systems, people refuse to give up their cars. It appears that the smaller, more fuel efficient automobile will continue to provide a vital link between the consumer and the retailer for the foreseeable future.

The automobile can be a curse to a retailer if too many are driven on poorly designed highway systems, with resulting serious traffic jams and poor store access. Thus, it is important for any shopping center to have adequate entries and exits available to and from a spacious, amply lighted parking lot. This will encourage customers to shop in the center, thereby potentially increasing customer density or "traffic" for most resident stores.

With increased pressure on people to become involved in more activities, both business and leisure, time has become a scarce commodity and convenience a necessity. Therefore, retail chains have followed migrating population to the suburbs to be near their market and to minimize customer travel and shopping time. In well-designed shopping centers such major stores have generated customer traffic that has given the small retailer opportunities to capture impulse buyers. New shopping centers in prosperous subdivisions do not spell instant success for all retailers, but they do increase the concentration of consumers with wants to be met.

Recent Federal Trade Commission hearings and related court cases have brought to light the fact that some large department or chain stores, usually referred to as "anchor stores," have in the past attempted to dictate the terms and conditions of the competition they would allow in a specific shopping center. Such action has been declared illegal under the terms of the Clayton Act. Additionally, large retail chains can be prevented from purchasing other retail outlets that sell similar merchandise in the same geographical area if such action is interpreted as an intention to reduce competition significantly. This restriction has been particularly important in the grocery industry over the last half century.

Place considerations should not be limited just to external or geographic alternatives. Interior design, or store layout, constitutes a vital consideration in conducting the ongoing business of the retail firm. A potential retail lessee may be offered a location in a shopping center that is quite attractive in terms of pedestrian traffic density but may find the interior space is unsuitable for the purpose. One national chain store accepted an anchor position at one end of a medium-size shopping center only to find that there was no way of utilizing the irregularly shaped space. Departmental isolation and poor traffic circulation resulted in substantially lower sales than had been projected on the basis of target market characteristics.

Another interior layout problem may result from critical placement of supporting structural members or columns. Recent developments in cantilever roof construction in new shopping centers have alleviated this problem to some degree, but the potential store lessee should still consider the usability of the space being offered.

Customer needs are relatively infinite, and customers are constantly searching for new modes of need satisfaction. Thus, they shop "where the action is" or "where things are happening." Innovative retailers should periodically consider interior store rearrangement as well as frequent changes of merchandise displays to create customer interest. Store layout will be explored in depth in Chapter 8, but it is important to note that the placement of a department's merchandise and its systematic rearrangement can serve a vital function in generating customer interest. Such changes also serve an important supporting role in an effective interior promotion program.

Channels of Distribution: Tapping Differing Target Markets

Many firms use different brand names on identical products to reach different target markets. General Motors has done this for years in their automobile production and sales. Evinrude and Johnson outboard motors are made by the same firm but have different suggested retail prices and different advertising appeals. McCulloch® chain saws are physically similar to Montgomery Ward chain saws, yet similar models sell at different prices through different channels with differing levels of supporting services such as parts availability. McCulloch® goes through wholesalers and retailers, while the Ward product is distributed direct from the manufacturer to the retail store or mail order desk.

The above examples demonstrate that distribution through differing channels can create a unique product. Services provided by channel members can transform similar physical products into different, distinct products in the marketplace. Customer service, credit, return privileges, and convenient location of an outlet can make one product more attractive than another when viewed in the light of the total product concept.

Price: Relative Value

Most consumers are concerned with one question when it comes to price: "How much does it cost?" The usual clerical reply is some dollar figure, which doesn't answer the full implication of the question. What the consumer is actually requesting is information to make a comparative decision. The complex question in the mind of the consumer is, "Are the benefits promised by this product or service worth the expenditure relative to other possible purchase or savings choices?" Actual total cost in dollar terms is not generally considered in isolation, as the original question would imply. The price question is just the top of a complex economic iceberg.

At this introductory point it would seem appropriate for students of retailing to note that the price variable is the least effective long-term competitive tool of the four Ps (product, place, price, promotion) available to the marketer. Any retailer can buy merchandise and "give it away" by reducing the price below that of the competition. Additionally, any competitor can duplicate any other competitor's price policy in the short run to attract or hold patronage. All across the country in every major metropolitan market one can turn on the television and hear automobile ads which say, ". . . We will not be undersold. Bring in any advertised price for the same model and we will meet or beat it or give you $100 cash on the spot. Now how can you beat a deal like that? . . ." Here the audience is told that the asking price is irrelevant. Other variables, such as large selection and friendly service, should be the deciding criteria for buying a new car through this agency.

Another example of price competition is demonstrated by grocers across America when they run their weekly ads in an attempt to attract a larger share of the consumer's food purchases. Does "everyday low, low prices" generate store loyalty? Most research seems to indicate that such pricing strategies are only effective in the short term with little residual patronage effect if prices do not remain competitive.

The classic presentation of price determination is usually based on such concepts of supply and demand. Retailers will supply goods and services only as long as they can recover their costs and make an acceptable return on their investment of time and money. This was graphically demonstrated during the late stages of Phase III wage and price controls in 1973. If producers and retailers could not raise prices to obtain an acceptable profit, they quit making the product and scarcities resulted. Similarly, consumers will buy goods and services only when they have resources (money and credit) and are willing to trade their scarce resources for goods and services that provide greater need satisfaction than investing for a high rate of return.

In summary, price is a very relative concept that helps consumers establish their priorities and levels of acceptable need satisfaction. Many different price strategies are available to retailers, but ultimately they must decide which strategy best fits their firm's image and its ability to best meet the needs of the target market.

Promotion: Providing Market Knowledge

Promotion is an all-encompassing term for ways of telling consumers what products and services are being offered to meet their needs. In addition, promotions may inform consumers of related product attributes, prices, and locations of goods and services, and may attempt to persuade them to take purchase action. The promotion process is perhaps the most researched and yet least understoood aspect of marketing.

Certain aspects of promotion, particularly advertising, have been—and are—under attack for creating or uncovering latent consumer needs that lead to wasteful uses of the nation's resources. Conversely, without advertising and other promotional processes consumers would not be aware of need-satisfying products unless they undertook a personal search of retail establishments. Most consumers have neither the time nor inclination for such activities. Complete discussions of the social benefits and liabilities of promotion can be found elsewhere; the task here is to discuss promotion as a retailing competitive strategy.

Retailers can implement the promotional process in a variety of ways, but it is helpful to separate promotional efforts into two classes. The first category contains those communicative efforts that are directed at a broad general class or target market by impersonal means through such mass media as magazines, newspapers, radio, television, billboards, car cards, handbills or circulars, point-of-purchase displays, window displays, and the like. A second type, personal promotional effort, is directed toward the individual, as with personal selling in a store, via telephone, door-to-door, or by in-home presentations by appointment (encyclopedia collections).

Regardless of the type or combination of types of promotion a retailer may choose, it is vitally important that the firm use a "rifle" instead of a "shotgun" approach to get the most effective return on its promotional investment. One is best advised to focus on the promotional tasks to be performed, establish priorities for each task, select the most appropriate promotional tool, allocate adequate funds to do the job, and then implement the plan. A follow-through evaluation will help determine the effectiveness of the firm's promotional strategy. Retailers can learn from past mistakes by keeping a daily diary of their promotional efforts and those of competitors. They might even keep an annual scrapbook of advertisements (both the firm's and those of its relevant competition), and perform a sales analysis correlating promotional efforts and gross sales. Admittedly, one cannot say with absolute assurance that an advertisement resulted in X dollars of sales, but some inferences may be made and insights gained about future promotional efforts.

It is important here to point out the connections between the promotional tools. Retail advertising should be focused on generating traffic. This can be accomplished by providing information on seasonal, consumer-wanted products or by reducing prices on regular merchandise for limited periods. Other useful promotional techniques include the purchase of special merchandise to sell at a "lower price" or using "give away" contests or drawings for prizes or cash. The essential point of retail promotions is to get people to frequent the establishment so that they may be exposed to merchandise the retailer has acquired for their need satisfactions. Additionally, sales personnel are given an opportunity to encourage, persuade, and convince potential customers that the firm's products best meet their needs. It should be noted that retail mass media promotions are aimed not only at retaining present patrons but also at attracting new customers. This latter function is particularly important when the selected target market includes young adults who display high geographic-economic mobility and a propensity to adopt new lifestyles.

Personal promotion in retailing is primarily limited to big ticket or high profit-margin items that require personal instruction, persuasion, or advice. Unfortunately, the "salesman" stereotype is not held in high regard by the general public because of past unpleasant experiences. Paradoxically, retail salespersons are both the lowest and the highest paid employees in business. Many retail clerks earn minimum hourly wages, while life insurance salespersons make tens of thousands of dollars per year. The retail firm must decide, in light of its target market's need characteristics, what balance of mass media and personal selling will best inform and motivate its potential clientele to patronize its establishment.

Strategic Positioning in Retailing

As the retail mix is implemented the retail store will acquire a certain image in the minds of the consuming public. Current and potential customers will consider patronizing those stores which are perceived to best meet their needs. Store patronage is the key to building unit volume and a profitable business.[29] Every major retail firm is currently reevaluating its customer and store characteristics to determine what should be changed in the 1980s.

According to Shirley Young, executive vice-president, marketing planning and strategy development, Grey Advertising, Inc., ". . . What is important for stores to understand is that their customers of the 1980s are formulating a new definition of 'value,' based on two factors: A greater concern with quality not just low price; and increasing importance attached to self-expression and personalization, demonstrated by their interests in intangible attributes beyond pure function." Successful product examples include designer jeans and fragrances. She continues, "The effect of this changing perception of value is that retailers must find new ways to add 'value' to their stores as a means to draw customers."[30] She concludes that the key factor that will spell success in the 1980s is the impression of the store that lives on in the mind and heart of the store's customers.

With this challenge, each major retail organization is trying to strategically position itself in the right markets in the right locations with the right merchandise and services with the right image to capture the major share of the retail business. If successful the store will be viewed as "the store" to shop for merchandise which is just right for the desired lifestyle. Bloomingdales has been singularly successful in its efforts to create such an image in the metropolitan New York City area for the last seven years.

A retail store may compete on the basis of its unique combination of location, store layout, organization, promotion, pricing, service, merchandise assortment, and buying. In so doing, it creates its own retailing mix.[31] Integrated decisions reached in each competitive area will collectively create the store image in the minds of the customers. Consumers consider patronizing that establishment which appears to be capable of most completely satisfying their needs. If the firm has anticipated the needs of the consumer in the past, a patronage motive or connective link has been made for associating need satisfaction with that particular store. Thus, an appropriate retail marketing mix creates a retail personality that will generate seller-buyer trust, loyalty, and good will.

In order to anticipate the target market's collective needs, a retail firm must engage in market planning and research. Each firm must segment its market and focus its efforts on a profitable but limited target market. However, even within this target market it may discover varying degrees of heterogeneity among its potential customers. While the major attribute of the target market will be its degree of common needs, selected individuals will have unique needs that the retail firm cannot afford to meet.

For example, suppose a woman's retail clothing boutique finds that it has two potential customers out of twenty possible customers that require a size 20 dress. The source supplies these dresses in a selected grouping and prices them by the dozen, with each dress retailing for $130. Should the boutique attempt to meet such customer needs? The answer, obviously, is no. Cost of inventory maintenance, loss of alternative use of rack space and its associated costs, plus ordinary fashion obsolescence of a single style, would make such a decision unprofitable. As a consequence, women's dress shops are specializing in complete ensembles, including accessories, in petite, junior, women's, or extra large sizes. In short, each fashion boutique has defined its market precisely and attempts to market a "look" or "image" for its chosen clients.

Such decisions may appear clear-cut, but as the number of diverse customers increases or their various needs become more commonly shared, the more difficult the decision becomes. This is the point where market planning really pays off. Instead of reacting to an individual and immediate customer demand and later regretting it, the effective retail firm delimits its market mix and *profitably adheres to it.*

However, such lack of response to market requests cannot be absolutely and blindly observed or the firm will not adapt to changing market needs. Constant market awareness through research begins to pay dividends in return for its costs. Properly designed and implemented market research will alert a retail firm to long run as well as fad trends that must be recognized and merchandised if it is to be competitive and profitable.

Marketing Research: Defining the Environment	Marketing research, as it is generally applied, had its origin in the early 1900s when marketers began to apply the principles of scientific investigation to marketing unknowns. Application of observation techniques, formulating hypotheses, testing hypotheses, and predicting the future has led to considerable insight into a more effective functioning of the marketing system.[32] Important areas of investigation have included (1) target market segmentation, (2) market forecasting and analysis, (3) market investment considerations, (4) customer behavior, (5) product development, (6) merchandising, (7) advertising, (8) pricing, (9) personal selling, and (10) physical distribution.[33]

This partial list of marketing research efforts gives some feeling of the complexity of the marketing process. While retailing is the terminal system of the marketing process, it contains micro examples of similar macro-marketing problems. The same techniques that are used to solve macro-marketing problems can be adapted and applied to similar retail situations. Territory decisions become location decisions; product development questions become assortment decisions, and so on.

Perhaps the most concentrated marketing research effort during the last decade has been focused on consumer behavior and is carried out primarily by advertising agencies and producer-sponsored university research. Generally, the retail industry has been reluctant to encourage or even permit experimentation in its stores. In reality, the store represents an ideal laboratory for the study of consumer purchase behavior; but in order to conduct such research the investigator would destroy the original environment. The retail industry should make more test stores available and should provide more active support of research to find out what the consumer needs are, rather than going to market and taking what the producers offer. Retailers should take a more active part in product development in order to better represent their customers.

Marketing Management: Effective Merchandising

The term **merchandising** means many things to different marketing practitioners. Merchandising is the planning and supervision involved in marketing particular merchandise or services at the place, time, price, and in the quantities that best serve to realize the business's marketing objective.[34] For the purpose of this text, we will consider merchandising to be the internal coordinative effort to meet customers' needs. Admittedly, external environmental conditions, influenced by international trade conditions and agreements, domestic suppliers, competitors, economic conditions, governmental regulations, product development, and consumer demands, will affect the merchandising effort. However, it is important to stress that just as no single customer will determine consumer demand, no single product or department will solely determine the viability of a retail operation.

As noted earlier, consumers have a mental image of a firm or its store, and this conditions their behavior. A retail operation is a composite blend of goods, services, prices, promotion, and personnel with certain personality characteristics. Merchandising ties these various qualities together to form a retail business. Differences in merchandising methods are not simply the result of outside factors affecting customer demand; they grow out of differences in the thinking of each store's management team and its degree of willingness to plan ahead in a systematic way.[35] Simply stated, that is the difference between a true merchandiser and a store owner.

The merchandiser fits complementary assortments of goods together in logically grouped categories in attractive store layouts. Prices provide quality satisfaction for the customer at a reasonable profit for the service provided, and the retailer anticipates customer needs for tomorrow. Store owners buy goods for people to buy today, based on their own personal choices and experience. Market management through merchandising is the route to retailing growth and survival.

Summary

The marketing concept represents a fundamental reorientation in the U.S. economic system. The industrial revolution emphasized mass production of uniform goods at prices that a wide segment of the population could afford. An age of relative scarcity during World War II gave way to an age of relative affluence that demanded new methods of product and service distribution.

The marketing concept was born in the mid-1950s and continues to gain acceptance in enlightened business centers around the world. The marketing concept stresses consumer need satisfaction through possession and use of goods and services. For example, instead of designing a car body based on aerodynamic characteristics or an automotive engineer's calculations, the Japanese automakers surveyed American consumer tastes and designed automobiles to sell in America. Their success speaks for itself.

Through the skillful blending of various combinations of product, place, promotion, and price, marketers everywhere are devising an almost infinite series of total need-satisfying packages to vie for customer dollars in the retail marketplace. Thus the retailer, the ultimate bridge between producer and consumer, bears the heavy burden of anticipating consumer needs and buying patterns and of transporting, financing, promoting, merchandising, and pricing goods and services. All of this is done in competition with other retailers in an attempt to serve consumers better, transforming them into repeat customers, thereby assuring the business of continued survival. The task of profitably meeting consumer needs has been made even more challenging with growing government intervention and regulation. Federal, state, and local laws increasingly reduce the retailer's sphere of free choice in the operation of the business.

Questions

1. According to Drucker, the mission of any business is "to create a customer." How does a retailer attempt to create a customer?
2. What level of profitability in a retail firm is needed to survive? Discuss.
3. What is a future planning gap and how can retailers use strategic growth strategies to bridge this gap? Explain.
4. What is strategic fundamentalism? Give an example.
5. Discuss the meaning of the marketing concept. Can you anticipate any future limits on the implementation of this concept?
6. What factors determine whether a retailer has an effective marketing mix?
7. How does promotion serve consumers?
8. Why do retailers generally prefer nonprice competition in their long-run plans?
9. What variables are at a retailer's disposal in deciding on a retailing mix?
10. Pick a consumer product that might be sold by a retailer and suggest a method of segmenting the market for that product.

Footnotes

1. Peter Drucker, *Management: Tasks, Responsibilities, Practices.* (New York: Harper & Row, 1974), p. 146.

2. Ibid., p. 77.

3. Peter Drucker, *Managing in Turbulent Times*, (New York: Harper & Row, 1980), p. 29.

4. Ibid., p. 36.

5. David J. Luck and O. C. Ferrell, *Marketing Strategy and Plans: Systematic Marketing Management*, (Englewood Cliffs: Prentice-Hall, 1979), p. 23.

6. Ibid.

7. Ibid.

8. Ibid.

9. George Sawyer, "Elements of a Strategy," *Managerial Planning*, (May–June, 1981): 3.

10. Ibid., p. 4.

11. Lauranne Gray Berliner, "Love It or Leave It Budget!" *Stores* (October 1981): 27.

12. Ibid.

13. Ibid.

14. Ibid.

15. Ibid., p. 28.

16. Ibid.

17. Albert D. Bates, "Ahead—the Retrenchment Era," *Journal of Retailing* 53 (Fall 1977): 48.

18. Ibid., pp. 42–43.

19. Albert D. Bates, "The Troubled Future of Retailing," *Business Horizons* 19 (August 1976): 27.

20. William R. Davidson, Albert D. Bates, and Stephen J. Bass, "The Retail Life Cycle," *Harvard Business Review* 54 (November–December 1976): 92.

21. Ibid., p. 96.

22. E. Jerome McCarthy, *Basic Marketing: A Managerial Approach* (Homewood, Ill.: Richard D. Irwin, 1971), p. 19.

23. Philip Kotler, *Marketing Management*, 2d ed. (Englewood Cliffs, N.J.: Prentice–Hall, 1972), p. 18.

24. Ray Geiger, ed., *Farmer's Almanac for 1976* (Lewiston, Maine: Almanac Publishing Company, 1975), vol. 159, p. 1.

25. Richard M. Bessom and Donald W. Jackson, Jr., "Service Retailing: A Strategic Marketing Approach," *Journal of Retailing* 51 (Summer 1975): 77.

26. William Lazer and Eugene J. Kelley, "The Retailing Mix: Planning and Management," *Journal of Retailing* 45 (Spring 1969): 34–41.

27. Joan Bergman, "The Man Who Turned May Around," *Stores* (December 1981): 51.

28. Rosalie Greenfield, "Target Customers: Age 25 to 45," *Stores* (November, 1981): 31.

29. Edgar A. Pessemier, "Store Image and Positioning," *Journal of Retailing* 56 (Spring 1980): 94–106.

30. "Building Brand Character," *Stores* (February, 1981): 36.

31. Ronald R. Gist, *Basic Retailing: Text and Cases* (New York: John Wiley & Sons, 1971), pp. 65–66.

32. McCarthy, *Basic Marketing*, p. 77.

33. Joseph C. Seibert, *Concepts of Marketing Management* (New York: Harper & Row, 1973), p. 364.

34. Ralph S. Alexander, ed., *Marketing Definitions: A Glossary of Marketing Terms* (Chicago, Ill.: American Marketing Association, 1960), p. 17.

35. John W. Wingate, Elmer O. Schaller, and F. Leonard Miller, *Retail Merchandise Management* (Englewood Cliffs, N.J.: Prentice–Hall, 1972), p. 16.

Case Study: Microland Computer Company

Jim Day was daydreaming one day as he rode home from his job in the company car pool. Jim worked very hard in his job as a computer program specialist with a large eastern firm. He was tired of the big city hassle, commuting in traffic jams, breathing polluted air, and paying high taxes to the state for very little in the way of services. He began to think how nice it would be to live in the West and own his own business. Just then he looked over at Bill who was attempting to read his Wall Street Journal in the crowded car. There on the back page was an advertisement offering franchises to qualified persons for Microland Computer Stores. When Bill got to his stop he left the paper behind, so Jim took it home and after dinner began to explore the offering with his wife Joan, who was a legal secretary.

Jim and Joan had both graduated from college four years ago, with Jim earning a B.S. in electrical engineering and a M.B.A. and Joan earning a B.S. in secretarial science. They had met two years ago at a mutual friend's party and after eight months decided to marry with the stipulation that they would both pursue their careers for the first five years. Over the years they had been frugal and saved their money and had a nice nestegg but not enough for the downpayment on a new home they both wanted. As the years passed they became frustrated with their situation and had talked about going into business for themselves somewhere in the West. Perhaps this was the time to seriously pursue that dream. After talking it over for three consecutive nights they decided Jim should call about the franchise and get more details.

Ten days after Jim called a large packet of information arrived in the mail from Microland. That evening was spent going over all the material, reading every word with great enthusiasm. The firm had franchise opportunities in Phoenix, Arizona; Boulder, Colorado; and Salt Lake City, Utah. Their firm would provide the location, two weeks of training, arrange financing, arrange for servicing of the microcomputers through factory representatives and coordinate national advertising for the chain. They had authorization to distribute Apple, Atari, NEC, and Commodore microcomputers and supporting software in each of these three regional markets. Competition was just beginning to surface with introduction of Xerox, Burroughs, and IBM machines which were primarily aimed at the small business market.

Each system ranged in price from a low of $1,200 for a basic machine to $10,000 for a complete system.

The situation was very attractive. Jim had the money needed for the franchise down-payment; he was an experienced computer programmer and had the necessary theoretical business background to start a business. Joan could continue her career in any of the three communities and provide some income during the lean early years. Jim had checked out Microland through Dun and Bradstreet and several local Better Business Bureaus and found it to be a reputable organization. The decision was made that they would become entrepreneurs.

The next morning on the way to work in the car pool Jim broke the news to Bill that he was quitting his job to become a Microland Computer owner-manager. Bill was surprised at the news but tried to be very positive and supportive, "Fantastic, sounds great the way you explain it." Then, from the front seat came a question, "Who ya goin' sell those toys to, Jim? When I looked at them they wanted $3,000 for an outfit. That's pretty expensive for just some space games for the kids. I'll just give them a handful of quarters now and then and let them play the ones in the arcade!"

After the laughter died down Jim began to think seriously about the question, "Who will be my target market in each one of those towns?"

Discussion Questions

1. Who is the target market for microcomputers? Is there more than one target market? What are the demographic characteristics of each of the target markets? Will they vary with the three separate prospective locations?

2. Should Jim and Joan accept the challenge of becoming a Microland Computer owner-manager? What further information do they need?

Chapter 3 | Understanding the Consumer

Learning Goals

1. To learn how economics affects consumer purchase behavior.
2. To discuss how social dimensions influence consumer buying decisions.
3. To understand how cognition, perception, motivation, and learning contribute to the consumer decision-making process.
4. To know how a retailer's attributes are evaluated by consumers.
5. To be aware of the effect that the consumer movement has had upon the retailing industry.

Key Terms and Concepts

substitute items
complementary items
nondiscretionary
   expenditures
discretionary expenditures
conspicuous consumption
reference group
social class
family life cycle
drives
cues

response
reinforcement
physiological needs
safety needs
social needs
esteem needs
self-actualization needs
cognition
perception
motivation
learning

The first two chapters stressed the need for retail managers to study consumer behavior to obtain an understanding of consumer habits and motivations. An improved understanding of the reasons consumers behave as they do can enable management to predict changes in tastes, behavior, and attitudes. These predictions can be used to plan a retail strategy that will reach the consumer more effectively and efficiently. Indeed, success of the retailing effort depends upon an understanding of consumer behavior. Effectiveness of retail merchandise assortments, price and promotion policies, and selection of store locations depends on how well management understands the needs, motivation, and habits of its potential customers.

    This chapter is devoted to setting forth some basic explanations for consumer behavior. It is concerned with the questions, "Why do consumers behave as they do? How do consumers

learn? How can consumers' impressions and opinions be modified?" Many large retail managers no longer have the time to
interact with many of their retail customers on a face-to-face
basis; nevertheless, these managers must understand consumers
in terms of the general concepts defining consumer behavior and
by undertaking specific marketing research projects (such as
those described in Chapter 20). Management can then use its understanding of consumer behavior as a basis for building a retail
strategy that will better meet the needs of the consumer group(s)
the outlet is attempting to serve.

General Approaches to Understanding Consumer Behavior

The study of consumer behavior will now be examined from four
different standpoints. These standpoints reflect the economic, social, psychological and sociopsychological aspects of consumer
behavior.

Unfortunately, none of these approaches offers a complete explanation of consumer behavior, but each approach provides a
partial explanation of consumer behavior in the retail environment.

Economic Aspects of Consumer Behavior

Economic aspects of behavior involve those elements of consumer behavior that are influenced by income or purchasing
power.

Maximizing Satisfaction

Traditional economic theory has focused on the belief that consumers act to maximize the satisfaction that they purchase with
available monetary resources. Despite some limiting assumptions, this theory suggests several useful behavioral explanations
of consumer buying behavior.

First—other things being equal—the lower the price of merchandise, the higher the sales level on that product. For most
items a price reduction increases the consumer's perception of
the relative value of the item and thereby generates increased
sales. This is a general rule which does not apply to all people or
all merchandise items. If some consumers buy a smaller quantity
as a result of a price decrease, they may believe that the quality
has deteriorated or that ownership of the item has less status
value as a result of the price decrease. Some items (diamonds,
jewelry, furs, boats, campers, and so forth) are used as status
symbols and are displayed to gain and maintain esteem. Severe

price reductions on these items may not stimulate sales but may merely reduce the value of the items in the minds of the consumer. In this case the consumer may not believe that the actual quality of the item has declined, but the display or status value has declined.

Price also appears to be directly related to the amount of searching that consumers do before they make a purchase. Searching activity includes store visits, exposure to promotions, discussions with knowledgeable people, and reading consumer publications. The direct relationship between the amount of searching done and the item's price simply implies that consumers spend more time evaluating expensive goods and services and less time evaluating inexpensive items. For example, about three-fourths of the clothing, fabrics, and small household soft goods are purchased in the first store that the consumer visits. However, the number of stores visited before a consumer makes a soft goods purchase increases with the price of the item and with merchandise involving fashion and style.[1]

A second implication of the economic model involves the interrelationship of merchandise items. Other things being equal, lowering the price on **substitute** (or similar) **items** will lower the sales of the item being observed. For example, a price reduction on the retailer's house brand of clock radios will probably cause an increase in the sales of that item but reduce the sales of the other brands of clock radios the store carries. Some items tend to generate sales for **complementary** items (companion merchandise), and the economic model predicts that lowering the price on one item will stimulate additional sales of its complementary products. For example, retailers may reduce the price and/or increase the promotion of a card table in the hope of stimulating sales of card tables *and* folding chairs.

The third implication of the economic model is that higher real personal income tends to result in higher sales of goods and services. However, the amount of increase varies among specific items and services, and two basic consumer expenditure patterns have implications for retailers. These are the nondiscretionary and discretionary patterns of income allocation.

A **nondiscretionary expenditure pattern** concentrates upon the consumer's monetary outlays on contractual, necessary, and habitual expenditures. Mortgage payments, installment debt, and insurance premiums are examples of contractual expenditures for which consumer commitment cannot be changed unless he or she wishes to lose some or all of the value of past payments. Necessary expenditures are those life-sustaining purchases that are made mostly for food, clothing, and medical care.

Habitual expenditures are the purchases made so frequently that the consumer develops a regular purchasing plan to acquire them. Daily newspapers, cigarettes, and beer are examples of habitual outlays of a relatively low unit value.

Discretionary expenditures are made for consumer purchases not motivated by a compelling need and not generally governed by habit, and which entail some deliberation prior to purchase. Many retailers depend upon discretionary consumer expenditures for their main source of business. Rising consumer income and increased consumer willingness to use credit have caused some retailers to concentrate on product and service offerings that capitalize on these trends.

Certainly the proportion of income spent for nondiscretionary goods and services tends to decrease as consumer income increases. Similarly, Engel's laws and the income elasticity concept can be used to identify those products and services that respond best to increases in consumer income. (These concepts are explained and illustrated in Chapter 6.)

Thus, income determines ability to buy. For this reason many retailers define their target market as consumers in the top half of the income distribution. This 50 percent of the people controls 75 percent of the total income and, hence, 75 percent of the buying power in the country. Therefore, it is relatively inexpensive to only have to serve half the people in order to reach three-fourths of the total buying potential.

Income also affects the way people shop. For example, people with higher incomes and more education, children, and fashion consciousness are greater users of in-home shopping methods such as mail order, telephone, and buying from door-to-door salespeople. Items that are easily standardized and identified are most likely to be purchased at home. But merchandise items such as clothing that must be offered in many different sizes, colors, styles, and so forth are less likely to be purchased in the home because they entail more risk of producing consumer disappointment.

Reacting to Expected Changes in Income

Another aspect of income that influences consumer behavior is expected changes in the consumer's income. Income expectations depend upon the percentage of chance that the consumers attach to the likelihood that their incomes will change in the near future. Expectations also depend upon the amount consumers believe their income will increase or decrease in the near future. Finally, expectations depend upon whether consumers view the anticipated change in income as a permanent or temporary change. Consumers who expect a temporary decrease in income usually do not immediately adapt their purchases to this reduced income level.

As income declines expenditures decline, but at a much slower rate than the decline in income would suggest. On the other hand, unexpected income (which consumers didn't believe they would receive in the near future) is usually spent fairly quickly.

Income Trends in the '80s

Aided by an increase in the number of working women, there has been a sharp rise in family income. During the 1965–1980 period, the real standard of living of the average American family rose 50 percent. The number of households having annual incomes of more than $25,000 (in constant 1979 dollars) about doubled during the 1970s. However, during recent years the growth rate of upper-income households has slowed due to a sluggish economy and a slow increase in middle-aged people who are traditionally high income earners. By 1980 about 15 percent of the American households had annual incomes of more than $35,000. This represented almost one-half of the total personal income. It is estimated that families earning over $35,000 will own 28 percent of all homes by 1990. Personal income obtained by families earning more than $35,000 is expected to increase by about 70 percent during the 1980s compared to a 35 percent increase in total personal income during the 1980s.[2] The high level of disposable income available to this group makes it a very attractive market segment for the retailer.

Although median family income has increased from $9,867 in 1970 to $24,036 in 1981, disposable real income has increased only slightly, from $8,528 in 1970 to $9,184 in 1981 (Figure 3.1). Higher federal income and social security taxes and inflation have squeezed the real purchasing value of consumer income during this period to the point that disposable income is not increasing for the total population. The poorest 40 percent of all families account for only about 20 percent of all retail sales. These families are being squeezed by inflation to the point that they are now spending 40 percent of their income for food and fuel compared to only 25 percent for the high income segment (Figure 3.2). Thus, the market segment of families earning over $35,000 per year is likely to become even more appealing during the 1980s.

People in this high income group are currently spending more than economists have been forecasting because of the rapidly expanding equity they have in their homes (most of which are financed on a low fixed rate mortgage). Consumer liquidity in this

Figure 3.1 The Two–Way Squeeze on Median Family Income

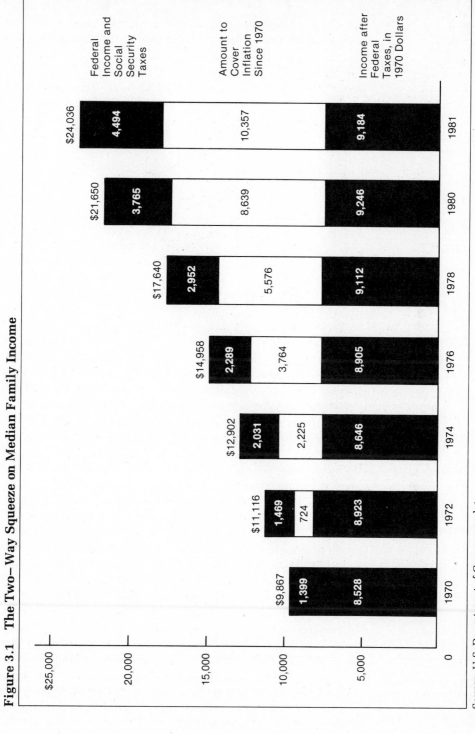

Source: U.S. Department of Commerce data.

Figure 3.2   Percentage of Retail Sales Made to Different Income Groups

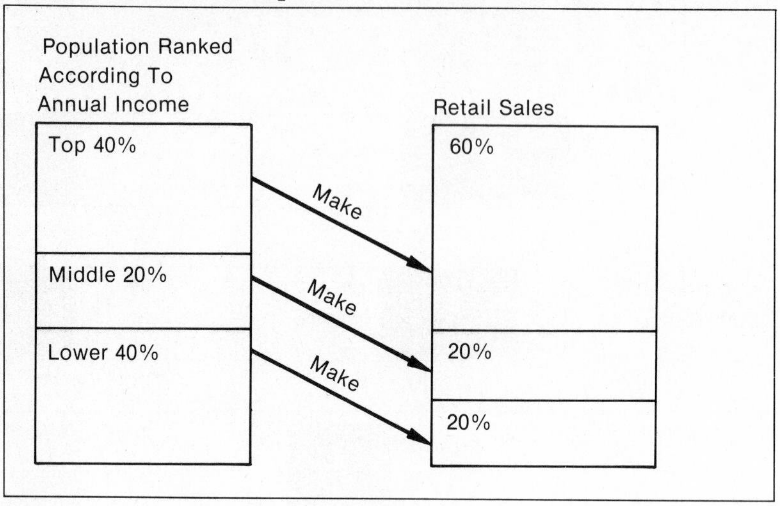

Population Ranked
According To
Annual Income

Retail Sales

Top 40%

60%

Make

Middle 20%

Make

Lower 40%

20%

Make

20%

Source: U.S. Department of Commerce data.

segment could get a further substantial boost if homeowners are given the opportunity to write checks against equity in their homes.

Deteriorating economic conditions such as inflation, recession, and rising energy costs have eroded the level of disposable income of the middle-American family so much that it has been forced to cut its spending to cover basic needs. This has caused many middle-income families to desert their favorite place to shop primarily because of the inability of these retailers to respond sufficiently to these new spending attitudes. Low-income families stayed with low-priced stores that offered lower-quality goods, and affluent consumers maintained enough disposable income to sustain their customary shopping habits. As a result both the low-price stores and the high-quality outlets remained healthy, but some department stores and mass merchandisers have lost customers to inflation. This has set the stage for a major battle to win the business of the middle-income consumer.

In 1980 some discounters began trading up and some department stores began trading down. Sears, K mart and Penneys broadened their merchandise offerings to include more fashionable higher-quality goods. But the results have been less than expected. Therefore, a new battle for middle-income consumers dollar is likely to be focused upon better promotions, assortments, presentation, and service to reach the new needs of this consumer.

Social Aspects of Consumer Behavior

Social dimensions of consumer behavior are implicit in those consumer actions that are related either to demographic matters or to reference group considerations. A demographic population study involves analysis of the effect that age, social class, education, geographical density characteristics, occupation, marriage status, and sex have upon purchase behavior. The term "reference group" refers to any group of people that is capable of influencing individual behavior.

Demographic Characteristics

Demographic characteristics particularly critical to retailers are population size, geographical distribution of the population, and social class. Trends in these factors have been discussed in Chapters 1 and 2. The importance of demographic characteristics is reflected by retailers who have learned that they must serve consumers from a location that is conveniently reached by the consumer. For example, suburban shopping centers are an outgrowth of population movements to the suburbs.

Not only is population increasing, but Americans have become a mobile people. About 20 percent change their address each year. About two-thirds of these moves involve relocation in the same county. The dramatic effect population mobility can have upon a store's customers during a four-year period is illustrated in Figure 3.3. The majority of the population in the key 20–34 age group moved during this period. In fact, one could conclude that unless a retailer is serving a target market consisting of people of 45 years or older, the majority of the firm's market would disappear during a four-year period.

Whenever people move they develop new store patronage habits. Thus, a retailer may continually lose 20 percent of the customers each year. However, the firm also has the opportunity of gaining at least an equal percentage of the consumers who are new to the area. The astute retailer will determine what goods and services these new consumers want and then adjust the firm's offerings to meet these needs. Sometimes retailers find that new consumers in the community are quite different from the previous consumers. For example, only young people from eighteen to twenty-two years old may be moving into the area to replace older families who are moving out of the area. If the magnitude of the shift is large, then the retailer will have to make radical changes in the firm's retailing mix. In this case the firm which was selling major home appliances may have to completely redefine its market and switch to handling more small appliances, stereos, and so forth that will better appeal to the new younger market. If the firm does not want to undergo such radical changes, then it may eventually have to consider moving to a new location.

Figure 3.3   Baby Boom Aging Heightens Population Mobility

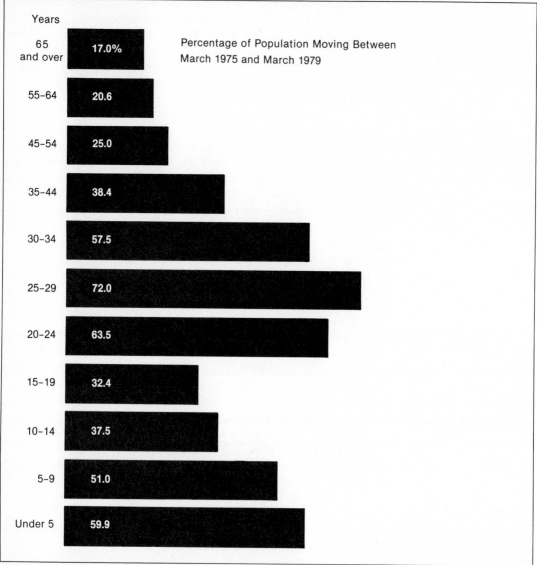

Source: Bureau of the Census, Report No. 353, as reported by Shearson/American Express as publisher of
Consumer Capsule, p. 22.

Major changes to occur in the age distribution of U.S. consumers during the 1980s will show (1) that the median age of the
population will continue to get older (Figure 3.4), (2) a dramatic
increase in people between 35 and 44 and a decrease in the
number of people between 14 and 24 (Figure 3.5).

Figure 3.4   Older Median Age of U.S. Population*

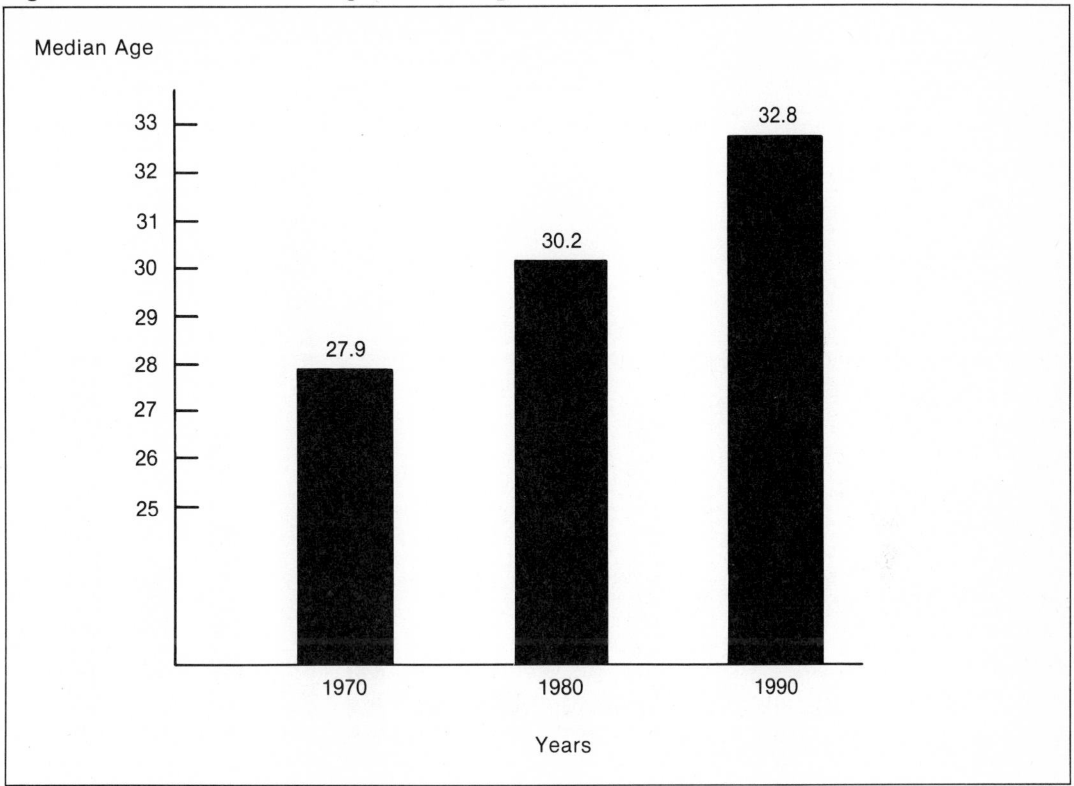

* 1980 and 1990 data are estimates based upon the middle of three estimated birth rates.
Source: U.S. Department of Commerce.

Since households headed by the 35–44 year group will increase by 42 percent in the 1980s, a key to consumer spending will be to figure out where these people spend their incomes.

For example, shifts demonstrated in Figures 3.4 and 3.5 are already changing the sales volume in diamond engagement rings relative to total sales of diamond rings. Engagement rings accounted for 35 percent of the diamond ring sales during 1976 and 1977 but only 19 percent of the diamond ring sales just two years later.[3] Shifts in buying habits of this magnitude can easily make or break a retail firm. Thus, jewelers should begin to upgrade their offerings to better reach the needs of the growing 25 to 44 year-old who spends more on jewelry than young adults. A 1979 industry study showed that the average price paid for diamond rings by customers in the 18 to 24 age group was $221. The average price paid by 25 to 34 year-old consumers was $413, but the 35 to 44 year-old customer paid nearly five times that of the 18 to 24 year-old, with an average price of $1,141.

**Figure 3.5   Projected U.S. Population Change
by Age Groups 1980–1990***

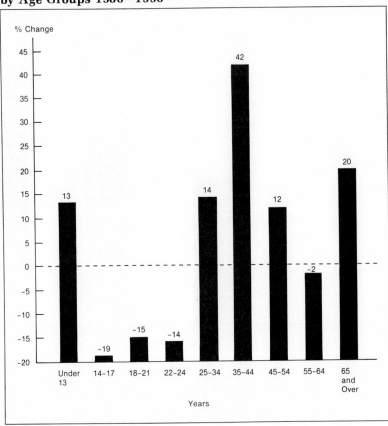

* Data are based on middle of three estimated birth rates.
Source: U.S. Department of Commerce.

Social Role

A consumer's social position and the perceptions of his or her role in society also influence retail buying habits. For example, isolated urban dwellers have been found to prefer making purchases in small stores because the small store provides them with personal contacts.

Conspicuous consumption, or the purchase and use of goods and services primarily to raise prestige rather than to satisfy material needs, is designed to gain acceptance from the consumer's reference group. Thus, the newly rich minority group member may be in a market group that is especially likely to buy large diamonds or fashion clothing because they offer visual proof that the individual has arrived. It is important that retailers identify purchases made for conspicuous consumption, because their pricing, advertising, merchandise selection, and packaging can be adapted to appeal to this consumer motivation.

Desire to improve one's quality of life and enjoy some luxuries has led to the human desire to always want the "new and improved" or the best and most unusual merchandise and services. Retailers of durable goods have capitalized on these conspicuous consumption desires by always trying to get consumers to purchase top-of-the-line merchandise because it offers more and better features than less expensive models. Other examples of conspicuous consumption include increased (1) frequency of eating out at restaurants; (2) demand for wines and gourmet foods; (3) attendance at live entertainment events; and (4) purchases of art, antiques, and precious minerals.

The individual's role in the family also has important implications for retailers. Some retailers' merchandising strategy may be oriented exclusively toward the actual buyer of the merchandise. Others may orient their merchandising toward users of an item. For example, a supermarket's breakfast cereal assortment may reflect the preference of children rather than the preference of the adult buyer.

Where, when, what, and how-much-to-spend decisions are not always made by the same individual and, in fact, may be made jointly. Purchase of expensive goods or services (such as autos, major appliances, and housing) that affect a number of family members is usually made after very careful planning and involvement of more than one group member. Most major joint purchases are heavily influenced by the person who knows the most about the items under consideration. For example, the husband may have more influence than the wife on when an automobile should be purchased, where it should be purchased, and how much should be spent on it, but the color, model, and make may be decided by mutual agreement. Similarly, the wife may have more influence in determining the style, color, and fabric of furniture purchases, but the how-much-to-spend, when-to-buy, and where-to-buy decisions may be made jointly.

It is important for retailers to realize who is buying and to identify the degree of influence the buyer receives from within or outside the family. If influences can be identified, the firm's promotion and merchandise assortment can be shaped to appeal to both the buyer and the influencing **reference group** (group of people that the individual aspires to belong to).

It is also important to realize that consumers may identify negatively with particular reference groups. That is, they avoid the unique behavioral traits of such a group. Thus, a store may have considerable difficulty appealing to two widely different consumer groups simply because members of each group perceive the store to be catering to the other group.

Social Class

Social class is another sociological consideration that has helped retailers better understand consumer behavior. All U.S. citizens do not have the same power and prestige. They are engaged in different occupations that are not equally prestigious. They do not have similar possessions or value systems. Thus, there is an informal ordering of individuals into relatively homogeneous groupings in terms of social status. A **social class** is a group of many people who are about equal to one another in prestige and community status. People within a social class regularly interact among members of their group and share the same general goals and philosophy of life.

Professor W. Lloyd Warner is largely responsible for development of a description of social stratification that divides U.S. society into six social classes (described in Exhibit 3.1). The major contribution of the study of social classes to a retailer's understanding of consumer behavior is that it provides a useful tool with which to segment the market into meaningful consumer groups.

Shoppers in various social classes seek retail outlets that make them feel most comfortable and that cater to their particular class. A lower-status woman may believe that if she enters high-status department stores, the clerks and the other customers will make her wait or will punish her in some other subtle way. This belief causes lower-status people to avoid upper-class stores. The result is retail institutions that convey a sense of different levels of social class and social prestige to their customers.

Such differences are more noticeable with some merchandise lines than others. Middle-class shoppers may patronize relatively low-status discount stores to buy large items (such as refrigerators, color television, washing machines, etc.) whose quality is "assured" by the brand name of a national manufacturer. Selection of the "right" store is much more important for items (such as clothing or furniture) whose style or taste is important to the consumer, because these items convey social awareness and values.

Preferences for different types of retail outlets are also related to social class membership. The lower-level working class tends to prefer neighborhood stores because they fear being snubbed or ignored if they go outside their neighborhood to a downtown merchant or large shopping center. Middle-class housewives are more confident in their shopping ability and are more willing to

Exhibit 3.1   Warner's Six Classes of Commonly Used Social Stratification

1. **Upper-Upper** or "Social Register" consists of locally prominent families, usually with at least second or third generation wealth. Basic Values: living graciously, upholding family reputation, reflecting the excellence of one's breeding, and displaying a sense of community responsibility. About ½ of 1 percent of population.

2. **Lower-Upper** or "Nouveau Riche" consists of the more recently arrived and never-quite-accepted wealthy families. Goals: blend of Upper-Upper pursuit of gracious living and the Upper-Middle drive for success. About 1½ percent of the population.

3. **Upper-Middle** are moderately successful professional men and women, owners of medium-sized businesses, young people in their twenties and early thirties who are expected to arrive at the managerial level by their middle or late thirties. Motivations: success at a career, cultivating charm and polish. About 10 percent of the population.

4. **Lower-Middle** are mostly non-managerial office workers, small business owners, highly paid blue-collar families. Goals: respectability, and striving to live in well-maintained homes, neatly furnished in more-or-less "right" neighborhoods, and to do a good job at their work. They will save for a college education for their children. Top of the Average Man World. About 30–35 percent of the population.

5. **Upper-Lower** or "Ordinary Working Class" consists of semi-skilled workers. Although many make high pay, they are not particularly interested in respectability. Goals: enjoying life and living well from day to day, to be at least modern, and to work hard enough to keep safely away from the slum level. About 40 percent of the population.

6. **Lower-Lower** are unskilled workers, unassimilated ethnics, and the sporadically employed. Outlooks: apathy, fatalism, "get your kicks whenever you can." About 15 percent of the population, but have less than half that of the purchasing power.

Source: Irving J. Shapiro, *Marketing Terms: Explanations, Definitions and/or Aspects* (Totowa, N.J.: Littlefield, Adams & Company, 1981), pp. 234–235. Reprinted by permission.

seek new stores and new shopping experiences. Lower-status consumers appear to prefer face-to-face contact with friendly local clerks whom they know and believe can be trusted to assist them in making purchase decisions. They also prefer to shop in stores that extend credit.

The difference in store choice by members of different social classes can be illustrated by consumer behavior in buying cosmetics. Upper-middle-class women buy their cosmetics in department stores while lower-class women prefer to buy cosmetics in variety stores. Drug stores appear to be equally suitable to all classes. When consumers from several different social strata buy in the same store, they are likely to purchase different items or to buy the same items for different reasons. For example, when the lower-class woman shops in a store patronized by middle-class women, she may be interested only in buying gifts for others and not in making purchases for herself.

One segment of the American social scene that is growing rapidly is the group who are committed to a simpler lifestyle. The person living the simple life tends to prefer products that are functional, healthy, nonpolluting, durable, repairable, recyclable or made from renewable raw materials, energy cheap, authentic, esthetically pleasing, and made with simple technology. There are currently five million people in this segment, and it is projected to grow to 25 million by 1987.

History indicates that existing merchants tend to miss new major markets that develop after their own basic operation is defined. If existing mass merchandisers miss this market segment, it will open up a real opportunity for small, independent outlets to serve.

Executives of large western supermarket chains are already noticing increased consumer interest in nutrition with more emphasis on "healthful" foods instead of products high in sugar, additives, or preservatives. An increased number of consumers are making their own granola, baby food, and baking their own high-fiber bread. The trend toward natural products (e.g., natural juice drinks) is also evident as is the move to ethnic foods. Management that keeps abreast of change in consumer preferences stands the best chance of serving the needs of this growing market segment.

Family Life Cycle

The **family life cycle** concept, which divides the population into different groups with each group representing a different stage in life, is also used to segment markets and identify market targets. Expenditure patterns and purchase motivations change over a consumer's lifetime. Market targets revealed by the family life cycle include clothing for fashion conscious singles. The young, married, no-children family is a good market for consumer durable goods. Change toward more youth-oriented products is apparent for full-nest stages. Empty-nest stages are identified as good markets for luxury goods and services and other quality merchandise. Some families in empty-nest stages are now moving to exclusive apartment buildings or condominiums that require little upkeep and are convenient to their places of work. This group of people represents a new market segment with new needs and purchase motivations. Alert retailers will respond to these needs and increase profits by recognizing this shift in consumer behavior.

Thus, changes in the social structure are just as important to retailers as are changes in the age of the population. The shift toward smaller family size has been the result of more people living alone or with friends either because they never marry or they become divorced or widowed. People are waiting longer to get married, then waiting even longer after marriage to have their first child and end up having fewer children. Statistics indicate the large magnitude of this trend. In 1960 only one of seven households consisted of unmarried adults living alone or with unrelated adults. By 1978 one household in four belonged in this "non-family" classification, and this statistic is projected to increase to one household in three by 1990.[4]

Another important shift that affects consumer behavior within the family life cycle concept is the strong trend toward more employed women (Figure 3.6). About one half of wives worked outside the home in 1980, but this percentage is expected to grow rapidly during the 1980s. In 1980, 44 percent of the unmarried women 18 or older were employed, but this percentage is expected to increase during the decade.

The effect these changes in social structure have upon retailers may be illustrated by the jewelry retailers who have discovered that employed women not only buy more than twice as much jewelry as nonemployed women, but they also spend more on each purchase. For example, a 1980 consumer market survey in-

Figure 3.6   Proportion of Husband-Wife Families with Two or More Workers and Labor Force Participation Rate of All Married Women

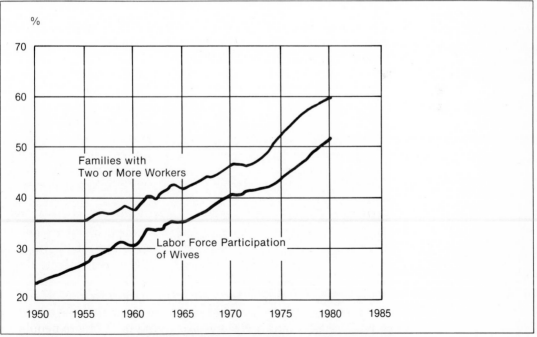

Source: Bureau of Labor Statistics as reported on p. 19 of "Consumer Capsule" by Carol Brock Kenney and Leslie J. Morgan (New York, N.Y.: Shearson/American Express), Vol. VII, No. 3, 1981, p. 19.

dicated that the average price working women paid for diamond rings was $385 while unemployed women paid an average of $311.[5] The increase in the percentage of "dating" buyers combined with the increasing demand of working women offers a bright future to retailers who can serve their needs. Jewelers could benefit by catering to working women by providing easier credit and being open longer hours in the evening and weekends. A 1980 study showed that 47 percent of all gold jewelry purchases made by women were impulse purchases which were frequently made at a department store where a charge card could be used.[6] Independent jewelers not offering credit to this consumer group are likely to lose their business.

Changing lifestyles are also influencing consumer behavior in food retailing. The trend toward two-income families has stimulated consumer interest in convenience foods and eating outside the home. A related change is toward more men cooking and taking an increasingly larger role in regular family shopping and meal preparation.

Psychological Aspects of Consumer Behavior

Several psychological concepts make important contributions to the study of consumer behavior.

Exhibit 3.2   Many psychological factors influence a consumer's retail buying behavior.

Source: Photo courtesy of K mart Corporation.

Pavlovian Learning Model

The Pavlovian learning model, as it has been modified over the years, is based on the four concepts of *drive, cue, response,* and *reinforcement.*

Drives are an individual's strong internal stimuli that impel them to action. Drives, or needs, may be either physiological (hunger, thirst, cold, pain, and sex) or socially derived motives (cooperation, fear, and acquisitiveness) which are learned.

Cues are weaker stimuli in the individual and/or environment that influence the consumer's response. For example, a McDonald's hamburger advertisement can serve as a cue that stimulates the hunger drive in a child. The response will depend upon the advertisement cue and other cues such as the time of day, the relative availability of other hunger-satisfying alternatives, and the like. A change in the relative intensity can frequently be more forceful than the absolute level of the cue. For example, a child who has only a small amount of money may be more motivated by a special price offer that is good for one day only than by the fact that the hamburger is usually low priced.

Response is the individual's reaction to all cues. The same relative arrangement of cues will not always produce the same response each time in the individual because the earlier experience may or may not have been rewarding. If the response generates a favorable experience, that response is strengthened or **reinforced,** and the response will probably be repeated when and if the same arrangement of cues reappears.

The Pavlovian model does not adequately treat concepts such as perceptions, the subconscious, and interpersonal influence. It does, however, offer some useful insight into consumer behavior. It provides guidelines in developing advertising strategy by suggesting that a single exposure to an advertisement is too weak a cue to stimulate a strong, favorable response. Thus, it is desirable to repeat advertisements because repetition reduces forgetting on the part of the consumer. Absence of a message would tend to result in a weakened learned response according to the Pavlovian model.

In addition, repetitive advertising provides reinforcement as the consumer becomes selectively exposed to the advertisement after making the purchase. The Pavlovian model also indicates that copy strategy must arouse strong drives in the individual if it is to be effective as a cue. The strongest item- or service-related drives must be identified and presented with the right words, colors, and pictures to provide the strongest stimulus to these drives.

Maslow's Hierarchy of Motives

Maslow's hierarchy of motives offers a good perspective for a better understanding of consumer behavior. Maslow believed that a person is a perpetually wanting individual. As certain needs are satisfied, the next most important need tends to dominate the individual's conscious life. Maslow considers **physiological needs** (hunger, sex, thirst, and so forth) to be the most basic type of needs. These must be satisfied before an individual can be concerned about other needs. When these physiological needs are satisfied, the buyer proceeds to second-level needs, which are **safety needs.** Safety needs consist of the desire for security, protection, and order or routine. Consumers satisfy their safety needs by means of savings accounts, insurance, pension plans, refrigerators, home freezers, and the like.

After physiological and safety needs are satisfied, individuals become concerned about **social needs** such as love needs, or the need for affection and belonging. To satisfy love needs, the individual strives to be accepted by the members of his family and to be an important person to them and to others who are close friends. The fourth need level, **esteem needs,** emerges as soon as the love needs are satisfied. Esteem needs are demands for reputation, self-respect, prestige, success, and achievement. Different status groups and symbols emerge as ways of satisfying this level of need satisfaction.

The fifth and last basic need is the desire to know, understand, organize, and construct a system of values that can be used to develop one's desire for self-fulfillment. These needs, called **self-actualization needs,** consist of developing one's self to the fullest.

Maslow's theory is based on the concept that people have these five kinds of goals or needs. People are motivated to achieve various conditions that provide satisfaction for their needs. The needs are related in order of importance in such a way that the most powerful need will monopolize the conscious thought process of the individual who will minimize the less pressing needs. When that need is satisfied, the next most powerful need emerges to dominate the individual's conscious reactions. Thus, a starving person (need 1) is not likely to be interested in whether he or she is breathing unpolluted air (need 2), or in how he or she is seen by others (need 3 or 4), or in a travel tour of Europe (need 5).

Socio-Psychological Aspects of Consumer Behavior

The socio-psychological concept of consumer behavior views behavior as the result of four factors: cognition, perception, motivation, and learning.

Cognition

Cognition is a process of making sense out of what is seen or perceived. It is an individual's total belief system, consisting of values, ideas, and attitudes. Cognitive processes assist people in achieving their needs satisfactorily and determining the direction to take to attain satisfaction of the initiating need.

Perception

Perception is what individuals "see" as a result of complex patterns of stimulation filtered through their own unique cognitive processes. Perception reflects a person's past experience, present attitudes, and inclinations. For example, a customer entering a store "perceives" things that are not "seen." The person "sees" the physical items such as the building, fixtures, merchandise, people, but the individual's perception is influenced by previous experiences shopping in the store, by conversations with friends, and the like. Thus, a person may perceive the outlet to be a warm, friendly place, conducive to shopping and lingering, if previous exposure has been pleasant.

No two people perceive a situation in exactly the same terms because people have different views of the world. Each person's view, or total belief system, is formed over time as a result of physiological abilities (eyesight, sense of smell, intelligence level, and so forth), psychological characteristics (personality and need-value systems), and past experiences.

The consumer's total belief system, or cognitive set, predisposes the person to receive and retain perceptions that he or she wants to see. Therefore, the consumer is a decision maker in the communication process. Consumers decide what messages to receive from their exposure to different kinds of media. They selectively decide what messages to receive from their exposure to different peer groups. They also decide what messages to perceive and retain on the basis of their attitudes, culture, and past experiences.

Risk is one element of perception that deserves further discussion. Any purchase competes with alternative uses of the same money, and any purchase involves a risk that the product will not work properly, that the consumer's friends may not approve of the selection, that the service was performed improperly, and the like. **Perceived risk** may exist when the consumer is not able to define buying goals and/or there are some unforeseeable consequences related to quality of the product or service and ability of the purchase to fulfill the consumer's psychological and social needs. Thus, the consumer may perceive risk to be the result of one or more of the following factors:

1. *She may be uncertain as to what buying goals are.* Would she rather have an outrageously expensive new dress or a new piece of furniture? If a dress, should it be the cocktail dress she has always wanted or a more functional wool suit?

2. *The consumer may be uncertain as to which purchase (product, brand, model, etc.) will best match or satisfy acceptance level of buying goals.* Should the suit be purchased at Lord and Taylor's or the local discount house? Will she really be more satisfied with a modern styling or a more conservative basic cut?

3. *The consumer may perceive possible adverse consequences if the purchase is made (or not made) and the result is a failure to satisfy her buying goals.* For example, she may suffer intense embarrassment if she buys her cocktail dress, and it is much too risqué at a party, or she looks fat, or it fits poorly.[7]

Consumer risk can be reduced by either decreasing the possible consequences or increasing the certainty of the possible outcome. Consumers read advertisements and *Consumer Reports,* examine merchandise, talk to friends, purchase items that have performed well for them in the past, buy advertised products, and buy at familiar stores to increase the certainty of the outcome of their purchases. Retailers can assist the consumer in reducing uncertainty by refusing to handle items that have not performed well for their customers. The rate of product returns and the frequency of consumer complaints will quickly identify these inferior-quality items that may have slipped through a buyer's careful selection process.

In addition, retailers can reduce consumer's perception of risk by providing a good warranty policy complemented by a good public relations policy in the consumer complaint or refunds and exchange departments. Retail advertising can also reduce consumer uncertainty by truthfully emphasizing styling, function, and performance attributes of merchandise or service. Retail salespeople can reduce a consumer's perception of risk by assisting the individual in defining buying goals or identifying problem(s) and then providing the best available solution. Handling nationally advertised, familiar brand name products also results in a reduction of the consumer's perceived risk.

Motivation

Motivation, the driving force behind consumer behavior, is aimed at attaining protection, satisfaction, and self-enhancement. Motives are the impulses or desires that initiate behavior. The major motives can be divided into physiological and psychological or social forces.

Maslow's hierarchy of needs, discussed previously, reveals that people first satisfy their physiological needs. The major motivating force is then channeled to satisfy the individual's next highest order need, according to Maslow's listing.

Retailing is a means by which consumers can reach their goals. In other words, retailing assists the consumer in satisfying the range of needs contained in Maslow's list. Maslow's ranking also indicates that a satisfied need is no longer an important consumer motive. Because most American consumers are able to satisfy their basic physiological desires, retailers should concentrate on strategies that satisfy consumers' social needs (love and belongingness), esteem needs, and self-actualization needs. Indeed, most consumers in American society appear to make discretionary purchases to satisfy social or esteem needs. For example, advertising does not emphasize the nutritional content of food items but concentrates on social messages that illustrate how well various products will be enjoyed at parties, by friends, and so on.

Learning

Finally, the socio-psychological approach views behavior as depending upon learning in addition to the cognition, perception, and motivation factors just discussed. **Learning** is the change in

Figure 3.7   Store-Choice Processes

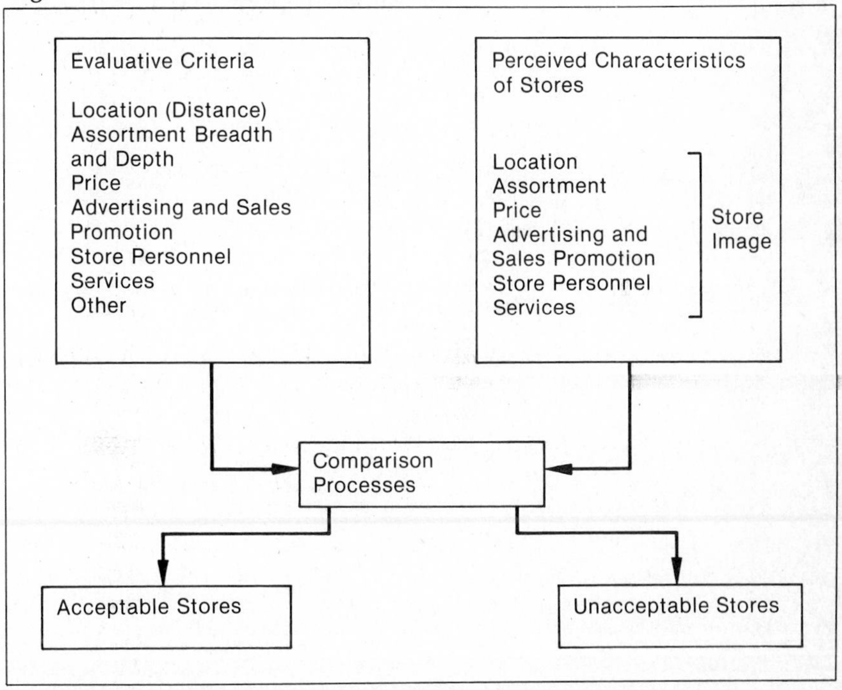

Source: James F. Engel, Roger D. Blackwell, and David T. Kollat, *Consumer Behavior*, 3d ed. (New York: The Dryden Press, Inc., 1978), p. 506. Copyright © 1978 by The Dryden Press, A Division of Holt, Rinehart, and Winston, Publishers. Reprinted by permission of Holt, Rinehart, and Winston, CBS College Publishing.

Table 3.1   What's Important in Choosing a Supermarket

Rank	Characteristic	Score	Extremely Important (% Rating)	Not Important At All (% Rating)
1	Low prices	5.83	86.5	—
2	Cleanliness	5.77	80.5	—
3	All prices clearly labeled	5.72	81.0	0.3
4	Good produce department	5.57	69.0	0.5
5	Accurate, pleasant checkout clerks	5.55	67.5	0.3
6	Freshness date marked on products	5.53	71.2	0.5
7	Good meat department	5.51	71.4	2.1
8	Shelves usually kept well-stocked	5.47	58.6	0.3
9	Convenient store location	5.42	59.2	0.3
10	Good parking facilities	5.40	60.3	1.3
11	Frequent "sales" or "specials"	5.31	60.3	1.6
12	Good dairy department	5.25	54.7	1.3
13	Good layout for fast, easy shopping	5.20*	49.1	1.3
14	Helpful personnel in service departments (meat, produce, deli)	5.20*	50.7	1.1
15	Short wait for checkout	5.18	50.3	1.6
16	Don't run short of items on "special"	5.16	54.7	2.4
17	Good selection of low-priced store brand items	5.04	50.5	2.4
18	Aisles clear of boxes	4.90	42.9	2.9
19	Baggers on duty	4.78	43.0	5.8
20	Good frozen foods department	4.74	39.2	3.7
21	Good selection of nationally advertised brands	4.72	34.1	3.7
22	Check-cashing service	4.66	45.4	12.1
23	Pleasant atmosphere, decor	4.57	30.0	3.9
24	New items I see advertised are available	4.49	27.9	5.0
25	Manager is friendly and helpful	4.39	34.3	9.3
26	Not usually overcrowded	4.38	27.1	6.1
27	Good selection of budget-priced generic (no brand name) products	4.35	31.9	9.0
28	Unit pricing signs on shelves (price per unit)	4.31	32.2	10.5
29	Open late hours	3.94	24.5	16.8
30	Good drugs and toiletries section	3.52	19.3	22.2
31	Good assortment of nonfoods merchandise	3.38	10.2	18.5
32	Carry purchases to my car	3.26	20.1	33.6
33	Have in-store bakery	3.25*	11.5	25.9
34	Have deli department	3.25*	13.8	27.1
35	Store has UPC scanning checkout (electronic) registers	2.90	13.0	39.3
36	Eye-catching mass displays	2.70	6.5	34.5
37	People know my name	2.52	8.5	43.7
38	Trading stamps or other extras	2.35	7.2	52.8
39	Sell hot foods to take out or eat in store	1.99	3.7	58.3

* = Tie score

Source: Reprinted from *Progressive Grocer*, with permission. (September 1981) p. 137.

the individual's response tendencies due to effects of his or her insight and experience. Experience may be a previous visit made to a particular retail outlet, a promotional message sent by a retailer, or merely a suggestion made by a friend. The person's response may be a strong inclination to return to the store the next time he or she needs the merchandise or service it offers, a weak inclination to return, or a strong inclination to avoid the outlet if at all possible.

The learning process involves the four concepts discussed previously in the Pavlovian learning model: drives, cues, responses, and reinforcement. In addition, learning involves restructuring of the individual's attitudes and beliefs about the environment. A consumer's learned response is thus based on insight and past experiences. The consumer's choice of retail outlets is conceptualized in Figure 3.7. An example of evaluative criteria listed in this figure influences the consumer's choice of a supermarket as illustrated in Table 3.1.

Market Segmentation: The End Result of Understanding Consumer Behavior

As illustrated in Chapter 1, retail management cannot appeal equally to all groups of people. Instead it needs to develop marketing strategies for reaching segments of the population called target markets. As stated in Chapter 1, this process of dividing a market into groups of people who have similar consumer characteristics and behaviors is known as market segmentation. Once different segments have been defined, the worth of each can be evaluated, target markets can be identified, and merchandise and messages can be tailored to best appeal to selected population subsets.

Consumer behavior plays a large role in properly defining market segments. Basic requirements for effective market segmentation are:

1. *Measurability* Each group must be capable of being both identifiable and quantitatively measured.
2. *Accessibility* Each group must be capable of being effectively reached and served by the media as well as by the retail offering.
3. *Substantiality* Each group must be large enough and profitable enough to be worth considering for separate marketing action.

The common bases for retail market segmentation are presented in Table 3.2 but any group of people can effectively serve

Table 3.2 Common Methods of Segmenting Retail Consumer Markets

1. **Geographic**
   a. *City Size* (Population under 5,000, 5,000–19,999, 20,000–49,999, 50,000–499,999, and 500,000 and up)
   b. *County Size* (Same as city size)
   c. *Region* (New England, Atlantic, North Central, Mountain, Pacific)
   d. *Climate* (Cold, tropical, arid)

2. **Demographic**
   a. *Sex* (Male, female)
   b. *Age* (Under 6, 6–11, 12–19, 20–34, 35–49, 50–64, 65 and up)
   c. *Family Size* (1, 2, 3–4, 5–6, 7 and up)
   d. *Annual Family Income* (Under $5,000; $5,000–9,999; $10,000–14,999; $15,000–19,999; $20,000–24,999; $25,000–29,999, and $30,000 and over)
   e. *Education* (Grade school or less, some high school, graduated from high school, some college, and graduated from college)
   f. *Occupation* (Professional, technical, manager, craftsman, foreman, clerical, sales, farmer, retired, student, housewife, unemployed)
   g. *Family Life Cycle* (Young-single, young-married with no children, married with youngest child under six, married with youngest child six or over, married with all children living outside the home, older-single)
   h. *Social Class* (Lower-lower, upper-lower, lower-middle, upper-middle, lower-upper and upper-upper)

3. **Psychographic**
   a. *Lifestyle* (Swingers, straights, longhairs)
   b. *Personality* (Outgoing, introvert, ambitious, lazy, leader, follower)

4. **Behavioral**
   a. *Benefits Sought* (Economy, convenience, prestige)
   b. *Rate of Use* (Light, average, heavy)
   c. *User Status* (Regular user, first-time user, potential user, ex-user, nonuser)
   d. *Loyalty Status* (None, average, strong)
   e. *Readiness Stage* (Unaware, aware, interested, intending to buy, not interested)

as a market target for a retailer if it is measurable, accessible, and substantial. Any of the factors presented in Table 3.2 may be combined to form one market segment. For example, an examination of changing values and lifestyles of U.S. consumers reveals that more are inner-directed consumers who are less materialistic than the traditional American consumer. This study was based on identifying the percentage of people in eight different market segments as presented in Table 3.3.[8]

The money restricted consumer segment consists of "households and individuals whose discretionary freedom in purchasing goods and services is severely restricted by lack of money. In general they are the least psychologically free Americans and are farthest removed from the cultural mainstream. They have low incomes, tend to be older and have little education; they live mostly in inner cities or in poor rural areas."[9]

There are three outer-directed groups—Belongers, Emulators and Achievers.

"The Belongers want to conform, to fit in, to be traditional, they do not want to stand out. They come mainly from rural areas or small towns; have low to middle incomes, and span all age groups, although the greatest proportion is middle aged. Many widows are in this category. Although they participate in fads, they are not the innovators; they join the fad in the third or fourth wave, largely because of the influence of the media. Their concerns are mostly associated with their families and with the local community."[10]

Emulator Consumers are very outer directed.

"They emulate the patterns of those they consider to be wealthier, or more successful than they. These people are on the climb, highly concerned with the impressions they make, and at the stage in life of high ambition and maximum social and job mobility. Generally they have good education, good incomes, and tend to live in cities."[11]

Achiever Consumers are the success driven persons who use most of their wealth and energy to obtain the good things in life.

"These are rugged individualists in the frontier tradition—competitive, self-confident, and willing to try the new, especially if it smacks of technological innovation. At the same time they do not want too much change because they are on top, and really radical change might shake them off. They are well educated, affluent, and influential. They are generally found at the top of business, politics, and the professions."[12]

The three inner directed groups are segmented as the I-Am-Me Consumer, the Experimental Consumer, and the Socially Conscious Consumer.

I-Am-Me people total about 17 percent of the adult U.S. population. They are young and individualistic individuals who are likely to pass quickly through this stage into the experimental consumer group.

"The Experimental individual is a person who seeks direct experience, deep involvement, intense personal relationships, and a rich inner life. They are young, well educated and affluent, belong to many of the avant-garde movements; they are active in 'far out' ideas, ranging from astrology to

Table 3.3 U.S. Market Segments as Suggested from Lifestyle Research

Consumer Group	Demographic Characteristics	Personal Values	Buying Emphasis	Current Adult Population (%)
Money Restricted Consumers	Low Income Older Little Education	Survival Security	Basic Needs Staples Functional Items Occasional Splurge	12
Belonger Consumers	Low to Middle Income Slightly Older Low to Average Education	Conforming Conventional Unexperimental Formal, Puritanical Sentimental Traditional	Family Home Fads Middle and Lower Mass Markets	38
Emulator Consumers	Good Income Young Middle Education	Ambitious Upwardly Mobile Status Macho Competitive	Display Oneself Conspicuous Top of the Line Highly Visible Items Voguish Fashion	10
Achiever Consumers	Excellent Income Wide Age Spectrum— Emphasis on Middle Good Education	Success Materialism Fame, Status Efficiency Comfort	Give Evidence of Success Top of the Line Luxury and Gift Markets "New and Improved"	24

I-Am-Me Consumers	Student or Young Professional Incomes Many Singles Good Education	Fiercely Individualistic Aggressive Dramatic Impulsive	Display One's Taste Experimental Fads Market Extremes Volatile Buying Patterns Source of Far-out Trends	17
Experimental Consumers	Bimodal: Low and Moderate Incomes Mostly under 40 Many Young Families Good Education	Participative Avant Garde Artistic Experimental Process over Product	Obtain Direct Experience Interaction with People Vigorous Sports "Making" Home Pursuits Outdoor Activities	6
Socially Conscious Consumers	Bimodal: Low and Good Incomes Mostly under 50 Excellent Education	Societal Responsibility Environmentalism Global Philosophy Smallness of Scale Inner Growth Simple Living	To Conserve, Protect, Heal Many Specific Concerns	5
Integrated Consumers	Good to Excellent Incomes Bimodal in Age Excellent Education	Sense of Fittingness Inner Assuredness Psychological Maturity Tolerant Self-actualizing World Perspective	Varied Self-expression Esthetically Oriented Ecologically Aware One-of-a-Kind Items	2

Source: Adapted from information and data presented by Arnold Mitchell and Christine MacNulty, "Changing Values and Lifestyles," *Long Range Planning*, Vol. 14, No. 2 (April 1981), pp. 37–41.

yoga—their desire for direct, often unusual experience leads them to such sports as hang-gliding and backpacking; to have pursuits such as winemaking, weaving, and gardening; and to such activities as volunteer social work. They are strongly person-centered, well educated, somewhat intellectual, aesthetically inclined, and with good financial prospects. As consumers they are highly experimental in 'establishment' terms, but may be rather conforming in terms of their peers."[13]

The size of this group is expected to double to about 12 percent of the adult population during the next ten years. Another group that is expected to double in size in the next ten years is the Socially Conscious Consumer. Most of these people are affluent and leaders or members of activist groups concerned with the physical environment. The Integrated Consumer segment is composed of psychologically mature people who are quite certain of their preferences. The greatest impact in the future is likely to come from the rapidly growing inner-directed groups which tend to be the best educated and most affluent members of the U.S. population. Inner-directed consumers buy to satisfy their own internal needs rather than buying goods which are identified with social status. Thus, they prefer high quality, durable goods and natural rather than synthetic goods. They also prefer do-it-yourself projects such as winemaking, knitting and sewing clothing, furniture construction, and artistic creations.

"Their attitudes also have an effect on the way in which products can be advertised and merchandised. Inner-directeds do not respond to advertisements which emphasize: bigger, better, new improved version, washes whiter than . . . and so forth. They want to know more about the actual products, what they are made from, by what process, what do they consume. They prefer small specialty stores to large supermarkets and department stores. Aside from wanting more personal, friendly service it facilitates the ordering of special brands and types of goods."[14]

Selecting Market Segments

Selecting market segments that will constitute target markets is a decision that may be made at corporate headquarters of large national chains. This practice leaves little discretion to local managers. On the other hand, managers of independent stores usually have complete discretion in choosing their target markets.

Target market selection involves consideration of many different factors. First, an estimate forecast of current and future attractiveness of various market segments can serve as a guide for selecting target markets. For example, the lifestyle research summarized in Table 3.3 indicates that inner-directed segments will double in size during the next ten years. The resulting increase in demand for certain types of merchandise is not likely to be met by current retailers unless they recognize the existence of this segment and act to serve its needs.

Second, an evaluation of trends in the technological, economic, social, and political environments can lead one to identify new market segments. For instance, advances in computer technology are reducing the prices of small computers to the point where many small businesses and households can afford to purchase them.

Third, an evaluation of existing competitors can provide clues that will help one make segmentation decisions by identifying target markets that are not being served and those that are being served by many powerful competitors. Retail management should position firm offerings so it can be shielded as much as possible from competitor actions. Thus, a major factor in selection of market targets is a thorough evaluation of the strengths and weaknesses of competition.

Finally, the budget can act to constrain the target markets selected. Firms with very limited resources may seek to attract broad numbers of people by using mass appeals. Certainly treating all segments as though they are alike has an appeal from the cost viewpoint. However, even at the local level each radio or television program and section of the newspaper has a different audience profile. Efficient allocation of resources requires use of research to determine the attractiveness of each target market segment and the best methods of reaching each segment.

Summary

Consumer behavior is subject to many influences. Consumers attempt to satisfy a variety of needs—physiological, safety, belonging, status, and self-actualization—with the financial resources available to them. There are different explanations of how they pursue these objectives.

Keeping abreast of changes in consumer attitudes and motivations is mandatory if a retailer is to develop effective merchandising strategies. Retail management should keep the following points in mind if it is going to effectively satisfy consumer needs.

1. Consumers are problem solvers, so the firms' activities should assist them in solving consumption-related problems.
2. Consumers seek to reduce the risk of making wrong purchasing decisions, so retailers must provide consistent and accurate information.
3. Consumers shop for many different reasons, so the retailer must identify these reasons and respond to them.
4. Variations in store choice and in-store behavior can be better explained by understanding consumer behavior. The consumer responds to a series of cues which the retailer needs to understand (and

generate) in order to develop strategies that will stimulate buying decisions. Retailers must realize that in today's market consumers are the bosses of the marketplace. Consumerism is a powerful political force that is influencing the enactment of numerous laws that regulate the activities of retailers.

Questions

1. Distinguish between complementary and substitute items in terms of price and demand changes. What relationship (if any) would you expect between an increase in the price of gasoline and the price of motor oil? Between a decrease in the price of butter and the demand for margarine?
2. What is meant by real personal income? How does inflation affect the discretionary and nondiscretionary patterns of consumer spending?
3. How important are reference groups in retailing?
4. What is conspicuous consumption and why is it important in retailing?
5. What social classes are most likely to patronize a store that is designed to attract members of some other social class? Which classes are least likely to make this changeover? What types of merchandise would you expect to sell to these changeover customers?
6. How would you use the concepts covered in question 5 to design a sales promotion plan for high-quality suits to be sold in a discount store in a major metropolitan area?
7. How does the concept of the family life cycle influence retailing decisions and long-range plans?
8. Consider each level of Maslow's hierarchy as a market segment and describe how you would go about marketing some product or line of products to each segment.
9. Many retailers define their target markets as being consumers in the top 40 percent of the income distribution. Discuss how these retailers can reach 60 percent of the total buying population potential yet only have to serve 40 percent of the people. What changes appear to be taking place to make this segment even more attractive for retailers?
10. Buying motivations arise from consumer wants. List five of the essential buying motives and discuss how each motive can be satisfied by: (1) a jewelry retailer, (2) a home furnishings retailer, and (3) a supermarket.

Footnotes

1. Matilda Frankel, "What Do We Know about Consumer Behavior?" in *Selected Aspects of Consumer Behavior—A Summary from the Perspective of Different Disciplines* (Washington, D.C.: National Science Foundation, 1976), p. 12.

2. Fabian Linden, "Demographically, 1980's Look Bright," *Marketing News*, Vol. XIII, No. 18, March 7, 1980, p. 2.

3. "The Customer of the 80's: Gearing Up for Change," Jeweler's Circular-Keystone, January, 1980, p. 66.

4. Ibid.

5. Ibid., p. 67.

6. Ibid., p. 68.

7. Adapted from Donald F. Cox, ed., *Risk Taking and Information Handling in Consumer Behavior* (Boston: Harvard University Division of Research, Graduate School of Business Administration, 1967), pp. 5–6.

8. Arnold Mitchell and Christine MacNulty, "Changing Values and Lifestyles," *Long Range Planning*, Vol. 14, No. 2 (April 1981): 37–41.

9. Ibid.

10. Ibid.

11. Ibid.

12. Ibid.

13. Ibid.

14. Ibid.

Case Study: Consumer's Cooperative Inc.

Consumer's Cooperative Inc. is a retail cooperative that sells a fairly complete line of gasoline, diesel, oil, tires, batteries, auto accessories, fertilizer, agricultural chemicals, animal feeds and tire repairs to local farmers, ranchers and the 500 residents of the small midwestern town where the firm is located. Consumer's Cooperative Inc. delivers about 75 percent of its gasoline, diesel, oil, and animal feed sales directly to the local farmers via its own bulk delivery trucks. The firm also offers on-the-farm tire repair for tractors and large equipment. The Cooperative owns twenty-two liquid fertilizer tank wagons which the farmers and ranchers pull to the field behind their own pickup trucks. It is difficult for the Cooperative to hire and keep good employees so the local manager is proposing that the hours of service be shortened from 7 A.M. to 6 P.M. for Monday through Saturday to 8 A.M. to 5 P.M. for Monday through Friday. Members of the Board of Directors are in favor of the reduced hours although they believe that their only local competitor will maintain his open hours of 7 A.M. to 6 P.M. for Monday through Saturday.

The cooperative is a profitable operation ($215,000 net profit during the last year) and currently obtains a 70 percent share of the local market sales dollar volume of about $4,000,000.

Discussion Questions

1. What alternatives does Consumer's Cooperative Inc. have? What affect will each action have upon both employees and consumers?
2. What do you recommend they do? Why?

Part Two | Developing a Retailing Mix

Comments from the CEO

Earle Ingalls
President
Porteous

Development and growth of America's retail industry can be compared to the nation's industrial complex. From the humble efforts of individuals like F. W. Woolworth, S. S. Kresge, and many others, we have the regional and multinational companies of Woolworth's, K mart, Sears, Filene's of today. Retailing diversity is unparalleled by any industry, and its complexity is hard to comprehend.

The roster of retail companies ranges from the small specialty store which sells a volume of $100,000 or less to the multinational Sears, Roebuck and Company which has sales of over $20 billion. The retail industry includes all sorts of special merchandise classifications, from work clothes to fashion boutiques from discount stores to the prestige department stores. Each store was founded on one business precept—the need to serve in their chosen market. Each store either succeeded or failed depending upon their ability to translate the market needs into goods and services. Successful stores have prospered and grown by establishing a reputation and personality in their market places.

To focus on a particular segment of retailing, my entire professional career has been with a family-owned department store. Our history has been somewhat the opposite of the growth patterns for most department stores. The company was founded in the late 1800s by John Porteous in Norwich, Connecticut. As with many of the early general merchandise companies, the founding store became the base for another store in another market. At one time Porteous, Mitchell and Braun had several stores stretching from Connecticut to Grand Rapids, Michigan. In 1906 Porteous decided to consolidate his retail holdings in Portland, Maine, and the Portland store has since been the headquarters.

With the growth of the Northern New England market, another store opened in a regional shopping mall in Newington, New Hampshire in 1974. Since then two more stores have opened in regional malls; the first in Bangor, Maine in 1978, and the second in Auburn, Maine in 1979. Porteous, Mitchell and Braun anticipates opening a fifth store in a regional mall in South Portland, Maine in 1983.

The growth and prosperity of a family-owned retail establishment has been accomplished only through the dedication of the family and its employees. Consistent planning and awareness of the market that we chose to serve has enabled the company to expand its market share and to finance its growth from one store to four.

While Porteous, Mitchell and Braun does not profess to have the sophistication of the huge retail companies, it is able to offer career opportunities to employees who are interested. We have always believed that the company's greatest asset is our people. The stores' merchandise mix is keyed to each market, but the personality and reputation is a product of human contact. The company's growth and success has been a product of the employees' efforts. Our stores have participated in civic activities within all market areas. The company's policies have been and will continue to be one of customer service, recognizing that "A store is more than just a store—it's part of the hopes and lives of people."

Chapter 4 | The Product and Product Planning

Learning Goals

1. To understand why a retailer must stock merchandise and offer services that satisfy the needs of the firm's target market consumers.
2. To be able to discuss methods retailers use to arouse consumer interest in the firm's offerings.
3. To be aware of current merchandising trends.
4. To be able to discuss the advantages and disadvantages of using space yield concept.

Key Terms and Concepts

total product
systems selling
augmented product
want slip
vendor
shopping the competition
shopping goods
specialty goods
convenience goods
width of merchandise
   assortment
merchandise line
merchandise assortment
depth of merchandise
   assortment

consistent merchandise
   assortment
inconsistent merchandise
   assortment
product life cycle
fashion cycle
fashion goods
staple goods
compatability of product
   lines
scrambled merchandising
turnover
gross margin dollars
return on investment
net space yield concept

A successful retail outlet must stock goods of a type and price level that are consistent with the target consumer's needs and the store's location and image. The discussion in the present chapter will concentrate on the importance of stocking a product line that will meet the needs of the retailer's potential or actual customers. It will examine the major merchandise policy decisions faced by retailers—those relating to the question, "What products should we stock?" The first section presents some basic product concepts. The second section examines the merchandise assortment decision—the range, kind, and brands of products the retailer should stock. This second section also examines the product elimination decision.

Total Product Concept

Product selection or rejection seems to be a simple concept. Actually, a retailer's selection of merchandise and service offered must involve a great deal of planning and study in order to estimate sales potential and to determine how successful the venture will be. Selection of the best product-service offering is the first step in the retail planning process (Figure 4.1). It is the first step because the retailer must know what is being sold before a determination about location or type of outlet can be made. Only after the strategic decisions contained in Figure 4.1 have been set can the retailer proceed to the more tactical retail decisions which can be changed relatively easily, such as pricing, personnel, advertising, control of merchandise and money, etc.[1]

The product-service offering is a strategic decision which involves the analysis of market and competitive trends hoping to identify gaps that create a market opportunity. Innovativeness is the key as the offering should be based upon filling unsatisfied consumer needs. This calls for a great deal of creativity as both consumer needs and competitors' offerings must be evaluated to yield an offering that can partially shield the firm from direct competition.

Defining a product is not an easy task, but one must begin with such a definition if he or she is to be truly creative in designing a good merchandise-service mix.

A product consists of more than the tangible, physical product that is offered to consumers. The **total product** is the tangible item combined with the whole set of services that accompany it when it is sold to the consumer. Total product sales can be accomplished by using either systems selling or suggestive selling.

The term **systems selling** is used to convey the idea of selling a total product. Additional elements contributing to customer satisfaction may include a formal written guarantee and assistance in product utilization or in its proper care and maintenance. When retailers fully appreciate the extended product concept, they profitably consider their potential customer's total consumption system. The consumption system describes the way a purchaser performs the total task of whatever it is that he or she is trying to accomplish when using the product.

An illustration of total product sales using suggestive selling is an observed reaction to an announcement of stricter enforcement of a local ordinance requiring metal garbage cans with lids. All retailers—except one—stocked many pairs of garbage cans and lids to sell to the consumers who would be "forced" to buy their product at a combined price of about five dollars. The astute exception stocked some matched garbage cans and lids, but rec-

Figure 4.1   Strategic Retail Planning Process Steps

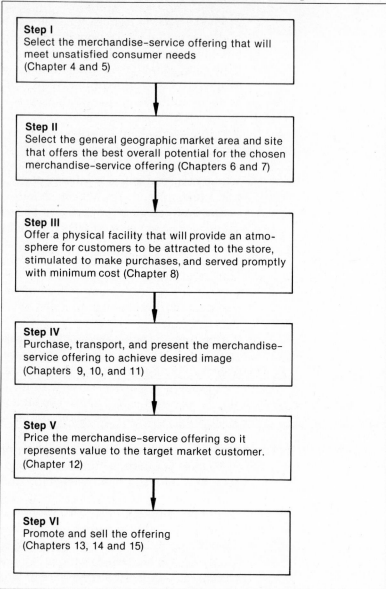

Step I
Select the merchandise-service offering that will
meet unsatisfied consumer needs
(Chapter 4 and 5)

Step II
Select the general geographic market area and site
that offers the best overall potential for the chosen
merchandise-service offering (Chapters 6 and 7)

Step III
Offer a physical facility that will provide an atmosphere for customers to be attracted to the store,
stimulated to make purchases, and served promptly
with minimum cost (Chapter 8)

Step IV
Purchase, transport, and present the merchandise-
service offering to achieve desired image
(Chapters 9, 10, and 11)

Step V
Price the merchandise-service offering so it
represents value to the target market customer.
(Chapter 12)

Step VI
Promote and sell the offering
(Chapters 13, 14 and 15)

ognized that the main consumer need was not for more cans but only for lids to cover their old garbage cans. He therefore stocked and sold lids separately (at about $1.19) to a volume market. Of course, this retailer did not make a fortune from the sale of lids, but through suggestive selling, he sold chains to fasten the lids to the garbage cans so they could not be lost again. Profits derived from the combined sales were not large, but his recognition of this consumer need attracted several hundred new customers into his store for the first time.

This kind of creative merchandising can have a tremendous long-run impact upon business. Satisfied consumers who give word-of-mouth reference for a retailer can influence more consumers to shop at that store than any single expenditure in the mass media.

Total product selling can also treat an item as **an augmented product.** The augmented product is not the item itself but the essential benefit that the buyer expects to gain from the product. Consumers will be looking for different benefits depending upon their needs. The augmented product idea implies that benefits, not product features, should guide the retailer's strategy.

Cosmetic retailing can be used to illustrate the function of the augmented product concept. In this case, the tangible product, the cosmetic, is in a strictly physical sense a product possessing a specified set of chemical and physical attributes. But the tangible product is not what the consumer is buying; she is buying beauty. Thus, retailing the augmented product involves selling beauty—not lipstick or eye shadow—to provide the essential benefit expected by the potential customer. Once retailers recognize this, they begin to provide beauty counselors to assist women to become (or remain) beautiful by suggesting purchase and use of certain cosmetics that would go well together and be tailored to suit individual needs.

Clothing retailers can use the same reasoning to sell color-coordinated ties, suits, shoes, and socks. In summary, the total product concept involves using the whole product—tangible product, service, warranty, and psychological contributions—to coincide with the benefits that a group of potential consumers expects to receive from a product.

Merchandise Line Decisions

Current Customer Need Satisfaction

Customer needs are the most basic considerations in establishing a retailer's product line policy. Customers' preferences with regard to the price class of goods, quality, styles, colors, and the like determine if products will sell well or will not sell at all. In an economy where discretionary consumption is quite prevalent, the task of anticipating consumer preferences successfully is quite difficult. Information on consumer preferences can be obtained through research conducted within the company and from outside sources.

Data from Company
Sources

Analysis of past sales records provides one of the best estimates of consumer preferences for all items, including those that are subject to changes in demand because of preference switches made on the basis of fashion, style, or whatever. Analysis of a retailer's past sales data, adjusted for seasonal fluctuations, indicates consumer preferences for size, color, style, quality, or brand labels. This information allows the retailer to identify those items that are most likely to be best sellers.

Returned goods and adjustment data also contain information pertinent to product line decisions. Frequent consumer complaints and/or frequent returns of an item indicate some fundamental weakness in that item's ability to give satisfaction under normal use conditions. Such negative feedback should be given more serious weight than it might at first appear to deserve because only a few of the dissatisfied customers will make the effort to complain and/or return merchandise. Severely dissatisfied consumers are also likely to classify all of the store's merchandise in the same category as the inferior items. This can lead to a switch in store patronage and cause the store to lose many previously loyal customers. Thus, products made of inferior material or with poor workmanship should be eliminated from the product line as soon as their inferior qualities are discovered.

A record of items requested by potential customers but not carried by the store is an excellent source of new product ideas. This record could be maintained on a form located near the cash register. The request record or **want slip** should be sufficiently detailed to include a description of the items desired, plus other consumer-provided information on color, size, style, price, and so forth (Figure 4.2). This type of form is frequently contained in a *want book* with perforated pages that can be easily torn out and sent to merchandise buyers.

Salespeople may be encouraged by certain incentives and regular supervision to suggest alternative merchandise that is currently in stock. If such substitutes are not acceptable, the originally requested item should be reported. Usually sales clerks are also able to make good suggestions on the types of products that should be stocked. Because salespeople have the most direct contact with customers, they are good sources of product ideas.

Careful consideration should be given to want slip informa-

Figure 4.2 Sample Want Slip Form

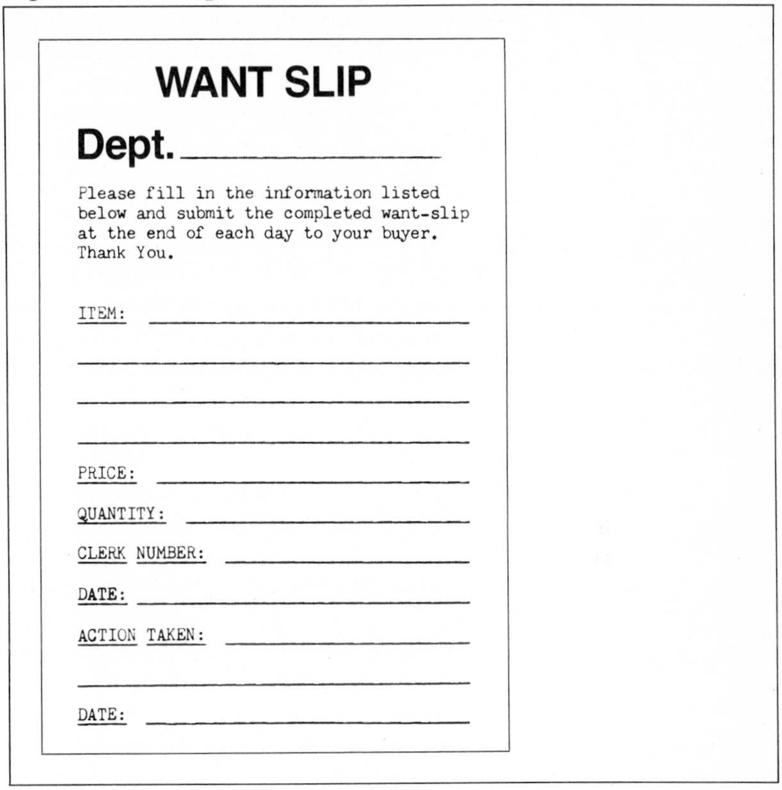

```
                 WANT SLIP

  Dept._____

  Please fill in the information listed
  below and submit the completed want-slip
  at the end of each day to your buyer.
  Thank You.


  ITEM:     _____

  _____

  _____

  _____

  PRICE:    _____

  QUANTITY: _____

  CLERK NUMBER:  _____

  DATE: _____

  ACTION TAKEN:  _____

  _____

  DATE: _____
```

tion. Requests for fad and/or fashion items require an immediate decisive response. The greatest risk is getting too much merchandise too late to capitalize on the item profitably. Fast twenty-four to forty-eight hour delivery can spell success in these situations.

Customer inquiries for additional staple items require a different retailer response. The danger in meeting isolated, individual requests is accumulating slow-moving inventories and overstock. Most merchandise is packaged in multiple units that require special orders and entail delays. Unless the customer makes a significant deposit, he or she may be tempted to purchase elsewhere, leaving the merchant with excessive stock.

Remember, the retailer must be responsive to target market needs but cannot be "all things to all people."

Information from Outside Sources

Retailers can obtain estimates of consumer demand from the wholesalers, manufacturers, jobbers, and others who sell merchandise to the store. Accuracy of such estimates is dependent upon the amount of consumer research conducted by these sellers. Some **vendors** (as these sellers are commonly called) provide bulletins or computer reports that indicate past sales for items they are selling. Franchise vendors usually provide sales estimate data to their outlets to assist their client-partners in maximizing profitability.

Retailers may observe product lines offered by other retailers with the idea that successful outlets have already identified the items that are selling well. Such visits to other local stores and similar stores in other areas are made by retail management personnel, who may even purchase merchandise for the purpose of making a detailed comparison with their store's offerings. These visits also provide retailers with an estimate of the competition intensity they are likely to encounter on each item.

Many retailers are successful because they offer unique product lines. **Shopping the competition** (allowing store employees to make price and product comparisons in competitive outlets) is done by all types of retailers, but especially by small retailers who cannot afford more costly methods of demand estimation. These smaller retailers are more likely to carry unique merchandise because they are not bound by established product line policies as are some large chain stores. Store visits are also used by retailers who are opening a new outlet in the area and lack past sales records for the target area.

Trade magazines, newspapers, and other publications also contain information on the items, styles, colors, and so forth that consumers appear to prefer or are likely to prefer in the near future.

Consumer surveys can be used by large retailers to provide preference information on fashion items. Such surveys could be conducted in person, by telephone, or by mailing questionnaires to the store's current or potential customers. The store's credit and customer records could serve as a mailing or telephone listing. These surveys should be designed and analyzed by knowledgeable persons who are familiar with proper survey procedures, since the use of improper survey techniques can lead to incorrect decisions.

Several "outside" agencies conduct customer surveys that provide retailers with information on consumer purchasing habits. The A. C. Nielsen Company and the R. L. Polk Company are sources of detailed consumer buying data. Newspapers such as the *Denver Post, Chicago Tribune, New York Times*, and many smaller newspapers also sponsor periodic research on consumer buying patterns.

**Interest Arousal
with Merchandise
Assortment**

Retail competition frequently involves market segmentation based on merchandise assortment. Retailers use market segmentation by planning their merchandise assortment to meet the demands of some particular subgroup of consumers who have similar motivations. One of the first requirements for successful market segmentation is to identify the consumer group or groups that appear to offer the best potential market. The retail merchandise assortment can then be altered to meet the needs and preferences of these target market groups.

Just as it is necessary to segment the market to improve retailing efficiency, it is also important to classify products according to the amount of time and effort spent by the average consumer in seeking to purchase the product (Table 4.1). Three broad categories of consumer goods are: (1) shopping goods, (2) specialty goods, and (3) convenience goods. The basic goal of retailing is consumer satisfaction. Thus, this classification of goods and services focuses on the consumer, not on the products themselves. Since the consumer is the focal point for the entire retailing program, retailers should use this classification of products concept when they make decisions not only on merchandise but on all elements of the retailing mix.

Stores selling **shopping goods** (goods the consumer usually purchases only after making several comparisons on quality, price, and style) usually make the most distinct segmentation appeals. The merchandise assortment in stores selling mainly shopping goods such as furniture, clothing, shoes, used automobiles, and major appliances may be selected to appeal to a specific market target, which may be the youth market, a specific ethnic group, an extremely high income group, and the like.

Shopping goods are products about which the consumer does

**Table 4.1 Consumer Goods Classification Based on Degree of
Consumer Prepurchase Planning**

	Classification of Goods		
	Convenience Goods	Shopping Goods	Specialty Goods
Degree of Prepurchase Planning Made by Consumer	Little	Some	Considerable
Degree of Brand Preference	Little	Makes brand comparison	Insists on specific brand
Amount of Shopping Effort Used by Consumer	Minimum	Moderate	Maximum

not have thorough knowledge. The consumer shops for this information by making several trips to various stores to compare one product with another. Because the price of shopping goods is relatively high and because the item may account for a relatively high percentage of the individual's budget, the consumer purchases shopping goods much less frequently than convenience goods.

Frequently the consumer buys shopping goods on the basis of the best price, delivery, and customer service available. Independent shopping goods retailers have become successful by offering delivery, repair, return, credit, installation, and other customer services along with the product. This combination is frequently preferred by consumers who like to have their products serviced by the retailer where the item was bought. For this reason shopping goods lend themselves to a franchising arrangement between a local retailer who can provide the service and a national company which can provide a well-known quality product.

Retailers of shopping goods usually try to locate near one another so that consumers who want to go from one store to another to seek advice and information may do so with a minimum of effort.

Stores selling **specialty goods** (goods that are sufficiently unique or have strong enough brand identification to entice a significant group of buyers to habitually make a special purchasing effort) can also benefit by developing a merchandise assortment to reach one or more market segments. Some retailers of photographic equipment, hi-fi components, sporting goods, and men's suits, for example, carry only exclusive, high-quality brands to cater to the very quality-conscious segment of the market.

There is generally a strong brand preference for specialty goods, and the consumer has a fairly complete knowledge of the product. The consumer tends to accept no substitute for this brand but continues to shop for the specific brand he or she prefers. Frequently, when he or she finds a retail store which offers this favorite brand, the consumer continues to patronize that store because the item can be purchased without using any extra effort to find it elsewhere. It is important to note that the brand name serves as the basis for the consumer selecting one outlet over other outlets. Generally there is only one retailer offering specialty goods in a given trading area during any one point in time. This gives the competitive advantage to the retailer who does not have to compete with other local stores on this particular brand. Thus, specialty stores can also lend themselves to a franchise agreement between a local retailer and a supplier of a well-known branded product. Under such a contract, the retailer may be guaranteed the right to be the only outlet allowed to handle the specified brand in a certain geographic area.

Segmentation is used to a lesser extent by stores that primarily sell **convenience goods** (goods the consumer usually purchases with minimum effort at the most convenient and accessible place). Stores stocking only well-known branded merchandise appeal to a different market group than do stores that stock mostly unadvertised brand items or private brand items that are associated with the retailer or some wholesaler instead of with a nationally known manufacturer. Soap, personal care items, packaged food items, other staple items, and impulse goods are examples of convenience goods.

Retailers who sell convenience goods must place emphasis upon the proper location of their outlets. Convenience goods are purchased frequently, and usually the consumer has only a slight brand preference. Consumers of convenience goods generally spend only a minimum amount of effort on making their purchases. They are likely to make most of their purchases of convenience goods at the nearest outlet that sells acceptable merchandise. Thus, the same brand of goods may be sold in many different retail outlets.

Advertising and promotional efforts on convenience goods will not be as likely to lure customers from long distances as similar efforts featuring shopping goods. Retailers who offer mostly shopping goods may therefore be better able to use promotional appeals to overcome a less than optimal location.

Types of Merchandise Assortment

The merchandise assortment decision involves three dimensions—width, depth, and consistency. The **width,** or breadth, **of merchandise assortment** refers to the number of different merchandise lines a store may carry. **Merchandise line** refers to a group of products that are closely related because they satisfy a single class of needs, are used together, or are sold to the same consumer groups. A **merchandise assortment** is composed of a series of demand-related merchandise items that is unique and distinguishable as a separate entity. A supermarket's merchandise assortment typically consists of hundreds of merchandise lines (soft drinks, for example). However, a supermarket generally carries over 10,000 different merchandise items (such as Coke, merchandised in sixteen-ounce bottles in a carton of eight bottles).

Stores offering many merchandise lines (supermarkets, for example) are said to offer a wide line of goods. Stores selling only one line, such as Shakey's Pizza, are said to offer a narrow specialized line.

Merchandise assortments also differ in respect to their depth. **Depth of assortment** refers to the number of items offered within each merchandise line. A shallow assortment is an offering of several items within a product line. A deep assortment involves stocking many different items within a merchandise line.

Maintaining a deeper merchandise assortment generally results in a larger trading area for a given store (Figure 4.3). In addition, a higher percentage of the store's customers is satisfied since they do not have to go to another store to buy that type of merchandise. For example, stocking an adequate supply of many different brand names, each offering a good selection in color, style, and size, will please nearly all customers. However, it also results in a large investment in inventory. If sales volume is not large enough to warrant this huge investment in inventory, then the firm's profits will be adversely affected. In addition, the store's limited selling space forces its management to either not stock many merchandise categories with a deep assortment or use only a few merchandise categories.

Figure 4.3   Relationship Between Depth of Merchandise Line and Distance Consumer Is Willing to Travel to Reach a Store

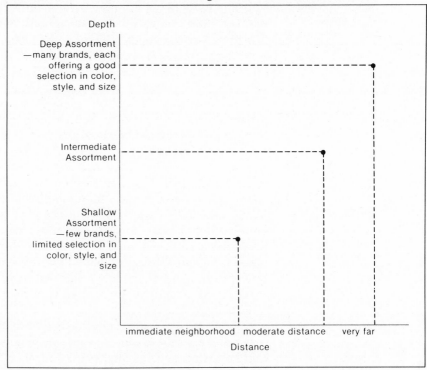

Consistency of the merchandise assortment (the degree of relationship between various merchandise lines in terms of consumer end use) is also an important aspect of merchandise assortment planning. Merchandise assortments that are very closely related in use are highly consistent. Liquor stores that sell only liquor and mix items offer a highly consistent merchandise assortment. An **inconsistent merchandise assortment** exists when the merchandise lines offered are not related to one another in terms of consumer usage. Proper grouping of related merchandise within departments, as well as logical arrangement in a store layout, enhances the possibility of additional impulse purchases by customers.

The appropriate assortment is affected by the estimate of marketing opportunity and by the image the store wishes to project. A store that emphasizes "one-stop shopping" or "full-service merchandise" advertising themes is likely to offer complete merchandising assortments—wide merchandising lines with deep assortments of goods and services that complement one another. Other retailers who find a small market segment to serve usually offer more narrow merchandise lines and more shallow merchandise assortments because their offering is reduced to the most popular items that appeal to their target market.

For example, if a retail manager of such a store finds that three-fourths of his store's sales in a certain merchandise line originate from only four of the fifteen items carried, he is likely to decide that it is not worth the extra effort and expense to stock and maintain eleven extra items. On the other hand, a store that has a "one-stop shopping" or "full-service" theme is more likely to carry all fifteen items because of its different management philosophy. Neither policy is incorrect because merchandise assortments must be based on company goals and objectives and on consumer preferences.

Adding and Dropping
Merchandise Lines

Retailers are continually besieged with offers of "new" merchandise. This merchandise may be considered new because it is an entirely new technological development or merely because it is a substitute "me-too" product (one that is similar to those already on the market) being offered for the first time by a particular manufacturer. This continuous stream of new product offerings and a rapid decline in the popularity of some current product offerings force retailers to develop systems that will assist them in identifying the products that should be discontinued. The same systems could be used in the selection of new merchandise lines. Some large firms have developed elaborate point systems, based on projected volume, gross margin, turnover, and so forth, which they effectively use to make their product line decisions.

Growth Potential The growth potential of a new merchandise line should be evaluated to determine how the proposed line compares to other lines in terms of expected performance. Some product sales (those with high income elasticities as outlined in Chapter 6) respond better to increases in consumer incomes than do other products (those with low income elasticities). Accelerated growth potential is indicated on merchandise lines having a high income elasticity (those products for which a relatively higher percentage of income is spent as consumers' incomes increase).

Radios, television sets, foreign travel, sporting goods, and toys have responded very favorably to the income increases that occurred between 1948 and 1965. Items that are associated with the rise of leisure time have recently experienced relatively significant growth. The most spectacular increase is in the purchase of products used in the pursuit of pleasure and relaxation. Items such as bowling balls, color television sets, camping vehicles, cameras, and boats are faring quite well in this boom. Expenditures related to the use of these goods, such as traveling and vacationing, also are increasing rapidly.

Merchandise line growth is also affected by the age of the product line being considered. Products age and their sales decline over time. The product life cycle concept can be used to provide some insight and guidelines to assist the retailer in making merchandise assortment decisions. The term **product life cycle** suggests that products move through success stages of sales and profit conditions: introduction, growth, maturity, and decline. Figure 4.4 is a graph of a product life cycle.

Retailers frequently incur losses in the introduction phase of a product life cycle because many risks are associated with products in this stage. Generally the price is relatively high, and the item may be merchandised only by exclusive outlets. Sales volume is normally low. Low sales volume and a high degree of risk influence the retailer to carry only a relatively low level of inventory for the product positioned in the introduction phase.

The growth phase begins when sales start to rise rapidly. The retail merchandise assortment usually increases as more models, styles, colors, sizes, and so forth are manufactured to meet increased consumer demands. A buildup of larger retail inventories is needed to lessen the possibility of being out of stock. The rate of growth begins to decline at the start of the maturity phase. Sales continue to increase but at a decreasing rate. Com-

Figure 4.4 Product Life Cycle

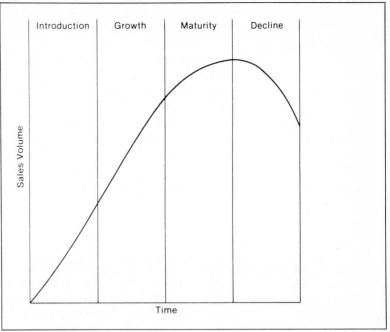

petition also begins to intensify as more me-too products are introduced. This causes a decline in prices, which requires a more careful balancing of retail inventories. Retailers may also attempt to capitalize on the product differentiation and packaging innovations offered by leading suppliers during this maturity stage of the cycle.

Merchandise sales start to turn downward at the beginning of the decline stage. The product is making continually smaller contributions to retail profit primarily because of lower sales volume. Retailer's responses made at this stage include reexamination of required inventory levels and a decision on the appropriate time to close out the remaining product stock.

The **fashion cycle** concept is also important to retailing since the fashion-minded consumer is a prime target market for the retail industry. **Fashion goods** are associated with frequent changes in style, color, or design. The other merchandise term, **staple goods**, refers to standardized items that change slowly over time. Increasing emphasis on new products, colors, and unique designs is making it more difficult to distinguish staple goods from fashion goods. However, staple goods are necessity items. As incomes increase, the relative importance of fashion goods increases.

The length of the fashion cycle is affected by the same factors that affect the product life cycle, and the same four stages can be defined. However, the fashion cycle can repeat itself continuously over a period of time for the same item or style, because the decline phase may be temporary. It is followed by an upswing and a new cycle. A successful fad product may also follow the typical product life cycle, but its sales usually rise faster, reach a peak (as opposed to a plateau), and then fall more abruptly (Figure 4.5).

As noted earlier, retail managers should consider the fashion cycle concept when they are planning their merchandise assortment. Certain types of stores are more appropriate than others for merchandising a given fashion through each of its four stages. If the store is to project its desired image, its management should balance the store's merchandise assortment of fashion items with its customers' shopping attitudes and practices.

Compatibility with Other Merchandise Lines. **Compatibility of product lines** refers to the degree that either current or planned lines meet the needs of the market segments being served by the store. The trend toward **scrambled merchandising** (unrelated

Figure 4.5   Life Cycle for Fad Product

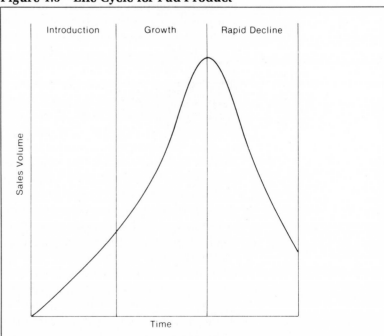

merchandise sold by the same store) may have decreased the relative importance of this compatibility consideration. However, merchandise lines must agree (in terms of quality, style, color, size, and so forth) with preferences of the target market customers.

Some of the merchandise lines available to the store are simply consumer substitutes for one or more of the store's existing lines; that is, consumers use several products for the same purpose. Products may be identical except for brand name or color, or they may differ in some slight way. Stocking similar, or me-too, merchandise lines usually causes most sales to originate from the brand that is considered superior by the store's consumers. One brand begins to divert sales from the others.

Because a store's selling space is limited, each item's sales must be evaluated to determine if it is worth handling. In cases where one item is superior to other similar items, the inferior items may be pared from the offering.

In some instances, however, consumers do not consider one item to have a market superiority over other so-called substitute items. If this is the case, total store sales volume can increase because the consumer responds favorably to a wider merchandise selection.

Merchandise lines can also complement one another. Perfectly complementary items are usually sold together because the sale of one necessitates the sale of the other if the first item is to be used immediately. For example, the sale of a camera necessitates the sale of appropriate film before the consumer is able to take pictures. Sale of a fishing pole can be combined with sales of a reel, fishing line, and lures because the customer ultimately will need to acquire these items before he or she can use the fishing pole.

Stocking complementary merchandise lines is usually desirable because the sale of one item can stimulate the unplanned purchase of several complementary or accessory items. Moreover, the customer is likely to be less sensitive to higher price tags on smaller complementary items such as film. Ties, belts, and shoes that are color coordinated with a sport coat that has just been purchased are also examples of accessory items that can be merchandised successfully because they complement a larger item.

Other merchandise lines that are neither substitutes nor complements for existing merchandise lines should generate sufficient sales to be profitable by themselves. In other words, items that are unrelated to the rest of the merchandise assortment can increase store profits and remain in the merchandise line only if they make a positive contribution to overhead. If such products do not generate traffic for complementary, accessory, or substitute products, the stocking decision must be based solely on the items' own merits.

Competitive Conditions Competition is another consideration in the task of evaluating new merchandise line worth. If a retail outlet can obtain an exclusive geographical right to carry an item, this agreement would minimize direct competition with other local retailers. Retailers may also prefer to handle a specific item if the estimated sales volume appears to justify its addition to their lines and if the manufacturer is going to spend a considerable amount of money promoting the item. It is a risky practice not to handle popular well-promoted new items because consumers will be drawn into stores by national advertising, and it is difficult to tell these customers (who may be regular customers) that such an item is not carried by the store. They will probably go to a competitor to make that purchase. Once they enter a competitor's store, they may make price, merchandise, and service comparisons that may result in the loss of their patronage.

Profitability of Merchandise Lines Direct profitability is one of the most important considerations in merchandise planning. Evaluating profitability of a proposed merchandise line generally involves use of some estimated elements. Manufacturers may offer retailer clients test market results that estimate dollar sales based on store size or volume. Estimated unit sales can be multiplied by the gross margin percentage to obtain estimates of future total receipts. The expenses associated with the item can be subtracted from total receipts to obtain the item's contribution to overhead.

Retailing expenses vary from item to item depending on how much time is required for their sale, the amount of service they require, the amount of money required to carry an inventory, and the amount of shelf or floor space required to stock the items. However, from the store management point of view, profitability resulting from addition or deletion of an item is the change in contribution to store profit resulting from the decision to stock or not stock the item.

More conventional ways of determining an item's profitability involve a series of techniques such as calculating indices of turnover rates, gross margin dollars, return on investment, and dollar margins per linear or cubic foot of shelf space.

Turnover data are usually obtained by dividing total dollar sales volume by the average retail price value of inventory. **Gross margin dollars** refers to the dollar difference between per unit

selling price (retail) and purchase price (wholesale). Both turnover and margin influence a good's profitability.

Return on investment (ROI) is an important measure of effective capital utilization. It indicates profitability as a percentage
of the amount of money invested in the store. It can be calculated
using the following formula:

$$\text{ROI\%} = \frac{\text{Profits \$}}{\text{Tangible assets \$}} \times 100$$

Tangible assets include the value of the store building and
equipment (counters, cash registers, and so forth), the amount of
money owed the store on credit sales (accounts receivable), and
the store's investment in inventory.

The **net space yield concept** is a more complete approach in
determining product profit that considers handling costs, space
costs, and margins. The concept is based on the fact that the exposure area of a store (the area exposed to the shopper) must be
used in the most productive way.

Under the net space yield concept, space dimension is considered in exposure area terms because:

1. Different stores use different shelf depths. Exposure (facing)
area is more likely to be uniform.
2. Exposure area can be studied from photographs and easily
charted on graph paper.
3. Manufacturers can compute the necessary exposure area for
their own products. All they need know is the number of facings
required.
4. Store personnel think in terms of facing or exposure.
5. Companies using computers can determine exposure area by
item and insure adequate shelf allocation from store to store.[2]

Table 4.2 shows the necessary measurements that must be completed so that space yield can be calculated for three merchandise categories. The handling cost per case is the cost of handling from warehouse through checkout. Handling cost can be
estimated by retail management, or it can be obtained by using
secondary estimates available from retail trade associations.

In Table 4.2 handling cost for vegetables is estimated to be 95
cents per case. This figure, multiplied by the number of cases
sold per week, gives the total weekly handling cost. Linear display of vegetables is measured as 40 feet long and 5 feet wide, so
that the total exposure and display area in square feet is 200.
"Occupancy" cost for vegetables is estimated to be $60, based on

Table 4.2   Net Space Yield Calculations for Three Merchandise Categories

A. Handling Cost per Case (¢)	B. Cases Sold	C. Total Handling Cost ($) Equals (A × B)	E. Exposure Area Display · (sq. ft.)	F. Occupancy Cost $ Equals (30¢ × E)	Merchandise Category	G. Gross Margin (%)	H. Weekly Dollar Sales	I. Gross Margin Dollars Equals (G × H)	J. Net Gain $ Equals (I) Minus (C + F)	K. Net Space Yield ($) Equals (J/E)
95	210	200	200	60	Vegetables	27	3500	945	685	3.43
55	142	78	100	30	Baby food	15	1100	165	57	.57
84	116	97	140	42	Health and beauty aids	40	3200	1280	1141	8.15

a 30 cents per square foot occupancy cost. Occupancy cost is derived by adding the estimated annual cost for rent, utilities, and depreciation, and dividing the result by the square feet of exposure area in the store.

The gross margin percentage obtained by merchandising vegetables is 27 percent and weekly sales have averaged about $3,500, so the gross profit for vegetables is $945 (gross margin percentage × dollar sales). Net gain is the sum of the total handling cost and occupancy cost, subtracted from the gross profit: $945 − ($200 + $60) = $685. To obtain the net space yield, the net gain is divided by exposure area display in square feet, giving a value of ($685/200 ft. = $3.43), the net profit yield per square foot in the area occupied by vegetables.

This procedure is repeated for all of the merchandise lines the store carries. In this example, baby food items contributed only 57 cents per square foot of exposure area—considerably less than the $3.43 yield on vegetables and the $8.15 on health and beauty items. Thus, the health and beauty line appears to be the most profitable. The high gross margin percentage (40%) obtained on the health and beauty line combined with a good weekly sales level ($3,200) to make this a very profitable line. Baby items, on the other hand, have a low gross margin percentage (15%), combined with low weekly sales ($1,100), to considerably reduce their profitability.

The net space yield concept provides the basis for the following recommendations:

1. Give profitable categories more display space.
2. Give the profitable categories more desirable locations.
3. Prune variety in low-yield categories.
4. Enrich variety in high-yield categories. Retailers will want to consider something even more basic. They will want to set in motion a dialogue with suppliers to learn what can be done with low yields. Together with suppliers, they will try, among other things:
   a. To reduce handling costs.
   b. To reduce bulk wherever possible and urge redesign of hard-to-handle packages.
   c. To shed more light on the relative impact of couponing and deal promotions.[3]

Thus, in our three-category example, the health and beauty aid line could be expanded by adding more items that provide the consumer with more variety. Display space could also be increased for health and beauty items, and they should be given a desirable, high-traffic location in the store. If possible, some items might be pruned from the baby food category.

However, even a low profitability does not automatically indicate that those lines should be severely reduced or eliminated. Baby food is an essential product that will be purchased *somewhere* by a specific segment of the market. A severe reduction in item variety could easily result in loss of sales for other items or even store patronage. The more practical alternative would be to reduce the display space devoted to baby food and place this category in a less desirable location, which will raise the net space yield and redistribute customer traffic past impulse items.

The net space yield concept can be altered in many different ways to more accurately reflect current economic conditions and the specific environment in which the firm is operating. For example, with retail rental rates and interest rates increasing so rapidly, it may be better to use a net yield measure from that of a cubic foot of exposure yield to a yield per square foot of selling space, as rent is usually paid on the basis of square footage of floor space. Interest charges could also be deducted before the net dollar yield is obtained in step J of Table 4.2.

Merchandise Lines Must Change over Time

Consumer desires and needs change not only seasonally but also over long periods of five- to ten-year cycles. For example, automobile preferences of Americans have changed over the last twenty years. The '60s began with great consumer interest in foreign and American compact cars, but gradually the consuming public expressed its preference for larger, better-equipped, full-size units. With the advent of pollution controls and fuel shortages, the current auto buyer is showing great interest in subcompact cars loaded with luxury accessories such as power steering, air conditioning, and so forth. It is even predicted that the true full-size auto will not again be available in the United States.

It should particularly be noted that even though a cycle has seemed to repeat itself, there have been subtle but profound changes in the merchandise offerings that reflect the needs and preferences of today's consumer. Every retailer must be aware of these attitudinal changes and make appropriate adjustments in merchandise offering.

Many of these attitudinal changes are traceable to the consumer's changing demographic characteristics. For example, currently there are indications that department stores may be losing their leadership position for women's clothing. A 1979 survey conducted for the Newspaper Advertising Bureau, Inc. revealed that 39 percent of American women made their most recent dress purchase from a department store, 29 percent from a specialty store, 13 percent from a national chain store, and 10 percent from a discount store. An October 1981 followup survey indicated that 5 percent more women (29%) were shopping in specialty stores and 10 percent fewer (29%) were shopping in department stores, while national chains (15%) and discount stores (9%) remained near 1979 levels.[4] Specialty stores are most preferred by younger and single women as a source of dresses and separates.

Changes of this magnitude illustrate the need for a continual reevaluation of the merchandise assortment to ensure that the store is stocking items that satisfy consumer demand. With the clothing example, the single greatest source of dissatisfaction that women have with department stores as their apparel source was the quality of sales and service help. Besides improving sales/service assistance, other suggestions that consumers had for improving department store offerings were to: (1) arrange clothing by size, item, and style so the consumer could find merchandise easier, (2) provide a bigger and better variety of sizes and styles, (3) use more sales with lower prices, and (4) provide better physical features such as lighting and elevators.

Supermarkets have also had to change their offerings to better meet customer needs. A declining birthrate, plus demographic changes such as more working women and the decline of the conventional family, has put the traditional supermarket in competition with fast-food restaurants and, to a lesser degree, with convenience stores for a share of the consumer's food budgets.

Americans now eat 18 percent of their meals away from home but spend 36 percent of their food dollars doing so. Sales of the nation's convenience stores account for more than 5 percent of the consumer's food dollar. Some industry experts believe that the number of convenience food stores, which offer a limited line of groceries but stay open at odd hours, will soon outnumber the nation's supermarkets.

Thus, supermarkets are placing more emphasis on nonfood items as a way of maintaining sales and profits. In some areas overbuilt supermarket facilites, high grocery inventory, and increased competition from fast-food and convenience outlets have caused the supermarket to not make any money on traditional food items.

Selling nonfoods in supermarkets is nothing new, but the wide assortment of nonfood items currently offered by supermarkets is new. Many new supermarkets devote about one-third of their selling space to nonfood sections such as appliances (television sets, coffee makers, hair dryers, and so forth), hardware, housewares, and auto products. It is now getting to the point that in many areas the grocery business is just a drawing card for the general merchandise business.

Supermarkets are also beginning to meet the fast-food competition head on with expanded deli sections (some of which feature in-store seating and offer specialty items such as teriyaki rolls, barbecued chicken, and lox), in-store restaurants, and even cocktail lounges. Generally these deli and restaurant sections cater to the store's specific target market. For example, Ralph's Grocery Co. stores in the Los Angeles area offer their Oriental population special frozen shrimp and crab dishes which are flown in from Japan.

The extremely wide line of goods offered by these new huge supermarkets is designed to compete directly with fast-food, convenience grocery and general merchandise stores. Management frequently believes that if the customer comes into the store wanting fifteen items but only finds twelve, he or she may not return. These managers believe that the curve outlined in Figure 4.6 represents the relationship between the number of

Figure 4.6   Relationship between Width of Merchandise Line and Percentage of Nonreturning Customers

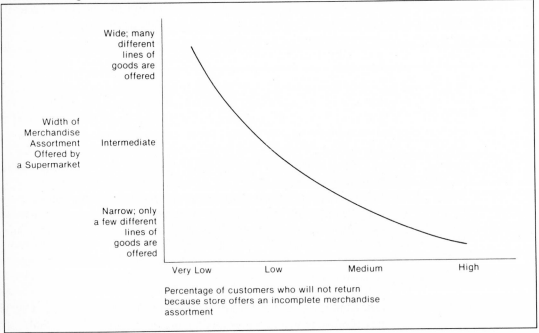

merchandise lines stocked and the percentage of customers who will not return to the store because of an incomplete merchandise assortment. Supermarkets also use private label items (products which carry no association with a nationally advertised manufacturing company) to increase their selection.

Survival Rates by Kind of Retail Business

Little hard data exist on the life expectancy of retail firms in the United States because comprehensive statistics on entry and exit rates of retail firms are seldom available. Perhaps the most useful data available on survival rates for various kinds of retail firms are presented in Figure 4.7 and Table 4.3. These data were developed by tracking 17,252 Illinois retail firms that commenced operation in 1974 and were registered to do business in Illinois. The firms were observed by using records of the Illinois Retailers' Occupational Tax which is administered by the State Department of Revenue. The percentage of firms surviving during

Figure 4.7   Continuing Illinois Retail Firms Started in 1974

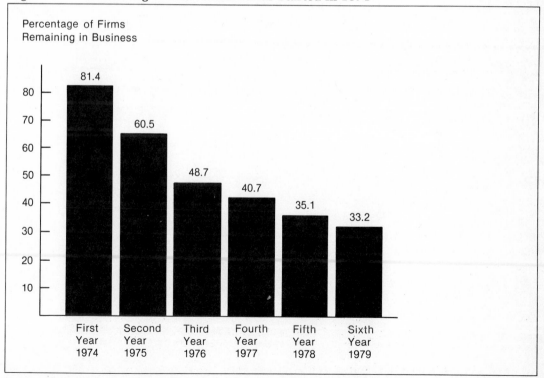

Source: Alvin D. Star and Michael Z. Massel, "Survival Rates for Retailers," *Journal of Retailing*, Volume 57, Number 2, Summer 1981, p. 93.

Table 4.3 Survival Rates by Kind of Retail Business in Illinois*

Kind of business	Number started in 1974	Percentage active in October 1979
Farm equipment dealers	110	63.6
Motor vehicle dealers (new and used)	127	55.9
Lumber yards and other build. materials dealers	116	53.5
Farm and garden supply stores, n.e.c.**	83	53.0
Hay, grain, and feed stores	66	51.5
Drug stores	203	50.7
Hardware stores	230	49.1
Drapery, curtain, and upholstery stores	95	46.3
Shoe stores	88	44.3
Furniture stores	149	44.3
Misc. automotive dealers	241	44.0
Jewelry stores	170	43.6
Book and stationery stores	168	43.5
Household appliance stores	76	43.4
Tire, battery, and accessory dealers	279	43.4
Paint, glass, and wallpaper stores	68	42.7
Antique stores	501	42.5
Florists	221	42.1
Men's and boys' clothing and furnishing stores	109	41.3
Liquor stores	234	40.2
Used-car dealers	465	38.9
Dry goods and genrl. merchandise stores	68	38.2
Sporting goods stores and bicycle shops	406	37.7
Eating and drinking places	745	36.5
Music stores	151	35.8
Food stores, n.e.c.	109	35.8
Misc. stores, general merchandise, n.e.c.	224	35.3
Misc. home furnishings stores	114	35.1
Automatic merchandising	134	35.0
Radio and television stores	164	34.8
Misc. retail stores, specialized, n.e.c.	2061	34.2
Floor-covering shops	157	33.8
Misc. apparel and accessory stores	125	33.6
ALL RETAIL	17,252	33.2
Women's ready-to-wear stores	192	31.8
Drinking places (alcoholic beverages)	1403	30.5
Direct-selling organizations (including door-to-door)	949	30.0
Family clothing stores	92	29.4
Mail-order houses	199	29.2
Gift, novelty and souvenir shops	572	28.9
Meat and fish markets	143	28.7
Secondhand stores	193	27.5
Limited price variety stores	62	27.4
Grocery stores	962	27.0
Dairy products stores	175	24.0
Gasoline service stations	908	23.6
Retail bakeries	115	23.5
Eating places (no alcoholic beverages)	2347	23.0
Candy, nut, and confectionery stores	93	22.6
Fruit stores and vegetable markets	160	20.6

* Only categories with 50 or more new starts in 1974 are listed.
** n.e.c.: not elsewhere classified.

Source: Alvin D. Star and Michael Z. Massel, "Survival Rates for Retailers," *Journal of Retailing*, Vol. 57, No. 2 (Summer 1981): 92–93.

each of the six years that were observed is presented in Figure 4.7.

Survival rate for each type of retail business is presented in Table 4.3. Although many successful retail firms may have sold out for a profit, the relative stability of each type of retail category is expressed by the percentage of the firms started in 1974 that were still "in business" six years later. During the 1974–1979 period, the highest survival rates were for farm equipment dealers and new (and used) motor vehicle dealers. Both of these categories probably were hard hit by the recession of 1980–1981. Thus, selection of a different time period may alter the survival rates of any given category and prospective retailers should be aware of the effect that changes in the economic environment may have upon the success of their business.

Outlet types having the lowest survival rates are: (1) fruit and vegetable markets; (2) candy, nut, and confectionery stores; and (3) eating places without an alcoholic beverage license. These data do not suggest that a profit cannot be made in these lines of retailing, but that competition and the nature of the market are such that a very good marketing plan is needed in order to be successful. For example, the data reveal that adding alcoholic beverages to the product offering of an eating place will increase the firms' chance of survival.

Summary

Retailers' merchandise/service offerings must meet the needs of their target market consumers. They should analyze the way potential customers use the merchandise in order to offer a goods/service mix that reflects customer demand. This can be accomplished by evaluating the offering in terms of the benefits desired by the consumer, which may go well beyond the tangible products themselves. Thus, the offering should provide assistance to the consumer in item usage, maintenance and repair service, and warranties. Delivery and credit also should be provided, but only if the consumers want and are willing to pay for these extended versions of the product. The merchandise assortment must provide the quality, style, color, size, and variety that target consumer groups demand. A deeper merchandise assortment can increase the distance that consumers are willing to travel to reach the outlet.

Store shelf and floor space limit the width and depth of merchandise assortment an outlet can offer. Outlets that sell shopping and specialty goods may benefit by using their limited selling space to concentrate on meeting the needs of a single, narrowly defined target group. Stores that sell convenience goods generally define their target market in broader terms to include numerous market segments.

Each merchandise line should be evaluated on the basis of its current sales, growth potential, compatibility with other merchandise offered, profitability per unit of selling space, and availability in competitive stores. Profitability criterion indicates that more profitable merchandise lines should be given relatively more display space in more desirable locations. This will allow retailers to enrich the variety of their offering in the higher profit categories.

Questions

1. What internal and external sources of information are available to help retailers make product line decisions?

2. Briefly segment the market for tooth brushes and stereo systems. For which of these two products does segmentation seem most effective? Why? What are the implications of this phenomenon for promotion and store location?

3. What is meant by a wide line of goods? A narrow line? A deep line? A shallow line? Cite real or hypothetical examples of each.

4. Discuss the concept "consistency of merchandise assortment." In what types of retailing would you expect the assortment to be consistent?

5. What factors would you consider in deciding whether to add a new product line to your merchandise? Why would you expect the margin to be high on a new product?

6. Discuss the concept of complementary goods and cite examples of such goods. Discuss and cite examples of substitute goods. What are the retailing implications of these concepts?

7. A company has a $100,000 inventory and sales of $20,000 per month.

> **a.** Find the turnover.
>
> **b.** If inventory is increased by 10 percent and turnover remains constant, what is the new sales volume?
>
> **c.** Assuming the same turnover rate, what margin is required if management decides it must have a 20 percent return on investment?
>
> **d.** If management finds that it must maintain a 5 percent margin on a certain product line, and turnover is 5 percent, what is the ROI for this product line? What would you recommend to management in this situation?

8. Why is the measure of gross margin dollars usually a poor method of measuring product line profitability? In what cases would this criterion be an adequate measure of profitability?

9. Why is net space yield considered to be the most reliable measure of product line profitability?

Footnotes

1. Albert D. Bates, *Retailing and Its Environment* (New York, N.Y.: D. Van Nostrand Company, 1979), pp. 82–109.

2. Paul J. Cifrino, "Cifrino's Space Yield Formula," *Chain Store Age*, (November 1963):32–34.

3. Ibid.

4. Alfred Eisenpreis, "Marketing Clothes to Women," A speech given to the National Retail Merchants Association Convention, New York, N.Y., January 12, 1982.

Case Study: Sears Roebuck

Sears Roebuck plans to open five business-machine specialty stores and eventually establish a nationwide chain. The stores, to be separate from its retail outlets, will sell small computers, typewriters, word processors, and other office equipment under both the Sears name and other labels.

Discussion Questions

1. How do you think Sears should proceed with this new product venture? How would you analyze the situation?

<table>
<tr><td>Chapter 5</td><td>

Franchising: A Predetermined Marketing Plan

</td></tr>
</table>

Learning Goals

1. To be aware of the current trends in franchising
2. To discuss the advantages and disadvantages of franchising

Key Terms and Concepts

franchising
territorial franchise
operating franchise
manufacturer sponsored
   franchise systems

wholesale sponsored
   franchise systems
service sponsored franchise
   systems

Franchising represents one instance when the merchandise line decision is usually accepted or rejected in its entirety. The current popularity of franchising warrants a detailed discussion of this important product decision. **Franchising** is a joint venture or cooperative agreement between an owner of a product/service and a dealer. It is a form of licensing by which the owner (the franchisor of a product or service or method) obtains distribution at the retail level through retail distributors (franchisees). The product, service, or method to be marketed is usually identified by a brand name and associated trademarks, uniform symbols, standardized equipment, common storefronts, and stores that operate under a set of standardized policies and procedures. While the franchisee is usually given exclusive access to a relevant target market, the franchisor maintains some degree of control over the operational aspects of marketing the product or service.

Franchise agreements exhibit a wide range of permissions, prohibitions, and statements of duties and responsibilities on the part of both the franchisor and the franchisee. In many cases the relationship extends beyond mere licensing, as is noted by the International Franchise Association when it defines franchising as "a continuing relationship in which the franchisor provides a licensee the privilege to do business, plus assistance in organizing, training, merchandising, and management in return for a consideration from the franchisee."[1]

Basic Franchise Forms

Franchise agreements can be divided into two fundamental types—those that are based on territorial considerations and those concerned with operating aspects.

A **territorial franchise** provides the franchisee with the exclusive right to develop the market potential in a given area. The expectation is that the individual or firm already possesses the necessary skill and resources to proceed on its own with the development of that area for that product or service, bound only by certain basic policies and understandings. Such territorial franchises may encompass a country, a state or region, a city, or a section of a community. Quite often such firms or individuals subfranchise their region and act as the resident management for the parent franchisor.

A territorial franchisor often obtains a percentage of the sales volume made by other franchised units in the territory. A territorial franchisor usually establishes, trains, and occasionally, finances sub-franchises. An example is a branded oil company jobber who owns his own service stations and leases them out. The territorial franchise is granted by the parent franchiser, the oil company.

An **operating franchise** is normally a single unit located on a specific site such as a McDonald's restaurant. The more popular operating franchise agreement concentrates on attracting individuals who qualify for franchisee training and have access to sufficient investment or risk capital. In this case the franchisee receives training, guidance, and assistance from the parent franchisor in return for his or her own work and a share of the gross sales. Franchisors consider their fees as operating expenses of the franchisee and thus receive their remittance on gross sales whether the outlet is profitable or not. Some alternative variations frequently found in franchise agreements are presented in Table 5.1. A classification of different franchise business organizations and representative franchise firms for each category is contained in Table 5.2.

The three major types of franchise systems are:

Sponsored by manufacturers,

Sponsored by large wholesalers, and

In the service industry.

Manufacturer sponsored franchise systems give the franchises the right to manufacture a product or line of products via a specified process. Most manufacturers who market their products

Table 5.1   Variations in Franchise Agreements

Variation in Agreement	Description of Arrangement in Franchise Agreement
1. Distributorship	Franchisee who is the distributor takes title to goods and redistributes goods to subfranchisees who sell goods to consumer.
2. Leasing	Franchisor leases buildings, equipment, and/or land to franchisee.
3. Manufacturing	Franchisor gives franchisee the right to manufacture its product via the use of a specified process. Franchisee distributes product using franchisor's practices.
4. Licensing	Franchisor gives franchisee a license to use franchisor's trademarks and business practices. Franchisor may supply product or give franchisee a list of approved suppliers.
5. Service	Franchisor specifies methods that the franchisee can use to supply the service to consumers.
6. Co-ownership	Franchisor and franchisee share the investment and profits.
7. Co-management	Franchisor retains major part of investment and partner-manager shares profits based on a predetermined percentage.

through franchises do not charge a franchising fee. However, they do expect the franchisees to live up to their operating guidelines and carry their merchandise lines. Some distributors handle several lines; others have an exclusive franchise and handle only one merchandise line. Although these retailers may carry several brand names of merchandise, the dealer who carries only one brand of an item can frequently obtain better manufacturer support than can a multiline dealer. Examples of manufacturer sponsored outlets are retailers who sell B.F. Goodrich tools, Schwinn bicycles, John Deere implements, Ford auto dealers and Conoco oil products.

Wholesaler sponsored franchise systems are common in the grocery, drug, hardware, and automotive parts and accessories industries where franchise dealers are usually organized as voluntary chains. Volume purchasing, private branding, and chain store operating procedures are the major reasons former independent outlets have decided to belong to some type of chain organization. Examples of wholesale sponsored outlets are Western Auto, N.A.P.A. Auto Parts Stores, Ace Hardware, True Value Hardware, Gambles, Walgreen's Drug Stores, Rexall Drug Stores, I.G.A. Grocery Stores, and Associated Grocers.

Service sponsored franchise systems differ from the other two types of franchise systems in that service franchisors generally charge a franchising fee. The main goal of manufacturers and wholesalers is to sell merchandise, so they usually do not charge a franchise fee. The service franchisor's main contribution is the goodwill created by the franchisor, so a fee is charged to the franchisee to pay for this intangible item (goodwill). Examples of

Table 5.2 Categories of Franchise Business Organizations with Representative Firms

Classification	Representative Firms
Automotive Products/Services	AAMCO Automatic Transmissions, Inc.
	B.F. Goodrich Tire Company
	Western Auto
Auto/Trailer Rentals	Budget Rent-A-Car Corporation
	Hertz Corporation
Beauty Salons/Supplies	Edie Adams Cut & Curl
Business Aids/Services	H & R Block, Inc.
	Business Consultants of America
Campgrounds	Kampgrounds of America, Inc.
Clothing/Shoes	Just Pants
	Mode O'Day Company
Construction/Remodeling Materials/Services	Munford Do-It-Yourself Stores
Cosmetics/Toiletries	Color Me Beautiful Cosmetics
Drug Stores	Rexall Drug Company
Educational Products/Services	Evelyn Wood Reading Dynamics
Employment Services	Dunhill Personnel System, Inc.
Equipment/Rentals	United Rent-All, Inc.
Foods–Donuts	Dunkin-Donuts of America, Inc.
	Spudnuts, Inc.
Foods–Grocery/Specialty Stores	The Circle K Corporation
	Hickory Farms of Ohio, Inc.
	Baskin-Robbins, Inc.
Foods–Pancake/Waffle/Pretzel	Village Inn Pancake House, Inc.
Foods–Restaurants/Drive-ins/Carry-outs	A & W International, Inc.
	Burger King Corporation
	McDonald's Corporation
General Merchandise Stores	Coast-to-Coast Stores
	Gamble-Skogmo, Inc.
Health Aids/Services	Health Clubs of America
Home Furnishings/Furnishings/ Furniture–Retail/Repair/Services	Amity, Inc.
Laundries, Dry Cleaning Services	Dutch Girl Continental Cleaners
Lawn and Garden Supplies/ Services	Lawn Medic, Inc.
	American National Service Corporation
Maintenance/Cleaning/ Sanitation–Services/Supplies	
Motels, Hotels	Days Inns of America, Inc.
	Holiday Inns, Inc.
Paint and Decorating Supplies	Mary Carter Industries, Inc.
Printing	Kwik-Kopy Corporation
Real Estate	Century 21 Real Estate Corporation
Recreation/Entertainment/ Travel–Services/Supplies	Billie Jean King Tennis Centers, Inc.
Security Systems	Dictograph Security Systems
Soft Drinks	Bubble-Up Company
Swimming Pools	Sylvan Pools
Tools, Hardware	Snap-On Tools Corporation
Transit Service	Aero Mayflower Transit Company, Inc.
Vending	Ford Gum & Machine Co., Inc.
Water Conditioning	Culligan International Company

Source: Summarized from U.S. Department of Commerce, *Franchise Opportunities Handbook, 1977* (Washington, D.C.: Government Printing Office, 1977), pp. 75–86.

service sponsored franchise systems are Pizza Hut, Kentucky Fried Chicken, Wendy's, Burger King, and McDonald's.

Historical Perspective on Franchising

Even though current interest in the franchise industry and its expansion might lead one to believe that franchising is a twentieth-century innovation, historical evidence indicates that limited franchising was practiced in the early 1800s. Modern franchising, as practiced today, really dates back to 1898, when it was introduced by General Motors. This pioneering effort was followed by Rexall (1902), Western Auto (1909), A & W Root Beer (1919), and Howard Johnson (1926), plus innumerable petroleum, soft drink bottling, variety, grocery, drug, hardware, motel, and fast-food merchandisers through the intervening years.[2]

Aspiring small business retailers were given new hope of success following World War II. In the 1950s a new application of an old idea burst on the American scene—business format franchising. For the first time in recent history the latent entrepreneur could participate as a full partner in the creation of new markets and achieve a long cherished dream of personal independence. As a franchisor, each person could create a new product or service and see their creation replicated in every town from border to border. Alternately, franchisees could acquire a fully integrated package of product, service, trademark, a marketing strategy and plan, operating standards, procedures, and quality controls as well as an information system to measure their success. The potential for overcoming the major causes of small business failures seemed to be at hand.

During the 1960s the term "franchising" became a pseudonym for small business. The widespread use of the automobile, combined with significant disposable incomes, created ready markets for fast food, lodging, and travel franchises. These new channels of distribution fit with the emerging lifestyles of purchasing experiences instead of material goods. America was on the move, both economically and geographically. New market opportunities were found in every city, town, and suburb. Potential franchisees, seeing the successes of the fast food chains, mortgaged their futures and became instant franchised business persons. The franchisor, with limited personal capital, could create a large chain in a short time by selling a packaged business format.

The franchisee provided the capital for the franchise facility, equipment, and labor force. Both parties viewed this as a winning combination.

In the late 1960s franchising experienced major trauma as about fifty entire restaurant franchise systems went out of business in a two-year period, raising serious questions about franchising as a viable mode of distribution.

Frail franchisor organizations, based primarily on celebrities' names but little else, were among the first to go under. History shows major causes of failure were lack of adequate franchisee training and capitalization, poorly chosen locations, and meager continuing managerial support after franchises were established.

Compounding matters, franchisors began to compare the fees they received from successful franchisees as opposed to getting the full return as sole owner. Gradually the firms began to exercise dormant buy-back clauses in the franchise agreements of their more lucrative outlets. Franchisees saw their hard-earned businesses being "repossessed" at a fraction of their current market value. Some of the less successful franchisees found themselves stuck with large plant and equipment investments along with prohibitively high fee schedules, loan payments, and tie-in supply purchase contracts.

Such "abuses" did not go unnoticed by both state and federal governments. Twenty-three states passed fair practice acts in the 1970s. Somewhat belatedly the Federal Trade Commission issued "Disclosure Requirements and Prohibitions Concerning Franchising and Business Opportunities" which became effective on October 21, 1979. Unfortunately the federal rule only deals with fair disclosure before buying into a franchise agreement and does not adequately deal with continuing relations between the parties after the initial contract is signed. Seven states, noting this loophole, have passed legislation specifically addressing the practices in the operation and termination of the franchise agreement.[3]

As the decade closed the franchise industry seemed to have stabilized with smaller franchisors being forced out of business due to the high costs of legal fees and registration costs.

Economic concentration was rapidly taking place in the fast food industry, motel chains, and gasoline service stations. High inflation rates resulting in lower consumer disposable incomes combined with rising interest rates seemed to slow the rate of industry expansion.

Franchising Sales Trends in the 1980s

Franchise sales of goods and services have increased from $156 billion in 1973 to $333 billion in 1981. Not only have sales increased, but so have the number of franchised businesses. In 1971 some 431,000 franchisors were engaged in a wide variety of business activities, and their number has continued to increase to at least 476,000 in 1981.[4]

While the spotlight of public attention has focused on the newer methods of franchising, the traditional forms (such as automobile dealers, service stations, and soft drink bottlers) still represent the backbone of the industry. These traditional franchisees seem to have reached a maturity plateau and are decreasing in numbers of outlets (especially auto and truck dealers and gasoline stations), but they still serve a vital retail function and are obtaining an increased sales volume (Figure 5.1).

Franchising's hopes for future growth would seem to lie in areas which utilize the newer methods of retail merchandising. Among the newer franchising fields the fastest growing sectors include business aids and services, equipment rentals, fast food operations, and recreation, entertainment, and travel.

Between 1970 and 1976 receipts of franchised business aids and service establishments more than doubled and reached an estimated $1.6 billion. In 1981 receipts were expected to reach nearly $9 billion. Real estate franchising continues to be the fastest growing sector of the franchising system in number of units. The high level of interest rates and a turndown in the economy in 1980 and 1981 slowed housing sales. However, during 1980 almost 3,000 independent real estate brokers joined the franchise system, which showed a sales gain of 12 percent in gross commissions from 1979. Under real estate franchise agreements brokers receive guidance in office management and personnel training; benefits of bulk purchase of stationery, signs and forms; as well as access to finance, insurance, escrow, and computer services. Other growth areas in franchising in the business aids and service field are employment agencies and printing and copying services.

The biggest growth sector of the restaurant industry continues to be the franchised food business. Fast food restaurant sales have increased from $14 billion in 1976 to $31 billion in 1981. Stepped-up activity is also evident in such areas as increasing consumer traffic, introduction of new products, store modernization programs, and expanding menus to include breakfast items as well as other new foods. The number of franchised restaurant units is expected to grow at an average annual rate of about 8 percent over the next few years. This growth will be due to population growth and increased spending for food and beverages outside the home.

Strong growth is also being experienced by convenience stores which provide the many "fill-in" items that consumers need between their regular excursions to the supermarkets. More convenience stores are obtaining extra sales by installing

Figure 5.1 Franchising Encompasses 32% of Retail Sales in 1981

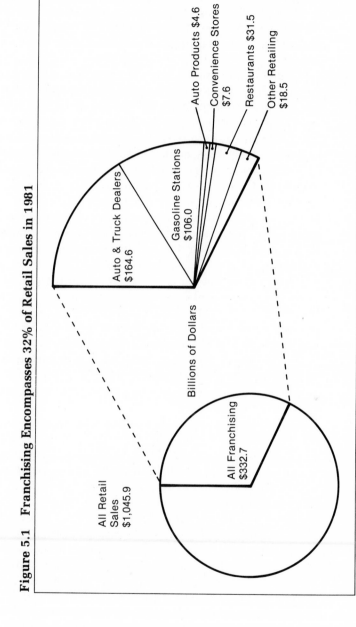

Auto Products $4.6
Convenience Stores $7.6
Restaurants $31.5
Other Retailing $18.5

Auto & Truck Dealers $164.6

Gasoline Stations $106.0

Billions of Dollars

All Retail Sales $1,045.9

All Franchising $332.7

Source: U.S. Department of Commerce, *Franchising in the Economy 1979–1981* (Washington, D.C.: Government Printing Office, 1981), p. 12.

self-service gasoline pumps and offering a wider variety of take-out foods such as hot and cold sandwiches, coffee, chicken, hot dogs, and other foods that are precooked by the supplier and then reheated in a microwave oven located in the store. Specialized franchised food outlets such as donut shops and ice cream parlors are also obtaining annual sales increases of more than 10 percent.

In the nonfood area receipts of franchised auto products and services increased over 10 percent from 1980 to 1981. Retail outlets of tire manufacturers lead the auto product and service field with nearly 37 percent of total sales in 1980. Higher costs of automobiles and auto repairs are encouraging more car owners to undertake their own repairs, a fact that provides considerable opportunities for merchandising the many tools and items needed by the home auto mechanic.

Other growing franchises in the auto products and services category include small and specialized car washes, parking services, brake parts, and diagnostic shops. The major thrust behind this growth is a rising demand for service and consumer convenience.

Another area that has experienced rapid franchise growth is the leisure and travel area. Shorter workweeks, longer vacations, increased number of holidays and days off, and earlier retirement have all contributed to the success story in this sector that includes hotels and motels, and a variety of entertainment, recreation, and travel businesses. Sales were estimated at $8.8 billion in 1981 and are growing at more than 10 percent annually.

Hotels and motels in 1979 enjoyed a 71 percent occupancy rate. This was their highest occupancy level in 20 years. The hotel and motel industry should show continued strength during the next few years, reflecting a concerted effort for accommodating the international traveler as well as travelers of specific age groups. In 1980 franchised hotels and motels accounted for an estimated 31 percent of employment and receipts of the entire hotel and motel industry.

Franchised campgrounds have also grown in numbers and sales and receipts reached about $121 million in 1981. Other franchising firms that are engaged in the recreation, entertainment, and travel business received sales of $433 million in 1980, compared with $360 million in 1979. Sales in 1981 were expected to climb to $544 million, a jump of almost 21 percent over 1980.[5]

Some of the underlying reasons for this phenomenal increase in franchise growth are:

1. Technological advances in equipment and systems have been perfected that reduce product variability and provide uniform products/services. Also, certain products can more effectively be merchandised as a product group rather than in combination with other products. (Example: Amway, Avon, Tupperware, etc.)

2. Businesspeople realize that national saturation of product/service potentially produces better profit returns, but the cost of creating and maintaining the necessary nationwide network of outlets is prohibitive. Thus, through franchising they can tap the savings and credit capacity of small investors who may want to be "independent" but lack the proven product/service or the demonstrated managerial skill to pursue an entrepreneurial career. Such an arrangement assists producers in reaching their goal while maintaining some degree of control over the distribution of products/services.

3. The American dream of independence through "owning your own business" supplies motivation for many people who actually work harder for themselves than for an employer. Such perceived "independence" is economically and psychologically rewarding to the franchisee while providing the franchisor with, perhaps, the best sales force available (provided, of course, that appropriate selection procedures are followed and adequate training and support are continually supplied).

4. Recent economic reverses have resulted in selective massive layoffs, creating doubt in the minds of the affected employees about the future security "in working for someone else." Unfortunately, some unscrupulous franchise promoters have capitalized on such fears and promised financial security for a relatively worthless franchise opportunity. Be that as it may, many professional and skilled employees have sought personal security on the perceived independence of becoming franchisees.

5. Urban "sprawl," or decentralization, has created a need for more small retail establishments, particularly those specializing in convenience goods and services which franchising is adapted to market effectively.

6. As our population has increased its geographical mobility, it has created some psychological uncertainty about meeting everyday basic needs of food and shelter while traveling. Creative modern franchising has met this need by providing a certain level of homogeneous quality in its product or service so travelers (or newcomers to the community) can depend on, with some degree of certainty, these retail merchants to meet their needs. For seasoned travelers, this "sameness" of Holiday Inns or McDonald's, while reassuring for others, may be dissatisfying. Which target market do you wish to please? At the moment, gross sales figures would indicate the former represent the majority of the consuming public.[6]

Factors That Breed Franchise Success

Significant product characteristics that best lend themselves to distribution through franchising are:

Products and Services

1. The product is sufficiently distinctive and identifiable by brand or trademark, and consumer acceptance has reached a point where customers will search out the product when it is needed.
2. The product cannot be offered along with similar products and still have public acceptance, i.e., prepared foods, rugs and upholstery cleaning services.
3. The product has unique qualities that require special handling or preparation for proper product consistency and satisfaction when sold to the consumer. (Example: Shakey's Pizzas, Coca-Cola, etc.)
4. The product-service requires installation, periodic service, and a stock of locally available parts such as automobile repair services.[7]

Franchisor-Franchisee Qualifications

Specific qualities that are desirable for potential franchisees are good health, outgoing personality, good credit and financial standing, sufficient educational level, stable and productive work experience, and the ability to manage people and operations.

A potential franchisor should be evaluated on the basis of

Table 5.3   Franchising Considerations

Advantages
1. Greater chance for success than as an independent businessperson.
2. Franchisors may provide management training programs and management advice.
3. Franchisors normally develop advertising and share the cost of advertising and sales promotion programs.
4. Franchisors usually extend credit for merchandise and financing for buildings and fixturing.
5. Products and services are presold because potential customers are familiar with franchisors' brand names.
6. A uniform quality product-service offering appeals to consumers.

Disadvantages
1. Many franchisors charge a substantial fee for the use of their name.
2. A franchise agreement requires the franchisee to follow prescribed operating procedures; thus, the franchisee loses some independence.
3. If the franchisee wants to sell the business, the prospective buyer may have to be approved by the franchisor.
4. Nationwide operating procedures may not be suitable for local situations.
5. Franchisors may attempt to require the franchisee to purchase supplies from franchisor.
6. Multilevel or pyramid franchisee plans work against franchisee.

Exhibit 5.1   Criteria for Determining Whether a Franchise Should Be Located in a Community

---

(1) The community met a specific population size.
(2) There was an adequate supply of labor available.
(3) The income level in the community was the type to create an active market for the product.
(4) Property in a good site location was owned or could be acquired.
(5) There appeared to be little competition for the product in the area.
(6) A good franchisor (franchisee) was available in the community.

The franchisor and franchisee ranked the six criteria as to which they felt were the most important. The results were that they both agreed on a top three and bottom three but the order within the two areas was different.

Source: Ronald F. Bush, Ronald L. Tatham, and Joseph F. Hair, Jr., "Community Location Decisions by Franchisors: A Comparative Analysis," *Journal of Retailing* 52 (Spring 1976): 33–42. Reprinted by permission.

knowledge of financial requirements, fairness, expected profitability, the training programs provided, the reputation and progressiveness of the firm, and consumers' demand for the product or service.

A person considering investing in a franchised business should consider both the advantages and disadvantages of franchising before making a decision. (Table 5.3).

The six criteria that have been rated by both franchisors and franchisees to be most important to franchise success are presented in Exhibit 5.1.

The Other Side of Franchising: Disadvantages

Without a doubt, one of the most discouraging influences on the growth of franchising has been the problem of "exclusive dealing arrangements" or "tying contracts," which are expressly prohibited by the Clayton Act. Franchisors argue, and with some justification, that such contracts can *potentially* result in cost savings to their franchisees due to bulk purchases and resulting quantity discounts. Second, and particularly in the fast food segment of the industry, in order to maintain consistent product quality throughout a wide geographic area a franchisor should be able to control the quality of the raw material and supply inputs by supplying all these items and assuring their proper use through frequent visits to the various locations.[8]

From the franchisee point of view, such an argument represents a two-edged sword. Indeed, if the franchisor really had the best interest of the franchisee at heart and attempted to maximize the gross profits through such suggested economies of scale, then such practices should be encouraged. However, in most situations under such tying contractual arrangements, the franchisor negotiates the price of the raw materials and supplies with outside vendors, adds its expenses of handling and distribution, plus a profit margin for its "managerial" activities, and then charges the entire cost to "its" franchisees. In short, the franchisees represent a captive market that the franchisor can monopolize. The franchisor is free to charge virtually any price for the basic ingredients that the franchisee must have in order to operate. From a macro point of view, such exclusive agreements would preclude local competition for the franchisee's purchases, which is anticompetitive. This issue, particularly in fast-food franchise arrangements, has yet to be clearly resolved.

Despite the legal uncertainty of franchisors furnishing franchisees with supplies, sales of supplies by franchisors to franchisees amounted to a $6.5 billion business in 1981 (Table 5.4).

Table 5.4   1981 Product and Service Sales by Franchisors to Franchisees[a] ($1000)

Kinds of Franchised Business	Total	Merchandise (Nonfood) for resale	Supplies (Such as paper goods, etc.)	Food Ingredients	Other
Automotive Products and Services	2,112,429	2,083,854	6,477	0	22,098
Business Aids and Services	57,173	13,854	24,271	0	19,048
Construction, Home Improvement, and Cleaning Services	195,427	174,495	13,802	0	7,130
Convenience Stores	172,529	325	20	171,384	800
Educational Products and Services	6,685	2,142	4,543	0	0
Restaurants (All types)	1,045,288	43,146	345,009	622,543	34,590
Hotels and Motels	11,423	279	10,884	260	0
Campgrounds	883	572	311	0	0
Laundry and Drycleaning Services	785	5	100	0	680
Recreation, Entertainment and Travel	3,853	3,245	125	0	483
Rental Services (Auto-Truck)	14,135	0	14,135	0	0
Rental Services (Equipment)	28,870	1,764	25,616	0	1,490
Retailing (Nonfood)	2,150,087	2,083,919	62,126	0	4,042
Retailing (Food other than convenience stores)	694,408	15,803	26,972	633,709	17,924
Miscellaneous	37,425	22,431	6,311	0	8,683
Total–All Franchising[b]	6,531,400	4,445,834	540,702	1,427,896	116,968

[a] Estimated by respondents.
[b] Does not include Automobile and Truck Dealers, Gasoline Service Stations and Soft Drink Bottlers for which data were not collected.

Source: U.S. Department of Commerce, *Franchising in the Economy 1979–1981* (Washington, D.C.: Government Printing Office, 1981), p. 34.

Another problem pertains to the right of the franchisor to re-purchase the franchise after the franchisee has made the outlet successful. Many franchise agreements have guaranteed repur-chase clauses, permitting the franchisor to repurchase the outlet after some period of time, say two to five years. At first glance, potential franchisees might view such a provision as being to their benefit if they should want to sell out or the business turns out to be less profitable than anticipated. Actually, the guarantee is exercisable only by the franchisor at its option, which will be exercised only if the guaranteed price is less than the value of the going business.

Most startup and buildup headaches are borne by the fran-chisee. The person who can raise the considerable capital (Table 5.5) needed to start a franchise can get sick and tired of that bus-iness and sell it back to the company. Thus, many stores are really owned by the franchisor and not the person running his or her own business. In some industries (for example, automobile and truck dealers, automobile products and services, construc-tion, home improvement, maintenance and cleaning services, fast food restaurants, hotels and motels, campgrounds, and rental services) the franchisor has managed to own the high sales vol-ume outlets while letting the franchisee own the lower sales vol-ume outlets (Table 5.6).

Another problem is maintenance of exclusivity in a geograph-ical area. Many franchisees have found that their "exclusive ter-ritories" shrink in size or are carved up by the franchisor so as to increase the level of product or service saturation. The franchisor will not suffer, because it still reaps its collective share of the gross sales, but the franchisees may find their markets too small to sustain the needed profit levels for their personal indepen-dence.

A serious problem that seems to be a major point of contention in most modern franchise relationships is the matter of initial and continuing managerial training and assistance. Many poten-tial franchisees have little or no business or managerial experi-ence. (If they had such abilities and capital, they would have their own retail operations.) While most franchise agreements provide for some initial managerial training, they do not guaran-tee success or, for that matter, make any statement about the quality of the training or continuing assistance. If the franchisor is primarily interested in making money by charging a sizable fee for setting up franchise outlets and using the franchisees' cap-ital and borrowing ability, little or no assistance may be expected after the "grand opening." Alternatively, a change in the fran-chisor ownership or top management may result in a deempha-sis on training and development. In any event, the potential

Table 5.5 Total 1979 Investment and Startup Cash Required[a] ($1000)

Kinds of Franchised Business[b]	Number of Firms	Number Reporting	Total Investment Company Owned			Total Investment Franchisee Owned			Startup Cash Franchisee Owned		
			Lowest	Highest	Median	Lowest	Highest	Median	Lowest	Highest	Median
Automotive Products and Services	127	107	10	500	80	5	450	50	2	150	25
Business Aids and Services											
Accounting, Credit, Collection Agencies and General Business Systems	17	13	5	50	25	5	100	20	3	20	10
Employment Services	72	43	10	200	35	10	150	30	2	80	20
Printing and Copying Services	15	13	30	108	50	29	108	54	10	27	20
Tax Preparation Services	14	11	3	15	6	2	15	5	2	8	3
Real Estate	66	33	12	200	30	3	50	10	1	35	5
Miscellaneous Business Services	71	48	5	200	30	3	200	25	2	100	15
Construction, Home Improvement, Maintenance and Cleaning Services	133	76	10	1,000	43	5	750	30	2	300	10
Convenience Stores	25	17	20	250	99	20	250	81	6	50	20
Educational Products and Services	47	29	5	150	20	1	150	20	1	50	10
Restaurants (All types)	399	239	22	1,000	240	18	1,200	155	5	500	50
Hotels, Motels and Campgrounds	36	20	450	2,800	850	164	2,800	950	75	700	55
Laundry and Drycleaning Services	15	13	65	200	90	17	90	60	10	30	20
Recreation, Entertainment and Travel	33	20	15	1,000	75	13	900	50	5	300	25
Rental Services (Auto-Truck)	17	10	100	750	123	75	550	100	25	60	50
Rental Services (Equipment)	19	10	10	30	70	60	175	115	5	75	40
Retailing (Nonfood)	207	120	10	350	70	5	350	60	1	140	30
Retailing (Food other than convenience stores)	96	58	15	1,000	70	6	480	70	1	160	20
Miscellaneous	50	33	12	150	55	5	150	50	3	60	25

[a] Investment and start up cash represent averages reported by responders.
[b] Does not include Automobile and Truck Dealers, Gasoline Service Stations and Soft Drink Bottlers for which data were not collected.
Source: U.S. Department of Commerce, *Franchising in the Economy 1979–1981*. (Washington, D.C.: Government Printing Office, 1981), p. 42.

franchisee should be aware of these and other pitfalls before becoming an "instant entrepreneur."

One type of franchise to avoid is the multilevel (or pyramid) plan. This form of franchising has come under considerable attack by consumer groups and legal authorities. The multilevel plan was used in the retailing of products and services. This plan called for many levels of investors to buy in at a certain level in the corporate pyramid. An individual could buy in at one of the upper positions such as a distributor and then in turn sell positions such as an area sales position to others.

Under the multilevel plan the franchise fee paid by each entrant might be split among those in levels above him or her. Also, each entrant was usually required to purchase a certain amount of merchandise.

At first this might not seem to be different from the pyramid type of organization within any large corporation. One difference is that the pyramid organization within most established firms represents positions which are earned rather than purchased. Moreover, the individuals in those positions are commonly paid a salary by the corporation. In the case of the multilevel plan, a position in the pyramid or territory was purchased. Those purchasing the position may or may not have any experience or ability to perform the task.

As previously discussed, Federal and State laws have been passed to eliminate gross abuses in the franchise industry, but every potential franchisee should exercise considerable caution and seek legal advice before making any major commitment to participate in a franchise venture.

The Future of Franchising

The future of franchising seems bright and promising. It is generally agreed that the modern forms of franchising have grown and continue to grow in number and sales volume at a remarkable rate. Some segments of the industry have yet to experience the "shake out" of marginal product/service ideas and selling firms that will inevitably occur as this form of franchising matures. Cyclical economic events may take their toll as rising prices make consumers more aware of the costs of specialized services and prepared foods. The same effect may result during a significant economic slowdown when every consumer's penny counts.

It appears that "franchising will continue to be a driving force in the business world, especially in the business format franchise sector of the retail and service industries during the 1980s. Pav-

Table 5.6 Average 1979–1981 Sales per Establishment ($1000)

Kinds of Franchised Business	1979			1980[a]			1981[a]		
	Total	Company Owned	Franchisee Owned	Total	Company Owned	Franchisee Owned	Total	Company Owned	Franchisee Owned
Automobile and Truck Dealers[b]	4,713	4,710	4,713	4,436	4,435	4,436	5,145	5,100	5,146
Automotive Products and Services[c]	160	521	124	163	519	125	164	534	125
Business Aids and Services	153	148	154	155	163	154	167	181	165
Accounting, Credit, Collection Agencies and General Business Systems	43	131	42	42	144	40	44	148	42
Employment Services	333	484	280	345	518	285	364	549	302
Printing and Copying Services	117	120	117	129	133	129	133	144	132
Tax Preparation Services	29	32	27	32	36	28	35	39	32
Real Estate[e]	209	570	205	202	611	197	210	641	206
Miscellaneous Business Services	82	505	70	85	541	73	94	587	82
Construction, Home Improvement, Maintenance and Cleaning Services	98	410	85	96	388	84	100	402	88
Convenience Stores	418	366	524	445	396	542	462	412	560
Educational Products and Services	99	123	93	103	133	97	103	136	96

Restaurants (All Types)	420	478	397	440	500	416	459	523	435
Gasoline Service Stations[b]	436	436	436	608	608	608	697	697	697
Hotels and Motels	1,241	2,009	1,068	1,324	2,334	1,103	1,371	2,467	1,134
Campgrounds	106	427	101	113	475	107	113	516	107
Laundry and Drycleaning Services	100	390	93	105	480	98	111	553	102
Recreation, Entertainment and Travel	84	332	79	97	345	92	111	433	104
Rental Services (Auto-Truck)	387	936	202	396	970	211	425	1,077	222
Rental Services (Equipment)	170	489	132	175	499	137	177	502	140
Retailing (Nonfood)	242	288	221	255	320	226	267	348	233
Retailing (Food other than convenience stores)	419	1,809	344	470	1,933	362	484	1,977	374
Soft Drink Bottlers[b,d]	6,253	11,373	6,049	7,646	13,200	7,412	8,960	15,053	8,695
Miscellaneous	145	211	140	147	202	142	148	215	144
Total–All Franchising	690	464	742	728	544	770	790	591	835

[a] Estimated by respondents.
[b] Estimated by BIE based on Bureau of the Census and trade association data.
[c] Includes some establishments with significant sales of non automotive products such as household appliances, garden supplies, etc.
[d] Includes soft drinks, fruit drinks and ades; syrups, flavoring agents and bases. Data do not include figures for independent private label and contract-filler bottling companies which account for 22 percent in 1979, 22 percent in 1980 and 22 percent in 1981 of the value of shipments of the total industry.
[e] Revised.
Source: U.S. Department of Commerce, *Franchising in the Economy 1979–1981* (Washington, D.C.: Government Printing Office, 1981), p. 35.

ing the way for franchising's continual growth is an increasing population with more leisure time and with stronger inclinations towards recreation activities of all types. Ethnic food restaurants are expected to move into the market place in large numbers, along with hair styling salons, retail stores featuring technological items such as home computers, and franchises that concentrate on convenience and specialization.

The 1980s should see a greater influx of foreign franchisors penetrating the U.S. market, mostly from Canada but also from the United Kingdom, Continental Europe, and Japan; they will be specializing in restaurants, clothing, furniture, and automotive products and services. The acquisition pace in franchising remains strong as large corporations and conglomerates intensify their attempt to take over independent franchising chains. Diversification into franchising is becoming a key strategy for these large organizations.

Within the United States more and more firms will look to franchising as the ideal method of growth. Regional firms seeking national markets faced with high financing costs will find franchising attractive. Investor groups seeking high rates of return will seek master franchises for financial reasons. New business format ventures which have passed modern stringent marketing criteria will have to pass the financial tests of projected yields, leverage opportunities, stock appreciation, and special tax considerations.

Increasingly, potential franchisors will seek subsidiary corporations which will build and own all of the franchise units. By using corporate financing rather than mortgage financing the costs of implementing a new franchise system are expected to be lower. Continuing the same logic, if the franchisor group who acquires the property contracts for future improvements and has the unit operated by a lessee rather than a franchisee, it will have greater managerial control.

Additionally, if the franchisor can reduce the rental requirement needed to justify the investment, the market for their financial instruments may be broadened. More lenders may be found who will be willing to finance many units rather than just one, which has been the traditional practice. Thus, the organization costs are reduced, making franchising more attractive. Lastly, from the real estate investment perspective, such financing modes will make the sale of single parcels or groups of properties to individual investors or pension funds much more likely. If these financing schemes become widespread, in the future the classical franchisee will cease to be a source of capital and will revert to the status of lessee/employee.

The 1980s do not bode well for current or aspiring small business franchisees. Profitable units will be increasingly bought back at fair market value and turned into franchisor owned units managed by firm employees. Nonprofitable units will close after the franchisee's equity and credit sources dry up or become prohibitively expensive to continue financing through external sources. Also, as consumers change their purchase patterns, product/service packages will have to be adjusted which will impact heavily on some franchised retailers both quantitatively and qualitatively such as in the petroleum distribution networks. Many national refiners such as Texaco, Shell, and Mobil have withdrawn from some segments of the country, leaving franchisees or lessees the option of closing or seeking different sources of supply. In some cases the national firms have decided to change over to volume operations using self-service and competitive pricing techniques to survive, forcing out the franchisee who wishes to continue offering full service to an established clientele. Such abandoned market segments may present new opportunities to reconstitute a new channel of distribution with franchising playing a new role.

As the franchising life cycle begins to repeat itself, most new ventures in the 1980s will be characterized as high-risk opportunities. Risk-assuming small business persons interested in participating in the franchise system may increasingly choose the franchisor rather than the franchisee role because of projected changes in the franchise relationship. In either case, the entrepreneur must adopt a combined marketing/finance decision matrix with much greater emphasis on the financial criteria, with payback periods with a maximum of three to five years. Any longer maturity will not be risk acceptable. One might suggest that further research be done in this area to develop more specific detailed financial decision rules for aspiring small business franchise prospects.

The most significant trend in franchised regulation is a renewed effort by state franchise law administrators and the Federal Trade Commission staff to make state registration and disclosure (where applicable) more uniform and less costly to franchisors. The franchise committee of the North American Securities Administrators Association, comprised of administrators from states that have franchise laws, has adopted uniform registration guidelines which are expected to be approved by the individual states. Also, under development is a revised "universal" disclosure document. When accompanied by a "state addendum" this document should be acceptable to all franchise regulatory authorities.

Greater numbers of companies still look to franchising as an ideal system for growth, while both men and women look upon franchising as a means to become independent entrepreneurs under the protective umbrella of a firm that can offer instant identification. Consequently, the net number of franchisors entering the franchise system has been growing steadily and is expected to continue to do so in the early 1980s."[9]

Summary

Franchising represents a rather unusual product decision because in many cases the retailer is under contract to sell only products associated with a particular franchise. Persons considering the purchase of a franchise outlet should make a thorough investigation of contract terms, market potential, cost structure, and pay-back period before they make any commitment. Failures occur in franchise outlets despite the current increase in the number of franchise outlets in operation. The franchise concept perhaps exemplifies the ultimate in a total product designed for a narrowly defined market.

The 1980s promise to be a time of change and challenge for the franchising mode of distribution in the United States. Established franchises based on business format ideas will continue to be operated by small business franchisees who will have opportunities for success and independence. Their ranks will be thinned as parent franchisors assemble new corporate funding and exercise their repurchase privileges. New entries in the industry will be high-risk, requiring the new small business person to consider the situation as an investment decision with supporting marketing documentation. Increasingly this same group of venture enthusiasts will move away from franchising as traditionally practiced and create a new form of distribution which will be a hybrid of franchising and licensing. Research will be needed to assist small business persons during this transition period as the projected new form of marketing distribution evolves on the American scene in the 1980s.

Persons seeking detailed information on individual franchises should obtain a January issue of *Entrepreneur* magazine as this is their special franchise edition which includes a rating of 500 franchises in 27 different fields. Other sources of information are: *The Franchise Opportunity Handbook* published by the Department of Commerce; *Franchising in the Economy* published by the Department of Commerce; *Franchising Annual* published by Info Press, Lewiston, New York; *Directory of Franchise Organization* published by Pilot Books, New York; and *Guide to Franchising* published by Dow Jones Irwin, Homewood, Illinois.

Questions

1. Define franchising in your own terms.
2. Contrast the difference between a territorial and operating franchise and give examples of each.
3. How important is franchising to the U.S. economy in terms of retail sales? What is the future for franchising?

4. What are the advantages for a small businessperson to operate as a franchise rather than completely independent? What are the disadvantages?

5. How does the main objective of manufacturer and wholesaler sponsored franchise systems differ from the main objective of service industry franchise chains? How does this difference affect the way each type of system operates?

6. Investigate the desirability of starting a new fast food franchise in your area. Where would you obtain data? How would you reach a conclusion as to whether it would be a good idea or not?

Footnotes

1. U.S. Department of Commerce, Bureau of Domestic Commerce, *Franchise Company Data: For Equal Opportunity in Business* (Washington, D.C.: Government Printing Office, December 1970), p. xi.

2. Aaron M. Rothenberg, "A Fresh Look at Franchising," *Journal of Marketing* 31 (July 1967):52–53.

3. John R. Nevin, Shelby D. Hunt, and Robert W. Rueckert, "The Impact of Fair Practice Laws on a Franchise Channel of Distribution," *MSU Business Topics* 28 (Summer, 1980):27–37.

4. U.S. Department of Commerce, *Franchising in the Economy 1979–81* (Washington, D.C.: Government Printing Office, 1981), p. 2.

5. Ibid., p. 17.

6. Jack M. Starling, "Franchising," *Business Studies*, (Fall 1970): 10–16.

7. Robert J. Mockler and Harrison Easop, "Guidelines for More Effective Planning and Management of Franchise Systems," Research Paper 42, Bureau of Business and Economic Research, Georgia State College, Atlanta, May 1968, pp. 14–16.

8. Red Rock Bottlers Inc. v. Red Rock Cola Company, 195 F.2d 406 (CA-5, 1952).

9. U.S. Department of Commerce, *Franchising in the Economy 1979–81* (Washington, D.C.: Government Printing Office, 1981), p. 4.

Case Study: Chocolate Chips Inc.

"Tourists love our cookies. Now we are looking for the best way to sell them to residents of Jackson, Wyoming. Once we have learned how to develop that market we plan to expand.

"We could start a franchised chain of stores like Baskin-Robbins or even hook up with a firm like Frito Lay to distribute our cookies."

As Debbie spoke, it was obvious she meant to succeed in a big way. She has been in business only three months and had already received excellent publicity in the local newspapers. Her location in a tourist shopping plaza meant that about 90 percent of her customers were visitors.

The smell of chocolate chip cookies fresh from the oven plus the assortment of sizes proved to be powerful merchandising tools.

In addition to her retail store, Debbie sold packaged cookies at wholesale prices to several specialty stores in Jackson. Many small retailers such as restaurants, coffee houses, and ice cream parlors expressed interest in selling her cookies.

Debbie delivered cookies herself. The trouble was that these tended to be small accounts and required considerable work for relatively few sales. There was also a problem of collecting from one or two.

"I'd really rather deliver to one large account than fifty little ones but that's going to take time and a strategy. I believe that chocolate chip cookies can be sold as a fashionable item at a premium price in major retail outlets. Hard work doesn't scare me. I want my own business more than anything."

Debbie had developed a Chocolate Chips Inc. plastic tote bag which she also sold. She was convinced that it was necessary to merchandise her business, not just sell cookies.

At $3.50 per pound, cookies from Chocolate Chips Inc. were priced as a top-of-the-line item. Debbie recognized that the price probably limited sales to certain market segments. She also felt that the success of her retail store proved the existence of a market. Now she needed to decide upon a direction for growth and develop appropriate strategies.

Discussion Questions

1. What other factors might account for the initial success of Chocolate Chips Inc. besides Debbie's hard work and the smell and assortment of her cookies?

2. Why has Debbie been able to sell cookies at $3.50 a bag?

3. What value do you think the free publicity in newspapers has been to Debbie?

4. What are the possible advantages and disadvantages in developing a market among small retail stores?

5. What are the advantages and disadvantages of the two strategies Debbie is thinking about, i.e., developing a wholesale market in the Jackson area or developing a chain of franchised retail stores?

Chapter 6 | Store Location Considerations

Learning Goals

1. To understand why a retail outlet's success depends upon how many of its target market people reside in the trading area.
2. To discuss the methods retailers use to evaluate a town or city as a possible location site.
3. To discern characteristics of different types of retail locations: free-standing, business-associated, and planned shopping centers.
4. To list the advantages and disadvantages of locating in a shopping center.

Key Terms and Concepts

general trading area
buying power index
understored
overstored
index of retail saturation
free-standing site
business-associated site

planned shopping center
neighborhood shopping
   centers
community shopping centers
regional shopping centers
lead tenants
tenant mix

A retailer's merchandise may be easily duplicated. Promotions can be imitated. Prices can be matched. But through a good location the retailer achieves a unique advantage. Once a site has been selected and secured, the space cannot be occupied by a competitive retailer. This chapter examines the factors that retailers should consider when choosing a general trade area to locate an outlet. Specifically, the chapter discusses two of the three basic phases involved in selecting a location for a new store or reevaluating the location of an existing store. The two phases discussed in this chapter are: (1) evaluating the general trade area in regard to its market potential, and (2) investigating the type of location that would be most appropriate for the intended type of store. Steps involved in the third phase of the process—that of selecting a specific site within the general trade area—are discussed in Chapter 7.

Location influences all other elements which the retailer uses to attract customers. In a poor location a retailer will have to spend additional effort persuading people to seek out the store. This may simply mean that more will be spent on advertising and promotion. Added drawing power might also be obtained by lowering prices or increasing service—all of which costs money. Thus, a good location can save future expenditures that might otherwise be needed to attract customers to the store.

Most site evaluation work consists of careful investigation of a new store location. However, changes in consumer behavior may make a once suitable site suddenly unprofitable. For example, deterioration of a neighborhood or opening of a new freeway often causes a change in consumer demand that calls for a site (or at least a consumer target) reevaluation. Therefore, present sites must be continually reevaluated.

A particularly crucial location decision arises every time a retailer signs a new lease. By signing a lease he or she commits the store to continue operations from the same location for a specific period, ranging from six months to twenty-five years. It is advisable to analyze the current location every year or two with the same care as if a new store location decision were being made.

These periodic analyses allow the retailer to spot current or potential deficiencies in market saturation and thereby anticipate the need to change the location to meet changing consumer demands. Although the following discussion is conducted in terms of a new store, the factors involved are also applicable to appraisal of an established store.

General Trading Area Evaluation

An evaluation of the **general trading area** (the entire city or county in which the outlet may be located) is needed before the specific site is selected. Often this evaluation of the city or trading area is omitted because the retailer believes that it is convenient to locate in a certain area. This can be a tragic mistake, as competitive or environmental conditions may cause the business to fail even if the best site is chosen. Thus, the evaluation must be objective and include an analysis of the general trading area as well as the specific site. Profit potential in different areas can be compared. The retailer can then choose the opportunity that appears to offer the best profit potential. The factors to consider when evaluating a community as a possible retail location are presented in Table 6.1.

Selection of a City or Town

The number of people in the general trading area and their age distribution determine the number of potential customers of retail stores of a particular type. Generally, the purchase rate of most retail products responds favorably to population increases.

Table 6.1   Factors to Consider in Selecting a General Trade Area

People Living in or Coming into Trade Area	Community Environment	Business Growth
Population	Legislative restrictions	Present industries
Trend in population	Taxes	Proposed new industries
Income or purchasing power	Competition	Area promotions
Distribution of income	Number of independent firms	
Seasonalty of income	Number of chain outlets	
Stability of income	Advertising media available	
Trend of income	Transportation facilities	
Purchasing habits	Banking and credit facilities	
Lifestyle	Insurance rates	
Social class	Protection from fire, theft, and the elements	
Age	Rental cost	
Race	Availability of employees	
Nationality	Availability of community facilities	
Religion		
Living status (home owner, mobile home owner, renter, etc.)		

Population

The average population served by retailers has increased by 41 percent during the 1948–1977 period as annual sales volumes have increased (Table 6.2). However, the total number of retail establishments increased only 5 percent from 1948 to 1977. These trends would indicate that a retailer would want to locate in areas where the average population served per store was (or will be) above the national average population served per store as reported in Table 6.2.

City and town population data are available from the U.S. Census Bureau. Detailed demographic data are collected every ten years and are available by state, county, and city in the *County and City Data Book: A Statistical Abstract Supplement*. This supplement is published by the U.S. Department of Commerce every five years. *The Editor & Publisher Market Guide* and *Sales and Marketing Management* also provide annual population estimates by town and county. If current secondary population data are not available, the number of new residential electrical connections has been found to provide reliable estimates of an area's population growth. The last known number of people per household for the area (generally obtainable from census data) can be multiplied by the number of new residential electrical connections to provide an estimate of population growth.

Data provided by most sources do not account for seasonal

Table 6.2 Comparison of Sales Factors for Selected Retail Outlets in 1948, 1972, and 1977

Type of Retail Outlet	Number of Stores (1,000)			Sales ($1,000,000)			Average Population Served per Store[a]			Average Annual Sales per Store[b]		
	1948	1972	1977	1948	1972	1977	1948	1972	1977	1948	1972	1977
Retail trade, total	1,773	1,912	1,855	130,521	459,040	723,134	82	106	116	74	240	390
Hardware stores	35	26	26	2,494	3,957	6,087	4,213	7,727	8,135	72	150	230
Department stores (including mail-order sales)	3	8	9	10,645	51,084	76,909	56,125	26,391	24,435	4,125	6,634	8,732
Variety stores	20	22	17	2,507	7,344	7,095	7,229	9,322	12,384	124	337	408
Grocery stores	378	194	179	24,774	93,327	147,759	386	1,046	1,203	125	480	826
Gasoline service stations	188	227	176	6,483	33,655	56,468	776	897	1,219	34	149	320
Total apparel and accessory stores	115	129	140	9,803	24,741	35,564	1,268	1,572	1,535	85	191	254
Eating and drinking places	347	360	368	10,683	36,868	63,276	422	565	584	31	103	172
Drug and proprietary stores	56	51	50	4,013	15,599	23,196	2,618	3,946	4,341	72	303	468
Sporting goods and bicycle shops	9	23	32	549	2,538	4,655	21,057	9,032	6,827	79	113	148
Jewelry stores	21	25	34	1,225	3,118	5,429	6,869	8,032	6,310	58	123	159

[a] Average population served per store is total U.S. population divided by the number of stores; population figures used were 146.1 million in 1948, 203.2 million in 1972, 215.2 million in 1977.
[b] Obtained by dividing total sales by number of stores. Sales are reported in $1,000.
Source: U.S. Department of Commerce, U.S. Census of Business, Retail Trade (Washington, D.C.: Government Printing Office, 1948, 1972, and 1977), various pages.

shifts in population. Some trading areas gain people during the summer and lose them during the winter. Some communities, located in states such as Colorado, Wyoming, and Michigan, have a large influx of tourists and summer residents who increase the potential number of customers for the summer months. Other communities in Arizona, California, and Florida obtain temporary population gains during the winter months. In some locations tourists and temporary residents may arrive at a fairly constant rate throughout the year. College and university towns benefit from increased student populations during the September to June period. Whatever the seasonal pattern may be, the amount of business generated by these people must be added to the resident business potential to obtain a valid estimate of potential business for the general trade area.

Long-term trends in population growth must also be considered, because a store is expected to generate sales and profits far into the future. The U.S. population is expected to grow by about 1 percent per year during the 1980–1987 period.[1] However, not all areas will grow during the next five years, so retail managers must keep abreast of population trends in each possible area they are investigating as a location. Detailed state-by-state population increases and retail sales estimates are available from *Sales and Marketing Management.* Of course, some towns and cities within the same state will grow faster than others. Proximity to a large population center will encourage growth in the nearby towns. The attractiveness of the city or town is enhanced by good schools and churches, health facilities, parking, shopping, and entertainment facilities. The town leaders' positive attitude toward attracting new industry is also a must if an area is to achieve its share of population growth.

An increased trading area may be obtained by sponsoring civic and merchant events, conventions, and the like that draw people from the fringe of the trading area into town. Improved public transportation and good highway and street systems can increase the size of the trading area by reducing the time required to reach the shopping area. As traffic becomes more congested, consumers tend to think more in terms of the additional driving time required to reach their destinations than in terms of the actual distance involved. Population changes and accessibility to population have a great influence upon retailing since people tend to shop at the nearest, most convenient location.

Major chain retailers and franchisors have established a minimum population that an area must possess before they would consider locating an outlet in that area. The exact size of the minimum population requirement varies from firm to firm. Recent reports indicate that some retailers are lowering their specified population. Apparently large retail organizations are beginning to realize the potential that smaller communities offer. One big advantage that many chains and franchise organizations have discovered is that competition from other chains or franchise outlets is absent in smaller communities. The result is they can capture a very large share of the market and do not have to divide it up with ten or fifteen closely competing franchise or chain outlets.

Kentucky Fried Chicken, which would not consider locating outlets in towns under 35,000 population ten years ago, now has over 890 outlets in towns of less than 10,000 population. In fact, one of their most successful outlets is located in Harlan, Kentucky, a town of 3,300 population (but the trade area consists of about 30,000 people).

Most of these national retailers use a scaled-down version of urban outlets to serve these smaller communities. McDonald's Corporation, which would hardly look into the establishment of an outlet in a town of under 30,000 population five years ago, is now expanding into small towns with its Mini-Mac outlet that is smaller than its traditional outlets. Pillsbury Company's Burger King chain is also establishing forty- to fifty-seat restaurants (instead of the hundred seats usually placed in an urban outlet) to serve smaller towns. Pizza Hut Inc. has also done extremely well in towns of 5,000 to 10,000 people. Chain outlets benefit from the national advertising and from competing only with the local mom-and-pop operation which usually does not offer any special image appeal to the consumer.[2]

Even K mart has discovered that it can conduct business profitably in a smaller town. From its inception in 1962, K mart constructed its new stores in the path of growth around major metropolitan areas. The basic K mart store that serviced these heavily populated communities ranged from 65,000 square feet to 96,000 square feet. In 1974 the company introduced a 40,000-square-foot store to serve smaller more rural markets. These stores were opened to supplement their primary program of full size stores for medium size cities and major metropolitan markets.

K mart expansion has recently moved into intra-urban sites located in high density areas where the population varies from 350,000 to 750,000 in a primary trade area. These locations are sometimes twice as costly to acquire as are the typical suburban locations. However, the intra-urban sites generally offer less retail competition than do the suburban sites.

These examples illustrate that the required population differs from one firm to another and even within the same firm according to the size of the outlet.

Income or Purchasing
Power

Population influences the sales of all products and services, but
it relates more directly to sales of products that are frequently
purchased (such as groceries) than to seldom purchased durables
(autos), semidurables (clothing or small appliances), or services
(insurance). Spending on all but frequently purchased goods is
influenced by the level of disposable income, which is the money
that families have available to them to spend. So population,
while still important, may not be the dominant factor affecting
sales.

As family income increases there are pronounced shifts in the
relative demand for different categories of goods and services. In
1857 Ernst Engel observed that although rising family income
tended to be accompanied by increased spending in all product
and service categories, the percentage spent on housing and
household operations remained constant, while the percentage
spent on health and savings tended to increase. These findings
have been validated in budget studies.

Increases in income that have occurred in the United States
since 1965 have resulted in a proportionately higher percentage
of a person's income being spent for autos and parts, furniture
and household equipment, other durable goods, gasoline and oil,
and household operation services.

Product lines that benefited least from the increase in disposable income included foods and beverages, clothing and shoes,
and transportation services. Because of their low response to increases in disposable income, sales of these items may be more
dependent upon population growth than upon increases in income. Thus, the demand for these products is not likely to increase as rapidly as sales of products that are favorably related to
higher incomes.

There is no simple measure of income or purchasing power
that can completely describe the consumer's ability to buy merchandise. Average family income and per capita income are provided in several sources such as the *Editor & Publisher Market
Guide* and *Sales and Marketing Management*. The **buying power
index** provides an approximate value for the ability of an area to
purchase consumer goods. For example, Anaheim, California had
a buying power index of 0.1131 in 1980. The projected buying
power index for Newport Beach, California was 0.0542. Thus, the
market potential in Anaheim is estimated to be approximately
double the market potential in Newport Beach. This index is
most applicable to mass market products (as contrasted with
items not sold on the mass market) that are sold at "popular"
prices. These index calculations provide a good estimate of the
level of income available for spending, but they do not take into
consideration the following factors:

1. *Distribution of income* Distribution of income is important because average per capita income can be distorted by a few individuals with very high or very low incomes. More importantly, the dispersion of income can be estimated from the proportion of families that are homeowners, the average value of single-unit dwellings, the number and make of automobiles registered in the area, and per capita retail sales.

2. *Stability of income* Income is generally more stable in areas with diversified industries than in areas dominated by one industry. Of course, some areas that are dominated by one employer offer a strong but stable economy. Washington, D.C. and the small-town locations of large colleges and universities are examples of areas that usually have relatively strong but seasonally stable retail sales. Retail sales in areas dominated by employers whose sales are affected by seasonal or economic conditions are likely to fluctuate with the decline and expansion of these industries.

The quality of the labor-management relationship also affects stability of income and hence retail purchases. Constant labor strife and periodic strikes may result in violent fluctuations in retail sales and may also require merchants to overextend credit during strikes.

3. *Trend of income* For most retailers it is desirable to be located in areas where consumers' incomes are growing at a faster rate than the national average annual increase in income. However, some retailers prefer to appeal to the low-income market segment and thus locate stores in low-income areas offering a narrow merchandise assortment and high-risk credit terms.

Purchasing Habits of Potential Customers

Purchasing habits must be investigated to determine if potential customers are likely to do their buying at the most accessible locations. If the majority of people rely mostly upon mail-order purchasing or like to combine a shopping trip with a pleasure trip and travel many miles, it will take some additional advertising and promotional expenditures or price reductions to influence these consumers to change their buying habits. These differences in purchasing patterns may correspond to group differences in social class, age, race, nationality, or religion.

The basic industry upon which the town depends for the majority of its income influences the type of retail outlets that will be most successful in the area. Thus, retailers who are planning to expand into new areas must analyze the character and industrial base of the communities they have under consideration. Lifestyle is also an important factor for retailers to consider when they locate a new outlet.

Better estimates of an area's sales are obtained if the prospective retailer is personally familiar with the buying habits, preferences, and prejudices of the people residing in the trading area. Familiarity with potential consumers' purchasing patterns will also make it easier for the prospective retailer to estimate the importance that consumers give to services and to wide and deep merchandise assortments. This knowledge is useful not only in the site selection process but also in decisions on what products and services the retailer will offer.

Legislative Restrictions

The legal environment influences profitability of any store and may determine its existence or nonexistence. Local zoning ordinances limit the number of sites that are suitable for retailing. Municipal or state regulations relative to the hours of business may limit night and Sunday openings for many types of retail outlets. The location decision is also influenced by the tax and license structure in the particular area. The relative level of sales tax charged in nearby areas is particularly important to retailers who sell shopping goods. For example, the difference between a 3 and 6 percent sales tax on a $1,000 stereo system is $30. Such marked differences can influence consumer buying habits toward making purchases in a lower tax area.

Competition in the Area

Choice of a location is influenced by the number, type, location, and floor space of competing stores. Competition should be evaluated to determine to what extent its merchandise and service mix meet the desires of the prospective consumers.

The trend toward scrambled merchandising—selling many unrelated lines in a single outlet—has made this evaluation more difficult. Today much of the competition for items that used to be sold in specialty stores is not derived from other specialty stores but from chain, department, discount, grocery, drug, or hardware stores. Thus, the study of competitors must be based on a realistic estimate of the share of the total market that can be obtained when one faces this vigorous competition.

Store Saturation

Preliminary estimates of how much the competition has already obtained the retailing opportunities in the trade area can be obtained from several sources.

County Business Patterns, which is published annually by the U.S. Department of Commerce, uses a classification system called the Standard Industrial Classification (SIC) to classify most manufacturers, wholesalers, and retailers into designated categories for each geographical area. Using this information, one can determine the number of retailers doing business in the trade area. State sales tax revenue offices sometimes summarize and make public the number of retail outlets doing business in each county and also provide information on the volume of business obtained by each type of outlet (as defined by the SIC code system).

No matter which source is used, the SIC system of trade area appraisal has several weaknesses. It is difficult to identify the precise activities of a particular firm because some retail outlets sell wide assortments of merchandise. Then, too, the mere number of a specific type of store in an area does not give an evaluation of the aggressiveness of the outlets.

A more precise measurement tool, called an index of retail saturation, can determine if the stores in a trade area supply consumer needs adequately or inadequately. When an area has too few stores to meet the needs of the consumer community satisfactorily, an **understored** condition exists. This situation presents the best retailing opportunity for new stores to satisfy consumer needs.

If an area is **overstored** it has more stores than are needed to satisfy consumer demand. This situation would probably result in a low return on investment for the retail outlets operating in the area. It would not represent an opportunity for a new store unless the new store could serve consumer needs much more effectively than the current outlets. In such a case some of the current outlets would probably be driven out of business.

The **index of retail saturation** can be calculated by dividing estimated consumption by the ability of current retailers to satisfy consumer needs. In formula terms, that calculation could be obtained as follows:[3]

$$\text{Saturation Index} = \frac{(C)\,(RE)}{RF},$$

where C is the number of prospective consumers of the proposed product, RE is the average expenditure for the proposed product line for a selected period of time, and RF is a measurement of competing (and planned) retailing facilities in the trade area, measured in square feet of space devoted to the proposed merchandise lines.

This index may be illustrated by the following example. Saturation index calculations could be made for several different areas to indicate which area offers the most potential for a proposed supermarket. There are 50,000 consumers in area A. The average consumer in the area spends $12 per week in supermarkets. The six supermarkets serving area A have a total of 60,000 square feet of selling area. The index calculation is:

$$\text{Saturation Index} = \frac{(50,000)\,(\$12)}{60,000} = \frac{\$600,000}{60,000} = \$10$$

The $10 sales per square foot of selling area can be measured against the sales needed per square foot if the business is to just break even. The $10 calculated sales per square foot could also be compared with the index figure for other possible location areas. The highest index would indicate the area with the best potential. It does not indicate that the area will be a profitable location unless the highest index is higher than the break-even sales needed per square foot, and even then it does not guarantee success because the outlet must be well managed, competition may change, and so on.

This index of saturation is an excellent measure of potential sales (per square foot) because it uses both consumer demand and competitive supply to evaluate the trading area. However, the index does not reflect the quality of the competition in each trade area. Some areas may have more progressive merchandisers than others, and this difference may not appear in the square footage measurement of competitive strength used in the denominator of the formula. Thus, qualitative evaluation of competition should also be made to determine if and to what degree competitive strength differs from the assumed power made on the basis of square feet of selling space.

Retailers can develop other indices to evaluate competition. Their own experiences in the industry can determine which of these measures can yield a reliable assessment of the competitive environment. Other factors that can evaluate the level of retail saturation in an area are:

The number of persons living in the area divided by the number of competing retail outlets in the area

The population in the area divided by store front footage of competing outlets

Annual category retail sales in the area relative to amount of competitor's advertising

Counts of pedestrian and vehicular traffic going past competitor's location

Number of salespeople on the floor of competitor outlets during a specified time period

Number of checkout counters in use at competitive outlets during peak business hours

Number of autos in competitor's parking lot during peak business hours

Size and quality of competitor's inventory

Assortment of competitor's merchandise

Percentage of retail facilities that are vacant

The appearance of a leading department store in a community

Another factor retail managers must remember when using the index of saturation is that managerial decision variables, such as merchandise assortment and service levels, also may have a substantial impact upon consumer expenditure in their type of retail outlet. For example, a recent study has shown that department store expenditures per household can be strongly influenced by the marketing actions of department store managers.[4] If demand is subject to retailer influence, managers should carefully evaluate each location using the retailing mix that they would most likely employ at that site.

Location Considerations

After the retail manager has evaluated a trade area and determined its potential to support a store, the most suitable type of location within that area must be determined. There is a wide selection of alternatives to choose from including: (1) **free-standing** sites (where a store is not located near other retail outlets), (2) **business-associated sites,** and (3) **planned shopping centers** of varying sizes. A retail outlet's type of location has a strong influence upon the size and shape of the trading area that the store is able to serve. Type of location also determines the degree to which a store is able to penetrate its market area.

Lastly, which location is best suited for a particular retailer depends upon the type of merchandise sold.

Generally, shopping goods stores require a location near other shopping goods stores so they locate in planned shopping centers or in the downtown business district where consumers can easily do considerable comparison shopping (Table 6.3). However, scrambled merchandising strategies have led shopping goods stores to carry some items that some consumers consider convenience goods. For these convenience goods it would be better to be located near the consumer but not too near the competitive outlets. Such a location benefits the consumer and the convenience goods store (Table 6.3).

Table 6.3   Suitable Locations for Various Store Types

Store Classification	Type of Merchandise Sold	Consumer Purchasing Behavior	Most Suitable Type of Location
Convenience store	Convenience goods	Consumer buys most readily available brand at most accessible store	Neighborhood business district near target market population, away from competition, and in heavy pedestrian traffic areas
Convenience store	Shopping goods	Consumer selects purchase from assortment carried by most accessible store	Neighborhood business district near target market population and away from competition
Convenience store	Specialty goods	Consumer purchases favorite brand from most accessible store carrying the item in stock	Planned neighborhood shopping center or downtown central business district
Shopping store	Convenience goods	Consumer is indifferent to the brand of product but shops different stores to secure better buy	Neighborhood business district near target market population
Shopping store	Shopping goods	Consumer makes comparisons among both outlet and brand	Planned shopping center or downtown central business district near similar outlets
Shopping store	Specialty goods	Consumer has strong brand preference but shops a number of stores	Planned shopping center or downtown central business district near similar outlets
Specialty store	Convenience goods	Consumer prefers a specific store but is indifferent to the brand	Free-standing site—consumer preference for outlet is stronger than brand preference
Specialty store	Shopping goods	Consumer prefers a specific store but is uncertain as to which product he will buy	Free-standing site—consumers will search for outlet
Specialty store	Specialty goods	Consumer has preference for a particular store and for a specific brand	Highway, free-standing site—consumers will search for outlet

Source: Table is based upon consumer goods classification concept developed by Louis P. Bucklin, "Retail Strategy and the Classification of Consumer Goods," *Journal of Marketing* 23 (January 1963): 50–55. Reprinted with permission from *Journal of Marketing*, published by the American Marketing Association.

Meanwhile, the convenience store also sells goods which some consumers consider specialty goods. For this merchandise the store may have a much larger trading area because consumers will spend considerable time and effort searching for the outlet.

Because the consumer will search for the particular store, the specialty goods store can locate in a free-standing site which does not require foot traffic (Table 6.3). Thus, the site location decision is strongly influenced by the specific target market which the retailer chooses.

Other factors that influence location choice are: cost of the site, location strategies of key competitors' consumer shopping patterns, and the retail firm's strategic marketing objective. In some retail fields it has become traditional for everyone to choose a particular type of location. For example, most new department stores are located in planned suburban shopping centers. Marketing objectives of a firm frequently dictate the type of location because the target market consumer must be reached in the most efficient manner. For example, retailers who stress low prices as their major marketing strategy usually select less than prime locations so operating costs may be reduced. Their target market consumers must prefer the lower price enough to accept the reduced accessibility provided by the inconvenient site.

A more detailed discussion of the various types of location available to retailers is needed to better understand what each provides as a retail environment.

Classification of Location Types

Locations may be either *free-standing* or *business-associated* sites. Most locations are business associated as a part of either a planned shopping center or an unplanned shopping district. Characteristics of both store location types are:

1. **Free-standing**
   a. Neighborhood—an isolated retail outlet which serves the needs of a small portion of the town.
   b. Highway—an isolated outlet located on a highway.
2. **Business-associated**
   a. **Unplanned shopping center**
      1] Downtown—the traditional commercial core of town. It may contain department, variety, apparel, and food stores plus many offices and service shops.
      2] Edge of downtown—the area located at the edge of the downtown area.
      3] Neighborhood business district—small parts of a town that are usually defined by social, economic, or geographic boundaries. A neighborhood business district contains small stores with nothing larger than a supermarket or variety store.
      4] Secondary business district—a small-scale downtown area usually bounded by major street intersections. It must contain at least a junior or general merchandise department store and a variety store and some smaller retail and service shops.
      5] Highway business string—an elongated area which contains several retail businesses. Extensions of the string down perpendicular streets are very shallow.[5]
   b. **Planned shopping center**—location, size, type of tenants, and parking space are the result of conscious planning by the developers. Expansion of this type of retailing has been continuing. Retail shopping center sales have expanded from

about 20 percent of the total retail sales in 1964 to more than 40 percent of all current retail sales in 1980 (Figure 6.1). The three types of planned shopping centers are:

1] **Neighborhood shopping centers**—oriented toward convenience shopping, so they contain nothing larger than supermarkets, variety stores, or small department stores. Total (gross area) store space in the center ranges from 25,000 to 75,000 square feet. The supermarket or the drug store is the leading tenant in a neighborhood shopping center. This type of center generally serves about 10,000 people. A typical neighborhood center uses about six acres of land.

Figure 6.1   U.S. Retail Sales Made in Shopping Centers 1964 – 1980

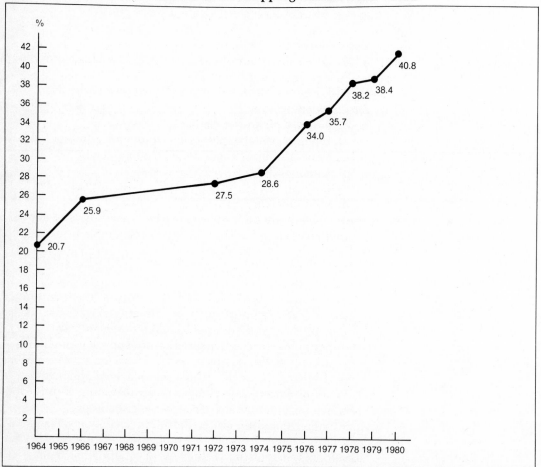

Source: Figure created from data supplied by International Council of Shopping Centers, New York.

2] **Community shopping centers**—can serve both the convenience and shopping goods needs of a city and a few of its suburbs through its larger junior department store, smaller branch stores and specialty shops. The community shopping center offers wider style assortments, wider price ranges, and more stores designed to attract more impulse sales than stores located in the neighborhood shopping center. Total store space in a community shopping center usually ranges from 75,000 square feet to 300,000 square feet. With an average size of 150,000 square feet, a typical site requires about twenty acres of land to serve a population of 20,000 to 100,000.

3] **Regional shopping centers**—larger centers that contain over 300,000 square feet of gross store area. The average size is about 400,000 square feet of gross floor space. At least forty acres are required for a regional shopping center, but some large centers use more than one hundred acres for their buildings, parking areas, and landscaping. Regional centers feature at least one full-line department store and a range of department, variety, apparel, and miscellaneous stores. Smaller tenants are selected to offer a variety of complementary goods and services formerly found only in the downtown area. Many regional centers are now featuring an enclosed mall for year-round shopping comfort. This type is designed not only to shut out the weather but also to provide psychological integration. Such climate-controlled malls give the impression of one giant store with individual shops. As a result, it often serves an even larger trade area than other regional centers.

Shopping Center Location Considerations

Trends in planned shopping centers are contained in Figure 6.1 and Tables 6.4, 6.5, and 6.6. Both the number of centers and the gross leasable area have about tripled during the 1964–1980 period. Moreover, sales have increased by nearly five times (Table 6.4) and the share of the market obtained by shopping centers has doubled from 20 percent in 1964 to over 40 percent in 1980 (Figure 6.1). By 1990, industry experts expect shopping centers to account for half of all retail sales.

"Industry forecasters, however, agree that shopping centers will look and act differently in the future. For one, developers will tailor the complexes to more human dimensions—no more megamalls of 2 million square feet, no more energy-inefficient designs, no more big parking lots for gas guzzlers.

Table 6.4   16 Years of Progress for American Shopping Centers

	Number of Centers	Total Gross Leasable Area (Square feet)	Gross Sales	Average Size (Square feet)
1980[a]	22,050	2,962,701,000	$385,501,000,000	134,363
1978[a]	19,201	2,498,303,000	$283,050,000,000	130,113
1976[a]	17,458	2,277,930,000	$211,504,000,000	130,480
1974[a]	15,074	1,874,259,000	$153,087,000,000	124,337
1972[a]	13,174	1,649,972,000	$123,159,000,000	125,245
1964[b]	7,600	1,010,000,000	$ 78,700,000,000	132,985

[a] Based on SCW's Biennial Census of the Shopping Center Industry.
[b] Based on a survey conducted by SCW's Editorial Consultant, S. O. Kaylin.
Source: "Fifth Biennial Census of the Shopping Center Industry: Center Industry Has Grown to Major Proportions," *Shopping Center World* (January 1981): 80. Copyright *Shopping Center World*, a publication of Communication Channels, Inc., Atlanta, Georgia.

"Shops will be smaller, with emphasis on boutiques rather than full-line department stores. Nestled between the boutiques will be discounters, cataloguers, mail order firms, and warehouse outlets—store-sized survival kits of the future.

"Also, there will be a smattering of larger stores that will endure by scaling down operations. Certain lines that require vast amounts of space, such as appliances and furniture, will be eliminated. Diversification will continue as shopping centers evolve into community centers with more space devoted to entertainment, health, and recreation. . . .

"Perhaps most importantly, as America's population growth becomes stunted, shopping center developers must rely more on marketing, advertising, and promotion to insure future profitability. Mall retailers, who today spend about 3% of sales on ads and promotion, will increase that percentage as competition becomes keener."[6]

The average size shopping center has not changed much during the 1964–1980 period (Table 6.4), but the most rapid rate of gain during the 1979–1981 period was in centers having more than 400,000 square feet of space (Table 6.5). Although the small center of less than 100,000 square feet of space is the slowest growing type of shopping center, it still accounts for 66 percent of the number of centers in the United States (Table 6.6). This small center also accounts for 31 percent of all sales made in shopping centers and the highest sales per square foot ($148) of any of the shopping center categories (Table 6.6).

A few new shopping centers are conceived as integral parts of new developments and are becoming hubs of community social

Table 6.5 Shopping Centers and Sales Made in Six Sizes of U.S. Shopping Centers

Size of Center (Square feet)	January 1, 1981			January 1, 1979			% Gain 1980 vs. 1978		
	Number of Centers	Total GLA (Square feet)	1980 Sales ($)	Number of Centers	Gross Leasable Area (Square feet)	1978 Sales ($)	Number of Centers	Total Gross Leasable Area (Square feet)	Annual Sales
10,000–100,000	14,586	798,470,000	118,677,000,000	12,964	707,979,000	90,230,000,000	12.5	12.8	31.5
100,001–200,000	4,420	643,755,000	81,203,000,000	3,699	541,362,000	59,073,000,000	19.5	18.9	37.5
200,001–400,000	1,695	483,066,000	58,646,000,000	1,449	414,569,000	44,331,000,000	17.0	16.5	32.3
400,001–800,000	839	486,562,000	58,457,000,000	696	403,053,000	42,618,000,000	20.6	20.7	37.2
800,001–1,000,000	242	218,197,000	26,984,000,000	190	171,363,000	18,299,000,000	27.4	27.3	47.5
More than 1,000,000	268	332,651,000	41,534,000,000	203	259,977,000	28,499,000,000	32.0	28.0	45.7
Total	22,050	2,962,701,000	385,501,000,000	19,201	2,498,303,000	283,050,000,000	14.8	18.6	38.2

Source: "Fifth Biennial Census of the Shopping Center Industry: Center Industry Has Grown to Major Proportions," *Shopping Center World* (January 1981): 80. Copyright *Shopping Center World*, a publication of Communication Channels, Inc., Atlanta, Georgia.

Table 6.6   Categorical Analysis of American Shopping Centers[a]

Size of Center (Square feet)	% of Total Centers	% of Total Gross Leasable Area	% of Total Sales	Average Size	Sales per Square Foot
10,000–100,000	66.2	27.0	30.8	54,742	$148.63
100,001–200,000	20.0	21.7	21.0	145,646	$126.14
200,001–400,000	7.7	16.3	15.2	284,995	$121.40
400,001–800,000	3.8	16.4	15.2	579,931	$120.14
800,001–1,000,000	1.1	7.4	7.0	901,641	$123.67
More than 1,000,000	1.2	11.2	10.8	1,241,235	$124.86
Total	100.0	100.0	100.0	134,363	$130.19

[a] Percentage figures represent each size category's share of the total.
Source: "Fifth Biennial Census of the Shopping Center Industry: Center Industry Has Grown to Major Proportions," *Shopping Center World* (January 1981): 80. Copyright *Shopping Center World*, a publication of Communication Channels, Inc., Atlanta, Georgia.

activities. The centers may include as many as five department stores, many smaller stores and services, plus hotels, apartment houses, office buildings, cultural centers, churches, and theaters. This type of center is also made more attractive by using fountains, waterfalls, and landscaping. Size of such centers is also becoming larger.

The expanded form of a regional shopping center integrates all of the retail and commercial functions plus activities in areas of entertainment, health, shopping, eating, and education. These larger regional shopping cities are growing in importance, although only a few of the 22,000 U.S. shopping centers could currently be classified as shopping city centers. Such large centers have an added impact beyond their numerical importance, because large city centers outdraw smaller centers and can pull shoppers from much longer distances.

The trading area differs for each of these location types and even for each store in the center. Store size and operating procedures differ markedly from one company to another, so it is impossible to make accurate statements about trading areas for all companies. Experiences of two eastern companies provide an example of the drawing power of each location type for a supermarket (Table 6.7).

Shopping center characteristics attract customers who like the convenience, parking facilities, and variety offered by the wide assortment of stores located in the center. Factors that consumers rate as the most important drawing attractions for large shopping centers are presented in Table 6.8. Consumer preferences and shopping habits are summarized in Table 6.9. Of the twelve

Table 6.7 Comparison of Trading Areas for a Supermarket Situated in Different Location Types

Location Type	Primary Trading Area Size (Radial dimension: miles)	% of Total Sales (0–1 Mile Area)
Neighborhood free-standing	½–¾	65–70
Central business district	½–¾	70–75
Neighborhood business district	¾–1	60–65
Secondary business district	¾–1	60–65
Highway business string	1–1¼	60–65
Highway free-standing	1–2	55–60
Edge of downtown	1½–2	40–45
Community shopping center	1½–2	50–55
Regional shopping center	1½–2½	35–40

Source: Bernard Kane, Jr., *A Systematic Guide to Supermarket Location Analysis* (New York: Fairchild Publications, 1966), p. 91. Reprinted by permission.

reported habits and preferences, eight have undergone significant changes between 1978 and 1981. Major shifts seem to be taking place which, if they continue, will have long-range implications for large mall managers and retail tenants.

It is evident that some large shopping centers also provide social drawing power. Teenagers, particularly, are drawn to these centers on Saturday, not to shop, but to socialize. Some centers sponsor community activities such as dog shows, flower shows, and art and other special exhibits to increase their appeal to all

Table 6.8 Most Important Consumer Rated Characteristics of Shopping Malls or Large Shopping Centers

Factor	Percentage of Consumers Rating Factor as Extremely or Very Important	
	1981	1978
Reasonably priced merchandise	89	78
Wide variety/selection	82	78
Adequate parking space	76	71
Convenience/ease of getting there	73	70
Knowledgeable sales help	67	73

Source: "Surveying Consumer Attitudes: Why They Shop Some Centers." Reprinted by permission from *Chain Store Age/Executive* (© September 1981): 60. Copyright Lebhar-Friedman, Inc., 425 Park Avenue, New York, NY 10022.

Table 6.9 Comparison of Consumer Shopping Habits and Preferences for Large Malls or Shopping Centers

Percentage of Sample	1978	1981
Shopping at a mall or center at least once a week	60	37
Believing that their favorite mall or center contains too many stores of the same type	18	68
Visiting a large mall or center during the last six months	85	69
Visiting small centers during the last six months	94	55
Shopping small centers more than large centers or malls	61	37
Saying availability of restaurants or fast food outlets are important in a center	50	25
Saying mall promotions are important	8	16
Saying store reduced-price sales are important	62	26
Saying convenient evening hours are important	54	40
Saying "too far away/inconvenient location" was main reason they stayed away from a large center	43	70
Saying they always shop with planned purchases in mind	79	63
Average number of stores visited per trip to shopping center	4.5	3.8

Source: "Surveying Consumer Attitudes: Why They Shop Some Centers." Reprinted by permission from *Chain Store Age/Executive* (© September 1981): 57–62. Copyright Lebhar-Friedman, Inc., 425 Park Avenue, New York, NY 10022.

age groups. Merchants who are deciding if they should locate in a center must weigh these positive characteristics against the higher rental costs in such centers and the limitations placed upon them as center tenants. The shopping center tenant must pay its prorated share of all joint center promotion efforts. The shopping center retailer must also keep store hours, light windows, and place signs in accordance with center regulations.

Historically developers and owners of shopping centers wanted to attract a wide assortment of successful retailers. Their initial selections were likely to include one or two prestige merchants (usually large chain stores or large department stores) as their **lead tenants** (retailers who provide major consumer attraction). Then at least one daytime restaurant and other complementary types of stores (usually small, independent retailers) was selected so that the center achieved an appealing **tenant mix** (the combination of all outlets operating from a shopping center) and offered a varied array of merchandise. The developer needed leases from companies with strong credit ratings to be able to obtain financing prior to construction, and most lenders favored tenant rosters that included the best of the national chains. However, the average developer also preferred to devote at least 40 percent of its store space to specialty or other shops on short-term leases.[7] This provided the developer with some protection against inflation because many specialty shops paid a percentage on their sales as rental. Big chains usually would not agree to share a percentage of their sales with a developer. Specialty shops also carried a merchandise assortment which could be adjusted to draw additional customer traffic. In addition, an overbalance of major chain stores could be detrimental to small merchants' sales because of their rather complete merchandise assortments.

The tenant mix of shopping centers is changing. The latest trend appears to be toward including off-price/factory-outlet retailing firms in shopping centers. Consumers like bargains and the developers of shopping centers are beginning to cater to this motivation by clustering factory-outlet stores and other "off-price" discounters in a shopping mall. These lower price stores appeal to economy minded consumers by offering prices 20 percent to 60 percent below those offered by department stores. Construction of no-frills, off-price centers has increased rapidly from about twelve in 1979 to about forty-five in 1980 and one hundred were planned for 1981. Many of these future off-price centers will consist of conversion of a failing shopping center into a center with factory outlets. Rouse Company has successfully transformed two small malls near Philadelphia and one in Charlotte, North Carolina to include off-price outlets.

Competition between off-price and regular merchants can be intense. For example, the Jack and Jill shop in Memphis has carried the Health-tex line of children's clothing. Health-tex opened its own factory outlet in a Memphis mall in the Spring of 1981 and began selling the same merchandise at 50 to 60 percent of the price charged by Jack and Jill. Eventually the Jack and Jill outlet dropped this brand of merchandise.

Pressure to expand sales will likely result in more and more manufacturers using factory outlets in an increasing number of shopping malls. This will have a very adverse effect upon small retailers who sell the same brand name merchandise in any nearby site.

The retailer who is considering locating in a shopping center has several major items to investigate. First, an objective trading area analysis (including an evaluation of competitive outlets analysis) must be performed. Second, an analysis of merchandising characteristics of the stores must be conducted. Selection of stores should be sufficient to meet the needs of the area's customers. Arrangement of the stores should give the retailer's store at least an equal chance of obtaining passerby pedestrian traffic. Ideally, every retailer would like to be located between the stores with the greatest customer pull. Third, total rent should be evaluated in making the decision, and this includes maintenance of common areas, the dues paid to the center's merchants' association, and the minimum lease guarantees—typically 5 to 7 percent of gross sales.

The retailer must evaluate these costs with the additional profits she or he believes can be obtained by locating in a center. A center location could be chosen if a reasonable projection showed that the added profits would be greater than the added costs.

Summary

Considerable care must be used to select and review the general area where a retailer could locate a store. The population must be sufficient to support a new store that carries the proposed merchandise assortment. Thus, competition must also be evaluated to determine if an area has too few stores to meet the needs of the community's consumers satisfactorily.

If the current or projected population is not large enough to support an additional store, a new or proposed store will have to rely upon other elements of the marketing mix (such as low price, heavy promotion and advertising outlays, better service, a larger merchandise assortment, and so forth) to drive current competition out of business. This could result in continual low profit margins, even if the new entry is successful in eliminating an established outlet.

Income level of the people living in the area will also influence retail sales. Retailers who stock shopping goods such as radios, TVs, sporting goods, and other items that are extremely sensitive to changes in income must place relatively more emphasis upon the area's income level than retailers who carry merchandise that does not appear to respond much to income changes. Other factors that must be considered are the purchasing habits of potential consumers, the legal environment, and the progressiveness of the community in attracting customers.

Type of location must also be evaluated, because stores located in shopping centers may have a much different trading area from stores that are located downtown or in neighborhood business districts. The trend is toward extremely large shopping centers that draw customers from a large trading area for entertainment, health, education, eating, and shopping purposes.

Each retailer must make an independent judgment, weighing all the variables, and then select the type of location that will provide the firm with the best possible chance of success.

Questions

1. Why is population an important factor affecting sales? For which types of merchandise is it most important? Discuss.
2. What factors do buying power index calculations fail to take into consideration?
3. Why does the legal environment influence profitability and determine the existence or nonexistence of any store?
4. Describe the three major types of planned shopping centers.

5. What are the major items that the retailer who is considering locating in a shopping center has to investigate?

6. What strategies are available to retailers who find themselves in an overstored area? Would you expect an understored situation to continue in the long run? Why?

7. Suggest several reasons why retail shopping center sales have expanded since 1965. Would you expect this trend to continue? If so, for how long? Why? What types of shopping centers will expand fastest in the future? Why?

8. Since lead tenants are considered so important in drawing customers to a shopping center, why would a shopping center developer want to devote at least 40 percent of his floor space to specialty shops?

9. If you were offered very low-cost financing to open a retail store in Watts, Harlem, or some similar inner-city low-income area, how would you decide exactly where to locate and what to sell? Develop a complete retailing mix for whatever type of establishment you would suggest and give your reasons. What major problems would you anticipate in the first year of operation?

10. Some cities and states (Boulder, Colorado and the state of Oregon, for example) have made deliberate attempts to limit population and/or economic growth. Considering the retailing industry as a whole, what are the implications of these limits? What line of merchandise and what retailing mix would you suggest for a potential retailer in these areas?

Footnotes

1. Projection Series II from U.S. Census Bureau.

2. "Fast-Food Chains Deserve a Break Today, So They Are Moving into Smaller Towns," *Wall Street Journal*, 21 April 1976, p. 36.

3. B. J. LaLonde, "New Frontiers in Store Location," *Supermarket Merchandising* (February 1963): 110.

4. Charles A. Ingene and Robert F. Lusch, "Market Selection Decisions for Department Stores," *Journal of Retailing* 56 (Fall 1980): p. 40.

5. This classification was obtained from J. Ross McKeever, *Factors in Considering a Shopping Center Location* (Washington, D.C.: Small Business Administration), Aids No. 143, p. 3.

6. "Shopping Centers Will Be America's Towns of Tomorrow," *Marketing News*, Vol. XIV, Nov. 28, 1980, p. 11.

7. "Shopping Centers Grow into Shopping Cities," *Business Week*, 4 September 1971, p. 37.

Case Study: Smith's Supply Store

Smith's Supply Store operates two general merchandise retail outlets which serve two different rural trading areas. The main store (unit one) is an established profitable outlet, and the second outlet (unit two) is just becoming a profitable operation after opening in that area three years ago. Annual sales volume obtained in 1981 in unit one was $2,135,000, and $758,500 sales was generated in unit two.

Smith's would like to open another outlet but doesn't know if it should do so or not. The firm is studying two possible locations. Possible unit 3 is located near unit one so it will share the current trading area served by the main store. Possible unit 4 is situated in an entirely new trading area.

The firm's present sales are equally divided between general merchandise sales (for which it mostly competes with K mart and Gibsons) and supply sales to agricultural firms.

Smith's has conducted research to determine if either potential unit 3 or 4 would have a market sufficiently attractive to justify the profitable operation of a Smith store. Data collected appear in Tables 6.10–6.16.

Table 6.10   Smith's Supply Stores Retail Sales and Population Summary under Different Location Strategies

Strategy 1—Continue Serving Consumers from Unit 1 and Unit 2

	1982 Population	1982 Estimate of Disposable Personal Income ($1,000)
Unit 1	34,454	$259,094
Unit 2	15,205	$105,041
Total for area served by Smith's Supply	49,659	
% Unit 2 store is of Unit 1 store	44%	41%

Strategy 2—Add Unit 3 Outlet to Unit 1 and Unit 2 Outlets

	1982 Population
Unit 1	23,257
Unit 2	15,205
Proposed unit 3 store	11,197
% of population currently served by unit 1	32%

Strategy 3—Add Unit 4 Outlet to Unit 1 and Unit 2 Outlets

	1982 Population	1982 Estimate of Disposable Personal Income ($1,000)
Unit 1	34,454	$259,094
Unit 2	15,205	$105,041
% Unit 2 store is of unit 1 store	44%	41%
Proposed unit 4	39,074	$260,743
% Unit 4 store is of unit 1 store	113%	101%
Total for area served by Smith's Supply	88,733	

Table 6.11   1982 Estimate of Disposable Personal Income

Area	1982 Estimate of Disposable Personal Income ($1000)	1982 Estimate of per Household Income
Served by Smith's unit 1	$259,094	$20,550
Served by Smith's unit 2	105,041	19,360
Served by proposed unit 4	260,743	21,519

Table 6.12   Estimated Retail Sales

	Total Retail Sales Volume ($1000)		1982 Estimate of Retail Sales ($1000)		
Area	1981	1982	Lumber and Hardware	General Merchandise	Apparel
Served by unit 1	100,910	131,176	13,869	15,564	6,297
Served by unit 2	46,801	75,925	6,318	4,701	4,145
Served by unit 4	119,499	193,011	22,902	12,488	10,138

Table 6.13   1982 Value of Agricultural Production

Area	Number of Farms	Total Market Value of All Products Sold ($1000)	Value of Crop Production ($1000)	Value of Livestock Production ($1000)
Served by unit 1	1090	$81,520	26,221	55,298
Served by unit 2	330	46,253	10,616	35,638
Served by unit 4	757	32,951	6,651	26,300

Table 6.14   Estimate of Relative Attractiveness of the Three Trading Areas

Area	Index for Population Served[a]	Index for General Merchandise Sales[b]	Index for Agricultural Sales[c]	Overall Index[d]
Unit 1 trading area	100	100	100	100
Unit 2 trading area	44	49	44	47
Unit 3 trading area	32	32	20	26
Unit 4 trading area	113	120	55	88

a. Source data as reported in Table 1.
b. Average of sales tax collections as reported in Table 3.
c. Average percentage of farms and of total market value of all agricultural products sold as reported in Table 4.
d. Average of the index figures for general merchandise sales and agricultural sales.

Table 6.15   Evaluation of Competition for Smith's Outlets

Major Retailers in Area Served by Unit 1	Major Retailers in Area Served by Unit 2	Major Retailers in Area Served by Unit 3	Major Retailers in Area Served by Unit 4
Gibson's	C.R. Anthony	K mart	K mart
Big Anthony	Gambles	Pamida	J.C. Penney
Coast-to-Coast	J.C. Penney	2 Corral West	J.M. McDonald
Gambles	Jones	2 Lumber & Hardware	Pamida
2 Auto Parts Stores	Pamida	3 Auto Parts Stores	Woolworth
2 Lumber Yards & Hardware	Town & Country	Coast-to-Coast	Bi-Rite
War Surplus		Gambles	Gambles
3 Major Implement Houses		Horse Care Center	Coast-to-Coast
4 Tire Centers		2 Tire Centers	C.R. Anthony
1 Livestock Sale Barn		No Major Implement Houses	Wards
Co-op			4 Auto Parts Stores
			Sears
			5 Lumber & Hardware
			3 Appliance Stores
			5 Clothing Stores
			Woolworth
			2 Western Clothing Stores
			4 Major Implement Houses
			4 Furniture Stores
			8 Oil Well Supply Outlets
			1 Livestock Sale Barn
			Co-op
			Farmer's Exchange
			Livestock Supply
			2 Home Related Specialty Stores

Table 6.16 Retail Establishments and Employees in General Merchandise Outlets and All Retail Outlets

Area	Employees for All Retail Outlets	All Retail Establishments
Served by unit 1	2039	281
Served by unit 2	942	121
Served by unit 4	2394	264

Discussion Questions:

1. Based on the data presented, what would you recommend for Smith's? Why?

2. What other data would you like to have before you make a decision, and how would you obtain these data?

Chapter 7 | Factors in Retail Site Evaluation

Learning Goals

1. To understand the techniques retailers use to define the size and shape of an outlet's trading area.
2. To estimate the population within a store's trading area and the dollar value of potential merchandise purchases originating in that area.
3. To discuss the factors that influence the share of purchases that an outlet can obtain.
4. To learn to estimate sales volume of a proposed store.
5. To list the advantages and disadvantages of buying or leasing retail land and buildings.

Key Terms and Concepts

trading area
trading area overlays
credit record analysis
license plate analysis
customer interview
percentage of income method
percentage of retail sales
  dollar method
per capita method
market share

compatability of nearby
  business
generative business
shared business
incidental business
market share to selling space
  share ratio
payback period
storing land
economic value

Specific site selection must be made after the general trade area has been evaluated. Discussion in this chapter will concentrate on this process which is critical to the successful operation of a retail business. The most significant factors retailers should consider when evaluating a site are summarized in Exhibit 7.1. Although no standard evaluation procedure is used by all retail firms, the selection of a specific location within the chosen trading area can be determined by considering the following location principles.

Defining the Trading Area

A **store's trading area** is that geographical area in which about 70 percent of the store's customers reside. Measuring the trade boundaries for existing retailing facilities is much easier than es-

Exhibit 7.1   Evaluation Factors for Selecting a Retail Site

A. Population residing in primary and secondary trading areas
B. Product line purchases made in primary and secondary trading areas
C. Share of market firm is likely to obtain, involving analysis of:
  1. Competition
      a. Nearby independent outlets
      b. Nearby chain or franchise outlets
  2. Compatibility of nearby businesses
  3. Traffic flow
      a. Auto
      b. Pedestrians
      c. Hours of peak movement
      d. Traffic patterns
  4. Transportation availability
  5. Parking facilities
  6. Physical facility
  7. Accessibility of site to residents of trading area
D. Estimate of sales volume at site
E. Buy, lease, build, or do-not-enter-market decision

timating the trade area for proposed stores. However, studies of the trading area for similar existing stores can provide an excellent measure of the probable trading area for a proposed store. Chain retailers who must use more than one outlet to reach most of a city's population utilize **trading area overlays** to determine how well their stores are serving the consumers (Figure 7.1). Each store's trading area is plotted on a transparent plastic sheet and placed over a city map to spot geographical areas from which the chain is not drawing customers. A new store that is located in such an area could be a profitable addition to the chain's current list of outlets.

Trading area analysis also allows the firm to prevent trading area overlap which results in higher retailing costs by having an excessive number of small higher-cost, lower-volume outlets. In this case, the less profitable stores may be eliminated by building larger stores with more complete merchandise assortments which better serve most of the customers. This type of trade area analysis offers more benefits to chain retailers whose outlets have a relatively small trading area. Grocery stores are examples of stores whose trade areas are relatively small.

The hypothetical trade area analysis in Figure 7.1 contains trade areas for the two chain A stores numbered 1 and 2 on the map. The trading area for each store would be drawn independently so that about 80 percent of each store's customers reside within the outlined trade area designated for that store. This analysis indicates that the two chain A stores are not drawing

Figure 7.1   Using Trade Area Analysis to Identify Store Coverage

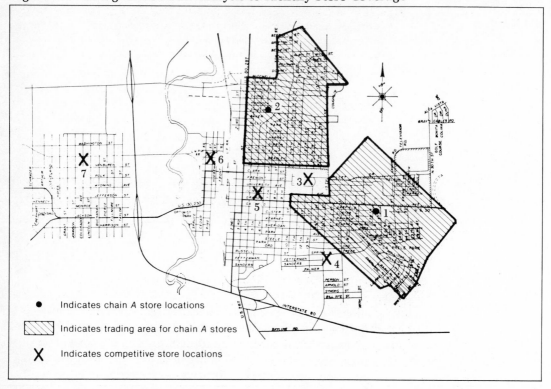

●   Indicates chain *A* store locations

▨   Indicates trading area for chain *A* stores

✗   Indicates competitive store locations

customers from the extreme west side of the city (from the area surrounding competitor store number 7) or from the south central part of the city in the area surrounding competitor stores 4, 5, and 6. Chain A would be able to expand its sales if it would locate a new store in each of these areas. However, this is only the preliminary step in retail site evaluation. It must be determined if either of the new stores could generate enough sales to operate on a profitable basis.

    The following techniques can be used to measure the boundaries of the trading area for retail outlets.

Store Credit Record Analysis

The observational technique of store **credit record analysis** consists of examining store credit records for data on the residences of the store consumers. It is relatively inexpensive and can produce acceptable results if the credit customers' store patronage patterns do not differ from the store selection habits of non-credit-using customers. Credit usage may vary among different consumer groups residing in an area, and in these cases the addresses of cash customers must be obtained if the trade area is to be accurately defined. Addresses of cash customers may be obtained by analyzing the addresses on checks written by cash customers. Addresses of cash customers may also be obtained from delivery tickets or cash sales slips. After a representative sampling of the store's customers has been made, the addresses of the clientele are plotted on an area map with dots or pins.

The trading area is then determined and area boundaries are defined. The intensity of a store's penetration within its trading area usually diminishes with increased distance (measured in travel time) from the store. The entire trading area can then be divided into primary, secondary, and fringe trading areas. All three areas should be defined in statistical and geographical terms. The primary trade area is usually determined on a population basis. For example, the area could be defined so that 55 to 70 percent of the customers reside within its boundaries. The secondary trade area could contain about 70 to 90 percent of the customers, and the fringe area, which will probably be widely dispersed, will contain the remaining customers. A similar analysis can be made by using telephone numbers (obtained when making reservations) cashing checks, and so forth.

License Plate Analysis

License Plate Analysis, another observational technique, consists of inconspicuously recording the license numbers of cars in the store's or shopping center's parking lot. The county treasurer's office or some other appropriate county office is then contacted to learn the addresses of the owners of the automobiles. The addresses of these customers are then plotted on an area map to define the trade area.

This is a fairly inexpensive technique that yields, as does the credit record analysis, a list of customer names. These names can also be used for other research purposes such as determining store image, improving store service, and so forth.

The person who records the license numbers should be certain that the person is a customer and not a store clerk or a patron of a different store in the same area. This may be done if the recorder watches the entrance and exit doors and records only the license numbers of persons passing through these doors during business hours.

Another precaution is that license numbers should not be collected during times when an atypical representation of consumers might be chosen. For example, large conventions, sporting events, or special sales could temporarily overstate the actual trading area.

Customer Interview   Interviews with people residing in an area can also be used to identify the trading area. These **customer interviews** can be conducted by mail questionnaire, personal interview in the respondent's home, or telephone. Cross-reference books provide listings of telephone numbers by address so that persons in any selected area may be interviewed. These data collection techniques are discussed in detail in Chapter 20.

In addition, a short questionnaire may be placed in customers' shopping bags. A high percentage of the customers will return these questionnaires if the return postage is prepaid and if there is some incentive to return them. A contest or offer of a small prize is usually a sufficient stimulus to induce a good return rate of 60 to 70 percent of the customers receiving the questionnaire. This approach allows the store to obtain additional information on demographic characteristics such as age, family size, educational background, and the like.

The chief disadvantage is that the sample selected in this manner may not be representative of all customers. Middle-income customers are likely to be overrepresented among those who respond to the questionnaire. In general, higher-income customers do not like to take the time to complete and return questionnaires. Lower-income customers are sometimes afraid to cooperate because of fear that a hidden commitment is involved or because of fear of revealing their lower level of formal education. The extent to which these types of biases occur should be determined carefully by examining the response rate. Last, many shoppers do not inspect the bags at home but simply remove the merchandise and discard the bags.

Household shopping surveys are also used to estimate trade areas for proposed outlets. They can provide detailed insight into consumer purchasing patterns. However, caution must be used when analyzing the results since about 30 percent of all people will say yes to anything.

A study of the proposed outlet's trading area is important because it reveals information about the consumer groups from which management of the outlet will select its target market. It also allows retail management to make a more careful analysis of the market segments toward which the outlet will direct its merchandising efforts. This should allow the firm's management to satisfy the demands of its consumers better.

It is necessary to analyze two other trading area characteristics, size and shape, to ensure that a realistic trade area is employed in the planning process.

Trade Area Size

Size of the trading area must be related to the size of the proposed outlet. Other things being equal, a larger store will attract
consumers from a larger trade area than a smaller store.

The size of the urban area in which the store will be located
also affects the size of the trading area. Larger populations attract
a greater number of the same type of stores in the same general
area. Clustering of competitive outlets results in a larger trade
area for the retail cluster. It also diminishes the share of business
that the store can obtain from the trading area.

In addition, a higher income level for the population surrounding the outlet results in a larger sized trading area. Higher income people tend to be more mobile and travel longer distances
to shop in areas of greater merchandise depth and assortment.
The advent of higher gasoline prices has recently placed even
more emphasis upon the ability and willingness of consumers to
drive past convenient shopping to get to an outlet offering more
depth, assortment, or some other appeal. Further gasoline price
increases or a limited supply of gasoline could rapidly alter the
management plans of a proposed outlet which is counting on
these people for a portion of its target market.

Finally, size of the trading area is affected by the ease of entering and exiting from the outlet. The more accessible the site, the
larger is the size of the outlet's trade area. Natural or artificial
barriers that impede movement of traffic to the site can greatly
restrict trading area size.

Trade Area Shape

Theoretically, if consumers want to minimize driving time and if
there are no barriers to traffic, the trade area around each shopping outlet would be a circle. The radius of the circle would reflect the optimum travel time for the consumer. The outlet would
sell its products outward in all directions from its location to a
point where the consumers are indifferent as to whether they
shop at this outlet or at some other competitive outlet located
outside the trade circle.

However, in the real world the shape of a trade area is influenced by more than distance. The trade area can be shaped by
variations in land formations, the nature of transportation routes,
political boundaries, and the power of competing retail facilities.
As a result the shape of store trading areas is typically elongated
in the direction of consumer movement, which may parallel a
superhighway or a mass transit route. Certainly the existence of
good roads and mass transit facilities will greatly affect the size
and shape of the trade area.

A recent study indicates that consumers consider a combination of retail center characteristics (such as merchandise assortment, center design, pricing, hours of operation, and informal and uncrowded atmosphere) and transportation considerations (such as safety, convenience, reliability, clean and attractive atmosphere, and cost) in their decision to patronize alternative retail areas.[1]

Determining the Total Population of the Trading Area

The total population residing in the primary trading area may be estimated by taking a personal survey of the area and counting all the dwellings. If the proposed site is located within a standard metropolitan area, the U.S. Bureau of the Census provides detailed population and demographic data by census tract. Municipal agencies are usually able to provide an estimate of the number of water hookups in an area, which gives a rough estimate of the number of families residing within an area. Local utilities (power, gas, telephone) might be able to provide a more reliable estimate of the number of families residing within an area because each family is more likely to be billed separately for these items than for water and sewage.

To refine population estimates, one must determine how well the residents of the area fit the description of the retailer's target market. Further breakdowns made on the basis of age, income, nationality, and lifestyle can be matched against the store's merchandising plans to provide a more accurate estimate of potential sales volume.

Determining per Capita Product Line Purchases in the Trading Area

Per capita purchases are usually available from trade sources or from publications such as *Sales Management's Survey of Buying Power, Editor & Publisher Market Guide,* and other secondary sources. The latest *Census of Business* provides data on sales made by various types of retail outlets in standard metropolitan areas. The annual total sales made by different types of retailers may also be available from the state department of revenue. Whatever secondary source is used, the total sales may be divided by population to obtain an estimate of per capita expenditures on the proposed service or line of merchandise.

Consumer surveys or "diary" studies may be used to estimate

per capita expenditures if the data are not available from secondary sources. (A diary study consists of a sample of typical consumers who record all their purchases for a week or month in a diary which is then returned to the researcher for analysis.) A crisscross directory can be used to select the sample of "typical consumers" residing within a specified area, and the selection of an area can be based upon differences in consumer income, age, education, and the like.

The crisscross directory, which is usually available from a city office or public utility company, lists all the active addresses in an area. It also provides the names of the persons residing at each address. (A diary study is a fairly expensive method unless purchases of several product lines are observed simultaneously, allowing the cost to be shared by several retailers.)

The chief difficulty associated with consumer surveys that rely on querying consumers on past purchases is the inability of respondents to recall all the purchases they made during the previous month. Thus, the best estimates of purchases are sometimes made when the respondents are asked to recall last week's purchases with the aid of a prepared list of possible purchases. The short time period and the memory-enhancing list are especially important if consumers are asked to recall purchases of lower-price items. Of course expenditures on major items such as autos, furniture, and appliances are remembered for a much longer period of time.

Determining Total Product Line Purchases Made in the Trading Area

Total purchases can be obtained simply by multiplying the population by per capita consumption of the product line. This step answers the question, "If we obtain all the business available in this trading area, how large would our sales volume be?" The remainder of the volume estimation analysis has to determine how much of the total business can be obtained by the proposed outlet.

Frequently, the trade area may consist of an entire town or county. If so, secondary sources such as the *Editor & Publisher Market Guide* or *Sales and Marketing Management's Survey of Buying Power* provide current estimates of total retail sales as well as sales in the five or six major retail categories. In addition, state sales tax agencies generally have a breakdown of retail sales into many different categories. Thus, one may be able to obtain an estimate of the total product line purchases made in the trading area directly from these sources.

Other calculations may be required if the exact product line sales for the trade area are not available from these sources.

The **percentage of income method** estimates category sales in the trade area by using the percentage of current income spent on the particular merchandise category. In formula format the calculation procedure is:

$$\begin{matrix} \text{\$ Spent Annually} \\ \text{on Specified} \\ \text{Merchandise Category} \end{matrix} = \begin{matrix} \text{\$ Total Annual} \\ \text{Personal Income} \\ \text{in Area} \end{matrix} \times \begin{matrix} \text{\% of Annual} \\ \text{Personal Income} \\ \text{Spent in the} \\ \text{Specified} \\ \text{Merchandise} \\ \text{Category} \end{matrix}$$

Secondary sources, *Editor & Publisher Market Guide* and *Sales and Marketing Management's Survey of Buying Power,* provide the current estimate of annual personal income by county and town. The percentage of annual personal income spent in different retail merchandise categories is presented in Table 7.1.

To illustrate how this method can be used to estimate sales, suppose one wanted to locate a hardware outlet which would serve an entire town. If the estimated 1981 personal income for people living in the town is $817,114,000, data in Table 7.1 indicate that on the average 0.4 percent of personal income is spent in hardware stores. Thus, one can estimate that if national average conditions hold for this area, annual sales can be computed for the town as: $817,114,000 × .004 = $3,268,456. Of course, this calculation yields just a rough estimate of category retail sales in an area. It does represent an initial forecast that can be adjusted or refined to better reflect the deviation of local conditions from the national average.

The **percentage of retail sales dollar method** of estimating category retail sales in the trade area follows a similar logic. The calculation procedure is:

$$\begin{matrix} \text{\$ Spent Annually in} \\ \text{Specified} \\ \text{Merchandise} \\ \text{Category} \end{matrix} = \begin{matrix} \text{\$ Total Annual} \\ \text{Retail Sales} \\ \text{in the Area} \end{matrix} \times \begin{matrix} \text{\% of Annual} \\ \text{Retail Sales} \\ \text{for the Specified} \\ \text{Merchandise Category} \end{matrix}$$

Secondary sources such as *Editor & Publisher Market Guide, Sales and Marketing Management's Survey of Buying Power,* and state sales tax collection records provide the current estimates of annual retail sales in the area. The percentage of retail sales for different retail merchandise outlets is presented in Figure 7.2.

Thus hardware outlets, serving an entire town, could forecast 1981 sales by multiplying the total retail sales for the town

Table 7.1   Percentages and Expenditure Associated with Different Merchandise Categories[a]

Type of Retail Outlet	% of Personal Income Spent in Category	Annual $ per Capita Expenditures in Category
Retail trade total	47.0	3,360
Lumber and other building dealers	1.6	115
Hardware stores	0.4	28
Department stores	5.0	357
Variety stores	0.4	32
Grocery stores	9.6	686
Automotive dealers	9.8	697
Auto and home supply stores	0.8	60
Gasoline service stations	3.7	262
Apparel and accessory stores	2.3	165
Women's clothing, specialty stores, and furriers	0.9	63
Men's and boys' clothing and furnishings	0.5	32
Family clothing stores	0.5	37
Shoe stores	0.4	26
Furniture, home furnishings, and equipment stores (total)	2.2	154
Furniture stores	0.9	65
Home furnishings stores	0.4	29
Household appliance stores	0.3	22
Radio, TV, and music stores	0.5	38
Eating and drinking places (total)	4.1	294
Eating places	3.6	258
Drinking places (alcoholic)	0.5	36
Drug and proprietary stores	1.5	108
Liquor stores	0.8	60
Sporting goods stores and bicycle shops	0.3	22
Jewelry stores	0.4	25

[a] Personal income for 1977 is estimated to be $1,537,000 million according to 1977 *Editor & Publisher Market Guide*. Retail sales were obtained from *U.S. Department of Commerce, Bureau of the Census, 1977 Census of Business, Retail Trade* (Washington, D.C.: Government Printing Office, 1977).

($301,042,000) times the 1.2% obtained from Figure 7.2 to equal $3,612,504.

A third approach to forecasting category retail for a trade area is to use the **per capita sales method.** The calculation is:

$$\begin{matrix} \text{\$ Spent Annually in} \\ \text{Specified Merchandise} \\ \text{Category} \end{matrix} = \begin{matrix} \text{\$ Annual per Capita} \\ \text{Expenditure in} \\ \text{Specified Category} \end{matrix} \times \begin{matrix} \text{Number of} \\ \text{People Residing} \\ \text{in Trade Area} \end{matrix}$$

Figure 7.2   U.S. Merchandise Line Sales of Retail Establishments: 1977 (% of total sales)

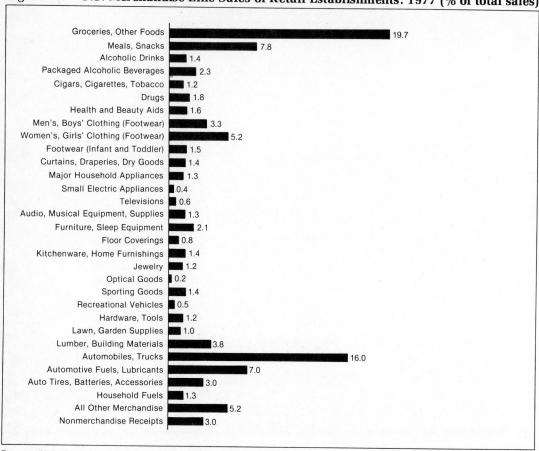

Groceries, Other Foods	19.7
Meals, Snacks	7.8
Alcoholic Drinks	1.4
Packaged Alcoholic Beverages	2.3
Cigars, Cigarettes, Tobacco	1.2
Drugs	1.8
Health and Beauty Aids	1.6
Men's, Boys' Clothing (Footwear)	3.3
Women's, Girls' Clothing (Footwear)	5.2
Footwear (Infant and Toddler)	1.5
Curtains, Draperies, Dry Goods	1.4
Major Household Appliances	1.3
Small Electric Appliances	0.4
Televisions	0.6
Audio, Musical Equipment, Supplies	1.3
Furniture, Sleep Equipment	2.1
Floor Coverings	0.8
Kitchenware, Home Furnishings	1.4
Jewelry	1.2
Optical Goods	0.2
Sporting Goods	1.4
Recreational Vehicles	0.5
Hardware, Tools	1.2
Lawn, Garden Supplies	1.0
Lumber, Building Materials	3.8
Automobiles, Trucks	16.0
Automotive Fuels, Lubricants	7.0
Auto Tires, Batteries, Accessories	3.0
Household Fuels	1.3
All Other Merchandise	5.2
Nonmerchandise Receipts	3.0

Source: U.S. Department of Commerce, Bureau of the Census.

Sources used in the percentage of income and percentage of retail sales approaches can be used to provide the current estimate of population in the trade area. The annual per capita dollar sales for different merchandise categories is presented in Table 7.1. For example, annual per capita expenditure in hardware stores was $28 in 1977. If per capita hardware sales have increased in proportion to inflation in consumer prices, they increased by 44 percent from 1977 to 1981 to $40 per capita. Thus, the per capita method would indicate that annual hardware store sales in the town can be computed by multiplying the number of people (95,753) times $40, resulting in $3,830,120.

Frequently estimates obtained by using the percentage of income, the percentage of retail sales dollar, and the per capita methods are quite close. If so, one may be more confident that the estimate is relatively accurate. Other times the three methods give widely divergent estimates. If this happens, the basic information going into each method should be reinvestigated to determine if it is accurate. If all of the input data appear to be reasonable, then the three estimates can be averaged to provide a single estimate. The range between the smallest and largest sales estimates can be used to establish the range of possible sales volume. In the hardware example, the $3,268,456 estimate from the percent of income approach is the lowest estimate and the $3,830,120 estimate obtained from the per capita method is the highest. The average of the three estimates is $3,570,360. This average might be the best estimate to use because it takes population, income, and other retail sales into consideration at one time. However, the most conservative estimate is the lowest of the three values or $3,268,456. Prospective retailers frequently overestimate the size of the market and their share of it. Use of the lowest figure will provide a little cushion and not allow would-be retailers to get carried away with their emotions.

Both the volume of total sales and sales by type of outlet obtainable in a shopping center can be determined by the following analysis:

1. A priori establishment of a tentative trade area for analysis. 2. Creation of a conceptual image of the completed shopping center in order to determine the strength of attraction which would be exerted by the envisaged facilities. 3. Determination of the gross personal consumption expenditures of the residents of this area through population tabulation, income analysis, and consumer expenditure studies. 4. Study of consumer movements, characteristics, and attitudes—both within and outside of competitive centers—to determine the probability of patronage from various segments of the subject trade area. 5. Derivation of quantitative sales expectancies and spatial requirements for specific retail facilities within the subject center.[2]

Determining the Share of Total Trading Area Purchases

The **market share** (percentage of category sales obtained by the store) that a new firm will be able to obtain is based upon many factors. Frequently prospective owners of independent outlets merely judge how well competitive stores are doing and then evaluate how well their proposed entry can fare against these competitors. If it is believed that the new outlet will be able to attract a normal portion of the market, then the firm's market share will be:

$$\text{New Firm's \% Market Share} = \frac{1}{\text{Total Number of Similar Outlets in Trading Area}} \times 100$$

Usually this figure is adjusted to account for the many other factors that influence the consumer's decision on where to shop. A prospective merchant may ask wholesale suppliers for their best judgment. Chain or franchise firms often prepare their market share estimates by comparing the planned store with other company outlets of a comparable size and type in cities of about the same population size, social class, and competitive environment. Skilled management is required to adjust the share estimates for any observed differences between the situation facing the proposed outlet and the supposedly similar existing outlets. Frequently these judgments focus upon the accessibility to the site itself.

Evaluation of Site Accessibility for Residents of the Trading Area

Passing foot and car traffic can be counted to determine how accessible the site is to a potential customer. A foot and car traffic count (which shows the number of passersby during a given period) can be made several times at the proposed location and at successfully operating stores. The comparative passerby traffic count at successfully established stores and proposed new sites provides a relative measure of accessibility. Passing foot and car traffic each offer customer potential that a good promotional merchandising effort can turn into business.

The minimum traffic count needed to indicate that the site has substantial potential will depend upon what type of retail or service outlet is being proposed. Outlets which depend upon shared or suscipient business will require a higher traffic count than outlets which depend upon generative business. Passing traffic must also be evaluated on a qualitative basis. Daily commuters going to and from work are much less valuable than passing pedestrian traffic.

Ease of entrance to and exit from the site must also be evaluated. Passing auto traffic offers no potential if it cannot enter the retailer's location with a minimum of accident risk and with little effort and time. A list of physical factors that must be evaluated for each site being considered is presented in Exhibit 7.2.

Evaluation of the Compatibility of Nearby Businesses

Compatibility of nearby businesses occurs when two adjacent businesses have a larger sales volume together than they would have if they were located in separate areas. Compatibility may be

**Exhibit 7.2 Physical Factors to Be Evaluated before
Determining Retail Site Potential**

Quantity and quality of nearby businesses and institutions
Quantity and quality of auto traffic passing site
Quantity and quality of pedestrian traffic passing site
Adequate traffic direction and control (e.g., stop lights)
Visibility of site to passing traffic
Ease of entrance to site
Ease of exit from site
Quantity and quality of parking
Quantity and quality of sidewalks, walkways, and bicycle paths
Availability of public transportation
Freedom from unpleasant noise, smell, and dust
Alternative availability possibilities (rent vs. buy)
City planning and zoning restrictions
Vulnerability to negative changes in physical environment (e.g., those
relating to weather such as closed streets, floods, etc.)

caused by the two firms' selling complementary product lines or
services. For example, a prescribing doctor's office and a phar-
macy offer complementary services. Compatibility also occurs
when firms sell competitive goods of different styles, lines, and
prices. A drug store and a supermarket, for example, may benefit
by being located next to one another, even though they carry
many of the same product lines.

Generative business, which is produced by the store itself
through an effective promotion and merchandising effort, can be
calculated for each segment of the trading area. Retail outlets
that must generate all of their own business should be located in
the most accessible location commensurate with cost.

Shared business, which is secured by a retailer as the result of
the generative pulling power of nearby retailers, can also be isolated. This business is represented by customers who are in the
area primarily because they want to visit a neighboring store or
service agency. Much of the prescription business of a drug store
located near prescribing doctors' offices will be a shared business.

Incidental business comes from people whose principal purpose for being near the retail outlet is *not* because the store or its
neighbors attracted them; thus, a newsstand at a commuter railroad station or an airport does mostly suscipient business. It
does not generate any of its own business but merely offers a
service to people who are at the location for another purpose—
transportation to another destination. Some downtown stores
specifically serve people working in the area. Because these
stores do not attract people directly from their homes, the acces-

sibility requirements can be so specific that they can be satisfied only by an outlet located within walking distance of the work area.

The volume of business done by most retailers and service suppliers is composed of all three types of business; therefore, evaluation of a site's accessibility must take all three business types into account. Estimates of the amount of business that is believed to be available from each source can later serve as a checkpoint to determine if a store is realizing its full potential.

Compatibility has contributed to the success of the planned shopping center and to well-designed downtown and suburban shopping areas. Compatibility is important because a number of stores dealing in the same lines of shopping merchandise will frequently do more business if they are located near one another than if they are widely scattered. Clustering of stores increases the drawing power of the stores in the retail center. This is the reason for large department stores being located near one another in the downtown areas and for the trend toward more regional shopping centers having two or more department stores as their principal tenants instead of just one.

In addition to business interchange, a group of negative factors can be used in measuring compatibility. These variables tend to reduce the business of nearby retailers. Interruptions in pedestrian traffic flow can reduce business interchange with adjacent stores. Interruptions may be caused by "dead" frontage spots which cause a shopper to lose interest in continuing to walk farther in the same direction. Driveways and other physical disruptions in the sidewalk and heavy vehicular or pedestrian cross traffic tend to create congestion and cause interruptions. Other items that interfere with traffic flow are associated with hazard, noise, unpleasant odors, unsightliness, or other inhibiting qualities. Nearby businesses whose customers require an extremely long parking period will also minimize traffic flow.

It is extremely important that the layout of the shopping area ensures that consumers pass the specialty outlets on their way to the chief drawing attractions, which usually are major department stores. In the layout of a regional shopping center in Figure 7.3 note that the focal or anchor spots are located at the outer extremities of the center. Convenience shopping stores (supermarket, drugstore, variety store, and so forth) are dispersed among the comparison shopper type outlets such as the department store, clothing, shoe, jewelry stores. The major retail attractions in the convenience shopping area are the drugstore and supermarket.

Customer surveys have revealed that anchor stores have a relatively stronger customer drawing power (they attract consumers

Figure 7.3 Typical Planned Shopping Center Layout with Anchor Stores Located in Positions A, B, and C and Convenience Shopping Stores Located in Positions D, E, and F

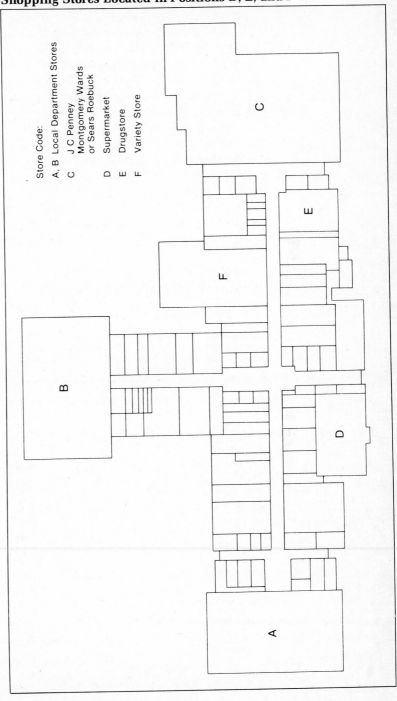

Store Code:

A, B Local Department Stores

C J C Penney Montgomery Wards or Sears Roebuck

D Supermarket

E Drugstore

F Variety Store

from farther geographical distance) than convenience stores such as supermarkets. Surveys have also indicated that half of the customers in drawing stores also shop in one or more of the other stores.

The trend appears to be toward more major stores anchoring large centers. For example, Southwest Plaza, a new facility containing 1.4 million square feet of retail space located in the Denver area, will have The Denver, Joslins, May D & F, Montgomery Ward, and Sears Roebuck & Co. as anchors. These five department stores have not previously shared space in the same mall.[3]

The typical tenant profiles of six types of shopping centers are presented in Table 7.2. Despite the tremendous drawing power of chain outlets, merchants who operate specialty shops tend to produce per square foot sales that far exceed the performance of national chains. For example, local entrepreneurs operate nearly all of the men's wear shops in Northbrook Court near Chicago. Their sales exceed the $175 per square foot of the center as a

Table 7.2   Tenant Profiles of Six Shopping Center Types*

Category	Urban			Nonurban		
	Under 100,000 Square feet GLA	100,001– 500,000 Square feet GLA	Over 500,000 Square feet GLA	Under 100,000 Square feet GLA	100,001– 500,000 Square feet GLA	Over 500,000 Square feet GLA
Department stores	N.A.	16.20%	32.07%	1.52%	10.17%	32.85%
General merchandise	N.A.	18.18	22.89	N.A.	11.54	21.82
Discount store	5.62	10.65	0.91	9.21	10.06	1.51
Variety store	4.85	3.29	2.19	2.42	3.43	1.18
Catalog showroom	0.61	0.86	0.19	0.67	1.58	0.21
Supermarket	28.56	8.04	2.00	35.38'	14.24	1.85
Drug store	11.89	3.61	1.64	8.96	5.07	1.49
Large specialty store	N.A.	2.29	1.21	0.48	0.99	1.28
Women's apparel	2.79	4.61	7.23	2.16	5.07	6.92
Men's apparel	3.48	2.06	2.33	1.04	1.59	2.93
Other apparel	1.73	1.95	1.57	2.20	2.08	1.98
Shoe	0.50	2.15	2.51	1.89	2.62	2.90
Jewelry	0.44	1.19	1.07	0.36	0.86	1.23
Card and gift	1.18	1.78	1.34	2.43	1.85	1.42
Service shops	5.86	5.14	1.83	10.15	4.64	1.44
Entertainment	3.16	1.95	1.91	0.88	2.46	1.93
Recreation	0.25	1.88	1.07	2.30	1.27	1.07
Fast food	2.16	1.38	1.63	2.50	1.40	1.15
Sit-down restaurant	4.24	3.27	2.29	4.64	3.17	2.42
All others	22.69	9.56	12.11	10.82	15.91	12.41

N.A.—Sample too small to be statistically significant.
* Expressed in terms of % of total GLA.

Source: Reprinted by permission from *Chain Store Age/Executive* © (December, 1980): 36. Copyright Lebhar-Friedman, Inc. 425 Park Avenue, New York, NY 10022.

Exhibit 7.3   Del Plaza Atrium—A Focal Point in a Retail Shopping Area.

Source: Photo courtesy of The Center Companies.
This area in the Detroit Plaza Hotel provides a soaring meeting place for some 12,000 business and professional people who work in the surrounding four office towers and frequent the "World of Shops" in Detroit's Renaissance Center.

whole by averaging $200 per square foot.[4] Thus, not only do the specialty stores lend character to a mall, but their extensive selection of merchandise and good customer service offering yield above average sales on a per square foot basis.

The Taubman Company has developed a process of evaluating the tenant mix for stores in shopping centers. They use experienced retailers to evaluate merchandise assortments, category breakdowns, representations of price lines, displays, store design, and store layout. They also survey consumers to obtain their evaluation of a store on these factors as well as the treatment they received to determine how each store compares with its competitor. This allows the center developer to assess the pluses and minuses of each potential tenant in a new development. In an existing center, analysis would focus on what's already being offered in the center and would include a consumer survey to determine what is missing.[5]

Evaluation of the Physical Characteristics of Location

The size, shape, and frontage of a building can increase its visibility and thereby have a significant influence upon drawing traffic into the store. Also, proper interior layout can stimulate impulse sales after potential customers have entered the store. (A detailed discussion of store layout is presented in Chapter 8.) Parking space must also be analyzed to determine if it is sufficient to provide customers with parking near enough to the store so that it will be more convenient to stop and shop than to go to the next trading area.

Modern shopping centers provide a minimum of about four times as much parking space as store floor space to ensure adequate nearby parking facilities. A lower ratio is usually found in downtown shopping locations since shoppers are expected to park in some commercial facility and shop at several stores on foot. Observation of parking opportunities and shopping patterns can indicate if there is likely to be a parking problem near a new store.

Remodeling projects are increasingly being implemented to expand the drawing power of both older shopping centers and central business districts. Older retail facilities are affected by: (1) economic blight which occurs because of less consumer purchasing power available in the area; (2) physical blight which takes the form of structural deterioration of buildings caused by age and lack of maintenance; (3) functional blight which is caused by the obsolescence of older retailers' businesses who do not use mass-merchandising techniques and/or are affected by increased consumer mobility made possible by automobiles or a new mass transit system; and (4) frictional blight which is caused by adverse environment effects such as traffic congestion, litter, and vandalism.[6]

Redevelopment needs are frequently just as pressing for older shopping centers as they are for the downtown metropolitan areas whose leaders may believe that they have to offer the same amenities that are available in suburban shopping centers. For example, management of The Galleria in Fort Lauderdale, Florida estimates that a major remodeling and enlargement project will generate average sales of $141 per square foot, compared to $120 per square foot sales obtained prior to remodeling.[7] The Galleria stands on the site of the former Sunrise Shopping Center, which has been a hub of shopping activity since the 1950s. The old center, which consisted of 450,000 square feet, was partially razed to accommodate the new Galleria, which contains 150 stores on 1.1 million square feet of gross leasable area. The new center is following the trend of including five major anchors— Jordan Marsh, Saks Fifth Avenue, Burdines, Nieman-Marcus, and Lord & Taylor—to increase the merchandise assortment and draw more people to the center.

Evaluation of Competition

Other things being equal, people will seldom pass a store to get exactly the same product at a more distant location. Thus, the location of the new store relative to the population density of the trading area and to competitive locations has a very significant influence upon what share of business can be obtained by the new store. It is easier to stop potential consumers en route than to pull them away from their normal traffic patterns.

Prospective retailers can improve their position relative to competitors by selecting locations near most of the potential customers (or their normal traffic routes) but near as few competitive sites as possible. They may also be able to protect their locations in the future by gaining control or by designating the use of unoccupied sites for noncompetitive purposes through restrictive lease provisions.

A key factor to consider in selecting shopping center sites is the tenant mix, which is the combination of business firms that occupy selling space in the shopping center. If a large center is properly planned, its tenant mix should satisfy the needs of the consumers in the trading area with no duplication of offerings. Factors to be considered by shopping center developers in relation to tenant mix include:

1. The total amount of space allocated to each major line of trade within a shopping center. This should bear a reasonable relationship to the amount of space allocated to every other major line of trade. These relationships are established after analysis of consumer needs in the trade area, competitive facilities, existing or anticipated for the future, and the availability of tenants acceptable to financing institutions, the developer, and the community.

2. The relationship that space allocated to an individual merchant bears to the total space allocated to his specific line of trade and to closely related lines of trade. This relationship in a tenant mix must consider the requirements of the various prospective tenants and the limitations in accommodating all competitive merchants within the shopping center.

3. The exact location of each retail store in relation to every other retail store within a shopping center. This is closely tied to shopper convenience and shopper traffic patterns, and hence to the objective of optimizing sales for all merchants.

4. The minimum rent and the average rent, year by year, projected for each merchant. Rent projections, however, must also consider financing requirements, since tenants from whom high rents might be obtained may not be acceptable to financing institutions. Thus, the amount and proportion of retail space allocated to prospective tenants in relation to their financial standing must be balanced to optimize rent, without impairing the ability of the developer to borrow funds with which to construct and operate the center.

5. The retail sales projected for each line of trade and for each individual merchant. This provides a basis for projecting revenues. Total revenues, of course, also take into consideration projected average rentals.[8]

One method used to forecast a center's sales for each retail line is to multiply the square footage of retail space devoted to each line times the median annual sales per square foot for similar lines in comparable centers.

The center's projected sales for each retail line are useful when forecasting future sales for an outlet located in a center. Most shopping center planners conduct surveys of consumers' purchasing patterns for those people residing in the center's defined trading area. The findings are presented by the center's developers to financial institutions for projections upon which loans are obtained. Thus, these forecasts are likely to be optimistic but fairly reliable.

Conditions change, however, and the final tenant mix can deviate from the original or "ideal" tenant-mix plan. Although the number of competitors may vary, the total amount of space allocated to each major retail line usually departs relatively little from the original plan.

A fairly comprehensive list of factors that should be investigated by a retailer who is considering a shopping center location is presented in Exhibit 7.4.

Exhibit 7.4 Evaluating Shopping Center Locations

1. Who is the shopping center developer?
2. How long has he been in the business of developing real estate?
3. What are his financial resources?
4. With whom has he arranged for the financing of the center?
5. What is his reputation for integrity?
6. Who performed the economic analysis? Does the report cover both favorable and unfavorable factors?
7. What experience has the economic consultant had?
8. Has an architectural firm been retained to plan the center?
9. Has the architect designed other centers? Have they been successful from a retailing standpoint?
10. Who will build the center? The developer? An experienced contractor? An inexperienced contractor?
11. Has the developer had experience with other centers?
12. What is, or will be, the quality of management for the center?
13. Will the management have merchandising and promotion experience? (Some developers are large retailers rather than real estate operators.)
14. What percent of the leases have been signed? Are they on a contingent basis?
15. Has every facet of the lease been carefully studied?
16. Is the ratio of parking area to selling area 3 to 1 or more?
17. Has sufficient space (400 feet) been assigned to each car?
18. Is the parking space designed so that the shopper does not walk more than 300 to 350 feet from the farthest spot to the store?
19. What is the angle of parking space? (Ninety degrees provides the best capacity and circulation.)
20. What is the planned or actual car turnover? (3.3 cars per parking space per day is the average.)
21. Is the number of total spaces adequate for the planned business volume? (Too many spaces make the center look dead; too few openly invite competition around the center.)
22. Does the parking scheme distribute the cars so as to favor no one area?
23. Is there an adequate number of ingress/egress roads in proper relationship with the arrangement of parking spaces?
24. For the larger centers, a ring road is preferable. Is this the case?
25. Is the site large enough for the type of center?
26. Is the size sufficiently dominant to forestall the construction of similar shopping centers nearby?
27. Is the center of regular shape? If not, does the location of the buildings minimize the disadvantage of the site's shape?
28. Is the site sufficiently deep? (A depth of at least 400 feet is preferred; if less, the center may look like a strip development.)
29. Is the site level? Is it on well-drained land?
30. Can the center be seen from a distance?
31. Are any structures, such as a service station, located in the parking area? (If so, do they impede the site's visibility?)
32. Is the site a complete unit? (A road should not pass through the site.)
33. Are the buildings set far enough back on the site that the entire area may be seen?
34. Are all the stores readily accessible to each other, with none having an advantage?

Source: J. E. Mertes, "Site Opportunities for the Small Retailer," *Journal of Retailing* 39 (Fall 1963): 44. Reprinted by permission.

**Estimation of
Market Share**

The amount of business that a store obtains from a given area can be divided by the total amount of business conducted in the area in the specified category. The result multplied by 100 equals the percentage share of market obtained by the store. An estimate of the market share must be made after all of the previously discussed factors have been evaluated. Subjective judgment and experience can then be used to adjust the share estimate.

The **ratio of market sales share to selling space share** can be used to estimate the market share that a new store can obtain, provided additional information is available from stores currently operating in other areas. If the new store is affiliated with a chain, or if it can obtain information from similar independent stores, this same ratio can be used. This ratio provides a measure that is most useful in forecasting shares for new stores.

The share of market sales volume is usually measured by dollar sales; the share of selling space is usually calculated on a square footage basis. Reliability of this ratio has been proved over years of research in the grocery industry. If a store obtains a 25 percent share of market in an area and has a 40 percent share of the total selling space for the product line in the area, then the ratio of the market share to selling space share is 25/40, or 0.625. The average ratio for similar existing stores and the share of selling space to be occupied by the proposed store can be used to forecast the market share that a proposed store can obtain. Both figures can be inserted into the ratio formula to obtain this estimate of market share.

For example, if the average market share to selling space share ratio is 0.625 for similar stores and the proposed new store will occupy 20 percent of the selling space in the area, its estimated market share (X) would be $X/20 = 0.625/100$, or X equals 12.5 percent of the forecast market share. The estimated share projected from this ratio can then be adjusted to reflect the deviations from the average in regard to the quality of competition, the physical characteristics of the location, the compatibility of nearby businesses, and the accessibility of the site to the trading area.

Estimating Sales Volume of the Proposed Store

Estimating sales volume for a new store can be found by multiplying its estimated market share by the total product line purchases made in the trading area. Another method of estimating the sales volume that can be obtained by the new store is to multiply the number of square feet in the store times the average annual sales per square foot for that type of store. Average annual sales per square foot are presented in Table 7.3.

In calculation format this procedure becomes:

$$
\begin{matrix}
\text{Estimate of Annual} \\
\text{Sales for Specific} \\
\text{Outlet}
\end{matrix}
=
\begin{matrix}
\text{Number of} \\
\text{Square Feet} \\
\text{in Specific Outlet}
\end{matrix}
\times
\begin{matrix}
\text{Average Annual} \\
\text{Sales per Square} \\
\text{Foot for Outlets in} \\
\text{This Specific} \\
\text{Merchandise} \\
\text{Category}
\end{matrix}
$$

For example, suppose a new hardware outlet were to occupy 4000 square feet of selling space. Estimated annual sales for the outlet would be 4000 × $67 = $268,000. Thus, the new outlet would have to obtain annual sales of at least $268,000 to reach the sales per square foot sales level reached by an average hardware store. This value should then be compared to the other estimates of sales volume for the outlet. If it is larger than other estimates, chances for establishing a successful outlet are less than average. If other sales estimates are larger than $268,000, then the outlet has a better than average chance of being successful.

The previous discussion reveals that the site selection decision involves many factors which frequently interact with one another. Sales estimates for a specific site consume a considerable

Table 7.3   Square Footage to Sales Relationships for Different Outlet Types

Type of Retail Outlet	Annual Dollar Sales per Square Foot of Selling Space	Selling Space Percentage of Total Floor Space	Average Square Footage of Under Roof Floor Space
Hardware stores	67	73	6,064
Department stores	125	68	103,640
Variety stores	57	74	11,780
Miscellaneous general merchandise stores	99	72	8,718
Grocery stores	237	74	6,503
Apparel and accessory stores	112	71	3,819
Furniture, home furnishings and equipment stores	71	74	6,520
Drug and proprietary stores	135	78	4,678

Source: U.S. Department of Commerce, *1977 Census of Retail Trade*, Volume 1, Summary and Subject Statistics (Washington, D.C.: Government Printing Office, 1977): 83.

amount of time and money. Frequently, retail management wishes to evaluate many different sites in an area to determine which site offers the most retail potential. In this case the problem may become so complex and time consuming that a computer may be required.

One such computer analysis is being conducted by Dunning Brothers, a firm specializing in commercial operations analysis.[9] This computer analysis is based upon the assumption that the consumer is attracted to each retail outlet in varying degrees, depending on the travel time to each store. Travel time is computed for each quarter-mile-square section. Then the percentage of the proposed outlet's share of the trade in that area is computed and an index describing potential sales is developed for that quarter-mile area. Every quarter-mile square is considered as a hypothetical store location. Each possible site is then rated according to its net trade area value. The net trade area value at any point is that portion of all surrounding buying power allocated to that particular site. Sites with the highest trade area values are those most advantageously located in the travel network serving the consumer field. Lower net trade area values indicate either a remoteness of customers and/or excessive existing store saturation.

Use of this and similar computer analyses to select the best available retail site is likely to increase in the future as increases in land and building costs make the location decision even more critical to the success or failure of a retail operation. For example, multiple regression analysis has been adapted successfully to evaluate new sites and assess existing stores to determine if they should be closed, relocated, or expanded.[10]

Determining Sufficient Estimated Volume to Support a New Store

Costs must be examined and compared to expected profits to determine which proposed site will yield the most profit. Industry sources will usually provide estimates of the average rent expense for leased stores. For example, average rent expense for new supermarkets is about 1.5 percent of sales. If the estimated weekly sales volume is $32,000, then 32,000 times 0.015, or $480 per week, could be spent on the site if the store wanted to pay no more than average leasing rates for its facilities.

If the building and land price (or leasing) cost (not including equity buildup in land and buildings) is less than $480 per month, the proposed store should be more profitable than the average supermarket. If the cost exceeds $480, these extra costs must be overcome by reduction in other costs such as labor and transportation. If these costs are not reduced, the profit margin will be below the industry average.

The **payback period**—the estimated period of time in which a project will generate cash equal to its cost—should also be calculated if store owners are going to buy the land and building. If the annual cash inflow is estimated to be received in equal annual amounts, the payback period (in years) equals the cost of the project divided by annual net income after taxes and depreciation. For example, if a retail building project costs $100,000 and is expected to yield an annual net income after taxes and depreciation of $10,000, the payback period would be $100,000 divided by $10,000, or ten years.

There is no common agreement on how many years it should take a building and land to pay for themselves from the revenues generated from the store. Selection of the appropriate payback period is influenced by the cost of obtaining money (interest rates) and alternative uses of the investor's money. Most realtor investors have said that a building should receive 1 percent of its cost per month as payment for its rental (or lease) value. The land should receive 0.5 percent of its appraised value as its monthly payment. This means that the building should pay for itself in 100 months, or 8⅓ years.

In speculative types of retailing where market and environmental changes occur quite rapidly, the desired payback period might be much less—say five years. The higher the degree of uncertainty and the cost of obtaining money, the lower the desired payback period will be. Under interest rates of about 16 percent, a minimum payback period of five years is frequently required to make a project an economic success.

Of course, site evaluation analysis must also project future potential sales and profits. A growth area will be much more attractive than a declining area. A growing profit trend can legitimately be incorporated into the payback period analysis because, hopefully, the store will be generating profits over at least a five- to ten-year period. If the annual cash inflow generated by the building is not received in equal amounts, one may compile a list of cumulative cash gains expected to originate from the project until the year in which the running income total is equal to the amount of the expenditure.

Deciding to Buy, Lease, or Build

Another important aspect of the site selection problem is to determine if the firm should buy the property outright or if it should lease the facility. As noted earlier, some retailers prefer not to own property because of the high fixed costs involved and the uncertainty of future market potential. If the dollar return in inventory investment is greater than the dollar invested in real estate, it is usually desirable to lease instead of purchase.

Leasing terms vary by location, type of store, and numerous other considerations. Supermarkets usually generate an annual sales volume of from $1 million to $3 million. Because of their low profit margin, supermarket rents are generally comparatively inexpensive on both a percentage of sales (1.5 percent) and square footage ($1.50 to $4) basis. Large, full-line department stores have a higher profit margin, but they also have a great deal of bargaining power. This usually results in a rent of 2.5 percent of gross sales. Specialty stores, which have the highest markups and the least bargaining power, usually pay a higher percentage of their gross sales as rent. A summary of rental rates for selected store categories is presented in Table 7.4.

Lease rates in a major midwest regional shopping center vary from a low annual cost of $1.17 per square foot for a major anchor department store to $60 per square foot per year for a small keymaking outlet. Most of the tenants paid between $6 and $10 per square foot per year. Rental rates also vary slightly from one area to another.

The rental policy of shopping center developers is designed so that operating expenses (mostly maintenance, utilities, and upkeep) are only 15 to 18 percent of total gross rental income. Data contained in Table 7.5 detail where shopping center operational dollars are spent.

Some land developers and some retailers are now using a philosophy of **storing land.** This involves purchase of vacant land in the development path of a city or suburb on which low-cost business structures are erected. Taxes and interest payments can be made from the income generated by these buildings, and the buildings are constructed so that they can easily be torn down when the land becomes a desirable site for a major retail development. This practice is based on the belief that development land values will rise faster than interest costs and taxes. Site selection that is based upon projected population movements involves the additional risks associated with imperfect foresight. It also involves a high fixed cost. However, retailers should plan ahead so that consumers can be served near their places of residence. Storing land can be a part of expansion planning, since it can guarantee a location in areas where real estate is expected to become difficult to acquire.

Generally, developers have only a small percentage of equity in a shopping center or large retail building. Lending institutions usually mortgage up to 75 percent of the **economic value** (the value of the project based upon future estimated earnings) of

Table 7.4   National Percentage Lease Ranges for Selected Store Categories

Store Category	1950	1960	1970	1976
Art shops	8–10	6–10	6–10	6–10
Auto accessories stores	4–8	2–5	3–5	3–6
Barber shops	10–12	8–10	6–10	5–10
Beauty shops	10–15	8–10	6–12	5–10
Books and stationery stores	8–11	5–11	4–10	5–8
Candy stores	8–12	5–8	6–10	6–12
Department stores	3–4	2–3	1.5–4	1.5–3.5
Discount department stores (over 75,000 square feet)	NA[a]	1–2.5	1–2	1–2.5
Discount department stores (under 75,000 square feet)	NA[a]	NA[a]	NA[a]	1–4
Drug stores—independent	6–8	3–6	3–8	2.5–6
Drug stores—chain	3–6	2.5–4.5	2.5–5	2.5–5
Drug stores—prescription (medical buildings)	8–12	5–10	5–10	5–10
Electrical appliance stores	4–7	2.5–5	3–6	3–6
Five and dime stores	4–6	3–6	3–6	3–5
Fabric (yard goods) stores	NA[a]	NA[a]	4–6	4–6
Florists	8–10	6–10	6–10	6–10
Furniture stores	4–8	3–7	3–8	3–6
Gas stations (costs per gallon sold)	1–1.5¢	1–1.5¢	1–2¢	1–2¢
Gift shops	7–9	5–9	6–10	6–10
Supermarkets	0–1.5	0.75–1.5	0.5–2.25	1–2
Convenience food stores	NA[a]	NA[a]	NA[a]	2–3.5
Hardware stores	5–8	3–6	3.5–6	4–6
Hosiery and knit goods stores	6–8	6–8	6–10	6–10
Jewelry stores	8–10	3–8	4–10	4–10
Luggage/leather goods stores	7–10	5–9	5–10	5–10
Liquor and wine stores	6–8	3–8	4–6	2–6
Men's clothing stores	6–8	4–8	4–8	4–8
Men's furnishings (haberdashery) stores	6–10	5–10	4–10	5–8
Motion picture theaters	14–25	8–18	8–15	7–15
Radio, TV, and hi-fi stores	NA[a]	NA[a]	4–8	3–8
Record shops	NA[a]	NA[a]	5–7	5–7
Restaurants	6–8	5–7	3–8	5–9
Restaurants—liquor	6–10	6–8	4–10	6–10
Sporting goods stores	6–8	5–8	4–8	3.5–8
Women's ready-to-wear stores—chain	5–8	2.5–6	4–8	3–6
Women's ready-to-wear stores—independent	7–9	4–8	4–10	4–8
Women's furnishings/accessories stores	NA[a]	4–10	5–10	5–8
Women's shoe stores	6–8	4–7	5–8	5–7

[a] NA = not available.

Source: Nathan Schloss, "Inflation Proofing Retail Investments with Percentage Leases." Reprinted with permission from *The Real Estate Review*, 7 (Winter 1978): 37. Copyright © 1978, Warren, Gorham and Lamont Inc., Boston, Mass. All rights reserved.

Table 7.5   Where Operational Dollars Are Spent[a]

	Urban			Nonurban		
Category	Under 100,000 square feet GLA	100,001– 500,000 square feet GLA	Over 500,000 square feet GLA	Under 100,000 square feet GLA	100,001– 500,000 square feet GLA	Over 500,000 square feet GLA
Promotion	$0.22	$0.15	$0.28	$0.17	$0.18	$0.21
Interior Maintenance	0.24	0.14	0.37	0.05	0.11	0.44
Exterior Maintenance	0.18	0.13	0.47	0.33	0.22	0.44
Security Personnel & Monitoring	0.25	0.20	0.21	0.06	0.03	0.14
Utilities	0.40	0.26	0.26	0.28	0.22	0.59

[a] Expressed in terms of dollars per square feet of Gross Leasing Area.
Source: Reprinted by permission from *Chain Store Age/Executive* (© December 1980): 57. Copyright Lebhar-Friedman, Inc., 425 Park Avenue, New York, NY 10022.

a shopping center. The economic value of a well-planned center will usually be 25 to 33 percent higher than total building costs.

For example, the developers of Willowbrook Center in New Jersey were able to build their $23 million center by using only $500,000 as their own cash equity.[11] The other $22.5 million came from an insurance company that made a twenty-nine year loan at 7½ percent interest. An estimated net economic value of nearly $32 million was calculated by capitalizing on an estimated annual net profit of $2.7 million at the going interest rate of 8½ percent. The insurance company loaned about 70 percent of the estimated economic value ($32 million), but the loan ($22.5 million) amounted to nearly 98 percent of the total project cost ($23 million) in this case. Wouldn't today's retailer like to obtain a long-term loan made on a good retail facility that contains a low fixed-interest rate charge for using someone else's money? Unless individual stores develop their own centers or build their own large stores, they will not be able to obtain such low equity financing. Instead, they will have to pay rental fees similar to those in Table 7.4.

However, long-term leases also offer some advantages. Currently retailers are benefiting from having very favorable lease rights. Leasehold rights have recently become valuable property because of:

1. The time factor. Whereas the development time for a new store may exceed two years, an acquired site can be converted in a few months.
2. The cost factor. Given the favorable terms of older leases, along with the skyrocketing prices for land, labor and materials, the cost advantages of a leasehold purchase can be considerable.

3. The location factor. Many sites—especially in malls or densely populated areas—are considered irreplaceable, and retailers are interested in other locations to protect their markets.

With the prime rate still at astronomical levels, retailers are increasingly anxious to keep store development periods to a minimum, and that is where the purchase of leasehold rights comes in. An acquired unit can be converted in a fraction of the time needed to build a new store, where regulatory and financing delays protract the scheduled opening.[12]

Purchase of a lease from an existing retailer is probably most enhanced by a high prime interest rate and high construction costs that are encountered in building new retail facilities. Table 7.6 contains the breakdown of 1980 construction costs for developing shopping centers of various sizes. These data indicate that construction costs alone account for about $20 to over $34 per square foot of gross leasable area (GLA).

Table 7.6   Expenses of Current Projects[a]

| | Urban | | | Nonurban | | |
| | Under 100,000 square feet GLA | 100,001–500,000 square feet GLA | Over 500,000 square feet GLA | Under 100,000 square feet GLA | 100,001–500,000 square feet GLA | Over 500,000 square feet GLA |
Category						
Predevelopment costs	$3.80	$1.40	$ 4.00	$0.68	$ 3.58	$ 1.00
Offsite allowances	1.00	0.95	2.00	0.18	0.87	2.00
Shell/frame	5.50	6.10	15.00	8.33	11.93	13.50
Plumbing	1.27	1.70	3.00	1.30	3.43	2.50
Flooring/floor covering	1.13	1.50	1.00	1.07	0.85	2.30
Ceiling	N.A.[b]	0.60	0.98	0.68	0.85	1.00
Roofing & skylights	N.A.[b]	1.60	1.82	1.43	1.80	2.01
Electrical & lighting	1.75	2.20	2.51	2.57	2.90	2.50
Parking lot lighting	0.20	0.20	1.03	0.50	0.70	1.10
Signs and graphics	0.28	0.33	0.21	0.43	0.47	0.20
Elevators/escalators	N.A.[b]	1.10	1.43	N.A.[b]	N.A.[b]	0.99
Interior wall covering	0.89	0.80	0.67	0.68	1.25	1.01
Exterior wall	N.A.[b]	1.50	2.89	3.60	4.70	3.50
HVAC equipment	2.50	2.00	2.26	2.84	3.18	3.00
Fire detection/ security systems and hardware	0.95	1.10	1.55	0.90	0.06	1.30

[a] Expressed in terms of expenditures per square foot Gross Leasing Area.
[b] N.A. = Sample too small to be statistically significant.
Source: Reprinted by permission from *Chain Store Age/Executive* (© December 1980): 46. Copyright Lebhar-Friedman, Inc. 425 Park Avenue, New York, NY 10022.

These high construction costs have caused retailers to decrease every aspect of a retail property. In shopping centers this means decreasing store size, building smaller common areas such as making the aisles narrower, and downsizing center court focal points. For example, in the early 1970s, Lord & Taylor units averaged 148,000 square feet but their comparable outlets in the 1980s will operate from 104,000 square feet.[13]

Additionally, high construction costs are causing an increase in the ratio of selling to total building space. This is accomplished by eliminating unproductive departments and reducing service, office, receiving, storage, and handling areas.

Retailers have also adopted more of a "fewer-frills" approach to fixturing and construction to combat the high cost of construction. They do this by using less expensive materials and offering fewer skylights and fountains and keeping to a simple interior.

Such factors as the financial condition of the company, the profitability of the business, and the degree of growth orientation in company philosophy determine the proper investment that should be made in buildings and real estate. Thus, each retailer must make commitments based upon his or her financial and marketing situation at the time a site is available.

Summary

Evaluation of a specific site requires a detailed study of the current or proposed outlet's trading area. Size and shape of the store's trading area must first be determined. This can be done by studying store sales records, conducting a license plate study, or interviewing consumers.

This trade area is then studied intensively to reveal its population level and characteristics, purchasing power, competitive outlets, accessibility to consumers, and compatibility with other business firms. An estimate of the total retail business potential for the site is then made. This is usually accomplished by using the percentage of income method, the percentage of retail sales dollar method, and the per capita sales method to provide a range of sales estimates for the specified category in the defined trade area. Then a realistic estimate of the firm's market share is made. These two factors (total category retail sales and the firm's market share) are then multiplied to give an estimate of the firm's expected sales at the site. Computer analysis is currently being used to evaluate sites and provide related sales estimates for each site. These data can be used to establish expansion priorities for a firm considering building several new stores in the near future. Finally, these same data can be used in the firm's critical decision to buy or lease a new building on a selected site.

Questions

1. Discuss the concept of trade area and describe how it is used.
2. How can you measure the current trading area for a grocery store? Discuss the usefulness of the method you describe.

3. How would you suggest defining the trade area for a discount store? Explain your reasoning.

4. What are the factors that can be used in measuring retail compatibility?

5. Describe the differences between generative business, shared business, and incidental business.

6. How can two adjacent stores selling goods competitively be considered compatible?

7. What is the value of the market share ratio to selling space share? If a retailer estimates 18 percent of the market is needed to break even and the ratio is 0.5, what percent of the selling space is required if all other variables are held constant? What other factors must be considered?

8. If the average rent paid out in an area is 3 percent of sales and estimated annual sales are $1,600,000, how much monthly rent can a retailer with these sales expect to pay? If rent is expected to increase at 5 percent per year (that is, 5 percent of the previous year's rent), what level of sales would be required for the first three years? (Assume all other variables to be held constant.)

9. What factors influence the payback period? What other factors must be considered in purchasing a store? Why should the payback period be shorter for high-risk locations?

10. How does "economic value" differ from building cost?

11. Describe the philosophy and practice of storing land.

12. How have rapidly rising construction and land costs and a high interest rate affected a retailer's location decision? Discuss fully.

13. What factors would you consider if you were making the buy, lease or build decision for a retail firm? Discuss fully.

14. Computer site selection techniques are being used to evaluate retail locations. What factors should be included in such an evaluation if the store were a grocery store? What factors should be analyzed if the store were a department store? Where would you obtain the necessary data needed to determine each factor?

Footnotes

1. David A. Gautsch, "Specification of Patronage Models for Retail Center Choice," *Journal of Marketing Research* XVIII (May 1981): 162.

2. William Applebaum, *Shopping Center Strategy* (New York: International Council of Shopping Centers, 1970), p. 74.

3. Willard Haselbush, "5 Major Stores to Anchor Mall," *The Denver Post*, February 18, 1981, p. 30.

4. "Creative Approach Crucial for Good Tenant Mix," *Chain Store Age/Executive*, (December 1980): 35–44.

5. *Ibid.*

6. Ross L. Davies, *Marketing Geography with Special Reference to Retailing*, (Corbridge, Northumberland, England: R. P. A. Books, 1976), pp. 170–71.

7. "Remodeling Projects Designed to Extend Markets," *Chain Store Age/Executive*, (January 1981): 114–115.

8. Applebaum, pp. 111, 113.

9. "Computer Analysis Aids Strategic Site Selection," *Stores* (May 1976): 25–27.

10. J. Dennis Lord and Charles D. Lynds, "The Use of Regression Models in Store Location Research," *Akron Business and Economic Review*, 12, (Summer 1981): 13–19.

11. "Shopping Centers Grow into Shopping Cities," *Business Week*, 4 (September 1971): 37.

12. "Lease Rights Become Valuable Assets," *Chain Store Age/Executive*, (January 1981): 59.

13. "Cutting Space, Increasing Productivity," *Chain Store Age/Executive*, (December 1980): 45–47.

Case Study: Midwest Grocery Company

Mr. Kent, owner of Midwest Grocery Company, is considering building a new store one block from his present site. Midwest Grocery Company is not affiliated with any grocery chain organization. It has been operating from a leased building in a neighborhood shopping center that contains a drug store, doctors' offices, a restaurant, and a barber shop. The center is four years old and is located near a new upper middle-class residential area. Sufficient parking space has been provided in the center's parking lot. Auto traffic appears to flow smoothly in and out of the lot.

Mr. Kent is not satisfied with his present weekly sales of $41,000. He believes that sales could be increased if he built a larger store. The present store contains 4,700 square feet of selling space in a brick building of 7,000 square feet. The new outlet would contain 10,200 square feet of selling space in a 15,000 square foot building. Mr. Kent can renew the lease on the old building for the next five years at the present rate of $15,000 per year. The cost of the land for the new location is $200,000; the construction cost is estimated to be $500,000.

Midwest Grocery Company's trading area is believed to be centered in the 10 square block area surrounding the store. The nearest competitive store is run by a small, independent grocer who operates in a 2,500 square foot building with no off-street parking. The main competitor is a supermarket 15 blocks away. However, another chain supermarket is building a new outlet 10 blocks away from the present Midwest Grocery Company location.

Discussion Question | **1.** What action do you recommend Mr. Kent take? Why?

Chapter 8 | Attracting with Atmosphere

After a site has been selected the retail building must be constructed or remodeled and fixtures and equipment purchased and arranged so that customers will be attracted to the store, stimulated to make purchases, and served promptly with minimum cost. This chapter is devoted to a discussion of factors for retailers to consider when they build, remodel, or rearrange their outlets.

Psychological Impact and Store Image

The image a store projects to its customers is one of the most important influences contributing to a retailer's success. It is also the most difficult variable to control, to measure, and, indeed, to define. If **store image** may be defined as "the aggregate stimulus value the company, store brand, or product has for a particular individual or group,"[1] it is obvious that a store's image may be seen somewhat differently by each person. Nevertheless, for a particular group of like customers or a market segment, a store's image may be fairly similar. A store such as Saks Fifth Avenue or Tiffany and Company may be thought of as ultraexpensive and out of reach by low-income persons, while more affluent individuals may think of them as stores with excellent quality products and service to match a sophisticated taste.

Another way of looking at image is to view it as the overall personality of the store. This personality is always present, regardless of whether or not it was planned by the management. Just as the personality of an individual attracts or repels certain types of people, so too does that of a store.

This is not to imply that a store's personality or image remains the same over time. It is often a shock for us to encounter a high school classmate several years after graduation and to witness the change in his or her personality. Some grow old before their time; others seem to develop a wit and charm they never had in school. For this reason it is not uncommon for old friends to discover at a class reunion that they no longer have much in common and that others, whom they scarcely knew, have become interesting and attractive individuals.

This analogy also holds true for retail stores. A store always has a personality, even if that personality reflects blandness, a lack of creativity, and general sterility. A store manager who feels that a store's image is a concern only for the supersophisticated, or who says, "I only worry about price and quality," is naive. Knowingly or unknowingly, he or she is developing an image for the store.

Consumers' patronage patterns and perceptions differ from one type of retail outlet to another. Data contained in Table 8.1 reveal the perceptions that consumers have of discounters, department stores, and specialty chains as sources of men's wear. Consumers have also been found to patronize a supermarket primarily because of its location and the low prices it offers. Consumers for women's clothing fashions were found to select their outlet on the basis of the best value for the money, the largest overall assortment, and the highest quality clothing.[2] Thus, management for each store must determine what image that individual outlet should project to the consuming public.

To provide the proper image, stores have to be remodeled to meet changing customer desires. Management can only change lights, fixtures, and other flexible elements for a certain period of time. Then they must remodel or they will lose sales. Store design itself is frequently found to be a fashion item that attracts consumers. For example, store remodelings stimulate sales by creating consumer interest. People who may not otherwise look into a particular window suddenly become sidewalk superin-

Table 8.1   Evaluations of Store Types Based on Patronage Determinants by Shoppers Who "Last Shopped" at Each Store Type

(Type of store last shopped for men's wear)				
Determinant of Patronage	Discounter/ Mass Merchandiser Average	Department Store Average	Midrange Fashion Specialty Chain Average	High- Fashion Specialty Chain Average
1. Easiest to get to from home	41%*	48%	32%	14%
2. Lowest prices	60	30	26	12
3. Highest quality	2	17	34	51
4. Best value for the money	47	54	50	43
5. Most knowledgeable, helpful salesclerks	21	38	50	65
6. Largest overall assortment/selection	27	43	33	20
7. Most exciting display	14	31	29	52
8. Best advertising	18	39	18	28
9. Best for conservative everyday men's wear	31	43	35	27
10. Best for current, up-to-date men's wear	21	29	31	63
11. Best for very latest most fashionable men's wear	9	19	26	58

* READ: On the average, among those respondents who "last shopped" at a discounter/mass merchandiser, 41 percent also said the discounter/mass merchandiser was the "easiest to get to from home," and 60 percent said the discounter/mass merchandiser had the "lowest prices."

Source: Charles W. King and Lawrence J. Ring, "Market Positioning Across Retail Fashion Institutions: A Comparative Analysis of Store Types," *Journal of Retailing*, 46 (Spring 1980): 61. Reprinted by permission.

tendents. Retail managers can tie many good promotions into the remodeling projects. Some stores have found that if they place the merchandise from areas being remodeled out on the selling floor in stacks of cartons, consumers will search through the inventory to find bargains. The temporary stacking of merchandise in cartons creates a "priced to go" impression even if markdowns are minimal.

A remodeled building provides an excellent opportunity for redefining the target market and creating a place the customers call "their store." The target market should be redefined in terms of such factors as income level, race, price consciousness for the products to be sold, geographical location, seasonality, age, and other important variables.

An example of a firm that used a remodeling program to better reach its redefined target market is the Mi Amigo chain of stores in Guatamala City, Guatamala. This chain began as a children's store but gradually added new merchandise lines and new stores. The new stores were located in different income areas ranging from high to low. The corporate logo, a stork carrying a baby, seemed dated and did not represent the stores.

When the two sons of the original owner accepted full management responsibility, a series of studies were begun. The young management team hired a marketing research firm to conduct image studies. They also carefully studied the sales contribution from each product line and each store. They reviewed the outside and inside appearance of each store and came to the conclusion that a dramatic change was needed.

An architect was hired and their stores were remodeled to resemble a circus or amusement park. A target market of children up to twelve years of age was selected. This meant designing an atmosphere that would appeal to both the mothers and the children.

The store became a setting that children enjoyed visiting and that said "We like babies and kids and want to please you."

A decision was made to turn the store in the low-income area into another type of store. Its logo was changed, salespeople were retrained, and even management thinking changed.

High interest and construction costs which appear to be key elements in the economic environment of the 1980s are also causing more emphasis of remodeling by both individual stores and entire chains. It is usually less expensive to purchase and remodel an existing outlet than to build a new store. For example, it took Crowley, Milner & Company only nine months to remodel a 103,000 square foot closed-down discount store in Universal Mall in Warren, Michigan into one of its most productive branches. The department store organization, based in Detroit, accomplished the task of creating such a pleasant appearance and consumer convenience that it is credited with making Universal Mall competitive with Oakland Mall, an extremely large regional mall located three miles away.[3] Crowley's did this at a relatively low cost (Table 8.2).

Crowley's visual merchandising program involved input from the store's buyers on location relative to other departments, fixture types and capacities, staffing plans, and setting up of feature displays. This interaction resulted in an environment in which Crowley's customers are exposed to the teaser treatment as they move through the outlet. This is due to three design factors:

> "Looped aisles that are broken up into angled stretches, from each of which the customer gets a complete view of an organized segment of merchandise plus a peek into something of interest lying beyond. All but four departments are located directly on an aisle.
> Carpet, walls, and columns have blending yet distinctive coloration—taupe, plum, gray or beige. These variations,

Table 8.2 Cost Breakdown, Crowley's 103,000 Square feet Store (1980 Reconstruction of 14-Year-Old Premises)

		$/Sq. Ft.
Demolition and clean-up	$ 17,510	$ 0.17
Bricking in exterior glassed window areas, glazing parking lot entrance and all exit doors	14,420	0.14
2 exterior signs above entrances	13,390	0.13
Re-working HVAC, plumbing, sprinklers	43,260	0.42
Electrical lights and signals	168,920	1.64
Ceiling repair, drywall construction, metal studs	297,670	2.89
Wall hardware, recessed standards, brackets, rods, and waterfall attachments	88,580	0.86
Floor coverings, mainly cut-pile nylon broadloom, some ceramic tile selling area; vinyl reinforced tile aisles	112,270	1.09
Painting, wall-papering	78,280	0.76
Floor fixtures, standard and custom: millwork, custom decor, furniture	616,970	5.99
Installation, floor fixtures, and perimeter wall hardware	96,820	0.94
Design and planning fee	103,000	1.00
Exact total of outlays for materials and services bought through Jon Greenberg and Associates	$1,651,090	$16.03
Approximate total of other costs assumed by landlord or Crowley's, including: 43 POS terminals, receiving dock enlargement, display manikins, incinerator, office furniture, alterations equipment, employee cafeteria equipment, stockroom shelving, toilets reconditioning	406,850	3.95
Approximate grand total	$2,057,940	$19.98

Source: Reprinted from *Stores* Magazine, March, 1981, p. 34, © National Retail Merchants Association, copyright, 1981.

combined with contrasts in illumination—about 45 foot candles at walls and on aisles, and 30 on midfloor areas—give individual identity to merchandise groupings, while also flagging shopper attention to adjacent groupings.

A carefully calculated 2'9″ gap between the top of interior walls and the 13'9″ ceiling gives the shopper promise of "something beyond."

This third element is less important than the first two, since design effort has been primarily to minimize ceiling area impact and to keep customers looking mainly in the merchandise stratum of from 30 inches to seven feet above the floor.

The store's lighting system is simple, subtle, and energy efficient. General illumination comes from strategically positioned ten-tube banks of 35-watt fluorescents, relatively inconspicuous thanks to flush-mounted paracube louvres."[4]

The philosophy of Crowley's store design in this unit may be summarized:

"The important thing is that, within a theme of storewide unity, merchandise presentations must vary in each section so as to create an individualized impact every 30, 48, or 60 inches to capture the attention of shoppers and subtly lead them to virtually every bit of merchandise. The more people see, the more they buy."[5]

Another advantage of retail renovation projects that retailers are finding is a quicker and better return on investment through major renovation of existing units. Complete store renovation projects can be done in stages so the unit continues to do business while remodeling produces an almost entirely new store.

Department store retailers frequently get a 10 to 20 percent larger store by reclaiming excessive nonselling space that was designed into the original store. In addition retailers are usually able to reallocate space to those departments which are most profitable. For example, Macey's has been increasing the space devoted to its men's store by 50 to 80 percent and its cosmetics by 20 to 100 percent and decreasing the space allocation for children's departments, furniture, and leisure/recreation (books, toys, luggage and sporting goods) departments.[6]

| **Store Image and Consumer Psychographics** | The target market for a store is normally described in terms of **demographics** such as age, income, race, sex, and so forth. These are useful descriptions of the profile of a target market but they are incomplete. They are incomplete because two persons with identical demographic profiles may exhibit very different shopping habits and preferences. |

In an attempt to describe the target market better, the concept of psychographics was developed. **Psychographics** attempts to describe lifestyle characteristics of the consumer that can be used by the retailer.

The management of Northpark Shopping Center in Dallas used psychographics to aid them and their retail merchants in the center with marketing planning. The center contained three major department stores—Neiman-Marcus, Titches, and Lord & Taylor. There was a question as to whether the three stores were attempting to share the same market segment or were appealing to different segments. Demographic results had failed to answer this question satisfactorily.

A psychographic study was then conducted among target group consumers to determine lifestyle characteristics. Sample characteristics studied included conservative or liberal attitudes, outdoor or indoor orientation, intellectual or nonintellectual orientation. Results showed psychographic differences for these stores as well as for other department stores not in the center.

In spite of the usefulness of psychographics, the following problems are connected with its use:

1. *Deciding upon which lifestyle characteristics to include.* It is often quite difficult to decide upon the type of psychographic characteristics that should be included. As an example, is a measurement of conservatism or a measurement of a person's interest in outdoor activities really meaningful to a retailer?
2. *Deciding upon how to use results.* It is sometimes difficult for a retailer to know exactly how to use demographic statistics. The problem is compounded with psychographic data. For example, the management of a large service firm conducted a psychographic profile of its customers and found that they were more likely to drive sports cars than customers of competitive services. The management was then left wondering how to use these data.

Undoubtedly, psychographic information can be used by a creative advertising department or as a basis for store remodeling decisions. Use of psychographics often demands new habits of thinking on the part of management. An unresponsive management may dismiss the data as meaningless information.

For a moment, recall the notion of image and note that it is defined as the aggregate stimulus value the store has for an individual or group. It is apparent from this definition that image is a result of all our sensory reactions. Thus, each reaction should be considered in the image-planning process.

Scent Considerations

Retail stores that sell food, flowers, perfumes, soaps, candles, and even automobiles need to be constantly aware of the effect that odor has upon overall image. Anyone who has passed a Karmel Korn store or a fresh roasted nut and coffee establishment in the heart of a city can attest to the value of smell. Fans that are placed to carry the aroma of these products to the sidewalk are not accidentally placed. Used-car dealers sometimes have been accused of spraying their near-new automobiles with a heavy spray to represent the odor of new cars in an attempt to change consumer images. Imagine the negative effect that stale cigar smoke would have in a dress shop or even in a shoe store. New cars and new car showrooms are expected to have a new car smell. Strong disinfectants, greasy smells, and other foreign odors can adversely affect the image of many establishments.

Sound Considerations

The tinkling of Chinese wind chimes in an import store immediately sets the stage for image creation. Even the background noise of elevated trains, freight trains, or shopper congestion can add a vital ingredient to the image of a store. The "believability" of a freight salvage store may be enhanced if the sounds of switching trains and semi-trailer trucks are audible to shoppers.

Other stores depend upon the almost total absence of extraneous sounds. Many exclusive dress and fur shops eliminate unwanted sounds through heavy carpeting, multiple partitions, low ceilings, and the low-key, hushed tone of sales personnel. Yet only a short distance away, on the same shopping mall, other retail establishments such as teen shops depend upon loud noises, including recordings of the latest hit group.

It is a costly mistake for a retailer to overlook the effect of sounds on store success. Appropriate background sounds or music convey the message, "Things are happening here. Stop, look, see what's going on." In fact, many stores deliberately start a retail day by eliminating the "dead store" silence when they turn on lively music. Activity generates customer interest.

Touch Considerations

We tend to say, "Let me see that, please," when we really mean, "Let me touch that, please." Many objects are meant to be touched and can best be sold after they have been touched. Imagine the success an automobile dealer or furrier might have if no one were allowed to touch their products until after the purchase. Furs are irresistibly touchable. Toys are meant to be handled, books to be looked through, and cars to be sat in—with doors to slam and tires to kick.

As important as touch is, far too many retailers place artificial barriers in the path of the natural and desirable reaction of the customer to touch the merchandise. It is highly probable that the "Do Not Touch" or "Touch at Your Own Risk" signs in tourist and curio shops have caused lost sales far in excess of the breakage they have prevented. Small children cannot read these signs so they touch anyway, but shoppers—with dollars to spend—may be frightened away. The recent practice of covering books with cellophane or plastic may also be questioned, particularly if no sample books are provided.

Certainly there are places where touching must be prevented, as in art galleries featuring original oils, but in many other cases the touching of merchandise may be desirable and profitable. Displays and samples may be arranged in a store in a way that invites touch. In these cases only the samples may be soiled or damaged, and they can be inexpensively replaced.

Although the term *sensuous* is sometimes applied to a person, it is also applicable to some retail stores or sections within stores. The products sold within these stores appeal to our needs for love, affection, sex, and perhaps even religion. These stores should be designed to promote a feeling of sensuousness in the customer. The proper use of touch in these stores can add to the desired image. There's an old saying that sums up the discussion: Put the merchandise out where the customers can feel it and steal it so they will try it and buy it.

Sight Considerations

No one can deny the importance of sight. Yet thousands of retail stores each year are established without attention to sight. The visual impression that is imposed upon customers by signs, sidewalks, window displays, awnings, parking lots, and every nut and bolt of the building is of the utmost importance.

Visual merchandising is a combination of every factor that can affect the consumer's visual perception of the store. Moreover, visual merchandising is the utilization of every square inch of the building, inside and out, to sell the company and its products.

Visual merchandising is more than image building; it is the conscious recognition of the fact that a consumer is in one's store to buy goods and services. Therefore, each moment that a consumer is the guest of a retailer, he or she should be exposed to planned visual merchandising. The same retailers who spend hundreds of thousands of dollars a year on advertising, catalogs, and other material designed to bring the customer to them often neglect the importance of a total selling environment once the customer is in their store.

Because store layout usually concentrates on developing optimum traffic patterns, important areas are planned with total disregard for visual merchandising. Elevators and escalators are planned only for the function of hauling bodies from one floor to another. Yet, in each case the customer is in a captive position for several seconds to several minutes. Why shouldn't this time and space be utilized to sell the products and services of the store? It would not be difficult to line the walls of the elevators with samples of carpet, wall paper, fabrics, or other goods sold in the store.

Many other store areas are traditionally treated as nonselling areas. These include the credit department, the employment and personnel department, and the rest rooms. Is it really too extreme to consider visual merchandising of toiletries, cosmetics, facial tissues, and other products in the rest rooms?

Today, companies such as Susan Crane Packaging are entering the field of visual merchandising. These companies manufacture and sell an integrated program to aid in visual merchandising. Such firms are able to provide supporting assistance with visuals from window dressing to tote bags. However, their effectiveness is limited by a store's commitment to visual merchandising as a concept and as a continuing program.

The appearance of the store can seldom be divorced from that of its neighbors. It might be impossible for a retailer of high-quality jewelry to convey such an image, regardless of the creativity in design, if the store is surrounded by discount record shops, fast-food drive-ins, and a pawnshop or two. It might be equally difficult for a low-margin retailer to establish an appropriate image in an area known for its appeal to the affluent carriage trade which is conscious of good taste and proper style regardless of cost.

In most cases errors in location and their effect upon image are not as extreme as those described in these examples. Exorbitantly high rents, zoning restrictions, shopping center restrictions, and common sense prevent such glaring errors. Nevertheless, errors are made. This can be easily proved by observing the variety of stores in one's area.

Small-town department and clothing stores sometimes feel compelled to try to be all things to all people. A department store in a small Michigan town was once observed to feature in its front window men's work overalls and women's formal dress. The end result of such image building is often a loss of customers to the nearest metropolitan shopping center.

Of course image impression through sight extends beyond the appearance and location of the building, equipment, and signs. Dress, personal grooming, and composition of the labor force are equally important. It is not enough to consider simply the sales force, since the appearance of delivery crew, credit personnel, and many others leaves strong impressions upon customers and potential customers. The fact that a particular store employs members of minority groups only as janitors and shipping clerks can be a strong negative factor for customers from these racial groups.

Employees' mode of dress is of particular importance in the case of high-quality merchandise, since the total image of the store can be lowered by even one employee. While the problem of dressing below the image of the store appears to be most common, the reverse situation can also be true. Stores that specialize in products such as feed, fertilizer, auto parts, and plumbing supplies generally expect their sales personnel to dress in work clothes for practical as well as image-building purposes. Individuals in these types of retail establishments often perform laborious and dirty tasks.

Wearing a coat and tie may also place a barrier between the customer and the retailer, for it is not uncommon to find among middle-class consumers a distrust of those who wear a suit and tie. As retailers grow larger, they often hire salespeople and troubleshooters to call on their customers in the field, and when these persons are hired they sometimes assume that a coat and tie is the proper dress. This, however, is usually incorrect; they will be calling upon contractors, farmers, ranchers, and others who are seldom dressed in suits and ties and who often resent such attire in the sales representatives who call on them. Thus, the sight-image impression that customers hold of a retailer extends well beyond the confines of the retail store.

Image Control

Development and control of image creation cannot be planned for a store opening and then forgotten. It is an ongoing and everyday function of retail management. It requires a coordinated effort from all areas: promotional mix, personnel policy, pricing, location, and indeed every function of retailing.

In a very true sense image creation and control is what retailing is all about. It has allowed retailers such as Saks Fifth Avenue, Tiffany's, Neiman-Marcus, and other firms that are known for their quality and high prices to grow in the face of discount houses and other mass merchandisers.

Land Utilization Considerations

The increased price of energy has resulted in rapidly increasing building costs. This, in turn, is creating pressure for more concentrated designs. These designs limit open space and encourage building of more multilevel buildings that occupy less land space.

Choice pieces of land are valued at a high rate; therefore, the retailer must decide carefully how much space should be allocated to the building and how much to parking and other open, landscaped space. Although the cost of providing a one-car parking space may amount to $2,000 in downtown areas and about $50 in suburban shopping centers, consumers may demand the convenience associated with nearby parking availability.

The amount of land required for a parking area varies according to the type of retail outlet. Shopping centers usually provide four square feet of parking space for every square foot of selling space. Outlets that cater to consumers who spend only a short amount of time in the store can provide less parking space. However, stores such as supermarkets, whose customers typically spend about twenty minutes per store visit, must provide parking space if a large volume of consumers is to be served.

Outlets that wish to create a more prestigious image will probably need to allocate more space to open landscaped areas, fountains, and so forth, than will discount or bargain-image retailers (see Exhibit 8.1).

Exhibit 8.1 Shopping Center Focal Point.

Source: Photo courtesy of The Rouse Company.
This fountain in a multilevel mall serves as focal point for the shopping center.
Such a focal point and open-space surroundings create a prestigious image for
all of the stores in the center.

Stores

The exterior physical appearance of a store also creates images that influence a consumer's decision of whether or not to enter the facility. Major exterior factors that affect a consumers perception of an outlet are summarized:

1. Physical structure of building
   a. Size
   b. Type of building materials used
   c. Architecture
2. Exterior store signs
3. Store entrance(s)
4. Store windows

Building Exteriors

High interest rates, rising construction costs, new construction materials and techniques, and rising crime rates have caused numerous changes in the type of buildings used as retail outlets. Retailers have attempted to reduce building costs by reducing store size, increasing the ratio of selling to nonselling space by reducing service areas and office space, and by using more multistory outlets, some of which are windowless at least in the upper-floor levels. The absence of windows also improves security and reduces heating and air conditioning costs.

Retailers have also begun to adapt a less frills approach to construction by using simpler exteriors and less expensive building materials wherever possible. A summary of the construction activity of 19 major retailers is presented in Table 8.3.

The storefront should convey the impression that the outlet is permanent, stable, and progressive. It should also clearly identify the store. Customer entrances should be wide enough to prevent consumer congestion and inviting enough to attract walk-in trade. Curtains of warm or cold air may serve as doors during store hours, and this increased ease of entering may attract some consumers who might otherwise hesitate to enter through a revolving or regular door (Exhibit 8.2).

Despite their cost, display windows continue to be used to attract consumers into stores. In fact, many stores use an open or all-glass store front through which the consumer can see even the store's interior displays. The visual store-front allows the consumer to view most of the store's merchandise offering at a glance. Other stores may use a closed-background show window display, which lets the consumer see only the specially prepared window display and shuts off the interior view of the store com-

Table 8.3 Summary of Construction Activity for Major Retailers in 1980 and 1981

Firm	Stores in Operation at End of Calendar Year 1980	1981	Total Stores Added in Calendar Year 1980	1981	Square Footage Added in Calendar Year (millions) 1980	1981	Number of Stores Enlarged or Remodeled 1980	1981	Number of Stores Closed 1980	1981	Square Footage Lost Through Closings (millions) 1980	1981	Total Capital Expenditures ($ millions) 1980	1981
K mart	2,232	2,367	193	165	10.9	8.5	NA	450	30	30	0.7	0.7	275	250
Sears, Roebuck and Co.	854	861	36	31	5.0	4.5	8	3	31	24	2.8	1.2	344	300
Kroger	1,245	1,335	118	110	4.0	4.3	40	60	86	75	NA	1.4	239	275
J. C. Penney	2,119	2,179	89	60	6.4	4.0	0	0	81	NA	1.4	1.1	295	250
Wal-Mart	330	395	57	65	3.0	4.0	20	18	0	0	NA	NA	49	55
Safeway	2,416	2,500	160	146	5.0	3.9	69	NA	169	NA	3.6	NA	475	400
Federated Dept. Stores	358	377	26	29	2.7	3.4	6	7	12	10	0.4	1.3	313	450
Dayton Hudson	831	935	134	105	3.4	2.8	NA	NA	4	1	0.0	0.0	265	300
Woolworth	4,317	4,637	386	357	3.0	2.3	NA	92	76	37	1.0	NA	150	240
Lucky	1,511	1,617	146	159	3.0	2.1	6	6	101	53	NA	NA	147	150
Jewel	1,248	1,405	105	146	1.6	2.0	NA	NA	51	46	NA	NA	90	116
Revco	1,540	1,670	105	130	1.4	1.3	30	15	4	NA	0.0	NA	NA	NA
Winn Dixie	1,216	1,241	84	50	1.8	1.3	70	20	60	30	NA	NA	95	85
Montgomery Ward	411	411	28	13	3.3	1.2	13	1	36	13	2.3	NA	230	176
Albertson's	396	420	24	30	1.0	1.2	21	21	12	6	0.3	0.1	37	50
R. H. Macy	87	92	5	6	0.9	1.0	2	0	1	1	0.1	0.1	116	116
May Department Stores	1,156	1,281	172	125	1.2	1.1	NA	NA	0	0	0	0	180	200
American Stores Co.	1,136	1,154	52	30	1.6	1.0	5	4	14	12	0.2	0.2	140	110
Allied Stores	226	240	14	15	0.8	0.9	NA	NA	1	1	0.6	0.1	60	115

Source: Data summarized from information presented in "Tight Money Slows Big Builders' Pace." Reprinted by permission from Chain Store Age/Executive © September, 1981: 66–94. Copyright Lebhar-Friedman, Inc., 425 Park Avenue, New York, NY 10022.

Exhibit 8.2   Illustration of Doorless Design

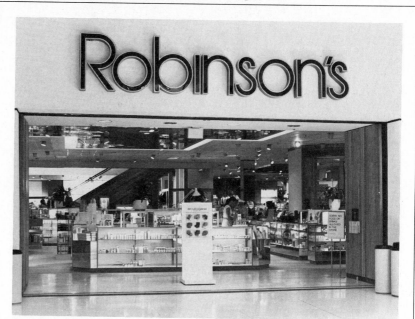

pletely. This practice allows merchants to focus consumer attention on displays which can convey either a quality or popular price image.

Higher building and land costs and effective display techniques have caused more retailers to use inexpensive out-of-door merchandise displays. These displays may be erected in the parking lot or in a specially designated space that is incorporated into the building and landscape design plans. The displays are generally crude in construction, so care should be taken that they do not detract from the permanent exterior appearance. The merchandise that is sold from these exterior displays is usually bulky, seasonal merchandise, such as lawn and garden-care products in the spring, boats in the summer, Christmas trees in December, and so on.

Building Interiors

The interior design of retail facilities should be designed to maximize visual merchandising. Visual merchandising is the integration of display and visual presentation with elements of merchandise management (Chapter 9). Visual presentation personnel develop ways to present, display, and sell the firms' products and services. They do this by creating the appropriate store image that will change customers' minds and create a desire to buy.

The interior of a building must be attractive to the consumer. This may be accomplished by providing good lighting, colorful walls, attractive floors, colorful displays, ceilings of a proper height, and by arranging store fixtures and equipment in a manner that will accommodate anticipated consumer traffic.

Factors that influence a consumer's perception of a retail facility's interior are:

Fixtures

Equipment

Color

Design

Lighting

Central theme

Consumer traffic patterns

Merchandise groupings and display

An outlet's interior appearance and its effectiveness in servicing customers in an efficient manner are strongly influenced by the fixtures and equipment in its retail operations. *Fixtures* are usually defined to mean any durable good that the retailer uses to display, store, protect, or sell merchandise. Items included as fixtures are: shelves, counters, cases, display cabinets, racks, tables, and freezers. *Equipment* is any durable good used in or outside the store to facilitate both retail selling and nonselling activities. Equipment items are: cash registers, delivery trucks, elevators, escalators, and air conditioning units.

Fixtures and equipment should be selected that will be most consistent with the expectations of the store's target market and the degree (self-service vs. full service) of the outlet's service offering. Fixtures and equipment should blend in with the interior environment and not divert the consumer's attention away from the merchandise. The fixtures and equipment selected should be appropriate for the type of merchandise handled so as to provide protection from spoilage or theft but still display the merchandise in the most attractive manner possible. The trend in fixtures and equipment selection is to use as much portability and flexibility as possible. Finally, fixtures and equipment should be selected upon the basis of the item's cost and its expected maintenance cost.

One type of equipment that deserves special mention is the equipment that is used to move consumers from one floor to another floor. Few people realize how large a problem it is to move 250,000 people efficiently over eight floors on a daily basis. Yet this is what most large department stores must do.

Stationary stairways are frequently found to be adequate to handle the consumer traffic that goes up or down one floor from the main floor. Elevators and escalators must be used if the store consists of more than three floors. Elevators are usually more advantageous than escalators in smaller stores because only one or two elevators may be required. The space required for two elevators is considerably less than the space required for one escalator. In addition, the installation cost is lower for two elevators than for one escalator.

Escalators are considered a must for large, multilevel stores. The escalator offers: (1) a reduction of crowding and congestion, (2) fast transportation between floors, (3) a low use of power, (4) the use of less space when many elevators would be required to move people, and (5) a maximum view of the merchandise as consumers pass slowly by or over the selling area. Despite all of these advantages, larger stores also provide a minimal elevator installation to satisfy consumers who prefer not to use an escalator or who want to move up or down several floors at a time. Elevators are also necessary to transport the handicapped, ill, and older customers.

The color of a store's interior can enhance the store's appearance and emphasize its individuality. Color and design patterns can be used to direct consumers to specific areas and to put them in a buying mood. A different color scheme is likely to be most appropriate for each department, or perhaps even for each merchandise line. The men's section of Neiman-Marcus reflects a man's color preference with a combination of deep blue and oak wood. Only a few feet away, the children's section offers a contrast in light pastels and designs that incorporate movement. Even different floor tile designs can be used to differentiate departments.

Every retail facility must be properly lighted to direct or attract the consumer's attention to the desired areas of the building. Lighting can be an effective sales tool to highlight different types of merchandise. A qualified lighting engineer can provide suggestions about colored lights, as well as on the physical arrangement of lighting fixtures. Lighting can also be used to increase employee productivity by properly illuminating the checkout, storage, receiving, and other work areas.

Consumer buying decisions are the result of seeing. The shopper's eye is attracted to the brightest thing in its field of vision, so the lighting on a display should be between two and five times stronger than the light in the room. The brightest light can draw attention to special retail displays that may occupy different locations from time to time. This gives consumers something new to look at and enhances shoppers' interest. However, strong light alone will not induce consumers to buy. Lighting must also have the quality and color which brings out the best features of the merchandise. Effective lighting catches the consumer's eye and encourages the consumer to examine and buy the merchandise that is featured to its best advantage.

Retail managers must realize that the purpose of lighting is to bring attention to the merchandise. The amount of light must be varied to attract attention, pull shoppers to the desired areas of the store, and create the desired impression. Colored lamps and soft lighting can be used to create a buying mood that will encourage the consumers to "see" that living room set in their home. Lighting tips for specific types of merchandise are presented in Exhibit 8.3.

Interior Layout

The **layout** of a retail store refers to the plan that designates the specific location and arrangement of equipment, fixtures, merchandise, aisles, and checkout facilities. Store layout automatically and instantly invites or repels a customer the moment the customer looks through the window or passes through an entry. This may be the most crucial moment in consumer shopping behavior, particularly in modern shopping center malls where dozens of stores stand one against the other.

There is only one universal law in layout that applies to all retail stores: each store must have a distinctive layout. Plan it with the store's clientele in mind and make certain it reflects the desired image and personality of the store.

Strategies of presenting merchandise to gain a desired store image include:

1. *Eyeball merchandising* Presenting merchandise at eyeball level to induce maximum consumer exposure on high margin and impulse items.

2. *Space productivity ratios* Using net space yield concept (Chapter 4) or return per square foot of selling space to allocate selling space and make merchandise arrangements.

3. *Free-flow layout pattern* Incorporating much open space to obtain high quality image in department stores, gift shops, high fashion stores, etc.

Exhibit 8.3 Lighting Tips for Specific Merchandise

1. Use large area lighting fixtures plus incandescent downlighting to avoid heavy shadows when displaying major appliances and furniture.

2. Use general diffuse lighting, accented with point-type spotlights to emphasize the beauty of china, glass, home accessories, and giftware.

3. Bring out the sparkle and luster of hardware, toys, auto accessories, highly polished silver, and other metalware by using a blend of general light and concentrated light sources—spotlights.

4. Use concentrated beams of high brightness incandescent sources to add brilliant highlights to jewelry, gold and silver, or cut glass.

5. Highlight the colors, patterns and textures of rugs, carpets, upholstery, heavy drapes, and bedspreads by using oblique directional lighting plus general low intensity overhead lighting.

6. Heighten the appeal of men's wear by using a cool blend of fluorescent and incandescent—with fluorescent predominating.

7. Highlight women's wear—especially the bright, cheerful colors and patterns—by using Natural White fluorescents blended with tungsten-halogen.

8. Bring out the tempting colors of meats, fruits, and vegetables by using fluorescent lamps rich in red energy, including the deluxe cool white type. Cool reflector incandescent lamps may also be used for direct type lighting.

Source: Charles B. Elliott, "Pointers on Display Lighting," *Small Marketers Aids No. 125*, Washington, D.C. (November 1972), p. 5.

4. *Grid layout pattern* Routing consumer traffic by designing aisles and fixtures to maximize selling space in supermarkets, discount stores, general merchandise outlets, etc.

5. *Organized clutter or "dump displays"* Encouraging the sale of "special" items by piling merchandise on a table, rack, or bin in the belief that consumers like to search through the pile to discover "their bargain."

Retailers have discovered that it is impossible to design a general layout that works for all types of retail stores in all areas. A certain degree of uniformity is possible within a single chain or a single industry, but strict adherence to a generalized model even within a single chain usually leads to disaster. The layout that is best suited for a store in Skokie, Illinois, may be completely out of character in Honolulu.

There is a basic conflict in all mass merchandising layouts for which a compromise must be reached. The customer wants a layout that does not cause undue inconvenience, or take added time, or tend to hinder shopping. The retailer wants a plan that exposes the shopper to the maximum amount of merchandise.

In the case of existing stores, **in-store traffic pattern analyses** should be conducted before remodeling to determine the natural flow of customers. In such studies, the percentage of consumers who pass or buy from each merchandise area is recorded by interviewers, who plot the paths of a consumer sample on a floor plan similar to the one in Figure 8.1. Retailers believe that those

Figure 8.1   Consumers Passing Different Supermarket Sections

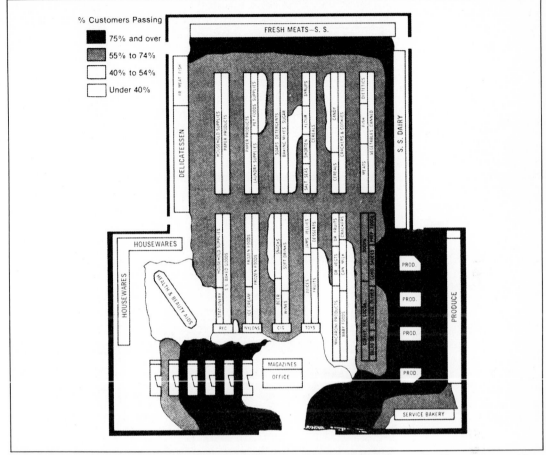

Source: "Colonial Study," *Progressive Grocer* (1964), p. C 90. Reprinted from *Progressive Grocer*, 1964, with permission.

merchandise lines which have high passing or buying percentages should be dispersed about the store so that consumers are exposed to more merchandise lines.

A scientific study of this nature usually is not available to new retailers, but observation of the patterns followed by shoppers in similar and competing stores is possible and desirable. Although the layout requirements facing retailers tend to vary, there are basic and common considerations.

Planning Layouts
with Customers
in Mind

Various social, age, and race segments exhibit different shopping habits and have individualized needs. Thus, the store's layout must be designed to meet the needs of the customers in its target market. For example, elderly people may prefer not to use an escalator or a curved, underground parking ramp, so a department store that caters to this group of people would have to use more elevators and more above ground parking facilities.

Promoting a Buying Mood

It is important to establish a buying mood. This is the sum total of what layout is all about. The most creative designs and the best research are valueless unless an effective environment for buying can be created.

Using a Simple Layout

In general, the more simple and natural the layout, the more the likelihood of success. Consumers object to being treated like mice in a laboratory maze. They express their objections in a silent but forceful manner: they do not return to the store! Have a well-defined entrance to the sales area. Again, this goes hand in hand with a simple layout (Exhibit 8.4).

Exhibit 8.4   Illustration of a Well-defined Entrance to Sales Area

Note how the floor pattern is used to direct consumer traffic.

Exhibit 8.5 Flexible Fixture Usage

Source: Photo courtesy of Pay'n Save Corporation, Public Relations.

Using Color, Design, and Lighting

Design patterns and color combinations should be planned on the layout so that they can effectively direct the attention of consumers to a particular location in subtle and attractive ways. Color and lighting can be used to create the effect of a separate department without using permanent walls or fixtures. Built-in fixtures and permanent walls are difficult to change if remodeling becomes necessary. An illustration of portable designs and fixtures is presented in Exhibit 8.5.

Lighting should also be planned as part of the layout. Lights are not simply fixtures that provide illumination; they create moods and atmospheres. Only certain types of lighting are appropriate for particular retail stores. Neglect of this results in consumer fatigue, improper reflection, and shadows on merchandise. Additionally, the shade of fluorescent lights must be considered, particularly in apparel shops. In artificial light a beautiful blue sweater may appear to be purple. Lighting, in both quantity and quality, is of paramount importance.

Planning Definite Themes

Layout and decor should not be simply brought together in a haphazard fashion. A definite theme is more effective. A central theme, such as a North Woods, Mexican, or Hawaiian setting helps give the store a personality and set the pace for departments within the store.

There are mixed feelings as to whether the theme of the store should follow the general theme of the shopping center. In general, if acceptance of the shopping center theme will tend to make the store another me-too retailer, it is wise to select something else. In many cases a slight variation from the central theme can achieve the desired results without a "sore thumb" effect. An overall North Woods shopping center theme might be varied by using a ghost town or Alpine village theme. Such a change is distinctive, yet it complements the overall theme.

Avoiding Natural Shoplifting Areas

A layout can be designed to minimize shoplifting. Secluded areas or areas that do not lend themselves to observation by store personnel are open invitations to shoplifters. Store fixtures and related displays should be kept low so that maximum customer visibility is maintained.

Capitalizing on the Flow of Traffic

The entire display layout should be neither too random nor overly rigid. Two major patterns are used in planning store layouts that follow the natural flow of traffic. The **grid pattern** routes consumer traffic in a manner similar to that of the rectangular street plan of a city (Figure 8.2) and creates a series of aisles similar to those found in most supermarkets, where customers' movements are directed by the aisles and fixtures. A warehouse image may also be created by the grid layout pattern unless colorful walls and fixtures are used to enhance its appearance.

The grid layout is designed to promote retailing efficiency, since it maximizes the use of selling space and simplifies security. As noted in Figure 8.2, customers are practically forced to pass by the bakery, produce, meat, dairy, and frozen food departments. This is a major characteristic of a grid layout in a mass merchandise outlet. In such cases the grid design pulls the maximum number of customers past the sides and back of the store. In department and specialty stores, the grid pattern is usually designed to draw consumer traffic down the main central aisles. In these cases high demand merchandise is placed near the sides of the building to draw consumer traffic to these otherwise slow-moving areas.

The **free-flow pattern** allows consumers to form their own traffic patterns and browse within the outlet. It is a more casual pattern, since right angles are eliminated (Figure 8.3). It is most appropriate for shopping goods and specialty stores in which the

Figure 8.2 Supermarket Design Using Grid Layout

Other space includes areas used for mezzanines, conference rooms, employees' lounges, restrooms, compressor rooms, janitor closets, etc.

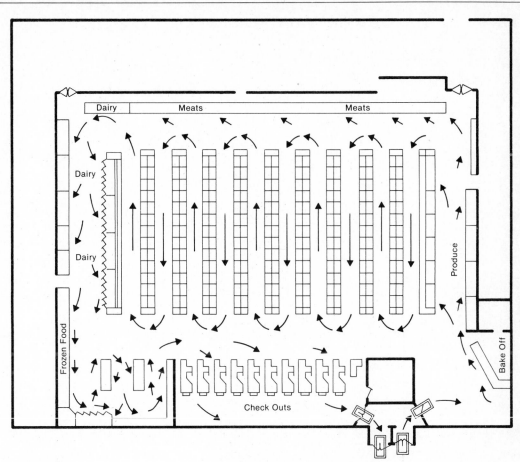

Space Allocation

Proportionate Allocation of Total Store Area:

Sales Area 71%
Backroom Area 29%

Proportionate Allocation of Total Sales Area:

Product Sales Area 91%
Front-end Area 9%

Proportionate Allocation of Product Sales Area:

Grocery Sales Area 83%
Meat Sales Area 6%
Produce Sales Area 11%

Proportionate Allocation of Backroom Space:

Product Storage and Preparation 80%
Other 20%

Features of this suggested supermarket layout are:

1. A right-hand single traffic pattern for customer shopping. Studies continue to show that this pattern minimizes shopping congestion, allows for a relatively smooth flow of traffic, and enhances maximum product exposure.

2. The attractive, high impulse bakery (including rolls, pies, cakes, cookies, doughnuts, etc.) and produce departments are located first and second respectively in the shopping pattern.

3. The attractive natural color, and freshness of the fresh fruits and vegetables, along with a good margin, help the produce department to attain either the first or second location in the shopping pattern.

4. The meat department is located across the back of the store. This location gives the department repeated exposures as the shopper travels the grocery aisles, encourages wider aisles in the meat area, and greater customer convenience.

5. The dairy department is located next, about as far from the entrance as possible, because nearly 80 percent of the shoppers will shop in this department. This location assures that the shopper will be exposed to a wide variety of other merchandise while making a dairy item purchase.

6. The frozen food department is placed near the end of the shopping pattern to minimize the chances of the product thawing with resulting quality depreciation. Placing it last also serves to eliminate some doubling back in the shopping pattern by customers as is presently the case in many stores.

7. As much as possible, the back room storage and preparation areas should be located so they are immediately back of, and supporting their respective sales display areas. All doorways for handling the receiving products should be at least five feet wide to accommodate materials handling equipment.

Source: Clyde R. Cunningham and Harold S. Ricker, "Supermarket Guidelines—Store Design and Layout," Manual 84, a cooperative report by the University of Missouri-Columbia and the Agricultural Research Service, Agricultural Marketing Research Institute, Beltsville, Maryland June (1973), pp. 29–32.

Figure 8.3   Free-Flow Layout Pattern in a Department Store

customer wishes to compare and evaluate products in a relaxed atmosphere. Less merchandise and fewer fixtures can be placed per square foot of space in the free-flow pattern than in the grid pattern; however, the more favorable consumer impression generated by the free-flow pattern offsets the higher display costs in stores where relaxed shopping is important.

Rising space costs have forced even the most exclusive department stores to discontinue using free-flow arrangements on their prime first floor selling space. Thus, one currently finds the grid layout being used on the main floors of multilevel department and specialty stores. These same stores may use the free-flow arrangement in other areas where the space cost is less and where it is important to maximize consumer convenience and allow the consumer to browse and make impulse purchases in a more relaxed atmosphere.

Supermarkets and other outlets where customers make frequent repurchases of the same items can use the grid pattern more effectively. In these stores consumers follow the same traffic pattern regularly and become familiar with the location of various products. Customers want to make their purchases with a minimum amount of time and effort, and the grid pattern layout is both efficient in displaying products and convenient for consumers with these shopping motives.

Most stores use some combination of these two basic layout patterns to display various types of merchandise better and to serve the different target market customers. The "shoppe" or **boutique concept** utilizes the free-flow pattern within a department that sells related merchandise. In effect, boutiques become small specialty stores within a large store. These individual specialty shops are targeted toward a particular market segment.

Thus, the boutique arrangement brings complete offerings together in one department instead of having the merchandise displayed in many separate departments. This allows the shopper with a particular interest to shop in one location for a complete assortment of related merchandise. For example, a ski boutique in a department store will feature not only skis, ski boots, and ski poles but also warmup boots, sweaters, pants, goggles, gloves, socks, and other appropriate clothing.

The boutique concept is growing in popularity because it allows retailers to use visual merchandising to provide a clear focal point for consumers who are interested in a specific line of merchandise, and because it is very flexible. Once a boutique has been established, its character can quickly be changed. With slight modifications, the same fixtures can be adapted to feature different merchandise. Colors, display decor, graphics, etc. can be altered with each new concept without making major changes to the basic store layout. For example, the progressive clothing retailer should re-evaluate their boutiques at least weekly to be sure that they are projecting an up-to-the minute "fashion" image and highlighting their best promotional stores and selling opportunities. The major disadvantage of the boutique layout is that it does not utilize space in a very efficient manner.

Grouping Merchandise

Assemble together items of merchandise that carry a natural association. Hammers and nails, syrup and pancake mixes are examples. A close examination of merchandise may reveal some related items and chances for extra sales previously not considered. Studies by *Progressive Grocer* have demonstrated that sales were nearly twice as great for pretzels and potato chips when these items were displayed near complementary products such as soft drinks as when they were near noncomplementary items such as milk and cheese.[7]

Departmentalize when possible. Form sections of the store into departments such as shoes, men's clothes, bakery goods, and auto parts. Departmentalization personalizes the store and tends to reduce the feeling on the part of both consumers and store personnel that they are numbers in a vast wilderness of merchandise. Also, management planning and control are facilitated if operating expenses and receipts are maintained separately on a departmental basis. However, because of increased labor costs and computerized merchandise control, central "cash-wrap" stations on the floor are diminishing the importance of departmental considerations.

Several criteria can be used to group merchandise into departments. Generic merchandise (such as footwear, or health and beauty aids) is one criterion. Other criteria considered when grouping merchandise are:

Functional merchandise (e.g., dairy, meats, housewares, etc.)

Target market groups

Lifestyle groupings (e.g., skiing, modern apartment living, etc.)

Demographics (e.g., teenagers, female, local, etc.)

Social class (e.g., lower middle, upper middle, lower upper)

Economic grouping (e.g., economy-minded consumers may be served from a bargain basement)

The location of the various departments depends on such considerations as the size and shape of the building, the type of clientele, the nature of the merchandise, and the value of the floor space. In a single-floor outlet, the most valuable space is the area nearest the store entrance. This is the area with the heaviest consumer traffic. Floor space decreases in value as one moves from the entrance to the rear of the building. In a multifloor building, the space decreases in value as one moves up or down from the main floor.

Managers of one-floor retail outlets can use the **50%–33%–17% concept** to allocate space. This concept (Figure 8.4) indicates that the front one-third of a one entryway outlet should ac-

Figure 8.4 Illustration of the 50%–33%–17% Concept

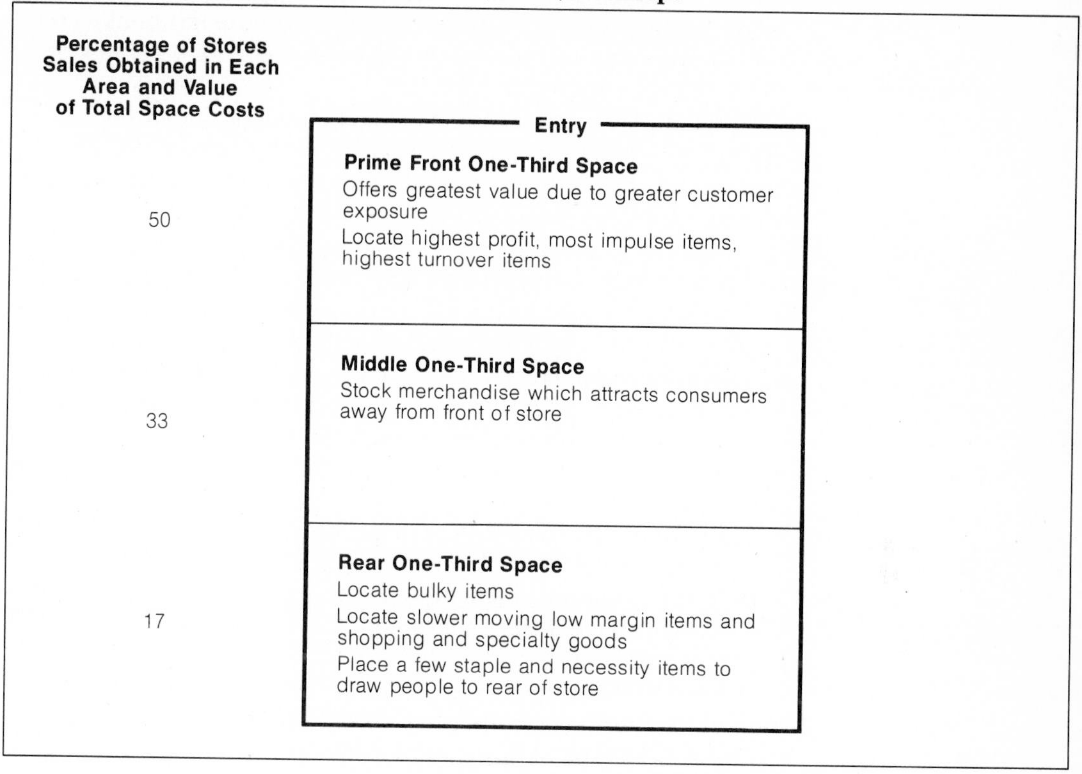

**Percentage of Stores
Sales Obtained in Each
Area and Value
of Total Space Costs**

— Entry —

Prime Front One-Third Space
Offers greatest value due to greater customer exposure
Locate highest profit, most impulse items, highest turnover items

50

Middle One-Third Space
Stock merchandise which attracts consumers away from front of store

33

Rear One-Third Space
Locate bulky items
Locate slower moving low margin items and shopping and specialty goods
Place a few staple and necessity items to draw people to rear of store

17

count for 50 percent of all retail sales. The middle third should account for 33 percent and the rear one-third of space should contain 17 percent of all sales. Rental and building cost may also be allocated according to this concept to calculate the profitability of departments or different lines of merchandise. For example, if a retail outlet occupied 3,000 square feet of selling space for which an annual rental of $20,000 was paid, 50 percent of the rent or $10,000 would be allocated as a space cost for the front one-third (1,000 square feet) of the store. Thus, the rent per square foot of selling space in this prime area would be the $10,000 rent divided by the number of square feet (1,000) or $10 per square foot. The rent allocation for the middle of the store would be 33 percent of the $20,000 total rent or $6,600 equals 6,600/1,000 or $6.60 per square foot. The rear one-third of space would account for 17 percent of the total rent or $3,400 which amounts to $3.40 per square foot. The advantage of using this concept is that it allows one to subtract a more relevant rental cost from the contribution made by each department. This yields a more realistic appraisal of each department's profitability than merely subtracting a flat rental fee from each department's gross contribution and recognizes that different locations in the store have different economic values.

Merchandise departments usually are located according to their sales-generating capacity relative to the value of the space occupied. Frequently-purchased items and high profit items usually are given the most favored space allocations. However, the nature of the merchandise also must be considered. Impulse items, high-rate replacement items, and convenience goods, such as cigarettes, should be located in the heaviest traffic areas because consumers will not search them out. Shopping goods, such as furniture and specialty goods (such as sporting goods), can be located in less heavily traveled areas because they will pull traffic to outer locations. Bulky merchandise, such as large appliances or boats, generally are located in less heavy consumer traffic areas.

If possible, it is advisable to locate departments with different seasonal sales patterns adjacent to each other. An exchange of selling space among adjacent departments can provide more efficient use of space if the departments have different seasonal selling peaks.

A store that merchandises on many levels may display a portion of its offerings on the main floor. Impulse items and a small sample of the type of merchandise that a consumer can expect to see in the primary location are also usually displayed on the main floor. This main floor display can encourage consumers to make a trip to the primary department location.

Department stores provide an example of the most extreme use of departmentalization. Each department is set up almost as an individual store, with separate merchandise and expense budgets, individual accounting statements, and inventory control. Such departmentalizing frequently results in duplication of lines in the various departments of the store. This is done not only to reach different market segments but also to promote in-store competition among the buyers and managers of the various departments. For example, ladies' blouses are carried in fourteen different departments (basement blouses, first floor blouse bar, budget blouses, better blouses, junior sportswear, misses sportswear, couture blouses, collegiate shop, and so forth) in one large eastern department store.

Planning Perimeters and Crosswalks

Perimeters are the heaviest customer traffic area in the store and should be planned to accommodate those items that account for a store's major revenue. Unduly wide aisles within perimeters can create consumer dissatisfaction because of the need to cross continually from one side to the other. Narrow aisles create a feeling of claustrophobia in many consumers, particularly when merchandise is stored above eye level.

Crosswalks are often considered poor merchandising areas, but they can break up the canyon effect of long perimeters. Crosswalks and escalator exits also are effective locations for end-of-the-aisle displays of weekend specials and so-called impulse items.

Planning Midstore
Sales Appeal

Many retailers have found that the middle of the store is a poor merchandising area. As a result, it is necessary to examine carefully and relist the type of merchandise that sells best in this area rather than to stock indiscriminately (see Table 8.4.)[8]

Designing "Eyeball"
Merchandising

Studies and experience have demonstrated that merchandise displayed at eye level sells better than merchandise at either a very low or high level. **Eye-level merchandising** should be planned for a retailer's "bread and butter" lines. Retailers can locate brands and items within a merchandise category to maximize profitability. Per unit margins, sales volume, and the sales sensitivity of each brand and/or item must be considered. Brands and/or items providing the highest profit contribution as calculated by margin times volume divided by space used should usually be given the eye-level shelf space. An exception to this rule would be an item whose popularity is so strong that consumers will search for the item no matter what height level it occupies.

Table 8.4   Supermarket Items Found to Be Best Customer Attractors for Midstore Location

Product Group	Percent of Total Store Traffic Attracted
Coffee	66
Cookies and crackers	65
Canned vegetables	62
Baking needs	60
Paper products	59
Canned soup	58
Laundry supplies	55
Cereal	55
Sugar	55
Salad dressing and oils	53

Shelves should not be more than fifty-four to sixty inches high, or they will block the view of consumers. And, of course, sales will suffer if the consumer cannot see the merchandise. In the case of mass merchandising displays, consideration should also be given to peripheral vision since few consumers walk sideways down a shopping aisle.

Planning Return per Square, Linear, or Cubic Foot

Plan the **return per square foot** of selling space. A dollar return per some measurable unit of space is the most common measurement used by retailers to establish rental rates and to gauge merchandising success. (This concept is discussed in detail in Chapter 4). While it should always remain in the back of the retailer's mind, it should not be overemphasized in the planning of layout. For example, if a retailer finds that men's undershirts return more per square foot than any other product, should the store stock contain nothing but this item? Unless there is sufficient demand for a specialty retail store of this nature, the answer is obviously no. Yet if reliance upon return per measurable unit of space is the sole consideration, dangerous merchandising errors such as this can occur. Likewise, complete dependence upon other considerations involved in layout can result in stores that are works of art but have a very low dollar return.

Sales of most items will increase if more shelf space is devoted to that item. Because space is so expensive and limited, existing retailers can expand the space allocated on only a few items. Items which frequently seem to warrant more space are:

Private-label merchandise because of higher margin and excellent response to increased consumer exposure.

Impulse items because sales respond well to increased space.

Fast-turnover items because sales increase even more when more space is allocated to them.

New products because more shelf facings are perceived by consumers as an indication that the item is popular with other consumers.

High margin items because if combined with a high turnover rate they generate the most profit.

Although these suggestions can guide space allocation, frequent shifts in store display and layout should be avoided as they only confuse the consumer and can actually result in sales reduction.

Planning Locations of Sales-Supporting Areas

Plan the locations and space occupied by sales-supporting and sales-generating equipment. Multifloor outlets require stairways, elevators, or escalators to move customers from one floor to another. Stores that have merchandise from the ground level, basement, and only one floor above the ground level can often provide only a stationary stairway. Larger stores must provide some more elaborate system. Customers do not like to wait for elevators or escalators or to climb steps; so adequate facilities must be provided if consumers are to be attracted to another floor.

Sales-supporting equipment and space must be arranged so that goods can be received, inspected, marked, and placed on the shelves with minimum effort. Mechanical handling equipment, communication devices, and other labor-saving equipment should be considered and incorporated into the store layout if economically feasible. The storage and work areas should be located in nonprime areas, but they should be easily accessible to the selling areas. These storage and work areas are generally located at the rear of single-floor outlets and not on the ground floor of multifloor outlets.

Higher retail land values and increased building costs have caused some retailers to reduce the amount of nonselling space in the retail outlet or to move the nonselling area to less valuable space, such as mezzanines. Faster and more frequent delivery and labor-saving techniques, such as prepackaged and premarked merchandise that is ready for display when it arrives at the store, are being used to reduce the amount of space devoted to nonselling activities. Even so, from 25 to 50 percent of the total floor space in most stores is used for nonselling activities (Table 8.5). In today's high cost economy, the goal is to increase selling space as a percentage of total floor space to as high a percentage as possible without interfering with the essential nonselling activities.

These nonselling activities can be grouped into four categories: (1) those that must be located in some particular area of the store, such as receiving docks; (2) those that relate directly to certain departments, such as the kitchen adjoining the restaurant; (3) those that do not require any particular location, such as executive offices; and (4) those that involve direct customer contact, such as escalators, dressing rooms, and rest rooms.

It should be noted that only categories three and four allow for much flexibility as far as location is concerned. The nonselling activities described in category three offer the most flexibility. For this reason, executive activities are usually performed in the lowest-value areas such as upper floors, away from the consumer traffic.

Table 8.5   Capital Expenditures Made by Different Retail Groups

Retail Group	Average Store Size (1000 square feet)	Average Size of Store Built in 1977–1978 (1000 square feet)	Selling Space % of Total Floor Space	1978 Capital Expenditures per Square Foot		Fixture Expenditures $ per square foot
				Including Labor	Excluding Labor	
Drug stores	18.8	19.7	81.8	$22.13	$15.50	11.45
Supermarkets	25.9	34.2	73.6	$29.5	$18.12	20.54
Department stores	114.2	106.3	83.0	$28.33	$19.17	19.05
General merchandisers	82.5	103.7	83.8	$31.90	$22.50	10.57
Home centers	30.0	33.5	66.0	$37.02	$26.10	9.67
Discount stores	69.1	77.5	80.6	$24.98	$15.49	11.14
Specialty stores (shoes)	3.0	2.6	70.1	$37.43	$24.45	8.35
Specialty stores (auto)	6.5	7.0	48.8	$29.8	$21.34	5.40
Specialty stores (apparel)	3.8	3.9	83.5	$27.9	$18.14	14.30

Source: *Chain Store Age Executive Edition*, (August 1978), pp. 42–127. Copyright Lebhar-Friedman Inc., 425 Park Avenue, New York, NY 10022.

The other area that would appear to offer some flexibility in layout involves those activities that involve direct consumer contact. The complex nature of each activity influences where the facilities are located and how they are operated. The following discussion points up factors to consider in planning these consumer contact centers.

Checkout Areas Plan the placement and size of checkout areas. There is no other single area in a store more important than the checkout counter. Once customers have decided upon their purchases, they want to make the purchase transaction as quickly as possible.

Most of the problems at the checkout counter can be controlled only by providing adequate checkout facilities and by careful scheduling of clerks, but the location can have important bearing on the efficiency of operation. If the checkout stand is designed so that incoming and outgoing customers mingle in traffic jams, customers will be dissatisfied, and there is a good chance that shoplifting will increase.

At best, a checkout counter necessitates a short wait. The checkout area should be planned with a layout that incorporates attractive **impulse items** (items bought on an unplanned basis) in point-of-purchase displays (Exhibit 8.6).

Dressing Rooms and Rest Rooms Incorporate dressing rooms and rest rooms in the plan. Unless they are incorporated in the original layout and overall theme, they tend to become conspicuous boxes and can easily detract from the overall purpose of creating a favorable buying mood. For security reasons, only one entrance should be provided to the dressing room. This entrance should not be located near a stockroom, stairwell, rest room, or outside exit.

The overall store theme should give the planner many ideas for creative design for the dressing room and rest room areas. In a circus theme, the dressing rooms might be identified and designed as the "magic show." These areas should be used to sell merchandise, but the dressing rooms in most stores are hardly designed to encourage purchases. It is difficult for the most expensive suit or dress to complement the wearer in a coffin-like upright rectangle complete with faded mirror and unpainted walls. A dirty, unkempt, barren rest room can suddenly reduce the image of any store to little more than that of a backwoods filling station.

The problem of rest room security is becoming increasingly serious. Rest rooms located in large, busy retail stores have been the scenes of assaults and robberies that have occurred during prime daytime hours. This has caused the management of some stores to use security guards in the rest rooms.

Exhibit 8.6   Placement of Impulse Items at Checkout Area

Source: Photo courtesy of K mart Corporation.

Planning for
Dead Areas

Regardless of the best planning, dead spaces are likely to occur within the store. Such areas as corners often become dead areas. These can be utilized for vending machines, a play area for children (complete with toys), or for other functions that attract customers and add directly or indirectly to sales.

Retailers should consult the Small Business Administration, industry trade associations, and similar stores in other locations when they begin to plan a layout. The entire physical project (including outside surroundings, parking lot, exterior building appearance, and interior layout and appearance) creates an overall store personality for consumers. Each consumer will perceive the store image differently, so the entire project should be designed to appeal to the store's selected target market group. A list of items that the Small Business Administration believes must be planned into the proper retail image creation process is presented in Exhibit 8.7.

Exhibit 8.7   Checklist for Interior Arrangement and Display

Layout
1. Are your fixtures low enough and signs so placed that the customer can get a bird's-eye view of the store and tell in what direction to go for wanted goods?
2. Do your aisle and counter arrangements tend to stimulate a circular traffic flow through the store?
3. Do your fixtures (and their arrangement), signs, lettering, and colors all create a coordinated and unified effect?
4. Before any supplier's fixtures are accepted, do you make sure they conform in color and design to what you already have?
5. Do you limit the use of hanging signs to special sale events?
6. Are your counters and aisle tables *not* overcrowded with merchandise?
7. Are your ledges and cashier/wrapping stations kept free of boxes, unneeded wrapping materials, personal effects, and odds and ends?
8. Do you keep trash bins out of sight?

Merchandise emphasis
1. Do your signs referring to specific goods tell the customer something significant about them, rather than simply naming the products and their prices?
2. For your advertised goods, do you have prominent signs, including tear sheets at the entrances, to inform and guide customers to their exact location in the store?
3. Do you prominently display both advertised and nonadvertised specials at the ends of counters as well as at the point of sale?
4. Are both your national and private brands highlighted in your arrangement and window display?
5. Wherever feasible, do you give the more colorful merchandise in your stock preference in display?
6. In the case of apparel and home furnishings, do the items that reflect your store's fashion sense or fashion leadership get special display attention at all times?
7. In locating merchandise in your store, do you always consider the productivity of space—vertical as well as horizontal?
8. Is your self-service merchandise arranged so as to attract the customer and assist her in selection by the means indicated below:
   a. Is each category grouped under a separate sign?
   b. Is the merchandise in each category arranged according to its most significant characteristic—whether color, style, size or price?
   c. In apparel categories, is the merchandise arranged by price lines or zones to assist the customer to make a selection quickly?
   d. Is horizontal space usually devoted to different items and styles within a category (vertical space being used for different sizes—smallest at the top, largest at the bottom)?
   e. Are impulse items interspersed with demand items and not placed across the aisle from them, where many customers will not see them?

Source: U.S. Small Business Administration, "Small Store Planning for Growth," *Small Business Management Series No. 33* (Washington, D.C.: Government Printing Office, 1966), pp. 98–99.

Summary

Each retail outlet has an image. Retail management must discover what factors are most important to the firm's target market customers. The store's entire merchandise and promotional offering and its physical appearance must be coordinated to achieve the image demanded by its target market customers. Stores that have a more distinctive image are more likely to appeal to a specific market segment.

Retail outlets are being remodeled more frequently to meet the changing needs of their customers. Remodeling may take the form of a major renovation or it may merely represent a facelift. Regardless of the extent of change, it must be planned from the viewpoint of the consumers' sensory reactions to scent, sound, touch, and sight. The image control process includes using land properly. Using a lot of open space and fountains creates a more prestigious image, but it also increases the cost for land. This increased cost must be passed on to the consumer. Attractive building exteriors are a good investment since they can increase the outlet's consumer traffic.

Interior fixtures and equipment must be selected to go along with the rest of the store, so they must be coordinated with the interior lighting and color scheme. The arrangement of the fixtures, merchandise, and equipment should be designed so that consumer exposure is maximized. The two major forms of store layouts are the grid pattern and the free-flow arrangement. Most mass merchandisers use the grid layout because it allows a maximum amount of merchandise to be displayed from a given floor space. Department stores are also using the grid layout on their main floor, but they may use a free-flow arrangement in other areas to increase consumer convenience and allow the consumer to browse and make impulse purchases in a more relaxed atmosphere.

Consumers must be able to locate merchandise with a minimum of effort. Retailers have established separate departments and boutiques to make this an easier task for consumers. Placing high demand and high margin merchandise at the consumer's eye level and in prime space areas also allows consumers to find the merchandise more easily and increases store profits.

Effective retail managers realize that presenting the proper retail atmosphere and displaying merchandise correctly are factors that make or break many a retail firm. Intelligent investment in more effective merchandise display usually leads to huge increases in profit.

Questions

1. Considering the general advisability of diversified merchandise, how would you account for the existence of stores that sell only ties or only shirts. Where are stores of this type usually found? What generalizations can you make about this type of retailing with regard to risk, target segment, marketing mix, location, and so forth?
2. Distinguish between the grid pattern and the free-form pattern of store layouts. In what types of stores is each pattern most useful? Why?
3. What factors might cause a retailer to want to change an image? How would a retailer go about deciding whether it would be beneficial to do so?

4. Considering as many variables as you have studied (location, layout, risk, retailing mix, and so forth), suggest a store design given the following parameters: supermarket in a middle-class suburb; private bookstore in a college town; sporting goods store in a wealthy suburb.

5. What advantages and disadvantages does the boutique concept offer a retail outlet? For which types of outlets does it appear to be best suited?

6. How can the 50%-33%-17% concept be used to allocate rent and space to different merchandise departments?

7. Why are more retailers remodeling old outlets today than ever before? What are the advantages and disadvantages of remodeling?

8. What factors affect a consumer's perception of a retail facility's exterior? Discuss.

9. What factors affect a consumer's perception of a retail facility's interior? Discuss.

10. Discuss some alternative strategies that retailers can adapt to present merchandise to gain a desired image.

11. What types of items frequently warrant allocation of more shelf space? Why?

Footnotes

1. William J. E. Crissy, "Image: What Is It?" *MSU Business Topics* 19 (Winter 1971): 77–80.

2. Stephen J. Arnold, M. A. Sylvia, and Douglas J. Tigert, "Comparative Analysis of Determinant Attributes in Retail Store Selection," *Advances in Consumer Research,* Proceedings for the Association for Consumer Research, 1978, pp. 665–666.

3. "Total Re-Do At $20/sq. ft." *Stores* (March 1981): 31.

4. *Ibid.,* pp. 34–35.

5. *Ibid.,* p. 32.

6. "Renovation for Faster ROI," *Stores* (May 1981): 44.

7. *Consumer Dynamics in the Super Market* (New York: Progressive Grocer, n.d.), p. 2.

8. Ibid.

Case Study: Convenience Stores

A traffic flow study was conducted in two convenience stores located in the same town in the northwestern United States. The study was designed to answer two major questions:

1. Which layout exposes the customer to the most types of merchandise?

2. Does increased exposure lead to more sales for the store as a whole?

In each of the stores 180 customers were observed as they shopped, and their paths of travel through the store were traced on individual layout maps. Data were also collected on number of items purchased,

Figure 8.5 Store A Customer Traffic Patterns

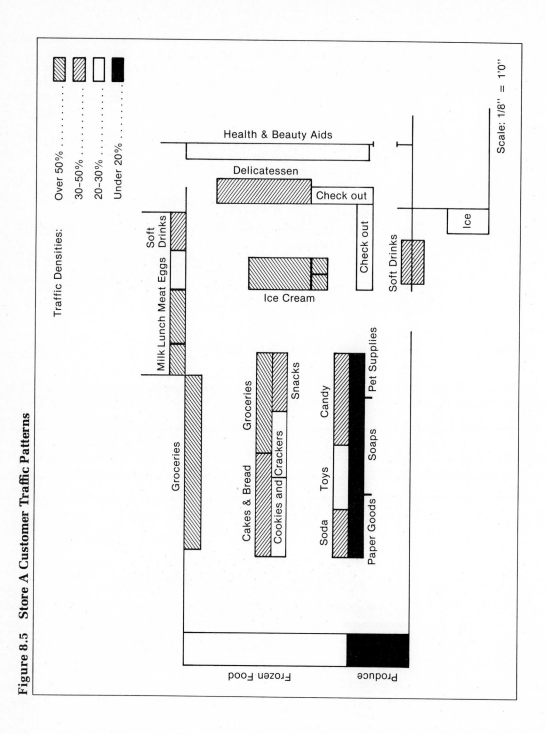

Figure 8.6 Store B Customer Traffic Patterns

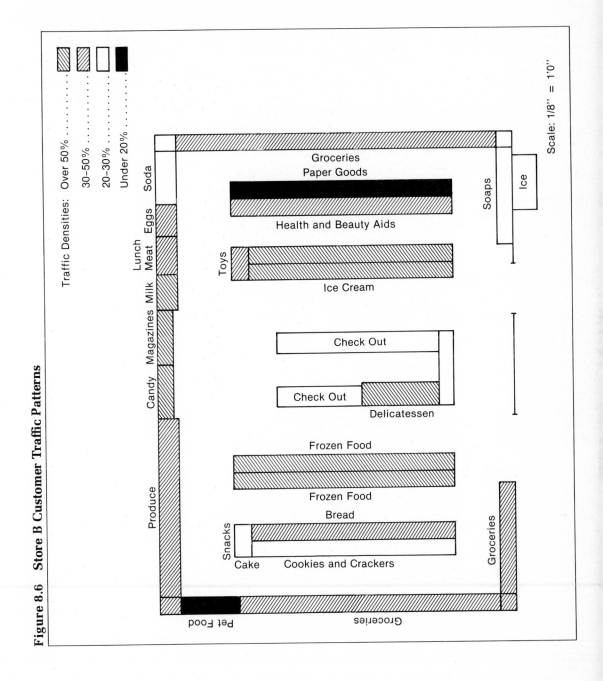

types of items purchased, and amount of total sales check. The average customer in this study was exposed to 6.20 departments in Store A and 7.98 departments in Store B. The shopper in Store A was exposed to significantly fewer departments than the shoppers in Store B. Spending for the average customer in this study was $3.26 in Store A and $3.07 in Store B. The average customer in this study purchased 3.26 items on their shopping trip. The number of items varied from store to store. In Store A 3.50 items were purchased, while in Store B 3.01 items were purchased. Department traffic densities for each store appears in Figures 8.5 and 8.6. The maps are coded to indicate the percentage of shoppers in each store who passed each department.

Discussion Questions

1. What conclusions can you draw from the study? Which type of layout should the firm adopt in their next store? Why?
2. What other information would you like to have before you make your decision? Specifically how and where would you obtain it?
3. What suggestions do you have to improve each design? Why?

Chapter 9 | Merchandise Management

Learning Goals

1. To understand how concepts such as the merchandise budget, stock turnover analysis, and other methods are used in merchandise management.
2. To discuss methods employed in determining how much merchandise should be bought.
3. To learn when merchandise should be purchased and how to plan inventory levels.
4. To be aware of electronic checkout systems in merchandise management.

**Key Terms
and Concepts**

merchandise budget
annual sales forecast
seasonal sales forecast
monthly sales index
basic stock method of
   planning inventory
percentage deviation method
   of planning inventory
weeks' supply method of
   planning inventory
stock to sales ratio method of
   planning inventory
model stock
never-out merchandise

marginal analysis method of
   planning inventory
retail reductions
open-to-buy amounts
initial markup percentage
physical inventory
perpetual inventory
overage
shortage
universal product code (UPC)
stock turnover
gross margin return on
   inventory (GMROI)

Merchandise management, one of the most critical areas in retailing, is defined in this book as the activities involved in balancing inventories to meet expected consumer demands. This process is depicted in Figure 9.1. Major merchandise policy decisions or those decisions relating to the question, "What products do we stock?" were discussed in Chapter 4. This chapter concentrates on the other major merchandising issues—how much to buy, when to buy, and merchandise planning. Several techniques (such as the merchandise budget and stock turnover analysis) that can be used by retail management and buyers to plan and control inventory levels will be presented in this chapter. These techniques can simplify many of the activities associated with merchandise planning and control by establishing routine pro-

Figure 9.1   Merchandise Management Process

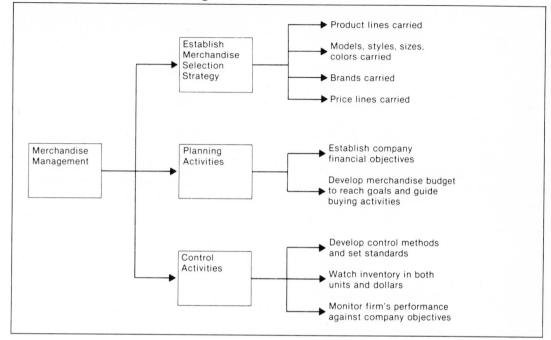

cedures. A discussion of the remaining buying issues—how to buy, organizing for buying, sources of merchandise, buying negotiations, and legal considerations—will be presented in Chapter 10.

Merchandise Planning

Retailers should recognize several factors that determine whether their merchandise plans are providing the optimum balance between inventory levels and potential sales. Planning and control methods are simply aids to the buyer's judgment. Such planning and control methods provide data that must be analyzed and interpreted in light of the buyer's previous experience and knowledge. Frequent review of planning and control techniques must be made to ensure that such tools provide realistic information. Planning and control procedures are usually designed to provide information that is realistic only under a specific set of assumptions about the environment. Retail situations change quite frequently, so the planning and control procedures must be reviewed to be certain they are the most practical means of providing the desired information.

Planning and control procedures are effective only when information is analyzed and translated into action. The merchandise control process involves taking steps to bring actual results closer to stated retail objectives. The trend toward larger retail organizations, combined with the tendency for the consumer environment to change more rapidly than ever, has made some type of control process essential. However, changes in consumer preferences also have necessitated flexibility in allowing individual store managers to adjust their merchandise assortment to reflect the needs of their specific trade area more quickly.

Small owner-operated retail outlets have fewer formal control problems than large chain retail outlets. However, even the small retailer can make profitable use of such tools as merchandise budgets and stock turnover analysis to simplify buying procedures and to meet the needs of potential customers. Even the smallest retailers need to plan their sales, stocks, purchases, reductions, and margins by reviewing past records and observing inventory levels on a periodic basis.

Basic Merchandise Information Procedures

Efficient merchandise management involves the use of the most detailed, accurate, and current information that is available. The merchandise budget is one management tool that can be used for both planning and controlling inventories.

Merchandise Budget

The **merchandise budget** can be applied to plan and control sales efforts, markups, purchases, markdowns, and shortages. It usually consists of:

1. A forecast of sales for given periods
2. A plan for the stocks to be carried at the beginning of each period
3. Planned retail reductions
4. Planned purchase quantities
5. A planned profit margin

Such a budget enables the retailer to buy merchandise of the kind and quantity that better reflects potential customer needs. By identifying fast-moving and/or highly profitable items, it provides information that the retailer can use to plan promotional efforts more efficiently. The merchandise budget contains a record of both actual and predicted past sales which can be used to evaluate the performance of both the budget procedure itself and the store's merchandise buyers.

The budget can be constructed on a weekly, monthly, quarterly, semiannual, or annual basis. However, the longer the time period covered by a budget, the more difficult it is to obtain accurate forecasts. Frequently, the budget is made for six months or one year in advance and is revised each month. A normal sequence in merchandise budgeting is presented below. Deviations from the sequence of activities are both appropriate and common if other, relevant information is available.

Step 1: Forecasting Sales

Either unit or dollar sales are forecast for each merchandise type for the specified time period. Past monthly (or weekly) sales performance should be recorded and analyzed to identify trends and seasonality patterns. Estimated sales volume is a critical element in the merchandise budget because an error in the estimated sales figures can cause a serious error in the projection of the firm's profitability.

Annual sales forecasts must consider such factors as past trends in store sales as well as local changes in (1) population, (2) income, (3) employment, (4) competition (both in number and in action), (5) consumer preferences, (6) the general price level charged by the store, and (7) any of the other internal elements used by the store to attract customers.

Annual sales forecasts may be made simply by estimating a "reasonable" change from last year's sales or by using more complicated statistical forecasting techniques, such as multiple regression analysis (discussed in Chapter 20). Several prewritten computer programs are available at reasonable cost, so a commercial service bureau, such as Statistical Tabulating Corporation, may be able to provide annual forecasts less expensively than the individual retailer can.

Seasonality of sales differs by the type of merchandise being sold; so **seasonal sales forecasts** must be made for each different merchandise category on a monthly, weekly, or sometimes even a daily basis (Figure 9.2). In some cases an entire selling period, such as Christmas or Easter, can be analyzed separately. Monthly sales indexes can be used to forecast monthly sales. Monthly sales can be forecast by dividing the estimated annual sales by twelve to obtain the *average* monthly sales estimate. Past monthly sales records can then be used to obtain a **monthly sales index** for each merchandise category. The monthly sales index is calculated by dividing each month's sales by an average month's sales and the result is multiplied by 100. In formula format:

$$\text{A month's sales index} = \frac{\text{that month's sales}}{\text{an average month's sales}} \times 100$$

For example, suppose sales data for the past five years indicated average sales in January were $10,000, and the five-year annual average sales were $240,000. In this case the average previous monthly sales would be $240,000 divided by 12, or $20,000. The January sales index is ($10,000/$20,000) × 100, or 50.

Each monthly sales index is calculated in a similar manner, so an index of 100 represents sales made during an "average" month. The percentage that a monthly sales index deviates from 100 is the percentage deviation of that month's sales from the sales of the average month. In the above example, the 50 index for January indicates that January sales are 50 percent *below* average. An index of 110 for May would indicate that May sales

Figure 9.2 Seasonal Sales Patterns

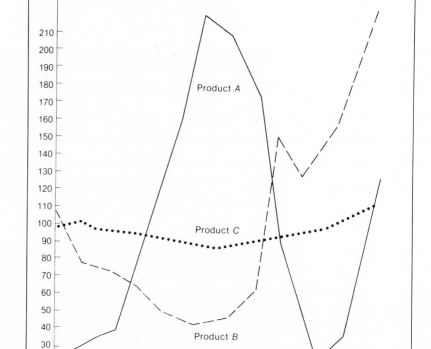

are 10 percent *above* an average month's sales (because 110 is more than 100).

Once the value of the monthly sales index has been determined, it can be divided by 100 and the result multiplied by the average estimated monthly sales to provide an estimate of that month's sales for the upcoming year. For example, suppose the forecast sales level for the upcoming year is $300,000 and the January sales index is 50. The forecast January sales is the estimated average monthly sales, or $300,000/12 = $25,000 × (50/100), or $12,500.

Even the best estimates must be revised to account for unanticipated developments such as abnormally severe weather, epidemics, and so forth. However, the seasonal index approach can make accurate sales forecasts by comparing against similar pay periods, holidays, etc. Of course, the occurrence of a holiday in a different week or month from year to year must be accounted for in making weekly or monthly forecasts. This adjustment in forecast sales may consist of simply adding and subtracting the normal value of that holiday occurring or not occurring during the specified period. For example, forecasts should reflect the fact that Easter occurs during one week one year and another week the following year. The presence of any other high sales generating period, such as five weekends in a month, should also be noted and sales adjusted to provide more accurate month-to-month sales comparisons.

Step 2: Planning Inventory Levels	Inventory levels should be planned to maintain the necessary depth and breadth in merchandise assortment that will meet expected customer needs. However, the investment in inventory should also be held low enough to allow a sufficiently high inventory turnover.

Several methods are frequently used to plan needed inventories. The **basic stock method** involves ordering sufficient stock to begin the month (or any other specified selling period) with an inventory that exceeds estimated monthly sales by some "basic stock amount." The basic stock amount is really a basic inventory level or safety stock below which the retailer would not like to fall (Exhibit 9.1).

The **percentage deviation (variation) method** involves ordering stocks so that the beginning monthly inventory fluctuates from the planned average stock by 50 percent of the sales fluctuations from the average monthly sales (Exhibit 9.2). This method is usually used when an outlet's inventory turns over at least six times per year. Experience has shown that in stores that obtain a high inventory turnover, the change in inventory should gener-

Exhibit 9.1   Planning Inventory Levels by the Basic Stock Method

In this method planned sales for each month are added to a basic stock to obtain the stock on the first of each month. Thus, basic stock equals average stock for the season — average monthly sales for the season.

A. Calculation formula:
Retail stock at the first of a month=Estimated sales for the month+(Average stock for the season−Average monthly sales for the season).

B. Example Data:
Estimated sales for May= $35,000, average monthly stock for April, May and June= $40,000, and average monthly sales for the April, May and June quarter is $30,000.

Calculation: Stock needed on May 1= $35,000+($40,000− $30,000) or $45,000. In this example the basic stock is $40,000− $30,000 or $10,000.

ally be one-half of the planned increase or decrease in sales as provided by the method.

In fact, inventory turnover can establish the average stock level for any specified time period. For example, in Exhibit 9.1 the average monthly stock for April, May, and June is $40,000, which is equal to

$$\frac{\text{Sales for the season}}{\text{Estimated number of inventory turns}}.$$

Quarterly sales are $30,000 × 3 months = $90,000 and the store is estimated to obtain an annual inventory turnover of 9, or a

Exhibit 9.2   Planning Inventory Levels by the Percentage Deviation Method

In this method the stock is increased or decreased from the average stock desired by one-half the percentage variation in sales from average monthly sales.

A. Calculation Formula: Retail stock at the first of the month =

$$\text{Average stock} \times \tfrac{1}{2}\left(1 + \frac{\text{Sales for month}}{\text{Average monthly sales}}\right)$$

B. Example: Average monthly stock for year = 40,000, Estimated May sales of $35,000 and Average monthly sales for the year = 45,000

Calculation: stock needed on May 1 = $40,000 \times \tfrac{1}{2}\left(1 + \dfrac{\$35,000}{\$45,000}\right)$

$$= \$35,555$$

quarterly turnover of 9/4, or 2.25. Thus, the $40,000 average monthly stock was obtained by dividing $90,000 quarterly sales volume by the 2.25 quarterly stock turn.

Another technique, the **weeks' supply method,** consists of inventory being planned on the basis of a predetermined number of weeks' supply with some stock turnover as a goal (Exhibit 9.3).

This method is used when sales and stocks are planned on a weekly basis instead of monthly, as is the case with the other inventory planning methods. This method is administered in planning stocks for staple merchandise, not fashion, fad, or general departmental inventories where sales may fluctuate widely. The reason the method is not usually applied with nonstaple merchandise is that stock levels may become much too high when sales are considerably above average. This is caused by a rapid rise in planned stocks which rise in proportion to expected increases in sales. Stocks also can become much too low when sales are considerably below average because there is no provision for a minimum basic stock when sales are low.

The **stock to sales ratio method** also assists decision making on inventory levels. Generally the stock to sales ratio is used to plan monthly stock levels for highly seasonal merchandise. It can, however, also be successfully applied to staple stock merchandise (Exhibit 9.4). This method involves multiplying the es-

Exhibit 9.3   Planning Inventory Levels by the Weeks' Supply Method

Based on planned turnover, the number of weeks' supply to be carried is determined and sales estimated for this number of weeks ahead.

A. Calculation Formula: Retail stock at first of the month = predetermined number of weeks' supply based on desired stockturn.

B. Example: Desired annual stockturn = 10, Estimated sales for next 4 weeks = $35,000, Estimated sales for next 8 weeks = $65,000 and Estimated sales for next 12 weeks = $90,000. Stock needed on May 1 = 52 (number of weeks in a year)/10 (Desired annual stockturn) = 5.2 weeks.

$$\text{Stock needed on May 1} = \text{Sales estimate (Average weekly sales}^a \times 5.2) \text{ for 5.2 weeks}$$

$$= \frac{\$35,000 + \$30,000/4}{5} \times 5.2$$

$$= \frac{\$42,500}{5} \times 5.2$$

$$= \$8,500 \times 5.2$$

$$= \$44,200$$

[a] Average weekly sales for the period is obtained by using the $35,000 for the first four weeks plus an average week taken from the second four weeks ($65,000–$35,000)/4.

Exhibit 9.4   Planning Inventory Levels by the Stock to Sales Ratio Method

This method yields a planned ratio between the stock on hand on the first of any given month and the sales for that month.[a] This ratio is multiplied by the planned sales for that month.
A. Calculation Formula: Retail stock at first of the month = Estimated sales for the period × Desired beginning of the month stock : sales ratio.
B. Example of Desired monthly stock : sales ratio = 2.0 and Estimated sales for May = $35,000.

Calculations: Stock needed on May 1 = $35,000 × 2.0 = $70,000.

[a] The monthly stock : sales ratio =
$$\frac{\$ \text{ Value of Inventory on Hand at Beginning of Month}}{\$ \text{ Sales Expected for That Month}}$$

timated sales volume for the month by the planned beginning-of-the-month stock-sales ratio to obtain the amount of inventory to be carried at the beginning of the month. In formula form,

Estimated sales for the period
× desired beginning-of-the-month stock-sales-ratio
= retail stock to be carried at the beginning of the month.

Retailers can analyze their past stock-sales ratios or use the stock-sales ratios of similar retailers to determine the desired stock-sales ratio. Stock-sales ratios are available from several trade publications, such as *Departmental Merchandising and Operating Results of Department and Specialty Stores*, published by the National Retail Merchants' Association in New York.

Stock-sales ratios need to be computed on a monthly basis when turnover varies considerably throughout the year. Each of the four methods provides a different solution to the inventory problem. The stock level indicated by the basic stock method is usually larger than the inventory level given by the stock-sales ratio method. Each method has the major disadvantage of not considering such serious factors as net margin contribution, perishability, fashion influences or style obsolescence, lead time needed before a new order can be received, and the effect that an out-of-stock condition can have upon regular consumers' store preference patterns.

Model stock represents a quantity of basic merchandise that should be stocked to satisfy normal customer demand for the item. In addition, the inventory level should be based on the lead time it takes to receive the merchandise from the vendor. Thus, if a store usually sells 100 units a month of an item and the vendor normally requires three weeks to replenish the item, a total of 100 units expected sales plus 100 × 0.75 or 175 units would be needed in order to maintain a cushion consisting of a month's supply.

The job of writing an order is simplified when a model stock is incorporated into the inventory sheet. In this case the model stock represents the order up to quantity. For example, if the model stock of an item is 100 units and 70 units were calculated as having been sold, then a reorder is placed for 30 units.

Never-out basic items are those items which management believes must always be in stock (e.g., all common sizes of underwear). Never-out items require more followup and usually require a larger investment in inventory in order to assure an in-stock condition.

Determining Inventory Levels on Perishable and Fad Items A relatively simple method, termed **marginal analysis,** can determine the quantity of goods that should be stocked. This method is appropriate for goods that are either perishable (such as Christmas gift boxes of fresh fruits) or that are likely to become obsolete because of time (such as newspapers, magazines, or fad items). It can be used to examine the retail price, wholesale cost, and reduced price that can be obtained for perishable or out-of-date goods if they cannot be sold before they lose quality or become obsolete.[1] The marginal analysis method gives the retailer the minimum percentage chance of selling the *additional* unit added to inventory before that unit can be profitably stocked.

Marginal analysis involves the calculation of p, which represents the minimum percent chance of selling at least an additional unit in order to justify the stocking of that unit. The value of p is found by using the formula

$$p = \frac{ML}{(MP + ML)} \times 100$$

where ML is the marginal loss or the decrease in profit resulting from stocking an additional unit that is *not* sold at the retail price, and MP is the marginal profit or the increase in profit resulting from stocking an additional unit that *is* sold.

Marginal analysis can be illustrated in the following example. Suppose an item is purchased at wholesale for $4 per unit and is resold at retail for $10 per unit. If the product cannot be sold to a retail customer within a stated period of time, it can be sold to an industrial user for $1 per unit. The per unit profit obtained by stocking and selling the item is the marginal profit (MP), which is the retail price ($10) minus the wholesale cost ($4), or $6. The marginal loss (ML) is the per unit wholesale cost ($4) minus the reduced per unit price that the product can be sold for in the secondary market ($1), or $3. The calculation of p is [3/(6 + 3)]

100, or 33 percent. Thus, a retailer would have to be at least 33 percent certain that the additional unit of stock can be sold before it will be profitable to purchase that additional unit. Previous sales records could be checked to determine at what stock quantity one is 33 percent sure of selling the last unit stocked.

For example, suppose the previous sales records follow the pattern in Table 9.1. The retailer would stock 16 units in this situation because there is a 39 percent chance of selling at least 16 units. It will not pay to stock the 17th unit because the percent chance of selling 17 or more units is 23 percent, which is less than the calculated 33 percent.

It is important to note that the retailer expects to sell about 15 units (the average weekly sale) but is stocking 16 units. More units than can be justifiably stocked are expected to sell because the per unit marginal profit ($6) exceeds the per unit marginal loss ($3). The retailer can afford to take more risk whenever marginal profit is greater than marginal loss. This is the case for items that carry a high markup on cost. The reverse also holds: if marginal profit is less than marginal loss, the retailer will want to stock less than he expects to sell if consumers do not become so dissatisfied with the outlet that they discontinue shopping in

Table 9.1   Illustration of the Marginal Analysis Approach to Determine Optimal Retail Inventory

Level of Past Weekly Sales in Units	Number of Weeks When Sales Level Occurred[a]	% Chance of Sales Level Occurring[b]	Cumulative % Chance That Sales Will Be at This Level or Greater
10 or less	0	0	100
11	6	3	100
12	18	9	97
13	26	13	88
14	34	17	75
15	38	19	58
16	32	16	39
17	26	13	23
18	14	7	10
19	6	3	3
20 or more	0	0	0
Total	200	100	

Average weekly sales = 14.93
Median weekly sales = 15

[a] Weekly sales level may have to be analyzed as "adjusted weekly sales level," where a seasonality adjustment is used to increase the forecast accuracy for products whose demand fluctuates on a seasonal basis.
[b] Percent chance of sales level occurring is obtained by dividing total sales (200) into the frequency (6 for the 11-unit level) and multiplying the result by 100.

that store. If the marginal profit and marginal loss are equal, the retailer outlet would stock exactly what it expects to sell (the average sales) because the calculated p value is equal to 50 percent.

The marginal analysis approach can be incorporated into computer programs, which can rapidly indicate the proper inventory level for any item, provided its average sales and the variation in average sales are known.[2] This marginal approach is limited by the assumption that a customer will not become dissatisfied enough to refuse to trade with the retailer after that consumer finds an out-of-stock condition on a product he had intended to buy. This assumption is not too unrealistic in situations where close substitute items are available from the same store or where high buyer loyalty to the store has been developed.

Determining Inventory Levels on Staple Items Large retail outlets will reorder thousands of staple items regularly, so it is essential to develop a systematic method of reordering merchandise. Several kinds of data are needed to determine the appropriate stock level on staple items whose demand is not subject to wide fluctuations in preferences. The data needed are:

1. S = the level of sales expected before the next order can be received
2. DP = the delivery period, which is the amount of time estimated to elapse between the time an order is placed and the time the merchandise is delivered and prepared for sale by the retailer
3. R = the reserve or safety stock needed to take care of deviations from expected sales
4. I = the level of stock currently on hand
5. O = the amount of merchandise currently on order but not yet received
6. The store's policy with regard to inventory review and reorder periods (where "review period" refers to the frequency with which inventories are checked to determine stock levels and "reorder period" (RP) is the time interval that normally elapses between orders).

Retailers need to order enough stock to meet the expected purchases during the combined delivery (DP) and reorder periods (RP) plus an additional "safety stock" (R) which is carried to prevent an out-of-stock condition if actual sales should exceed expected sales. The safety stock level, R, may be determined by observing the past sales fluctuations. A prespecified level of confidence can be used to correspond to the desired inventory condition. If a merchant desires to create an image of not being out of stock on staple items, he can set a goal for a safety stock that is intended to accomplish this result nearly all (say 97 percent) of the time can be set.

If sales of a staple item were distributed as indicated in Table 9.1, this would mean that a safety stock of 4 units (19 minus 15, which is the average) would be needed. If 90 percent protection is considered adequate, the safety stock would be 3 (18 minus average sales of 15 units), assuming immediate delivery can be obtained.

The order level on a staple item (following the sales distribution given in Table 9.1) for a firm which every two weeks reorders an item that requires three weeks for delivery and preparation for retail sale could be determined by a similar analysis of the distribution of sales over a five-week period of time—three weeks for the normal delivery period (DP) and two weeks for the reorder period (RP). The usual minimum stock level would be the number of weeks (three) required for delivery and preparation times the average weekly sales, plus the desired safety stock. This is the point at which another order should be placed to prevent an out-of-stock condition before the newly ordered merchandise arrives.

The maximum amount of stock (M) that a store should have on hand in inventory and on order at any point in time is:

Maximum (M) = [Reorder Period (RP)
+ Delivery Period (DP)] Rate of Sales (S) + Reserve Stock (R)

Suppose that an item is selling at the rate of seventy-five units per week, a thirty-unit reserve stock is desired, the delivery period is three weeks, and the reorder period is two weeks. In this case the combined maximum number of units that the store should have on hand and on order is:

$$
\begin{aligned}
M &= (RP + DP)\,S + R \\
&= (2 + 3)\,75 + 30 \\
&= (5)\,75 + 30 \\
&= 375 + 30 \\
&= 405
\end{aligned}
$$

Frequently, past sales information is not available on an item. Guidelines can reveal the safety stock needed for these items and for items whose past sales have changed enough to make analysis of past sales records unreliable. Table 9.2 contains safety stock formulas that provide varying degrees of protection from running out of stock if average sales levels can be forecast with reasonable accuracy. Data in Table 9.2 indicate a general stocking rule that the level of safety stock relative to sales needed is

Table 9.2   Safety Stock Levels Needed to Obtain Varying Degrees of Protection against Running Out of Stock

Approximate Safety Stock Level Needed to Obtain Stated Degree of Protection against Running Out of Stock If Expected Delivery and Reorder Period Sales Are		Retail Stock Policy: Approximate % Chance of Not Running Out of Stock	Safety Stock Level Needed to Obtain Stated Degree of Protection against Running Out of Stock
25	400		
12	46	99	$2.3\sqrt{\text{Forecast Sales Level for Delivery and Reorder Periods}}$
8	32	95	$1.6\sqrt{\text{Forecast Sales Level for Delivery and Reorder Periods}}$
5	20	80	$\sqrt{\text{Forecast Sales Level for Delivery and Reorder Periods}}$

Note: This table is applicable to situations where average sales can be forecast with reasonable accuracy. In such cases, the Poisson probability distribution appears to describe variations in retail sales appropriately. See John W. Wingate, Elmer O. Schaller, and F. L. Miller, *Retail Merchandise Management* (Englewood Cliffs, N.J.: Prentice-Hall, 1972), pp. 342–343.

usually lower on fast-moving merchandise than is the required safety stock on slow-moving items.

For example, the safety stock level of 12, when expected sales are 25, represents a safety stock of nearly 50 percent of expected sales to reach the 99 percent level of protection from running out of stock. When expected sales are 400, the safety stock required to provide 99 percent protection is 46 units, which is only 11.5 percent of the 400 units forecast to be sold.

Data presented in Table 9.2 can also determine the level of the reserve stock = $ required to maintain a specified percentage protection against running out of stock. For example, data in Table 9.2 indicate that the retailer could use a retail stocking policy of being about 99 percent sure of not running out of stock on a staple item by calculating the value for R in the following formula:

$$R = 2.3\sqrt{(RP + DP)\, S}$$

Thus, if the weekly sales are estimated to be 75 units, the reorder period is two weeks and the delivery period is three weeks:

$$R = 2.3\sqrt{(2 + 3)\, 75}$$
$$= 2.3\sqrt{(5)\,(75)}$$
$$= 2.3\sqrt{375}$$
$$= 2.3\,(19.4)$$
$$= 44.6 \text{ or } 47 \text{ units}$$

The same retailer could be about 95 percent sure of not running out of stock by calculating the value of R in the following formula:

$$R = 1.6\sqrt{(RP + DP)\,S}$$
$$= 1.6\sqrt{(2 + 3)\,75}$$
$$= 1.6\,(19.4)$$
$$= 31 \text{ units}$$

Or finally the retailer could be about 80 percent sure of not running out of stock by finding the value of R in:

$$R = \sqrt{(RP + DP)\,S}$$
$$= \sqrt{(2 + 3)\,75}$$
$$= 19.4 \text{ units}$$

These calculations illustrate a general rule in regard to establishing the reserve stock level on staple items; namely, if the retail policy is designed to be out of stock only one percent of the time, the required reserve stock will be 2.3 times the level of the reserve stock needed to be 80 percent sure that the item will be in stock.

Determining Inventory Levels on Fashion Items Fashion items such as apparel and home furnishings present the most complex and critical inventory problems because they are usually offered in many different styles, colors, sizes, materials, and so forth. The major characteristics of fashion goods are:

1. Short product life span
2. Relatively unpredictable sales level
3. Broad assortments needed to create favorable store image
4. Extreme amount of consumer emphasis on style and color
5. Consumer purchases made on impulse basis or on subjective evaluation of the item and its close substitutes.

Additional safety stock must be carried on fashion items, not only because of their wide fluctuations in sales but also because of a need to provide a broader merchandise assortment for fashion customers. The formulas in Table 9.2 can be used to determine the safety stock needed for fashion goods, but another reserve amount, called the "basic assortment reserve," must also be carried. The amount of the basic assortment reserve is based upon the buyer's judgment of the level needed to provide the basic merchandise assortment demanded by consumers. Thus, the total reserve stock of fashion goods will be larger than the safety stock level required of staple items.

There is some degree of predictability that can be used to estimate sales of fashion items. Because each retail outlet caters to a certain target market, the average-price merchandise sold within a merchandise line is not likely to change drastically over a short period of time. Thus, an apparel merchandiser's total sales on all different price lines can be predicted with considerable accuracy. Distribution of sales by size is also fairly constant from year to year, as the distribution of human body sizes and shapes does not change suddenly for the population as a whole.

Seasonal patterns also exist in fashion merchandise, so monthly sales indexes can be used to forecast the sales distribution by color and type of material. For example, black- and white-colored clothing sells better during the summer months, pastel and light-background prints sell better in the spring, and green and rust are preferred in the fall.

Step 3: Planning
Retail Reductions

Retail reductions can occur because of (1) markdowns and (2) stock shortages. Markdowns are price reductions that are used to stimulate sales of overstocked items and discounts that are given to employees or other specific customer groups, such as cash customers. Stock shortages are caused by pilferage, shoplifting, damaged merchandise, and the like.

Both markdowns and shortages are inevitable in retail outlets despite the efforts made to prevent them. Thus, these items must be included in the merchandise budget. Markdowns reduce the value of retail inventory because the retail price is lowered on the same number of physical units. Shortages reduce both the value of the retail inventory and the number of physical units as well, because some portion of the physical stock is no longer available for sale.

Every effort should be made to minimize the value lost by markdowns and shortages. The discussions of markdowns in Chapter 12 indicate that good sales forecasting will reduce the volume of marked down items. (The effect that good management and control practices can have on reducing shortages will be discussed in Chapter 11.) However, markdowns and shortages will occur in spite of even the most rigorous control methods. Therefore retailers should use their past experience, or that of similar stores, to provide an estimate of the value of the inventory loss. Reductions are usually estimated on a percentage-of-sales-dollar volume basis and entered as part of the store's merchandising budget.

Step 4: Planning
Purchases

The quantity to purchase is easily obtained if (1) sales have been forecast, (2) desirable inventory levels have been determined, and (3) retail reductions have been planned. If these data are available, the following formula can be applied to an entire store, department, or merchandise line:

Planned purchase quantity = desired inventory at end of period
+ estimated sales + estimated reductions
− inventory available at beginning of period

The dollar amount of allowable purchases that the buyer can make during the remaining portion of the period under a merchandise budget system that establishes maximum inventory levels and planned purchasing figures is called the **open-to-buy amount.** Thus, the open-to-buy device assists the buyer in determining how much merchandise he is able to buy during the remainder of any merchandising period and still remain within the guidelines established in the merchandise budget.

Open-to-buy amounts are usually stated in retail-price dollars. The open-to-buy concept can be illustrated by an example of a buyer who is making purchases for the month of September. Suppose that the merchandise budget calls for a planned inventory of $20,000 on September 30, estimated September sales are $40,000, the beginning inventory on September 1 was $22,000, the planned markdowns and shortages are estimated at 10 percent of retail sales dollar volume, or $4,000, and the planned initial markup on cost is 30 percent. Also assume that during the first ten days of September net sales amount to $18,000, markdowns or shortages amount to $2,000, $12,000 worth of retail goods (valued at retail prices) are delivered, and goods already ordered during September are valued at $12,000. The open-to-buy amount may be calculated as illustrated in Table 9.3, which indicates that the buyer can still purchase goods costing $12,600 at wholesale prices during the remainder of September and remain within the merchandise budget.

The open-to-buy figure should not be a set quantity that cannot be exceeded. Consumer needs are the dominant consideration. If sales of a product line, department, or store exceed the forecast, additional quantities should be ordered above those scheduled for purchase according to the merchandise budget. Thus, a buyer must have permission of the management to make occasional additional purchases of fast-moving goods whose demand has been underestimated. However, additional purchases of the same goods should not have to be made on a frequent basis. If this is the case, either the forecasting procedure is too conservative or the buyer is overbuying other goods that are not selling as well. Retail management should determine the causes of frequently overbought conditions and then take steps to prevent their recurrence.

Table 9.3   Illustration of Open-to-Buy Amount

Inventory Requirements		Available Inventory	
a. Desired inventory level, September 30	$20,000	e. Actual inventory, September 1	$22,000
b. Estimated sales for remainder of September ($40,000–$18,000)	22,000	f. Value of goods received during September 1–10	12,000
c. Planned markdowns and shortages for remainder of September ($4,000–$2,000)	2,000	g. Total inventory handled (e + f)	34,000
		Less deductions such as	
		h. Markdowns and shortages during September 1–10	2,000
d. Total Inventory Requirement (a + b + c)	$44,000	i. Sales during September 1–10	18,000
		j. Total Deductions (h + i)	20,000
		Plus	
		k. Value of inventory already ordered for September delivery	12,000
		Equals	
		l. Total Available Inventory (g + k − j)	$26,000

Total Inventory Requirement (item d or $44,000) minus Total Available Inventory (item l or $26,000) equals Open-to-Buy ($18,000) at Retail Prices. Open-to-Buy at Cost equals Open-to-Buy at Retail times [(100—markup percent)/100] or $18,000 [(100–30)/100] equals $12,600.

Note: All inventory, reductions, and sales are valued at retail prices.

The timing of merchandise arrivals needs critical attention. Ideally merchandise should be purchased to arrive in the store just before it is sold. If a big buildup of merchandise occurs too far ahead of the sales peak, then merchandise will not be fresh at and following its peak of popularity, even if the overall stock levels are about where they should be. The importance of good timing cannot be overemphasized. It is illustrated by the following letter received by an owner of a small maternity shop.

> Dear Sir:
>   Please cancel my order for the blue maternity dress. I delivered before your supplier could deliver the dress to you.
>   Sincerely,
>   Jane A. Customer

This is not an isolated instance. Customers usually will shop the competition if they cannot find the item they are looking for. Other negative effects caused by poor timing of merchandise arrivals are:

Merchandise received too early is perceived as old by customers before it becomes saleable.

Retailer has to pay bills for goods before they have a chance to sell.

Money is tied up in inventory not yet in season, resulting in either high interest costs or other store needs not met.

Employee morale may decline if items sell slowly because they arrive too early.

Selling space is poorly used if prime floor area is filled with merchandise that arrived too early.

When merchandise arrives too late in the season the limited selling time results in excess end-of-the-season merchandise which must be marked down or stored, resulting in an excessive investment in inventory.

Step 5: Planning
Profit Margins

The **initial markup percentage** (the percentage of the retail price that is not spent for merchandise) should be adequate to cover expenses, reductions,[3] and profits. It is usually planned on all the merchandise carried because detailed data on expenses and reductions are not available for each item.

The necessary markup percentage may be calculated by first forecasting the total sales for the store for the desired time period. Then expenses and price reductions needed to reach the sales goal can be estimated. And then a realistic profit goal can be established. These three components—expenses, reductions, and profits—are then added together and that sum is divided by the sum of sales plus reductions to give the required initial markup percentage needed to achieve the desired profit goals. The calculation for initial markup percentage is:

$$\text{Required initial markup percent} = \frac{(\text{expenses} + \text{profits} + \text{reductions})}{(\text{sales} + \text{reductions})}$$

For example, suppose planned sales are $500,000 annually, with estimated operating expenses of $100,000, reductions of $70,000, and a profit goal of $50,000. The initial markup percentage would be:

$$\text{Required initial markup percent} = \frac{(\$100,000 + \$50,000 + \$70,000)}{(\$500,000 + \$70,000)}$$

or 38.6 percent.

This same equation can also be used when expenses, reductions, and profits are planned in percentage terms instead of dollars. Sales simply become 100 percent in the equation in this case.

The remaining figures are expressed as percentages converted to decimals. In the previous example, expenses were estimated to be 20 percent of sales, the profit goal was 10 percent of sales, and reductions were estimated to amount to 14 percent of sales. Thus, the required initial markup percentage would be:

$$\frac{(0.20 + 0.10 + 0.14)}{(1.00 + 0.14)} = 38.6 \text{ percent}$$

This equation can determine what percentage markup a retailer must obtain on all purchases to cover expected expenses, reductions, and markdowns and still make the desired planned profit. It should be reemphasized that this calculation yields the overall, or average, markup on all merchandise. Markup used on each item or in each department will deviate from this average markup depending upon consumer demand, competition, and so forth. However, the formula is a useful guide that shows the average markup needed to generate the desired profit level.

The retail buyer should strive to attain the planned markup goals. Expense percentages have been rising during recent years, and unless sales can be substantially increased by using lower prices, a higher initial markup is required to achieve the target net profit. Thus, the basic merchandise budgeting problem consists of accurately forecasting a realistic initial markup percentage that will yield the desired net profit margin.

Use of the Merchandise Budget

Retail management can use the merchandise budget to determine how efficiently the retail operation is being conducted and to locate possible sources of trouble before they become too serious. For example, management can apply current and past merchandise budgets to see if the open-to-buy quantity is being frequently exceeded. If so, it can determine which departments have been guilty and identify who was responsible for the action. Merchandise budgets also allow management to check actual results against the planned figures. This will not only indicate which people are the most accurate planners, but it will also indicate which budgeted figures need to be revised. A form similar to the one presented in Exhibit 9.5 is frequently used to provide a summary of the data obtained by following the steps of the merchandise budget process.

The merchandise budget should be utilized as a management tool that improves the judgment of retail management who review it at frequent intervals. Although the merchandise budget is a useful tool, its benefits must be weighed against its costs to ensure that the time and effort expended are worthwhile expenditures. The budgeting process should remain sufficiently

Exhibit 9.5   Completed Six-Month Merchandise Budget

SIX-MONTH MERCHANDISE PLAN

STORE Downtown

DEPARTMENT Hardware

FROM January 1, 19___

TO June 30, 19___

		First Half / Last Half	Jan. / July	Feb. / Aug.	March / Sept.	April / Oct.	May / Nov.	June / Dec.	Total
Sales	Last Year		$42,315	$78,120	$65,100	$55,335	$52,080	$32,550	$325,500
	Plan		39,385	71,610	82,350	64,450	64,450	35,805	358,050
	Actual								
+ E.O.M. Retail	Last Year		186,620	173,600	163,835	160,580	141,050	162,750	
	Plan		155,155	165,895	147,995	147,995	119,350	143,220	
	Actual								
+ Reductions	Last Year		4,300	1,790	6,445	8,590	7,880	6,805	35,810
	Plan		5,728.80	1,718.64	4,296.60	7,161.00	7,447.44	2,291.52	28,644
	Actual								
− B.O.M. Retail	Last Year		150,815	186,620	173,600	163,835	160,580	141,050	
	Plan		122,930	155,155	165,895	147,995	160,580	119,350	
	Actual								
Purchases = Retail	Last Year		82,420	66,890	61,780	60,670	40,430	61,055	373,245
	Plan		77,338.80	84,068.64	68,746.60	71,611.00	43,252.44	61,966.52	406,984.00
	Actual								
Purchases Cost	Last Year		50,110	40,670	37,560	36,890	24,580	37,120	226,930
	Plan		43,696.42	47,498.78	38,841.83	40,460.22	24,437.62	35,011.08	229,945.95
	Actual								

Control Data

	Last Year	This Year
% Initial Markup	45.0	43.5
% Reductions	39.3	39.0
% Maintained Markup	1.5	1.0
% Alteration Expense	2.0	2.0
% Cash Discount	40.0	40.0
% Gross Margin	35.0	35.0
% Operating Expense	5.0	5.0
% Net Profit		
First Half Turnover	2.0	2.5

Planning and Authorization

Buyer _____

Merchandise Controller _____

Date Prepared _____

Date Authorized _____

flexible so that unique purchasing opportunities are not stifled and that changes in both the wholesale and retail marketplaces can be quickly identified and new estimates incorporated when preparing a revised budget.

Merchandise Planning and Control Systems

Merchandise planning and control techniques are related to both overall merchandise values (dollars) and to measurable quantities of goods or services (units). Unit controls are needed because the retail firm's buyer and the retail customer make their purchases in units. Dollar controls are needed because overall store sales, expenses, and financial reports are stated in dollars as well as in the quantity of physical units. Dollar control is the usual basis for establishing initial merchandise control systems.

However, the retail buyer must look beyond dollar figures to determine which sizes, colors, styles, and price lines are selling. This information is contained (both in dollar and unit terms) in the store's daily sales slips or records. In small stores, the sales data are likely to be recorded on sales slips or booklets. In large stores, cash registers are frequently linked to electronic computer systems which provide detailed information on inventories and sales for each item.

Sales and inventory information also is usually summarized and analyzed by classifying and categorizing the entire merchandise assortment into different subassortments, such as departments, merchandise lines, and so forth. Classification is needed in merchandise planning and control because it is easier to analyze smaller and similar types of products and services than the entire merchandise offering and then make inferences for the different merchandise lines. The split-total cash register, hooked up to a computer, is an efficient method of recording and analyzing data on large numbers of product categories. The categories may be defined by differences in color, price line, size, style, product content, and so forth, provided the appropriate key is pushed on the cash register.

The main point for the current discussion is that stores using such systems obtain their classification totals at the end of the day as a by-product of their normal sales-registering procedure. These totals can easily be posted manually to merchandise control records from the cash register tape, or the computer can automatically print out the desired control records.

Merchandise planning has traditionally been based on either a **top-down** or **bottom-up** approach. The top-down approach starts with a gross dollar value for departmentalized sales which the buyer allocates among the classifications. The bottom-up approach starts with an estimate of unit sales for each class of goods. The buyer then looks at price line history and translates unit sales into dollar sales for each classification. Total department sales are then obtained by summing all classifications.

An interactive approach which combines both top-down and bottom-up planning is being used more frequently. This involves top management examining economic trends, competitors' actions, and the firm's offerings to provide broad guidelines of dollar planning to the buying staff. The buying staff then reviews these guidelines by the bottom-up approach and the two get together to iron out any differences that may occur. Because both dollar and unit planning are so critical to successful merchandise management, it is essential to understand what is involved in each process.

Dollar Planning and Control

Retail buyers plan and control dollar inventory values because they need to keep the stocks of each department or merchandise category in line with its sales. Proper dollar planning and control procedures allow the buyer to minimize both stock shortages and the markdown pricing that is required if the inventory is too large relative to sales. The dollar control process also allows the buyer to identify easily those merchandise items or lines that have the largest inventory investment and those that have the highest dollar sales.

Dollar control is initially concerned with determining the value of the firm's inventory at any point in time. Without inventory valuation data, the buyer cannot plan or control any portion of the merchandise management process. Purchases, cost of goods sold, gross margins, and profit margins cannot be planned or determined until inventories are valued in dollar terms.

A periodic **physical inventory** count must be taken at least once a year to satisfy legal requirements. Counting of the actual physical inventory is a time-consuming process, so retailers use a technique called **perpetual inventory** to estimate inventory levels. Perpetual inventory results from recording the beginning inventory (counted at the start of the period), all purchases, and all sales in retail prices. The following formula is then used to estimate the retail value of the current inventory:

Retail value of current inventory = retail value of beginning inventory + retail value of purchases made during the period − retail value of sales made during the period.

The perpetual inventory method provides current useful information, particularly if it involves a computer-reported inventory system.

Reductions in inventory values resulting from pilferage, damaged merchandise, other forms of dishonesty, and price reductions do not appear on the perpetual inventory. Thus, despite the time required, retailers may decide to take a physical count more than once a year. Retailers of large items, such as automobiles, can afford to take physical counts quite frequently compared to retailers of many small items such as grocery stores that handle over 10,000 items at one time. Taking a physical inventory permits the buyer to determine the overage and shortage magnitudes by which the perpetual inventory deviates from the physical inventory.

Overage is the dollar amount by which the physical inventory value exceeds the perpetual inventory value. Such a discrepancy is usually caused by clerical error, such as overcharging customers on sale merchandise or marking merchandise higher than it is supposed to be marked. **Shortage** is the dollar amount by which the perpetual inventory value exceeds the physical inventory value. Such shortages can originate from both clerical error and retail reductions caused by markdowns and shrinkage.

The National Retail Merchants' Association has established electronic processing centers in New York and California to provide its member stores with a variety of reports for standard classification numbers. Stores send in their sales, purchase, inventory, and markdown data and receive dollar and unit information on merchandise sold, received, and held in inventory, as well as stock to sales ratios and gross margin percentages for each category. A report is sent to the participating stores on a monthly basis. The opening inventory figures in each category are reported semiannually or annually by the stores as they take a new physical inventory. The inventory for the intervening months represents estimated inventories calculated by the computer. Such a report can indicate merchandise categories in which inventories appear to be out of balance relative to sales. If the present percentage inventory distribution is much higher for a category than its percentage of sales distribution, the merchandise described in this category may be overstocked. Typical information contained in computerized retail inventory-management form can include:

Sales in dollars and units for a specified week this year, comparable week last year, and cumulative for this year to date, versus cumulative for last year to date.

Quarterly sales for this and last year and percentage change from last year.

Inventory levels for current week and comparable week last year, and last month.

Markdowns for current week, last three months, and similar periods last year.

Shipments en route from distribution center and vendors.

Gross margin on sales.

On the other hand, if the percentage of sales distribution for a product category greatly exceeds its present percentage of inventory distribution, the category would probably be understocked; so inventories could be built up in this product line. Of course, the gross margin and profitability ratios would also have to be considered to ensure that the retail outlet was not overstocking a low-margin category.

A comparison of the perpetual and physical methods of obtaining merchandise data by merchandise classification indicates that when a computer is available, the perpetual inventory method can function accurately and at a lower cost to provide a more current source of data than the physical method. When the computer equipment is not available, the periodic physical inventory method can be used profitably in merchandise planning.

Unit Planning and Control

Unit merchandise control is used to maintain ideal merchandise assortments by recording and reporting quantities in inventory, on order, and the rate of sale of individual items. Unit control procedures are needed if the buyer is going to be able to (1) identify the items that are selling best, (2) invest properly in inventories, (3) identify vendors whose merchandise is selling best, (4) identify price points around which sales appear to cluster, (5) identify colors, sizes and styles that sell well and should be reordered, and (6) use good buying procedures based upon the knowledge of what is needed and what has been selling. Merchandise controls are valuable aids to the decisionmaking process the buyer must use in developing purchasing strategy. Therefore unit control procedures should be designed to assist the buyer in his purchasing function.

Unit control involves the same general procedures as dollar control:

1. Implement some form of classification system.
2. Identify sources of all data required by the unit control system (e.g., sales, receipts, purchase orders, etc.).
3. Develop a flow of source data (and time schedule) to the person or department responsible for unit control.
4. Use either a perpetual or physical inventory system to provide unit inventory, order, and sales data.
5. Record all required data at defined regular intervals.

6. Summarize the data in a logical manner that lends itself to easy interpretation on a daily, weekly, or monthly basis.
7. Have buyers and merchandisers review and analyze these unit control reports.
8. Establish the ideal merchandise assortment to be carried and the unit levels of inventory needed to be stocked on each item.

Item inventory requirements are established only after considering such factors as the item's rate of sale, amount of time required to receive the item after it has been ordered, markup obtained on the item, effect an out-of-stock condition has on the retail customers, and so forth. Naturally, high inventory levels must be maintained on the faster-moving items if supplies are to satisfy consumer demand. Inventory levels will also be higher for items that require longer delivery periods, because a store manager does not want to be out of stock on an item for a long period of time. Higher inventory levels should also be established for high markup items because lost sales caused by such out-of-stock items decrease net profit considerably more than the same volume of lost sales on a low-margin item. A larger inventory level may be carried on unique items that the store stocks. If no close substitute products are sold by the store, other things being equal, management could justify a larger inventory on that item than on an item that is quite similar to several other items that are sold in the store.

Unit control systems are designed to minimize lost sales and consumer dissatisfaction caused by out-of-stock conditions and, at the same time, identify items or merchandise lines that are overstocked in relation to their consumer demand. In addition to periodic physical inventory counts and perpetual inventory methods, retail managers are also using unit control devices such as checklist systems, warehouse control systems, and requisition stock control.

Cash register systems hooked to electronic computers implement unit control procedures as well as cash control techniques. As the adoption of these types of systems spreads, the cost of implementing and using item control procedures will decrease. As a result, store managers will probably acquire even more unit control techniques as the basis for sounder merchandise management planning.

"A few leading firms in each retailing sector already have advanced information systems built around data capture at point-of-sale and point-of-receipt which demonstrate the practicality of such systems:

Food Stores Giant Foods has completely converted its stores to front-end scanning, significant commitments to automation through point-of-sale also have been made by Winn-Dixie, Ralphs, and Lucky Stores among others.

Home Improvement Centers Lowe's has completely converted to CRT point-of-sale terminals driven by in-store minicomputers. Busy Beavers uses optical character recognition (OCR) wanding to capture item movement.

Catalogue Showrooms Modern Merchandising's on-line point-of-sale terminals are driven by in-store minicomputers. This system is used to record detailed item information and produce picking tickets for the backroom warehouse. Store replenishment is based upon polling the in-store mini-computer by the corporate host computer. Other firms have made significant commitments including Consumers Distributing and Service Merchandising.

Specialty Stores Several companies have very compre-hensive installations. The limited stores use clamshell readers to capture item sales at point-of-sale, and a host computer polls each store so that central merchandising decisions can be made. B. Dalton Booksellers tracks the sale of 30,000 titles by store and communicates this information to a central buying staff which can react quickly to sales and inventory trends.

Discount Department Stores Target Stores appears to be the leader, but many other companies have made a serious commitment including K mart.

Conventional Department Stores Most federated divisions are using point-of-sale capture. Dayton Hudson has a major thrust under way. Wieboldt's has a well-developed, purchase order management system.

National General Merchandise Chains Both Sears and J. C. Penney are moving strongly toward complete credit and merchandise capture at point-of-sale."[4]

The **Universal Product Code (UPC)** was developed in 1973 to reduce operating expenses in supermarkets. This process uses a laser checkout scanner that contains a light source to illuminate and automatically identify each premarked item as it passes through the checkout facility. The UPC symbol is a unique twelve-digit item identification number that is marked both in decimal characters and in a bar coded form that is read by the laser scanner (Exhibit 9.6).

There were about 4000 supermarkets using the UPC system in 1981. These stores maintained instantaneous inventory records

Exhibit 9.6   UPC Product Code Symbol and Checkout Sales Receipt

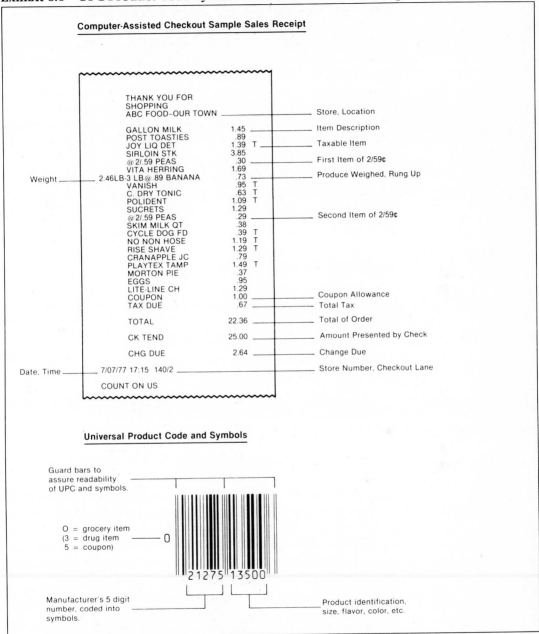

Computer-Assisted Checkout Sample Sales Receipt

THANK YOU FOR		
SHOPPING		
ABC FOOD–OUR TOWN		Store, Location
GALLON MILK	1.45	Item Description
POST TOASTIES	.89	
JOY LIQ DET	1.39 T	Taxable Item
SIRLOIN STK	3.85	
@ 2/.59 PEAS	.30	First Item of 2/59¢
VITA HERRING	1.69	
Weight — 2.46LB-3 LB @ .89 BANANA	.73	Produce Weighed, Rung Up
VANISH	.95 T	
C. DRY TONIC	.63 T	
POLIDENT	1.09 T	
SUCRETS	1.29	
@ 2/.59 PEAS	.29	Second Item of 2/59¢
SKIM MILK QT	.38	
CYCLE DOG FD	.39 T	
NO NON HOSE	1.19 T	
RISE SHAVE	1.29 T	
CRANAPPLE JC	.79	
PLAYTEX TAMP	1.49 T	
MORTON PIE	.37	
EGGS	.95	
LITE-LINE CH	1.29	
COUPON	1.00	Coupon Allowance
TAX DUE	.67	Total Tax
TOTAL	22.36	Total of Order
CK TEND	25.00	Amount Presented by Check
CHG DUE	2.64	Change Due
Date. Time — 7/07/77 17:15 140/2		Store Number, Checkout Lane
COUNT ON US		

Universal Product Code and Symbols

Guard bars to assure readability of UPC and symbols.

O = grocery item
(3 = drug item
5 = coupon)   — 0

21275 13500

Manufacturer's 5 digit number, coded into symbols.

Product identification, size, flavor, color, etc.

Source: Reproduced by permission from "Grey Matter," Grey Advertising, Inc.

because the system keeps track of each item's sales as well as its inventory level. This item movement data can be used by management to implement optimal inventory policies and produce better shelf allocation procedures that reduce stockouts, level of inventory required, and ordering costs. The value of benefits can be substantial. For example, Mr. Joseph B. Danzansky, President of Giant Food Inc., in testimony before the Maryland Senate, indicated that their average store, which has sales of about $140,000 per week, could save about $2,745 per month by using the UPC system. The savings could be attained in six areas:

Front-end productivity is an evaluation of the computer-assisted checkout's impact on the dollar savings that could result from more quickly processing our customers through the checkout operation.

Price marking is an evaluation of the labor dollars that could be saved if Giant was no longer required to maintain prices on the items stocked in the store.

Routine reordering is an estimate of the dollar savings if store personnel no longer have to manually reorder stock items.

Register balancing includes all of the cashier functions that can be automated by computer-assisted checkouts. These have been translated into man-hour dollar savings.

Under-rings refer to those errors caused by the checker or by mismarking which are in favor of the customer.

Register replacement is the cost avoidance of having to buy conventional registers.

The most significant savings is in front-end labor which accounts for 42 percent of the savings. Elimination of price marking accounts for 23 percent of the savings and register balance for 15 percent. Routine reordering accounts for 9 percent, under-rings for 8 percent and register replacement for 3 percent.[5]

The practice of marking all prices on the shelf but not marking the price on each individual merchandise item has been criticized by consumer groups. As a result, most of the super-markets using the UPC system are still maintaining the price marking on each individual item even though the laser-computer system does not use this price mark. Some supermarkets do not want to give up the significant savings that can be obtained by eliminating the price marks on all individual items. Thus, consumer acceptance appears to be an important factor in on how the UPC system will be adopted and used. Steinbergs, a grocery chain in Montreal, has come up with a method of reducing consumer resistance to the lack of marking on each item. After three months of operating its IBM system with UPC symbols, the chain was able to eliminate price marking without encountering any resistance from customers. It offered grease pencils, which shoppers could use to do their own price marking. No one took the chain up on the offer. The chain also used suggestions from independent consumer panels. For example, it indicated on the printed sales slip which items were sold at special sales prices.

Thus, by considering consumers as well as advances in technology, outlets can successfully implement more complex retail information systems.

Many stores do not use computer systems to assist their management in making merchandise decisions. In some cases both machine and training costs are too high to justify the implementation of a computer system.

A good noncomputer technique that can be used to implement unit control procedures involves perforated price tickets. Under this system, the salesperson tears off part of the ticket when the item is sold and deposits the torn-off section in a container. At the end of the day these torn-off portions are sorted and totaled by classification on either a manual basis or by the use of a tag reader system that reads the tickets automatically, tabulates the data, and prepares a printed daily, weekly, and monthly summary report.

The more mechanical assistance provided by the system, the higher the initial cost of establishing the system. This higher installation cost must result in reduced manual operating costs or improved accuracy if the more mechanical systems are going to be a profitable investment. Large retail chains can usually spread the setup costs of a sophisticated electronic system over enough stores and/or sales volume to justify the installation. Smaller independent outlets may be able to lease computer time, equipment, and so forth to reduce the cost and still justify the use of electronic systems.

Stock Turnover Considerations

Successful merchandise management involves the maintenance of adequate profit markups combined with an acceptable level of **stock turnover** (the number of times during the year that the average amount of inventory is sold). The rate of stock turnover may be calculated for any period of time, but it is usually computed on an annual basis. Good buying practices are reflected by high turnover rates, which indicate that the consumers are buying the merchandise purchased by the retail buyer. Relatively low stock turnover rates indicate that consumers' preferences do not correspond with the purchases made by the store buyer or that other elements of the retail marketing program are failing. A high stock turnover rate has other advantages such as reducing price markdowns to move stale or shopworn merchandise. Also, the return on investment capital is likely to rise in high turnover stores because fixed costs are spread over a high sales volume. Advantages of rapid stock turnover are that:

It usually results in an increase return on investment.

It usually results in fewer markdowns.

It reduces reordering costs.

It usually results in lower inventory costs because quantity purchase discounts can be obtained.

It usually results in lower transportation costs because bulk shipments can be used.

It usually results in a reduced per unit sold cost on the fixed costs such as space, utilities, insurance, property tax, etc.

Measuring Stock Turnover

There are three commonly used ways for calculating stock turnover:

1. On the basis of dollars in retail prices
2. On the basis of dollars valued at cost to the retailer
3. On the basis of units

These calculation methods can be illustrated by the example of a grocer who begins the year with 30 cases of brand X canned peaches which are sold for $10 per case and bought for $8 per case. If we assume no stolen or damaged merchandise and that no price reductions were necessary, the net sales of brand X peaches for the first half of the year consist of 600 cases, or $6,000. The grocer paid $4,800 for the 600 cases purchased during the first half of the year and $5,400 for the 600 cases purchased during the last half of the year. At the end of the year the grocer had seventy cases on hand, but the per case wholesale cost had just been increased to $9 at midyear, and the grocer had raised the retail price to $11 per case on July 1. The firm sold 560 cases @ $11 during the last half of the year.

The annual stock turnover rate calculated by the three different techniques is:

1. **On the basis of dollars valued at retail prices:**

   Opening inventory \$ value at retail (30 cases @ \$10) = \$ 300
   Closing inventory \$ value at retail (70 cases @ \$11) = \$ 770
   Average inventory \$ value at retail (300 + 770)/2 = \$ 535
   Net sales in retail dollars = \$12,160
   Annual stock turnover rate

   $$= \frac{\text{Net sales in retail dollars}}{\text{Average inventory at retail}} = \frac{\$12,160}{\$535} = 22.7$$

2. **On the basis of dollars valued at cost:**

   Opening inventory \$ value at cost (30 cases @ \$8) = \$ 240
   Closing inventory \$ value at cost (70 cases @ \$9) = \$ 630
   Average inventory \$ value at cost (\$240 + \$630)/2 = \$ 435
   Cost of goods sold (630 cases @ \$8; 530 cases @ \$9) = \$9,810
   Annual stock turnover rate

   $$= \frac{\text{Cost of goods sold}}{\text{Average inventory at cost}} = \frac{\$9,810}{\$435} = 22.6$$

3. **On the basis of units:**

   Opening inventory in units = 30
   Closing inventory in units = 70
   Average inventory in units = (30 + 70)/2 = 50
   Annual net unit sales = 560

   $$\text{Annual stock turnover rate} = \frac{\text{Annual unit sales}}{\text{Average unit inventory}}$$
   $$= \frac{1160}{50} = 23.2$$

Capital turnover is a ratio that is used to measure the number of times the cost of the average inventory investment is converted into sales.[6] Its value is calculated as follows:

Capital turnover
$$= \frac{\text{Dollar sales at retail prices during a specified period}}{\text{Average inventory dollar value at cost}}$$

Analysis of previous turnover ratios generated by a firm and comparison of these ratios with those of similar retail outlets provide a good basis for planning the inventory needed to meet consumer needs and still reduce inventory to a sufficiently low level that will generate a good profit. The stock turnover ratios should be interpreted with considerable caution. Management should be certain that both the sales and the average stock figures used in the stock turnover ratio calculation cover the same operating period and that both are quoted in the same dollar terms—either in retail price or cost of merchandise.

Another factor that can lead to incorrect analysis is determination of an atypical inventory level as the average inventory level in the calculation procedure. The average inventory must reflect the average inventory level for the period of time covered by the calculation. For example, seasonal items or merchandise lines that sell well only during summer months will show an abnormally high stock turnover ratio in an annual analysis that calculates only the beginning-of-year and ending-of-year inventory levels to calculate average inventory level. This illustrates the necessity of conducting more frequent (monthly or quarterly) stock turnover analyses to obtain a more accurate performance measure.

The net sales to inventory ratios, where inventory is valued at cost, presented in Table 9.4, indicate that turnover varies according to the type of retail line offered. Several factors are usually responsible for fluctuations in turnover ratios. Frequent consumer purchases result in higher stock turnover rates, as reflected by the high turnover rate obtained in grocery stores versus the low rate experienced by farm equipment dealers and jewelry stores.

Table 9.4   Median Net Sales to Inventory Ratios for Selected Retail Outlets, 1980

Retail Line	Net Sales to Inventory Ratio[a]
Auto and home supply stores	5.0
Children and infants' wear stores	3.7
Clothing and furnishings, men's and boys' stores	3.7
Department stores	4.5
Family clothing stores	3.3
Furniture stores	4.5
Gasoline service stations	22.6
Grocery stores	15.0
Hardware stores	3.3
Household appliance stores	5.2
Jewelry stores	2.4
Lumber and other building materials dealers	6.2
Motor vehicle dealers	6.0
Paint, glass and wallpaper stores	6.6
Shoe stores	3.3
Variety stores	3.4
Women's ready-to-wear stores	4.4

Source: "The Ratios of Retailing," reprinted with the special permission of *Dun's Review*, November 1980. Copyright, 1980, Dun & Bradstreet Publications Corporation.
[a] Net Sales to Inventory—the quotient obtained by dividing the annual net sales by the statement inventory. This quotient does not represent the actual physical turnover, which would be determined by reducing the annual net sales to the cost of goods sold and then dividing the resulting figure by the statement inventory.

Stores that sell the same types of merchandise may experience lower stock turnover rates because the store is located in a small town or community where trade is limited. Such stores may have to maintain a fairly high level of inventory merely to provide an adequate merchandise assortment. In these cases, store management might not be able to increase sales enough to raise the stock turnover ratio significantly. On the other hand, stores in high customer traffic areas will probably show high stock turnover rates because the required inventory level needed to meet consumer needs is not likely to increase in proportion to the increase in sales volume.

Stock turnover rates can be increased by changes in merchandise policies, such as eliminating slow-selling items, handling fewer sizes, colors, and styles, devoting more shelf space to fast-selling items, and maintaining only minimal inventory on slow-selling brands. Of course, stock turnover can also be accelerated by reducing the retail price charged customers or by using more advertising and price reduction promotions. However, turnover rates must increase considerably as a result of a price reduction or a promotion campaign if profit margins are to be maintained. Ways to improve merchandise turnover include:

Insisting all merchandise must be on the selling floor within 24 hours upon receiving it.

Admitting when you make a bad purchase and move the merchandise fast.

Giving valuable shelf space to fast selling items and items "in season."

Not overstocking.

Don't add a new item without discontinuing an old item.

Concentrating on a few lines and avoiding many complete lines and duplicate items.

Spending more time making buying plans and preparing merchandise budgets.

Keeping up-to-date on sales trends.

Believing in and using retail inventory management reports.

Not trying to be everything to everybody.

Manufacturers and wholesalers can also assist the retailer in achieving higher stock turnover ratios by reducing the delivery period needed to reach the retail outlet. New production and/or distribution techniques will allow more flexibility in producing merchandise required to meet specific and immediate needs of an individual retailer with regard to sizes, colors, and styles and can allow that retailer to reduce stock level and still meet consumer demands for a wide selection of merchandise. Using laser beams to cut material at a very rapid rate is an example of a process that can benefit the retailer. Through computers, conveyor belts, and so forth, material can be custom cut to meet specifications of an individual clothing merchant. Considerable decrease in time required to deliver items to the retailer allows both the manufacturer and retailer to sell more merchandise by reducing out-of-stock conditions on items that catch on in the fashion world. Without this system, a large volume of the same item has to be ordered before the manufacturer can justify a rerun based on needed qualifications.

Some manufacturers have also built shelf or free-standing displays which make better use of floor space and provide a clear view of the merchandise, arranged in an orderly manner. Other manufacturers provide merchandise guidelines that assist the retailer by setting up ideal stock levels in the pertinent category; they may also take inventory and offer to replace slow-selling items with fast-selling items. Small retailers may find such advice to be very worthwhile, providing the manufacturer and/or wholesaler does not try to overemphasize the importance of his or her products relative to those of other manufacturers or wholesalers.

There are, however, several conditions one must avoid in achieving high turnover. An extremely low inventory level will sometimes increase turnover but also result in many lost sales which can damage both the store's profit and image. Such hand-to-mouth buying will also increase bookkeeping, transportation and merchandise handling costs in addition to the loss of quantity purchase discounts.

Gross Margin Return on Inventory (GMROI)

For most retailers, turnover needs to be supported by **gross margin return on inventory** (GMROI):

$$\frac{\text{Gross Profits}}{\text{Total Sales}} \times \frac{\text{Total Sales}}{\text{Average Inventory}} = \text{GMROI}$$

The first part of the GMROI formula is an indication of gross margin which is one indicator of profit. Although business expenses such as utilities, rent, advertising, etc. are not deducted when arriving at gross margin, they give a fairly reliable measure of profits and can be measured with a high degree of accuracy. The second part of the GMROI equation is an estimate of inventory turnover where investment in the GMROI formulation is simply the number of dollars the firm has tied up in inventory.

Table 9.5 Items with Varying Gross Margin Percentages

Item	Gross Margin	×	Sales to Inventory	=	GMROI
A	50%		2.5		125%
B	40%		3.1		125%
C	30%		4.2		125%
D	20%		6.3		125%

For individual items or departments, inventory is frequently the only investment factor that can be measured with precision and directly controlled by the merchandise buyer. As a result GMROI is used by several department stores to evaluate buyers' performance.

The real value of GMROI is that it allows management to evaluate inventory on the return on investment it produces and not merely on margins. Table 9.5 contains data on four items.

Since all items produce equal GMROI percentages, they should be considered equally profitable. This type of thinking represents a deviation from traditional retail thought which places most of the emphasis upon gross margin percentage and ignores turnover. For example, many retailers would still suggest that product B is twice as profitable as product D because its gross margin is twice as high. GMROI calculations reveal that this is not true, and that all four items are equally profitable. GMROI is a merchandise management tool that measures the profitability associated with merchandising decision which in turn will maximize return on investment.

GMROI criteria in the merchandising decision process has yet to take the place of the "margin only" system used by many present day retailers. However, survival is forcing retailers to determine results by merchandise department on an individual store basis, which is, of course, the basis for GMROI.

Summary

Merchandise management consists of the activities involved in balancing inventories to meet consumer needs. The merchandising department usually supervises these activities.

The merchandise budget is frequently utilized to plan and control sales efforts, markups, purchases, markdowns, and shortages. It consists of:

1. A forecast of sales for given periods
2. A plan for the stocks to be carried at the beginning of each period
3. Planned retail reductions
4. Planned purchase quantities
5. Planned profit margin

Merchandise planning and control techniques use both unit and dollar measures. Unit planning is needed because both the retail firm's buyer and the retail customer make their purchases in units. Dollar planning is required by the firm's accountants and financial planners who work with overall sales dollars, expense dollars, and ratios between sales and expense dollars.

Electronic data processing equipment allows retailers to acquire more current retail inventory management reports and direct product profitability calculations (exemplified by the COSMOS and IMPACT systems) to increase profits.

Use of the Universal Product Code (UPC) and laser checkout scanners is increasing at a rapid pace. Main advantages of these systems are that: (1) they increase the speed of processing customers through the checkout operation, (2) price marking on each individual package is no longer needed, (3) routine reordering procedure can be established, (4) checkout cash registers can be balanced faster, and (5) fewer pricing errors are made at the checkout counter because the computer can remember prices better than people can.

UPC and laser scanner systems appear to result in improved merchandise management. The systems provide so much data so quickly that managers can soon identify problem areas in their inventory and adjust their purchasing plans to correct the situation.

Consumer reactions to the systems have been somewhat mixed. Shoppers in stores that use no price marking on individual packages complain unless the sales receipt contains a sufficient description of the item along with its price. A majority of the customers prefer the faster checkout procedure and the more accurate price recording at the checkout counter.

Questions

1. Develop a plan for implementing a merchandise budget in a new independent shoe store.
2. Discuss ways that the annual sales forecast can be developed for an established retail firm.
3. A retailer expects the firm's sales to increase by 20 percent during this next year. Last year the firm's sales were $400,000. The monthly sales index for January is 75; for February the sales index is 90. Calculate the sales volume you expect this retailer to have during the January 1 to February 28 period.
4. A grocery retailer has reviewed the firm's sales records for the past five years. Average monthly sales are: January, $150,000; February, $180,000; March, $190,000; April, $190,000; May, $200,000; June, $210,000; July, $230,000; August, $230,000; September, $170,000; October, $150,000; November, $170,000; December, $250,000. Calculate monthly seasonal sales index figures for each month.
5. What are advantages and disadvantages of using the various methods of planning inventory levels?
6. What average markup must a retailer use to obtain a profit of 20 percent of gross sales if the firm's sales are estimated to be $600,000, its operating expenses are expected to be $200,000, and its reductions are estimated to be $50,000?

7. What is the gross margin percentage for the retailer in problem six?
8. How can small retailers use the open-to-buy amount to guide their purchase activities?
9. Which is the more common occurrence in retailing, a shortage or overage? Explain why.
10. How can a retailer increase the firm's stock turnover? Should retail management always strive to get the maximum stock turnover that is possible?
11. ABC Retail Company estimates its February sales to be $90,000 and its average monthly sales for the first quarter to be $60,000. The average monthly stock for the first quarter is $80,000. Use the basic stock method to determine how much inventory the firm should have on hand on February 1. What is the dollar value of its basic stock?
12. The shoe department of a local department store has estimated its sales for next year to be $220,000. It estimates January sales to be $12,000. The firm wants to have an average monthly inventory of $20,000. Use the percentage deviation method to determine how much inventory the shoe department should have on hand on January 1.
13. Stock on hand, and the estimated sales for the next two months are as follows:

Week beginning	Sales
Feb. 1	$3,500
Feb. 8	2,000
Feb. 15	1,750
Feb. 22	3,200
March 1	1,900
March 8	2,500
March 15	3,400
March 22	3,800

Find the number of weeks' supply that the firm has on hand on February 1.
14. The following weekly sales estimates have been prepared for a supermarket:

Week beginning		Sales	Week beginning		Sales
February	1	$40,500	March	15	$48,300
	8	45,000		22	55,000
	15	42,500	April	4	44,200
	22	36,400		11	48,400
March	1	52,300		18	46,300
	8	50,100		25	41,200

Management of the supermarket desires to obtain an annual stock turnover of 15. Use the weeks' supply method to calculate the planned stock for February 1 and March 15.

15. A local retailer wants to hold the firm's inventory to a monthly stock to sales ratio of 2.0. Estimated sales are:

Month	Sales	Month	Sales
January	$15,600	July	$24,000
February	20,800	August	28,500
March	23,000	September	23,200
April	24,500	October	21,100
May	27,000	November	27,200
June	25,400	December	30,150

Use the stock to sales ratio method to determine how much inventory the firm should have on hand on January 1, April 1, July 1, and September 1. What annual stock turnover rate is this retailer expecting to achieve?

16. From the following figures find the open-to-buy amount for July:

Actual inventory, July 1	$40,000
Planned inventory on hand, August 1	55,000
Value of inventory on order for delivery in July	15,000
Estimated sales for July	40,000

17. A local retailer plans the following for the month of April: sales, $50,000; mark-downs and shortages, $4,000; beginning-of-the-month stock, $100,000; and planned initial markup, 20 percent of retail. Find the open-to-buy amount for April in dollars of retail value and in dollars of cost to the retailer.

18. The manager of a certain department of a general merchandise store believes that its annual sales volume will be $1,800,000 next year. Estimated operating expenses are $280,000 and estimated reductions are $96,000. The manager would like to achieve a profit of $18,000 next year. What percentage of initial markup must be used to reach this profit goal?

19. What is the value of inventory on June 30 for a retailer who is in the following situation: retail value of purchases made by the retailer during the January 1 to June 30 period was $97,000; retail value of sales made to consumers during the January 1 to June 30 period was $85,000; retail value of the beginning-of-the-month inventory in January was $33,000?

20. A local retailer has obtained net sales of $30,000 during the first three months of this year. The average stock for the firm has been

$60,000. What will the firm's annual stock turnover rate be if business continues at the rate it has been going during the three months?

21. A retailer obtained net sales for last year of $275,000. The retailer made purchases totaling $135,000 of cost to the firm during the year. A physical inventory was taken at the beginning of the year, again on July 1 and again at the end of the year. Inventory values for these periods are:

	Value of Inventory	
	in Retail Dollars	in Cost Dollars
Beginning of year	200,000	120,000
On July 1	220,000	130,000
End of year	180,000	110,000

What is the firm's stock turnover rate valued in retail prices? What is its stock turnover rate valued at cost?

22. Answer the following questions for a firm that has a July merchandise plan that shows: planned sales at $100,000, planned markdowns at $8,000, planned employee discounts at $2,000, planned shortages at $3,000, and planned end-of-the-month (EOM) stock at $300,000.

    a. What is its planned EOM stock to sales ratio for July?
    b. What is its planned markdown percentage for July?
    c. What are the total retail reductions for July?

23. If management has planned sales for the year at $35,000 and industry trends indicate an expected stock turn of at least three, about how much inventory will be needed to support sales?

Footnotes

1. Richard I. Levin and C. A. Kirkpatrick, *Quantitative Approaches to Management* (New York: McGraw-Hill, 1965), pp. 96–111.

2. Ibid., pp. 106–111.

3. Reductions include price markdowns, discounts to employees, and stock shortages.

4. Cyrus, C. Wilson and William D. Haueisen, "Retail Information Systems Can Help Provide Profits Needed for Growth," *Marketing News*, XIII, March 7, 1980, p. 5.

5. Testimony by Mr. Joseph B. Danzansky, President of Giant Food Inc., before the Maryland Senate Economic Affairs Committee, March 17, 1976.

6. Capital turnover, as used here, measures only turnover in capital invested in merchandise inventory, not total capital used by the retailer.

Case Study: Atkens Department Store

Atkens department store management delegates much authority and responsibility to individual store managers. Each store manager has considerable freedom to adapt merchandise offerings to meet local circumstances and to adjust operating procedures and methods to cope with special problems that they encounter. Store managers delegate as much authority and responsibility as possible to their assistants and department managers so that these people will develop as managers in accord with the company's general management philosophy.

A new and fairly large unit of the company is located in a planned suburban shopping center in a major metropolitan area. The operating results of the shoe department of this store have been a disappointment to the store manager during the past merchandising season.

Total sales volume for this store was about $4 million for the past year. The shoe department, which has consistently accounted for about 5 percent of total store sales, has been the source of 30 percent of all markdowns. The annual rate of stock turnover for the shoe department is 3.0 compared with a store average of 6.4 and a range from 1 on slow-moving lines (such as jewelry) to over 10 on fast-moving lines (such as some women's clothing items).

The shoe department currently handles men's work and dress shoes, children's shoes, women's casual shoes, and a very limited number of styles in women's dress shoes. Information about the shoe department's performance for the last year is summarized in Table 9.6.

With the exception of women's dress shoes, which offer an unusually high markdown risk, the department manager feels that she has a large

Table 9.6   Atkens Shoe Department Performance

Classification	Department Sales (%)	Gross Margin (%)	Range of Retail Prices ($)
Men's work shoes	30	35	$20–50
Men's dress shoes[a]	20	40	25–50
Women's casual shoes	20	35	15–40
Women's dress shoes	5	45	25–50
Children's shoes[b]	25	40	15–40
Total	100		

Classification	Number of Styles Stocked	Percentage Reductions Are of Category Sales Dollar Volume	Average Dollar Inventory
Men's work shoes	6	10	$ 8,000
Men's dress shoes[a]	16	20	$12,000
Women's casual shoes	10	20	$15,000
Women's dress shoes	4	25	$ 5,000
Children's shoes[b]	14	15	$20,000
Total	50		$60,000

[a] Includes boys' sizes, 4–7.
[b] Includes infants' shoes.

assortment of styles in each classification. Stock depth for each style has been limited, however, in an attempt to keep the total dollar inventory at a minimum level.

Purchase control for most departments in the store is made on the basis of each department manager's current inventory being the equivalent of the next two months of expected sales, and on having on order an additional amount equivalent to expected sales in the third month ahead. If the stock on hand plus stock on order exceeds estimated sales for three months, the department has no open-to-buy. In the shoe department, purchase control is made on the basis of having a seventy-five-day supply on hand and a thirty-day supply on order allowance. The greater on hand allowance is justified on the basis of the complex nature of size buying for shoes. The manager has felt the need for a seventy-five-day stock in order to keep all sizes on the shelf.

According to a recent national survey of a representative group of shoe stores and departments, about one half of all lost sales are due to being out of stock on the particular size at the time of potential purchase. This factor has been particularly important in the case of general merchandise stores, owing to the limited capital available for stocking a wide variety of styles in depth.

The department manager buys or orders shoes from a classification catalog which contains pictures of styles available, size information, retail price, markup, wholesale price, and a qualitative description. Inventory in each shoe classification is counted at sporadic intervals to determine movement of merchandise by style numbers since the last count, and this information is used as the basis for buying.

Since the shoe department has operated at a loss from the time of store opening, the store manager is most anxious to increase sales volume, reduce markdown losses, increase the rate of turnover, and begin to operate the shoe department on a profitable basis.

Discussion Questions

1. Analyze the inventory turnover for each merchandise classification.
2. Analyze the profitability of each merchandise classification.
3. What steps do you recommend that the store manager take to accomplish the objectives of increasing shoe sales, reducing markdowns, and increasing turnover and profitability?

Chapter 10 | Buying Merchandise

Learning Goals

1. To be able to discuss the buying process and the organization needed to implement buying decisions.
2. To be able to describe a system for successfully buying profitable goods at market.
3. To understand the procedures needed for evaluating merchandise.
4. To be able to assess the impact of vendors shifting the marketing functions of financing and inventory accumulation downward to retailers.
5. To understand and be able to calculate the various discounts offered to retailers.

Key Terms and Concepts

buying process	work the line
economic order quantity	negotiation process
marketing "intermediaries"	trade discounts
keystoning policy	Robinson-Patman Act

Four Phases of the Buying Process

The buying process consists of four phases: *search, evaluation, selection,* and *review.* **Search** activities involve determining what to buy and from whom it should be purchased. Ideally, the retail merchant should formulate a merchandise plan that best reflects the needs of the firm's target market and then seek suppliers who can provide the products in a timely, profitable manner. Unfortunately, in the short-run, the real world of retailing does not conform to the ideal model of marketing theory. Usually the search process is implemented by entering the market with a basic outline of desired products which is subsequently compared with what is currently available in the market. Some large retailers, such as Sears, Roebuck and Company can go directly to manufacturers and have products made to their exact specifications, thereby precisely implementing their merchandising plans. Small retailers may make suggestions to manufacturers' representatives that may result in ideal products being produced at some future date. However, for most retailers the actual merchandise assortment represents a calculated compromise between ideal requirements, supplier substitutes, and new innovative products selected to stimulate customer interest.

Evaluation activities involve specific analysis of merchandise and vendors on the expected performance each is likely to yield in terms of quality and service. Naturally, the cost of merchandise is also a prime consideration in the evaluation process, so alternatives are really evaluated on a benefit-to-cost basis.

The **selection** phase consists of the actual purchase of the merchandise from the chosen vendor after all available alternatives have been evaluated.

Review, the final phase of the buying process, involves the buyer's reappraisal of the activities in the previous three buying phases. This reappraisal is designed to identify trouble areas in the buying process so that mistakes are not repeated. The review process may also yield suggestions that can reduce the amount of time the buyer spends on the more menial and routine tasks, thereby allowing the buyer to spend more time on the important buying considerations.

Buying Merchandise

Buying merchandise is not an occupation for the timid or indecisive individual. Anyone who has difficulty making personal decisions probably has a limited future in retail management. Each decision situation will present certain alternatives that must be effectively evaluated in a short time frame and a choice or decision to be made expeditiously. Once the decision is made it must be implemented and the results evaluated. Anxiety or worry about past decisions is nonproductive and cannot be tolerated because it clouds present perceptions and impairs the quality of future decisions. Everyone makes mistakes; the effective buyer-manager recognizes mistakes, acknowledges and learns from them.

Determining the Reorder Quantity for Staple Merchandise

Staple merchandise is considered to be any good that the retailer must always have on hand in appropriate quantities to meet customer demand. Usually the rate of sale of this type of merchandise is stable and thus quite predictable. Occasionally changes in the product or in competition or vendor relations require a major adjustment in the staple merchandise line, such as the introduction of stretch socks. This innovation revolutionized the sock market in a period of approximately three years. Given this length of time, most merchants were able to gradually shift their purchasing emphasis to the new line and ultimately clear out remaining stocks through selective price reductions.

Reorders of staple merchandise represent periodic replenishment of current stocks to maintain a balance in sizing, color assortment, or price lining. The objective of this exercise is to balance opportunity costs associated with missing sales due to stock outs and the interest costs associated with carrying excessive inventory.

Assuming that the retailer has kept accurate detailed records of the previous year's sales of staple merchandise and related expenses, that person can determine fairly accurately when to place an order and how much to order using an economic order quantity model (EOQ).

Inventory Costs

The first preparatory step which the decision maker must make is to determine the cost of physically handling and storing the specific goods under analysis. Next the opportunity cost of capital must be calculated and added to the previous charges. Lastly, some factor must be added, based on historical records for shrinkage due to loss, damage, or theft, while the goods are being stored. The total sum of these variables represents inventory holding costs.

The second step is to calculate individual **order costs.** One must account for the time spent by the buyer determining "the buy," the clerk's time for order preparation and processing, plus the cost of paper, postage, telephone, and related expenses. It is quite common for individual order costs to approach $10.00. Most department stores will process hundreds of orders a week so the costs mount up in short order.

Demand for the Period

The last preparatory step is to determine demand for the staple merchandise under consideration. Even though staple merchandise is not seasonal in nature, customer demand will vary from month to month, year to year. In order to use the EOQ concept the **constant demand rate** must be determined. One simply sums the total sold for the previous period (year), adjusts for any known stock outs or anticipated increased demands and divides by the number of months in the period (12). The result is the constant demand rate.

Once these three data items have been computed the **Economic Order Quantity** (EOQ) which will minimize total cost can be calculated. The formula is:

$$Q_1 = \sqrt{\frac{2DC_0}{C_s}}$$

where:

Q_1 = Quantity to be ordered
D = Period demand in units
C_0 = Cost per individual order
C_s = Period holding cost per unit

How Much to Order

For example, suppose an order is placed for mens' stretch white crew socks. Looking up current vendor quoted prices, the buyer determines that they will cost $12 per dozen pair packed in gross (144 pair) lots. Reviewing prior associated cost data supplied by the controller, these goods are found to cost 15 percent of the cost price to store for one year. Thus, the annual cost of storing (C_s) each pair of socks is (0.15) ($1.00) = $0.15. The same cost report indicated that it cost $9.00 ($C_o$) to process an order regardless of how much was ordered at any one time. Reviewing the forecasted demand for the period, the buyer determines that the store will sell 6,000 pair and be out of stock with none on order. Thus:

$$Q_1 = \sqrt{\frac{2DC_o}{C_s}}$$

$$= \sqrt{\frac{2(6000)(9.00)}{0.15}}$$

$$= 849 \text{ pairs of socks}$$

Standard Pack

The calculated result is 849, but that exact number cannot be bought because the socks come packed in gross lots. Five gross (720 pair) or six gross (864 pair) must be ordered. What should be done? Most buyers would opt for six gross due to the fact that they are out of stock and have none on order.

Timing of Reorder

In this particular situation the buyer didn't know when to reorder. To reduce the possibility of future stock out situations one must establish reorder points when new orders should be placed. This decision is conditioned by the buyer's ability to accurately forecast demand in some future period and the amount of lead time needed to procure the needed replenishment stock.

From the previous EOQ calculation the relevant period demand in units has been forecasted. This aggregate estimate can be broken down to an average daily sale rate. Delivery speed is dependent on how quickly an order can be generated, processed, approved, and sent. One must add mail transit time, which varies from overnight to weeks. Once the vendor receives the order it must be processed in the plant or warehouse. If the vendor has readily available inventory and a slow season the goods can be picked, assembled, boxed, and shipped rather quickly, perhaps in two days. If any of these conditions do not pertain, restocking could take weeks or months.

Speed with which the goods reach the retailer is dependent on the mode of transportation chosen and the efficiency of the carrier. For most retailers some form of air express is the quickest if the store is near a major metropolitan airport. However, air transport generally costs twice as much as motor carriers and fifteen times more than rail transport. Within the motor carrier industry there are documented cases where identical shipments sent on the same day over the same route arrived seven days apart. Despite such disparities a buyer may review past order files and determine average replenishment time in days. Time to place an order then is determined by the formula:

$$T_R = \frac{365}{D/Q_1}$$

where:

T_R = Time to place an order
D = Period demand
Q_1 = Economic order quantity

$$T_R = \frac{365}{6000/864}$$
$$T_R = 52 \text{ days}$$

Previously it was noted that the period demand was 6,000 pair of socks and the EOQ was 849 pair of socks, but one must order 864 pair of socks due to packing limitations. This means that if seven orders were placed during the period the department would be overstocked by four dozen if demand forecasts materialize. Careful monitoring may be required to adjust the future quantity ordered to avoid this overstock condition. If one assumes that all 6,048 pairs are sold, then an order should be placed every 365/7 days. Thus, one complete order cycle time would be 52 days.

Safety Stock

As an added precaution most firms maintain additional quantities of staple goods which serve as a safety stock to prevent lost sales if the firm should experience a sudden surge in demand or suffer lengthening of the replenishment cycle. Figure 10.1 illustrates these points.

In modern transaction-center equipped stores these calculations are all made by preprogrammed computers. All staple merchandise is source-marked and all unit sales are either keyed in or optically recorded. Thus, perpetual inventories are maintained and replenishment orders are automatically generated, processed, and the goods arrive at the store without store management intervention.

In the event the store is not equipped to maintain a perpetual inventory system, stock must be physically counted at least once every 30 days to determine stock positions. Each item should be recorded on stock sheets with the lot or stock keeping unit (SKU), price, and current quantities of stock remaining by style, size and, if appropriate, color. In the interim between count periods, visual checks will reveal unusually high sale rate situa-

Figure 10.1   Economic Order Quantity Model

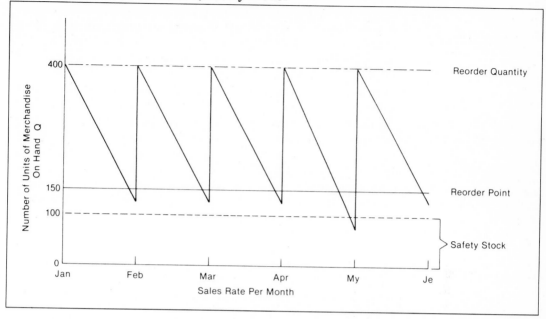

tions and a fill-in order may be placed or the vendor may be
asked to ship an advanced order at once. The important point is
not to miss sales in staple items due to stock outs nor to have too
much stock on hand even though it will eventually sell.

Fashion Buying and Merchandising

Fashion buying and merchandising has been the subject of thousands of articles and many books, yet it remains a lively subject.
"What will be hot this year?" remains the perennial question.
"Will it be a number one **checkout** (Will it be the best seller of
the season)? If so, where and when can we get it fast?" This dynamic suspense is the life blood of true merchants. Each new
season brings another opportunity for the buyers to demonstrate
their keen insight and understanding of what will sell in their
market. **Seasoned judgment** and an **experienced assertiveness** are
needed to pick the right goods, negotiate competitive prices, and
have the goods on the racks when the wave of acceptance hits the
store's community. If these qualifications are consistently
achieved over a period of years the firm becomes known as a
"fashion leader."

While space does not permit any significant exposition of the
fashion buying process, some rudimentary comments are appro-

priate. Fashion selling is time relevant. Fashion goods are highly perishable items which have product life cycles measured in days or weeks, at best. Thus, if the fashion merchandising phase of the operation is to be successful, the buyer must get the earliest possible feedback on the acceptance of the selection. When initial orders are placed the buyer must make a selling-season decision: "Do I sample the assortment and test the market, or do I trust my judgment and make a season commitment?" If one takes the conservative position one runs the risk of not being able to successfully reorder. Many manufacturers construct a fixed number of garments and when they are gone the firm turns its attention to the next new season. If one takes a calculated risk and "buys the season" he or she is assured of supply at a given price—both needed attributes for a profitable selling season in fashion merchandising.

Historically, successful fashion buyers have repeatedly displayed the following attributes: (1) a thorough knowledge of their target market, (2) a keen sense of economic and competitive conditions, (3) an unmatched sense of optimism and (4) a unique drive for achievement. Not all buyers match that stereotype, but then not everyone can be a fashion merchandiser.

Organizing for Buying

Every retailer, regardless of the size of the operation, must perform the buying process efficiently if the firm is going to remain competitive in the marketplace. The merchandise or service provided must be of the appropriate type, quality, and price demanded by the consumers. In addition, the firm's offerings must be available in quantities that will parallel consumer needs at the *time* customers want to shop for such goods or services. The offering must also be placed in the store in a way that customers can easily locate it. Both the manager of a small independent outlet and the merchandise division of a large retail organization usually perform the job of buying and maintaining merchandise that will satisfy these consumer demands.

Merchandise Division

The merchandise division of the large independent store does more than buy merchandise. Usually it is also responsible for selling, planning, and control activities. Buyers are generally appointed for each major merchandise line, so they buy, direct sales, plan, and control their activities in view of consumer demand and profit opportunities. Divisional merchandise managers supervise the activities of these buyers so that all departments reflect the image that top retail management is striving to achieve. This organizational plan allows the division merchandise managers to devote the majority of their time to activities that plan and control the merchandise assortment. Execution of these plans is left largely to buyers.

Central Buyers

By contrast, responsibility for buying and selling is usually separated in the chain store organization. Central buyers usually establish an approved buying list that contains new and regular items that the central buyers believe will enhance the chain's merchandise assortment. These same central buyers also make the decision of removing items from the approved buying list when they believe the items are no longer contributing to the overall merchandise assortment. The negotiation of terms is also handled by the central buyers. Individual store managers are then generally responsible for actually placing orders for specific quantities of each item and presenting the merchandise appropriately to stimulate sales.

The central organization in some chain systems may perform all of the buying and reorder activities. In this case, the store managers are responsible only for proper merchandise presentation, servicing consumers, and other selling-related activities. Merchandise planning is then performed by merchandise controllers, each of whom supervises one or more central buyers. These merchandise controllers plan stock assortment requirements for the entire chain after appropriate sales forecasts have been made. The central buyer(s) orders the specific items in the quantities required by the entire chain. The incoming merchandise is then allocated to individual store units by merchandise distributors.

Branch Stores

Branch store operators may follow a different approach in the buying process. A branch organization usually tailors its merchandise/service assortment to reflect differences in local market conditions. Chain organizations are more likely to provide a standardized merchandise/service assortment to all geographical areas. Variations in merchandise/service assortments are usually required to meet differences in consumer preferences for items such as better-quality jewelry, clothing, furniture, and so forth that are fashionable, distinctive, and subject to regional peculiarities. Individual outlet managers in such branch operations are given the authority to deviate from the centrally devised purchasing plan because the demand for some merchandise differs from one area to another. Central buyers usually plan the initial merchandise assortment, establish the prices, select the new items that are added to the approved buying list, and decide which items are to be dropped from the list. Individual branch managers generally place the reorders in the quantities needed to meet the special requirements of that outlet.

Centralized Buying Committees

A centralized buying committee is frequently used by both branch and chain store operations to allow regional representation in the buying process while maintaining the considerable buying power that is associated with volume purchases. A national buying committee may consist of approximately twenty persons who are mostly the "better store" managers from various geographical locations. The centralized buying committee determines which products are good for the entire nation and generally purchases the bread-and-butter items. Buying specialty, fashion, or fad items may be done by individual store managers who are in a better position to know which specific items are likely to appeal to their customers. Allowing the individual store manager to buy specialty items that best reflect unique consumer differences can allow the store to set trends with its merchandise assortment. This kind of leadership can generate a progressive image that cannot be established with a buying organization that is not in tune with local consumer demand.

A disadvantage of the centralized buying committee is that an overestimated demand can quickly generate a massive overbought condition in some, if not all, geographical areas. Inventory trading within the retail corporation is used to balance company inventory with consumer demand. The items that will not sell in one area or outlet frequently sell well in another (or even in a nearby outlet that serves a different type of consumer).

Centralized buying of some type usually is used despite the disadvantages cited. The discounts given for large-volume purchases are generally large enough to make it economically attractive. In addition, individual central buyers may believe that they must justify their existence by buying all items. Such buyers may hesitate to relinquish any outright buying functions to the individual outlet managers for fear of losing "political" power in the retail organization.

No matter what organizational system is adopted, sufficient flexibility must be maintained to allow the buyer to identify quickly new items that are being requested by consumers. Individual outlet managers can inform their district sales manager of consumer requests. The district sales manager can then check with other outlet managers to determine if it is a common demand. The best ideas can then be passed on to the central buyer, who can check with other district sales managers to determine if the new item has appeal in other areas. If the item appears to have sufficient consumer demand, a manufacturer could be contacted to produce the item.

This **customer feedback** system can provide very useful new merchandise ideas for a retailer in fashion and other fast-changing merchandise lines. This system can result in a progressive or new merchandise image for retail outlets affiliated with such a retail organization. Smaller, independent retailers also have the opportunity to identify consumer needs. They have an additional advantage in being able to react to these needs without having to go through a large retail organization before the product can be ordered.

Resident buying offices provide both independent and chain retailers with current marketing information that can enable the retail buyers to achieve higher stock turnover and better stock assortments. Both local and central retail buyers need a great deal of information because a single buyer or store system cannot keep up with changes in (1) types of new products being offered, (2) offerings of the numerous suppliers, (3) business levels, and (4) consumer preferences for different types of goods. The resident buying office usually makes such information available to retail buyers while serving as a source of training for the local store buyers. Resident offices may conduct training workshops, and their personnel may even shop with the retailer's local buyers when the latter come to the wholesale market. Some resident buying offices check on orders and even expedite deliveries on urgently needed merchandise. Resident buying offices may also provide assistance in planning promotional events.

The resident buying office may be either an independent office or a store-owned office. Independent offices can be either "salaried offices," which serve their clients on a contractual basis, or "merchandise brokers," who receive their payment (usually a 2- to 4-percent commission) from the vendor instead of the buyer. Hence, local buyers can receive free buying assistance from merchandise brokers. However, the retail buyers should be aware that the merchandise broker is also trying to present, in the most favorable way, the products from which the commission is derived.

Store-owned offices may be "private offices," which are owned and operated by and for a single retailer, such as the Neiman-Marcus New York City office, which assists only buyers in all Neiman-Marcus stores. If several different retail groups own the resident buying office, it is called an **associated office.** In this case the buying power and authority remains mostly with the individual buyers who use the service. The **syndicated office,** on the other hand, represents the chain store system in the ownership group situation; so the syndicated office purchase recommendations are usually adopted by local personnel.

The wide range of services provided by all types of resident buying offices is very helpful to both large- and small-scale retailers. Therefore, retail buyers should at least investigate the possibility of using a resident buying office to assist them in their buying procedure.

Sources of
Merchandise

The trend toward "scrambled merchandising" has complicated an already enormous problem for retail buyers. Merchandising many nonrelated merchandise lines requires that many different sources of supply be used to meet consumer demands. The magnitude of the problem of evaluating different supply sources is readily apparent for any large-scale retailer who handles over 10,000 different items. However, even small-scale retailers make an important decision when they select their suppliers.

There are three major sources of supply available to the retailers: middlemen, manufacturers or producers, and foreign exporters.

Vendor Sources

The different types of marketing intermediaries, the product lines they normally carry, and the type of retail outlet for which they are especially suited are described in Table 10.1. Intermediaries provide many services that are valuable to small and medium-size retailers who cannot afford to hire specialists in many different areas. However, retailers are getting themselves into the wholesale business by using many different retail-

Table 10.1 Characteristic Types of Intermediaries Serving Retailers

Type of Intermediary	Characteristics
Service (regular) wholesaler	Serves as the retailer's buying agent by assembling and collecting goods, storing goods, providing fast delivery, extending credit, and furnishing market information. These services appeal especially to small and medium-size retailers.
Limited function wholesaler	Charges less because less service is provided since generally credit is not granted or delivery service offered. Offers only fast-moving items; may do business only by mail.
Rack jobber	Supplies mainly nongood items to supermarkets, sets up displays, maintains merchandise assortment, and receives payment only on goods actually sold; thereby guarantees a prespecified percentage markup to the outlet.
Broker	Receives a commission to bring retail buyers and suppliers together; does not handle merchandise or take title to goods. Handles only a few lines— mainly grocery specialties, dry goods, fruits, vegetables, drugs, and hardware.
Commission agent	Similar to broker, except merchandise is handled although title is not taken to it; supplies mainly large retailers with dry goods, grocery specialties, and fruits and vegetables.
Manufacturer's agent (representative)	Renders services similar to those of a salesperson; is restricted to a limited territory and by limited authority to negotiate price and terms of sale; sells only part of client's output.
Selling agent	Similar to manufacturer's agent, except that a selling agent is responsible for disposing of entire client's output.
Auctioneer	Product is placed on display and sold to highest bidder. Used mainly to sell livestock and fruits and vegetables to small restaurants, large chains, or other wholesalers.

Co-op Buying Groups

wholesale combinations in which a group of retail outlets either owns the wholesale organization, as in the case of "cooperative chain" operations, or performs the wholesaling functions of assembling and collecting goods in chain distribution centers. Retailers also enter into group buying arrangements to perform some (if not all) of the functions normally performed by intermediaries.

Manufacturers

Retailers purchase their merchandise directly from manufacturers or producers for several reasons. First, manufacturers' salespeople can cooperate in training the retailers' salesforce to use proper selling and display techniques for the specific merchandise purchased.

Second, direct buying may reduce the time required for delivery of the merchandise because the shipments can be made directly to the outlets or sent prepackaged for each outlet to the chain's distribution center. This reduction in delivery time can be especially important for fad, fashion, or perishable items.

Third, retailers may buy direct because they can obtain lower net prices by not using the intermediaries. If some of the wholesalers' functions can be eliminated or absorbed by the retailer at a lower cost, direct buying offers an economic advantage.

Fourth, direct buying allows large retailers to purchase goods made according to their specifications. Consumer requests can be translated more easily into these specifications than in the case where the intermediary is also involved in the communication process. Many large retailers, such as Sears, Roebuck and Company, now specify the design of nearly all the items they handle.

Some large retailers have purchased manufacturing companies that produce sizable amounts of the merchandise they handle. Of course, this guarantees control over merchandise quality. In addition, it allows the retailer to reap more profits from the trend toward private label merchandise. Distribution costs frequently can be reduced because the products are placed in the mass market without incurring heavy advertising or sales costs. Per unit manufacturing costs may be reduced because high-volume sales allow spreading the fixed cost invested in machines, administration, and so forth over the many units sold.

Foreign markets are becoming a more important source of merchandise supply as countries, such as Japan, become more familiar with U.S. consumer needs. Foreign goods purchased by retailers pass through importers, who send catalogs and/or salesmen to retailers. Most importers are located in the New York area, the Pacific Coast area, Canadian and Mexican border towns, and several large metropolitan areas.

Importers

Some large retailers send their own buyers to foreign countries to negotiate purchases. An alternative is to make purchases from foreign buyers through resident buying offices. If a large retail firm buys large quantities of foreign merchandise, it may establish its own buying offices in the major foreign supply areas.

Many retailers elect to use the resident buying offices or regular wholesalers as their main source of merchandise. This is particularly true for small retailers who may not have sufficient volume or cash resources to take advantage of volume or cash discounts offered by manufacturers or primary sources. The retailer can save time and effort and gain financing by using the services of a regular wholesaler, but not without added cost. When the wholesaler performs these marketing functions and services, the retailer sacrifices a portion of the trade discount offered by prime sources, which in turn increases the merchant's cost of goods. The cost of goods is further increased by more frequent shipments of smaller quantities, which increases freight charges and handling costs. All of these factors lead to the need for relatively higher unit markups and tend to make these retailers less price competitive. The decision to depend on any marketing middlemen as a regular source of supply should be made only after weighing the costs and benefits associated with the services offered.

Supplier decisions should be reviewed periodically, because competitive pressures and marketing dynamics may make certain sources more or less attractive over time. Most authorities agree that the retailer should spread the firm's purchases among suppliers if possible. Such action spreads the risk of being temporarily without merchandise during periods of peak demand or tight supply situations. This wise advice should be used judiciously, because any attempt to spread buying orders usually results in smaller quantities being ordered from each source, with attendant higher costs.

Last, the retailer should not change sources of supply capriciously. One may be tempted to switch the business to alternate sources in search of lower prices or better service, but the retailer-buyer must remember that the supplier represents the lifeline to continued existence. Without a regular supply of needed goods the retailer cannot stay in business. Such relationships are partially based on a feeling of reciprocity. When times are good, supplies are widely available and intermediary competition is intense. The retailer may pay a bit more in price or tolerate less intensive service in the expectation that in the future when the retailer has problems, such as restricted cash flow or unexpected demand for merchandise, the wholesaler will extend "earned courtesies" to help out a loyal "good" customer. Ultimately the retailer must decide how valuable this tentative, un-

Wholesalers (margin note)

Periodic Supplier/Vendor Review (margin note)

stated relationship is in terms of dollars and cents or shipments promised but not delivered. In the long run, change can be the pathway to improved performance, and if suppliers are not competitive the retailer must search for better product/service offerings.

Evaluating Merchandise

Buyer Product Knowledge

Retailers must constantly remind themselves that customers buy products and services that will yield some form of satisfaction. Regardless of the services offered by a marketing intermediary, if the product does not live up to customer expectations the customer will not come back for further purchases. Therefore, successful retail buyers must be able to judge the quality of the merchandise to be certain their purchases will meet the needs of their customers. Hence, buyers need considerable knowledge about raw materials, manufacturing methods, workmanship, and current fashion trends. Merchandise may be evaluated by personally inspecting all of the goods purchased. However, this can be a time-consuming process when volume purchases are made, so a sampling procedure (evaluating only a portion of the merchandise to be purchased) can be used to reduce the time devoted to inspecting goods.

Standard Grades

Merchandise is also frequently purchased on the basis of a description of the item. U.S. government grades or standard industry definitions allow the buyer to make purchases on the basis of a description because the goods must meet prescribed quality standards to bear the label issued by the government or industry. The grading system used for beef is an example. Grocery outlets generally inform the meat suppliers of their needs in terms of both quantity and quality for a specified date. The quality description is merely a statement of which U.S. Department of Agriculture grade(s) a store desires to buy. Meat suppliers then respond with a bid price on the stated quantity and quality. Generally, the supplier who quotes the lowest price obtains the business for that specific period.

Testing bureaus also assist the buyer in making quality judgments. These bureaus may either be store-owned or independent commercial bureaus that charge a fee for evaluating goods. United States Testing Company of Hoboken, New Jersey, is an example of an independent commercial testing bureau.

Buying at Merchandise Markets

Regional merchandise showings are held in strategic locations throughout the nation. They provide excellent opportunities for small and medium-sized retail buyers to select their various lines and make their buying decisions based on their first-hand experience in comparing available goods. Usually these buying opportunities are referred to as regional shows or markets or marts. Periodically, either annually or semiannually, retail buyers gather at strategic regional centers in large auditoriums or in special showrooms with manufacturers' representatives and other intermediaries to buy their merchandise for the coming selling season.

Regional
Merchandise Markets

Most showings last three to five days in each location, usually over a weekend so small retailers can attend on Sundays while their stores are closed or when business is slow and they feel free to leave the store operation in capable hands for a few days. Admission is restricted to legitimate retailers who present business licenses or have permanent I.D. cards. The same merchandise offerings may be presented by intermediaries in similar markets in fifteen different locations during a buying season. An example of such markets is the international dress, western apparel, and equipment show held annually in early January in Denver, Colorado. Thousands of buyers from all over the nation attend. The 1981 show included buyers from nineteen foreign countries. During this five-day show it is not uncommon for western boot manufacturers to write over $4 million (wholesale prices) worth of orders. The pace is fast and an unprepared buyer can easily be persuaded to buy more merchandise than the store will need during the forthcoming selling season.

**The
Prebuying Process**

The merchandise manager and corporate retail management use dollars as the measurement unit in planning. The buyer must convert merchandising plans from dollars into units of merchandise. Actually, the buyer may first plan the unit sales and the unit assortment and then convert the figures into dollars to check against the merchandise manager's dollar plan.

Buyers often develop a "trip buying plan" which indicates the specific quantity of each item they intend to buy on a forthcoming buying trip. Several different forms can be used to coordinate the buyers' purchases with the merchandise budget and the firm's open-to-buy quantity. Figure 10.2 shows a trip buying plan form.

Regardless of store size or the merchandise line carried the same prebuying process should be followed. For the sake of simplicity the discussion will focus on the activities that should be undertaken by a small retailer with one to five individual outlets carrying merchandise that has seasonal characteristics.

Overview of Past
Sales Results

Complete, accurate, and appropriate merchandise records are the heart of any successful retail operation. They form the basis for sound buying decisions. Prior to buying any merchandise

Figure 10.2   Sample Trip Buying Plan Form

Department _____   On order for next month delivery _____

Store _____   Planned purchases next month _____

Date _____   Estimated sales next month _____

Buying trip to _____   Trip buying limit $ _____

Merchandise Code and Description	Units on Hand	Units on Order	Units Available for Sale	Forecast Sales until Delivery	Planned Stock at End of Month	Open to Buy This Month	Units Planned to Buy Now	Per Unit Cost	Planned Retail Price	Units Purchased	Dollar Amounts Purchases
(1)	(2)	(3)	(4) = (2) + (3)	(5)	(6)	(7)	(8)	(9)	(10)	(11)	(12)

Delivery date _____   Signed _____   Approved _____

(Buyer)   Merchandise Manager

from a traveling salesperson or attending a market, each retailer or buyer must systematically review the performance of past merchandise decisions from the previous comparable selling periods, such as "last spring sales." Admittedly such reviews take time and are sometimes psychologically painful, but the time will be well spent. Also, such critical analyses tend to preclude repeating buying errors of the past.

The process begins by taking inventory of the present merchandise on hand by type and vendor or seller. Any outstanding unfilled orders that have been invoiced or are likely to be shipped during the selling season are combined with the present inventory to create a total picture of the present and projected merchandise position in the store.

Forecasting the Firm's Future Sales

The next step is perhaps the most difficult and subjective step in the entire process—estimating the future selling season sales. How much will the store sell during the projected selling season? Past sales records may be helpful if one assumes the best predictor of the future is the immediate past. Unfortunately the competitive and economic environments in the last few years have been quite unstable, and retail sales have reflected this ebb and flow in consumer discretionary purchases. Competition seems to be constantly on the increase, and any future sales gains beyond those attributable to inflation must be aggressively earned by effective merchandising and tight cost control.

Forecast of Demand by Merchandise Line

Each retailer must predict the level of economic activity for his or her selling region and what share of the retail dollars the firm can expect to attract. Usually this is expressed as a certain "percent of gain" over the previous year's business. This figure will be affected by new competition, changes in traffic patterns, amount of disposable income, and so forth. Once this gross dollar figure is determined, it must be broken down by merchandise line. Some merchandise lines, such as western denims, will sell better one year than western shirts, due to new fashion acceptance or product innovations. Alternately, women's western hand-tooled handbags may be down this year while leather shearling coats may be up. Each line must be closely examined to assess its promise for the coming selling season.

Once the merchandise manager or owner/buyer has allocated the total gross sales dollars by merchandise category, the buyer must determine how much merchandise will be needed to generate the projected sales dollars. The number of buying dollars to be spent will be determined in part by the firm's markup policy. For simplicity, assume the firm has a keystoning policy of doubling its wholesale cost on all items purchased. This practice is not recommended as the optimum pricing strategy, but it is a common practice among retailers. Thus, if a merchandise line is projected to generate $50,000, the store must have $25,000 (at cost) of merchandise. Current inventory plus merchandise on order totals are subtracted from the total season's sales to create an open to buy figure to be allocated to future purchases.

Past Purchase Performance

Review of Past Sales Experience by Merchandise Line

At this point the buyer turns to past sales records, previous orders, or paid invoices of the relevant sales period, and any buying notes made at the last year's market. Often buying notes and unfilled orders can be particularly useful in selecting suppliers. Often manufacturers will make up special samples of merchandise for regional sales presentations to test the product's appeal among buyers. If the product finds poor order support, the firm will not put the item into production and cancel any existing orders. Alternately, some items will be a hit and enjoy such success that the firm is unable to deliver the merchandise as promised. If the buyer has committed a significant amount of purchase dollars to such items in the past, it may have cost the store valuable sales dollars, because the money was committed but no merchandise was available to sell. Past experiences of nondelivery must be known before going to market and may become important negotiating points and/or may affect vendor choice and requested delivery dates for the coming season. If an item is especially attractive, the buyer might move up the delivery date to be sure the firm is not shut out if demands do exceed supply.

What sold well last year; where did it come from? How many did we sell? Did we reorder? If so, how many? More importantly, what didn't sell? Why? These vital questions can be examined by reviewing the invoices and inventory recapitulations if accurate records have been maintained. Most large retail stores place most of this information (vendor number, lot number, date and quantity received) on a detachable price ticket and collect and record it as each sale is made. Small firms do not have either the time or facilities to maintain such complete records. However, elementary efforts in this area will pay significant dividends when buying is undertaken. In any event, the buyer should go to market with the past invoices, separated by merchandise line, to serve as a guide to selecting both vendors and merchandise to implement the buying plan.

Buying Procedures at the Market

An early arrival at the market prior to its official opening can be extremely beneficial in locating special promotional goods for the future selling season. Most manufacturers will set out sam-

Buying "Close-Outs"

ples of discontinued lines and cut the price to clear their stocks before the market officially opens. The buyer must be wary about overbuying such merchandise so that the bulk of the line will be purchased in new, fresh, current offerings. However, if an item has been a good seller and a few are needed to fill out a size run to be offered at a promotional price, such close-outs may represent good buys. Usually after the show begins these items are "put in the back room" if any remain and are only shown to special customers upon request. Additionally, these items must be paid for upon receipt of the invoice.

Getting the "Feel of the Market"

Once at the market the prudent buyer should not make any spontaneous decisions without surveying the entire market and the individual offerings. Some buyers will spend the first two days getting a feeling of the range and price of competitive offerings. What common themes are present? Is there an item or items that every vendor is selling? Who has the best quality for the best price? Can they deliver on schedule? Who offers the best terms on small and large quantities? Some buyers rely heavily on a salesperson they know personally and depend on that person's past experience and advice in making purchase decisions. Good salespersons will give sound advice on quantities and prices even if it means that the initial order is cut back or reduced. Salespersons know that if they load up the retailer they have made two sales, first and last, to that merchant/buyer. Future good will is always more valuable than immediate gain for the professional salesperson.

Narrowing the Alternatives for Price Lining

Range of Price Lines

The buyer must constantly keep in mind that customer needs and satisfaction are paramount and that the choices that must be made should not be based on "what I like" or "I like this so I'll buy it." Admittedly, many of the buyer's personal choices will be consistent with the firm's customer group, but it is quite easy to slip over the line separating personal tastes and customer preferences.

Another point to keep in mind, particularly for those buyers who have a small store or a few outlets, is that the buyer will often not be selling on the merchandise floor. The buyer must depend on a few key full-time salespersons to be so enthusiastic about the new offering that they will personally accept it and suggest it to their customers. Often buyers will take one or two of the professional, full-time sales staff to market to get their opinions of the new merchandise as well as to acquaint them with the challenges of the buying process.

The buyer must buy merchandise which will fit into a limited range of prices to reduce customer buying confusion. Each vendor will quote different prices for their goods, yet the buyer must mentally sort out which goods will sell well in the established price categories, such as $10.95, $19.95, or $29.95. Today with customers "trading up" for better quality items the buyer, after assessing the vendor offerings and his or her perception of the firm's target market, may elect to drop a low-price range and pick up a new, higher-priced range of goods. The astute buyer realizes that most of the business will be done in some middle-range price line, but the firm must offer upper- and lower-priced lines to capture "plus" business.

Working the Line

"Working the line" means to review past sales records and current stock positions systematically, to project sales estimates for the next sales period, and to determine the amount of "open-to-buy" for each merchandise line—all of which is stated in units and purchase dollars. Then, in consultation with the sales representative, the buyer reviews the current merchandise offerings. Past poor performers and discontinued items are deleted, new interest-generating goods are added, and the staple line is reordered. The end product is an order stating the specific quantities being ordered by lot number and size, the price, all terms and conditions of sale, and specific shipping instructions.

When the buyer sits down to write and work the line, the sharp salesperson will usually offer to provide the buyer with copies of the relevant past orders. Together the buyer and salesperson briefly review the past purchases and analyze the line results in terms of both units and dollars purchased. Demonstrated winners or staple items are usually reviewed first in depth. Most of the time certain styles or renderings are offered year after year but in new fabrics, colors, or with slight changes in design. Such items form the core of the line and are usually bought in depth (large quantities).

Standard Assortments

Most of this merchandise comes in ranges, or standard assortments, by the dozen or carton lots. The manufacturers know certain items in an assortment will sell better than others. However, when they are making up the samples, they cannot predict the number of styles or sizes which will be "1s or 2s," so they present what they think will be a balanced offering. Thus, the buyer is precluded from picking and choosing individual items. One either buys the range or passes up the merchandise. Some higher priced merchandise in all lines is available "by each," and often these items are added by the buyer to provide assortment recognition of local color or style preferences.

New Items

After the major staples have been selected by size, color, or range, the buyer considers new items that will add spice to the line or increase the attractiveness of the offering. Usually these items are purchased on a highly subjective basis because there are no sales records available to guide decision making. At this point the buyer must exercise intuitive judgment or gut feeling as the new items are presented. Some new items may have been introduced or test marketed on a limited basis earlier, and the salesperson will have those results available to help guide the buyer. Caution is advised in using the salesperson's verbal reports because the representative may be tempted to puff up the results or employ the standing-room-only sales technique to increase the order. Usually the new items are sampled on a limited quantity basis with subsequent reorders later in the season if the item enjoys early sales success.

Merchandise Assortment's Contribution to Store Image
 Each item purchased and each line worked must fit into a nebulous but vital concept of store image. Each decision represents a piece of the jigsaw puzzle that will ultimately become a completed picture. The buyer must constantly be thinking about such tangential issues as how the merchandise will look on display, how many will be needed to fill up a counter, whether the colors can be fashion coordinated with other merchandise, and so forth. Also, one must keep in mind the need to reserve a pool of purchase dollars to buy new items from new suppliers not currently patronized.

New, Innovative, Unique, Attractive Items

Experienced buyers know that the large major suppliers concentrate on accepted merchandise items with yearly touch-ups to create a fresh image on the old line. The new innovative ideas and products are usually brought out by new, small, fledgling firms that may only have one good item out of ten new offerings. The astute buyer identifies that *sleeper* from the other nine items and places a sample order for early delivery with the intent of placing early reorders in depth if the product is a success. The

Merchandising Fad Items
buyer knows that such fad items move quickly in the market and that the small supplier will be unable to meet all the reorders during the current selling season if the product is highly successful. Early recognition of such new items is essential if the firm is to get in and out before the item is widely imitated and readily available from competitors. The secret to success lies in widely but selectively sampling the new items, taking early delivery, and closely monitoring the daily sales of these items. Again, mistakes will be made, but over time the risk turns into profit, creates customer interest, and establishes the store as a place where the action is.

Buying Negotiations

The climax of a successful buying effort occurs in the negotiation process. Regardless of the development and use of elegant economic buying models, retail buyers must realize that the negotiation of prices and terms of sales remains an exercise in the skillful enforcement of relative economic power.

The negotiation process begins when the retail buyer has determined the type of merchandise needed and after a choice of suppliers appears to be acceptable. Price, of course, is one of the major elements to be negotiated. Each buyer must constantly be aware that today's customers are very value conscious. When a customer considers "investment purchases" of large ticket items he or she wants the maximum satisfaction at a reasonable cost. The buyer must realize that the lowest cost merchandise, particularly in clothing, may not be the best buy for that firm's target market. On the other hand, those firms which stress "low everyday prices" must achieve the lowest possible cost available in the market to survive. In this situation "value" means "lowest price." In summary, each buyer must be aware of the differing perceptions of value held by the focal target market which he or she attempts to satisfy. Regardless of the market served, the buyer must negotiate the best prices possible. Trade practices vary from industry to industry and price concessions among vendors in each industry change from time to time within the legal framework of the Robinson-Patman Act and subsequent judicial decisions.

Value Conscious Customers

Price Discounts

Quantity Discounts

The most common reduction from list prices is quantity discounts (Table 10.2). A quantity discount is a price reduction on each item when those items are purchased in designated bulk units such as dozens or case lots. For example, an auto supply dealer may be able to buy oil filters from vendors for $4.00 each, or $3.75 each in dozen quantities or $3.50 each in case lots (24 filters). These discounts can be justified through significant cost savings in order processing, handling, and shipping. One may recall that in the earlier EOQ example the cost to process the order was $10.00 regardless of the amount ordered. This same principle applies to the vendors' operation in that the economies of scale reduce the per unit price as volume increases. A portion of these cost savings can then be offered to the buyer in the form of quantity discounts.

The buyer must not be lured into creating dangerous, costly overstocked positions by concentrating on quantity discounts. The decision maker might be reminded that marketing functions are not eliminated, just shifted. Even though the quantity discounted price may be attractive, the buyer must realize that the firm's inventory cost will rise in proportion to the amount purchased. Fewer turns, higher interest charges, and loss may occur if the appropriate volume is not achieved. If the retailer has ready

Quantity Discounts
Countercosts

Table 10.2 Characteristics of Price Discounts Given to Retailers

Type of Discount	Description
Quantity	Price reduction given from invoice price because purchases are made.
	Amount of discount must be justified by either a reduction in cost associated with handling a larger quantity or by meeting a competitor's equally low price if retail buyer is to avoid prosecution under Robinson-Patman Act.
Trade (functional)	Price reduction is based upon the marketing activities performed by the buyer. Discounts are deducted from list price in order stated, so a trade discount of 20, 10, 5 would be calculated as 20% off the list price, 10% off the balance, and 5% off the second balance, and the retailer would pay 100% − 20% (= 80%), −8% (= 72%), −3.6% or 68.4% of the list price. Trade discounts may be given in addition to quantity discounts.
Seasonal	Price reduction given to encourage ordering during "off" seasons.
Advertising allowances	Price reduction made to retailers who promote a product or service for the supplier. Amount of allowance must be justified by being a reasonable payment for such promotions and by similar offerings made by the seller to competitive dealers if retailer is to avoid prosecution under Robinson-Patman Act.
Cash	Price reduction given if retailer pays his bills promptly.
	Cash discounts are usually stated as 2/10, net 30, which means that a 2% discount is given if payment is received within 10 days of the date of the invoice, and interest charges will not be added unless bill is not paid during the 30 day period.
	Other forms of cash discounts are: 2/10 (2% discount if paid within ten days, balance due in thirty days), 2/10—30 extra (2% discount is extended ten days to forty days), and 2/10 E.O.M. (2% discount runs for ten days after end of month in which purchase was made).
	Retailers should use cash discounts because they are profitable (even if money must be borrowed) and they promote vendor good will.

access to an adequate market, a portion of the savings realized from quantity discounts and freight rate reductions may be passed on to the customer, resulting in more business.

Cumulative Quantity Discounts

Some vendors offer cumulative quantity discounts or "differed" or "patronage" discounts to their customers in an attempt to increase their total sales volume per account. Annually or at the end of a specified accounting period vendors total up the actual value of the goods shipped to each account. Then, based on predetermined volume breaks, the vendor will credit each client's account with a sum equal to five or seven or ten percent of their purchases for that previous period. While cumulative discounts reduce the actual cost of goods to the buyer, as he or

Vendor Dependence

she concentrates purchases with a limited number of suppliers this dependence can be damaging if tight supply conditions develop and the favored vendors cannot meet the demands. Again it is evident that all retail decisions have risks and benefits which must be carefully weighed to derive the greatest benefits over the long term.

Not all quantity discounts are offered as direct cost deductions from stated prices. Some vendors will offer merchandise premiums such as video recorders, stereo systems, or vacation trips for buyers and their families if the buyer will swing business their way. Often the trips are described as "product seminars" or "annual showings" when in fact they are opportunities to vacation at a luxury spa or expensive mountain retreat at no cost to the buyer. Most of these offers border on being illegal but some buyers do succumb to these selling techniques.

Trade Discounts

Suppliers, in certain industries, offer **trade discounts** to different classes of marketing institutions. This functional discount is justified by the vendor by saying that some of the marketing functions are shifted to other members of the distribution system and, hence, they should be entitled to lower costs via trade discounts. For example, if you walk into an automotive supply house and order a set of spark plugs, you could be quoted four different prices depending on who you are or whom you represent. If you are a "do-it-yourselfer," you would pay full retail price of $1.50 per spark plug. If you are a service station mechanic, you would get a 20 percent discount off list price. If you owned an automobile agency you might get another 10 percent off the balance. Lastly, if you owned an automobile repair shop and did all your repair parts business with this one firm, you might get an additional five percent discount.

Chained Discounts

Trade discounts are quoted in chained figures, i.e., in the last case 20, 10, 5 or list less 20, less 10, less 5. The first buyer would pay $6.00 plus the appropriate state sales tax for four spark plugs, the service station owner would pay $4.80 (no sales tax), the automobile dealer would pay $4.32 (no sales tax), and the repair shop would pay $4.09 (no sales tax) for the same merchandise. In each of the latter three cases the merchandise is purchased for resale and the buyers will capture and remit the sales taxes in their final customer billings. Not all industries offer such extensive trade discounts but if they are available, the buyer should attempt to achieve the best position possible, given the firm's volume of business.

Seasonal Discounts

Many retail products experience seasonal ebbs and flows in consumer demand. In an attempt to even out production schedules and minimize inventory accumulation, some vendors will offer seasonal discounts to interested buyers. Farm implement manufacturers will offer substantial discounts during winter months to encourage farm implement dealers to take delivery prior to the growing season. Alternatively, many vendors will offer "end of season" discounts to clear leftover finished goods. Large chain stores will instruct their buyers in New York City to search the market for fresh, unsold merchandise which can be purchased at a substantial end-of-season discount in large job lots. As the season nears an end in the store, these goods are shipped out and used as special purchases to attract in-store traffic which will be exposed to all merchandise which did not sell at full retail and has been marked down to clear. All parties benefit because the vendor clears stocks, the merchant gets a reasonable markup, and the customer gets new fresh merchandise which can be used or stored for next year.

Seasonal Discounts Promote "Early" Sales

Advertising Allowances and Discounts

Coop Advertising Discounts

National manufacturers with established trade name recognition often wish to increase their sales volume or their market share at the retail level. They will have their advertising agencies design a coordinated national campaign which will include national magazine advertisements, TV spot commercials, local advertising, and point-of-purchase displays. These manufacturers know that their objectives cannot be achieved without the cooperation of retail outlets across the nation. Additionally, they know that local newspapers charge substantially lower rates for local retailers' advertisements than those placed directly by national firms.

Alternately, some manufacturers will not spend the necessary time or resources to develop national consumer recognition and approval. Such vendors often turn to prestigious local department stores and specialty shops to sell their merchandise. In each case the local retail merchant may be offered advertising discounts from the list price so that the retail merchant will run advertisements featuring the vendor's products over the name of the advertising retailer. Such coop advertising can potentially increase both the vendor's and the retailer's total volume in that product line increases in-store traffic and contributes to the profitability of both seller and buyer, but they must be proportionately equal to all buyers.

Cash Discounts

Cash discounts for prompt payment of vendor invoices have always been important to the retail industry. Under current high cost of capital conditions, cash discounts have become even

Traditional Cash Discounts

more important to vendors and buyers alike. For years buyers with good credit ratings could routinely expect to receive such terms as "2/10, net/30," meaning that if they paid the face amount of the invoice within 10 days the vendor considered it a cash transaction and paid in full. If the retail firm did not pay within this 10-day grace period a 2 percent interest charge was assessed on the bill for the remaining 20 days. Surprisingly, when this 2/10, net/30 term is annualized it turns out that the rate is 36 percent, which in bygone days seemed outrageously high; but it did permit some retail merchants to receive the merchandise, sell it, and pay the invoice without investing any of his or her own limited working capital.

Prepayment

Today, while some firms are still offering cash discounts, more and more vendors are demanding immediate payment on delivery (COD) regardless of the retailer's credit worthiness, and some have gone so far as to demand prepayment when placing the order. Such dire tactics have been leveled primarily against small retailers who possess little bargaining power in the negotiation process to make up for the excessive slow payment by some retail firms who often have to be threatened with law suits before they will honor their obligations. Small manufacturers who depend on such retailers for the sale of a major portion of their production have little recourse if they wish to retain that market outlet.

Order Dating

Another negotiation issue is **dating,** which determines when cash discounts may be received and when payment is due if an interest penalty is to be avoided. Terminology for cash discounts under several frequently used future dating statements, such as 2/10-net 30 and 2/10 E.O.M., is explained in Table 10.2.

Future-dating negotiations take many forms. The invoice date can be used as the base date, so that any cash discount and billing statement refers to the number of days after the invoice date. However, several other kinds of future dating are commonly used. End-of-month (E.O.M.) dating allows for cash discount and full-payment period to begin on the first day of the following month instead of on the invoice date. For example, 2/10, n/30, E.O.M. on an invoice dated any day in June indicates that a 2 percent cash discount may be received until July 10. The full amount of the invoice is due by July 31. If no net period is indicated, the full amount is usually due at the end of the next calendar month (July 31 if the purchase was made any time during June).

E.O.M.

R.O.G.

Under receipt of goods (R.O.G.) dating the period begins on the date that the goods are received by the retailer. Thus payment on merchandise received on June 10 with a 2/10, n/30, R.O.G. dating must be made on or before June 20 to obtain the 2 percent cash discount and by July 10 to avoid possible payment of interest.

Advance or seasonal dating specifies a date in the future when the terms become applicable. For example, an order placed July 20 and shipped on October 15 with a 2/10, n/30 as of November 1 dating would indicate that a 2 percent cash discount may be obtained if payment is made on or before November 11.

Future datings are advantageous from a retailer's point of view because they allow the firm to operate with a lower level of merchandise investment. As a result, the retail buyer will benefit from, and negotiate for, the type of future dating that will delay the cash discount payment date as long as possible. Some suppliers will not accept future dating dealings but insist on immediate settlement. In this case the merchandise is sold on a C.O.D. (cash on delivery) basis and discounts must be taken and payment made when the goods are received. C.O.D. shipments are not generally used unless the retailer has not established credit standing with the particular vendor.

Retail buyers may also negotiate for an extra cash discount, called an **anticipation discount,** if the bill is paid before the expiration of the cash discount period. This extra discount is generally calculated on the basis of a prespecified annual percentage rate which is determined by the going commercial loan rate. Anticipation payments are normally calculated on the number of days remaining until the end of the cash discount period.

For example, suppose an invoice for $5,000, issued with terms of 2/10–30 extra with a 9 percent prespecified anticipation rate, is paid in ten days. This invoice is anticipated thirty days (40 – 10) prior to the expiration of the cash discount period. In this case the buyer would be entitled to a 2 percent cash discount (5,000 × .02), or $100, plus an anticipation reduction equal to 9 percent interest on the balance ($4,900) for 30/360 of a year (360 days), or $36.74.

Some retailers may obtain external financing from vendors who do not allow either cash or anticipation discounts and who do not charge interest on the unpaid balance after a stated number of days. Retailers, in this case, intentionally delay the payment of bills for thirty to sixty days beyond the due date. The amount of money owed to vendors is used by the retailer at no interest charge, but long-term vendor relationships are likely to suffer by using this **delayed payment** approach. Large retailers, however, may be sufficiently important and their overall credit rating good enough to force the supplier to allow them to be continually behind in making their payments. The supplier will also

Advanced
Dating

be forced to maintain good service and speedy merchandise delivery to these retailers or risk losing their business.

The delayed payment approach is not likely to be successful for smaller retailers. These firms, as individual accounts, do not represent a significant volume of business to the supplier. In addition, their credit rating is likely to decline rapidly if they attempt to use the delayed payment approach. Thus, the supplier can reduce the level of service provided to the smaller retailers, or even cease to sell to them if they attempt to follow this method.

Currently some firms have begun to factor or sell accounts receivable the day after the due date. The factor buys the accounts at a negotiated discount and then turns them over to collection agents. Collection agents attempt to get immediate full payment of the account including a substantial collection fee. While such actions may be necessary for persistent slow paying accounts, this practice hardly seems justified in all cases. Factoring may increase cash flow and funds utilization, but it usually results in the long-term loss of some profitable business if applied without due consideration for the retailer's situation.

Transportation and physical handling considerations are still another set of items that need to be negotiated. Suppliers usually quote prices as:

1. F.O.B. (free on board) factory, which means the buyer pays all transportation costs from the supplier's delivery platform.
2. F.O.B. shipping point, which means that the supplier bears the transportation charges to a local shipping point, but the retailer pays all further transportation costs.
3. F.O.B. destination (or store), which means that the seller pays the freight.
4. F.O.B. (freight allowed), which means that title to the goods passes as soon as the freight agent picks up the merchandise at the plant or warehouse, but the seller absorbs all freight charges.

The F.O.B. point is critical because it determines the point of ownership transfer, the assumption of responsibility for freight charges, and any damage to the merchandise while in transit. For example, a furniture store might order a bedroom suite to be shipped F.O.B. destination, and after months of waiting it never arrives at the store. In this case, the retailer is not responsible for payment or freight followup because furniture ownership has not passed to the firm.

Buyers must be knowledgeable about freight and handling costs to make comparisons of prices quoted on different transportation terms which are discussed at length in Chapters 11 and

12. Extra physical handling services may also be provided by some vendors. Vendors who sort and package merchandise separately for each store in a chain (or branch) retail system are able to reduce the handling costs for that chain or branch store system. These and other vendor-provided services (such as prompt delivery of merchandise) are quickly reflected in the firm's net profit picture.

Unfortunately, in today's markets freight payment by the intermediary or manufacturer is rapidly disappearing. Most retailers now have to pay all freight charges.

Retail buyers may also want to negotiate a guaranty against future price changes. If such a **price guaranty** is granted, the retail buyer can benefit as well as current buyers do if the supplier lowers his price after the order is placed. If the vendor raises his price after the order is placed, the buyer has the benefit of the originally stated price under the provisions of the price guaranty. Price guaranties are used frequently on orders for seasonal merchandise and for staple goods during periods of price uncertainty.

Robinson-Patman Act The principal federal legislation which deals with terms of sale in buyer-vendor relations is the controversial Robinson-Patman Act enacted by Congress in 1936. The law was a product of national concern over the demise of small family grocery stores. With the advent of the Great Depression, new forms of distribution were created to increase the efficiency of the retail food industry. Supermarket chains were formed to streamline food distribution by buying in large quantities, eliminate traditionally labor-intensive practices, and sell food at lower prices.

Unable to compete, the small retail groceries sought and received federal relief in the Robinson-Patman Act. The act provides that sellers engaged in interstate commerce cannot legally offer or be induced to offer to sell goods of the same grade and quality to different retailers in the same retail class at different prices if the effect is to substantially lessen competition or tend to create a monopoly or injure, destroy, or prevent competition with sellers or buyers or customers of either party. Price differences can be granted only on the basis of demonstrable cost differences in the manufacture, sale, or delivery of differing quantities of goods or in a good faith attempt to meet an equally lower price offered by a competitor. The law applies to all discounts, rebates, datings, and allowances. Essentially, all buyers should be offered the same quantity of the same goods at the same terms of sale.

This does not preclude a large volume liquor dealer in the Rocky Mountains from selling liquor at lower retail prices than an adjacent state liquor commission can buy it at the wholesale level. The retailer buys by the carload; the liquor commission buys by the case. This is a classic case of legal price discrimination which the law was meant to encourage and yet give some reasonable protection to the small retailer.

Retail Prices Can
Legally Differ

Current Negotiation Considerations

The retail buyer must negotiate cost/price, delivery dates, and credit terms. All three elements are significantly interrelated because they affect the cash flow and profitability of the firm. For example, if the merchandise is delivered early, with credit terms that dictate payment before demand and sales develop, the retailer will be forced to use precious capital or expensive borrowed funds to pay for the goods. This adds to the cost of the merchandise and must be recouped in larger markups.

In the last few years there has been a marked trend by manufacturers to shift the marketing functions of finance and inventory accumulation downward to the retailer. In the past it was a common practice for manufacturers to accept orders for "at once" or "when ready" delivery and offer dating as the sales generated a cash flow. Now most large firms offer a maximum dating of sixty days, and the more common offer is "net thirty days" with no cash discounts.

Delayed Shipping

Additional pressure is being exerted by the manufacturers to take early or "at once" deliveries. Any order carrying a delayed shipping date carries the explicit condition that the order may not be filled. Thus, the retail buyer must weigh the consequences of having to borrow heavily at a high interest rate or risk not having adequate quantities of goods on the shelves and racks to sell.

Another problem associated with future order dating arises between large and small retail accounts. Informally, large manufacturers encourage their large accounts (volume buyers) to split their orders, placing some for "at once" and some for future deliveries. In this way manufacturers have firm orders and can give the large accounts assurance of steady periodic deliveries and a predictable cash flow. Any surplus production is then parceled out among the smaller volume buyers. In some cases, the smallest buyers do not receive any of their ordered merchandise until late in the selling season, and even then they may experience a large number of substitute nonordered items. If challenged, the manufacturers plead overselling and unexpected demand and note that buyers were forewarned of the risk when they placed their orders.

Advanced Shipping

Additional strains are being placed on small retailers' limited capital and plant as manufacturers shift the inventory storage function to the retailer. When merchandise is shipped early the retailer must rent additional storage space, hire more stockroom personnel to handle the flood of merchandise, and risk product deterioration while awaiting the major portion of the selling season. All these activities increase the financing requirements for the small merchant operating on limited invested capital.

Return Privileges or Charge Backs

During the negotiation process most alert buyers will reaffirm any prior return privileges agreements or attempt to gain such benefits. Usually these privileges are limited to defective merchandise that did not meet customer or buyer expectations. This return privilege is becoming increasingly important as retailers are asked by customers to assume their responsibilities under the Consumer Products Warranty and Guaranty Act. Usually manufacturers require that each retailer write for specific permission to return such goods for credit toward future purchases. Many retailers who have only a few such defective items simply prefer to charge them off (mark the item down to zero) and throw them away. Such decisions assume that the cost in clerical time and postage is not worth the credited amount. While this may be true, the retailer must realize that the entire cost of the item is lost and must be recovered from future profit margins on other products. Buyers should always seek and use such return privileges within the legal framework of the Robinson-Patman Act.

Credit Considerations When Buying

Astute retail buyers take time to prepare their credit plans as meticulously as they do their merchandise plans. If the firm is large enough to have a finance/controller department, the retail buyer should work out a detailed buying budget to assure prompt payment of invoices to receive any cash discounts that may be offered later at the market. If the firm does not have specialized functions, the buyer/manager should work closely with the firm's financial backers and commercial banks to assure that adequate funds are available when needed.

Lines of Credit

Before going to market the buyer must work out cash flow projections based on anticipated monthly sales and expenses. The buyer must constantly juggle the desire to have the new merchandise early to test customer acceptance with the stark realization that merchandise should not be received before it is needed. Usually the small retailer/buyer negotiates a loan large enough to cover the season's buying and operational needs. Specific details vary with the type of retail operation, the state of national and local business conditions, the local demands for loans, bank discount rates, and most importantly, the past repayment history of the retailer. The retailer will periodically draw funds against the loan balance as needed to pay the bills as they come due. In this way the interest charges may be minimized and the funds borrowed only as needed.

Credit Ratings

The next step is to accumulate supplier letters attesting to the firm's credit worthiness. Usually these come unsolicited if the firm pays its bills promptly and takes advantage of the available discounts. If the firm deems it useful, it might be helpful to establish a credit rating with Dun & Bradstreet, the national credit rating bureau for business firms. Armed with these credit references and a line of credit through the firm's checking account, the buyer is ready to go to the market and is not restricted to doing business only with past suppliers who know the firm's credit worthiness. The ability to open accounts with new suppliers on the spot is important when new, innovative goods are encountered. Some small manufacturers may be "cash short" or undercapitalized and request payment with the order. One should question such a shaky position because it might affect future delivery. The experienced retailer always carries a few spare checks for "instant opportunities."

Purchase Procedures

Once the details of merchandise assortment, terms, and delivery dates have been settled, the buyer must be sure the oral agreements are accurately transcribed into specific orders. Most salespersons prefer to take the working sheets and transcribe them onto order forms during nonshow hours, usually late at night. The following day the buyer returns, verifies the order, signs it, and receives a copy. One should always get a copy of the final order so that any future "misunderstandings" between buyer and seller can be avoided and, more importantly, when the buyers return home, they can complete their merchandising, promotional, and financial plans and create the necessary budgets to translate purchases into profitable sales.

Some retail buyers complete a **purchase order** form when all the negotiations have been completed. This form may be supplied to its buyers by the retail firm itself (Figure 10.3 is an example of such a form) or a vendor's order form may be used. Large retail firms are likely to use their own standard form because information can be printed in one location and on as many copies as the firm needs to handle and control merchandise internally. These same forms are also used to give vendors shipping instructions. The written purchase order is issued by the purchasing department of the retail firm to the vendor. Upon acceptance by the vendor, it becomes a legal, binding contract.

The vendor sends an **invoice** to the buyer after the vendor has

Figure 10.3 Sample Purchase Order Form

Purchase Order

THIS SPACE FOR OFFICE USE

Customer Number	Credit Department
Pairs	
Entered	

PLEASE PRINT CLEARLY

Charge to

Owner

Street

City State Zip Code

Customer Order No.	Date Ordered
Shipping Instructions	

SINGLE PAIRS OR LESS THAN THREE PAIRS OF ONE STOCK NUMBER $1.50 PER PAIR EXTRA
ORDERS FOR ONE ACCOUNT NUMBER FOR TWELVE PAIRS OR MORE BY SAME SHIPPING METHOD TO ONE ADDRESS NO EXTRA CHARGE
ALL SIZES 12½, 13, 13½, 14, $1.50 PER PAIR EXTRA. SIZE 15 AND UP $2.50 PER PAIR EXTRA. STOCK GOODS NET – NO DISCOUNT.

TERMS Stock Goods NET 30 DAYS. F.O.B. FACTORY.

This and each future order of the Purchaser must be specifically accepted in writing by the Seller to become binding. Acceptance of this or any other order will not constitute the Purchaser an agent of the Seller.

Stock Number	Width	5	5½	6	6½	7	7½	8	8½	9	9½	10	10½	11	11½	12	12½	13	13½	14	15	Total	Price
		5	5½	6	6½	7	7½	8	8½	9	9½	10	10½	11	11½	12	12½	13	13½	14	15	Total	Price
		5	5½	6	6½	7	7½	8	8½	9	9½	10	10½	11	11½	12	12½	13	13½	14	15	Total	Price

PLEASE CIRCLE ANY PAIRS ALREADY SOLD FOR WHICH CUSTOMERS ARE WAITING

PRICES SUBJECT TO CHANGE WITHOUT NOTICE

received the purchase order. The invoice is the itemized statement (or bill) containing the quantity, price, terms of sale, and other negotiated agreements on the merchandise being shipped. An example of an invoice form is presented in Figure 10.4.

Another step in the negotiation process involves the **transfer of title,** which usually occurs when the supplier releases the goods to a common carrier for delivery. If the goods are damaged in transit, the buyer's recourse is *generally* against the transportation firm, not the vendor. But there are two variations from this procedure.

Goods may be bought on a **consignment** basis. In this case, title to the goods remains with the vendor until the goods are sold by the retailer. The supplier agrees to accept the return of any merchandise not sold; so the retailer does not take any risks caused by merchandise obsolescence or price declines. The retailer, however, is liable if the product is not properly cared for or is inadequately merchandised. Thus, retailers should carefully evaluate the consignment merchandise and the vendor. New items are frequently introduced on a consignment basis because the retailer does not like to invest in a product that may not sell well.

Goods may also be purchased on a **memorandum buying** basis, which is a special form of future dating. In this case, the title to the goods passes to the retailer, who assumes all ownership risks but reserves the right to return any unsold portion of the goods to the supplier without payment. The retailer assumes little risk and is free to price the merchandise at any level. Memorandum billing is used frequently when goods are introduced on an experimental or test market basis.

Order Cancellation

A final area for examination is the process of order cancellation. A buyer should not hesitate to cancel orders if projected sales

Figure 10.4 Sample Invoice Form

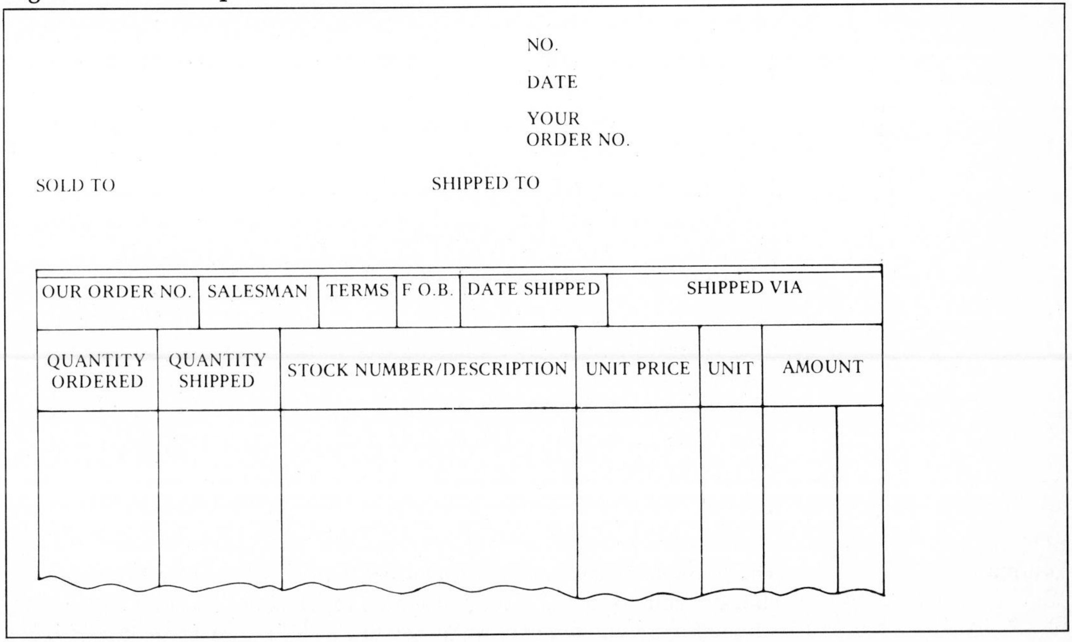
NO.
DATE
YOUR ORDER NO.

SOLD TO SHIPPED TO

OUR ORDER NO.	SALESMAN	TERMS	F.O.B.	DATE SHIPPED	SHIPPED VIA

QUANTITY ORDERED	QUANTITY SHIPPED	STOCK NUMBER/DESCRIPTION	UNIT PRICE	UNIT	AMOUNT

levels do not materialize or goods are late in arriving. Such action, if taken promptly, preserves valuable capital to be spent in more important ways. If sales are down markedly, the firm does not want to continue receiving more markdowns with the subsequent loss of money. Alternatively, if the supplier cannot deliver the merchandise, it is important to take corrective action and scramble for any available merchandise from other suppliers. In both cases future contractual obligations are terminated and a revised merchandise plan must be devised.

Cancelling Orders

In the first case, if the firm seriously overestimated the season's sales levels, then the buyer must go back through the outstanding orders and selectively prune the remaining orders. Mass cancellation of all orders will result in sure disaster, because the merchandise lines will be riddled with stock-outs in the best selling sizes, colors, and so forth. In order to stay in business and remain viable, the breadth of the assortment must be reduced through promotion and perhaps selective markdowns. Any resulting funds should be used to consolidate the assortment and reestablish some degree of merchandise depth. Fresh stock may temporarily revive customer interest and buy time for an orderly disposition of unsold seasonal merchandise.

In the second situation, missed sales are inevitable. The buyer must decide whether there is enough time to get merchandise and meet customer needs or lose the sales. The normal buyer reaction is to pick up the telephone and place orders for immediate delivery from distant suppliers or rush out to buy from local intermediaries. Hopefully such action will maintain customer loyalty and patronage. Nine times out of ten, however, such action results in losses because customers have already gone elsewhere and bought the needed goods. The buyer is best advised to put the cancelled order dollars in the next season's merchandise that can be brought in to test early customer acceptance. In any event, those suppliers who consistently do not deliver as promised should be dropped from any further consideration.

Retail buyers should attempt to purchase the desired merchandise at the lowest net cost, but should not expect unreasonable discounts or price concessions from the supplier. It is important to develop the respect of vendors who can aid the buyer by providing services, advice, and speedy delivery of merchandise. Thus, a long-run relationship, based upon mutual respect for one another, is desirable.

Summary

The previous discussion has examined the buying process in considerable detail. The general model that has been presented can be adapted to a wide range of retail situations. Large department stores, chain stores, and mass merchandisers have their own unique mode of operation, but the basic buying duties presented in the chapter must be accomplished if the firm is to obtain the best merchandise at the lowest costs. Particular attention was given to "market buying," which is a common practice for many small and medium retailers. Often the success or failure of the organization or store hangs on the quality of the decisions made in one to five days spent at the market. Buyers should always be alert for new and profitable products that fit into their assortment plans and complement their retail store image.

Merchandise buying is a risky, challenging profession that is fast paced and very demanding. However, the rewards, both in money and personal satisfaction, are significant. Positive professionalism seems to be the road to success for many aspiring retail merchandisers.

Questions

1. Define the types and characteristics of intermediaries serving retailers. Which one is most often used by small retailers? Why?
2. How can accurate, complete merchandise records aid buyers in performing their duties? Explain.
3. How should the buyer attempt to forecast a firm's seasonal sales? What variables must be considered? Why are they important?
4. What is meant by "keystoning" a product? Is this a good policy to follow in all situations? Explain.
5. What part should manufacturers' close-outs play in a retail store's merchandise program? Explain.
6. How can professional intermediaries and manufacturers' representatives assist the buyer in making appropriate buying decisions?
7. How should a buyer balance the merchandise assortment to both present staple items and add spice with new items? Explain.
8. What additional problems are experienced when suppliers shorten dating terms and demand "at once" shipping privileges? Explain.
9. How does cash flow generated by retail sales affect the buying process? Discuss.
10. Under what conditions should buyers cancel orders? What are the probable consequences of such action?

Case Study: The Cowboys Are Going to the Superbowl

Jim Adams was sitting in his office going over last month's sales reports. As general merchandise manager for the J. M. Department Store in Denton, Texas, he was responsible for the entire merchandise operation of the store. It was August and the store was right in the middle of its "back-to-school" rush and business was good. The spring season had also been good and they had successfully cleaned up the summer merchandise with few markdowns.

Just then his secretary-receptionist, Joan, came in with a business card from a salesperson who was seeking an opportunity to make a presentation on the "Silver Crush Bunch" promotion. Jim agreed to see the salesperson but only for ten minutes; he was a busy man.

Jayne Olsen walked into Jim's office with her sample racks and suitcases bulging with merchandise. After exchanging pleasantries Jayne began her sales presentation. "The Dallas Cowboys are going to the Superbowl this year and everyone will want to be a part of this super, super football season," Jayne said confidently. "The Dallas market has just gone wild already and we wanted your store to get in on this fabulous, profitable promotion," she said assertively. As the program unfolded, Jim was exposed to a complete array of Cowboy memorabilia ranging from ash trays to beer steins to T-shirts. The key to the promotion seemed to be the "Silver Crush" T-shirts. All loyal fans would express their support for the team by outfitting the whole family with a "Silver Crush" T-shirt and wearing them to all the games.

Jayne explained they had ten different standard packs of promotional items, each tailored for different types of retailers or each item could be purchased in gross lots separately. The T-shirts cost $30, $35, and $40 per dozen depending on sizes and were to be retailed at $5.95 for children's sizes, $6.95 for women's sizes, and $7.95 for men's sizes. The shirts could be delivered in ten days and all other items were available for immediate delivery. All shipments were freight prepaid with cash on delivery.

Nine minutes later Jayne went for a successful close by taking out her order pad and began saying, "Shall I put you down for our deluxe package or would you like to buy the items separately?" Jim leaned back in his chair, remembering that the Cowboys had been touted as a much improved team this year by the local sports broadcasters. There had been some mention of the Superbowl. Jayne stood quietly, awaiting his decision.

Discussion Questions

1. Are there enough Cowboy fans in his target market who will buy the merchandise? Will he have exclusive distribution of the promotion in town or will his competitors be offered the same deal?

2. If Jim does buy the promotion and the Cowboys have a losing season, what will happen to the merchandise?

3. If he did buy the promotion, where should he merchandise the goods? The firm did not carry sporting goods and was limited to men's, boys', girls', and women's departments.

4. Should Jim buy into the promotion? If so, should he carry the full line or just the T-shirts? Why or why not?

| Controlling Merchandise Handling, Theft, and Energy Consumption

Learning Goals

1. To become familiar with the various modes of transportation used in merchandise distribution.
2. To understand different freight rate classifications, how freight rates are determined, and how transportation costs can affect a retail firm's profitability.
3. To be able to explain the necessary storage and warehousing functions and the modern techniques of mechanization being employed in distribution centers.
4. To be able to discuss various methods of controlling loss through shrinkage, shoplifting, burglary, and internal theft.
5. To know how integrated merchandise handling systems can be coordinated with energy management systems to minimize energy consumption.

Key Terms and Concepts

freight classifications
freight rates
bill of lading
freight bills
computerized rate prerating and auditing

integrated POS systems
source marking systems: UVM, UPC distribution centers
EAS systems
false arrest civil suits
dishonesty exposure index

Handling merchandise is a multifaceted and heretofore often overlooked aspect of retail management. Many buyers have not concerned themselves with shipping rates, internal physical management, or merchandise theft. However, the informed retail merchant at all industry levels has begun to realize that any inefficiencies or waste in these areas contribute directly to the bottom line of profitability. While these "behind the scenes" activities may not be glamorous per se, each retail decision maker must be aware of the interrelationships found in handling merchandise at the lowest possible cost.

Each time an order is generated it sets in motion a complex series of interrelated activities. As noted earlier, the buyer must accurately anticipate the needs of his or her customers so that the store does not miss any sales to its target market yet not overcommit in inventory investment. When the buyer considers the

Inventory Level
Freight Choice
Interrrelationships

quantity to order, the person must consider the projected demand for a given period, current stock levels, any merchandise on order, any standard packing limitation *and* transportation costs.

Rail and motor transport companies charge customers on the basis of 100-pound increments up to 5,000 pounds. Therefore, a retail firm will pay exactly the same amount for a given shipment whether it weighs 100 pounds or 199 pounds. An astute buyer can often offset higher inventory costs of fast-moving, low unit weight items by carefully observing the "break points" of these and other common carriers, such as United Parcel Service (UPS), Federal Express, and Air Freight.

Determining optimal shipping instructions is a complex problem which each buyer must effectively resolve. Those fortunate enough to have access to a knowledgeable traffic manager will find the job much easier. The majority of buyers who must operate independently should have an elementary understanding of freight rate determination.

Regardless of the mode or modes of transportation chosen, certain basic truths do pertain:

1. High-speed freight movement or special services cost disproportionately more than low-speed, minimal service transportation.
2. Lightweight goods which have high-value density can be transported faster and further than bulky, heavy, low-value density items.
3. All forms of transportation are subject to unexpected delays ranging from acts of God to labor strikes. Losses incurred due to lack of products are not usually recoverable unless the retailer has specific insurance coverage.
4. Water transportation is the slowest and cheapest form of transportation. Rail transportation is the next least expensive, provided rail service is available near vendors and buyers. Motor carriers are only cheaper than air freight but provide maximum flexibility for shipments of less than 90,000 pounds. Air Express is the fastest, most expensive, and limited by the physical size and shape of the aircraft being used.

Relative transportation cost comparisons are difficult to generalize, but one recent study indicated that air freight was more than fifty times as expensive as shipment by waterways, fifteen times as expensive as rail, and two and one-half times as expensive as motor carrier (Table 11.1).[1]

Even though air transportation is the most expensive mode of shipment there are situations when that is the best solution.

Weight "Break Points"

Fastest May Be
Best Despite Cost

Table 11.1   Comparative Freight Rates Per Mile [a]

	Rail	Truck	Air	Waterways
1971	1.593¢	9.3¢	21.42¢	0.339¢
1972	1.618¢	9.5¢	21.52¢	0.328¢
1973	1.617¢	9.8¢	21.92¢	0.381¢
1974	1.853¢	10.6¢	24.87¢	0.492¢
1975	2.041¢	11.8¢	27.17¢	0.518¢
1976	2.191¢	12.2¢	29.22¢	0.507¢
1977	2.286¢	12.8¢	31.33¢	0.534¢
1978	2.370¢	13.6¢	33.65¢	0.569¢
1979	2.617¢	15.3¢	39.61¢	0.686¢
1980	N/A [b]	18.2¢	N/A	N/A

[a] One measure of freight rates, freight revenue per revenue ton mile, can also be used to determine how fast rates are climbing via different freight transportation modes.
[b] N/A = Not Available
Source: Thomas F. Dillon, "Freight Rates Will Rise But at a Moderate Pace," *Purchasing* July 9, 1981, p. 47. Information from Association of American Railroads, American Trucking Association, Air Transport Association of America, American Waterway Operators (1977–1979) and Transportation Association of America (1971–76).

Seasonal Business
Comes Once

Suppose you own a small department store in Billings, Montana and you get an unexpected snowstorm on September 10. The city is buried under a foot of snow; the children need new winter jackets and your initial shipment is sold out in the first hour of business. You know that this seasonal business only comes once a year and if you don't have the goods to sell, your customers will order the winter apparel from chain store mail order catalogs. A call to your vendor discloses that your entire order for the season can be filled and shipped at once out of New York City on an evening plane and be in your store ready for sale when you open at ten o'clock tomorrow. The freight cost will be $3.50 per jacket compared to $1.00 per jacket if sent by motor carrier which would arrive in a week to ten days. What is your decision? Most merchants would appropriately reply, "Let's go for it!" While the cost will cut into the markup margin, the store will not miss the vital winter business, and considerable goodwill can be created by meeting customer needs.

Freight rates are determined by a complex classification system and carrier tariffs or prices. Most merchandise moved by rail or motor carrier is charged on a **commodity rate** basis. Each carrier has a certain set of target markets in a specified number of cities which the firm attempts to serve. In order to attract business, each carrier sets up special low commodity rates on those items it wants to carry to optimally utilize its equipment over the designated routes. Most common carriers will accept other freight consignments which do not qualify for commodity rates. Shippers of these goods are charged **class rates** which are determined by consulting the Uniform Freight Classification, Consolidated Freight Classification, National Motor Freight Classification, or Coordinated Motor Freight Classification directories. Most generic products have a line designation in these directories which give a general description of the goods and list carload minimum weights in pounds, carload **(CL)** and less than carload ratings **(LCL)**. In the rare instance that some merchandise does not fit into a commodity or class rating, then it is assigned the "not otherwise indexed by name" **(NOIBN)** classification which is charged a single rate.

Calculating Freight Rate

Once the class and rating is known one must consult the carrier's freight tariff book which specifies that carrier's price for transporting the goods in certain mileage blocs, i.e., from Athens, Ohio to Atlantic City, New Jersey. These **line haul charges** are quoted on the basis of a "Class 100," which means that if a buyer wanted to ship 100 pounds of men's belts (NOIBN) in boxes from Boston to Atlantic City, he or she would determine the tabled value in the tariff book and then look up the actual dollar charge for that tabled value. If the weight of the shipment turned out to be 150 pounds, the rate would be doubled because the rates are based on 100-pound increments.

Alternately, line haul freight charges may be assessed by the volume shipped or by particular routing or on other miscellaneous bases.[2]

One rather unique rate has been developed to address the needs of freight forwarders, shipping associations, and distribution centers. **FAK,** or freight-all-kinds, is offered by major carriers to permit consolidation of small shipments into larger, more economical freight units. Thus, a number of small shipments from St. Louis bound for Dallas on the same day can be consolidated into one motor trailer load **(TL)** which will be billed at a lower price than a less than trailer load shipment **(LTL)**. The buyer gets the merchandise quicker and cheaper than contracting for transportation directly with the carrier. Also the risk of loss or damage is significantly reduced by using containers or just by less need for handling the goods. Large distribution centers, such as J. C. Penney, Montgomery Ward, and Sears, Roebuck and Company can apply for FAK rates to minimize their costs and still achieve large economies of scale in their operation.

Consolidation

Special Charges

In addition to these specific line haul charges, most transportation firms add charges for special services such as pickup and delivery by a local truck, spotting a rail car on a particular siding, or freight storage. Most motor carriers begin charging **de-**

murrage or storage fees if they cannot deliver to the merchant within eight hours after the goods are received at the terminal.[3] In practice, if the delivery person cannot make a successful delivery the first time he or she tries, the merchandise is returned to the terminal and storage fees are assessed as well as additional delivery charges.

Control of Merchandise in Transit

Bill of Lading

Each buyer should be familiar with three basic documents. The key element is the **bill of lading.** It acknowledges receipt of goods from the vendor to the carrier, specifies who has title to the goods, and delineates the legal conditions of transport agreed to by both the shipper and carrier. This document is particularly important when the vendor ships goods before complete payment is received or when freight claims for loss or damage to merchandise or overcharges must be filed.

Freight Bills

When freight is delivered dockside, the delivery person will present the **freight bill** for immediate payment unless prior credit arrangements have been made. Some motor carriers will extend credit up to seven days while rail carriers will only permit 96 hours on less than carload shipments. At the time of delivery each carton must be checked off the freight bill, making sure each one is destined for that particular store, and visually in-

Damage in Transit

spected for any external damage. If damage is detected it should be noted on all copies of the freight bill so that responsibility for loss can later be assessed.

Auditing Freight Bills

After freight packages have been checked in and opened to inspect for hidden damage, the freight bills should be checked for accuracy. Admittedly the small retailer does not have access to current rate and tariff books, but he or she can check for omissions, duplicate billings, and incorrect extensions. If everything seems in order they can be paid and set aside for later audit by firms specializing in freight rate overcharges. Any recovery is shared on a 50–50 basis between the auditor and retailer.[4] Even the best run traffic departments may experience recoveries of 1 percent of paid bills. Lastly, recovery can be gained up to three years after the overcharge was paid on interstate shipments.[5]

Damage Claims

Each carrier has different procedures for handling damage claims. Each bill of lading will stipulate the limit of liability as well as the conditions under which the common carrier will attempt to "reasonably dispatch" the shipment without loss or damage. Usually the damaged merchandise is set aside in the receiving area when unpacked, along with the damaged carton, and held until the carrier's claim agent arrives to assess damage. Once the assessment has been made the retailer negotiates a reasonable settlement ranging from complete reimbursement for cost of the item plus assessed freight charges to cost of repair of the item. In all cases the recovery is limited to the carrier's stated level of liability, which often is not enough to recover the value of fragile merchandise.

Limited Carrier Liability

Obviously making a wise transportation decision is a technically complex task. Large firms such as General Tire and Rubber Company and Lever Brothers have turned to outside firms which specialize in computer-based systems to prerate bills of lading and audit freight bills.[6] A firm called Distribution Services has developed an "Auto Rate" system which is reported to be the most comprehensive transportation rate database in the industry. Thirty files of information can be electronically searched for *the* optimal rate for any shipments sent by air, rail, motor carrier, or freight forwarder. Thus, the shipper is in control of freight operations subscribing to the service. If a firm wishes to perform the same computerized analysis in-house, such firms as Transportation Concepts and Services (TCS), Inc. will set up their program on the host firm's computer. Ore-Ida, a division of H. J. Heinz Company, installed the TCS system, called Compu-Rate II, in 1980 and anticipates they will save approximately $400,000 per year by using the system.[7]

Computerized Freight Billing and Audit

While there are no hard and fast rules about when to institute systematic freight audits there are some guidelines available. One authority, Harvey Cummings, traffic director for Woodward and Lothrop, suggests that when a store's freight bills average $40,000 a year or more it pays to have them audited. If one assumes that typical freight charges run 1.5–1.8 percent of gross sales, the store should be doing $2.2 to $2.7 million dollars a year. When a retail firm achieves $8.5 to $10 million, he advises the use of either an internal or external computerized system.[8]

When It Pays to Audit Freight Bills

Not all retailers can afford computerized systems or consultants. Some small firms may not have enough freight bills to warrant auditing. In these situations the retailer can acquire a copy of the *Manual for Reducing Transportation Costs*, published by the National Retail Merchants Association's Traffic Group, and become better informed on what to look for and how better to cope with rising transportation costs which can adversely affect vital cash flows and ultimate profitability.

Transportation Challenges

For many years retailers enjoyed predictable stable transportation service. Interstate carriers were controlled by the Interstate Commerce Commission (ICC) which granted route authorities and approved tariffs. Retailers could accurately forecast transportation costs and delivery schedules. Critics of the system said that it created unfair monopolies which resulted in inflated costs. The argument, in part, was quite valid. Revenues from profitable, high-volume long hauls were used to offset losses incurred in servicing smaller shippers in small towns across the nation.

Transportation
Deregulation

With the advent of deregulation of the airline and trucking industries in 1979 and 1980, respectively, the transportation industry was thrown into chaos with retailers sharing their full portion of challenges.

Almost immediately large long haul carriers filed to reduce or abandon the less profitable clients and communities. Secondly, these carriers, fully within the spirit of the law, filed for authority to "cherry pick" the better, more lucrative business of medium and small transportation firms. During 1981, many regional trucking companies failed, leaving small retailers without any common carrier service. Those fortunate enough to retain service began to notice major differences in the quality of service being given by the carriers.

Transit Times Vary

One recent study conducted by Woodward & Lothrop Department Stores in Los Angeles found that it took four working days and 15 hours to get a shipment from Los Angeles to Washington, D.C. using the motor carrier Roadway Express. Repeating the experiment Woodward found that the slowest time was eleven working days. All carriers had the same published rates.[9] In these days of tight inventory control, such variations in performance cannot be tolerated. Uncontrollable delays can wreck the best laid merchandising plans. Therefore the smart buyer is best advised to enlist the aid of the traffic department to determine

Choose the "Best" Firm

the "best" transportation combinations to minimize time delays even though it may cost more. A firm may wisely elect to funnel all its business through a limited number of proved transportation firms for better, reliable service. Some might counsel against this concentration strategy but in light of today's uncertain transportation environment it appears to be the best way.

Deregulation of the trucking industry has not been without some benefits for large chain retailers who operate their own trucking system. Historically, such retail firms as Safeway would receive carloads of foodstuffs at regional distribution centers, break down, store, and then reship the goods in mixed

Back-haul

truckloads to local supermarkets. This would mean that the trucks would return empty, hence, increasing the transportation costs. With the advent of deregulation these retailers are now permitted to solicit and carry freight in competition with other carriers on regular *back-haul* routes which potentially reduces operating costs. Not all retail firms have been successful in locating and negotiating regular freight contracts, but the opportunity to reduce costs is everpresent.

Warehousing

Remote Warehousing

When merchandise has been successfully shipped from vendor to retailer the focus of attention shifts to internal merchandise handling. The majority of freight shipments are shipped directly to the retailer's main retail location. Small retailers find that most of the goods can be adequately received and processed on-site without resorting to a separate warehousing facility. Certain small businesses such as automobile and appliance dealers may find it more economical to store some of their inventory off the premises in a lower rent section of the community. The merchant must decide the optimal use of the store's square footage. If warehouse space is costly or at a great distance from the store and frequent access is needed, then maybe warehousing on-site can be cost-justified.

Public Warehousing

Some retailers tend to forget that public warehousing is available in many metropolitan areas and can serve as a viable alternative to owning the storage facility. According to Mr. William Mischou, President of USCO Services, Inc., who operates a chain of 28 public warehouses across the nation, rising transportation, energy, and distribution costs are making public warehousing more attractive. In addition, most firms are unwilling to incur high debt charges for new buildings and are increasingly looking at the return on assets (ROA) rather than return on investments (ROI) as the appropriate measure of managerial efficiency.[10]

Full Range of Services

Such shifts in managerial thinking favor public chain warehousing. Modern public warehouses can offer a wide variety of services including storage, handling, bill of lading preparation, order entry, pool distribution and consolidation, import/export capabilities, pick and pack services, break bulk, bulk transfer and repacking.[11] While many of these services are particularly useful for marketing intermediaries, some large retailers may find it a better method of dealing with their merchandise handling functions than running their own operation, particularly during periods of low economic activity.

Distribution Centers

High volume retailers such as Safeway and J. C. Penney have taken the regional warehouse concept one step further and have discovered the advantages of using major distribution centers strategically located throughout the nation. In earlier times each store might have ordered goods from many separate vendors, received numerous small, high cost freight shipments, and employed stock room employees to process and store large quantities of merchandise at expensive retail sites. By centralizing most of these merchandise handling functions in selected locations in specially designed buildings in low cost industrial parks, the firm can use highly efficient mechanized systems which reduce handling costs to a fraction of former individual store operation's costs.

For example, K mart has eleven distribution centers located in eleven different states with 14.3 million square feet of warehouse space. By locating these distribution centers in optimal locations, 81 percent of the firm's stores will be within 250 miles of a distribution center, rather than hundreds of miles from individual vendors. By ordering and shipping in carload or truckload quantities, breaking bulk and using the automated equipment to sort and recombine the goods for shipment to their closely grouped stores, K mart will save transportation costs and reduce the level of in-store inventory without increasing the risk of stock-outs.

A wide variety of retailers has adopted and implemented the distribution center mode of merchandise handling. Some representative firms include Wal-mart, Lane Bryant, T. G. & Y., SupeRx Drug, O. J. Wilson, Lord and Taylor, and Burdines. Each organization's center has been custom designed to meet the individual retailer's particular needs. One firm, Lucky Stores, operates a highly mechanized 62,000 square foot frozen food warehouse in Buena Park, California. This integrated system picks 92 percent of all cases shipped and processes 23,000 cases per seven hour shift. Thus, the firm has the capacity to trans-ship over 2 million cases of frozen food a month at significantly lower costs than other competitive supermarkets.

Mechanized
Merchandise Handling

The key to efficient merchandise handling lies in mechanization. The most successful applications are found in the dry grocery distribution centers. As the shipping cartons are received they are placed on high speed conveyors and rushed to a sortation area where optical readers scan the special UPC labels and control high speed diverters which can process 100 cartons per minute. Operating at these rates Alpha Beta and Spartan Stores centers can routinely process 300,000 cartons a week. Such

Exhibit 11.1   Automated Sorting Equipment

Automated sorting equipment has reduced human resource requirements and increased distribution center capacities.
Source: Photo courtesy of Rapistan Division, Lear Siegler, Inc.

scanning-diverter systems can replace three employees who individually earned $40,000–$60,000 annually.[12]

Disposition of the goods after they have been sorted is determined by the distribution policy of the firm. Some goods are immediately picked and sorted for shipment to some smaller regional warehouse closer to the retail stores. If the goods are fashion garments shipped on hangers (GOH) or in cartons, they will be sent to preparation areas where the garments are unpacked, steamed if necessary, and hung on portable racks for delivery to the various stores which the distribution center serves. If the goods are source marked and packaged in cartons, they are sent directly to the stores or diverted to a warehouse area in the distribution center for future shipment.

Importance of Warehouse Design

Merchandise can be stored on flats, pallets, bulk or free standing. When new warehouse facilities are built the retailer needs to consider the kind of merchandise destined for storage and match it with the type of building and supporting mechanization. As land costs continue to increase, there is increasing pressure to build "high rise" storage buildings (Exhibit 11.2).[13] However, one must realize that there is a tradeoff between reduced floor

Exhibit 11.2   High-rise Storage

New materials management technology yields higher productivity per square foot of storage space.

space and increasing cost of heavier construction to support the added weight and inherent inefficiencies of vertical movement of goods compared with horizontal movement of goods. In short, there may be as many as four different ways to store the same merchandise but the constraints of the existing building will usually determine the optimal mode.

In-Store Merchandise
Handling

Once the merchandise from a mechanized warehouse reaches the store it must be distributed and shelved, assuming that UVM or UPC tickets or labels have been attached elsewhere. The modern supermarket is an excellent example of efficient in-store merchandise handling. One new California chain store unit contains about 33,000 square feet. Each week the store has 400–800 price changes on products which affect its weekly sales of $180,000. Twice each week department managers move through their sections with MSI 88-F portable inventory optical recorders

Exhibit 11.3   MSI/88f Alphanumeric Portable Terminal with Program-Loadable Memory

This MSI Data Corporation Series 88 model expands the portable terminal from its fixed-function, application-dependent operation into a multifunction, multiapplication system. The terminal has full alphanumeric capability and can provide wand scanning for UPC/EAN, MSI, Codabar and Code 39.
Source: MSI Corporation.

visually checking stock levels and keying in orders for needed merchandise. Each recorder holds up to 23,000 entries. When the orders have been entered on the recorders they are connected by telephone modems to the central warehouse computers. If orders are in by 11 a.m. the goods can be delivered by 10 p.m. that same day. Twice a week it takes 24 workhours to process the normal 1000 cases of new goods and "full-face" the store.

Automation Lowers
Labor Costs

In keeping with the modern practice of putting all the merchandise out on the selling floor, only 12 pallets of groceries can be held in the receiving area. Any shelf marked with a black diamond indicates that additional stock of that item is being held in the back room and none need be ordered. No goods are physically price stamped, which has led to the reduction of the stock crew to five members for the entire store. The complete inventory process at the store level has been so simplified that an entire new stocking crew can be trained and operating at optimal pace in less than five days. Thus lower handling costs can make the firm more competitive in a low-margin high volume industry.

Not every retail organization must be a grocery chain to benefit from some form of mechanization. For example, Montgomery Ward has experimented with a 350,000-square-foot small ticket distribution center in Industry, California which is designed to serve 132 stores in the area. The new facility uses a floor towline system which has a series of trucks integrated with a large network of conveyors.

Each system is coordinated with an automated sortation system.[14] The new system processes 40 cartons per minute instead of 30 cartons per minute under a comparable less mechanized system and has reduced labor costs about 32 percent.[15] The one weakness in the current system is that, due to the diversity of products carried by the firm, some orders have to be repacked to prevent some items from damaging others in transit. Because of this limitation the firm has adopted a "go slow" attitude in implementing the system elsewhere in the nation.

Mervyn's Integrated Merchandise Information System

Mervyn's
Integrated System

Perhaps the most advanced examples of use of modern merchandise systems can be found in both a regional and a national chain store operation. Mervyn's, a regional soft goods department store chain, has installed a completely integrated merchandise information system. The firm has eighty stores in eight western states with 3300 on-line point-of-sale (POS) terminals which record all sales data. As information is transmitted to a central computer, it is processed by four basic merchandising functions. The merchandise information interface (**MII**) follows all items in a stock keeping unit (SKU) level providing historical

Figure 11.1   Mervyn's Integrated Merchandise Information System

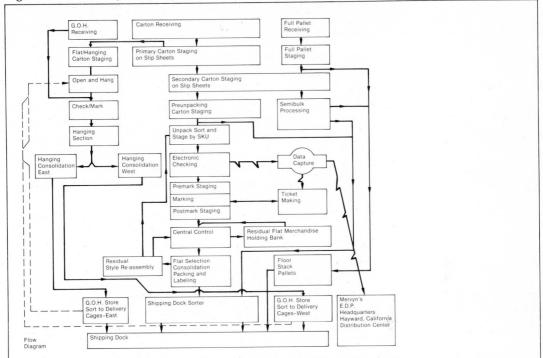

Source: Mervyn's, a wholly-owned subsidiary of the Dayton Hudson Corporation

and current stock information. Once the data have been processed by the MII unit, they are interconnected with Mervyn's automatic replenishment systems **(MARS)** which handles automatic re-orders of staple merchandise based upon predetermined optimal stock levels. Then the information is fed into the merchandise distribution interface **(MDI)** to coordinate the physical flow of merchandise in the system. The entire system is tied together by the merchandising processing system **(MPS)** which generates purchase orders, processes merchandise information, reconciles vendor terms of sales, arranges for accurate accounts payable processing, and compiles a list of all purchase orders outstanding by department. At any moment management can determine its merchandise position in the entire system while achieving high levels of cost efficiency in its merchandise handling system. The entire retail industry is following this major development with interest and perhaps it will become the model for integrated merchandise information systems in the '80s.[16]

Mervyn's is not alone in its interest to improve internal merchandise management. J. C. Penney is beginning to build a to-

J. C. Penney's
National Network

tally integrated electronic system in their full-line stores.[17] The system will be based around POS terminals placed in 517 of the 1700 units. Each designated store will have 30 to 80 POS terminals connected to either an in-store or remote minicomputer which will in turn be connected by ordinary telephone lines to a regional data processing center. The system will use IBM and NCR terminals which will gather the sales from optical character recognition (OCR) printed tickets via OCR wands. Experiments conducted by the firm indicate this method of data capture is more accurate and speeds up the cashiering operation approximately 30 percent.[18] According to Robert Capone, Vice-president and Director of Systems and Data processing, ". . . The justification (for this system) is based on building a totally integrated system to control the entire merchandise maintenance cycle. In doing so, we provide productivity improvements in all of the important elements of our business—people, capital and physical plant."[19]

Net Results Improve Productivity

These two detailed examples clearly point out that most experts agree that effective and efficient merchandise management begin at the point of sale. These transactions serve as the basic data source for control of the entire retail operation. When a sale is made, using either OCR or UPC data-equipped POS terminals, the firm can determine the vendor, the stock keeping unit (SKU), the date of receipt of the goods, the cost of the item, and the selling price with one pass of the reading instrument. Information is transmitted to a central location, usually after business hours, over ordinary telephone lines and is summarized in reports for decision making the next business day. Vital merchandise information on what is selling or not selling, in what colors and sizes, and in what stores is known immediately so appropriate action can be taken without delay. For example, Mervyn's found that

Gathering Basic Data

Timely Information for Action

Exhibit 11.4 Piece Goods Price Ticket

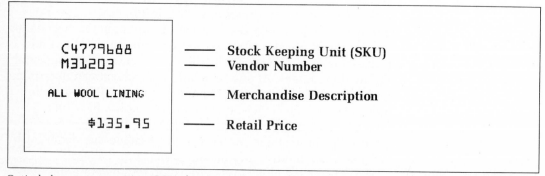

C477968B	——	**Stock Keeping Unit (SKU)**
M31203	——	**Vendor Number**
ALL WOOL LINING	——	**Merchandise Description**
$135.95	——	**Retail Price**

Optical character recognition (OCR) characters contain vendor, product, and date information which can be read by optical wands and entered by POS terminals.

their average merchandise cycle from register sale to stock back on the shelf was 34 days before they installed their integrated POS system. After the new system was installed and running the average cycle was reduced by 15 days.[20] Cost of the system was soon paid for by reduced investment in inventory without any appreciable increase in stockouts.

Despite such notable success stories one must hasten to note that new POS installations are not appropriate for all retail operations. In 1980 Woolworth-Woolco decided that the cost of $30,000 per store for its chain of 300 stores could not be cost justified.[21] If a grocery chain institutes a NCR full scan on eight checkouts in an existing building, the minimum costs in 1981 would have run $105,000 for the conversion. When a firm goes to a full-scan system, the checkout counters must be enlarged from their usual 8–10 foot length to 12–15 feet, which may necessitate remodeling the front end of the store at a cost of $35,000 to $70,000.[22] These costs do not include acquiring the processing hardware and supporting software. Clearly such installations are only practical where optical sensors can detect all relevant POS information encoded in either Universal Vendor Marking (UVM) or Universal Product (UPC) codes accurately and quickly, and there is an adequate transaction volume to make installations cost effective.

All automated systems depend on affixing uniform accurately coded information to every product carried in the store. Three coding systems are currently being used. General merchandisers such as J. C. Penney, Higbees in Cleveland, and The Fair in Beaumont, Texas use the UVM system coupled with OCR-A wands. Each ticket is magnetically encoded by special character inks with the relevant information. One advantage of this system is that, using the standard Font A format, the ticket can be read by both humans and machines.[23] The competing UPC system employs a series of black and white bars of varying widths to convey the same type of information. This system is currently being used primarily by supermarkets and discount chains where over 100,000 different products have the UPC symbol.[24] A third system, "Code 3 of 9," and a related "Code 39" are used in industrial situations.[25] One problem with all bar code systems, particularly the UPC system, is that the information must be printed on a nonporous surface so that the image is sharp enough for the laser reader to scan it accurately. Not all shipping materials possess this critical quality, which can limit usefulness of the bar code system.

For the small retailer who does not need a $2.5 to $4.0 million automated distribution center, there are some practical internal materials handling ideas which can contribute to the firm's

POS System Costs

OCR-A Coding

UPC Coding

Merchandise Handling
Ideas for Small Retailers

Exhibit 11.5   Automated Coding

Laser scanners and UPC marked merchandise speeds check-out and provides valuable data for tracking merchandise movements in retail food stores.
Source: Photo courtesy of Giant Foods Inc. Reprinted with permission from *Giant Food Inc. Annual Report* 1980. All rights reserved.

profitability. First, minimize the handling of the merchandise as much as possible. Some small firms assign certain members of the sales floor staff to report to the freight dock when merchandise is received. As each carton is removed from the truck it is placed on a cart and taken immediately to the floor for later checking and marking by the same crew during slow sales periods. If the goods are source marked by the vendor they can go immediately on the shelf for sale. This is particularly true if the goods have been tagged with OCR labels. If not, portable marking machines can generate the necessary price ticket which is placed on the goods as they are shelved.

Minimize Access to Storage Areas

Secondly, receiving areas are to be just receiving areas—not storage space. Merchandise only sells on the sales floor so it is vital to get the goods out as quickly as is practicable. When reserve stock is maintained off the sales floor, particularly bulky items such as bicycles in cartons or charcoal grills, the items should be stacked neatly and safely so that the sales staff can easily get them when a sale is made. Inventory storage areas should be secured at all times so that theft possibilities will be minimized. All rear exits should be secured as permitted by local fire codes so that unauthorized access will be detected by store security devices or security personnel and dealt with appropriately.

New Methods Must
Be Cost Effective

In summary, there is no one best way to handle merchandise in all stores. Each retailer must examine his or her own operation and look for ways to reduce replenishment time and costs more efficiently. Some retailers may be impressed with bright new digital gadgets and chrome plated equipment with all the "bells and whistles," but the successful retailer calmly calculates cost/benefit ratios and makes decisions accordingly. Every dollar spent behind the scenes must be recouped in profit dollars on the selling floor. If the new procedure or equipment will meet the objective of getting the goods to the floor faster with fewer errors or less chance of loss, it deserves the retailer's thoughtful consideration.

Merchandise Loss Prevention Considerations

Opportunities for
Shrinkage

The fundamental objective of effective merchandise handling is to move all goods from the vendor to customer as efficiently as possible. Each time items are moved or handled there is opportunity for some form of loss to occur. When merchandise is checked in, if the count doesn't match the packing slip or goods are mismarked there are opportunities to lose dollar revenues. When customers return merchandise for adjustments such as an exchange or replacement, if the transaction is not recorded properly shrinkage can occur. If merchandise doesn't sell at full markon, it is marked down for clearance and the SKU information and quantity must be carefully reported or losses will occur. If "charge-backs" (defective merchandise returned to the vendor for credit) are not vigorously and thoroughly processed the retail firm will lose money.

Even if all these activities are flawlessly performed there are still loss opportunities which can occur in the various functional offices. Incorrect extensions or mathematical errors which go undetected mean lost dollars. In all these situations one assumes any losses which might result are accidental or due to unintentional individual carelessness. Admittedly such oversights do occur and account for some small fraction of the shrinkage retail firms experience. However, deliberate, calculated theft by employees, customers, and burglars has become a multibillion dollar challenge for the retail industry.

Shoplifting Losses

According to Federal Bureau of Investigation 1979 statistics at least $8 billion of goods were lost to shoplifters and that figure was expected to reach $10 billion by the end of 1980.[26] In the past many retailers thought that most shoplifting was concentrated in stores located in downtown or depressed areas, but current data indicate the problem is universal, with suburbs experiencing the most significant growth rate in all categories of crime.

Shoplifting, historically the most common theft of goods from retail stores by concealment, is usually performed by amateurs of all ages. According to one expert, 80 percent of shoplifting incidents are impulsive actions.[27] When interviewed some convicted persons said they enjoyed the challenge of taking the merchandise and not getting caught. Some have an overwhelming desire for things they can't afford or don't want to pay for, so they conceal it on their person and attempt to walk out with the merchandise. Others, particularly young gang members, shoplift goods to resell them to support expensive drug or alcohol habits. Lastly, a small minority of the population has adopted the philosophy that society owes them the material goods of the "good life." When interviewed these people say they see nothing wrong in "eating their meals in a supermarket" or "borrowing" merchandise for their own use. In 1978 it is estimated that 30 percent of all theft losses were due to customer shoplifting and these losses were passed on to the remaining paying customers in the form of higher prices.

Attempts to Deter Shoplifting

Retailers across the nation have attacked this $8 billion problem in a number of different ways with varying degrees of success. Most security experts have long advocated a strong, consistent, prosecution policy not only to recover goods but to deter would-be shoplifters. However, recently retail executives have begun to question the wisdom of this approach on several grounds. First, most shoplifting cases require retail employee witnesses to be available for court appearances. With postponements and delays this could easily take 12 hours per case at the cost of $500 to recover a $5 to $10 item which has been impounded for five or six weeks. Even if the accused person is found guilty the penalty is considered so insignificant that any future deterrent value is totally lost.

Prosecution Problems

Threat of Civil Suits

Secondly, in 1980 a landmark court decision in California cast serious doubt on the retailer's ability to apprehend and successfully prosecute shoplifters without fear of being countersued for false arrest. The state supreme court ruled,

> "If stolen goods are not in 'plain view' at the time of apprehension, a suspect can be legally searched only if he first gives his consent."[28]

No knowledgeable thief would permit such a search to take place. Thus, if suspects can successfully conceal any merchandise they can walk out with the goods without any fear of apprehension. Even store security guards are bound by the same ruling because they are considered private citizens without police powers which permit personal search for probable cause.[29] Any persons apprehended or detained could successfully sue for false arrest with all the attendant notoriety and cash settlement losses. As a result shoplifting court cases were halved in six months. Legislation was introduced in the California legislature to change the law back so shoplifters could successfully be brought to the "bar of justice" but retailers in other states may soon face similar problems.

Theft Prevention Options

Store Design Aids Loss Prevention

Prevention of loss through theft is much more effective than remediation after the theft has occurred. Most authorities suggest that loss prevention should begin with store building design. Perhaps the leading advocate of this philosophy is Stanley Marcus of Neiman-Marcus. Under his direction the firm has developed a 13-phase program which covers an 18-month span from store design to poststore opening.[30] The program involves such items as checking employee locker locations, CCTV and lookout towers, fire and burglar alarm system design and installation, and selection and placement of interior store fixtures. Since the firm has initiated the program for new stores and retrofitted established units they report their loss rate is down to about one percent compared with an industry average of 2.21 percent of sales.[31]

EAS Systems

For retailers unable to structurally remodel their facilities to reduce theft, a first line of defense seems to lie in electronic article surveillance (EAS) installations. The system involves inserting tags, disks or new adhesive "teeny beepers" which set off an alarm when the customer leaves a protected area without having the device removed by a cashier. Major retail firms, such as Gimbels of Philadelphia, report a storewide reduction in shrinkage of 70 percent during the first year after the installation of such a system.[32] The Paul Harris Stores reported a reduction in inventory loss from 21 percent to less than five percent in six months when they installed their own customized EAS system.

One should not pretend that EAS systems will eliminate shoplifting, but it does put the potential thief on notice that the store will know if they try to steal merchandise. Some customers object to the inconvenience and discomfort of trying on garments with EAS devices attached, but most customers understand the retailer's dilemma. Most realize that rising theft costs must be recovered in higher prices and are willing to help in any way they can to combat the problem.

Some retailers such as Woodward and Lothrop say EAS systems are ineffective crutches.[33] They suggest that to be effective 95 percent of all goods must be tagged. When such a level of saturation is achieved the sales force tends to relax their visual observation which permits some thieves to mechanically defeat the tags and resume stealing the merchandise. Other critics point out that in the end the EAS program is only a more complicated deterrence system with its inherent prosecution problems. So far only five percent of the retail apparel firms have adopted the EAS approach, but as loss rates rise one can be sure more will install and actively use the system regardless of its shortcomings.

Burglary Challenges

Not all thefts are due to shoplifting. Increasingly would-be burglars are hiding in stores after closing hours, waiting until the employees have left, and the store is secured. Then, they prowl the store selecting high value, low bulk items and break out of the store before the security force or police arrive. Alternately stores in malls are increasingly being victimized by "smash, grab, and run" techniques which result in losses of $30 to $50 worth of merchandise. However when stores replace the smashed display windows management finds it costs hundreds of dollars per installation and results in higher insurance rates.[34]

Prevention Measures Costly

Retailers are fighting back with a wide variety of defensive measures. Ultrasonic and infrared detectors are being installed to alert security personnel if any movement is detected in a building after the store is secured. In Los Angeles, The Broadway, May Company, and others have installed iron gates on entrances and chained fire doors so that no one can get out of the building after it has been locked. Large exterior glass areas and interior jewelry cases are being fitted with shatterproof glass so that forced entry or "smash and grab" incidents will be reduced. Most department stores are now removing all valuable jewelry and furs from display areas and locking them in massive safes. In fact, Zales is redesigning its display trays to easily fit in custom made safes with a minimum amount of employee time or effort. Some firms have resorted to putting trained watch dogs in unattended stores, but most experts do not advise this measure unless the dogs are accompanied by a trained security person to alert police and call for backup assistance and arrest.[35]

Smaller retailers have relied on one-way mirrors, convex mirrors, and increased sales staff observation to deter shoplifting. Such measures have raised the employees' awareness of suspicious activity which may deter some would-be thieves. This is helpful but it has introduced another perhaps more critical problem which retailers haven't adequately addressed. What should employees do when faced with a blatant case of shoplifting or attempted armed robbery? With increasingly violent encounters becoming more common today, any staff member who challenges or threatens to challenge such often armed assailants may be putting themselves in mortal peril.

Employee Safety

In such cases most enlightened retail managements have set strict policies on how to handle these and other life threatening situations such as bomb threats. Without going into detail for obvious reasons, most retail employees have been instructed to comply with any request made by the threatening party but to carefully observe and remember all information relevant to the situation so that they can fully cooperate with authorities after the incident. A show of heroics is inappropriate and may cost the lives of innocent bystanders. The best advice is to be calm, cool, and comply as much as possible under admittedly stressful conditions and situations.

No Easy Answer

Most experts agree that even with all the modern detection equipment, increased security procedures and guard dogs will not deter the determined thief, given enough time. Therefore retailers are making it more time consuming and difficult so potential thieves will look elsewhere where it is easier to ply their trade.

Internal Theft Concerns

According to a Justice Department Law Enforcement Assistance Administration report in 1978, 65 percent or $6.5 billion in retail crime was attributable to employee theft.[36] One expert, Carroll E. Henkel, suggests that retailers should carry employee-dishonesty insurance to cover some of this risk. Henkel has developed a guide to determine the amount of insurance a firm should carry.

Dishonesty Exposure Index

He calls it the "dishonesty exposure index." The exposure index is calculated by adding five percent of the value of the goods on hand, 20 percent of the current assets minus the value of goods on hand, plus 10 percent of annual gross sales or income.[37] For example, if one determines his or her dishonesty exposure index to be between $1,000 and $250,000 the retailer should purchase an amount of insurance which is at least 25 percent of the exposure index plus an added $20,000 of coverage. The insurance rate quoted will be a function of the perceived risk in that particular situation. While some may quarrel with the figures, at least one can quantify the firm's internal theft risk exposure and take appropriate action.

Coping with Internal Theft

Internal thieves can create losses in hundreds of ways ranging from cashiers charging friends less than retail price to concealing goods in packages and walking out the employees' entrance with them. Management has retaliated with CCTV systems concealed in mirrored globes, installed 6½-foot hexagonal columns where security personnel can observe employees and customers to detect theft. Some are using polygraph and psychological stress evaluators (PSE) in prehiring interviews of potential employees and giving employee rewards for reporting peer theft. The last program seems to have had the greatest success. While few retailers will discuss their security program details, one executive did note that the only way to reduce internal theft is an integrated security system which includes checking potential employees' backgrounds, hiring very selectively, paying adequate wages, and rewarding those who report all suspicious activities which they may observe. One must be careful not to violate Equal Employment Opportunity laws in implementing these practices, but any dollars lost in any form of theft directly affect employees, managers, stockholders, and customers and must be dealt with effectively.

Check Employees before Hiring

Energy Management Considerations

Another major operations cost containment concern for most retailers is the soaring cost of energy. Increasingly retailers are systematically reviewing their energy consumption and trying to establish management procedures which will reduce future energy costs. As more and more large retailers install integrated systems which coordinate merchandise handling and security they are tying in heat, ventilation, and air conditioning (HVAC) control functions. During the 1970s when energy costs began their upward escalation, firms began to turn off the lights and darken their interiors. In the years since, firms have relied less on fluorescent lights and more on key spots to illuminate their stores. Then in the late 1970s, when the federal government institued public building temperature regulations, the large retailers began to systematically attack their HVAC power requirements. With solid state sensors and microprocessors companies can now monitor micro-climates throughout the store or even the entire mall for optimal energy consumption consistent with comfort, safety, and security.

Simple Methods

One company, Dayton Hudson Properties, has taken an aggressive managerial position in all the properties it manages and has achieved significant energy savings. By simply replacing exhausted insulation on steam and water pipes, effectively sealing and insulating shopping center entrances, enclosing high wind velocity entrances in building vestibules, and reducing the chill temperature in cooling systems the firm was able to reduce energy consumption by 10 percent while expanding the center's total square footage from 645,000 to 716,000.[38] In the firm's Westland center the firm converted mercury vapor parking lot lamps to metal halide lamps and increased the average level of illumination by 1.5 times without any appreciable increase in energy costs.[39]

Interior lighting costs were reduced in the Southland, Westland, and Genesee Valley centers by exchanging the traditional 150-watt incandescent bulbs with 75-watt mercury vapor lamps. Light output increased 20 percent and power consumption was cut in half.[40] Such energy conservation methods usually pay for themselves in 12 to 18 months after major changes are effected in the HVAC and lighting systems. With energy costs rising between 10 and 20 percent annually, no retailer can remain complacent and accept the higher bills. The technology is available today from such firms as IBM, Honeywell, and such smaller, well-known firms as Chillitrol, Inc. of Los Angeles, which can reduce and control energy costs and yet allow retailers to generate attractive, inviting, comfortable, safe environments which are needed to encourage people to patronize those stores and malls. Whether they like it or not, energy cost containment has become another challenging concern for all retailers regardless of size or geographical location.

Use Energy Only Where Needed

Summary

Retrospectively, retailers of tomorrow must be more adept at cost containment in all facets of their operations. This concern must begin at the point of sale and continue through arranging for the best transportation and optimal handling of goods between distribution centers or receiving rooms, to putting the goods on the shelf, integrating security to achieve maximum loss prevention, and controlling energy costs. These behind-the-scenes activities must be considered when new stores are constructed or old ones remodeled. Each dollar saved in these areas makes any sales floor profit dollars go further and yield a better return for the enterprising retailer.

Questions

1. How can a retailer increase the firm's profit potential by coordinating buying practices and freight handling decisions? Explain.
2. Generally, which is the cheapest form of transportation? Which freight classification usually carries the lowest charge? Does this rate apply equally to LCL and LTL shipments? Why or why not?
3. How can a retail firm benefit from using public warehousing rather than private warehouse operation? How does the retailer decide which form of warehousing to use? Explain.
4. How can a POS system contribute to a retail firm's profitability? When does it become cost effective to change to such a system? Explain.

5. Where should a retailer use an UVM rather than an UPC system once he or she has decided to install a POS system? Explain.

6. Under what conditions should a firm consider using a distribution center? What are the advantages and disadvantages of such a distribution system?

7. How can retailers deal more effectively with intentional losses in their organizations? What are the potential risks and benefits from such actions? Explain.

8. What should retail employees do when they observe unauthorized appropriation of merchandise in their organization? What should management do to cope with this problem?

9. What responsibility do customers and the general public bear in relation to the increase in retail theft? What can the public do to help retailers control and cope with merchandise losses through theft? Will they?

10. How can retailers contain their operation's energy costs? Suppose another energy crisis should occur worldwide and retailers are asked to reduce energy consumption by 10 percent. How would you suggest such a reduction be made? Explain.

Case Study: Larry Jones' Automation Decision

Larry Jones was justly proud of his accomplishment. He had begun ten years ago with one small supermarket in a small town of 15,000 people. He had successfully competed with Safeway and other small grocery stores by offering credit and had catered to local ranchers who bought their winter supplies by the pickup load. He was the first in town to carry canned goods in institutional sized containers and was the first to open a deli section.

The years had been good to Larry. He had worked hard and plowed all the profits back into the business and had expanded to two stores at opposite ends of the town, which had grown to a population of over 25,000. The local area was booming with energy exploration and development and the county population was expected to double in two years. During this period Larry had joined the Independent Grocers Association and enjoyed the benefits of bulk purchase, shared advertising, private brands, and the like.

Now he was faced with the most important decision in his business career. He was about to lose his lease on his small store and knew it had to be replaced with a new, larger unit. His competition had increased substantially to include a relatively new Buttrey's store and a Skaggs-Albertsons shopping center in the last four years.

Larry was convinced that he must build a new modern superstore to survive and hold his share of the local market. As he began to sketch out the new store he was faced with some major decisions. Over 100,000 items available to him were already source marked with UPC codes. Also, he was renting some low-cost storage space for dry groceries on the "other side of the tracks" in the industrial park. He had been notified that his rental charges for the storage were going up 12 percent in four months. He received deliveries twice a week and needed additional freight handling equipment to replace the one worn out forklift. With all these facts in mind, Larry set out to design his new store.

Discussion Questions

1. Should Larry install an integrated merchandise handling system or build a conventional supermarket?

2. If he does go "modern" how will this affect sales in his other store? What managerial problems might Larry anticipate using two different merchandise handling systems?

3. Will the automated store be cost effective?

Footnotes

1.   Thomas F. Dillon, "Freight Rates Will Rise But at a Moderate Pace," *Purchasing* 91 (July 9, 1981): 47.

2.   Ronald H. Ballou, *Basic Business Logistics* (Englewood Cliffs, N.J.: Prentice-Hall, 1978), p. 180.

3.   Ibid., p. 186.

4.   Lewis A. Spalding, "Dealing With De-Reg," *Stores* 63 (April 1981): 34.

5.   Ballou, p. 192.

6.   Tom Dulaney, "Computers Turn on to Rating and Routing," *Distribution* 80 (February 1981): 36–39.

7.   Ibid., p. 39.

8.   Spalding, p. 64.

9.   Ibid., p. 37.

10. "Shippers Should Review Numbers on Public Chains," *Distribution* 80 (June 1981): 90.

11. Ibid.

12. "Mechanization: Distribution Labor Costs Cut," *Chain Store Age Executive* 55 (June 1979): 52.

13. "Storage Analysis Uses the Head, Not the Heart," *Distribution* 80 (January 1981): 51.

14. "Mechanization: Distribution Labor Costs Cut," *Chain Store Age Executive* 55 (June 1979): 51.

15. Ibid.

16. Mr. John Shields, Vice President, Operations, Mervyn's, Los Angeles, California.

17. Marian Burk Rothman, "Retail Technology: Making It Work," *Stores* 62 (October 1980): 37.

18. Ibid.

19. Ibid.

20. Ibid.

21. Judith Morrison Lipton, "New Data: OCR-A Update," *Stores* 63 (July 1981): 47.

22. "Scanning Systems to the Forefront," *Chain Store Age Executive* 56 (August 1980): 140.

23. Lipton, "New Data," p. 47.

24. "Scanning Systems," p. 139.

25. Frederick W. Miller, "Magic Wand Comes of Age with New Uses," *Infosystems* 7 (1981): 42.

26. "Article Surveillance Gaining as Retailers Combat Pilferage," *Chain Store Age Executive* 56 (April 1980): 63.

27. Ibid.

28. "Zelinski Case Opens Retail Can of Worms," *Chain Store Age Executive* 56 (April 1980): 69.

29. Ibid.

30. "Neiman-Marcus Combines Security with Construction," *Chain Store Age Executive* 56 (April 1980): 78.

31. Ibid., p. 80.

32. "Article Surveillance," p. 63.

33. Ibid., p. 67.

34. Jack Blood, "Break-in, Break-out," *Stores* 63 (June 1981): 53.

35. Ibid., p. 56.

36. "New Openness Employed to Fight Internal Theft," *Chain Store Age Executive* 55 (July 1979): 24.

37. Carroll E. Henkel, "Dishonesty Coverage," *Chain Store Age Executive* 57 (June 1981): 12.

38. "Cost-Conscious Developers Seek Operations Efficiency," *Chain Store Age Executive* 55 (December 1979): 59.

39. Ibid., p. 61.

40. Ibid.

Chapter 12 | Pricing for Profit

Learning Goals

1. To learn how the concepts of break-even, markup, and elasticity are effectively used in establishing pricing strategies.
2. To understand how price levels are related to profit levels.
3. To become acquainted with the dynamic and psychological aspects of retail pricing.
4. To be aware of the complex legal environment that affects retail pricing activities.

Key Terms and Concepts

pricing strategy
merchandise costs
variable costs
fixed costs
break-even point
volume
markup dollars
markup percentage
markup percent of cost
maintained markup
retail reductions
markdowns
gross margin

price elasticity of demand
  coefficient
price lining
demand curve
unit pricing
private label pricing
odd pricing
markdown percentage
off retail percentage
low-price leaders
loss-leader pricing
bait-leader pricing
off-season pricing
preticketing

The heart of an effective retail operation is pricing the goods or services so that the customer sincerely believes that he or she has received fair value. This is accomplished by using an appropriate pricing strategy and is implemented through aggressive pricing tactics. This chapter examines the proper use of long-term pricing strategies, such as initial mark-ons and pricing elasticity, price lining, and the overall psychology of pricing. The chapter closes with an examination of such tactical pricing practices as markdowns and promotional pricing and, finally, the legal aspects of proper pricing.

Pricing Strategy

Pricing decisions are important because they can nullify the effect of intelligently conceived product, location, and communication programs. The retailer's **pricing strategy** is a form of market cultivation, but it is also a reflection of all the firm's actions. Pricing is symbolic of the kind of product strategy implemented by the retailer because the price tag conveys a mental image about product quality to the customer. Pricing may be used as a store location substitute in an effort to attract customers from greater distances.

Pricing strategy must be consistent with the retailer's communication appeal. Generally, a retailer who has low-price appeal must sacrifice some methods of demand stimulation, such as advertising. Rarely can large sums be spent on advertising and promotion if low price is the dominant appeal. Discount retailers may initially appear to be the exception. However, if advertising and promotion budgets are considered as a percentage of sales volume, most discounters spend relatively less on advertising than other retailers.

Price is the dominant factor that directly influences the retailer's profit or loss. Other things being equal, price can be lowered to increase sales. However, the increase in unit volume may not be sufficient to generate a higher level of profit. Thus, retailers must review price changes with regard to their effects upon both sales and profits. Many factors must be considered when determining the firm's retail pricing strategy (Table 12.1).

Pricing objectives of a retail firm are frequently twofold—to obtain a specified rate of return on the money they have invested in the firm and to retain or strengthen their position in the marketplace. The percentage return on investment obtained by typical firms in various lines of retailing is presented in Chapter 18. The new small independent retailer may use the average percentage return for typical firms in the industry as goals the firm wishes to reach. As the manager gains experience, he or she may alter this goal to better reflect local conditions. Large retail institutions develop an annual return on investment objective based upon past performance and general economic conditions.

The overall company objective is frequently applied to individual stores that are members of the chain. The store managers who exceed the specified target are then awarded extra compensation. This system works most effectively if store management has the responsibility of setting prices and selecting merchandise.

Retail firms also use the share of the market concept to determine if they are losing, maintaining, or increasing their position in the marketplace.

The goal of maintaining a *minimum market share* can conflict with a minimum rate of return on investment objective statement. The firm may find that it is necessary to reduce price (or

Table 12.1 Retail Pricing Strategy Considerations

Factors retailers can control
1. Pricing objectives of the firm—return on investment, share of market
2. Type of merchandise offered
3. Cost of goods sold
4. Business expenses
5. Firm organization structure

Factors retailers cannot control
1. Consumer demand
2. Competition
3. Federal, state, and local laws

Tools used to obtain pricing objectives
1. Markup formula
2. Price linings
3. Demand elasticity
4. Prestige pricings
5. Odd pricing
6. Multiple unit pricing
7. Markdowns
8. Leader pricing
9. Off-season pricing
10. Unit pricing

increase promotion) so much that the firm becomes less profitable. Thus, adoption of a high market share objective is frequently accompanied by that firm's intention to be the price leader in that line of merchandise. Price leaders are generally perceived by other retailers as being the outlets offering the customers merchandise at the lowest price in the area.

Some retailers, especially the small independent outlets, have difficulty getting data on their share of the market. The first difficulty is defining the exact market category. Large retail chains sell many different kinds of merchandise. Thus, it is difficult to estimate what dollar sales are for each category. For example, a small specialty store may be selling women's wear which is sold in similar competing stores, in department stores, and large chain outlets such as J. C. Penney, Montgomery Ward, and Sears, Roebuck and Co. It is just about impossible for the outlet to estimate accurately women's wear sales in these large stores. In this case, the outlet may be content to simply state its goal as 25 percent of women's wear sales in the nonchain and nondepartment stores.

Costs are another important factor that need to be considered in retail pricing (Figure 12.1). Retailers are concerned with three types of cost: cost of merchandise, variable costs, and fixed costs.

Merchandise costs consist of the price that the merchant pays for goods and services that he or she buys for resale to the ultimate consumer. Merchandise costs are the starting point in computing the general level of the retailer's price. Although the retailer may consider external factors such as consumer demand, competitor's strength, and so forth, he or she must still cover all of the firm's merchandise cost if the firm is to be able to meet other expenses and stay in business.

Fixed costs occur whether the firm is opened or closed. Costs such as square footage space costs, insurance, equipment and facility depreciation, a minimum level of employee and owner

Figure 12.1 Components of Retail Price

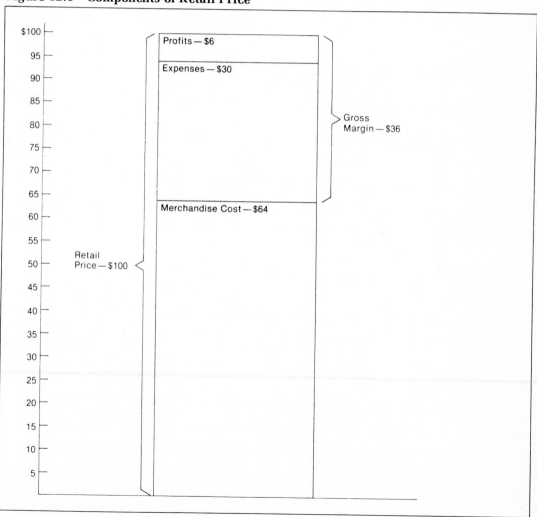

manager salaries, lights, heat, and utilities do not increase or decrease with changes in the store's sales volume.

Variable costs fluctuate widely with changes in the store's activities. These variable costs are the expenses that vary with the outlet's sales volume. Added sales may be obtained by advertising, adding more personnel to serve the higher sales level, keeping the store open longer hours, thereby requiring more utility charges, labor costs, and paying a higher rental cost because the property owner has specified that a percentage of the firm's retail sales be paid as rent.

For example, a department store may purchase a coat for $64 and sell it for $100. The gross margin for this item, which is sold at its original markup, is $36. But $30 of this gross margin goes for variable operating expenses such as wages, salaries, commissions, repairs, maintenance, advertising, delivery costs, bad debt losses, administration, and legal expenses; and for the fixed costs of rent, utilities, insurance, taxes, license fees, interest, and depreciation. This leaves only $6 for profit.

The distinction between these three types of costs is important to the retailer who is making pricing decisions, because one of the tools he or she may use is the break-even volume. This technique uses past cost data. The cost of merchandise figure is subtracted from sales, giving management an estimate of gross margin (the difference between what a retailer pays for the product and the price at which he sells it to the consumer), which must cover all of the firm's operating expenses as well as provide a profit to the owner.

Break-even volume is the minimum sales volume needed to avoid incurring a loss. Mathematically, break-even volume is calculated as follows:

$BEV = $FC/[(100% − %MC) − %VC], where
$BEV = break-even volume at which the firm neither makes a profit nor shows a loss
$FC = fixed cost in dollars
%MC = percent merchandise costs are of retail sales dollar volume
%VC = percent variable costs are of retail sales dollar volume

For example, suppose past retail records show that an establishment has incurred annual fixed costs (rent, utilities, a bare bones labor charge, depreciation, and so forth) of $100,000. The cost of merchandise has averaged 70 percent of retail dollar sales during the past five years. Variable costs (advertising costs, added labor costs, and so forth) have amounted to 12 percent of retail dollar sales during the past five years. This firm's break-even quantity is found by substituting these values in the above formula as follows:

$$\$BEV = \$100,000/[(100\% - 70\%) - 12\%]$$
$$= \$100,000/[(30\%) - 12\%]$$
$$= \$100,000/[18\%]$$
$$= \$555,556$$

Thus, the firm would have to sell at least $555,556 a year to cover all costs (Figure 12.2). If it can obtain a larger sales volume, then it begins to make a profit of 18¢ on each dollar of sales over the break-even volume. For example, if the firm gets annual sales of $800,000 then its profit is ($800,000 − $555,556) × .18, or $244,444 × .18 = $44,000.

If the firm cannot reach the break-even sales volume, it will incur a loss of 18¢ on each dollar below its break-even volume. For example, if the firm has annual sales of $400,000 then the loss would be ($555,556 − $400,000) × .18 = $155,556 × .18 = $28,000.

Figure 12.2   Break-Even Chart

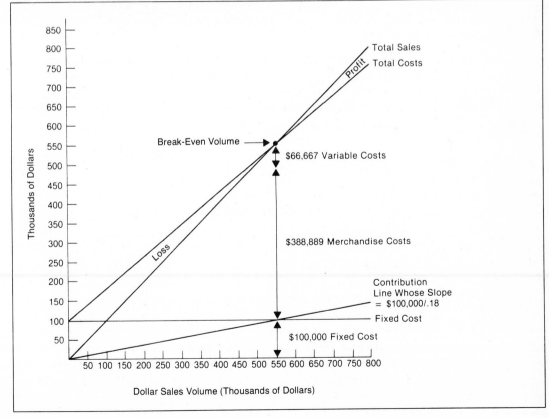

Managers of retail outlets can employ many different ways (increase promotion, reduce prices, and so forth) to increase firm sales above the break-even volume. However, all of these actions also involve some additional cost. Management must then determine if the increased sales outweigh added costs.

Thus, the establishment of the firm's pricing policy must be based on the break-even concept and attempts made to determine the optimum pricing strategy. Price changes can influence the firm's sales volume. However, the price change also affects the firm's gross margin. For example, a 10 percent price reduction will increase store sales (say by 20 percent), but it will also increase the firm's break-even volume. In the previous example, the 10 percent price reduction would affect the break-even calculation in the following manner: (1) The cost of merchandise has not changed, so it is still $70 of every $100 of the original sales. (2) However, because of the 10 percent price reduction, the same merchandise will now only bring in $90 to the retail firm. (3) The percentage merchandise cost is therefore increased to 70/90, or 78%. (4) The break-even calculation is changed to:

$$\text{\$BEV} = \$100,000/[(100\% - 78\%) - 12\%]$$
$$= \$100,000/[10\%]$$
$$= \$1,000,000.$$

Thus, the firm's break-even volume has nearly been doubled to $1 million from $555,556 just because it reduced prices by 10 percent. Management should be reasonably certain that the firm's sales volume would be in excess of $1 million before it reduces prices by 10 percent. These figures are typical for a general merchandise retailer.

Other studies have indicated that other lines of retailing face the same kind of relationship between price reductions and additional sales required to increase profits. One study in the food industry indicated that if prices were cut 7 percent to generate twice as many sales, the store would change from a profit producer to a loser.[1] Low gross margins in the grocery industry imply that price reductions must increase sales tremendously if profits are to be increased at all.

Thus, in order for a price reduction to be economically attractive, it must either result in a huge sales volume increase or be accompanied by a substantial cost structure adjustment that will change the economics of the firm. Since competitors are likely to retaliate if they observe a huge increase in volume caused by merely a price decrease, one can conclude that the retailers must make substantial changes in their cost structure if they are going to make a price decrease work.

One such move is to off-price branded stores which sell name brand apparel merchandise. Off-price sales amounted to about $3 billion or 4.5 percent of the nation's total apparel sales in 1979. It is expected to account for about $13 billion in sales and capture between 10 to 13 percent of the apparel volume by 1985. Off-price retailing currently consists of about 700 stores run by major chains, small chains, and independents dispersed around the United States and operating locally. Their decor is plain and the layout usually includes a piperack self-service arrangement with central checkouts. This supermarket type of operation has resulted in a reduction of between 6 and 12 percent in operating costs as compared to traditional apparel outlets. Leading off-price retailers are Melville Corp. (with Marshalls), Zayre Corp. (with Hit or Miss and T. J. Maxx), F. W. Woolworth (with J. Bannam stores) and Lucky Stores (with Pic-A-Dilly and It's-A-Dilly).[2]

As can be seen from the above examples, break-even volume estimates can play an important role in determining the pricing strategy of the retailer. This break-even concept should be considered when retail management establishes its markup pricing policies.

During the economic slump of the early 1980s retailers of all types cut prices to capture more consumer dollars. Even the most expensive department stores resorted to frequently having "a sale." More and more consumers began to recognize that the first price tag wasn't necessarily the last and as a result profits suffered.[3]

Markup Pricing

Most retail prices are determined by a cost-oriented markup. **Markup** is the difference between the cost of an item and its retail price. Cost, in this case, usually refers to the invoice cost of the merchandise, minus trade discounts, plus inbound freight paid by the retailer. Markup is generally expressed as a percentage of the retail price. In formula form:

$$\textbf{Markup percent} = \frac{\text{(retail price per unit)} - \text{(per unit cost)}}{\text{(retail price per unit)}} \times 100.$$

If, for example, an item costs a retailer $50 but is retailed at $75, the markup percent is ($25/$75) × 100, or 33⅓. Markup percent can also be calculated by using the following formula:

$$\text{Markup percent} = \frac{\text{dollar markup}}{\text{dollar retail price}} \times 100.$$

In the above example the dollar markup on the item is $75 − $50, or $25, so the markup percent = $25/$75 × 100 = 33⅓ percent. Markup can also be defined by using the cost as a base. Markup on cost is calculated by dividing the margin by the cost to the retailer. In formula form,

Markup percent of cost

$$= \frac{\text{(retail price per unit} - \text{per unit cost)}}{\text{(per unit cost)}} \times 100.$$

In this example the markup on cost percent would be $25/$50 × 100, or 50 percent. Markup percent of cost can also be calculated by using the formula:

$$\text{Markup percent of cost} = \frac{\text{dollar markup}}{\text{dollar cost}} \times 100.$$

In the above example dollar markup is $75 − $50, or $25, and the dollar cost of the item is given as $50, so the markup percent of cost = $25/50 × 100, or 50 percent.

In this text the term "markup percent of cost" will always be differentiated from markup as a percent of price. In the real world the reader should always check to see which markup is being used. Many retailers have gone broke because they misunderstood the difference between markup on retail and markup on cost.

One important point should be stressed when considering markups using both cost and selling prices as bases. A markup percent based on the retail or selling price will always be smaller than an equivalent dollar margin based on the cost of an item. A conversion from a given markup percent on cost to an equivalent markup on retail can be made by using the following formula:

$$\text{Markup percent} = \frac{\text{(markup percent of cost)}}{\text{(100} + \text{markup percent of cost)}} \times 100.$$

If the markup percent of cost is 20 percent, the comparable markup percent is equal to [20/(100 + 20)] × 100, or 16.7 percent. Table 12.2 contains equivalent markups, and may be used to convert markup percent into markup percent of cost. Markup percent of retail can be converted into markup percent of cost by using the formula:

Markup percent of cost

$$= \frac{\text{markup percent of retail}}{\text{(100} - \text{markup percent of retail)}} \times 100.$$

If the markup percent of retail is 16.7 then the equivalent markup percent of cost = 16.7/(100 − 16.7) × 100, or 20 percent. Retailers frequently want to determine what price must be charged on an item to yield a desired markup. The following

Table 12.2 Markup Table

Markup Percent of Selling Price	Markup Percent of Cost	Markup Percent of Selling Price	Markup Percent of Cost	Markup Percent of Selling Price	Markup Percent of Cost
4.8	5.0	18.0	22.0	32.0	47.1
5.0	5.3	18.5	22.7	33.3	50.0
6.0	6.4	19.0	23.5	34.0	51.5
7.0	7.5	20.0	25.0	35.0	53.9
8.0	8.7	21.0	26.6	35.5	55.0
9.0	10.0	22.0	28.2	36.0	56.3
10.0	11.1	22.5	29.0	37.0	58.8
10.7	12.0	23.0	29.9	37.5	60.0
11.0	12.4	23.1	30.0	38.0	61.3
11.1	12.5	24.0	31.6	39.0	64.0
12.0	13.6	25.0	33.3	39.5	65.5
12.5	14.3	26.0	35.0	40.0	66.7
13.0	15.0	27.0	37.0	41.0	70.0
14.0	16.3	27.3	37.5	42.0	72.4
15.0	17.7	28.0	39.0	42.8	75.0
16.0	19.1	28.5	40.0	44.4	80.0
16.7	20.0	29.0	40.9	46.1	85.0
17.0	20.5	30.0	42.9	47.5	90.0
17.5	21.2	31.0	45.0	48.7	95.0
				50.0	100.0

To use this table find the desired percentage in the left-hand column. Multiply the cost of the article by the corresponding percentage in the "markup percent of cost" column. The result, added to the cost, gives the correct selling price.
Source: NCR Corporation, *Expenses in Retail Businesses* (Dayton: NCR Corporation, n.d.), p. 45. Reprinted by permission.

formula makes this conversion:

$$\text{Retail price} = \frac{(\text{cost in dollars})}{(100 - \text{desired markup percent})} \times 100.$$

Thus, if an item were purchased by the retailer for $10 and he wished to obtain a markup of 50 percent, the calculation would be:

$$\frac{\$10}{(100 - 50)} \times 100 = \$20.$$

Initial Markup

In the above discussion we have referred to markup in a very general way—that is, the difference between the cost of an item and its selling price. It is now useful to distinguish carefully among three terms (initial markup, maintained markup, and gross margin) which are used to describe the difference between cost and retail price. The amount of markup on all items does not remain constant during the entire year. Some merchandise is always broken, damaged, or stolen. Other items are sold at reduced prices to employees and customers. Rarely will the first, full markup be realized. This first markup (the margin between cost and retail price) placed on merchandise is called the initial markup. The initial markup must be high enough to cover:

1. **Maintained markup** consisting of:
   a. Store operating expenses including payrolls, advertising, taxes, supplies, services purchased, travel, communications, pensions, insurance, depreciation, professional services, donations, bad debts, equipment rental, real property rentals, and interest payments, plus
   b. Alteration costs to goods sold, plus
   c. Expected profit, minus
   d. Vendor cash discounts
2. **Retail reductions** including:
   a. Markdowns, which lower the original price to promote merchandise sales
   b. Discounts to employees as a fringe benefit
   c. Shortages, which are the difference between the amount of merchandise that should be on hand and the amount actually on hand (the difference may be due to merchandise being lost, stolen, damaged, or improperly counted, or due to improper handling of cash or charge transactions)

Thus, initial markup measures what the retail manager hopes to retail the goods for. In percentage terms the initial markup can be calculated by using the following formula:

$$\text{Initial markup \%} = \frac{\text{maintained markup \% + reduction \%}}{\text{net sales \% + reduction \%}},$$

where maintained markup % = % store operating expense
$$+ \text{ \% alteration costs} + \text{ \% profit}$$
$$- \text{ \% vendor cash discounts}$$

and reduction % = % markdown + % employee discounts
$$+ \text{ \% shortages}$$

To illustrate this formula, suppose that there are no vendor cash discounts, expenses are estimated to be 33 percent, reductions are estimated to be 8 percent and profit is planned to equal 5 percent. Therefore:

Initial markup percent

$$= \frac{33\% \text{ expenses} + 5\% \text{ profit} + 8\% \text{ reductions}}{100\% \text{ net sales} + 8\% \text{ reductions}}$$

$$= \frac{.38 + .08}{1.00 + .08} = \frac{.46}{1.08} = .425 \text{ or } 42.5\%$$

This formula can also be used with dollar figures as well as percentages. For example, if the firm had sales of $100,000, no vendor cash discounts, expenses of $33,000, reductions of $8,000 and a planned profit of $5,000 the calculation would be:

Initial markup percent

$$= \frac{\$33,000 \text{ expenses} + \$5,000 \text{ profit} + \$8,000 \text{ reductions}}{\$100,000 \text{ sales} + \$8,000 \text{ reductions}}$$

$$= \$43,000/\$108,000 = .425 \text{ or } 42.5\%$$

Maintained Markup

Maintained markup has already been defined as being store operating expense + alteration expense + profit − vendor cash discounts. The above calculation indicates that the initial markup percent is a very useful planning tool that can ensure that maintained markup percentages exceed expenses by a preplanned percentage which represents profit to the firm.

Moving from Initial Markup Percent to Maintained Markup Percent

The relationship between initial markup percent and maintained markup percent can be used to determine what reduced price should be used to obtain a preplanned maintained markup percentage after a portion of merchandise has been sold at the initial markup. For example, suppose a retailer bought one hundred pairs of shoes at $14 a pair and sold eighty pairs at an initial markup of 33$\frac{1}{3}$ percent of retail, or at $21 per pair. The retailer then wants to reduce the price on the remaining twenty pairs but wants to achieve the planned maintained markup percentage of 30 percent. The calculation procedure is:

1. Determine actual dollar cost of goods = number of units purchased × per unit purchase price
= 100 × $14
= $1400

2. Determine dollar sales volume needed to obtain planned maintained markup percentage =

$$\frac{\text{actual cost of goods}}{(100\% - \text{planned maintained markup percent})}$$

$$= \frac{\$1400}{(100\% - 30\%)} = \frac{\$1400}{70\%} = \$2000$$

3. Determine dollar sales volume obtained at initial markup percentage = number of units sold at initial markup × initial price = 80 × $21 = $1680

4. Determine dollar sales volume still needed to achieve planned maintained markup percent

= required dollar sales volume (obtained in step 2) minus dollar sales volume obtained at initial markup (step 3)

= $2000 − $1680 = $320

5. Determine retail price for remaining units = dollar sales volume needed (step 4)/number of units left to sell

= $320/20

= $16 per pair

Gross Margin

The previous discussion has indicated that maintained markup is the markup obtained after retail reductions have been subtracted from the initial markup. Thus, maintained markup is really equal to net sales minus the gross cost of the merchandise. **Gross margin** is closely related to maintained markup in that gross margin = net sales − total merchandising costs. Thus, there are only two items (vendors' cash discounts and alteration expenses) that differ in the calculation of the gross margin and maintained markup figures. If a firm does not receive any cash discounts from its suppliers or make alterations on merchandise that is sold to its customers, then its maintained markup will equal its gross margin. This seldom occurs in the real world, since retailers rely on the cash discounts they receive on the merchandise purchased from their suppliers to increase profits. Most stores also find it necessary to incur some alteration expense which is needed to convert some merchandise into a form that better satisfies consumer needs.

The conversion formula for finding gross margin is:

Gross margin = maintained markup + vendor cash discounts earned − alteration costs

The interdependence of gross margin and maintained markup is illustrated by slightly altering this formula to find maintained markup.

Maintained markup = gross margin − vendor cash discounts earned + alteration costs

The following example illustrates the relationship between initial markup, maintained markup, and gross margin. Store X expects to obtain sales of $500,000 next year. Its operating ex-

penses have been equal to 15 percent of sales, its combined value
of employee discounts and markdowns has been equal to 7 percent of sales, its shortages have been equal to 3 percent of
sales, and alteration costs have been equal to 1 percent of sales.
Store management does not believe these cost relationships will
change for the next year. The store has been receiving 2 percent
of retail sales vendor cash discount and expects this to continue
next year. Store management desires to earn a 5 percent profit
on sales for the next year. Thus:

$$\text{maintained markup percent} = 15\% \text{ store operating expense}$$
$$+\ 1\% \text{ alteration expense}$$
$$+\ 5\% \text{ planned profit}$$
$$-\ 2\% \text{ vendor cash discounts}$$
$$=\ 19\%,$$

and initial markup

$$=\frac{\text{maintained markup} + \text{reductions}}{\text{net sales} + \text{reductions}}$$

$$=\frac{19\% + (3\% \text{ shortages} + 7\% \text{ markdowns} + 3\% \text{ discounts})}{100\% + (3\% \text{ shortages} + 7\% \text{ markdowns} + 3\% \text{ discounts})}$$

$$=\frac{32\%}{113\%}$$

$$=\ 28.3\%$$

and gross margin $=$ maintained markup $+$ vendor cash discounts
$$-\ \text{alteration costs}$$
$$=\ 19\% + 2\% - 1\%$$
$$=\ 20\%$$

**Advantages of
Markup Pricing**

Retailers use markup pricing because it is a convenient method
of pricing the very large number of items they stock. The retailer
generally cannot afford to spend time and effort to determine the
best price to charge on every item, although few retailers use the
same markup for all their goods. In fact, some retailers have different markup percentages for each merchandise department
and key each item's markup percentage into checkout facilities,
thereby identifying sales by department and maintaining a perpetual inventory in the process.

Retail merchants also use markup percentages as a negotiation
tool and as a control and planning device. The retailer can gain
significant benefits by using markup as a commitment to a
specific minimum markup policy of X percent on all lines
stocked in the store. Success of the commitment will depend
upon the ability of the buyer to communicate this commitment

to the supplier. A rigid markup schedule, if used by a retail outlet that dominates the trade in a locality, can help counteract the advantages otherwise held by a powerful supplier. Particular note should be made that such practices set only the minimum markup and still leave the retailer the option of increasing the markup.

Retail management can also adapt markup as a control and planning tool if it controls the level of markup required in each department. Markup pressures could induce department merchandise buyers to make purchases at the lowest possible price or to discover new products that yield more than the minimum markup. Management pressure for a minimum markup could also help top retail management protect the firm against a continually low sale-price policy that might injure the long-run image of a store selling high-quality merchandise. However, retail management should also realize that rigid adherence to a high markup percentage will not necessarily maximize store profits. At a lower markup, sales volume may increase enough to generate more profits than the firm obtained when a higher markup was used.

Factors Affecting Markup

Markup percentage rate is influenced by many factors including rate of turnover, product cost, branding policies, and the degree of retail competition.

Generally, the retail markup varies inversely with merchandise turnover. A higher markup is usually placed on products that sell less frequently. Slow-moving products generally occupy the same amount of selling space and require the same investment as fast-selling items. Thus, a higher margin is required on slow-moving items if these items are going to contribute an equivalent share to the retailer's profits.

This can be demonstrated by calculating the margin needed to return an equivalent profit on both fast- and slow-selling items. An item's gross margin can be determined by multiplying its per unit margin by its turnover. Suppose two products, A and B, each cost the retailer $500 and require about the same amount of shelf space, sales time, and investment. Suppose further that the retailer desires to obtain $1,000 annual gross profit margin from each product. Annual merchandise turnover is estimated to be 20 for product A and 4 for B. Per unit margins needed if each product is to contribute $1,000 gross margin can be calculated by using the following formula:

Annual gross margin = per unit margin × annual turnover.

The calculations for product A are:

$$\$1,000 = \text{(required per unit margin)} \times 20, \text{ or } \frac{\$1,000}{20};$$

so per unit margin is $50.

For product B:

$$\$1,000 = \text{(required per unit margin)} \times 4, \text{ or } \frac{\$1,000}{4};$$

so per unit margin is $250.

Therefore, to obtain an equivalent $1,000 gross margin, the per unit margin would have to be $50 on fast-moving item A, compared to $250 on slow-moving item B. The gross margin percent required would be (50 / 550) (100), or 9 percent for A, and (250 / 750) (100), or 33 percent for B.

The markup percent needed to obtain an equivalent $1,000 gross margin can also be calculated. For example, if total retail reductions (markdowns, discounts, shrinkage, pilferage, etc.) are estimated to be 5 percent of sales, the following formula can be used to determine the required initial markup percent:

$$\text{Initial markup percent} = \frac{\text{(gross margin + retail reductions)}}{\text{(100\% + retail reductions)}}$$

The calculations for product A are:

$$\text{Initial markup percent} = \frac{(9\% + 5\%)}{(100\% + 5\%)},$$

or 13 percent.

For Product B:

$$\text{Initial markup percent} = \frac{(33\% + 5\%)}{(100\% + 5\%)},$$

or 36 percent.

In this example, an initial markup of 13 percent is required to yield a gross margin of 9 percent on A. The initial markup of 36 percent would result in a gross margin of 33 percent for B.

In summary, per unit gross margin, gross margin percent, and markup percent must all be higher on the slow-moving item B if the item is going to generate the same annual gross profit margin as the fast-selling (high turnover) item A.

Higher-price items normally carry a lower markup percent than lower-price items. Consumers are likely to notice similar percentage price differences on higher-priced items, so competitive pressure may partially explain the lower markup percent on higher-priced items. For example, a 10 percent price difference (amounting to 3 cents) between two stores on a 30 cent item is less likely to be noticed by customers than a 10 percent difference (amounting to $600) on a new car selling for $6,000. Customers are likely to spend more time making purchase decisions (and to make more comparisons on prices and quality) on major items than on lower-price items that are purchased infrequently.

Branding policies also affect the level of markup. Higher markups are usually applied to private label brand items which a retail chain prices below the price for similar national brand items. Higher markups can be applied to private label items because their acquisition, distribution, advertising, and promotion costs are usually lower than comparable costs for national branded items. Thus, private label items are usually priced lower than national brand items, but they still provide the retailer with a product line that has a higher markup percent.

Retailers may change their regular markup policy to meet a competitor's price, but few retailers meet all prices of all competitors. However, most stores compare merchandise and prices in competing stores. Thus, the degree of retail competition in an area determines the markup level charged by its stores.

Other things being equal, more stores and more aggressive competition tend to produce lower markups. Larger stores generally use a slightly lower markup (and hence receive a slightly lower gross margin percent) on their merchandise than similar smaller stores. Average gross margin percent data for forty types of retail outlets are presented in Table 12.3.

Price Elasticity and Markup

Most of the factors that influence markup are considered in the calculation of the **price elasticity of demand coefficient,** hereafter referred to as E_d. The value of E_d indicates the percentage change in sales per 1 percent change in price, other things being held constant. The value of E_d, if known, can be used as a guide to determine markup for an item, group of items, or even a department in a store.

Price elasticity of the demand coefficient, E_d, may be calculated by the formula:

$$E_d = \frac{(Q_1 - Q_2)/(Q_1 + Q_2)}{(P_1 - P_2)/(P_1 + P_2)};$$

where Q_1 is the quantity sold when the price is P_1, and Q_2 is the quantity sold when the price is P_2. The value of the calculated

Table 12.3 Gross Profit Margin Percent for Different Types of Retail Outlets, 1980

Type of Retailer	Median Gross Margin Percentage for All Sizes of Firms, Year Ending 1980[a]
Family clothing	40.3
Furs	42.3
Infants' clothing	40.0
Men's and boys' clothing	41.4
Shoes	41.8
Women's ready-to-wear	40.8
Books and stationery	38.3
Office supplies and equipment	36.7
Building materials	26.7
Hardware	33.0
Heating and plumbing equipment	25.3
Lumber	24.2
Paint, glass, and wall paper	35.5
Cameras and photographic supplies	29.0
Department stores	34.1
Dry goods and general merchandise	33.2
Drugs	33.6
Farm equipment	20.9
Farm and garden supply	26.8
Cut flowers and growing plants	48.3
Dairy product—milk dealers	36.1
Groceries and meats	22.8
Restaurants	53.9
Floor coverings	30.0
Furniture	39.9
Household appliances	29.7
Radios, TV, and record players	33.5
Jewelry	47.1
Liquor	20.6
Luggage and gifts	44.0
Autos—new and used	15.8
Gasoline service stations	17.6
Mobile homes	20.4
Tire, battery, and accessories	33.0
Musical instruments and supplies	38.5
Sporting goods	34.2
Vending machine operators, merchandise	42.3

[a] Disclaimer statement: Robert Morris Associates cannot emphasize too strongly that their composite figures for each industry may not be representative of that entire industry (except by coincidence) for the following reasons: (1) Only member banks submit data, and only the most recent data are accepted. Thus, selection is not made by any random or statistically reliable method. (2) The included companies differ as to product lines, methods of operation, and demographics, but they are categorized by their primary product line only. (3) The size and variation of the sample can cause a disproportionate influence on the composite.
Source: Annual Statement Studies, the Robert Morris Associates, the National Association of Bank Loan and Credit Officers, Philadelphia National Bank Building, Philadelphia, Pennsylvania, 1980 Edition, pp. 231–279. Copyright © 1980 by Robert Morris Associates.

coefficient is nearly always negative because of the inverse relationship between price and quantity (an increase in price generally causes a decrease in the number of units sold).

The calculated value of the coefficient indicates if the price elasticity of demand is inelastic, elastic, or of unitary elasticity. If the calculated coefficient has an absolute value of less than 1.0, the demand is said to be inelastic.[4] The price increase (to the higher of the two prices—P_1 and P_2) will increase both total revenue (sales dollars) and profit if the demand is inelastic. If demand is found to be inelastic, then a new, higher price level should be tested in the next time period to determine if demand is still inelastic at a higher price level. Any calculated inelastic E_d indicates that prices must be increased even further to maximize profit. Thus, retail markups can be higher on products that have few substitutes, as indicated by an inelastic E_d. Stocking exclusive brands, obtaining a regional dealer franchise, and keeping the store open when other stores are closed are several ways of reducing the competition from substitute products or retail outlets.

Unitary elasticity is indicated when the calculated value of E_d is -1.0. Unitary elasticity maximizes total revenue but not profits. Thus, a price increase to the higher of the prices P_1 and P_2 would reduce total gross receipts, but would increase profit unless production and marketing costs are zero or there is a large difference between P_1 and P_2.

An *elastic demand* occurs when the percentage change in quantity is relatively greater than the percentage change in price. In this case, the calculated value of E_d has an absolute value greater than 1.0. A price decrease in the elastic section of the demand curve will result in an increase in the total revenue. Profit at the lower price may be either increased or decreased, depending upon margin and product marketing costs. One must analyze the costs and total revenue obtained under the two price levels before one can determine the effect a price change will have on profit in the elastic section of the demand curve. A very elastic E_d indicates that there are many close substitutes for the product, so the markup must be low to allow the retailer to remain competitive.

Retail markups should vary inversely with the price elasticity of demand if profits are to be maximized. High-profit stores have been found to price competitively on readily identifiable items with a high turnover rate and "known" prices. However, the high-profit stores also have used higher margins on less important merchandise. Thus, they could charge relatively high average prices but still give the appearance of competitiveness. In this same study, stores receiving lower profits tended to charge a higher price on items with a fast turnover and to charge a lower price on items with a low turnover. This pricing strategy can give the consumer the incorrect impression that the store charges high average prices.

Estimating Price Elasticity

Estimates of retail price elasticity of demand usually are based upon the experience of the retailer or upon representative markups charged by competitors or quoted by trade associations. There is no guarantee that any of these approaches will provide a reliable estimate of price elasticity for a specific product category sold by a specific store. Years of experience can provide the retailer with an approximate estimate of E_d, but it is a costly and time-consuming process. Several research techniques can be used to reduce the cost of making serious long-term pricing errors by analyzing sales data.

One way to measure price elasticity at the retail level is to change price and observe what happens to sales. However, care must be taken when interpreting the resulting sales since other factors, such as advertising, competitive actions, or seasonal fluctuations, may distort the sales data. A retailer should be able to control his advertising and promotion, or at least know that a promotion is planned, so that he can select a product line and time period when little abnormal promotional activity will be going on. Of course, retailers are not able to control competitive promotions. However, sales data obtained during weeks of abnormally heavy competitive promotion can be deleted from the analysis.

The effect that seasonal fluctuations have upon sales can be eliminated by comparing the weekly sales of a product during price changes with its weekly sales during previous years (Table 12.4). Other factors, such as shelf space devoted to the test products, sales personnel attention, shelf inventory on the test products, and so forth, also influence sales and should be controlled by calculating statistical experimental designs.

Price Lining

Price lining involves the search for merchandise that can be sold at previously determined retail price levels. It is contrary to markup pricing, which involves purchasing merchandise and adding a markup to arrive at the retail price. Price lining results in selling merchandise at only a few (generally three to five) price levels. For example, men's sport coats could be separated into $69, $59, $49, $39, and $29 classes.

The retailer who uses price lining implicitly assumes that his merchandise follows a **demand curve** (a schedule that indicates

Table 12.4   Determining Product Line Price Elasticity (or Department) by Changing Prices in 1982 and Comparing Sales with Previous Sales Levels

Product Line (Department)	Week	Price Level	Sales in Units 1982	Sales in Units 1979–1981 Average	1982 Index or Percent (1979–81 Sales Average)
Meat	May 1	No change	1,210	1,100	+10
	May 8	No change	1,080	1,000	+ 8
	May 15	No change	1,120	1,000	+12
	May 22	No change	990	900	+10
Preprice change average			1,100	1,000	+10
	May 22	Lowered by 10%	1,500	1,100	+36
	May 29	Lowered by 10%	1,536	1,200	+28
	June 5	Lowered by 10%	1,703	1,300	+31
	June 12	Lowered by 10%	1,501	1,200	+25
Postprice change average			1,560	1,200	+30

Calculation of $E_d = \dfrac{\text{Percentage change in quantity}}{\text{Percent of change in price}}$

$S_oE_d = \dfrac{\text{(Postprice change average index sales)}}{\text{minus (Preprice change average index sales)}}{\text{Percentage change in price}}$; or

$E_d = \dfrac{\text{(Plus 30) minus (plus 10)}}{\text{(Minus 10)}} = \dfrac{\text{(Plus 20)}}{\text{(Minus 10)}}$; or -2.0

the quantity of an item that can be sold at many different price levels) similar to the one presented in Figure 12.3. That is, the retailer believes that sales are not increased by making a *permanent* price reduction from $69 until the amount of the price reduction reaches $59. At that point sales increase from quantity A to quantity B. A further reduction of ten dollars is needed to increase sales. This decrease to $49 results in sales of quantity C.

Price lining is said to offer an advantage to the consumer. It reduces the number of product classes and thereby simplifies comparison shopping. If the consumer's decision-making process is simplified, sales might be increased on both the main item (men's sport coats) and on complementary items (ties, shoes, slacks, belts, socks).

Retail price lining simplifies buying, accounting, and pricing procedures for the retailer because it reduces the number of price levels. Price lining makes it easier for the retail salesmen to convince the customers they should purchase the highest-quality line they can afford. The limited number of price lines can easily be associated with different levels of quality by the consumer.

Different price classes may also provide convenient steps for making a price markdown if the merchandise does not sell. Care must be taken to ensure that the consumer actually perceives that the price has been reduced.

For example, men's sport coats that have been priced at $59 could simply be moved into the $49 line without advertising the price reduction. Price lining would make this more convenient. However, advertising a price decrease might be communicated more easily if the price were *not* reduced to exactly the level of the next price line ($49 in the case of a $59 sport coat). Full reduction to the next price level might confuse potential customers, who might think that the store is merely trying to advertise the $49 line and sell it at the regular price. Pricing the coat at $53 and/or careful advertisement writing could reduce this confusion.

Merchandise handling and sales training become easier with price lining. Stock checkers, markers, and sales personnel prefer

Figure 12.3 Demand Curve for Men's Sport Coats as Perceived by a Price Lining User

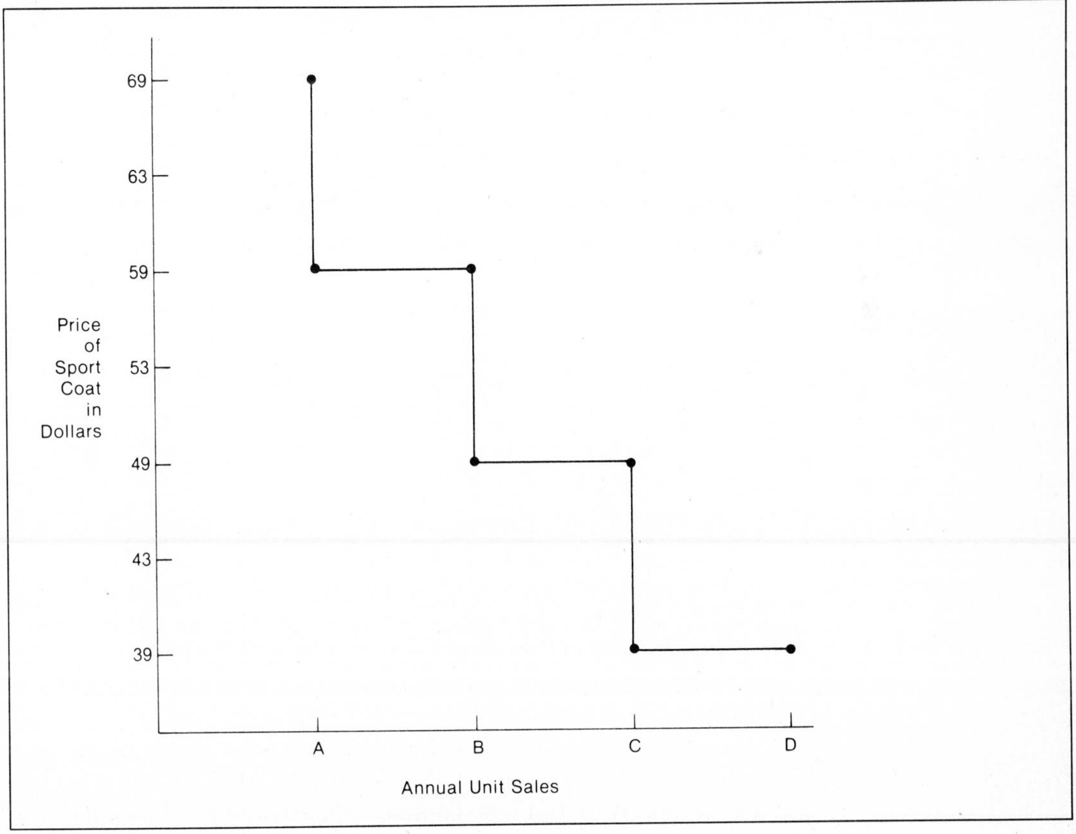

to work with the fewer different levels of price because it is easier to identify, classify, and mark the goods and to charge customers for their purchases.

Price lining also gives the retailer more merchandise depth and breadth with less stock because it forces the buyer to concentrate the merchandise into definite price categories. For example, stocking 200 units divided among ten price levels would give little breadth or depth at any price. However, the 200 units carried at only four price levels would provide about 50 units in each price line, and this would more than double the selection within each price line.

The merchandise buyer may also encounter problems associated with price lining. Products must not only be selected on the basis of style, color, quality, price, etc., but they must also fit into the previously determined price lines. Price lines must be upgraded continually to reflect increases in wholesale purchase prices and increasing preferences by consumers for items possessing more quality. If price lines are not upgraded by introducing a "new" top line and/or abandoning the lowest price line, markups will decline or quality must be reduced as wholesale prices increase.

Price lining is widely adopted despite the difficulties associated with it. However, the principles established in the discussion on markup pricing should establish that price lines best meet consumer needs. Usually, retailers survey competitive outlets to determine which of their price lines are strong and which are weak. They then carry the price lines that are not being well supplied by competitors or at least determine why the competitors are not emphasizing that line. Alternatively the retailer may battle competitors head on by emphasizing the same price lines that competitors are carrying in a full assortment. This policy requires that the retailer offer unique merchandise so the firm can capture a large share of that market and/or that the sales potential in that market be sufficiently large to be profitable.

Consumer Knowledge of Retail Prices

Reliable knowledge about consumers' price awareness is needed if an appropriate pricing strategy is to be established. If consumers do not know the price of any products, the price elasticity of demand is likely to be more inelastic since they are not aware that identical or close substitute items are available at different prices in other outlets. High markups would maximize profits in this case.

If consumers have a great deal of knowledge about prices on many products, price elasticity is likely to be elastic since consumers are aware of the existence of substitute products. Relatively low markups would result in maximum profits for those products.

Consumers' knowledge of prices is more likely to fall somewhere between the two extremes. They may know only the prices of a small number of frequently purchased items. In such cases it is even more important to determine which items' prices are known by consumers. These items could be priced lower to give a low-price or discount image. Items with well-known prices are also items that would respond best to advertised temporary price reductions.

Studies of consumers' knowledge of prices must be conducted separately for each type of retail outlet. Published results from such studies are very limited. A study of consumers' awareness of fifty-nine highly competitive and frequently advertised grocery items revealed that 71 percent of the consumers were unable to estimate within 5 percent of the actual price.[5] Responses from about 2,000 customers were obtained by placing unpriced products on tables in the store and asking the consumers what prices the products sold for. This study revealed that consumers were not aware of highly competitive and frequently advertised products. They were probably less aware of prices of other items sold in a supermarket. Consumer awareness can change over time and distance, so there is a need to conduct similar studies every two to three years.

Unit Pricing

Unit pricing is a system that displays both the price per standard unit of weight or measure as well as the common per package price. This allows the consumer to compare the cost of several items in terms of content volume per dollar spent, for example, 10¢ per ounce. It is most widely used when several competing brands of the same kind of product are sold in many different package sizes. The two prices, per package and the price per standard unit, are usually given on tags or stickers that appear on the shelves below the merchandise.

Unit pricing is a legal requirement for some types of stores in some states. Usually the requirement for unit pricing has been confined to food, health and beauty aids, and related products in large stores such as supermarkets.

Private Label Pricing

Unit pricing grew out of a desire to better inform customers of comparative purchasing values. Chain stores usually have benefited by this system as it shows customers that the per unit price of their private label products is lower than the store's prices on national brand products. Private label merchandise consists of items that are promoted under the retailer's own brand names, for example, Safeway's Townhouse, Sears' Kenmore, J. C. Penney's Towncraft, and Ward's Signature.

Most private label convenience items sell at lower prices than comparable brands because consumers will generally select the well-advertised national brand if prices are the same. Thus, retailers must price their own brands lower to generate volume sales. In addition, these low prices placed on the firm's private label merchandise help build an overall fair-price image among its customers. Finally, private label merchandise usually costs the retailer less to purchase than would a comparable national brand item. Thus, the retailer can mark up the purchase price by a greater percentage margin than can be obtained for national brands and still sell it to the consumer for a lower price. This can be done because of savings in transportation, advertising, distribution, and so forth.

Psychology of Retail Pricing

Markup pricing and/or price lining strategies can help establish a general price level. However, attention must be given to the psychological aspects of price when specific price is established.

Odd pricing, which uses prices like 39 cents and $4.95 rather than the nearly equivalent even prices of 40 cents and $5, is frequently practiced. A study of all products advertised by supermarkets in newspapers in twenty-three metropolitan areas revealed that 57 percent of all advertised prices ended in 9.[6] Another 15 percent of the prices ended in 5.

The practice of using odd pricing probably began as a safeguard against petty theft.[7] Even-price items tend to be paid for with the exact amount of cash, and the clerk can then serve other customers before ringing up a sale. This provides an opportunity for pocketing a portion of the proceeds. If every shopper demands a receipt, this type of theft can be prevented; but there are always a few customers—small children, for example—who don't obtain a sales slip. When odd prices are used, the customer is likely not to have the exact amount of cash, so the clerk must make change from the cash register. Some of the advantages of odd pricing have been lost by the universal adoption of local sales taxes, which tend to create similar change situations.

Retailers who uses odd retail price endings implicitly assume that their merchandise follows a demand curve similar to the one presented in Figure 12.4. That is, the retailer believes that sales are larger when the price ends in an odd number than when it ends in the next lowest number. In Figure 12.4 the sales at 59¢ are greater than the sales at 58¢ and greater at 57¢ than at 56¢, etc.

Figure 12.4   Demand Curve for Merchandise as Perceived by Odd Retail Price Endings User

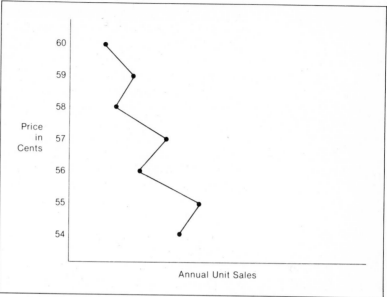

Actual impact of odd retail price endings on sales and profits is not determined in the published marketing literature. Experimentation is needed to determine if odd prices really promote sales. If they do not promote sales, they could be abandoned because they are "sticky" prices that could hinder profit-maximizing pricing decisions.

Multiple-unit prices are also used in selling frequently purchased items. The "two for 50¢" or "five for $1" multiple prices convey the impression of potential savings to the consumer. Generally, the multiple price ends in 9 (two for 39¢), so the consumer saves 1¢ by buying two items simultaneously instead of one unit at 20¢ on two different trips. The savings may be sufficient to persuade the customer to buy a larger quantity. However, the psychological aspect of buying a larger quantity may give the impression of additional savings.

This multiple pricing concept also works for larger items such as furniture. For example, Waldheim's Furniture of Milwaukee, Wisconsin has found that just one chair when advertised at a sales price might result in 100 chairs being sold, but when pairs of chairs are shown and priced together, 300 to 400 chairs may be sold. This concept also works on tables as the offering of any three tables for $299 will generate sales of 600 tables compared to sales of 100 tables under unit pricing.[8]

There appear to be several different types of psychological reactions to price. A **quantum effect** occurs when a certain price is the maximum that consumers will pay for any quantity of a product. For example, a product may not sell well at $1.05, but a package containing only four-fifths as much, clearly labeled as to quantity content, will sell well at 98 cents. In this case, $1 is a quantum point from the consumer viewpoint. This quantum psychological reaction may partially explain the popularity of using odd prices which are established just below the quantum point.

Consumers may also develop some idea of a fair price for many items. This results in a "best" price that will actually generate more sales than either a lower or higher price. A major retail chain discovered that a common hardware item sold better at $1.09 than it did at either 89¢ or $1.29.[9] Consumers apparently considered the 89 cents price too low to be attached to a quality item. The $1.09 price apparently reflected the image of a quality product to consumers.

Frequently, consumers think they can judge the cost of production. In this case their fair price standard is based upon the allowance of a modest profit, but no more. A lower markup usually must be charged when most consumers can accurately evaluate item production cost.

Dynamic and Tactical Aspects of Pricing

Retail pricing strategies function as planned only when they are implemented effectively. Many decisions have to be made during these implementation efforts. These tactical decisions are concerned with day-to-day decisions that should be made within the guidelines established when the pricing strategy was determined. Tactical decisions are therefore the short-run decisions needed to carry out basic pricing policy.

Many day-to-day pricing decisions are either passive responses to cost squeezes or estimated adaptations to what seem to be competitive market requirements. Many different price tactics can be utilized to make these day-to-day decisions more profitable. Familiarity with the different kinds of tactical price movements provides the background necessary if the retailer is going to expand or hold profitable markets.

Markdowns

Markdowns consist of a decrease from the original price of an item. The **markdown percentage** is usually stated as a percentage of the reduced selling price. In formula form:

$$\text{Markdown percentage} = \frac{\begin{array}{c}\text{(per unit original retail price)}\\ - \text{(per unit reduced retail price)}\end{array}}{\text{per unit reduced price}} \times 100.$$

For example, the markdown percentage on a sport coat originally selling at $49 but reduced to $40 would be ($9/$40) × 100, or 22½ percent.

The amount of the price reduction may also be calculated to reflect an **off retail percentage.** The off retail percentage is the reduction stated as a percentage of the original selling price—or ($9/$49) × 100 = 18.4 percent in the sport coat example.

There are many reasons why a retailer uses markdown pricing (Table 12.5). One objective of markdown pricing is to convert surplus merchandise into cash that can be reinvested in faster-moving merchandise or in some other demand-stimulating activity. Some markdowns are caused by an oversupply of merchandise which must be sold to reduce the store's inventory level. Oversupply may result from errors in purchasing merchandise, which can be "overbought" by an overly enthusiastic purchasing agent. Overbuying of an item can arise because of overly optimistic sales forecasting or because of an inappropriate merchandise assortment which does not meet consumers' needs or likes. Thus, overbuying is likely to occur with any merchandise that goes out of fashion (or never becomes stylish) because of preferences for different styles, color, size, etc.

Poor timing in the arrival of merchandise can also result in merchandise oversupply. This is especially true of seasonal merchandise which consumers buy only once a year to meet a specific need. If the store's supply has not arrived at the time of peak consumer demand, sales are likely to be lost. Antifreeze and winter overshoes are examples of products that are likely to be purchased over a short period of time. Therefore, timing is key to making markdowns. The more accurate one's timing is, the quicker the item sells and the more gross profit is obtained

Table 12.5 Reasons for Retailer Markdowns

Buying errors—Inappropriate sizes, colors, style, quantities

Timing errors—Merchandise delivery delayed, out-of-season, out-of-style, failure to spot slow sellers early, maintaining full assortments late in season

Selling and promotion errors—Rude sales practices, neglect to show some items, high pressure selling

Pricing errors—Initial markups too high

Deliberately planned—Assist in sales promotion to build image of meeting or beating competition on the transaction. Remember, a small markdown in season will move more merchandise than a large markdown out-of-season. Markdowns on seasonal, fashion, or fad items should be considered as soon as the selling activity on these items reflects customer resistance. The task then is to determine the highest price at which the item can still be quickly sold. This requires obtaining a great deal of retail experience and a feeling of how consumers perceive the item.

Markdowns may also be necessary when the correct quantity and quality merchandise is purchased, but the selling and/or promotion efforts are deficient. Selling errors can originate from poor department management, a weak sales force, or a poor promotion program. Poor management may be revealed by a failure to interpret sales records early enough to spot items that are not selling well. Some retailers are now using computer systems to provide reliable inventory and sales data quickly. The sales force may contribute to the overstock problem by not exposing all of the products in the category, so that some items are unexposed until it is too late to sell them at regular prices.

Markdowns are required even in cases where there are proper purchasing and selling procedures. Odds and ends merchandise gradually accumulates over time, so most retailers use markdowns to unload the least desirable merchandise from their shelves.

Many markdowns are deliberately planned price reductions, designed to assist in sales promotion and in generating an image of meeting competition. "Leader prices" are relatively low (or negative) markups on items that attract customers to the store where, hopefully, they will also purchase other regular-priced merchandise. Leader prices contribute little, if any, per unit profit, but they may make substantial contributions to dollar profits by generating added sales of products at regular prices. Leader items must be recognized as good values by customers since their principal aim is to draw customer traffic. Good leader items are products whose normal price is known by most potential customers. A good leader item is usually purchased frequently by a large number of consumers.

Using price leaders for a limited specified time as a promotional device appears to create less disturbance among competition than general price reductions. General price reductions are likely to initiate a price war because they offer the threat of a permanent price cut. Leader prices are more acceptable to competition because the prices are viewed as only temporary reductions and, hence, are considered part of the normal pricing routine.

Leader prices are generally assigned to high-frequency purchase products, and a good price leader is:

1. Well known, widely used, and appealing to many customers
2. Priced low enough so that many people can buy it
3. Not so low in price that price cuts will generate no interest
4. Not generally bought in large quantities and stored
5. Likely to have a high price elasticity of demand
6. Not in close competition with other products in the retailer's merchandise assortment.[10]

Types of Markdown

Leader prices can be classified by the degree of markdown and the purpose of the promotion.

Low-Price Leaders Low-price leaders are products whose prices represent bargain prices. Low-price leader items are not priced below actual cost to the retailer but merely represent a reduced markup percentage. The low-price leader does not violate the intent of most unfair trade practices acts, which usually prohibit sales of merchandise at less than cost when the intent is to injure competition. Often, large chains are able to make "special purchases" of seasonal merchandise at reduced costs which serve as excellent low-price traffic generators.

Loss Leader Pricing Loss-leader pricing involves sales of an item at a price below the actual cost to the retailer. The objective of loss-leader pricing is to attract customers to the store. A good merchandising program can then be used to stimulate consumers to make additional purchases of other regular-price items. Profit obtained from sales of the regular-price items must overcome the loss incurred on the loss-leader items. Proper placement of loss-leader merchandise within a department can encourage such additional purchases. Thus, loss-leader pricing is really a form of promotion, because loss-leader pricing costs the retailer money in the same manner as additional advertising.

The legality of loss-leader pricing must be established before it is used by retailers. Most states have passed laws prohibiting sales below cost and/or laws that establish a minimum markup if the intent of the pricing practice is to injure or extinguish competition. Exceptions are usually provided for specific merchandise which is sold for (1) clearance or close out, (2) charitable purposes, (3) liquidation of a business, or (4) liquidation of perishable, seasonal, or damaged goods.

Exhibit 12.1   Leader Pricing Illustration

Source: Photo courtesy of the K mart Corporation.

Bait-Leader Pricing Bait-leader pricing involves the use of an advertised price on an item that is not intended to be sold. It represents a very low price on a well-known item which is found by the customer to be relatively unattractive after arriving at the store. Bait-leader pricing could involve the advertising of a very low price on a relatively low quality (or small) item that is not likely to be purchased by a large percentage of the potential customers. After the consumer arrives at the store, the sales clerk uses persuasion to upgrade the consumer's purchase (at unreduced prices) to a better quality than was originally advertised. For example, USDA standard-grade beef may be advertised at $1.19 per pound, but the sales clerk would suggest that the good, choice, or prime grades are better-quality meats and would be better accepted by other family members.

Another version of bait-leader pricing involves advertisement of some central component item (for example, a new-model car) at an extremely low price. However, the price is quoted on only a portion of the total merchandise that is likely to be purchased. Accessory items are sold at the regular price, so the total "package" purchase price may not be lower than competitive prices.

Accessory items may take the form of both supplementary and complementary items.

Bait-leader pricing could also involve advertising an item that is in very short supply at a very low price and telling the customers who rush to the store that the last unit of the advertised item has just been sold. However, this practice has been made illegal and is policed by the Federal Trade Commission (hereafter referred to as the FTC). The FTC watches over deceptive acts by firms that do a substantial share of their business in interstate commerce. All firms may be required to make good on all offers made in advertisements, according to current legislation. The FTC publishes guides for business people who want clarification of the legality of related practices. Examples are *Guides Against Deceptive Pricing, Guides Against Bait Advertising,* and *Guides Against Deceptive Advertising of Guarantees.*

Firms should exercise care when any of the leader-pricing techniques are used. Low-price leaders and some forms of loss-leader and bait-leader pricing may be legal pricing practices, but they may strengthen customer support for the consumer movement. However, long-run businesses must be based upon providing consumer satisfaction. A poor postpurchase feeling, generated by a consumer belief of having "been taken," will not promote future patronage. Thus, leader pricing must be used in a way that will not offend or mislead consumers. The low-price leader and loss-leader are not likely to offend consumers if the featured items are always available for purchase in quantity and quality without special qualifications (coupon clipping, etc.). The consumer movement is here, and—like it or not—the trend is toward more consumer protection from deceptive pricing of all kinds.

Off-Season Pricing Off-season pricing is another form of markdown. Firms engaged in more seasonal service or retail businesses (for example, travel, resort, and tourist service) use off-season and special group-pricing practices to reach a different market segment from their regular-season customer. The off-season business may be promoted at the partial expense of the regular-season business, but the increased business volume may result in lower year-round average costs that justify price reductions.

Retail firms utilize special advertisements, mailings, and reduced off-season prices to generate a more constant sales level than they would otherwise attain. The more constant sales level reduces cost by better use of the somewhat fixed level of personnel who are needed to operate a retail outlet.

Farm machinery retailers have off-season price reductions during the fall and winter months to provide a more reliable sales forecast, which results in a more constant work load over the year. Sales are also promoted by offering a cash discount and delaying the payment until spring (the normal purchase period), with little or no interest charges being assessed.

Timing of Markdowns
The appropriate time to mark down the price on merchandise depends on many factors. Stores catering to the same clientele on a frequent basis will want to mark down prices early on items that are not selling well. Stores relying on sales made to different transient customers may delay price reductions and hope to make additional sales at regular prices.

Earlier markdowns are more likely to be taken on fashionable and/or perishable merchandise than on items that are not subject to sudden changes in fashion or spoilage. Taking early markdowns keeps a retailer's stock fresh and more in tune with the latest fashion preferences. Retailers may mark down a fashion item when its sales begin to decline if the outlet is estimated to be in an oversupplied condition. Seasonal items whose sales are dependent upon fashionability are usually reduced in price as soon as the rush of seasonal buying is completed and excess stock is estimated to be held in inventory. For example, ski equipment prices may be reduced in January, although sales are still made during February and March.

Staple goods prices are usually reduced if the supply is excessive or if the products have been on the shelf long enough that their appearance and/or quality are about to decline. Staple items whose demand fluctuates seasonally are usually marked down if the store does not have sufficient low-cost storage space to carry them until next year. An evaluation of the costs incurred in placing these items in inventory is needed before seasonal items are stored for nearly one year.

Fashion merchandise is not carried over, no matter how costly the markdown. If it did not sell now, it will not sell next year. Recognize the mistake, mark it down, take the bath, and get merchandise that will sell.

Some fashion retailers are even using automatic markdown policy. For example, all of the merchandise that remains unsold after twelve selling days in the basement store of William Filene's Sons Company of Boston is automatically marked down 25 percent. After eighteen days the unsold merchandise is repriced at 50 percent of its original price, and after twenty-four days the remaining merchandise is remarked at 25 percent of the original price.[11] This policy has developed a large and loyal customer group for the Filene basement. Most retailers prefer to use a more flexible plan of making markdowns. However, it is desirable to have some written markdown policy that has proven itself to be most appropriate for that particular store.

Mass merchandisers are also more likely to markdown earlier than are exclusive outlets. Exclusive shops prefer to delay price reductions to discourage bargain hunters (sometimes referred to as "cherry pickers") who select only markdown items and thereby detract from the stores' class appeal. If price lining is used, exclusive outlets can move slow-selling items into the next lower price line without advertising the price reductions. This practice is less likely to attract "cherry pickers," and could increase sales to their normal market segment.

Pricing for
Special Sales

Pricing for special sales poses particular problems of pricing for the retail operator. The amount of the markdown is not easily determined. Markdown level must be sufficient to generate sales on items that were not selling well. Department stores frequently reduce the retail price by about one-third on the first markdown. The retailer must consider the quality of the merchandise and its sales relative to other items sold in the store.

The retailer must evaluate the effect that advertising and sales effort have upon sales. Other things being equal, a large promotion effort can stimulate as many sales at a moderate markdown as a larger markdown promoted on a small scale.

Language that advertises special sale items usually involves hoopla and sensational-type advertising. Words and phrases such as "incredible," "unbelievable," "fantastic," "free," "2 for 1 sale," "1¢ sale" frequently describe promotional sales, but indiscriminate use of such terms has been overdone by too many retailers. The FTC has been increasing its regulation activity by forbidding deliberately deceptive language of special price promotions.

This increased level of regulatory activity, plus the consumer movement, are likely to result in a continual growth of informational advertisements. Such advertisements clearly state all the terms and conditions of the sale. Advertisements would answer such questions as, "What is the product? How can it be used? What does the price tag include and what is extra? Does it come fully assembled?" These important questions are being asked by both consumers and the government.

Pricing Restrictions

The retailer is not entirely free to set any price that is believed to maximize sales and/or profits. Manufacturers or distributors of well-known, branded products can strongly influence retail prices if they threaten to withhold products from retail outlets that do not comply with the manufacturer's pricing suggestions. Manufacturers and distributors control much of the marketing effort of franchised dealers (retailers) who represent the manufacturer or distributor in the market. Franchising allows manufacturers to restrict their products to a few outlets that are expected to price their products according to suggestions.

In nonfranchising situations, manufacturers sometimes preticket their products with "suggested retail prices." The retailer does not have to sell the item at the supplier's suggested price, but it is inconvenient to reprice the merchandise. In some cases, re-marking of "suggested retail price" items can lead to strained dealer-supplier relationships. Alternatively, reticketing to a lower price has been used by discount retailers to reinforce a low-price image.

The structure (number and size) of the local retail competition can influence a retailer to stress other nonprice sales stimulating devices. In some cases, smaller less powerful retailers may simply price their goods according to the price indicated by the dominant firm. The prevalence of price leadership of this type certainly impairs the effectiveness of the individual's price setting policy, which should be designed to maximize long-run profits. In other instances, several retailers of equal power may recognize that a reduction in price by any one of them will result in a retaliatory price reduction by the others. Such firms would probably attempt to prevent price wars by emphasizing nonprice competition. Nonprice competition has two general benefits: it may be longer lasting, and it is more difficult to imitate. For the retailer attempting to build a distinct store image both benefits are important. However, low profits by any of the current retailers or the entry of a new competitor will usually disturb static pricing after a period of time.

A retailer's freedom to establish prices is also limited by governmental authority at many different levels—local, state, and national. States and the federal government limit retailers' price-setting power by preventing the maintenance of high prices if retailers get together and make price-fixing agreements. Governmental authority can also impose minimum price levels that prevent a retailer from cutting prices too drastically.

Preticketing

Manufacturers still attempt to influence the retailer's price by suggesting specific prices for their items. They frequently even mark their suggested price on the good. This act of premarking the price on the merchandise is called **preticketing.**

However, manufacturers cannot legally force the retailer to use the preticketed price if the retailer owns the merchandise. Manufacturers must be reasonably certain that most of the retailers selling their products will follow their price recommendations before they preticket. This is because the FTC believes that a preticketed price is deceptive pricing if a substantial number of retailers sell the item for less than the preticketed price. Since some retailers believe that a reduction in price from a preticketed level offers proof to the customer that the outlet is offering low prices, manufacturers have little assurance that prices will not be cut. Thus, they are likely to incur the wrath of the FTC. As a result preticketing is on the decline.

Unfair Sales and Unfair Trade Practices Acts

Unfair sales and unfair trade practices acts establish a mandatory minimum price for all goods sold in states where unfair sales practices, unfair trade practices, minimum price, minimum markup, or sales-below-cost laws (known by some other name) are on the books. The unfair sales act in some states defines the minimum price as the cost of merchandise without the addition of markup. Other states require retailers to add at least a specified percentage of their invoice cost of goods. Usually the minimum retailing costs exceed the specified legal minimum markup percentage. Thus, unfair sales acts normally prevent the practice of drastic price cutting. However, unfair sales acts do not generally force an efficient retailer to raise prices above a low price level, based upon low cost of operation, low merchandise costs, and/or a low profit margin percentage on a large sales volume. This would not be true if the minimum specified legal markup is higher than the markup required for profitably marketing some items. In this case the unfair sales act can result in consumers paying higher prices than they would pay if this type of act were not law.

There are about twenty-five states that use unfair sales acts to establish a minimum price on retail goods. These acts are usually supported by small-scale independent retailers and wholesalers who wish to prevent or inhibit establishment of large-scale retailers. Minimum markup laws are designed to prevent predatory price cutting, which a large, powerful retailer could use to drive small retailers out of business. The large retailer may then increase prices above the original price level as soon as the competition is eliminated.

Predatory pricing of this kind is most likely to occur in areas where the retail competition is already weak. To be successful, this type of predatory pricing would not only have to eliminate current retailers but also discourage potential competitors from establishing a new outlet in the area. New retailers are likely to move into the area if the original predator uses an abnormally high pricing policy after eliminating all competition.

Unfair sales practices acts are also supported because they curb loss-leader pricing which may deceive customers into patronizing the store with drastically reduced prices on only a few items to which the consumer is price sensitive.

Deceptive Pricing The FTC regulates deceptive pricing that may mislead consumers into believing that they are getting a bargain.

Former-Price Comparisons Retailers can use former-price comparisons, which indicate that an item was formerly priced at a higher level but is now reduced to a new price level. To do so, however, they must be certain that the former price has been regularly used in sales during the recent course of business.[12]

Comparable-Price Comparisons Bargain advertising that offers a reduction from the price charged by other local retailers for either the identical or comparable merchandise is legitimate if the higher price is a genuine price, regularly charged by merchants in the local trade area.[13] Thus, advertisement of brand X cameras, "Price Elsewhere $75; Our Price $50," is legitimate if the higher price is truly established, and if brand X cameras are made available to the customers.

This type of price advertising has several advantages. The retailer does not have to establish the higher comparative price in his or her store, so the article may be introduced to customers at the lower price and the lower price may be maintained on a permanent basis or raised later. This type of comparative pricing also combines the pull of a brand name product with the lure of a bargain to generate additional sales.

Comparable merchandise pricing is allowed if it is made clear to the consumer that a comparison is being made with other merchandise of essentially similar quality that is regularly available in the local market area. The terms "comparable value $75" or "comparable retail $75" can be used if the comparable merchandise is "competing merchandise" of "like grade and quality." The FTC also permits the retailer to relate a bargain price to one being charged by him for other merchandise of like grade and quality. Thus, a retailer may compare the price of a private label brand with a higher-priced nationally advertised brand that is also carried, provided the private label product is of the same quality or quantity as that of the national brand.

Free Offers Offering and giving free goods is a very effective merchandising and advertising method for attracting customers.

The word *free* usually refers to an offer involving something other than an unconditional gift the consumer can receive without doing something or paying something. The "free" offer usually is an offer to give something if the customer purchases other goods or services for a stated price. In reality, most of these offers are merely price reductions, which are legal if the word "free" is not used in a deceptive manner.

Practices that are condemned by the FTC are:

1. Failure to fully disclose the terms and conditions of the bargain offer "at the outset"
2. Increasing the usual and regular price of the article to be purchased
3. Reducing the quality of the article to be purchased
4. Reducing the quantity or size of the article to be purchased.[14]

All bargain offers that are based upon the purchase of other items are judged on the basis of these four recommendations. The designation of the offer as "free," "buy one, get one free," "two for one sale," "half-price sale," "1 cent sale" or "50 percent off" does not influence the fact that the offer will be judged according to its adherence to the four guidelines.

An unconditional gift is not in violation of the FTC Act if it is truly a gratuity. Examples of such gifts are product samples received in the mail or distributed door to door, balloons and lollipops given to children who shop with their parents at a retail outlet, and coupons that must be mailed to a place of business. The inclusion in a "mail in" offer of a request for a small sum to cover handling and mailing costs is legitimate if the amount is no more than the actual cost to the distributor.

Cents-Off Pricing The FTC is also involved in ensuring honesty in "cents off" promotion pricing. Under current regulations, the manufacturer must print the amount of "cents off" on the label and the retailer must stamp the resulting price on the box. In addition, the store must post a shelf placard that contains the product's regular price in that store.[15] For example, a can of corn might be labeled "10¢ Off Regular Price." The store would stamp the can lid with the resulting price—say 20¢—and also post a shelf placard saying "Regular Price 30¢."

Price Ceiling Regulations

All deceptive pricing, fair trade, and minimum markup laws restrict retailer pricing freedom, but the other restrictions are associated with price freezes. During some of the various phases of 1971–1973, retailers' prices were both frozen at base period prices and controlled on the basis of customary percentage markups that were added to the cost of the merchandise or service. The absolute prices or the customary percentage markups were not allowed to exceed those prices or markups designated during the various base periods.

Price ceiling regulations provide another illustration of the trend toward more legal restriction on a retailer's freedom to determine price levels. The additional time and effort required to comply with price freeze regulations result in extra cost. If similar profit margins are maintained, this added cost eventually must be passed on to the consumer through higher prices. Apparently, governmental officials believed that price increases would be greater if free pricing prevailed than under controlled pricing, which requires more record keeping and new placard-posting costs.

Effects of Price Restrictions upon Retailers

The main feature of our free-enterprise economy has been competitive pricing. A major unanswered question now is, "How much can distributors' pricing freedom be limited if they are still expected to provide for an easy transfer of goods, service, and manpower?" On one hand, fair trade and minimum markup laws may prevent a retailer from being too competitive on the price variable. On the other hand, price ceiling restrictions limit the upward movement of retail prices. Considerable time must be spent making sure that the prices and communication of price level to consumers are permissible according to the latest legal interpretation. These additional costs will eventually be passed on to consumers in the form of higher prices unless profit margins are allowed to decline. Consumers are paying for more information which will presumably allow them to make more intelligent purchasing decisions.

These pressures result in a preference on the part of most retailers to concentrate on nonprice competition instead of outright price competition. Thus, we are likely to see more examples of Professor Malcolm McNair's wheel of retailing. The new retail firms are likely to appear first as low-margin, low-price establishments, but they will gradually upgrade their facilities and services and thus join the majority retailers by shifting to nonprice competition. The retail environment is again appropriate for the entry of new low-price retailers. (One of the major elements of nonprice competition—promotion—will be discussed in chapters 13, 14, and 15).

Summary

Generally, retailers use markup pricing because it is a convenient method of pricing the very large number of items they stock. Retailers cannot afford to spend the time and effort needed to determine the best price to charge on every item. However, few retailers markup the same for all items. General markup percentage varies inversely with merchandise turnover and the price of the item.

For maximum profits, retailer markups should also vary inversely with the value of the price elasticity of the demand coefficient. Estimates of retail elasticity of demand are usually based upon the experience of the retailer or upon representative markups charged by similar outlets.

Experimental techniques can also obtain elasticity estimates. Retailers can use these estimates to identify items whose sales are greatly influenced by price. Lower markups can generally stimulate greater profits on these items besides drawing additional consumers to the outlet. Retail managers can estimate the change in sales that is needed to make a general price level change profitable by calculating break-even volumes for each price level.

Consumers do not always perceive prices from an objective mathematical viewpoint, so the general price level must be fine-tuned to be compatible with consumer psychology. Multiple-unit pricing and odd pricing are two pricing techniques that might satisfy consumer preferences for certain exact prices.

It is important to note the relationship that exists between initial markup, maintained markup, and gross margin. Initial markup is the first markup placed on merchandise, so it must be high enough to cover the maintained markup (which consists of store operating expenses plus alteration expenses plus profits minus cash discounts given by vendors) plus all retail reductions (which include all markdowns, discounts given to employees, and all shortages). Thus, initial markup exceeds the maintained markup by the amount of the actual retail reductions incurred by the retailer. Gross margin is equal to the maintained markup plus any cash discounts given to the retailer by vendors but minus the amount retailers spend for alteration costs.

Retailers use markdowns to stimulate purchases of items that (1) have not been selling well, (2) are overstocked or (3) will draw potential consumers into the store, where—hopefully—they will purchase other, regular price merchandise.

Firms should use only pricing techniques that provide long-run consumer satisfaction. A postpurchase feeling of having been taken will not promote long-run purchases.

A price markdown is not likely to offend customers if the featured items are always available for purchase in the same quantity and quality, and without the consumer's having to meet special qualifications that are not clearly defined in the retailer's advertisements or price labels.

Some retailers are pressured by minimum markup laws to maintain their prices at high levels. Price ceiling legislation can be imposed to limit the amount of price increases that can be made by retailers. So, despite the apparent price-conscious mood of consumers, these legal pressures could cause well-established retailers to continue to rely upon nonprice elements of the marketing mix (such as advertising, service, and so forth) to attract consumers.

Questions

1. Distinguish between markup pricing and price lining. What are their advantages and difficulties?

2. What is the difference between markup percent and markup percent of cost? How do you make the conversion?

3. Describe the difference between initial markup and maintained markup.

4. Describe the difference between maintained markup and gross margin.

5. Briefly explain the four factors influencing the rate of markup percentage used by retailers.

6. How can retailers evaluate elasticity of demand coefficient, E_d, as an indicator in pricing strategy?

7. What are the objectives of retailers who markdown prices?

8. Which of the leader pricing techniques is most likely to offend or mislead customers?

9. A furniture buyer has a planned initial markup for the fall season (August 1 to January 31) of 40 percent. But on October 1, his figures in round numbers are as follows:

	Cost	Retail
Inventory, August 1	$285,000	$500,000
Inventory, October 1	250,000	440,000
Purchases, August 1 to October 1	200,000	325,000
Transportation charges	2,000	
Additional markups		1,000

Low markup on the purchases is due to August and September sales for which the furniture was closely priced. The planned purchase figure for the rest of the season, October 1 to January 31, is $400,000 at cost. What average markup should the buyer obtain on his purchases during the period October 1 to February 1 to get back his planned markup by the end of the season?

10. A book buyer makes the following purchases:

Number of Books	Unit Cost	Markup on Cost	Markup on Retail	Unit Retail
6	$2.00	25%	—	—
8	—	40	—	$2.00
4	—	—	24%	4.00
5	1.75	—	20	—
10	4.25	—	—	7.00
12	—	35	—	5.00
10	10.00	—	34	—

a. Fill in the blank spaces in the table.

b. Find the cost, markup in dollars, and the retail of the purchases as a whole.

c. Find the percentage of markup on cost and on retail for the purchases as a whole.

11. A retailer prices a coat so that the dollar markup amounts to $120. This is 40 percent of retail. What did the coat cost and what is the retail price?

12. A retail buyer informs one of her competitors that she was able to obtain a markup of 100 percent on cost for a certain line of merchandise. Since the competitor has always expressed her markup as a percentage of retail, she wishes to know what the equivalent markup on retail would be.

13. The retail price is $60; the cost markup is 40 percent. What is the cost?

14. Determine the cost and retail price on an item that you have purchased which will carry a markup of $90, or 30 percent markup as a percent of retail price. Calculate the nearest retail price.

15. What should the initial markup percent be in a store that has the following planned figures: expenses, $10,000; profit, $5,000; sales, $75,000; markdowns, $500; stock shortages, $250?

16. A ladies' wear buyer is able to purchase a line of ladies' dresses which will retail at $70 each. The manufacturer has offered these items to the buyer at a cost of $40 each. What is the retail markup percent that the buyer will achieve on this item?

17. An item has been marked down to $40 from its original price of $60. What is (a) the markdown percentage, and (b) the off-retail percentage?

18. A store has been able to purchase a color television set for $400 from a manufacturer. The retailer wishes to place a 40 percent retail markup on the item and has asked you to determine the retail price. What price will allow a 40 percent markup as a percent of retail price?

19. A markup of 28 percent retail is equivalent to what markup percent on the cost base?

20. A pair of shoes costs a retailer $25.00. If a markup of 40 percent on cost is desired, what will the retail price be?

21. A retail buyer calculates his markup on the basis of the cost price of the item. A vendor has informed the buyer that he will obtain a markup of 30 percent of retail on a certain line of items. Find the equivalent markup percent on cost for the buyer.

22. A shirt costs a retailer $10.00. If a markup of 50 percent of retail is required, what must the retail price be?

23. Suppose you purchase a line of ladies' dresses to retail at $80. Since the manufacturer has offered these dresses to you at a cost of $50 each, find the markup percent of cost that you hope to obtain.

24. A sporting goods store has purchased a number of golf club sets at a cost of $50 and wishes to place a markup of 50 percent of cost on the sets. Determine what the retail price of these golf clubs will be.

25. How much will a men's wear buyer have to pay for a suit that will retail at $150 and carry a markup of 35 percent on retail?

26. The markdown percentage for a suit originally selling at $120 but whose price is reduced to $90 is —?

Footnotes

1. *The Economics of Food Distributors* (White Plains, New York: General Foods Corporation, 1963).

2. Isadore Barmash, "How They're Selling Name Brands Off-Price," *Stores* (March 1981): 9–14.

3.   Jeffrey H. Birnbaum, "Can Retailers Afford to Keep Offering Sales?" *Wall Street Journal*, February 5, 1981, p. 25.

4.   The "absolute" value indicates that any value of E_d from 0 to minus 0.99 falls in the inelastic section of the demand curve. The demand curve indicates the quantity of an item that will be purchased, other things being equal, at various price levels during a particular time period. In graphic form, the demand curve generally appears as a downward-sloping curve.

   A more detailed explanation of the elasticity concept can be found in Richard H. Leftwich, *Introduction to Microeconomics* (New York: Holt, Rinehart and Winston, 1970), pp. 62–68.

5.   *Colonial Study* (New York: Progressive Grocer, 1962), p. C105.

6.   Dik Warren Twedt, "Does the '9 Fixation' in Retail Pricing Really Promote Sales?" *Journal of Marketing* 25 (October 1965):54–55.

7.   Ibid., p. 55.

8.   "Retailers Take a Look at a Challenging Decade," *The Competitive Edge*, (January 1980):68.

9.   Chester R. Wasson, *Managerial Economics* (New York: Appleton-Century-Crofts, 1966), p. 223.

10.   Roland S. Vaile, E. T. Grether, and Reavis Cox, *Marketing in the American Economy* (New York: Ronald Press, 1952), p. 447.

11.   "Filene's Basement, the 9th Wonder," *Women's Wear Daily*, June 14, 1973, pp. 1, 11, and "The Boston Supershoppers," *Time*, December 26, 1969, p. 27.

12.   Earl W. Kintner, *A Primer on the Law of Deceptive Practices*, 2nd ed. (New York: Macmillan, 1978), p. 672.

13.   Ibid., p. 673.

14.   Ibid.

15.   "Cents Off Rules Demanded," *Laramie* (Wyoming) *Boomerang*, November 26, 1971, p. 1.

Case Study: Ray's Men's Wear

Mr. Ray Snyder has been operating a men's wear specialty shop for the past five years. The outlet is located in a college town of 58,000 permanent residents and 20,000 college students. The nearest large competing town is 100 miles away from Ray's site. Although the first few years had its difficulties, Ray has finally gotten the firm into a profit-making situation.

   Recently Mr. Snyder has received some complaints from a group of male students enrolled in a local college. Ray is really concerned that this criticism might cause him to lose sales next year. The complaints have settled solely on Ray's prices, which the students claim are too high.

   Ray has achieved a 40 percent gross margin during 1982. He did this by using a 45 percent initial markup on every item. He surveyed the prices the local competitors charge and found that his prices are nearly identical to those of competition. When confronted with this information the students still persisted that Ray's prices were too high and that, in fact, all of the local merchants were charging too much for their merchandise. Ray replied that he would see if he could drop prices.

A meeting with Ray's accountant revealed that his estimated costs for 1983 are as follows:

Rent	$11,000
Utilities	2,200
Depreciation on fixtures and equipment	1,500
Wages for one full-time helper	10,000
Wages for part-time help	7,000
Insurance cost	800
Advertising	2,300
Supplies	700
Value of Ray's time spent in the store	14,500

Ray's sales for the 1982 year were $106,000 and its net profit was $5,300. Ray hopes to increase sales to $120,000 and obtain $8,000 profit in 1983. He thinks he will be able to reach his sales goal by reducing prices by an average of 5 percent, but he is not sure what effect this price reduction would have upon profits.

Discussion Questions

1. If Ray reduces his prices by an average of 5 percent and sales go to $120,000 what would his profit be?
2. How much must sales increase to make it worthwhile for Ray to reduce prices by 5 percent?
3. Do you think most of Ray's consumers will notice the price change?
4. Do you think the price change will influence Ray's customers to buy more of their clothing at Ray's?
5. How do you think the competitive outlets will react to the price reduction?
6. What should Ray do? Why?

Chapter 13 | Promotional Strategy

Learning Goals

1. To understand how environment influences development of a retailer's promotional strategy.
2. To be able to discuss the methods that determine promotional budget size.
3. To be aware of the factors that influence scheduling of promotional expenditures over time.
4. To learn the methods of allocating expenditures to the various promotional alternatives.

Key Terms and Concepts

institutional advertising
promotional mix
advertising
personal selling
sales promotion
publicity
self-analysis or retail audit
marginal analysis
experimental approach
objective and task approach

percentage-of-sales approach
competitive parity approach
return-on-investment approach
promotional calendar
cooperative advertising
selling process
cost per thousand potential customers criterion

Promotion is the marketing activity of communicating with an organization's customers through the use of advertising, personal selling, sales promotion, and publicity. Each year millions of dollars are spent on communicating by both private and public organizations in an attempt to persuade the American public to buy products and services, adopt or embrace a new idea, or contribute to a certain cause. In this advertising saturated environment, the advertiser/promoter must compete with thousands of others just to penetrate the consciousness of the citizenry. Thus, it becomes vitally important that each communicator have at least a working understanding of what constitutes an effective promotional strategy.

An effective promotional strategy must be based on extensive information gained through appropriate market research. According to Robert Gottlieb, Senior Vice President and Director of Marketing for Gimbels New York, "You can't produce ads for the sake of it. There must be a reason to advertise and a place to advertise so that the economic factors present a reasonable return. You have to know what you are in the eyes of the consumer, not what you think you are. The only way to find out is through market research. Qualitative research gives you descriptive information on consumers, their lifestyles, buying habits, and what they think of you and your services. Quantitative research tells you how many people you are reaching. Once you have done this research, you can segment your market and find those customers you want to reach. You'll know whom to promote to and merchandise for. You'll discover the most economical ways to advertise to those customers and what should be advertised to them."[1]

William McDonald, Vice President of Marketing for Woodward/Lothrop, a large eastern department store, explained his store's philosophy of promotion: "We approach most major projects from a marketing viewpoint. We look at the consumer and try to define the marketing opportunities that exist. The first thing we do for a promotion is to look at it in terms of the consumer, and whether it will work in the marketplace. Once we determine that there are sufficient reasons to go ahead, we begin the actual planning." In describing a major promotion called "On the Move," McDonald noted, "We did two things. First, we established a selling goal and determined initial budget parameters. How much money should be allocated for open-to-buy, how much for display, how much for promotion, and so on. Then we sent the merchants into the marketplace."[2] Interestingly, the firm sent its visual merchandise group on the same trip to the Orient so that they could develop the visual merchandising and display program while the buyers were making their selections. "When they returned, we had a series of meetings to develop promotional strategies based on the merchandise they bought. At that point, we solidified the budget parameters and came up with a specific program of advertising, promotion, special events, and collateral materials," McDonald noted.[3]

Major department stores are not the only retailers to be concerned about integrating their promotion plans. Lou Bremer, Manager of Marketing Communications, J. C. Penney Company, relates, "When our marketing team is developing a plan for the coming year, they will have a sales target and a resources target. They will ask the marketing research staff such questions as 'Is there an area that we want to enter or increase our share of market in?' 'How big is that business?' 'What are people looking for in that product?' For example, when we introduced the J. C. Penney battery a few years ago, we asked 'What do people want in a battery?' We found that besides wanting a battery that started the car every time, they wanted one that needs no maintenance. So based on that information, we developed the J. C. Penney 'no care' battery." Mr. Bremer continues, "Once the merchandise is developed, we evolve a marketing and promotion strategy. We may go back to marketing research and say, 'What is the most effective way to communicate what this does to the consumer?' 'What should we tell them about the merchandise?' "[4]

Penney's also pretests various elements in the campaign. Mr. Bremer relates, "We might want to know what would happen if we ran print, radio and TV, or print and TV only, or just print on this particular merchandise. Depending on the response, we might decide we want only one or two media."[5] Once the campaign is developed it is integrated into a total marketing strategy and annual promotional plan to support the strategy. In short, productivity of the dollars invested in promotion are significantly increased over similar funds invested in a random or haphazard fashion by individual stores.

These examples of promotional activities show the need to clearly define the target market and do the appropriate market research before beginning the planning of a promotion. Additionally, it is clear that if firms are to get the maximum productivity out of their promotion dollars they must carefully integrate all their channels of communication to the consumer and coordinate all their internal staff specialists to act in concert to make the promotion a success. If all the promotions are similarly planned, developed, and implemented then the firm may be successful in conveying its message to the chosen consumer group and establishing the desired position image in their minds.

Divergence between Theory and Practice

Not all retail firms have the resources to systematically acquire the necessary data bases to implement any significant market research. At best, small retailers may keep a diary and scrapbook of past newspaper advertisements. More often no records are maintained of past promotional activities, particularly in small entrepreneurial firms. Any energies diverted to gather and maintain such data are viewed as a "luxury" which the owner/manager "cannot afford at this time"—not realizing the long-term implications of such short-term acts.

In the near future this situation may change as progressive retailers introduce microcomputer technology into the management and operation of their businesses. As the cost of integrated electronic systems continues to decline and more retail software is developed, some merchants will request that promotional data be captured and stored for future analysis and decision making.

However, the vast majority of retailers will direct most of their efforts to improving their merchandising practices and improving cost control without reference to promotional concerns. One might suggest that the various media firms which serve this segment of the retail industry, particularly newspapers, might develop promotional research packages which could be offered to their retail clients so that both parties could benefit from more efficient use of promotional resources.

Function of Promotion

Retailers exert considerable effort to persuade prospective buyers that their merchandise or service offering is "right," that it is attractively priced, and that the circumstances surrounding its presentation will lead to purchase. It is the function of promotion to stimulate transactions by making a retailer's marketing inputs more attractive to potential customers who are currently engaged in the search process. Attracting consumers to a store by advertising is one function of this type of promotion. Another example involves a consumer who has visited a store in order to replenish stock of groceries and personal care items and who encounters a display of toothpaste that reminds him or her that the supply of toothpaste is low.

Promotion may also generate an attitude among consumers that will be conducive to making future transactions. Institutional advertising is designed to accomplish this objective. Instead of calling for direct purchasing action, **institutional advertising** stresses (1) the variety and depth of the store's merchandise; (2) the wide range of services offered; (3) the general high quality and good value of its goods, services and sales personnel; (4) the convenience of the store's location; and (5) the contribution that the outlet makes to the community. This type of advertising recognizes that a consumer's purchase of larger durable goods, such as furniture, may be the result of the cumulative effect of years of retail advertising. Even then, advertising may not have been received directly by the purchasing consumer. Instead, the customer may have received the message from others who passed the information along by word of mouth. Thus, retailers use institutional advertising to attempt to build long-run good will for the store and to generate shopping loyalty among consumers. Because all retail advertisements should attempt to build long-run consumer good will, all retail advertisements can be viewed as being, to at least some degree, institutional advertisements.

Communicating with Customers

Thus, promotion facilitates the flow of information from the retailer to the consumer concerning such bargaining issues as product features, price, service aspects, warranties, and so forth. A promotion program must make a retailer's goods and service offering meaningful to potential buyers. After all, consumers must see how products or services can be useful to them in achieving some personal or social goal before they will make the purchase.

In recent years the term **promotional mix** has been used to describe the combination of tools used to promote business firms, products, or services. Promotional vehicles available to retailers can be classified into advertising, personal selling, sales promotion, and publicity categories.[6] The promotional mix concept emphasizes the belief that each promotional vehicle persuades consumers more effectively if it is accompanied by some combination of the other methods. In other words, a retailer's promotional efforts are not likely to be effective if they are concentrated in advertising, personal selling, or any other single method. Instead, a combination of promotional methods is used because one method frequently complements another.

Before we proceed to a discussion of the promotional decisions facing a retail firm, it is essential to understand the definitions used to categorize the various promotional vehicles. The reader should be forewarned that while these definitions accurately reflect the current general usage in retail trade they are subject to change as the retail industry evolves. Therefore, one should not be surprised when a particular retailing term is uniquely defined by a particular firm or segment of the retail industry. The important point is that all persons using the term must have a common perception of what it means before effective communication can take place.

Advertising may be defined as:

. . . any paid form of nonpersonal presentation and promotion of ideas, goods, or services by an identified sponsor. It involves such media as the following:

Media

Magazine and newspaper space

Motion pictures

Outdoor (posters, signs, skywriting, etc.)

Direct mail

Novelties (calendars, blotters, etc.)

Radio and television

Cards (car, bus, etc.)

Catalogs

Directories and reference items

Programs and menus

Circulars

This list is intended to be illustrative, not inclusive. . . . Advertising is generally, but not necessarily, carried on through mass media.[7]

Promotion Modes

Personal Selling involves:
. . . oral presentation in a conversation with one or more prospective purchasers for the purpose of making sales.[8]

Sales Promotion includes:
. . . those marketing activities, other than personal selling, advertising, and publicity, that stimulate consumer purchasing and dealer effectiveness, such as display, shows and exhibitions, demonstrations, and various non-recurrent selling efforts not in the ordinary routine.[9]

Publicity involves:
. . . non-personal stimulation of demand for a product, service, or business unit by planting commercially significant news about it in a published medium or obtaining favorable presentation of it upon radio, television, or stage that is not paid for by the sponsor.[10]

The combination and volume of various promotional vehicles are problems that must be continually coordinated by retail management. Maximum returns from promotional efforts will not be achieved unless the purpose of the promotional mix is kept in focus constantly.

The promotional mix is used to achieve the overall corporate goals and objectives of the retail enterprise. Its purpose is not simply to serve as an outlet for creative talents, nor should it be viewed simply as a means to attract added customers for a "sale." If promotional goals and objectives have not been defined by management, the promotional efforts of the firm cannot be expected to serve at maximum efficiency or in a coordinated and meaningful pattern. They will, instead, tend to reflect either a "stone statue" or a "reed in the wind" position. On the one hand, promotional policies may become so rigid and unbending that it virtually takes a hurricane-force wind to change their direction. Or, like a reed in the wind, they may move first in one direction and then another at the slightest reason for change. Either position is damaging to the retailer and results in lost promotional opportunities and wasted dollars.

Advertising Objectives   The retail firm's advertising objectives depend on the nature of the firm itself, the market opportunity represented by its potential customers, the overall retail store image desired by retail management, and the nature of the goods and service assortment offered by the retailer.

A sound promotional policy must consider the correct proportion of each element in the promotional mix in view of the objectives to be met. Retailers should have realistic and specific ideas concerning the image they want to project to consumers.

Image   The first step involved in determining what image is best consists of an analysis of the outlet's target market consumers. Retailers need to identify their target market consumers by age, income, sex, family size, tastes, life style, place of residence, pay periods, and so forth. Only after retailers have decided who their customers should be can they effectively decide what kind of **image** they are going to present in their promotional activities and how they can reach the target consumers.

The next step involved in determining the appropriate image for the individual retail firm consists of making a thorough **self-analysis.** This analysis might consist of a complete *retail audit* (which is discussed in Chapter 21) or a comparison with competitive retailers in terms of (1) price policy, (2) merchandise quality, (3) brands of merchandise offered, (4) employees' attitudes, (5) employees' appearance, (6) store layout, (7) store fixtures and display, (8) store windows, (9) customer services, (10) advertising layout, (11) advertised price level, and (12) type of clientele.[11]

The self-analysis, or retail audit, allows retail management to identify and remedy the things that appear to be inconsistent with the desired store image. Self-analysis also provides an analysis of the reasons why regular consumers continue to make purchases at that outlet. These same shopping motivations may then be featured in the retailer's general promotional effort.

A brief discussion of the promotional factors that influence the store image is required to illustrate how each factor can be used to create the desired image. The relative price level can reflect a bargain basement or discount impression by using a "we will not be undersold" pricing policy. At the other extreme, a "you get what you pay for" impression may be achieved by using a relatively high price policy combined with relatively high quality merchandise.

Employee attitude and appearance are important factors in establishing a store image. Retailers who attempt to build a bargain basement or discount image may successfully hire employees who have gruff attitudes and overworked appearances.[12] On the other hand, retailers who desire to maintain a quality merchandise image must employ helpful, neat-appearing personnel, because the personalities of the employees influence the consumer's perception of the personality of the store.[13]

Kind and Quality of Service

The kind and quality of services offered influence the impression consumers get of the store. Few or no services suggests a bargain image. Offering many services, such as delivery, easy merchandise return, credit, carry-out service, and so forth, usually is associated with a prestige image.

Advertisements themselves can be prepared in such a way as to generate either a discount image or a high-quality, prestigious impression. Product display and advertising that are crowded and cluttered tend to make people think that the store is of the low-quality, bargain basement type. On the other hand, a clean, well-balanced advertisement, with considerable white space, can convey the opposite impression.[14] Cost considerations also enter into the layout decision, since more white space in an advertisement means less space for describing the products being sold.

A store's image is also influenced by its clientele. If the store's customers belong to one social group, the general population will tend to think that it is catering to that group. Thus, retail management must consider how the reputation of servicing its present customers will affect any new target market segment it may wish to cultivate.[15]

Promotional Expenditures

Retailers can begin planning their promotional programs after they have determined what their message is and who should receive it. Planning generally begins with a determination of how much to spend on promotion, when to spend the promotional funds, what merchandise to promote, and which promotional vehicles to use.

Promotional Budgets

Advertising must be considered as a prime ingredient in the process of image building and control. This is true even when advertising is seldom or never used by a retailer. Retailers who can afford to commit promotional dollars to advertising, but elect to spend little or none, may pursue this strategy for any or all of the following reasons:

1. They feel that their ad would be lost in the mass of ads by other retailers in the mass media—principally newspapers.
2. They believe that their customers represent a different type of person, one who seeks out special values in particular quality,

and may not even read the daily newspapers, listen to the radio, or watch much television.

3. They believe that their customers' shopping behavior is a result of their peer group association and that their shopping habits are directed by their social standing. It is felt that the customers are more apt to be affected by word of mouth and shopping patterns developed over years, or even generations, than by advertising.

4. They feel that their regular customers will be offended by advertising, since it might cheapen the store's image and place it in the class of all other retailers.

5. They are afraid that advertising might draw a different type of customer than their old customers and that this mixing of different social classes could cause their established clientele to shop elsewhere.

6. They believe the community they serve is so small that advertising is simply repeating things that people already know.

Changing Tradition

While any or all of these arguments may be valid for a particular retailer, they may prove to be dangerous myths in the long run. New generations within the old social class of dependable customers may change their shopping habits. They may become ardent television viewers. They may wish to break from tradition simply because they do not wish to follow exactly in the family footsteps. In addition, new social groups may emerge, armed with considerable purchasing power, and be "turned off" to the image and messages they receive from these retailers.

In addition, a policy of complete avoidance of advertising will cause retailers to overlook the growing segmentation of media. Thus, they may miss excellent opportunities to relate their message in specialized media directed specifically to their target market. One should not interpret these comments to mean that all retailers must advertise in traditional modes, but one must stress the need to use some promotional tools to communicate with their target customers.

Marginal Analysis

Several different techniques are used by retail management to determine how much should be spent on retail promotion. Among them, **marginal analysis** considers the additional increment of return that is earned as an additional increment of expenditure. This method is appropriate for determining the impact of hiring additional salespeople (permanent or temporary), using additional promotional expenditures, extending credit, and so forth. Marginal analysis is accomplished by comparing the change in store profit that may be attributed directly to a change in the expense item being considered, other things being equal. In formula form, the marginal return ratio equals the change in store profits resulting from the addition of the last unit of input divided by the change in store expenses resulting from the addition of the last unit of input.

For example, increasing the number of permanent salespeople by one may increase store expenses by $520 per month. If this change alone increases store profits by $1,060, the marginal return ratio for the added salesperson is $1,060/$520, or 2.04, and the store earns $2.04 per $1 of increased expenditure. A marginal return ratio of less than 1 indicates that the increased expenditure was not covered by the increased return. A ratio greater than 1 suggests there is money to be made through still greater expenditures. Promotional expenditures should be increased until the margin return ratio is "unity." In other words, retailers should continue to make additional promotional expenditures

Last Marginal Dollar   until the last marginal dollar spent generates one additional dollar of profit.

The marginal analysis rule requires accurate estimates of the sales-to-promotional-expenditure relationship. The character or shape of the sales-response-to-promotion curve is likely to conform with the law of diminishing returns. This law indicates that as equal additional promotional expenditures are added, while all other retail factors are held constant, the additional sales generated by each additional promotional expenditure will eventually be smaller than the sales response generated by the preceding unit. Thus, the sales response function is likely to follow the pattern in Figure 13.1. Sales in this figure expand at an increasing rate up to point A, then at a decreasing rate up to point B, when additional promotional expenditures do not influence sales at all.

Experimental Approach

Retail management can experiment with different advertising expenditures in the same way prices were changed in Chapter 12. Latin square and before-and-after designs can be used and sales comparisons can be made with previous sales levels as already indicated. This **experimental approach** to estimating sales response to promotional expenditures is likely to yield satisfactory results for promotional direct-action efforts. These efforts consist of promotion attempts to sell specific products or services by making a direct appeal to consumers to (1) come into the store and buy the product, (2) fill out a coupon and purchase the product by mail, or (3) purchase the product immediately by phoning the retail outlet.

Figure 13.1   Typical General Sales Response to Promotional Expenditure

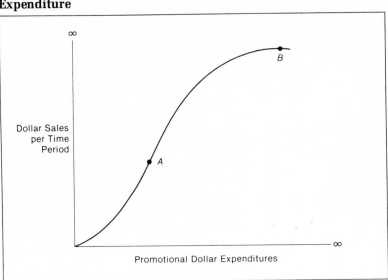

Mail-order advertisers can measure the short-run effect of their advertising by keying their ads so that each customer can be attributed to a particular advertisement. The short-run effect of changes in promotional direct-action retail expenditures can be obtained by comparing the sales level in the days following the appearance of a given promotional campaign with the sales level in previous periods when different promotional expenditures were made.

Long-run-effect measurement may not be necessary for a retailer because most of the value of retail advertising is received within a few days.[16] Long-run institutional advertising does not make a bid for direct consumer action. Instead, it uses the soft sell approach to stress the retailer's advantage in areas such as convenience of store location, the general high quality of merchandise, the wide range of goods and services offered, the friendliness and knowledgeability of personnel, and the like. Thus, institutional advertising attempts to build good will and create a favorable image. The lag between expenditure and eventual sales stimulation makes it considerably more difficult to estimate the sales response to this long-run type of advertising than that of promotional direct-action. For this reason, the objective-and-task approach may assist in evaluating the contribution of institutional advertising.

Institutional Advertising

Objective-and-Task
Approach

Under the **objective-and-task approach,** retail management defines the promotional objectives as specifically as possible. For example, an objective in institutional advertising may be to make 40 percent of the general population in the trading area aware of the fact that only XYZ Furniture Company carries brand X furniture. The tasks needed to be performed to achieve each objective are then listed, and management estimates the cost of performing these tasks. The promotional budget is then established by adding the cost of performing the necessary tasks for all of the objectives that are deemed worthy of pursuing on the basis of benefits derived from costs incurred. This method allows management to concentrate on achieving only those objectives that are most productive relative to their associated cost.

Percentage-of-Sales
Approach

Many retailers use a **percentage-of-sales approach** to determine the level of promotional expenditures. With this method, retailers budget their promotional expenditures at a specified percentage of current or anticipated dollar sales volume. For example, a retail firm may budget 2 percent of its forecasted sales of $1 million ($20,000) for promotional purposes.

Promotional Expenditure
Strategies

   This method of determining the level of promotional expenditures considers advertising to be a necessary cost, but it is difficult to support on the basis of logic. The percentage-of-sales technique lets the sales level determine the amount of money spent on promotion; however, the relationship should be reversed since the level of promotion is supposed to influence sales. If promotion does not influence sales, there is no reason to make promotional expenditures. Using the volume of retail sales to determine promotional budget size also ignores the marginal relationship of added promotional expenditures to added sales. The cost or worth of obtaining added sales is not considered under the percentage-of-sales approach. Nevertheless, the approach is widely used because many retailers are not able to estimate the sales-response-to-promotion relationship.

Competitive Parity
Approach

The **competitive parity approach** involves establishing a promotional budget that will match competitors' outlays for promotion. Industry figures are frequently available to indicate the percentage of gross dollar sales volume that similar retailers use in their promotional efforts (Tables 13.1 and 13.2), and knowing the level of promotional expenditure that competitors are using is helpful in establishing the promotional budget. However, it should not be followed blindly, since it does not account for differences in

Table 13.1   Percentage of Sales Dollars Spent on Advertising by the Top Twenty-five Supermarkets in 1980

Firm	Sales in Millions of Dollars	Expenditures on Advertising (Millions of dollars)	Percentage of Sales Spent on Advertising
Safeway Stores	$15,103	$151	1.0
Kroger Co.	10,317	121	1.2
Great Atlantic & Pacific Tea Co.	6,990	88	1.3
Lucky Stores	6,469	48	0.7
American Stores	6,260	70	1.1
Winn-Dixie Stores	5,389	43	0.8
Southland Corp.	4,783	28	0.6
Jewel Cos.	4,156	48	1.2
Grand Union Co.	3,527	53	1.5
Albertson's Inc.	3,039	17	0.6
Supermarkets General	2,629	33	1.3
Publix Supermarkets	2,168	17	0.8
Dillon Cos.	2,077	18	0.9
Stop & Shop Cos.	2,033	30	1.5
Von's Grocery Co.	1,650	19	1.1
Giant Food	1,484	14	0.9
Fisher Foods	1,413	13	0.9
Waldbaum Inc.	1,272	12	0.9
First National Supermarkets	1,260	18	1.4
S. M. Flickinger Co.	1,185	5	0.4
Pantry Pride Supermarkets	1,127	12	1.1
Borman's	984	10	1.0
Fred Meyer Inc.	973	18	1.8
Schnucks Markets	600	6	1.0
Allied Supermarkets	535	3	0.5

Source: Sales and advertising data obtained from "Here Are the 25 Top 1980 Supermarkets," *Advertising Age*, Nov. 2, 1981, S-2. Reprinted with permission from the November, 1981 issue of *Advertising Age*. Copyright 1981 by Crain Communications Inc.

location, reputation, opportunities, or company objectives. In addition, there is no reason to believe that the competition uses any logical method for determining promotional outlays.

Thus, the competitive parity approach can indicate only a starting point for determining the level of the budget. Changes in the budget can then be made and the resulting influence on sales observed to determine if promotional expenditures should be raised or lowered.

Return-on-Investment Approach

The **return-on-investment approach** is another method of determining the size of the promotional budget. This approach treats promotion primarily as a capital investment rather than a current

Table 13.2 Percentage of Sales Dollars Spent on Advertising by the Top Twenty-five General Merchandisers in 1980

Firm	Sales in Millions of Dollars	Expenditures on Advertising (Millions of dollars)	Percentage of Sales Dollar Spent on Advertising
Sears, Roebuck & Co.	$16,990	$708	4.2
K mart Corp.	14,204	319	2.3
J. C. Penney Co.	12,806	320	2.5
F. W. Woolworth Co.	7,218	170	2.4
Federated Department Stores	6,301	189	3.0
Montgomery Ward & Co.	5,497	182	3.3
Dayton-Hudson Corp.	4,034	85	2.1
May Department Stores	3,150	98	3.1
Wickes Corp.	2,877	44	1.5
Carter Hawley Hale Stores	2,633	69	2.6
Rapid American Corp.	2,604	16	0.6
R. H. Macy & Co.	2,374	114	4.8
Allied Stores Corp.	2,268	107	4.7
Associated Dry Goods Corp.	1,952	129	6.6
Walgreen Co.	1,850	43	2.3
Zayre Corp.	1,798	61	3.4
Wal-Mart Stores	1,643	26	1.6
Gimbel Brothers	1,321	30	2.3
Mercantile Stores Co.	1,108	20	1.8
Marshall Field & Co.	1,013	27	2.6
SCOA Industries	942	16	1.7
G. C. Murphy Co.	880	21	2.4
Caldor	667	15	2.2
Roses Stores	526	17	3.2
Levitz Furniture Co.	525	41	7.9

Source: Sales and advertising data obtained from "Top 25 Retailers in General Merchandising: 1980," *Advertising Age*, November 2, 1981, pp. S-2. Reprinted with permission from the November, 1981 issue of *Advertising Age*. Copyright 1981 by Crain Communications Inc.

expense. Determination of the amount of promotional spending then becomes a problem of capital expenditure budgeting, and the promotional budget must compete for funds with other kinds of internal investment on the basis of prospective rate of return. Each piece of promotion affects current sales and also builds good will to increase sales at a later date.

The relative importance of the two effects can vary tremendously according to the type of promotion used. At one end of the spectrum is institutional advertising with its long-term orientation, which reflects an almost pure capital investment. At the other end are promotional direct-action efforts such as advertising a special sales event. This type of promotional expenditure usually represents only a small portion of capital investment.

Isolating the portion of the promotional budget that can be considered a capital expenditure and then estimating the rate of return that can be obtained on the capital expenditure are difficult tasks, but not impossible.[17]

Strategic Considerations of Cooperative Advertising

Every retail firm must address the question of the strategic use of cooperative advertising. Many producers and vendors offer cooperative advertising incentives and programs to increase their products' visibility and sales volume. This is particularly true in the retail grocery business. Traditionally, local newspapers offer significantly lower rates to local advertisers than to national advertisers. Thus, when vendor and retailer combine their advertising resources they get more return on their investment than advertising individually. However, the retailer must realize that such cooperative packages have varying conditions attached to them such as certain minimum order quantities, annual volume purchase requirements, and reporting requirements which must be observed. Additionally, adoption of a heavy reliance on cooperative advertising may cause the retail firm to lose effective control of its promotional programs which may have negative effects on the overall image of the firm.

Today most retailers engage in horizontal cooperative advertising to promote local events. Shopping center tenants become members of the center association and join with their center's retailers to promote center patronage and increase the center's traffic especially during the major buying seasons. Mall merchants are assessed fees to cover such events and must budget for them in addition to their own individual store promotional effort.

In summary, a cooperative advertising strategy has benefits and costs which must be realistically considered. Conditions change so the policy decision must be periodically reexamined. The appropriate answer to the question of how to best use cooperative advertising is, "It depends on the situation."

Concluding Remarks

The previous discussion has centered on the various methods to determine the size of the retail promotional budget. Deciding how much to spend on promotion is a continual problem, because none of the approaches discussed is likely to yield an exact estimate of sales response to promotional efforts. Many factors, such as media effectiveness, the effectiveness of the promotional appeal, competitors' promotions, consumer attitudes, and so forth affect the sales-to-promotional-expenditures ratio. These factors are considered to be important to many retailers who believe that either the percentage-of-sales or the competitive parity approach provides an acceptable way of determining the level of the promotional budget. These retailers believe that attempting to measure sales response to promotional expenditures requires too much time, expense, and mathematical proficiency.

There are several fundamental considerations no matter what method is employed. The level of promotional expenditure will need to be higher for outlets that operate from less favorable locations. In addition, stores that operate in areas of exceptionally strong competition are likely to have higher promotional expenditures to combat the promotional efforts of competitors. New and expanding retail firms must use larger promotional expenditures to make consumers aware of their existence and merchandise offering. Higher advertising expenditure may also be required by stores that continually stress low price in their campaigns.

The list could continue, but the point of this discussion is to indicate that each retailer operates under unique conditions. Thus, promotional expenditures must be tailored to fit the situation. If the promotional expenditure appears to be low, it might be raised a little at a time and the results observed to see if added sales contributed enough profit to more than cover the added promotional expense.

The essential steps used in planning and evaluating the retail promotional budget are summarized in Figure 13.2.

Scheduling Promotional Expenditures Over Time

Timing Promotional Expenditures

Timing of promotional expenditures over seasons, months, weeks, and days must be determined after the promotional budget level has been established. Some components of the promotional mix, such as personal sales, require fairly constant expenditures throughout the year. Certainly part-time salespeople can be added during extremely busy sales periods such as the Christmas season. Overtime payments can be paid to regular employees during these peak periods, but otherwise the level of expenditure for personal sales is likely to remain fairly constant.

It is much easier to change the level of retail spending for advertising and sales promotion, because advertising media and printing companies do not require a constant expenditure as do store salespeople. Some media contracts contain cancelable clauses that may be used if it is necessary to reduce expenditures. Media options may be passed up to provide additional

Figure 13.2   Planning and Evaluating the Advertising Budget

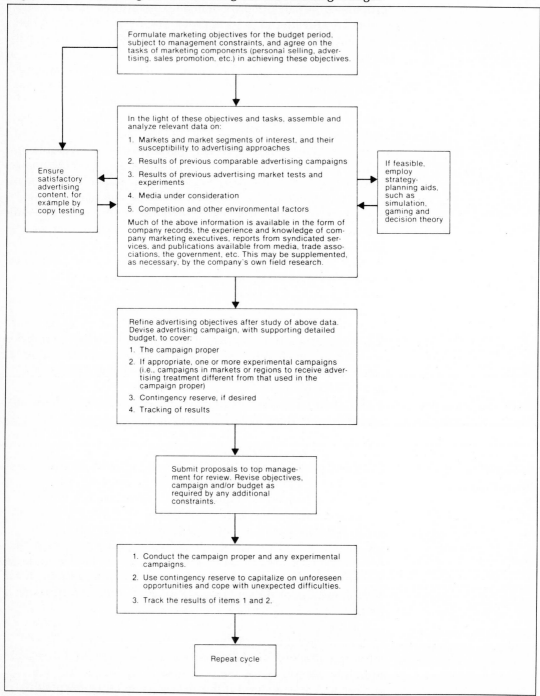

Source: *Some Guidelines for Advertising Budgeting* (New York: The Conference Board, Inc., 1972), p. 38. Reprinted by permission.

flexibility. Finally, a portion of the annual advertising and sales promotion budget is not contractually committed and hence can be shifted to a cash account if this is necessary to improve the short-run financial condition of the firm. On the other hand, when an unanticipated competitive threat develops, intensification of the advertising effort may be the easiest method of retaliation. Thus, it may be argued that advertising and sales promotion are the most flexible retail marketing factors.

Flexibility vs. Consistency

Despite the flexibility, retailers are likely to benefit more from spending smaller amounts of promotional money on a frequent basis than from spending a considerable amount on promotion for infrequent, special occasions. **Consistency** of promotional effort reinforces the store's image in the minds of consumers. It also reminds consumers of the outlet's advantages and merchandise/service offerings.

This is not to say that advertising and sales promotional budgets should be the same for all months of the year; it merely suggests that some minimal promotional expenditure be made each month. The level of total advertising and sales promotion budget will probably vary from month to month because of holiday, seasonal, and other special promotions, and it is a common practice for retailers to divide their monthly advertising and sales promotion expenditures into amounts that parallel expected sales patterns.[18] Actual promotional advertisements may be placed just before the expected peak in sales. For example, supermarkets spend a large percentage of their advertising budgets on Wednesday advertisements, which influence shopping on the high-volume days of Thursday, Friday, and Saturday. The same principle can be used to allocate promotional dollars during any period of time. Figure 13.3 illustrates the best division of a promotional budget over months of the year. In this case, promotional expenditures are higher just prior to periods for which higher sales estimates have been made.

Promotional Plans

Allocating promotional expenditures in this manner allows the retail firm's communication to reach the consumers when they are beginning to make purchasing decisions. Heavier promotion can also be scheduled to reach the consumers when they will be able to react to the promotional activity. For example, response to an advertisement placed just prior to pay day may be considerably better than the response obtained from an advertisement placed just after pay day.

Promotional plans are generally made on a planning form, or **promotional calendar,** such as the ones in Table 13.3 and Table 13.4. Such planning must be coordinated with merchandise planning, which is discussed in Chapter 10. Normally, retailers prepare the promotional budget, promotional calendar, and mer-

Figure 13.3 Allocation of Promotional Expenditures in Relation to Retail Sales Volume Estimates

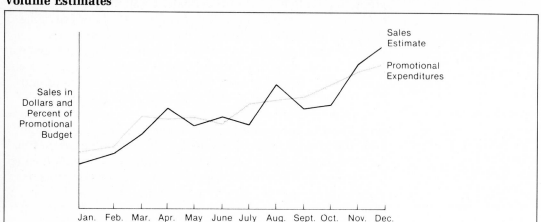

chandise budget simultaneously because of their interrelatedness. Distribution of promotional expenditures during each month should be scheduled to take advantage of the payroll days of important area firms, days of the week in which sales and traffic are normally highest, national and local events, night openings, and seasonal merchandise sales patterns. These calendars can be used when planning future promotional expenditures, provided such factors as last year's sales figures, this year's sales figures, weather conditions, unusual competitor promotions, and so forth are recorded.

Allocating Promotional Expenditures to Departments and Merchandise Lines

Another important decision involves the determination of how much should be spent promoting each merchandise line and each department. One method of attacking this problem is simply to allocate promotional expenditures to the departments in proportion to their contributions to total sales. For example, if the hardware department is expected to generate 9 percent of the store's total sales volume next month, about 9 percent of next month's promotional budget is allocated for promotion of the hardware department. Another approach is to allocate promotional expenditures in proportion to the department's contribution to total profit.

Promote to Generate Traffic

Either approach is insensitive to the fact that promotion of some departments and merchandise lines creates more store traffic than others. Since the main purpose of promotion is to attract consumers to the store, the heavy traffic-generating departments should have a more than proportional share of the promo-

Table 13.3 Worksheet for Preparing Monthly Promotional Budget

| | Sales Volume | | | | | | | Promotional Expenditures | | | | | | |
| | In $ | | | Percent of Total Annual Sales | | | | In $ | | | Percent of Total Promotional Expenditures | | |
Month	Two Years Ago	Last Year	Esti-mate for This Year	Two Years Ago	Last Year	Esti-mate for This Year		Two Years Ago	Last Year	This Year	Two Years Ago	Last Year	This Year
January	___	___	___	___	___	___		___	___	___	___	___	___
February	___	___	___	___	___	___		___	___	___	___	___	___
March	___	___	___	___	___	___		___	___	___	___	___	___
April	___	___	___	___	___	___		___	___	___	___	___	___
May	___	___	___	___	___	___		___	___	___	___	___	___
June	___	___	___	___	___	___		___	___	___	___	___	___
July	___	___	___	___	___	___		___	___	___	___	___	___
August	___	___	___	___	___	___		___	___	___	___	___	___
September	___	___	___	___	___	___		___	___	___	___	___	___
October	___	___	___	___	___	___		___	___	___	___	___	___
November	___	___	___	___	___	___		___	___	___	___	___	___
December	___	___	___	___	___	___		___	___	___	___	___	___

Table 13.4 Sample Promotional Calendar

Planned Promotional Expenditures: During Week _____ During Month _____

Week of _____

Type of Promotion	Sales Volume Data — In Dollars				Sales Volume Data — Percent of Annual Sales				Date Used	Merchandise or Theme Featured	Cost		Promotional Expenditures — In Dollars				Promotional Expenditures — Percent of Total Promotional Expenditures				Less Discounts and Coop Funds Reimbursed / Actual Promotional Cost	
	Two Years Ago	Last Year	Estimate for This Year	Actual This Year	Two Years Ago	Last Year	Estimate for This Year	Actual This Year			Last Year	This Year	Two Years Ago	Last Year	Estimate for This Year	Actual This Year	Two Years Ago	Last Year	Estimate for This Year	Actual This Year	Last Year	This Year

1. Advertising
Newspaper
Radio
Television
Outdoor
Direct Mail
Circulars
Other Advertising
(List Type Used)
   Total Advertising

2. Personal Selling

3. Sales Promotion
Displays
Demonstrations
Other Sales Promotions
(List Type Used)
   Total Sales Promotion

4. Publicity (List Type Used)

5. Weekly Totals
Planned Promotional Expense for Week
Actual Promotional Expense for Week
Deviation from Promotional Expenditure Plan

tional budget. For example, many supermarkets allocate more than proportional advertising funds to the meat and produce departments. Since the same brands of canned, frozen, and packaged goods are available in most outlets, management believes that the perishable commodities give the outlets a unique chance to differentiate themselves from their competitors. Intensive promotion of the perishable items also is defensible on grounds that the consumer is likely to plan menus around the meat and produce items that are featured in the advertisements. Consumers are likely to purchase, at regular prices, the staple items that are used with the featured meat and produce items during their visit to the outlet. Other departments that frequently are believed to be heavy traffic generators are ready-to-wear apparel, furniture, and appliances.

Department stores have varied their emphasis on different product groups over the period 1976 to 1980 (Figure 13.4). Men's apparel had consistently received less than 3 percent during the period. However, reflecting the new customer interest in "up-scaling" their home environments, the stores had responded with significant promotional support. Generally, these goods carry a comfortable markup and hence increase the overall profitability of the firm. Thus, as the customer interest changes, the firm should reallocate their sales promotional efforts to take advantage of different promotional opportunities.

Allocation of promotional expenditures to various departments should promote the heavy traffic-generating departments by granting them a more than proportional allotment of the budget. Another consideration in the allocation process involves the relationship between each department's inventory level and its expected near-term sales. Some departments may require heavier promotional expenditure to clear overstocked merchandise because its selling season is nearly over or it is in danger of going out of style. New products and new or expanding departments may also require a more than proportionate share of the promotional budget to make consumers aware of their existence.

Promote During Peak Demand Periods

It is important to realize that specific merchandise lines and departments benefit most from promotion during times when consumer demand is at its peak. Past sales patterns can be used to make allocations to departments in a way that will better balance departmental promotional expenditures with expected departmental sales. A special effort might be made to identify the best traffic pullers for each month. Promotion of these "hot items" attempts to match promotional expenditures with expected sales volume. The promotional campaign then tells customers that the store is offering those items that the consumer is seeking.

Figure 13.4   Sales Promotion Costs for Department Stores (Five-Year Patterns)*

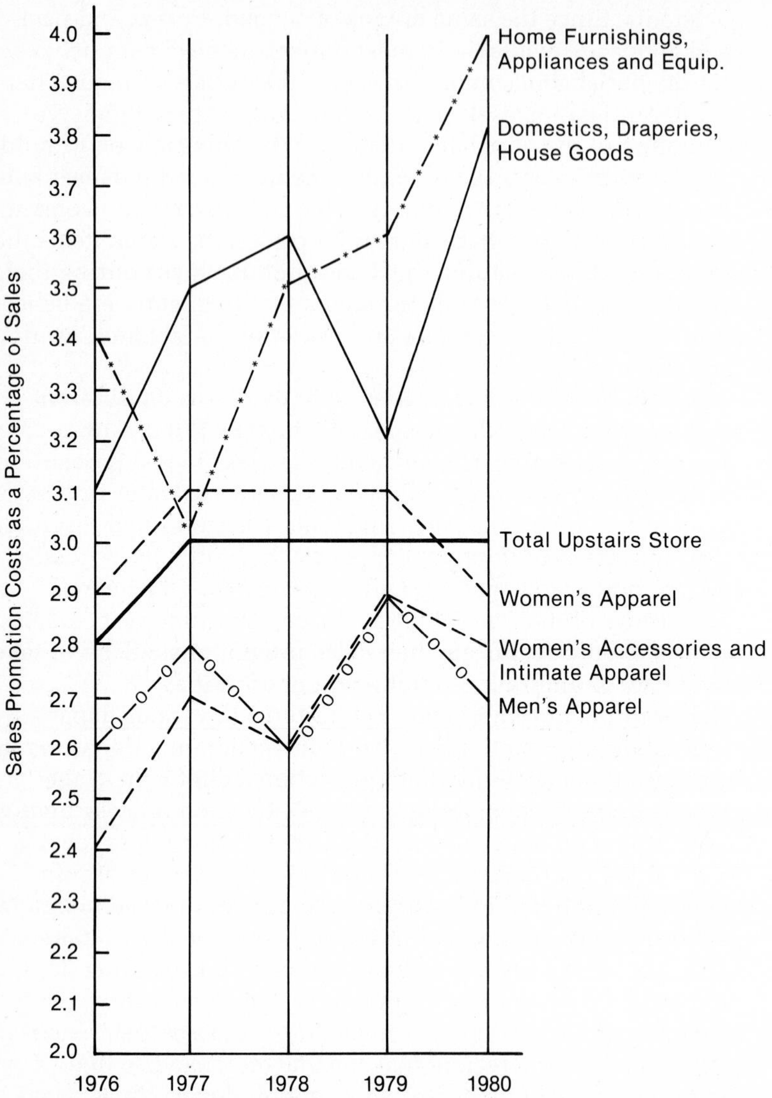

* Stores doing over $1 million annual volume
Source: Lance Ringel, "Department and Specialty Store Data MOR," *Stores*, (October 1981): 14.

Thus, the retailer's promotional efforts should concentrate on the goods and/or services that most of its customers want. This results in attracting maximum consumer traffic to the outlet.

Consumers' want change over time. Therefore the promotion plan must be flexible to accommodate these variations in demand. At the beginning of a season most people are interested in the new goods or services, so the promotion should feature the latest fashion, style, or technology appropriate to the new season. When the season is nearly over, promotions can feature special purchases or markdowns because consumers are looking for value and savings.

Another important consideration in deciding what items to promote involves the effect the promoted item will have upon the store's image. Is the promoted item consistent with the desired price and quality image? Is the promoted item likely to appeal to a desired group of consumers? Is there an adequate quantity on hand to meet anticipated consumer demand? These questions should be considered when items are selected and promotions are prepared.

Promote Prestige Brands

Research has shown that a high-prestige store obtains more favorable results when its promotional efforts feature either highly prestigious brand names or no brand names at all. Consumer reactions are less favorable when it features low-prestige brand name merchandise.

Low-prestige stores featuring high-prestige brands produce the most believable advertisements. Consumers perceive they can get a good value for their money when these low-prestige stores advertise high-image brand names. When these stores advertise unknown brand names or low-prestige brand merchandise, the promotion takes on a negative image.

When a retail store has no established image in the consumer's perception, it can make its message more believable by featuring high-prestige brand name merchandise. Consumers also believe they get more value for their money when high-prestige brands are featured by these stores.[19]

Promote Good Value

The promoted items should also represent a good value from the consumer's point of view. It may not be the lowest priced, but by offering better quality, guarantees, service, advice, and so forth the consumer should see the total product/service package as the best buy among the alternatives. Efficient use of this concept requires consumer knowledge of prices on different items. Price reduction advertising is likely to be more effective if it features an item whose price is known by most consumers. This simply makes the advertising more believable, since consumers can verify from their own experience that the price has been reduced.

Promote to Clear Stocks

Promotion plans are often formulated to deal with periodic merchandising crises such as reducing overstocked positions, clearing large quantities of unsold seasonal goods, or just improving the short-term cash flow to pay current payroll and rent expenses. There are old maxims in the trade that say, "Usually merchandise does not improve with age," and "There are times when one has to eat their mistakes." When such situations arise, the wise merchant allocates limited promotional funds combined with judicious markdowns to clear unwanted merchandise and invests the sales dollars for new open to buy positions in new more salable merchandise.

During the early 1980s many retail grocers included coupons which would double or triple the value of manufacturer product coupons in their weekly food advertisements. In this way they attempted to increase their instore traffic and market shares. In addition they often included special coupons which would reduce the price of certain items. Such "in-ad" coupons are authorized and paid for by the manufacturer; however, these coupons are distributed in the context of the retailer's own weekly newspaper ads. In-ad couponing has been successful in moving large amounts of merchandise. Retailers like these coupons because they can cooperate in the actual merchandising of the product, and because the redemption rate of coupons is increasing.[20] The need for more couponing stems from strong customer acceptance of coupons, which help reduce household expenditures. Departments that can take advantage of cooperative allowances are frequently promoted more heavily because of reduced cost to the retailer.

Departmental managers may be asked to prepare their own promotional plan on the basis of their knowledge of monthly promotional requirements. The budget amount, media usage, and general theme may be worked out with the store manager, merchandise manager, or sales promotion director and may reflect the planning done on the promotional calendars. The decision as to which products and merchandise lines to promote within a department is likely to be made by the department head, who may be better informed on inventory levels, consumer preferences, seasonal patterns, and the like.

In-Ad Couponing

Allocating Expenditures to Promotional Alternatives

Allocation of expenditures to various promotional alternatives is an ongoing process because both costs and audiences change over time. Costs have risen most dramatically for television and least for radio advertising. Audiences also change over time, so retailers who stay with the same media expenditures will not be spending their promotional dollar in the most efficient manner.

Ideally, the promotional budget should be allocated among advertising, personal selling, sales promotion, and publicity in a manner that yields equivalent marginal profits on the last dollar spent in each of these four areas. To implement this principle, a retailer has to determine the dollar sales and profit response obtained by each promotional method. He or she then selects the alternatives that give the highest marginal return ratio until all the ratios for all methods are equivalent at the value of 1.0. At this point the retailer is maximizing profits by using each type of promotion until the last expenditure is just covered by the increase in profits that it generated.

This reasoning simply involves the marginal analysis approach to budgeting discussed earlier in the chapter for each type of promotion. The same reasoning can also be used when allocating expenditures within media by choosing the vehicles that generate the largest marginal profits per added dollar expenditure until marginal profits no longer cover marginal costs for each vehicle. This marginal analysis principle must be continually followed in making allocation decisions if unprofitable promotions are to be avoided. Measurement of the marginal sales and profit response to each alternative promotional vehicle is a complex and time-consuming procedure. Therefore the marginal analysis principle is likely to consist of a managerial judgment as to whether the added benefits derived from the additional promotion exceed the added promotional costs.

Marginal effects of each vehicle depend upon the retailer's objectives, opportunities, and the constraints he or she faces. Different promotional mixes may be used successfully by similar retailing organizations; different tasks must be accomplished before sales can be generated; and each promotional tool differs in its ability to perform these tasks. The **selling process** may be considered to follow four steps: creating awareness; developing customer comprehension of the product/service offer; producing customer conviction that the offer is a good offer; and encouraging customer investigation that leads to purchase.[21]

Awareness is probably obtained most efficiently through publicity and advertising. For example, opening a new retail outlet or handling a new line of merchandise will probably require heavy advertising and publicity to make consumers aware of the change.

Developing customer comprehension of the product/service offer may require a combination of all four types of promotion. The most effective techniques would probably vary from one retailer to another, depending upon the quality of the sales personnel and the complexity of the product/service offering. Retailers who sell complex merchandise and services will have to place more reliance on salespersons to explain the advantages of their offering.

Personal selling is usually more effective in instilling consumer conviction of a good offer, especially for technical goods. However, extensive low-price advertising of national brand or private-label items may be the most efficient method of establishing conviction among a price-conscious segment of consumers.

Personal contact of some type is also influential in triggering the purchase act, even in self-service outlets where clerks may only provide information on merchandise location and availability.

The extent to which retailers should use each promotional vehicle depends on the target customer's reading, listening, watching, and shopping habits. The selected vehicles should reach the target customers at the lowest possible cost per potential customer. In addition, the vehicles' effectiveness for presenting the merchandise/service offering must be considered. Various media provide different opportunities for presenting demonstrations, conveying visual descriptions and impressions, providing explanations, and so forth.

The problem of allocation among various advertising media is complicated by the fact that they have overlapping audiences. Therefore it is difficult to determine which sales are attributable to each method. For this reason allocation among promotional vehicles is usually based upon a judgment of the media believed to reach the largest number of target customers, as many times as possible, as steadily over time as possible, and with the minimum cost.

At this point the retail promotional planner begins to investigate specific alternatives in terms of which programs, newspapers, and so forth offer the best promotional purchase. Analysis will center on the characteristics of each vehicle, its coverage, the nature of its audience, and how these factors relate to the outlet's promotional objectives.

The **cost-per-thousand-potential-customers criterion** is frequently used to compare the effectiveness of the numerous vehicles in reaching the target market consumer. With this approach, retail promotional planners calculate the cost per one thousand potential customers reached by each vehicle. For example, suppose a retailer could reach 100,000 potential target market customers with a full-page newspaper advertisement costing $2,000. The cost per one thousand target market consumers reached would be $2,000 divided by 100, or $20, because 100,000 target market customers are contacted with the $2,000 expenditure. The promotional planner would make similar calculations for each vehicle and rank them according to the lowest cost per thousand. Advertisements would be placed in those vehicles with the lowest cost per thousand target market homes reached. It is important to use the target market concept in making cost per thousand calculations because total readership, viewership, and/or listenership does not represent only potential consumers. The exposure value of each vehicle depends upon how closely the audience's characteristics match those of the target market. The cost per thousand in the target market calculation takes this into account.

Using cost per thousand in the target market concept requires data containing detailed demographic and geographic breakdowns. Pulse Inc. and individual newspapers provide detailed newspaper readership information for 157 cities. In addition, Standard Rate and Data Service publishes *Newspaper Rates and Data* and *Weekly Newspaper Rates and Data,* which provide six-month average summary circulation information. In the daily publication, circulation is divided into "city zone," "trading zone," and "other." In the weekly publication, circulation data are separated only into "paid" and "nonpaid." *Newspaper Circulation Analysis* breaks down the circulation of daily papers by county of distribution and makes a report for each county in which a newspaper achieves more than a 5 percent penetration of households.

Both Radio Advertising Bureau and Pulse Inc. provide detailed audience listenership data.[22] The *Nielsen Station Index* contains detailed viewer profiles for television audiences in over 200 markets.[23] Estimating the cost per thousand potential customers appears to be most appropriate when comparing two or more vehicles in the same medium (for example, several newspapers that claim to serve the trading area).

Estimating Relative Media Efficiency

The larger problem of determining allocation to each medium (for example, radio versus newspaper) is a more complex decision, involving considerations beyond the cost per thousand potential customers. The following factors, not considered in the cost per potential customer calculations, should be analyzed:

1. *Lead time,* which is the length of time between submission of the finished advertisement to the medium and the time when the advertisement will appear.
2. *Life of the advertisement,* which is the length of time that a consumer will be exposed to an advertisement.
3. *Intimacy,* which describes the consumer's degree of confidence in the medium which is being used.
4. *Editorial climate,* which refers to the degree that articles or programs are used to support the advertisements.
5. *Repeat or multiple exposures to the advertisement,* which is the number of times that a consumer may be exposed to the same advertisement.

6. *Type of advertisement,* which refers to product or promotional direct action advertising versus institutional advertising.

7. *Competitor's use of the medium.*

8. *Availability or appropriateness of the medium.*[24]

Analysis of all these factors and a review of the calculations of the cost per thousand potential consumers reached is time consuming, but the results can be rewarding.

Another measure of the relative efficiency of each advertising medium can be obtained by determining which media attract customers to the store.[25] This data can be obtained simply by asking each customer (or a random sample of customers if the number is large) how he or she happened to come into the store. A summary of their responses can be recorded for each type of advertising. Weekly records can be kept to indicate the number of people attracted to the store by each type of advertising. Sales slips can also contain sales volume for each consumer and can be totaled by category. The week's results can then be compared with costs. If the relative amount spent on each medium is not changed for several months, a retailer should have a fairly good estimate of how much it costs to attract a customer with each medium. Then expenditures can be changed in one medium for about a month and the results observed.

By carefully changing expenditures and analyzing results, retailers are able to judge the relative efficiency of each medium. They may also be able to determine if there is a significant carryover of their advertising in each medium. Most retail advertising does not generate a significant carryover effect because sale or promotion direct-action advertising is remembered for only a short time and does not generate a continual purchasing habit.

Both the cost-per-thousand-potential-customers approach and the analysis of relative media efficiency provide estimates that should be used with caution. These methods should be used to assist retailers in making allocations to the various promotional media and vehicles. They do not provide absolute answers on media effectiveness. It may take a considerable length of time to develop the skill needed to interpret the data. In addition, data provided by asking consumers why they came into the store may not reveal the true reasons. People are influenced by a combination of factors, but they tend to mention only the ones to which they have been most recently exposed. Despite these limitations, retailers can benefit by using all or portions of both techniques when they plan their promotional expenditures.

How Stores Spend Their Advertising Dollars

Newspapers have historically obtained the majority of the retailer's advertising dollar. However, there appears to be a shift
toward a belief that some mix in the media is desirable and a
feeling that each medium is supportive to other media. The large
national chains also have made changes in their usage of the
media (Table 13.5). Although K mart, Sears and Penney all use
newspaper advertising as the predominant medium, they are increasing their inserts in newspapers. These inserts provide more
control over the editorial content and allow economic produc-

**Table 13.5   A Comparison of K mart, Penney, and Sears
National/Local Advertising Expenditures for 1979 and 1980
(In Millions of Dollars)**

	1979	% of Ad Budget	1980	% of Ad Budget
K mart				
Newspapers	$250.00	86.8	$275.00	85.5
Spot TV	16.28	5.7	18.48	5.7
Spot radio	5.73	2.0	8.55	2.7
Network TV	8.09	2.8	5.06	1.6
Network radio	2.85	0.9	4.50	1.4
Magazines	5.16	1.8	9.91	3.1
Outdoor	0.03	—	0.15	—
Total	$288.14	100.0	$321.65	100.0
Sears				
Newspapers	$437.19	81.0	$456.33	76.2
Spot TV	17.05	3.2	15.55	2.6
Spot radio	0.31	—	2.54	0.4
Network TV	65.98	12.2	86.95	14.5
Network radio	5.43	1.0	5.37	0.9
Magazines	13.82	2.6	32.06	5.3
Newspaper supplements	—	—	0.09	—
Outdoor	0.12	—	0.71	0.1
Total	$539.90	100.0	$599.60	100.0
Penney				
Newspapers	$ 75.27	61.7	$ 69.11	64.0
Spot TV	16.91	13.9	14.65	13.7
Spot radio	—	—	0.15	0.1
Network TV	21.37	17.5	18.58	17.2
Network radio	0.86	0.7	0.32	0.3
Magazines	7.46	6.1	5.08	4.7
Outdoor	0.13	0.1	0.11	—
Total	$122.00	100.0	$108.00	100.0

Source: "100 Leading National Advertisers as Per Cent of Sales," *Advertising Age*
(September 10, 1981): 102–103, 120, 134.

tion efficiencies because one run can be used in several different newspapers. Readership does not appear to be reduced, but a longer lead time may be required to prepare the insert.

Major gains in the battle for large chain retailers' advertising dollars appear to be made by television, which has overcome increases in cost to provide a complement to these firms' heavy newspaper advertising campaigns.

Promotional Ethics

The consumer movement has brought about the passage of laws which make false, misleading, and deceptive advertising illegal. While it is true that enforcement agencies cannot monitor the advertising of all retailers, it is equally true that consumers today will not tolerate being misled. Thus, retailers must prepare their promotional campaigns in such a way that consumers are not given misleading information.

Promotional claims must be established as true before the claim is made. These claims should be made available to consumers who request them. Retailers can create a good long-run image in the eyes of consumers by promoting factual information on health and safety matters and on performance comparisons for their merchandise and service. Since promotion is the most common way that the retailer can use to inform consumers of the benefits of the store's offerings, it is important that high ethical standards be maintained in the promotion program. Failure to do so will only undermine the consumer's confidence in the reliability of the outlet. Ultimately it will lead to a decline in sales as more and more consumers distrust the firm's offerings.

Summary

A retailer's promotional mix must assist in achieving the firm's unified goals. Thus, the promotional mix will depend upon the nature of the firm's merchandise/service offering, the needs of its target consumers, and the overall retail image desired by management. Promotion can generate either a quality image or a discount image, whichever is desired. Retailers can increase the believability of their advertisements by including highly prestigious brand items in their advertisements.

The level of promotional expenditures can be determined by marginal analysis, experimentation, the objective-and-task approach, the percent-of-sales method, the competitive parity, or the return-on-investment techniques. Marginal analysis and experimentation appear to offer the most logical approach to the problem, but both require considerable time, effort, and expertise. Thus, many retailers use either the percent-of-sales method or the competitive parity technique.

Supermarkets spend a fairly consistent 1 percent of their sales volume on advertising. General merchandise stores spend a considerably larger percentage of their sales dollar on advertising, with the exact percentage varying from store to store. Advertising expenditures as a percent of sales for these general merchandisers usually varies from about 2 percent up to 7 percent.

Growth in retail advertising expenditures has been paralleling growth in retail sales. Advertising costs in television and newspapers have increased dramatically since 1967, while costs for radio advertising have increased at a much slower rate. Although most retail advertising is conducted in newspapers, a trend is developing toward the increased use of radio and television. This shift in media is occurring because of the very rapid increase in the cost of advertising in newspapers relative to radio. It is also due to the desire of retail managers to better complement their newspaper advertisements with television and radio promotions.

It is common for retailers to divide their promotional expenditures into amounts that parallel but precede expected sales patterns. This allows the firm to send more of its message to consumers when they are beginning to make their purchase decisions.

The cost-per-thousand-potential-customers approach is one method that can be used to guide expenditures to vehicles within any promotional medium. Other considerations, such as the permanence of the advertisement and the need for the merchandise to be displayed visually or demonstrated, also must be made when allocating expenditures among media.

In conclusion, promotion is an inexact science that is highly dependent on the situation, personal experience, and proper timing. Ultimately, each promotion program must be tailored to each retail unit in order to reflect the uniqueness of the outlet's target market.

Questions

1. Why would a retailer use institutional advertising? Is it a worthwhile expenditure of the firm's money?
2. What percentage of a retailer's advertising budget do you think goes for institutional advertising? Is the percentage of the firm's advertising budget that is spent on institutional advertising higher for retailers or for manufacturers? Discuss.
3. What are the first steps a retailer should always take when the firm begins to develop its promotional strategy?
4. Which methods can a retailer use to determine the level of the firm's advertising budget? What are the advantages and disadvantages of each?
5. Why do so many retailers apply percentage-of-sales approach to determine the level of their promotional budget? Does it make sense to use this technique?
6. How can the promotional calendar be used by retailers?
7. What are the advantages and disadvantages of a retailer participating in cooperative advertising?

8. How can the four steps in the selling process be employed by retailers in selecting the promotional tools that are most effective?
9. Why is the cost-per-thousand-potential-customers criterion a useful tool for retailers when they are selecting media? What are its disadvantages?
10. What are the advantages that a retailer gains by applying the analysis-of-relative-media-efficiency concept to select advertising media? What are the disadvantages? Under what conditions should this method be adopted?

Footnotes

1.   Doreen Mangan, "Marketing Research Gaining as a New Retail Sales Tool," *Stores* (May, 1979): 37–40.

2.   Ibid.

3.   Ibid.

4.   Ibid.

5.   Ibid.

6.   Jerome B. Kernan, William P. Dommermuth, and Montrose S. Sommers, *Promotion: An Introductory Analysis* (New York: McGraw-Hill, 1970), pp. 11–13.

7.   Ralph S. Alexander et al., *Marketing Definitions: A Glossary of Marketing Terms* (Chicago: American Marketing Association, 1960), p. 9.

8.   Ibid., p. 18.

9.   Ibid., p. 20.

10. Ibid., p. 19.

11. Laurence W. Jacobs, *Advertising and Promotion for Retailing* (Glenview, Ill.: Scott, Foresman, 1972). pp. 6–15.

12. Ibid., p. 7.

13. Ibid.

14. Ibid., p. 10.

15. Ibid., p. 13.

16. Julian L. Simon, *The Management of Advertising* (Englewood Cliffs, N.J.: Prentice-Hall, 1971), pp. 14–15.

17. Joel Dean, "Does Advertising Belong in the Capital Budget?" *Journal of Marketing* 30 (October 1966): 15–21.

18. Jacobs, *Advertising and Promotion*, pp. 88–97.

19. James G. Barnes, "A Hierarchical Model of Source Effect in Retail Newspaper Advertising," *Advances in Consumer Research*, Proceedings from the Eighth Annual Conference of the Association for Consumer Research, Vol. V (Ann Arbor: Association for Consumer Research, 1978), pp. 235–241.

20. *Editor and Publisher*, March 6, 1971.

21. Philip Kotler, *Marketing Management, Analysis, Planning, and Control* (Englewood Cliffs, N.J.: Prentice-Hall, 1967), p. 453.

22. The address of the Radio Advertising Bureau is 555 Madison Avenue, New York, N.Y. 10022.

23. The address of the A. C. Nielsen Company is 2101 Howard Street, Chicago, Ill. 60645.

24. Jacobs, *Advertising and Promotion,* p. 128.

25. Ibid., pp. 132–133.

Case Study: B & B Menswear

B & B Menswear was a small men's wear shop located in a large local shopping center in suburban Houston, Texas. The store was successfully launched in 1977 by Bill Rose and Bob Kilgore after they decided to be "their own boss." Both men had spent five successful years with a national retail chain store learning the business and accumulating personal capital to start their own business.

The five years since they opened the store had been good years. Even though the shopping center had been anchored by two major chain stores and a large suburban store of a local department store, they had prospered by offering a unique selection of dress and casual clothes for the young professional. However, things were changing. When a regional women's wear chain failed, the vacant mall space was taken over by a factory outlet which sells "off-priced, branded apparel" for men including suits, sportswear, pants, and shirts. The new store offers merchandise at 20 percent off regular retail prices on major brands. They do not offer layaway, cash refunds, free delivery, or free alterations, but they will accept major bank cards.

At first Bill and Bob weren't too concerned because they had built up a loyal clientele by offering full services including free alterations. However, in the last two months they had noticed a drop in sales. Occasionally they would drop into the factory store to see what was going on and they began to notice some of their better customers making purchases in the new store.

When Bob approached one and asked why he was not shopping at B & B the customer was apologetic but said that the factory store offered a better value because he only needed a few alterations and he could save 20 percent.

Both Bob and Bill began to wonder if their strategy was appropriate for the times. They decided to try to promote their unique store offering but they weren't sure how to get the most out of their limited advertising budget. Should they use local newspapers, spot radio, or even spot TV? What would you advise?

Discussion Questions

1. Devise a promotion strategy for B & B stressing service.
2. What media should be used, singly or in combination, for the next two months?
3. How can B & B determine if the promotion program is paying off?

Chapter 14 | Promotional Mix

Key Terms and Concepts

print media
direct mail
coupons
Yellow Pages
broadcast media
AIDCA process

white space
position media
point-of-purchase promotions
window displays
specialty advertising

The discussion in Chapter 13 centered on the financial aspects to consider in developing a promotional strategy: level of expenditure, proper scheduling, in-store allocation, and appropriate media. Chapter 14 looks more closely at each promotional medium and focuses upon the considerations necessary to establish a promotional mix that will be consistent with the retailer's objectives and effective in reaching target market customers. Discussion of two other important elements in the promotional mix—personal selling and consumer services—is presented in Chapter 15.

Advertising

Perhaps the most difficult task in all marketing is the continuous problem of advertising faced by retailers. In most cases, stores are too small to purchase large amounts of advertising in any media. In addition, they usually serve a relatively small area, such as a suburb of 50,000 persons. There may not be a good local paper serving their trade area. Persons who live in the store's trading area subscribe to major newspapers and listen to the major radio stations. A small retailer usually cannot afford to buy time and space in these media, since that would mean paying for coverage in areas outside the firm's market perimeter.

Faced with these problems, retailers should be aware of the characteristics of each medium so that they can make appropriate promotional appeals and audience and cost comparisons.

Printed Media

Because they are durable, all **print media** vehicles (any vehicles that are printed on paper and distributed to the consumer's home) allow consumers more freedom in translating the meaning of advertisements into something that is meaningful to them personally. Consumers can read and look at the advertisement at their own pace. If necessary, they can reread the advertisement to understand its message more clearly. In general, print media, because of their durable nature:

> (1) Provide greater opportunity for the consumer to translate the advertisement's message with more careful thought. (2) Allow for group participation in translating the advertisement's message. Members of a family can study a print advertisement together in a way that is not possible for radio or television advertisements. (3) Offer increased opportunity for consumers to make comparisons, by looking back and forth between pages, of the product-service offerings made by various retailers.[1]

The various kinds of print media possess different characteristics (Table 14.1). Therefore each will be discussed separately.

Newspapers

Although retailers may purchase all forms of mass media advertising, the primary promotional tool used by most retailers is the local newspaper and its supplements. The local newspaper offers retailers the opportunity to reach a large percentage of their customers at a comparatively low cost with an extremely short lead-lag time between preparation of the ad and exposure to the customer. It also allows customers the opportunity to compare prices, shopping hours, and other differences between competitive retailers, if that is desired. Newspapers are sufficiently timely that retailers can tie their advertisements to current events, such as a forecast of the first freeze of the year.

Broad Appeal

Newspapers appeal to a broad range of customers, and local newspapers are perceived by the consumers as factual.[2] Newspaper advertisers regard newspaper advertising as being easily understood. It is believed that advertisements are read most closely by consumers who are in the process of making a pur-

Table 14.1   Comparison of Major Print Media Used by Retailers

Medium	Market Segment Reached	Type of Retailer Particularly Suited for	Advantages	Disadvantages
Daily newspaper published in metropolitan area	General population above age sixteen located in metropolitan area and its suburbs	Mass merchandisers serving entire metropolitan area	1. Graphic potential can illustrate merchandise 2. Advertisement is easy and inexpensive to prepare 3. Requires little lead time until advertisement appears	1. Competition for readership of advertisements is keen 2. Short life of advertisement 3. Waste circulation occurs because circulation covers wide area
Daily and weekly newspapers published in smaller towns	General population in immediate community	Local retailers of all types	Items 1, 2, and 3 above 4. Local identification	Items 1 and 2 above 4. Limited coverage for national chains and mass merchandisers
Shopper handouts	Most households in immediate shopping area	Neighborhood retailers	Items 1 and 2 above 5. Written from a consumer viewpoint	Items 1 and 2 above 5. A give-away is not always read
Magazines	Special interest groups in metropolitan areas	Mail order firms, specialty outlets and mass merchandisers	Items 1 and 2 above 6. Long life span for advertisement 7. Provides a loyal, special interest audience	Item 1 above 6. Waste circulation if special segmented group is not reached 7. High production costs in preparation of advertisement
Direct mail including coupons	Most segmented coverage since advertiser controls circulation	Mail order firms, new firms, catalog firms	Items 1, 3, and 4 above 8. Provides personalized approach 9. High percentage of personalized mail is read	Items 2 and 6 above
Yellow Pages	Active shoppers; brand loyal customers	Retailers of brand name merchandise, specialty retailers, service firms	Items 1, 2, 4, 6 above 10. High percentage readership 11. High percentage of purchase item	Items 1 and 3 above

chase decision.[3] Another advantage of newspaper advertising is that the makeup of a typical advertisement requires less technical skill than the creation of advertisements for most other media.[4]

Short Life

The short life of a newspaper is one of the disadvantages of newspaper advertising; consumers tend to spend only a little time reading each issue, and then they discard it. Another disadvantage for retailers who serve a small area is the wasted circulation resulting from the wide geographical distribution of the large city papers. Finally, the quality of reproduction in newspapers is generally low because they must be printed at high speed.

The type of newspaper can be selected for effectiveness in reaching the target market customer. Morning papers in most cities have a masculine image, with emphasis on sports and business. Advertisements in the morning paper frequently are read shortly before the consumer makes the purchase (later in the day).[5]

Evening papers are experiencing a major readership decline in urban markets as readers depend more on evening television broadcasts for the news of the day. As a result, major retailers are gradually moving their advertising dollars to the more modern morning newspapers which employ high technology presses turning out updated formats.

Sunday papers are read in an even more thorough manner, but are even larger in size than evening papers. Circulation is also expanded on Sundays, so that retailers may be able to place their advertisements in a specialized section of the paper. The disadvantages of the Sunday paper are the increased competition from rival retailers and the larger circulation, which may raise advertising costs. It is easy for an advertisement to become practically unavailable to the reader when the paper is very large and a particular location within it cannot be specified. This is the case when run-of-the-press rates are obtained.[6]

Specialized papers with relatively small circulation are increasing in popularity because they reduce waste circulation by aiming at a specific group of people. Such papers may limit circulation to only a small geographical area or reach only a specific religious or occupational group. The cost per potential customer is frequently lower on specialized papers because wasted circulation is reduced.

Magazines

Magazine advertisements have a longer life and better-quality reproduction than newspapers. Consumers are likely to read and reread the copy at a leisurely pace and examine the pictures in more detail in magazine advertisements. This repeated exposure is a unique feature of magazine advertising. As such, magazines are well suited for the creation of the desired store image or institutional type of advertising. Because different moods are created by the content of each magazine, advertisements can illustrate how the outlet or selected merchandise fits this consumer mood.

For example, city magazines are frequently used to promote entertainment facilities, restaurants, and so forth. Both the number and the circulation of local magazines have increased in urban areas. The largest local magazine is *New York*. Other large local magazines are *Philadelphia, Palm Springs Life, D Magazine* and *Chicago Magazine*. These magazines reach higher-income consumers who have the ability to make large purchases.

Despite these desirable characteristics, magazines are not used extensively by retailers because even specialized magazines are likely to have a high level of wasted circulation. Specialized magazines appeal to a specific group, but their per square inch advertising rates are usually higher than newspaper rates.[7] In addition, magazine editors require a much longer lead time for an advertisement to be included in a particular edition.

Direct Mail

Direct-mail promotion includes any literature that is sent to customers or prospective customers through either the U.S. or a private mail system. Although the cost of postage and handling has increased markedly in recent years, so too have the possibilities for using direct mail effectively. This may be attributed to the growth of credit sales, the increased use of the computer, and zip code mailing.

Quality Mailing List

Direct mail is most effective when the retailer is catering to a small, well-defined segment of the market. In this case the cost per potential customer reached may be lower with direct mail than with other media. Success of direct-mail advertising depends on the quality of the mailing list, which should be selective, so that all names should be potential customers for the product/service being offered. Mailing lists may be developed by a retailer from the credit department records. These can be further segmented through development of a computer program to group customers on the basis of similar characteristics. Although the initial development of this system may be expensive, it allows a retailer to pinpoint the market and thus save on future promotions.

Zip code data and a crisscross directory, which contains names corresponding with the occupant of addresses grouped by area, enable the retailer to stratify mailings by income area and by areas of high social or ethnic concentration. Direct-mail promotion can then be employed using a rifle method of hitting a target market rather than a shotgun approach.

Advances in printing have allowed the retailer a great deal of flexibility and much room for imagination. Samples of products (such as fabrics) have long been sent to prospective customers. Now it is also possible to appeal to the customer's sense of smell through direct mail. New perfumes and colognes may be introduced through a process that impregnates the scent in the direct-mail piece.

The nature of the sample must, however, be carefully considered in any direct-mail piece. A manufacturer of razor blades included a new blade in the evening edition of urban newspapers, only to get a rash of serious complaints by homeowners—children and dogs discovered the blades before the adults. It is a dangerous—and sometimes unlawful—practice to distribute samples of many products in a direct-mail campaign. Premium coupons, rather than the sample product itself, should be used for products such as razor blades, medicines, and other potentially dangerous products.

Another advantage of direct-mail is that the advertisement does not compete directly for attention with other advertisements, since most mail is opened and at least scanned by the consumer. Thus, consumers may pay more attention to direct-mail advertisements than to other forms of advertisements. Retailers should nevertheless be aware that consumers frequently

Occupant Mail

discard third class "occupant" mail without opening it. Personalized first class mail increases attention, but costs more than third class mail.[8]

Several different forms of direct-mail advertising are sent by retailers. Personalized letters are designed to be similar in appearance to personal correspondence; and the more personalized the letter, the higher the readership—and the cost.[9] Cards are frequently sent out to introduce a sale; although the cost of mailing them is relatively inexpensive, they do not have a confidential or impressive appearance. Circulars, leaflets, and folders can reach the audience at a low cost, but they suffer because they are not personalized. Catalogs and coupons are other forms of direct mail that, because of their importance, deserve a more detailed discussion.

Catalogs

The first things that probably come to mind when catalogs are mentioned are Sears and Montgomery Ward; yet the use of catalogs as a promotion and sales tool is by no means limited to the giants of retailing. Nor is it strictly limited to mass merchandise items. Thousands of firms rely heavily upon their catalogs for promotion and for direct sales. Moreover, catalog usage is increasing rather than declining, in spite of bigger and better shopping centers. Catalogs are usually quite expensive to produce and mail, but they have an extremely long life.

Expansion of catalog advertising is particularly noticeable in industries that sell specialized products to a particular market segment. The leisure industry is indicative of this increase. There has been a growth of specialty retailers selling items such as back-packing equipment and precut vacation homes.

Catalogs are also important promotional tools for carriage trade retailers, such as Neiman-Marcus. Customers look forward to viewing the Christmas catalog of Neiman-Marcus to discover what exotic new gifts are being offered for sale. These have included Egyptian mummy cases for him and her and his-and-her Chinese junks. Neiman-Marcus has been able to develop a suspense buildup in the introduction of these gifts, complete with all the secrecy that automobile manufacturers use with yearly model changes. At the correct moment, the catalogs are released and the press is informed of the his-and-her gifts for the coming Christmas. This promotional technique dramatically ties together catalogs and publicity to enhance the overall image of Neiman-Marcus.

An entire mailing program could easily be a disaster if the tone of the catalog does not meet the image goals of the retailer. As a result, special attention is paid to layout, copy, color, and the overall esthetic appeal of the catalog. It is not simply a directory of products and prices, but a carefully planned promotional arm for the company. Unfortunately, the catalogs of many retailers are poorly planned and do not reflect an image consistent with that desired by the retailer. This is often true with small retailers who sell high-quality merchandise but feel they cannot afford the services of professionals in the design and layout of their catalogs. As a result, most of the planning is left to the sales manager and printer, who may only incidentally possess artistic talents.

Small retailers who are faced with this problem should give special thought to the possibility of selling their catalogs. Precut home manufacturers and many other retailers have demonstrated that consumers will pay over $1 for professionally designed catalogs. Such a program will enable a retailer to hire the services of professionals to produce a catalog consistent with the corporate image. The catalog must appear to be worth the charge. If it does not, customers will feel they have been taken and that the products sold by this retailer must also be overpriced. Retailers who sell their catalogs also believe that this policy results in a more careful reading of their information and a longer shelf life; that is, customers are reluctant to dispose of the catalog. They may also be more prone to show it to their friends than if it were acquired free.

Coupons

Coupons are a promotional tool that is widely used throughout the nation by manufacturers and retailers of supermarket items. **Coupons** include small cards or cutouts that are found in magazines, newspapers, direct-mail envelopes, selected editions of the *Yellow Pages,* and retail outlets. Coupons offer the consumer a savings on a particular product or service when they are redeemed at the cash register. They may be valued at as little as a few cents to as much as two items for the price of one.

New Products

Although coupons have been distributed for a variety of products, they are used predominantly by manufacturers of branded products that are frequently repurchased such as detergents, personal care products, and foods. Coupons are also a popular promotional tool for local retailers of services and prepared foods. Even the smallest pizza shop or beauty parlor generally can afford the costs of printing and distributing coupons door to door. Retailers and manufacturers have discovered that coupons are effective marketing tools when used in the following ways:

> (1) In the introduction of a new or improved product; (2) Introducing a product into a new market; (3) In obtaining broader distribution of a product by using the coupon program as an inducement for more stores to carry the product; (4) Reducing excessive inventories of a product; (5) Equipping salesmen with an additional sales tool; (6) As a marketing research tool.[10]

Marketing executives have found that coupons have the side benefit of being a marketing research tool. Since coupons can be coded by area, it is possible to derive such information as trading patterns, the effect of different types and values of coupons upon sales, generalized consumer profiles, and other important data.

It is obvious that a coupon is valuable as a promotional medium only if it is redeemed. In a study of coupons by the A. C. Nielsen Clearing House, five factors appeared to influence the redemption rate of coupons:

> **1.** *Method used to distribute the coupon* The use of direct mail and inproduct coupons resulted in a higher redemption than magazines or newspapers.
> **2.** *Size of the product class* As the rate of sale per $1000 increased, the redemption rate of coupons also increased.

3. *Rate of discount* The rate of discount relative to the price of the product also seemed to affect redemption rate. Although consumers may not know or calculate the exact percentage, they apparently recognize better discount values.
4. *Face value of the coupon* Consumers were influenced by high face values on the card, particularly when these reflected high discount values.
5. *Brand distribution* As can logically be expected, redemption rate increased as the distribution of the brand increased. Consumers can't buy a product if they can't find it.[11]

Although couponing can be an effective promotional tool for retailers and manufacturers, it is not without problems for both. Retailers often find it difficult or impossible to check purchases against coupon redemption. As a result, the manufacturer may redeem coupons for cash when in reality the product was never purchased. In addition, the sheer volume of coupons creates additional work and control problems for both parties.

In recent years a problem of counterfeiting has occurred in some areas. This is not a problem as long as the coupon is redeemed upon purchase of the specific product or service; it becomes a problem when coupons are redeemed for cash without proof of purchase.

Yellow Pages

One of the best advertising media available to small retailers is the *Yellow Pages* of the local phone book. According to the American Telephone and Telegraph Company, corporate parent for the *Yellow Pages*, the directory is used nationally 17 billion times a year. On the average, each adult in America refers to a *Yellow Pages* directory 117 times per year. Without doubt the *Yellow Pages* have become a pervasive medium.

In 1982 the *Yellow Pages* were experimentally increased in five major markets to include 16 pages of four-color inserts. Consumers in Denver, Atlanta, Boston, Chicago and a borough of Manhattan have an opportunity to preview the new innovation. According to Ross Brown, Division Manager of Directory Marketing for A.T. & T., "We think it offers an exciting new and colorful dimension to a proven and much used advertising medium. It offers regional and national companies an excellent new opportunity to promote their products and services, while at the same time providing a telephone number for 'where-to-buy-it' information through local dealers and outlets."[12] In earlier tests, color ads were inserted in 7,500 randomly selected directories. When recall tests were made months later, 17 percent of the experimental group were able to name a number of advertisers and 35 percent had read the color segment in the last three months.[13]

Advertisements in the new color segments will vary with the directory's circulation. For example, if a retailer wanted to place an ad in the Chicago edition with a circulation of 1,600,000, the merchant would have to pay $34,000. If the test market experiment proves a success the color inserts will begin to appear in other markets in 1983.

In recent years the *Yellow Pages* have been the subject of some criticism from the retail community. Some Bell systems have elected to segment the traditional *Yellow Pages* in business and consumer editions noting that the single volume was too large and thick to be effectively used by the public. Such actions have forced the potential retail advertiser to either purchase space in the "Consumer" edition or the "Business" edition or both. Some advertisers have complained that they thought such Bell actions were not in the best public interest. Additionally, the cost of purchasing advertising space in the *Yellow Pages* has increased to the point that some advertisers feel the medium is no longer worth the cost and have elected to buy a larger print entry in the regular white page directory. Whether such a decision is appropriate or not depends on the firm's name recognition in the community, and the amount of additional advertising needed to gain and maintain customer awareness of its existence and product/service offering. Regardless of the ultimate decision, a large segment of the consuming public still relies on the *Yellow Pages* as their directory to locally available consumer products and services.

Broadcast Media (Radio and Television)

Retailers utilize both radio and television advertising to relay their messages to consumers. Characteristics of both media are presented in Table 14.2. Both media reach a large number of people at a low cost, since nearly every home has at least one radio and one television set. But the amount of wasted circulation is also high, unless the retailer is large enough to serve the entire broadcast area. If the retailer serves only a small segment of the population reached by the broadcasts, the waste circulation problem could be serious enough to render broadcast media uneconomical. Some radio and television stations counteract this objection by scheduling programs that appeal to specific consumer groups. Retailers who cater to these groups can then advertise on these programs at a lower cost per potential customer simply because wasted circulation has been reduced.

Another problem shared by both radio and television is that each medium presents many advertisements that are unrelated to the purpose for which the consumer is tuned to the medium. Television and radio audiences are normally in a mood for diversion, but unfortunately that mood usually has only a slight

Table 14.2   Comparison of Broadcast Media Used by Retailers

Medium	Market Segment Reached	Type of Retailer Particularly Suited for	Advantages	Disadvantages
Radio	Different programs reach distinct market segments	Retailers and service firms catering to a specific market segment and mass merchandisers catering to general audience at low cost	1. Requires very little lead time before advertisement is heard 2. Advertisement can be prepared easily and inexpensively 3. Advertisement can be altered quickly 4. Local identification on local radio stations 5. Can provide a loyal, special-interest audience 6. Personalities (D.J.s) provide believable advertisements 7. Low cost per minute of advertisement	1. Advertisements must be repeated to be of value 2. Wasted coverage for small retailers located in a metropolitan area 3. Message must be brief 4. Can cover too large a geographic area for small retailers 5. Absence of photos and illustrations
Television	General audience	Mass merchandisers and chain outlets; retailers of demonstratable merchandise	8. Low cost for mass merchandisers	Items 1, 2, 3, and 4 above 6. High cost of preparing good advertisements 7. High cost of television time

connection with the accompanying promotional message.[14] Despite the fact that consumers do not appear to give radio and television advertisements as much attention as they do to advertisements in print media, it appears that they remember a surprisingly large part of the former's commercial messages.[15] In general, the length of time that a television commercial is remembered is longer than that of a radio commercial, but shorter than that of a newspaper advertisement.[16]

One of the largest problems associated with radio and television advertising is that consumers frequently use these media as "background noise" and may not hear or see the presentations. A high level of creativity in advertisement writing and preparation and considerable repetition of these advertisements may be required to reach the consumer effectively.

Effective Use of the Local Radio Medium

Retailers across the nation are discovering that by using local radio they can effectively reach many different segments of the consumer market. Comprehensive quantitative data concerning local radio promotions is difficult to obtain. However, some specific examples of local radio campaigns may give the reader an appreciation of how this medium can be used as an important part of the promotion package. According to Harry Spitzer, Vice President and Sales Director of the Southern California Broadcasters Association, local and retail radio advertising in Southern California has increased 190 percent in contrast to a national increase of 90 percent during the decade of the 1970s.[17] This same trend has been noted by Jim Haviland, President of the Radio Broadcasters of Chicagoland and Vice President and Manager of WLAK. According to Haviland, WLAK has experienced a 25 percent increase per year for the previous three years in retailer advertising. Retail chains are also spending advertising dollars in local radio advertising. K mart allocated 3 percent or $8,500,000 in 1980 for spot radio time to promote new store openings and merchandise.

Local radio advertising offers considerably more than just informing its listeners of new store openings. Jan Zechman, President of Zechman & Associates, Chicago, and the agency for Carson Pirie Scott & Company commented, "Print is a very price-item oriented type of vehicle. Radio offers you another element. It's a personality. You have an opportunity with radio to create and reinforce a feeling, a personality, for the store."[18]

Perhaps local radio advertising works best with what might be called the "donut style" advertisements.[19] This type of ad has a generic beginning and ending but leaves space for a live announcer or a prerecorded message to key in a specific sale message. Sally Ann Lowry, Division Vice President of Advertising Administration for Broadway, a southern California department store chain, adapted this approach very effectively in a six-day Columbus Day promotion. "This year we developed a whole bank of jingles based on the same theme, 'You can be what you want to be at the Broadway,'" noted Ms. Lowry. "We developed it into a jazz format, a classical format, and a western format. It's the same music. We've done it for 30- and 60-second commercials. So whatever we do, we get a consistent sound and instant recognition. And it will fit any kind of need we have."[20]

The Broadway's promotion provides one of the best examples of local radio's effectiveness as a promotional tool in retailing. Fully realizing that more than 90 percent of the cars in the Los Angeles area have radios and that at any one time there are at least two million people on the freeway system in the Los Angeles basin, Ms. Lowry worked with the Southern California Broadcasters Association to create a formula for the Columbus Day event which eventually cost $90,000. Some of the radio commercials were combined with a special newspaper preprint which heralded two private days at the beginning of the sale.

Exhibit 14.1   How to Buy Radio Time

Radio is a selective medium that reaches different kinds of people through different kinds of programming. The following is a very quick outline of Radio buying to reach your best customers most effectively.

Station Programming Spectrum

In most every city and town you'll have a choice of Radio stations. In order to attract their own audiences, stations will program differently, so your choice of Radio stations may include:

- Middle-of-the-road stations
- News stations
- Conversation stations
- Country music stations
- Talk stations
- Contemporary stations
- Progressive rock stations
- Classical stations

- Ethnic stations
- Variety stations

And many variations of the previous items. From a programming point of view AM and FM stations are similar since these days FM stations have formats that include all of these items rather than just "good music" which used to be the case. All stations in your market should be considered on the basis of the kind of audience they deliver, the size of their audience, and whether or not this audience will be interested in the merchandise you're selling.

How Time is Priced

The price you pay for commercials on stations is related to the size of your market, the number of people the station reaches, the kind (age, income, family size, etc.) of people reached and also the selling power of the station's on-air personnel. Radio stations can't expand the number of commercials they broadcast like newspapers can expand their ads—newspapers simply add more pages—because Radio stations limit the number of commercial minutes they broadcast each hour and the Radio day cannot be lengthened. This argues for planning Radio as far in advance as possible.

Source: Radio Advertising Bureau, Inc. Reprinted by permission.

Then the rest of the radio advertisements were backed up with regular newspaper ads and direct mail. The event was so successful that Ms. Lowry said the firm will increase its radio advertising much more in the future.[21]

The per minute cost of advertising is much lower over radio than on television. A retailer can take advantage of this relatively low cost and combine it with an advertising schedule that is designed to reach the target market group in an effective promotional campaign (Exhibit 14.1).

Television as a Viable Retailer Communication Tool

Television advertisement uses both sight and sound to take the retailer's appeal to the consumer. Indeed, its ability to show certain products that require demonstration may necessitate television advertising. Because consumers spend many evening hours relaxing before a television set, advertisements reach these people when they are more susceptible to new ideas.[22]

Television also provides the flexibility needed if advertisements should be changed suddenly. For example, spot antifreeze advertisements can sometimes be inserted into a weather program when the retailer perceives a sudden change in temperature is coming.

High Cost

The disadvantages of television include a high cost for advertising time and the relatively high cost required to prepare a good television advertisement. In addition, small retailers encounter much waste circulation because television does not generally offer as selective an appeal as radio. The total television audience in any area is also likely to be less segmented than the radio audience because there are fewer television stations. For these reasons, it is difficult for a small retailer to reach a target market through television.

Spot Television

Retailers across the nation are beginning to realize that the television spots in local markets can make an important contribution in their attempt to properly position the firm in the minds of their target customers. Food retailers, such as Safeway, are using the medium for image advertising. In the first six months of 1981, Safeway spent approximately $9 million on their new "Answer Man" campaign which expressed the firm's involvement and active concern for a better, cleaner community by buying and recycling aluminum cans. Such advertising goes beyond the previous price-item orientation of traditional retailer messages and is designed to create a "high-awareness" among the consuming public that the firm is concerned with their needs. Additionally, according to Mr. Bert Bremsen, Group Account Manager at Barickman Advertising, Kansas City, who designed the "Answer Man" promotion for 138 Safeway stores, the campaign is designed ". . . to touch upon the feeling that people have when shopping at a supermarket. This (campaign) gives the viewer a remembrance of habit—a feeling that it's safe and comfortable to shop at the same place, perhaps for generations."[23]

This image trend is also found in department store television promotion. According to Gordon Cook, Senior Vice President of Sales Promotion, Bloomingdale's, the firm has used a spokeswoman since 1977 and now is considered a part of the Bloomingdale image. "With the spokeswomen there is no need to build up a 'this is a Bloomingdale's commercial' identification. She epitomizes the aggressive and active style that we want associated with Bloomingdale's," he observed.[24] Other large eastern department store chains are moving beyond their traditional commercials and are presenting "inforercials" which are composed of 30-second informational spots followed by 30-second commercials. Gimbel's use this format and call it their "Fashion Report," with outstanding vendor and customer success. Abraham & Strauss, realizing that their customer's profile was very similar to that of soap opera viewers, have called their effort, the "Soap Opera Moment."[25]

General merchandisers and discount stores are also rediscovering television. One reason for this resurgence of interest may

be attributed to rising newspaper advertising costs and the fact
that the newspaper medium may only cover 35 to 40 percent of
the retailer's market. In any event, Woolworth/Woolco is returning to television with an emphasis on "the telling of events."
According to Tom McGoldrick, Vice President with Sawdon &
Bess, New York, who handled the Woolworth/Woolco account,
"Instead of showing random items, Woolworth's will pull a
range of products together and present them for Mother's Day or
Valentine's Day."[26] Regardless of the approach it is apparent that
the increasing use of television medium, including over-the-air
broadcasts and cable systems, will continue into the foreseeable
future. Each retailer should review the promotional options open
to the firm and select the combination which will best serve the
stores' needs. Often retailers are tempted to copy another store's
promotional approach, particularly if that store is highly successful. Unfortunately, such "me-too" approaches are rarely
successful. Each store must create its own image by designing
its own unique print and broadcast advertisements.

Creating Print and Broadcast Advertisements

Effective advertisements are created not made. Significant
amounts of time and effort must be invested both by the advertiser and the medium sales specialist if an advertisement is
going to accomplish its intended purpose. This is particularly
true for small retailers who may lack access to an in-house advertising department or an advertising agency. Regardless of resources available, all advertisements should have certain basic
characteristics. First, the message must speak for the retailer in
tone and content that match his or her objectives. Thus, the retailer must:

1. Identify the target market customers.
2. Identify the reasons for advertising, be they stimulation of
immediate purchases, changing of consumers' shopping
habits, enhancing the store's image, informing consumers
about the store's continued existence, the merchandise
[and/or] service offerings, etc.
3. Determine the unique selling features that are most likely
to appeal to the target market group. Seeing things from the
point of view of the target market customers can generate
unique selling features. Talking to customers and surveying
consumers by the use of questionnaires can give retailers
ideas on the desires of [their] target group.
4. List the benefits that should be featured in the
advertisements. Consumers want to know "what does this
advertisement offer me?" Facts (such as a large number of

automobiles on hand) mean little to the consumer until they are turned into benefits for the individual by emphasizing that they can choose from a large selection of automobiles. **5.** Develop the theme for the advertisement by taking the above factors into consideration.[27]

Converting the theme into an advertisement should follow the **AIDCA process.** This consists of attracting *attention,* stimulating *interest,* creating *desire, convincing* the consumer that the merchandise/service offering will provide the best solution to the problem, and, finally, suggesting that the customer take *action.* When one uses these simple guidelines, advertisements can become more effective in communicating the retailer's message.

Print Media

Headlines are used to capture the reader's attention. On the average, five times as many people read the headline of an advertisement as read the body.[28] Therefore, if retailers do not "sell" a benefit in a short simple headline, they waste 80 percent of their money. "Benefit headlines" are designed to answer the target consumer's question, "What does this advertisement offer me?" The good quality of the store's merchandise and service should be stressed relative to the most important consumer benefits that the merchandise and service provide.

Attention

Illustrations, if used, should reinforce headlines to capture the reader's attention. Usually photographs attract more readers, are more believable, and are better remembered than drawings.[29] Captions should be placed below a photograph because, in general, twice as many people read the captions as read the body of the advertisement.[30] More awareness can be obtained if each caption is considered to be a miniature advertisement containing brand names and benefits.

Stimulate Interest

The headline and illustration should capture the **attention** and stimulate the *interest* of the readers. The text, or copy, is used to create the *desire* for the product or service and to **convince** the readers that the advertised merchandise/service offering is best in light of their needs.

Convince

Copywriting is truly a creative process, but several concepts may be helpful. First, the message should include the benefits that are likely to appeal to the target group. Second, the writing should be phrased in the type of language that is most familiar to the people in the target group. The arguments should be presented in terms to which target consumers can relate. Third, the benefits should be presented in simple words and short sentences that get the ideas across quickly and clearly. The creative element is involved in using words that arouse interest and encourage people to read an advertisement to its conclusion. Readership falls off rapidly during the first 50 words, but it drops off only slightly between 50 and 500 words if the copy is well written.[31] Decline in readership means that the most important ideas should be presented first in copy.

Advertisement layout involves visually fitting together the lead line, illustration, copy, and a signature or logotype, which may include the store name, location, store hours, and phone number. Whenever advertisements are printed special care should be given to the mechanics of producing the best layout for the money. For an advertisement of a given size, this involves careful consideration of the following details.[32]

Amount of White Space Retailers should consider the image that they want to project and allocate more **white space** (the lack of print in an advertisement) to expensive quality merchandise if they wish to project a prestige image (Exhibit 14.2). If they wish to project a discount-price image, they will want to reduce the white space and use a more crowded cluttered layout.

Placement Regular advertisers will find that newspapers are generally willing to place their ads on desired pages or sections. Retailers should give serious consideration to the correct area, even if a small premium is required to reserve space in this area. Many small retailers sell specialized products, such as women's wear, wigs, sporting goods, and pet supplies, that coincide well with such special areas as the sports or the women's section.

Print Style A retailer may wish to purchase a print type not carried by the local newspaper. This can be kept on stock at the newspaper and used only by the retailer. Although difference is desired, an extreme can actually work to the detriment of the retailer.

Slogan A good slogan can aid in establishing an image and in repeating a message to the customer. It should contain the name of the firm and/or the merchandise or service offered. It should also have recall value; arouse curiosity; and serve as a focus point for the advertising policy of the firm.

Sponsor Identification A signature in the form of a logo or distinctive design can help improve identification. It does no good to advertise if the reader cannot remember later which store it was that was having the sale or confuses it with a competitor. Signature "cuts" may be purchased through engraving companies and stored with the local newspaper or printer.

Exhibit 14.2 "Sale" Advertisement Example Conveying Prestige Image Using White Space

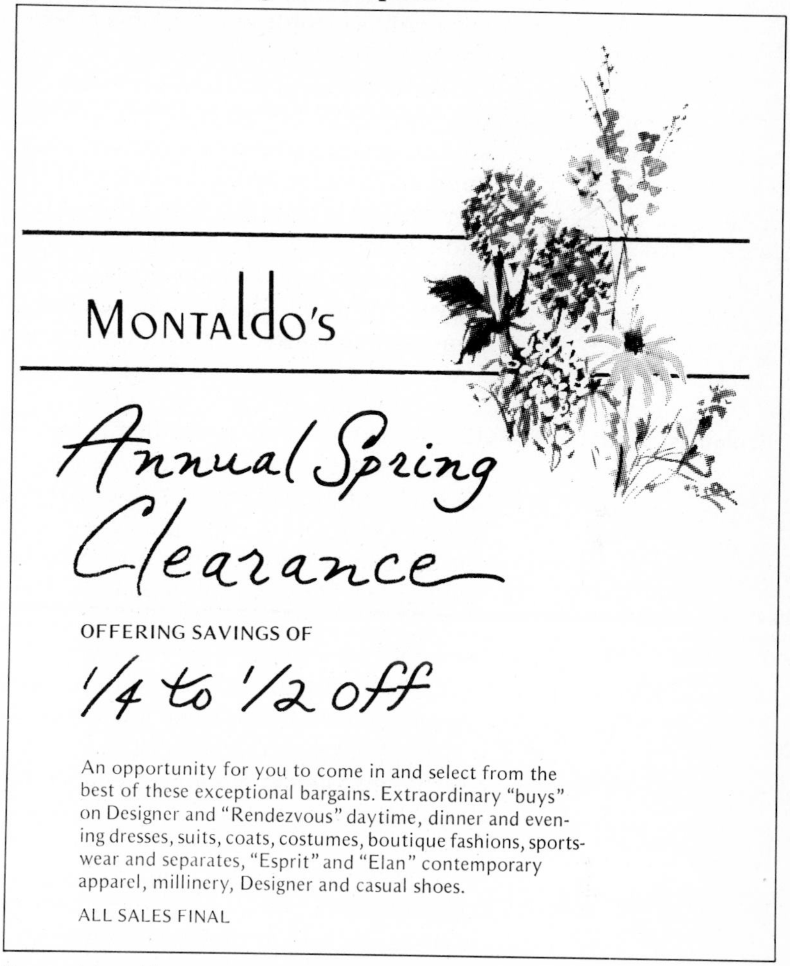

MONTALDO'S

Annual Spring Clearance

OFFERING SAVINGS OF

1/4 to 1/2 off

An opportunity for you to come in and select from the best of these exceptional bargains. Extraordinary "buys" on Designer and "Rendezvous" daytime, dinner and evening dresses, suits, coats, costumes, boutique fashions, sportswear and separates, "Esprit" and "Elan" contemporary apparel, millinery, Designer and casual shoes.

ALL SALES FINAL

Source: Montaldo's Denver. Reprinted by permission.

Human Interest Illustration Illustration can add to the interest in the ad if well done. Newspapers carry a catalog of illustrations that may have applicability. A special illustration, to be used in a recurring theme, should be custom made and kept on file with the newspaper or printer.

Advertisement Guidelines

Check the Advertisement before Printing Each advertiser should check the advertisement to be certain that (1) the advertisement is easily recognizable, (2) a simple layout has been designed, (3) a dominant element, such as a headline or illustration, presents a benefit to the consumer, (4) the amount of white space is consistent with the store image, (5) the copy is complete, including the store name, (6) possibly related items are included in the advertisement, (7) wording is simple and excessive claims are not heralded, (8) the advertisement urges readers to buy now.

Mr. Sandman (furniture gallaries) is an example of a retailer recognizing that innovation can be promoted through newspaper advertisements to create a desired image. The firm took a new approach to advertising modular furniture. "By introducing and continually promoting a new line of rugged and durable sleep-and-storage units, Mr. Sandman became synonymous with 'maximum living in minimum space.'"[33] The firm's advertising states, "We think ahead." This continual innovative promotional approach converted the firm into the leader in their market.

Broadcast Media

Broadcast media present difficult creative problems because consumers must understand the message the first time. They cannot go back and reread the message as they can in print advertisements. Only a very short message can be communicated because the consumer's attention is not completely focused on the advertising presentation. Both television and radio commercials can suffer from wordiness. One-minute radio commercials should present between 120 and 150 words.[34]

There are different types of radio commercials.[35] A **straight announcement** involves an announcer's delivering the commercial without music or any backup noise. The personality of a regular announcer attempts to make the commercial more believable. Use of celebrities, who are not connected with the offering, may only steal attention from the message.

A **dramatization** is a commercial playlet, which is a good attention getter but is also expensive to produce. Normally, a realistic consumer problem is posed and the sponsoring store eventually solves the problem in a believable way. The problem that is selected should be based upon some unique merchandise/service offering available at the store. A good **dialogue** commercial involves a realistic conversation between several announcers.

Good **jingle** or **singing commercials** and musical advertisements where the announcer reads the advertisement with a musical background are quite effective in gaining a listener's attention. However, they should be well done or they may irritate the listener and adversely affect the store's image. A checklist for writing radio copy is presented in Exhibit 14.3.

Television commercials employ the same techniques as radio, but also allow visual demonstrations. If they are honest and believable, these demonstrations are quite effective ways to com-

Exhibit 14.3   Checklist for Writing Radio Copy

Here are some suggestions to help you write effective Radio copy.

1. Write conversationally. Radio is a human being talking to another human being, not a novelist or poet writing to a reader.

2. Talk about benefits. Tell listeners what store or merchandise will do for them . . . . fast. Here are some benefits: economy, health, good looks, current fashions, quality, etc.

3. Be direct and go straight to the point. Short sentences are better because they can be absorbed easily through the ears.

4. Repeat the store name, the price, the comparative, the benefits as many times as you can to register the points you want to make.

5. Know what you're writing about. Use fact sheets from manufacturers, national ads, actual experience to make the merchandise come alive on the air.

6. Try out your script before airing. Read the copy over or, better yet, have someone else read it or read it into a tape recorder. This way you'll hear if any phrases are stilted, hard to read, or unbelievable.

Source: Radio Advertising Bureau, Inc. Reprinted by permission.

municate with customers. Animated and cartoon commercials can be effective in reaching children. They are less persuasive than live commercials in reaching adults, who cannot identify with the character in the cartoon.[36]

Natural Simple Language

Broadcast advertisements require natural simple language that will appeal to the target consumer group. The desired store image and its merchandise/service offering must then be turned into consumer benefits and presented in a short amount of time. Generally this means that the advertiser should try to communicate only one idea during a commercial. The more ideas presented, the less consumers remember about the content of the commercial. The name and address of the store should be repeated several times during the commercial. Musical jingles or spoken slogans that rhyme with the name of the store can assist the memory of consumers. A strong windup, calling for consumer action, is also desirable.

Position Media

Position media include all types of signs, posters, programs, menus, directories, skywriting, and transportation advertising, such as the signs that appear on the back of taxicabs or inside public vehicles. The characteristics of billboard and transit advertising are presented in Table 14.3.

In-Store Signing

For many years large retail stores who have stressed self-service have been strong advocates of in-store point-of-purchase signing. Some firms use fixture signs with "card-toppers" to

Table 14.3   Comparison of Major Position Media Used by Retailers

Medium	Market Segment Reached	Type of Retailer Particularly Suited for	Advantages	Disadvantages
Billboard	Pedestrians, commuters, and motorists who pass by the specific location	Services, tourist attractions, amusements, retailers of brand name merchandise	1) Long life span for advertisement 2) High percentage of passersby read advertisement 3) Humor can be used	1) High cost 2) cannot be changed quickly 3) Competition for readership may be keen 4) Limited to short message Item 4 above
Transit	Urban pedestrians, commuters, workers	Local retailers and service firms	Repetition of exposure to advertisement	5) May provide limited audience unless advertisement moves around the city on the back of a bus or taxi

communicate selling points of regular merchandise while others have limited their in-store signing to just advertising sale merchandise. In 1979 a group of researchers, after reviewing the literature, set about evaluating the effectiveness of in-store signing in home centers, drug/discount, department, and specialty stores and came up with startling results.

Based on 881 product days of observation they concluded: "Descriptive signing of regularly priced merchandise results in a 30 percent increase in units sold, while sale priced merchandise resulted in a 24 percent increase."[37] Kelly and associates continued, "Descriptive signing appears to be most effective for stores:

(1) in mall and strip locations; (2) with moderate to heavy store traffic; (3) where previous signing policies were heavy, moderate or nonsign user; (4) when products signed are on end caps or the perimeter of the store; (5) where the quantity of product on display is either a heavy or medium quantity."[38]

Overall, stores increased their sales by an average of 26 percent under all conditions. Department stores benefited the most with a 32 percent increase in sales during the test period using in-store signing.

This systematic study combined with other less rigorous experiments demonstrates the necessity of having timely, accurate, well-designed, strategically placed signs to increase customer communication and optimize total sales.

Outdoor Signs

Advertising by means of outdoor signs is more suitable for institutional image promotion than for product-direct-action promotion because it is difficult and expensive to change the message continually. Thus, position media are generally used to reinforce the messages presented in other media or other signs. The content of the former generally consists of no more than eight words, unless the sign is presented on the inside of a bus or train.[39] In the latter cases, the sign may contain up to fifteen words, since a consumer frequently has nothing better to do than read the advertisement.

It is becoming increasingly clear that decisions concerning outdoor signs are no longer strictly the province of the retailer. Legislation regulating outdoor signs is almost certain to increase in amount and severity. The more vociferous antisign groups argue that if all signs were removed, no single company would have an advantage. Unless this viewpoint gains more support, the argument will remain academic. In the meantime, retailers will continue to utilize signs.

Images and Logos

In recent years, corporations have placed increasing importance upon their images and logos. Gasoline retailers have been particularly concerned with the image portrayed through these signs. This reflects the fact that a logo must give quick and positive identification to the viewer and means that every aspect of such signs must be given careful consideration. The color, shape, size, and type of illustration also have taken on increased importance. For this reason, it is advisable to use the services of professional design firms.

Point-of-Purchase Promotions

Point-of-purchase promotions (P.O.P.) range from a simple counter display with a sign to free samples distributed by women in bikinis accompanied by a brass band. Point-of-purchase advertising

> sells both by reminder and by impulse. When selling by reminder it utilizes the impact already made by other advertising media, serving as a link between them and the place where sales are made. When selling by impulse it also appeals independently. In either case, it is a potent instrument in clinching the sale. It asks for the order.[40]

Point-of-purchase promotions exist to strengthen overall retail promotional strategy. A great quantity of the point-of-purchase material available to retailers is furnished by the manufacturer. These displays may have been designed to tie in with a current promotional theme by the manufacturer, but may be completely out of place in the retail store. Retailers have both the right and the responsibility to reject any P.O.P. material they feel is damaging to the store's image. Unless P.O.P. material is planned around the habits, needs, problems, and fears of the retailer, it is almost assuredly headed for the trash can.

Even the best planned and most creative P.O.P. display is destined for a short life. This is the very nature of P.O.P. material. Since the marketing and creative staffs of manufacturers and retailers continually create obsolescence in P.O.P. material, a precise classification is impossible. Retailers are, however, beginning to demand more quality and longer lasting promotions from manufacturers. Retailers no longer want a last-one-week display, but expect a display to last six to eight weeks. This means the displays must be better constructed than previous displays. If this is done, retailers can use longer advertising periods to complement the P.O.P. display. Such a promotional program could feature common theme (for example, Hawaiian) displays of several different manufacturers. Consumers have been shown to spend more time in a store that offers a consistent theme on its P.O.P. material.[41]

Certain types of P.O.P. displays have emerged over time. These should not be considered totally independent classifications. Creative P.O.P. designers purposely blend one type with another to create hybrid displays. One such effort was demonstrated by Sears in 1981 when they used video disk machines as P.O.P. display units. Similar applications of video, tape, and movies have helped sell millions of dollars worth of merchandise.

Cut-Case Displays

The simplest type of P.O.P. display is made from the shipping container. The carton is designed to be cut along dotted lines to form a display case. Cut-case displays have widest application in the mass merchandising field, particularly in food stores, variety stores, and discount houses. In addition, they are often used by liquor stores. Other retailers, including department stores, use these displays during heavy buying periods, such as Christmas.

This type of display is simple to assemble and often comes with a "riser" card to be attached as a poster. Cut-case displays fit in nicely as end-of-aisle displays, and may form temporary partitions to direct shopper traffic patterns. They can also be displayed near cash registers for so-called impulse items.

Dump-Bin Displays

As the name implies, dump bins are tubs, boxes, wire baskets, or any other container in which products are dumped in a random method. Although brands and varieties may be mixed, the dump bins furnished by manufacturers usually lend themselves to a particular brand. Dump bins are used in the same way as cut-case displays.

Mobile Displays

One definition of a mobile is a sign or figure that is generally suspended from the ceiling. It is widely used by supermarkets to direct customers to a specific brand. Another definition refers to any movable P.O.P. display.

Counter Displays

The checkout counter represents the last selling opportunity in the store and is an excellent location for impulse, or unplanned purchase, items. As a result, many manufacturers supply special racks or other display units specifically designed for the counter. Items commonly sold at this counter range from penny mints in restaurants to expensive hosiery in women's style shops. Although items such as gum and cigarettes "sell themselves" in this manner, the sale of many others should be helped by suggestions from the cashier.

Silent Suggestive Sales Tools

The old question, "Will there be anything else?" is practically useless as it is sure to be followed by the programmed response, "No, I don't think so." However, if a salesperson suggests that a new pair of shoes needs the protection of wax or that a new pair of hose would complement the shoes, the chances for success are infinitely greater. This last-minute selling effort is made considerably easier by the careful placement of a counter display to remind both the salesperson and the customer.

Permanent P.O.P. Displays

The term "permanent display" should not be taken literally. Unless the life of the retail store is extremely short, virtually no display is permanent. "Permanent" expresses a relative measure, compared to many dump bins and other P.O.P. displays that exist only a few weeks. Most of the so-called permanent P.O.P. displays are furnished by manufacturers in an attempt to gain more shelf space. Over the years, three common types of P.O.P. units for displaying merchandise on a shelf have emerged. These are shelf dividers, and shelf extenders.

Shelf Dividers

This device usually sits on the shelf and contains notches into which the merchandise is placed. They are generally designed to display merchandise at an angle most appropriate for lateral vision.

Shelf Extenders   This is a small tray that is fastened to the shelf and extends beyond it to give additional shelf space.

Posters   Posters are undoubtedly the most common form of P.O.P. material in retail stores. They can be printed in an infinite variety of
sizes and materials. They may take the form of a banner or as it is
sometimes called streamer. The low cost and storewide applicability of posters ensure their popularity with retailers. Posters
may also take the form of counter cards when mounted on a pa-
perboard back. These are generally placed in store windows or
on the counter.

Easy to Read   Traditional rules for the design of posters have called for a
clear style with easy-to-read numbers and letters combined with
an easy-to-understand message and illustration. It has also been
felt that a poster should not attempt to relay more than a single
message, such as "Fire Sale," "Vacation in Hawaii," "Fresh
Peaches," or other simple messages.[42]

In recent years the growth of pop art, black-light posters, soul
messages, and similar forms of expression has shown that traditional rules may be broken with success. This is not to say that
overnight acceptance of such P.O.P. material is a wise policy for
the retailer. However, if the retailer sells pop records or clothing
oriented to young customers these posters may be absolute
necessities.

Window Displays   An effective window display has the following objectives:

1. To increase the drawing power of the store by attracting the
attention of passing consumers
2. To achieve an attractive presentation of merchandise and
services
3. To project a fashion or quality image
4. To convey a value or price image
5. To support other promotional activities of the firm
6. To show the consumer the merchandise and service selections
offered by the firm
7. To arouse consumer interest so that needs are suggested

The method of constructing window displays is based on (1) attracting the attention of consumers, (2) identifying with consumer needs, (3) conveying the appropriate message, and
(4) providing an attractive presentation. It should be noted
that the aesthetic aspect has been placed last. This is done
deliberately to demonstrate that the window display must be

a commercial means of communication with the future buyer, not merely a work of art.

Attracting Attention

The use of lighting, color and movement are the three methods of attracting the attention of passing consumers. A well-lighted window attracts attention. A brighter lighting intensity or the use of colored lights can add a great deal to the attention-getting power of a window display. For example, a specially placed spotlight can emphasize important areas of a display.

Color is another significant factor in creating a unique atmosphere. Most consumers are sensitive to colors, so retailers can choose colors that are appropriate for the season. Blues, yellows, green and pink reflect a spring theme, and brown, tans and orange create an image of fall.

Almost any form of movement also captures the attention of passersby. Animated displays, toys, or other types of moving devices can attract attention.

Identifying with Consumer Needs

A well-designed window display must stimulate the consumer's interest by arousing imagination. It must promote satisfactions that parallel the consumer's needs and not merely present goods for sale. Thus, a good window display should serve as a mirror in which future customers can picture themselves. Naturally, consumer needs vary with the season so window display themes must also vary with the season. A seasonal theme should be developed from the viewpoint of personal situations that correspond with the seasons—return to school, graduation, gifts for Christmas, Mother's Day, Father's Day, Easter, and Mother-in-law Day. The reader may note that some holidays and special days have been created to encourage retail sales.

Conveying the Appropriate Message

A window display might include a written message to be better understood by consumers. A short text written in large type is frequently used to deliver a special message. For example, an office supply store may incorporate a professional activities theme to guide its window display. The written message may read "For your profession: A calculator that works for you." The products displayed might be game type calculators for children, inexpensive calculators for younger students, scientific calculators for advanced students, financial calculators for business students and business people, printing calculators for accountants, and so forth.

A retailer can change window displays regularly and use them to show merchandise that is considered to be "the newest" to accomplish the objective of projecting a fashion or quality image. If the objective of the window display is to project a value or price image, the store's best buys can be prominently displayed in the window along with price tags that are clearly visible to the consumer.

Window displays can support other promotional activities of the firm. For example, the window display can feature both the merchandise and the store's latest newspaper advertisement.

They can also convey the store's message concerning merchandise and service selection. The window displays do this if a selective rotation of goods and services are features in the ever-changing store windows.

Providing an
Attractive
Presentation

Attractive decorations can communicate the sales message as well as be aesthetically pleasing. Window displays should contain suggestions instead of including all types of merchandise in the display. The most important objective of a window display is to encourage consumers to enter the store. A window display that conveys the impression that everything of interest is contained in the window leaves little incentive for the consumer to enter the store. It is therefore suggested that only a modest number of items be exhibited in the window. This recommendation is consistent with the belief that an uncluttered display helps to improve the presentation of merchandise and allows consumers to picture themselves using the product. Inclusion of too many items in a window simply creates the impression of confusion and disorganization.

The window display should appear to be balanced. Poorly balanced arrangements appear to be untidy and disorganized. Balance is obtained by placing items of equal size at equal distances from the center of the display.

Backgrounds for window displays may be full, partial, or open. A full background, which blocks off the view of the store, can provide an attractive setting for the display. The background should not be left bare but should hold signs, posters, decorative material, or display props. Merchandise can then be suspended from the background or leaned against it. A display positioned against a full background frequently generates more consumer attention because there are no in-store distractions present.

Partial backgrounds allow consumers to see inside the store. The goal is to get consumers to look at the display, then follow their impulse to join the in-store crowd.

The display is shown against the background of the store's interior in the open background display. This type of window display must blend in with the rest of the store. It does give the consumer an invitation to inspect interior displays and purchase goods to meet their needs.

Specialty Advertising

Specialty advertising consists of matchbooks, calendars, blotters, paper clamps, and other novelty items that are frequently used to keep the name of the retailer in front of consumers. This type of reminder advertising is best suited for outlets where consumers shop infrequently. The institutional message, of no more than five to ten words, should communicate that the outlet is ready to meet consumer needs in specific merchandise-service areas.[43]

Reminder Advertising

This type of reminder message can usually indicate only who the retailer is, where outlets are located, and what is sold. Short reminder messages of this type are usually supplemented with other forms of promotion which contain a more detailed message.

Specialties are generally more effective in keeping customers than in attracting new customers. These specialty items represent an invitation to continue to buy and a token of appreciation for the consumer's patronage. The effectiveness of a specialty item depends upon the attractiveness of the item to the consumer and upon its distribution. Items that are unusual but that can help solve small customer problems are likely to be used and valued more by the consumer. Because the message is presented each time the item is used, retailers should give items that will be used more often than those that are given away by their competitors. The items may also be associated with the business. For example, a gasoline service station may give away a free ice scraper imprinted with its name, address, telephone number, and store hours.

Matchbooks, calendars, pens, and pencils are the most frequently used specialties. Specially designed covers on book matches and calendars can increase the exposure of a retailer's advertisement by being used and displayed by consumers instead of being discarded. The effectiveness of such calendars, pens, and pencils is likely to depend on who receives them. A homemaker will probably use these items because she is seldom oversupplied with them. Businesspeople probably receive many of these items from other sources and may not use them unless they possess some unique feature. A calendar, if displayed in a popular place of business consistent with the retailer's image, can be an effective but inexpensive type of advertising. The trick is to get the calendar displayed in other places of business that serve your target customers.

Sales Promotion Techniques

It should be recalled that sales promotions are different from advertising in that mass media are not used. Sales promotions include premiums, such as stamps, free gifts, contests, and so forth. Sales promotions also include consumer services such as packaging, alterations, wrapping, delivery, refunds and exchanges, and credit. The various types of sales promotion are designed to encourage the immediate sale of merchandise or service and to keep customers loyal to the store.

Premiums

The major appeal of premiums is that the customer believes he or she is getting something for nothing. Stamps and small gifts are thought of as being free. Even contests and sweepstakes give the consumer a chance to win something for nothing. Some of the more frequently used gifts include the following.

Giveaways or
Traffic Builders

These are small items, such as a piece of candy or gum, a trash bag, and so forth, which are given away with each purchase.[44]

Referrals

"Thank you" gifts are given to customers who send their friends to your outlet.

New-Customer Gift

These are small, free gifts that are given to new customers the first time they enter the outlet.

Continuity Program

Given one at a time, matched glasses, chinaware, towels, and so forth, keep customers coming back to complete the set.

Trading Card

Customers can collect a free gift when their card is completely punched out—after making the necessary amount of purchases. If the free gift is some service—say a free car wash by an automatic machine—it can be a real benefit to the customer and still increase retail costs only slightly.

Trading Stamps
and Games

Trading stamps and games, which promote retail sales, have been historically linked to supermarkets, service stations, and an assortment of small retailers including a few small, independent department stores. These promotional techniques were never adopted in significant numbers by large department stores, discount houses, car dealers, furniture outlets, and many other types of retailers. There have been a few exceptions in almost every retail category, but they are the exception rather than the rule.

History shows that national diffusion occurred in the period 1951–1962 for trading stamps and in the period 1962–1966 for games. After these periods, the popularity of both methods declined.[45] The decline of both promotional techniques may be traced to several developments.

1. The industry became saturated with both techniques. As a result, little or no competitive advantage was left.

2. Discount houses and other retailers who had not accepted stamps offered increasingly heavy competition to those with stamps. In fact, advertising campaigns were built around the fact that a particular store did not give stamps and thus offered consumers a savings.

3. In some areas, retailers were forced into stamp wars in which a significant number of extra stamps were given for purchases.

4. The attitude of shoppers changed. People actually formed protest movements in certain areas against stamps, games, and other promotional techniques.

5. Stores that had dropped stamps and games reported initial losses, but then reported profit gains without giving stamps. Stamp companies charge the retailer between 1.5 and 3 percent of sales volume.[46] For many retailers, the expense associated with stamps is greater than their entire advertising expenditure. Recently some retailers have again started to use trading stamps and games to attract customers.

The history of these promotional techniques offers retailers several important lessons concerning these and other new promotional techniques that may occur in the future. These may be summarized as follows:

1. Promotional techniques that are readily available to other retailers cannot replace sound retailing/merchandising strategies and planning.

2. Consumer preferences and response to promotional techniques may shift in short periods of time so that what was in vogue last year is the villain this year.

3. The first retailers to use new promotional techniques may easily capture larger market sales and gain greater profits in the short run; however, once the technique becomes widespread, they may easily be in a worse competitive condition than other more powerful retailers who adopt the same technique.

4. Dependency upon a promotional technique overlooks the fact that strong new retailers and retailing concepts may emerge while the older retailers are engaged in a competitive promotional battle.

5. It is evident that a particular market segment is attracted to stores that offer particular promotional techniques such as stamps and games. As a result, it may be possible for certain retailers, particularly independent stores and chains, to use these techniques as long as large competitors do not adopt the practices. This is particularly true after larger competitors have tried and discontinued the techniques.

Publicity

Nonpaid Communication

Unique approaches are required to get favorable publicity for retail outlets. Since the retailer does not have to pay for the coverage, the media programmers and writers must believe that the item appeals to the general population. Consumerism and ecological and minority opportunity program campaigns may be used to bring the retailer's name before the public. No matter what the appeal, a skilled writer and speaker is usually required to place the item in the media.[47]

Many retailers seem to feel that by hiring a specialist in publicity, or a public relations director, they have satisfied the need to "do something" about publicity. Publicity extends well beyond placing free articles in newspapers. In fact, the values to be obtained extend beyond those of the promotional mix. They have a direct bearing upon employee morale, motivation, and education.

A large department store is faced with an abundance of publicity opportunities. Nearly every department will find there are clubs, fraternal organizations, and consumer groups that are interested in knowing more about their particular products. Art groups and garden clubs are examples of types of organizations with special interest in particular products. Yet all too often the only contact a retailer of garden supplies or art goods has with these groups consists of sending a $10 item to the yearly benefit auction.

The growing interest among American consumers in wines and specialty foods provides invaluable publicity opportunities. Retailers have found they can sponsor wine-tasting parties at a cost to the customer. These are excellent opportunities to educate the customer concerning wines—at cost—and at the same time subtly sell one's products. Retailers who sell baby goods might profit through infant-care sessions for expectant mothers. Auto supply stores might find a full house for a profitable evening on the need for high-quality motor lubricants.

We are an affluent nation—a nation of consumers—in which one of the most popular pastimes is shopping. In this environment, there is little reason to believe that consumers will not respond to well-planned informative sessions on the products retailers sell. The success of many retailers in this area has proved that the problem is not lack of consumer interest, but rather a lack of employee time to honor all the speaking opportunities they would receive.

Major Store or Group Promotions

Retail outlets that are located within close geographical boundaries may group together and organize an area retail promotion. Downtown merchants, especially those located in smaller towns, often use the Chamber of Commerce as the organization that plans the promotion by establishing the theme, coordinating the advertising and store hours, and so forth. Two of the more popular promotions take the format of a "Crazy Daze" where prizes are given to the retail clerks who wear the "best" costumes and prizes are given away to customers, and "Moonlight Madness" where the stores offer prizes and lower prices on merchandise during the late evening hours, 8 p.m.–11 p.m.

Shopping centers usually have a promotional director who plans and implements the major promotions for the center. The promotions are scheduled to coincide with peak sales periods such as the Easter, back-to-school, and Christmas seasons. The promotions may feature a circus, a clown, a carnival, or any other attention-attracting activity. Large department stores today have an executive who usually goes by the title of Director of Special Events. Neiman-Marcus has its world-renowned Fortnight promotion. Macy's has its Thanksgiving Day Parade. Better stores feature designer trunk showings, noon fashion shows in the tea room, bridal fashion shows, cooking schools, and so forth.

Summary

Selection of the media that will most effectively reach the retailer's target market consumers must include consideration of the characteristics of each medium. Retailers rely heavily upon printed media and radio for their promotional efforts. Some newspapers have the advantage of serving a specific geographical group of people, so they can reach the local target market with minimal wasted circulation. Direct mail, including catalog mailings, can reach a specifically defined target group if a good mailing list is available. Coupons are frequently used to promote sales of special items that are designed to draw customers to the store. The *Yellow Pages* serve as reminder advertising and provide a listing to attract new customers. The chief advantage of

Yellow Page advertising is the continuous exposure offered for a long-life period of one year.

Radio is one of the most flexible media in that many different stations offer many different programs at any time of day. Also, its per minute cost of advertising is relatively inexpensive. Thus retailers can use radio to reach their target market at a fairly low cost. Repeated radio advertisements may be required to be effective, however, since listenership changes nearly every hour and the message is presented for only a few seconds at a time. Television is a useful medium for large retailers who serve most, if not all, of the area reached by the television station.

Advertising by signs is more suitable for institutional image promotion than for product—direct-action promotion because it is expensive to change the message. Point-of-purchase (P.O.P.) promotions create a buying mood after the consumer reaches the outlet.

Nearly all retailers use window displays to attract the attention of passing consumers and show them a limited selection of the type of merchandise and service offered by the firm. Retailers use lighting, color, and movement in their window displays to attract consumer attention.

Sales promotions use the appeal that the consumer believes he is getting something for nothing. The first retailers to use new promotional techniques can gain short-run sales increases until competitive outlets adopt similar techniques and a promotional war begins.

Individual retailers and groups of retailers are the sponsors of many major promotions that usually coincide with a peak sales season such as Easter, back-to-school, Christmas, and so forth. Downtown retailers usually organize such promotions through the local Chamber of Commerce. Most shopping centers provide a full-time promotional director to organize these promotions. The Director of Special Events in most large department stores organizes the store's promotional efforts.

Questions

1. What are the advantages and disadvantages that a small independent retailer obtains from using newspaper advertising?
2. When should newspaper advertising be used by a retailer? When should it not be used?
3. What are the advantages that direct mail advertising offers to retailers? Under what conditions should direct mail advertising be used by retailers?
4. Why do most retailers advertise in the *Yellow Pages*? What percentage of its advertising budget would you recommend that a small, independent repair shop spend in the *Yellow Pages*? What percentage of its advertising budget would you recommend that a large supermarket that is affiliated with a large national chain organization spend in the *Yellow Pages*?
5. What factors should one consider when creating a print advertisement?

6. What factors should one consider when creating a broadcast advertisement?

7. What are the advantages of radio as an advertising medium for retailers? What are the disadvantages? Under what circumstances should radio advertising be used by retailers?

8. What does television advertising have to offer retailers? Under what circumstances should it be used?

9. What are the current window treatment trends in your community? What message is being conveyed to consumers by the window displays? Is the treatment effective?

10. Why do sales promotions appear to be most effective for the first retailer to use them?

Footnotes

1. Jerome B. Kernan, William P. Dommermuth, and Montrose S. Sommers, *Promotion: An Introductory Analysis* (New York: McGraw-Hill, 1970), pp. 11–13.

2. Ibid., p. 203.

3. Ibid.

4. Laurence W. Jacobs, *Advertising and Promotion for Retailing* (Glenview, Ill.: Scott, Foresman, 1972), pp. 6–15.

5. Ibid.

6. Ibid., p. 118.

7. Ibid., p. 124.

8. Ibid., p. 119.

9. Ibid., p. 120.

10. A. C. Nielsen, Jr., "The Impact of Retail Coupons," *Journal of Marketing* (October 1965):11–15.

11. Ibid.

12. Louis A. Fanelli, "Yellow Pages Expand Color Ad Test," *Advertising Age*, April 20, 1981, p. 6.

13. Ibid.

14. Kernan et al., *Promotion*, p. 205.

15. Ibid., p. 207.

16. Jacobs, *Advertising and Promotion*, p. 123.

17. Jane Goltermann, "Radio Ads Come in Louder and Clearer," *Advertising Age*, November 2, 1981, p. S–16.

18. Ibid.

19. Ibid.

20. Ibid.

21. Ibid.

22. Ibid., p. 123. Jacobs, *Advertising and Promotion*, p. 123.

23. Abbe Wichman, "In the Image of Television," *Advertising Age*, November 2, 1981, pp. S16–17.

24. Ibid.

25. Ibid.

26. Ibid.

27. Ibid., p. 156. Jacobs, *Advertising and Promotion*, p. 156.

28. David Ogilvy, *How to Create Advertising that Sells* (New York: Ogilvy and Mather Advertising Agency, n.d.), p. 1.

29. Ibid.

30. Ibid.

31. Ibid.

32. Adapted from Jacobs, *Advertising and Promotion*, p. 161; Carl W. Birchard, "Distinctive Advertising for Small Stores," *Journal of Retailing*, Spring 1964, pp. 23–29, 50; Harry W. Hepner, *Effective Advertising* (New York: McGraw-Hill, 1949), pp. 558–560.

33. Richard Elkman, "Positioning: Wave of the 70's," *The Competitive Edge* (October 1977): p. 90.

34. Jacobs, *Advertising and Promotion*, p. 174.

35. Ibid., p. 174.

36. Ogilvy, *How to Create Advertising that Sells*, p. 1.

37. J. Patrick Kelly, E. Doyle Robison and Gary F. McKinnon, "Sales Effects of In-Store Descriptive Signing: A Field Study," paper presented at National Retail Merchants Association Annual Conference, January 15, 1980, p. 15.

38. Ibid.

39. Jacobs, *Advertising and Promotion*, p. 125.

40. Association of National Advertisers, *Advertising at the Point of Purchase* (New York: McGraw-Hill, 1957), p. 1.

41. "Supermarket Panel Cites Growing Interest in P.O.P.," *Advertising Age*, 30 August 1972, p. 2.

42. Harvey Offenhartz, *Point of Purchase Design* (New York: Reinhold Book Corp., 1968), p. 111.

43. Jacobs, *Advertising and Promotion*, p. 126.

44. William C. Battle, "Attract—and Hold—Customers with Premiums," *Motor*, September 1967, pp. 80–81.

45. Fred C. Allvine, "The Future for Trading Stamps and Games," *Journal of Marketing* 33 (January 1969): 45–52.

46. Jacobs, *Advertising and Promotion*, p. 126.

47. A list of dos and don'ts that can guide the nonprofessional in preparing publicity releases is presented in Harold L. Jenkins, *Action Marketing for Savings Institutions* (Chicago: Savings Institutions Marketing Society of America, 1972), pp. 168–169.

CASE STUDY: Winterglen Motel

In 1978 Glenn James decided to give up his job as a computer programmer for a large firm in Chicago because of the long commuting times and general hassle of urban living. For two years prior to his decision he had taken his family out to Colorado for a two-week ski vacation and really envied people living and working in such nice surroundings. When his wife received a significant inheritance they decided to buy a motel which was for sale in Winterglen, Colorado. The motel was situated between a large lake and a major highway which connected Denver with Salt Lake City, Utah. The motel had been built in the 1960s and had been kept in good repair. The main structure contained forty units on two levels and was about fifty yards from a small boat dock and marina where persons could launch their boats or rent small sailboats during the summer season. The motel was about a ten-minute drive from one of the major Colorado ski areas. The ski area was one of the first to open in the winter and the last to close in the spring due to their extensive use of snow-making equipment.

Winterglen was populated with a number of independently owned motels, a general store, two service stations, a combination snowmobile/boat shop, a postoffice and a family-style cafe. The ski area had two ski rental shops, two small gift shops, a convenience store, a liquor store/lounge, fifty condominiums, and an expensive modern ski lodge which operated all year. The James family was delighted with the prospect of living and working in this "wonderland" even though they had no experience in motel operation. They looked forward to the new challenge.

When Glenn and Joan James arranged to purchase the motel they had insisted that the Smiths, the former owners, stay on for two months and teach them the "ins and outs" of running the motel. Glenn felt this was vital because even though the inheritance had been large they still had to take out a loan for $100,000 at 15 percent for ten years. This meant that the motel had to have a high occupancy rate to succeed. One day, after the checkout rush was over, Glenn asked Bob Smith what he had done for promotion or advertising in the past. Bob just smiled and said, "Glenn this place has been such a gold mine I haven't spent anything on ads. The people just show up and we rent them rooms." Glenn felt a cold chill go down his back when he heard the remark but he thought, "After all the Smiths had spent 10 good years here so why shouldn't we?"

In January, 1982 the recession was felt across the country. Everyone was beginning to "feel the pinch." As Glenn looked over the registry book after turning the "Vacancy" sign off at 1 A.M. with only 10 rooms occupied, he began to recall Bob Smith's words, "Glenn this place has been such a gold mine I haven't spent anything for promotion or advertising in the past." Glenn thought, "Boy, Bob got out at the right time. He didn't have to contend with a recession, high unemployment, high gasoline prices, and blocked roads because of the worst winter in a century. Even if the skiers wanted to get here they couldn't. Even the lodge is off 25 percent!" As Glenn turned off the light and settled into bed he couldn't sleep and began to wonder what kind of promotion plan would be needed to get people into their motel during the coming spring-summer season.

Discussion Questions

1. What can the Jameses do to attract more motel patrons?
2. Who is Glenn's target market? How does he reach them?
3. Should Glenn try to advertise alone or should he try to form a cooperative promotion group with the other Winterglen retailers, including the ski area proprietors, and promote the whole area?
4. Devise a promotional package which will attract people to the Winterglen Motel for the following year.
5. Devise a promotional campaign for the Winterglen area for the coming spring-summer season.

Chapter 15	# Personal Selling and Consumer Services

Learning Goals

1. To understand the role professional salespeople play in retailing.
2. To describe the appropriate orientation for retail sales staffs and define common job tasks.
3. To discuss the retail selling environment including the selling process, training and evaluation of sales personnel, and appropriate compensation systems.
4. To be aware of the profitability of merchandising customer services.
5. To understand the role of consumer credit in retail sales management.
6. To identify the critical elements in a customer complaint system designed to provide customer satisfaction.

Key Terms and Concepts

marketing concept
selling process
trading up
straight salary

customer service policies
Consumer Products Warranty
   and Guaranty Act of 1970
delivery service

This chapter focuses on the two elements in retailing that the consuming public finds unsatisfactory most often: the quality of personal selling and consumer services. These two topics are discussed together to emphasize that personal sales efforts are often needed to sell a firm's consumer services. Additional sales of consumer services can result in increased profit dollars for an innovative retail firm.

Personal Selling

Personal selling is the heart of all retailing. Advertising can attract consumers to the store, but the face-to-face communication that occurs in personal selling provides unique opportunities. As salespersons talk with customers they can read the customers' reactions and identify individual consumer needs. Salespeople then can tailor their message to meet the specific needs of that customer. Face-to-face communication also allows salespeople to provide information that will reduce consumers' uncertainties about the product/service offering. Only through personal selling can customers receive individualized feedback from the retailer.

Decline of the Selling Profession

Traditionally, personal saleship has been the final vital link in the distribution process. Drummers, peddlers, and traveling salespeople sold the industrial output of this nation from its birth. However, immediately following World War II and during the Korean conflict the demand for goods far exceeded the nation's capacity to produce the needed goods. Few salespersons were needed because merchandise was either rationed or allocated. However, in the late 1950s supply exceeded demand and a new method to stimulate consumer consumption was needed. A partial answer was found in the marketing concept.

The **marketing concept** suggests that profitable consumer consumption should begin with the determination of customer needs and follow with the design of a package for goods and services that best meets those needs.

As an outgrowth of marketing concept application, mass media gained widespread acceptance both by consumers and producers as the most efficient means of moving merchandise. Significant research was undertaken in the applied behavioral sciences to determine why people purchased goods. Almost simultaneously the technologies of radio, television, and modern printing made great strides in providing excellent vehicles to present newly devised promotion strategies. "Preselling" and "self-service" were the bywords of the day. Mass media could sell anything to anyone given appropriate consumer research, product strategy, promotion design and enough money for implementation. Salespersons were viewed as a nonessential relic of bygone days.

Some twenty years later certain segments of the retail industry began to realize that not all products could be successfully merchandised through mass media alone. Custom stereo systems sales require human interaction if the customer is to achieve the best sound reproduction available within a given budget constraint. In every sector of our retail system, products have become so complex that the average layperson cannot make buying decisions independently. For a period of time the consumer relied on the old but not necessarily true maxim, "You get what you pay for." Price became the rule-of-thumb short-cut criterion for making purchase decisions. Unfortunately, some unscrupulous merchants noted this inclination and put high prices on products of inferior quality. Some people would argue that this practice is still in vogue.

Another semisuccessful technique for supplying buying information without using salespersons resulted in detailed package labeling. The federal government endorsed this action and together with industry convinced many consumers to read labels and do comparative shopping for the best buy.

Comparative Shopping Process

Comparative shopping involves going to different stores and comparing similar products. Suppose you want a pair of jeans at a price you can afford. What characteristics must the jeans you purchase possess? Some criteria might include proper fit, weight of denim, regular or fashion cut, zipper versus button closure, and relative price. Once the criteria are specified they must be put in order of importance. Which quality is most important? Usually the purchaser selects either price or fashion as the most important, followed by the other items which represent personal preferences.

Next, the purchaser must limit his or her search pattern. With the cost of transportation increasing, one may want to minimize costs and time by making all purchases on one shopping trip to a regional shopping center where different stores will carry a broad assortment of goods on the shopping list. Once at the center, one simply goes from store to store noting the differences in merchandise based on the previously prepared criteria. Ideally, the purchase decision will be made easier by such objective preparation, but most of the time consumers are swayed by current stocks, size and style availability and where they can use a credit card. The retailer equivalent of this practice is called "shopping the competition." Criteria on products remain much the same; but additional factors of display, interior location, and fixturing become items of competitive interest. This latter practice should be carried out by every retailer regularly in order to be aware of what is going on in the market.

Not all products lend themselves to easy comparison. A growing consumer movement is actively advocating the purchase and use of generic pharmaceutical and food products. Generic products do not carry a brand name but are labeled with a list of ingredients. Usually these products sell for substantially less because they bear no advertising costs. Entire research laboratories and magazine empires were built by far-sighted business persons to test competitive products and report their findings. All of these actions, while laudable, are not enough to instill the degree of consumer confidence that a good salesperson can generate in face-to-face contacts. Thus, retailers have begun to realize there are a limited number of situations where there is no acceptable substitute for dedicated, honest professional sales personnel. As a result some firms are belatedly beginning to recruit, train, and reward career retail salespersons and view them as valuable professional team members who can make a significant profit contribution to the organization.

Ethical Considerations: Salesperson versus Con-Artist

Hype-Specialists

At the outset of this discussion it is critically important to differentiate between salespersons and "hype-specialists." Unfortunately, few true salespersons are active in the current marketing system. A salesperson is an individual truly interested in matching consumer needs and product characteristics for optimal customer satisfaction, organizational profit, and personal gain—in that order. Hype-specialists attempt to prey on the gullible and put their own self-interest ahead of their customer's satisfaction. They profit in the short run but must move often to work new territories as their reputation becomes widely known. In contrast, salespersons view the occupation as a career and attempt to establish a reputation for honesty and integrity that generates repeat business and a personal following.

Somewhere in the middleground one finds "cash register clerks" and "sackers." The former usually inhabit central cash-wrap stations and are trained to make a high volume of transactions in the shortest period of time. "Sackers" usually only handle cash transactions in express checkout lines and "sack" the merchandise. Management has not trained these clerks to sell or give more than rudimentary information. Such is in keeping with the self-service concept which strives to keep personnel costs to a minimum. While a discussion of detailed sales training is beyond the scope of this book, it should be noted that an individual does not become a salesperson overnight. Various organizations, particularly house-to-house distributors, give intensive training in high-pressure selling techniques before the representative is placed in the field. In contrast, many of the life insurance firms spend considerable sums on training effective salespersons who take time to tailor their proposed insurance packages to the needs and goals of their clients. Other firms may hold periodic sales training sessions that stress both product knowledge and motivation. Perhaps the most important traits of any successful salesperson include acute perception of individual human behavior, personal positiveness that comes across as confidence rather than arrogance, and physical stamina which permits the long hours required in pursuit of sales. These traits will not make a salesperson, but they are benefits to be developed on the road to a profitable sales career.

In summary, salespersons are motivated to spend time and personal effort to either help the customer identify specific needs or present available merchandise/service offerings that will best meet the customer needs. Such efforts will entail considerable personal interaction, patience, and positive product presentations to achieve satisfactory merchandise/service matches. Occasionally, after a fair effort the salesperson must candidly admit that other products/services are better choices than he or she can offer and accept the loss of a sale. If this should occur, the salesperson should report these product/service deficiencies to top management so that adjustments in the marketing mix can be made and the offering restored to its competitive position. Thus, sales personnel provide a vital marketing service feedback so that the consumer will have greater choices in the future.

Retail Selling Environment

Major elements involved in a retail sale are the outlet and its policies, its merchandise, its promotion policies, its customers, and its salespeople. Salespeople need to be familiar with the store and its policies before they can offer the customer any reliable advice. First, the salesperson must know the types, price ranges, and quality of merchandise that the outlet has available. Second, the individual must know what services the store offers to its customers. A salesperson must be knowledgeable about the firm's delivery, credit, adjustment, and product/service offerings to serve customers effectively. A working knowledge of entire store layout is helpful in locating merchandise for consumers who have difficulty finding specific items.

The store's promotion policy should be another vital area of concern to the sales staff. The sales organization should understand the promotion mix concept so they know that advertising, sales promotion, and personal selling require coordinated teamwork to communicate with consumers successfully. The sales personnel should keep informed of the store's promotional activities by previewing and reading its advertisements, looking at its displays, and attending promotion meetings.

Credibility

Useful merchandise information may be found by the salesperson on the label, tag, or package of the product and in wholesale or retail catalogs. Salespeople who represent manufacturers and wholesalers are excellent sources of information. Independent testing bureaus are another good informational source because their findings can be quoted to customers to enhance the credibility of the presentation.

The customer should be the focus of attention in every sale. The salesperson should realize that when a sale is made, the consumer must be pleased with the approach used and relatively satisfied with the outlet's merchandise and services if the sale is going to be of long-run benefit to the store. Thus, salespeople need to sell from the consumer viewpoint. To do this, the salesperson must be aware of consumer psychology and buying motives. Merchandise is purchased because it satisfies some consumer need for beauty, pride, romance, feeling important, comfort, convenience, durability, safety, health, or economy. Salespeople should attempt to identify each consumer's primary buying motives and determine what pleases or irritates that person.

Customers may be happily surprised when sales personnel have a thorough knowledge of the store's merchandise. The amount of information needed varies with the type of merchandise sold and the clientele served. High-priced products, such as automobiles, generally require the salesperson to be more knowledgeable. The salesperson should know the identity of the manufacturer, the ingredients or raw materials in the merchandise, its construction, color, size, model, and so forth. In addition, the salesperson should know what the product is used for, how it should be used, how it performs, and how much care and service it may require. Knowledgeable salespersons will acquire appropriate competitive product knowledge through their comparative shopping efforts so that they may answer customer objections and highlight their product's superior points.

The salesperson is the final element in the retail sale. Characteristics that are associated with successful retail salespeople may be discussed under five categories: objectivity, personal appearance, sociability, maturity, and mental alertness.[1]

Objectivity refers to the ability of salespeople to understand consumers from the individual consumer's point of view. By being objective, the salesperson can empathize with customers and then interpret their needs. Subjective salespersons are more concerned with forcing their own values and solutions on consumers than with solving the consumer's problems. Thus, subjective salespeople are not likely to be successful retail sales generators.

A good personal appearance is required to make a good initial impression on the consumer. The salesperson who is well groomed, poised, and uses correct speech and a pleasant tone of voice creates a good impression and gains the respect of consumers.

Sociability

Sociability—the traits required to create an atmosphere in which consumers enjoy making purchases—includes the enthusiasm displayed by salespeople and the ability to deal tactfully and courteously with consumers without offending them. Friendly retail salespeople make consumers feel welcome and greet them by name if possible. Salespeople who are confident about themselves give consumers the impression that they are receiving worthwhile opinions and suggestions.

Emotionally mature salespeople handle unpleasant situations

smoothly because they are more understanding. They listen without judging and are better able to interpret the consumer's needs. Mature salespeople are also more dependable and industrious in being on the job and working hard to generate sales.

Mentally alert salespeople help make a sale by remembering customers and being knowledgeable about the features of the product/service offering that would best meet their demands and purchase capabilities. Salespersons must also use their imagination to interpret customers' needs in terms of the available merchandise/service opportunities. Retail salespeople must also be accurate in their handling of countless details and still remain courteous to all customers.

Selling Process

After the salesperson has an understanding of the retail selling environment, he or she should consider the selling process. The selling process is a systematic series of steps needed to make a successful sale. These steps include: the approach, the sales presentation, handling objections, and the close.[2] Each segment of the process must be well planned and executed if the salesperson's time and efforts are to be rewarded with sales and satisfied customers.

Prospecting: Identifying Potential Customers

Retail salespersons must tailor their initial customer contact methods to suit the buying habits of their target market clients. "Big-ticket" items such as automobiles, home furnishings, and insurance require salespersons to "prospect" or find the majority of their clients outside of the confines of a store and persuade them to "invest" in new retail products. Names and addresses of potential prospects can be gained through the purchase or rental of magazine lists, automobile registrations, and business or entertainment and travel charge account lists. Additional names may be gathered by regularly checking school graduation lists, and engagement, wedding, and birth announcements in the local newspaper as well as by checking the public records of real estate transactions.

Additional prospect leads may be acquired through company advertising, promotional contests that require participants to register for a prize, and referrals from friends, acquaintances, and satisfied customers. Most of these prospects may have to be contacted off the premises, while others will present themselves by walking through the doors of the establishment. Regardless of the sales contact locale, each potential prospect must be systematically evaluated, or qualified, so that the limited time and energies of the salesperson may be used to best advantage.

Prospective Buyers

Qualifying Prospects: Lookers vs. Buyers What characterizes a good prospect? A good prospect must be reasonably easy to approach or contact, be aware of unmet personal needs or wants, have the ability to buy, have authority to buy without restrictions from important "others" such as wives or husbands, be capable of legally contracting to buy, and be able to reasonably view the salesperson's products as satisfying his or her needs.[3]

As an illustration of how qualifying factors work, any male appearing alone in an automobile showroon wearing a wedding band is considered a marginal prospect for the immediate sale of a new car or truck. Research has shown that most automobile decisions in a family are a collaborative effort. The male may determine the brand and technical product attributes while the female may decide body style, exterior color, and interior decor, although these decision areas often shift from one partner to another. Thus, a married couple would constitute a better opportunity or prospect for a sale than the lone married male.

Qualifying information is gained usually by conversation over the telephone or in the establishment during the initial encounter between the salesperson and the potential customer. Salespersons who attempt to sell products that require considerable expense or decision time will usually qualify their clients before they initiate the first contact by checking with friends, business associates, and others to determine the target client's "ability to deal."

Approach: Bridging the Gap between Salesperson and Client

Most in-store contacts require quick prospecting, qualification, and choice of a proper approach. Usually people visit a store for one of two purposes: (1) to make a specific purchase, or (2) to browse, "kill time," or "just shop." Experienced salespersons have learned to respond differently to a variety of initial customer requests. When customers ask to see a specific item, the product approach is used. The salesperson immediately moves to the merchandise requested and lets the product sell itself. One assumes that customers have clearly perceived their needs and are interested in making the purchase. The objective of the product approach is to get the item in the potential customer's hands so that he or she can feel the potential psychological value associated with possessing the item. When the customer is made aware of the psychological satisfaction and the physical utility of the item, the urge to purchase becomes almost irresistible.

Alternately, if the initial customer response is one of uncertainty, but general interest is expressed in a product line, the service approach is appropriate. The main objective of this approach is to focus the customer's need and direct attention to the firm's specific product that will best meet this need. Quite often this approach is used by saying to the customer, "May I help you?" "Do you need help?" or "What do you want?" Unfortunately each one of these opening questions can be answered with an emphatic negative, which terminates the sales contact. An alternate set of questions might be "What may I show you?" or "How may I help you?" The questions clearly convey the desire to be of service as well as eliciting information that may lead to the sales presentation.

Browsing Customers

The browsing customer represents a challenge because that individual is primarily spending leisure time and is only marginally interested in specific products. Suggestive selling leading to an impulse purchase will require the customer-benefit approach.[4] As the customer wanders through the store, the salesperson should select some new unique item that might appeal to the customer and direct his or her attention to the unique product benefits without mentioning price. This approach requires a low keyed, helpful, informative approach such as, "Have you seen the new _____?" Here, a "no" leads into a sales presentation and a sale because the benefits are undeniable.

In summary, a good approach should attract the potential customer's attention in an appropriate manner, encourage the potential buyer to focus attention on a specific need-satisfying product, and provide a direct entry into a sales presentation. A successful approach concludes the first third of the path to a satisfying sale.

Sales Presentation

Showcase Selling

The sales presentation is the "showcase of selling." The product's most beneficial attributes are stressed and the negative factors minimized. A successful sales presentation is based on a positive, enthusiastic attitude toward the product being displayed or demonstrated. The salesperson should invest his or her personal credibility in each sales presentation. Such an approach stresses factual information, personal experience, and customer satisfaction features. The sales presentation must convey to the potential customer the sincere conviction that the salesperson has the best product for the individual's needs.

The purchase decision is a complex phenomenon. One authority postulates that the buying decision is composed of five separate stages.[5] The first stage is usually characterized by the customer's overt recognition of a need or a problem that is important enough to require attention. This recognition leads to implementation of a search process to find satisfaction.

In the pursuit of satisfaction the customer searches for products or services that will yield adequate satisfaction at an affordable price. In order to arrive at a satisfactory solution to their problems, customers seek information, advice, and personal assurances that products will meet their needs. As the search process begins the customer enters the second buying stage which is typified by the statement, "I'm interested in hearing what you have to say about my problem."[6]

The salesperson's role consists of translating the merchandise/service features into individualized consumer benefits and advantages. The salesperson must be able to talk and listen well in this consumer problem-solving approach. The sales presentation should be short enough to make shopping a pleasant but businesslike experience. Naturally, arguments should be avoided and the consumer's feeling of risk in buying reduced by assurances that the store is reliable, the brand is dependable, and the salesperson has a personal interest in seeing that the customer is properly served. It is the salesperson's job to make the customer feel important. The consumers must believe that they are **buying,** not being *sold.*

Exhibit 15.1   Retail Salespeople Are Vital to Retailer's Promotional Efforts

Source: Photo courtesy of Pay'n Save Corporation, Public Relations.

The salesperson should present merchandise that reflects what he or she perceives will satisfy the customer's needs. A request to see a certain item simplifies the interpretation process and the salesperson can immediately show the desired item. In most cases the consumer may be a little vague. If this is the case, the salesperson must present merchandise that seems to satisfy the consumer's desires. The first merchandise shown is usually medium-price items.

Then the salesperson must decide whether to attempt **trading up.** Trading up consists of selling either a better-quality item or a larger quantity than the consumer intended to buy. Frequently, better-quality merchandise will last longer and/or need less service and thus generate more long-run consumer satisfaction than the lower-quality item requested by the customer. To use trading-up selling, a salesperson must know the product line and be able to point out the benefits of buying better merchandise. The approach should not be misleading or dishonest but an objective evaluation of the item's future benefit for the customer.

When the store is out of stock on the item requested, the consumer should be informed of the unavailability of the item immediately. If the outlet has something in that line which will satisfy the consumer, that item should be presented to the consumer when the out-of-stock condition is determined. The requested product should not be criticized but the benefits of the in-stock item should be pointed out.

Demonstrating or showing merchandise involves several considerations. First, it is desirable to obtain consumer participation by asking the person to handle or operate it just as he or she would in normal use. Second, the way the salesperson handles the merchandise shows personal respect for the item. The demonstration should also show the advantages promised by the salesperson. This stage concludes with the effective salesperson summarizing his or her case as convincingly as possible so that the potential buyer will arrive at the third stage of the buying process.

If the salesperson has a thorough knowledge of the product and its appropriate application, and conveys these need-satisfying qualities in an effective persuasive manner, the customer will become convinced that "I need this product."[7] The alert salesperson can sense this third stage by picking up such cues as facial expressions, voice inflections, and other body language signs. These same indicators can signal negative responses or objections to the product being presented. Every salesperson must be prepared to deal with customer objections.

Meeting Objections

Consumer uncertainty in areas of product, price, and time gives rise to most buying resistance. Thus, the salesperson is frequently dealing with a customer who is not completely certain that the product under consideration is the best buy.

Good salespeople learn to anticipate consumer objections and incorporate answers to the objections into presentation of the merchandise. By presenting the most appropriate items from a consumer viewpoint, the salesperson reduces the amount of product objections. By pointing out all the benefits offered by the item, the salesperson reduces the importance of the price objections by emphasizing value instead of cost.

Time objections usually come in the form of a customer's saying, "I'll have to think it over." The salesperson might agree that some thought is desirable before making the purchase, and then point out that the store allows merchandise to be taken home on approval or on credit with a liberal return policy.

Frequently, time objections are excuses that are supposed to conceal the real reason the consumer does not want to make the purchase. Such excuses are more difficult to handle than real objections because they do not reflect the honest opinion of the customer. Thus, the real objection is not defined so that the salesperson can meet it. Further questions may be asked in an attempt to identify the objection. If this fails, the salesperson should not argue or belittle the customer's opinion.

The entire process of meeting objections should inspire consumer confidence in the quality of the merchandise and the knowledgeability of the salesperson. Additionally, finishing this phase will complete the second third of the road to a successful sale.

Closing the Sale

Closing the sale involves the last two stages of the buying process. The customer mentally says, "I want to buy this product now" and "I will buy this product now from this salesperson."[8]

Acquiring the Sale

Successfully meeting all of the customer's objections leads the customer to accept the product as appropriate, useful, and affordable, but does not guarantee a sale. The gentle art of persuasion must lead the customer skillfully to actually implement the purchase. Mentally agreeing with persuasive arguments is a significantly different act involving a lesser degree of personal commitment than signing a check or a credit agreement or counting out the cash. Thus, closing or asking for the order is a complicated process in itself and must be considered an art that is developed after much experience.

All closing techniques rely on the assumption that all

product-related objections have been answered and a sale will take place if the appropriate implementative actions are taken. Professor Buskirk proposes six different closing approaches to be used in differing situations. These assumptive closing approaches include: (1) the physical action, (2) closing on an objection, (3) SRO (standing room only), (4) closing on a minor point, (5) the inducement close, and (6) asking for the order.[9]

Briefly, the physical close simply requires the salesperson to put his or her body in motion to implement the sale, such as marking any needed clothing alterations so the merchandise will better fit the buyer. Closing on an objection is often used by car salespersons by having the customer sign an offer to purchase that is lower than the list price. Then the salesperson goes to the sales manager who usually agrees and accepts "the deal." This approach quickly separates the lookers from the buyers and saves the salesperson valuable sales time to devote to other customers.

SRO

The standing room only (SRO) close technique stresses the need for immediate action to secure the last item of a limited supply of the product. Urgency is stressed, with the implication that if the customer is not willing to accept the proposition the next person standing in line will be delighted to accept the offer. Admittedly, this close seems more appropriate as products become scarce. This is a risky close because the customer has the opportunity to say, "No, thank you." On the positive side, such a close does force an immediate decision.

Closing on a minor point approach is often appropriate when the customer has difficulty selecting between two equally favorable products that the salesperson has presented. Usually these closes take the form of a question such as, "Which color do you like best, the metallic brown or the blue model?" One should note that the question contains the implicit assumption of purchase and the only decision left to be made by the customer is which one will best meet his or her tastes or needs. Most importantly, such a question is not answerable with a simple no, which keeps the potential sale alive.

Inducement

The inducement close is usually based on the "bargain" philosophy. Such concession closes usually are made by increasing the product's seeming value by throwing in or offering something for "free" or immediate delivery which will appeal to the buyer's possession need. Such gestures of good will often result in significant sales at a considerable profit with minor cost or inconvenience to the salesperson or employing firm.

The last and most direct close involves directly asking for the purchase or order.[10] This direct approach is the most risky but is often appreciated by time-conscious customers. Once they have been persuaded to purchase the item, the actual transaction is anticlimactic and a nuisance to be handled expeditiously. If a person starts reaching for a wallet, purse, or pen, the sale should be closed by asking for the order.

In summary, the selling process provides a mechanism to examine buyer-seller relationships. Each transaction is unique, but the negotiation process follows predictable buying stages. Salespersons must use all their skill and knowledge to be sure each stage is successfully negotiated. The end result should be personal satisfaction for the customer, a feeling of accomplishment for the salesperson, a profit for the firm, and the continued functioning of our complex marketing-distribution system.

Developing Customer Good Will

A sincere expression of gratitude for the purchase is required before the consumer departs. In addition to indicating it was a pleasure to serve each consumer, the customer might be sent away by name. Attempts should be made to follow up on major purchases to determine if the customer was really satisfied, and why or why not. Consumers should be thanked for their interest even though they may not have made a purchase. Such actions promote customer good will that has a long-lasting effect.

Telephone Selling

Reminder Call

Telephone selling is used by retailers and service firms to generate additional business and smooth the work schedule of sales and service personnel. Service firms benefit by making a "reminder call" the day before an appointment is scheduled to assure a full schedule the next day. Reminder telephone calls made by firms selling merchandise or services that are purchased on a regular basis can stimulate additional sales from regular customers who should be ready to repurchase the item or service. For example, dentists can call regular customers after a proper interval has passed and remind customers to have their teeth cleaned and checked. Appointments can be scheduled for hours and days when the dentist is least busy. The same type of reminder system can be used by auto service stations that know the proper interval for oil and lube jobs, tune ups, and seasonal changeovers for individual customers.

This process requires a detailed follow-up file of index cards that identify the consumer, the last date of purchase, and the type of item or service purchased. The solicitation is brief and friendly. The call should be made at a time when it is convenient for the consumer to talk. House persons should not be called at hours when they may be preparing meals. Naturally, solicitations should be made from a telephone other than the one designated to receive the firm's incoming calls.

**Personal Selling
Outside the Store**

Contacting Newcomers

Welcome Wagon, Howdy Pardner, and other organizations are engaged in acquainting newcomers with local retailers. These organizations send their representatives to the homes of new residents to give them free gifts from numerous local retailers. The cost of sending their representatives to consumers' homes is spread over all participating retailers. Providing free gift coupons to those new consumers in the trading area is a good way to introduce these people to a firm's location and its merchandise/service offering. It is important that the regular in-store clerks accept the gift coupons with a high degree of enthusiasm. Poor follow-through at the store level will negate any good will obtained by the initial contact.

Because store loyalties are frequently established soon after the newcomer has relocated, getting the consumer's attention during this crucial period can yield good results. Approximately 20 percent of the U.S. population moves during a year, so the size of this mobile market segment is substantial.

Successful sales can begin in a store and conclude in the home. Many large department and some chain stores employ salespersons as interior decorators or coordinators. They take various samples of carpeting, draperies, and paint to the home at convenient times to work out custom applications of ready-made merchandise. Limited custom fitting is also available on such items as draperies, slipcovers, and tile installations. In the future this kind of additional service, for home decoration in particular, should become more prevalent and profitable as the number of new household formations increases.

**Evaluation of
the Personal
Sales Program**

Every store should have a continual training program for both new and experienced salespeople. Sales records offer an overall indicator of a person's performance. Dollar volume of sales, units sold, number of completed transactions, and gross margin contribution can indicate the sales performance of employees and identify any need for specific training. In addition, the percentage of consumer contacts that resulted in purchases can be obtained by dividing the number of transactions by the number of customer contacts. A dollar per consumer contact figure can be calculated by dividing the dollar sales volume by the number of consumer contacts.

Regardless of the type of evaluation, it is necessary that the evaluation procedure be based on job-related criteria and be thoroughly understood by each salesperson. It is also important that the method of evaluation be seen as objective and fair by all employees. This may be difficult because some retail salespeople do more than merely sell. They may provide customer service, handle complaints, accept merchandise returns, stock shelves, wrap merchandise, and perform other housekeeping duties.

Compensating Salespeople

Retail salespeople are usually paid a **straight salary,** which is either a prespecified monthly salary or a predetermined hourly wage. The straight salary approach allows the store manager to direct a salesperson's activities more closely, and includes more shelf stocking, price marking, and so forth. However, it may not provide much incentive for the salesperson to make sales.

Rewarding Behavior

The **straight commission** method of compensation rewards salespeople only on the basis of their sales volume. At the end of a pay period, an employee's sales are multiplied by the pre-specified percentage commission rate to determine his or her earnings. This plan provides considerable incentive for salespersons because their earnings are solely dependent on making sales. The commission method also allows dollar selling expense to be more flexible from a retailer's point of view. Employee compensation is reduced when sales volume declines and increased when sales volume increases. Reduction in compensation during a period of slack sales is not desirable from the employee's point of view because income is uncertain. Thus, the salesperson may ask to borrow from a drawing account against anticipated commissions. In addition, it is difficult to encourage a salesperson who is compensated on a straight commission basis to perform housekeeping duties that do not directly increase sales.

Combination salary and commission or bonus plans are frequently used for compensating salespeople. The bonus or commission added to a straight salary provides an incentive to make sales and still maintains control over employee activities. The bonus may be a cash bonus or a premium bonus of merchandise or a service—anything from clocks to a television set to an automobile. The premium bonus is an especially attractive incentive for higher-paid employees, who may be influenced by members of their family who want to use the premium. The cash bonus may be more appealing to lower-income employees, since their need to purchase necessities may be quite high.

Fringe benefits are another way to compensate employees. Employee discounts on in-store purchases, medical and life insurance, savings plans, and profit-sharing plans may all be used to better compensate the employee. Fringe benefits can increase employee morale and encourage store loyalty. Deferred profit-sharing and savings plans encourage good salespeople to remain with the retail organization.

In review, the authors feel that the art and skill of personal selling is woefully deficient in our retail institutions. A combination of forces has led to the present state of cash-wrap transaction specialists. While such depersonalization and the mechanical approach to sales transactions seem to reduce selling costs and increase the dollar per square foot of sales for presold products, many profitable dollars are to be made in rendering a personal selling service in narrow-line, big ticket, fashion-oriented, specialized stores. The consuming public who patronize these establishments will recognize professional expertise and reward the individual and store with personal referrals. A career in retail selling can be personally satisfying and economically rewarding if the aspiring candidate chooses the proper segment of the industry and plies the trade diligently.

Customer Services

Customer services are designed to custom tailor a product offering to the unique needs of a customer. Credit extension, garment alteration, appliance installation, product repair, gift wrapping, and delivery are all services rendered by employees of a retail firm. These are people-to-people transactions. Therefore, each employee becomes a potential salesperson as they interact with their customers. The execution of each customer's transaction reinforces or contradicts his or her previous image of the firm. Hence, every employee who comes into contact with the retailer's customers must act in a professional, efficient, effective manner so that the customer will be satisfied and continue his or her patronage.

In these inflationary times, retailers are experimenting with the concept of "unbundling" their services. In simple terms, they feel that customers should only pay for the services they require. For example, if Texaco customers want to use a credit card they are charged three cents a gallon more than those customers paying cash. Similarly, if an alteration is needed on a garment the customer should pay for that service. Retailers hope that the net result will be moderated price increases in the future, thus attracting a larger share of the target market.

Some retailers have gone beyond the philosophy of "breaking even" on customer services and have adopted the philosophy that each customer service must be viewed as a profit center. If the service can't create a satisfactory return on the invested resource, the service is either leased out or discontinued. As a result, large retailers are making major changes in their customer service offerings and enjoying considerable customer acceptance and approval.

Regardless of a retailer's position on charging for services the firm should establish customer service policies and procedures. These policies must reflect the fact that some services are required to meet offerings by the most competitive outlets. Often the type of merchandise carried influences the degree of service required in the offering. Bulky, high-value items that need to be installed and repaired by experts require more service than small, low-cost items that require little or no maintenance. Higher-quality merchandise is generally associated with higher prices and more service to appeal to the quality-oriented consumer group. On the other hand, bargain merchandise is usually sold with little service. Business hours such as late-morning openings, evening and limited Sunday hours are often required to blend with the customers' shopping patterns. Customers' lifestyles may dictate offering child-care facilities for shopping mothers, a package checkroom, personal shoppers, party counseling and catering services, entertainment ticket facilities, travel bureaus, and post offices on the premises.

Store location may dictate that the firm must provide services to meet the needs of its customers. For example, a furniture store that is located far from the residences of its target market may have to offer delivery services.

The retailer must choose the firm's service offerings from the consumer's point of view and cast them within the parameters of certain federal government edicts, particularly in the areas of credit and warranty maintenance. In general, inclusion of certain service components enhances the perceived utility of products and services and often becomes an integral part of a product purchase decision. Free coffee in a small consumer lounge area, clean rest rooms, free minor repairs, and so forth cost little but generate considerable good will. Other services, such as maintenance contracts for major appliances, package and gift wrapping, delivery, credit, and merchandise refunds and exchanges represent larger monetary expenditures and thus require further discussion.

Credit

Consumer credit in retail stores is now almost an institution. Barring serious social or economic disturbances such as a depression, it is almost a permanent retailing tool. Although credit sales have grown tremendously since World War II, they are not new to retailing but, instead, have changed in form and amount. Retailers have discovered that credit can be a powerful merchandising tool.

Credit Advantages

Customer convenience in paying for an item or service can be as important (or more important) a selling tool as advertising, personal selling, or promotion. Sometimes credit can be the major difference in influencing the decision to shop one store instead of a competitor's. More generous credit terms may make a prospective customer consider the retailer's total product more favorably. The advantages of using in-house credit are:

1. A more personal relationship can be maintained with credit customers who feel they are part of the firm.
2. Credit customers are likely to be more loyal than cash customers who tend to go where bargains are the greatest.
3. Credit customers tend to be more interested in quality and service than in price.
4. Good will is built up and maintained more easily when credit is used.
5. Goods can be exchanged and adjustments made with greater ease and, if necessary, goods can also be sent out on approval.
6. Credit account records provide valuable market information which will allow the firm to:
   a. have a permanent mailing list for special sales promotions or research projects.
   b. discover opportunities for suggesting the purchase of certain items considered appropriate in the light of previous purchases, buying habits, and so forth.
   c. gather material concerning sales by department or by individual sales personnel.
   d. detect any decline in purchases that might suggest a drifting away from the firm.
7. The firm's return on investment can increase if credit stimulates sales, because additional business can be secured and sometimes handled at practically no additional expense thereby reducing per unit costs.[11]

Whenever credit is extended by the retail outlet, it costs money. However, many retailers believe that credit extension is both necessary and attractive. Apparently, many target customers find immediate possession important enough to outweigh any extra costs.

Increase Sales with Credit

Individual retailers have demonstrated that demand for their products and services can be increased with credit. In addition, total retail industry demand has increased through the use of credit. Whereas other promotion techniques, such as trading stamps, simply shift purchase patterns from one retailer to another, credit increases total demand for goods and services.

Without credit, the demand for consumer durables such as refrigerators, boats, and automobiles would shrink markedly. The establishment of an installment credit department, General Motors Acceptance Corporation (GMAC), by General Motors played an important part in the tremendous marketing success of this firm.

Commercial bankers traditionally have been slow to finance new consumer durables, particularly when the payback period seemed long. However, this policy is changing rapidly, and the progressive banks and credit unions are broadening their loan portfolios and extending gradually lengthening maturities.

A sales program aimed at acquainting bankers with the merits of a new consumer durable should be a first-step combination effort of retailers, the trade association, distributors, and manufacturers of these products. This is of particular importance to independent retailers who operate without the benefit of a credit plan backed by the manufacturer. Retailers of mobile homes, campers, sailboats, and snowmobiles are examples.

Credit Disadvantages

An ill-conceived credit policy is responsible for an increasing number of business failures. Dun & Bradstreet has found that receivables difficulties rank first as a fundamental cause of business failures.[12] Poor credit and collection practices have contributed a disproportionate share to the unchecked upsurge in receivables. Proper evaluation of the credit policy is essential if it is to be implemented in a profitable manner.

Some other disadvantages of using in-house credit are:

1. The firm's capital is tied up in merchandise bought by charge customers.
2. If the merchant has borrowed the extra money required when credit is granted, the interest is added to the cost.
3. Some losses from bad debts and customers with fraudulent intentions are bound to occur.
4. Credit customers feel more at liberty to abuse the privileges of returning goods and having goods sent out on approval.
5. Credit increases operation and overhead costs by adding to the expenses of investigation, bookkeeping, sending out statements and collecting payments.[13]

Deciding Whether to Offer In-House Credit

Credit can stimulate sales, but its profitability is influenced by:

1. How much sales are increased by using credit.
2. How large the gross profit margin is on the goods being sold.
3. How fast the money on credit sales is received by the retailer.

4. The cost of financing this credit balance.
5. The cost of maintaining the credit system.
6. The loss incurred by bad debts.[14]

Gross Profit Margin

One of the most significant factors that influences the decision to grant credit is the gross profit margin received on the store's merchandise. Other things being equal, credit is more likely to be profitable if the profit margin is high. Thus, credit must stimulate sales considerably if credit usage is going to be profitable in retail outlets that have a low profit margin.

Naturally, proper handling of accounts receivable is required to keep consumers current on their payments and to reduce bad debts. (Accounts receivable records are discussed in more detail in Chapter 18.) Screening applicants for credit by checking with the local retail credit bureau can also reduce the incidence of bad debts and result in faster recovery of the retailer's money.

Other factors, such as the amount of capital available to the retailer, the credit policies of direct competitors, and the general consumer insistence that credit be granted also influence the retailer's decision of granting or not granting credit.

Kinds of Retail Credit

If the retailer decides to offer credit, the firm must evaluate the different types of credit available and choose the one that best meets its needs.

Bank credit plans, such as VISA and Master Charge, allow retail customers to use a credit account they have established with a financial institution. Customers can charge purchases at any participating outlet. Billing, recordkeeping, and collection activities are performed by the financial agency. This arrangement costs the retailer from 2 to 5 percent of the credit card sales volume. The exact rate depends upon the bargaining position of the retailer and the degree of competition between various bank credit card agencies. In return for this charge, a retailer transfers the work involved with offering credit and the responsibility for collecting unpaid bills to the financial institution. The retailer receives cash for bank credit card purchases when the charge slips are deposited in the participating bank.

The **thirty-day open account plan** is administered by the retailer who allows consumers to charge merchandise and pay the full amount within thirty days of the billing date. Interest is usually not charged unless a payment is not received when it is due.

The **revolving credit plan** divides the unpaid account balance into equal monthly payments, but approximately 1½ percent per month interest charge is made on the remaining balance if the account is not paid in full by the stated due date. Each customer has a credit limit that cannot be exceeded, but otherwise customers can charge and make payments to meet their needs, provided a minimal payment is made each month.

Deferred payment plans allow purchasers of large items to make equal monthly payments for the value of the merchandise, plus a carrying charge. Because the agreement involves only the particular item purchased, a separate agreement must be made on each item. Installment contracts, which are one type of deferred payment agreement, let the title to the goods stay with the retailer until the provisions of the contract have been fulfilled. Under installment contracts, payments are scheduled so that the remaining balance due is always less than the current market value of the depreciated merchandise.

Merchandising Maintenance and Repair: Service Contracts

Many large chain stores have found that it is profitable to be in the repair and home improvement business. Partially in response to passage of the Consumer Products Warranty and Guaranty Act of 1970 and in an effort to find additional sources of profitable merchandising, they have begun to actively promote their "service contract" product. Usually, as part of a closing approach for complicated expensive appliances, salespersons are encouraged to suggest the purchase of a service contract that covers the product for one, two, or five years from the date of purchase.

Service contracts provide varying degrees of guaranteed product performance at a range of competitive prices. For example, a customer can purchase a service contract at the time of product purchase that will guarantee product replacement for a year for a nominal $20 to $25. As contract life and replacement provisions are extended, the cost of the contract rises substantially up to a limit of five years. Thereafter, the useful life of the product is assumed to be realized and the customer assumes the full risk of repair or replacement.

Obviously, the rates for service contracts have been carefully calculated and related to average product life so that the odds of having to pay off are stacked in favor of the retailer. However, many customers would prefer to have such guaranteed protec-

In-Home Service

tion, which often includes in-home service, than be bothered with seeking out competent technicians and possibly be deprived of that appliance while it is in the shop for repair. Accurate cost/profit data on this new service are not available, but increasingly more large retailers are experimenting with this and other customer services such as home decoration, insulation installation, fence construction, reroofing, and auto repair as another means of providing customer satisfaction in a profitable fashion.

**Packaging and
Gift Wrapping**

A discussion of retail packaging cannot be confined to the product as it arrives from the manufacturer. In the long run, the retailer may have an important influence over the shape, size, color, and weight of the packaged product. However, in most cases the firm is relatively powerless to change the manufacturer's package. Thus, the primary responsibility for branded product packaging rests directly upon the manufacturer. It is critical for manufacturers to understand the problems and complexities of retailing so that their package designs can meet these needs.

There are, however, two areas of packaging over which certain retailers can exercise substantial control: gift packaging and bulk in-store packaging. The department store, in particular, has discovered a rich opportunity for increased profits, customer good will, and image building through use of these services.

The practice of offering free gift wrapping service for purchases can help create a favorable image of the store through the color and style of the package and may aid in establishing repeat sales or new customers. Nevertheless, this traditional approach

Cost versus Profit Center

to gift wrapping must be viewed as a cost center rather than profit generation. Many of the traditional gift wrapping centers also suffer from a lack of coordination as part of the store's total objective. They are simply areas of the store in which pretty wrappings are placed on merchandise.

Maximum benefits to a store can never be gained with this view of gift wrapping. Instead, gift wrapping must be viewed as a coordinated and integral part of the entire retailing system within a store. A coordinated and professional approach to gift wrapping can bring major rewards to retailers.

The package will become an integral part of the total image desired by a store. It can say much more than "I am a pretty package." By identifying the outlet tastefully on the wrapping, it can convey a store's total image of good taste, fashion, and styling—and to an audience far in excess of the buyer. Such packages will be seen by guests at showers, weddings, graduations, and dozens of other gift-giving occasions.

The package may be a part of the point-of-purchase display area. Wide lines of designs and materials are available to retailers from predesigned package manufacturers. Retailers can now buy packages just as they do the merchandise to fill them. These are professional designs, which generally are sold to a retailer with the guarantee that the store will have exclusivity on this design within a particular market area. Yearly package designs are made incorporating new trends and fashions. Professionally styled packages add to the point-of-purchase appeal of products and also help to differentiate departments or areas within departments.

The package itself can be sold at an excellent margin of profit. Thus, what was once a cost center can become one of profit, while corporate goals are enhanced.

Reinforce Store Image

Bulk, in-store packaging is of growing importance to the department store retailer who is facing a serious problem of maintaining a unique image. With the growth of shopping centers, many retailers have tended to become more alike in appearance. In addition, manufacturers have altered or eliminated their policies of brand exclusivity. Moreover, it must be admitted that competing brands have taken on an appearance of similarity. Brand names that at one time meant exclusivity and uniqueness now are simply competing brands.

Several leading department stores have discovered that a new and unique package can be created in the store by packaging several items together in a box, bag, tote bag, or other container. As an example, selected brands and scents of toiletries may be placed together in a unique box and sold as a single item. In this way the retailer is able to sell multiple products at one time in a container that is unique. In addition, the retailer is able to incorporate the price of the box with full markup into the total package price. The obvious problem with this is the selection of the right merchandise for the package at the right price.

Delivery

Offering delivery service to customers can be a competitive tool that can create a unique image for the retailer. Many customers do not like to carry large packages while they are moving from one store to another. Urban customers who depend on public transportation and older or physically disabled consumers are likely to respond favorably to a retailer's delivery service. Therefore delivery service can be an important part of the retailing effort in reaching these market segments. Delivery service can also expand a retailer's sales if the delivery person is alert and can recognize additional consumer needs.

When delivery service is indicated, the firm must make two decisions: (1) will they charge for the service, and if so, what will the service cost, and (2) how will the firm implement the service decision, that is, will they own it, contract it out, or use a co-op system? Each option has associated advantages and disadvantages and all options will involve significant added cost of operation. The simplest mode of delivery for a small store is to put the merchandise in the owner's vehicle and make the delivery. In many states this pragmatic approach may be technically illegal because the vehicle becomes a commercial carrier subject to commercial licensing and can only be operated by a person with a commercial license. If the private vehicle should be in an accident while being commercially operated, the litigation could become very expensive.

Once a firm outgrows the single vehicle delivery system, it usually turns to contracting for the service as needed. Perhaps the best known and most used contractors are the United Parcel Service (UPS) and the U.S. Postal System. The main advantage is that actual delivery costs are known and little managerial time is devoted to overseeing this facet of the operation. Disadvantages include loss of control over the quality of handling the merchandise will receive on the way to the customer; increased chance for theft, breakage, or loss of goods; and an increased opportunity for customer dissatisfaction as a result of untimely deliveries or discourteous, inconsiderate delivery people.

When contract delivery becomes unsatisfactory, many firms attempt to establish a cooperative arrangement to share costs while retaining control of the service. Specific legal agreements must be drawn up to assign certain responsibilities and costs, rent trucks, and hire delivery personnel. Usually this is a short-term arrangement on the road to individual ownership of delivery fleets as the demands of each cooperating firm change.

When a large retail firm with multiple units or several branch stores offers delivery services, the firm must consider the costs of buying or leasing a commercial fleet of trucks; employing and training commercially licensed delivery people; planning timely, appropriate, and efficient delivery routes and schedules; and incurring the full cost of operation and maintenance of the fleet. Offsetting these costs are the advantages of convenient transfer of goods between stores; direct authority to control theft, loss, and damage of delivered merchandise, and direct expense control. Maximum utilization is needed if the optimum benefit is to be achieved. In any event, delivery costs can quickly exceed profit margins and what started out as perhaps a limited, free service becomes a pervasive and prohibitive expense. At this point retail firms usually either institute a competitive service charge for delivery services, which may not cover the entire cost but will make a sizable contribution to offset the incurred costs, or offer discounts for customer pick-up.

In the final analysis, if the decision to offer delivery services is made, the kind and geographical scope must be determined only after careful, thorough cost/benefit analysis and then there must be periodic reviews to determine if the costs truly represent a competitive advantage or disadvantage for the firm.

Parking Facilities

Plentiful, well-lighted, and well-maintained parking space costs retailers untold dollars. Original land and construction costs for a large shopping center parking area are significant. Careless patrons, vandals, and ordinary wear and tear take their toll, and periodically the area must be resurfaced and refixtured. This "free" service is often taken for granted and expected by the consuming public. In fact, some studies indicate that certain shopping centers have flourished partly as a result of readily available, convenient, noncongested parking facilities.

Downtown merchants are at a distinct competitive disadvantage because of limited, costly, inconvenient parking and general traffic congestion. Parking space in some downtown areas may be so limited that retail firms may have to join together to purchase vacant buildings and convert them into parking facilities to encourage increased patronage. Alternately, when public transportation is available, downtown merchant associations may sponsor reduced fares during off-peak hours to encourage senior citizens and others to shop downtown. Even then these efforts have been negated by an increasing number of crimes and purse snatchings in which older citizens and women are primary targets. Increased police protection and urban renewal have been partial answers to these problems, but big city core retailers continue to labor under considerable disadvantages.

Procurement and Management of Leased-Space Customer Facilities

Often large department and chain stores find a need for a customer service that they do not feel is within their expertise nor one that they wish to develop, but it does offer a possible profit center if managed effectively. The classic example of such a venture is the leased-spaced optical department in most large Sears and Roebuck stores. The space is leased to an optician who provides the equipment and supplies for dispensing eyeglasses. Often the same vendor will provide the supportive staff during extended store hours to handle broken glasses or replacement orders that customers drop off during their regular shopping. Usually lease arrangements provide for Sears to receive a minimum space rental fee plus a percentage of the gross sales. In return the independent vendor gets high volume traffic, accepts Sears credit cards, and participates occasionally in the regular Sears promotion program. All three parties seem to benefit: the customer, the chain or department store, and the independent service operator.

Customer Consumerism

Retailers are becoming increasingly aware of the need to practice effective consumerism. Woodward and Lathrop demonstrated its concern for the customer by putting its furniture service center in its main downtown store just adjacent to the retail furniture department. It was staffed by fifteen employees who handled 96,000 customer complaints in one year alone.

Such customer service interests are not limited to department stores. A special section of one edition of *Sales Management* was devoted to customer service management. Such large firms as Honeywell, Otis Elevator, RCA, Maytag, International Harvester's Agricultural Equipment Division, Singer's Business Machines Division, B. F. Goodrich, and United Airlines all have instituted some form of formal organizational mechanism to handle customer complaints effectively.[15]

This rising interest in consumerism has led to the formation of the Society of Consumer Affairs Professionals (SOCAP) and the National Association of Service Managers (NASM) which, between them, have 1400 members spread across the nation. The officer ranks are filled with the Who's Who of industry, including top officers of Bell and Howell, Sears and Roebuck, Montgomery Ward, Firestone Tire and Rubber, and Coca-Cola.[16] The bulk of the memberships is made up of service managers for both large and small firms across America. Perhaps the essence of this movement was captured by Executive Director Marvin Lurie when he remarked, "There's a strong trend in every industry to make service executives responsible for managing [service departments as] profit centers . . ."[17] When viewed in this light, effective customer service and practical consumerism make good dollars and sense for all parties.

Customer Complaints

The way complaints are handled affects the store image and either serves as a way to gain loyal customers or negates any good will built up by various promotional activities. Thus, retailers should establish adjustment procedures that ensure that each dissatisfied customer receives understanding attention.

Complaints arise because of faulty merchandise, unsatisfactory installation or fit, delayed or incorrect delivery, damaged merchandise, errors in billing charge accounts, resentment with credit collection methods, and dissatisfaction with salespeople.[18]

Naturally, a store is obliged to make satisfactory adjustment when the consumer has a legitimate complaint based on any of these reasons. Even if the consumer has no legitimate complaint, complaining consumers nearly always are convinced that they should receive adjustment. Therefore, it is better for a retailer to let the complaining consumer have all the time needed to explain the problem. The adjuster should not argue with the consumer but should suggest that some sort of adjustment can be made.

Generous Adjustment

It is better to give generous adjustment to the customers than to irritate them. Customers who are dissatisfied with an adjustment generally inform their friends of their dissatisfaction, whereas satisfied customers recommend the store to their friends. If possible, many retailers try to satisfy customers with replacement items (which reduces the adjustment cost by the amount of the retail markup). However, the customer must be satisfied, so the adjuster should ask if the adjustment is fair.

Most consumers try to be fair if they believe the adjuster understands their problem and is trying to solve it. A few consumers, of course, are habitual complainers who can never be satisfied. Adjustment records can reveal the identity of such individuals, and they can be discouraged from trading at the outlet.

Retailers should keep detailed adjustment records, not only to identify habitual complainers but also to identify poor merchandise, poor delivery and credit procedures, poor performance in salespeople, and to show compliance with the law. For every reasonable complaining customer, there are likely to be numerous customers who encountered the same problem but simply chose to discontinue trading at that store as a silent protest.

Summary

Each retailer must devote considerable time and resources to personal selling and customer services. These two elements should be effectively integrated into a well-planned promotional mix that insures that a consistent message is communicated to customers.

Perhaps the major message contained in this chapter is that the effort put forth to do a good job of personal selling and the rendering of prompt, efficient customer service can put more dollars in the cash register and contribute profits to the "bottom line." When customer services cease to be viewed as a "free, menial, must-do-grudgingly task" and become an "opportunity to exploit a profitable product," retail employees and customers alike will see customer service as a product to be effectively merchandised and effectively consumed.

Questions

1. Many customers express the opinion that personal salesmanship and helpful customer service is a relic of the past. Should retail managers be concerned? Why or why not? Explain.
2. What role does face-to-face communication play in a successful sales program for retail stores?
3. The concept of self-service pervades large areas of retailing. Is there any need for personal saleship in retailing? Explain.
4. What are the major elements of a retail sale? What role do professional sales personnel play in the transaction process?
5. What are the five stages in buying? How can the sales staff use this information to improve their sales presentations?
6. What is the purpose of a selling approach? How can the different strategies be applied to advance a sale to a successful close?

7. How does a salesperson choose a proper closing strategy to improve the chances for a successful sale?

8. What impact has the Product Warranty and Guaranty Act had on retailers in regard to providing customer services?

9. Can customer services be profitably merchandised? If so, how? Explain.

10. What factors should a small retailer consider in deciding whether to accept bank credit cards to set up the store's own in-house credit operation? Should the firm extend credit both ways?

11. What impact has consumerism had on retail firms, particularly in the area of postpurchase service? Explain.

12. What major points must be considered when a retailer sets up a specific process for handling customer complaints? What should be the ultimate goal of such a program?

Footnotes

1.   Karen R. Gillespie, "Revitalize Personal Selling in Your Store," *Small Marketers Aids Annual No. 9* (Washington, D.C.: Small Business Administration, 1967), pp. 82–89.

2.   Richard H. Buskirk, *Retail Selling: A Vital Approach* (San Francisco: Canfield Press, 1975), pp. 75–166.

3.   Carlton A. Pederson and Milburn D. Wright, *Selling: Principles and Methods.* 6th ed. (Homewood, Ill.: Richard D. Irwin, Inc., 1976), pp. 216–218.

4.   Buskirk, *Retail Selling,* p. 75.

5.   Ibid., pp. 69–73.

6.   Ibid., p. 70.

7.   Ibid., p. 71.

8.   Ibid.

9.   Ibid., pp. 160–165.

10. Ibid., p. 165.

11. John E. Payne, "What the Vice-President of Sales Wants from the Credit Department," *Credit and Financial Management* 69 (January 1967): 15–17; Pearce C. Kelley and Kenneth Lawyer, *How to Organize and Operate a Small Business* (Englewood Cliffs, N.J.: Prentice-Hall, 1961), pp. 491–521; and Wallace Reiff, "Capital Allocation in Credit Decision-Making," *Credit and Financial Management* 69 (September 1967): 20–23.

12. Merle Welshans, "Using Credit in Profit Making," *Credit and Financial Management* 69 (February 1967): 18–27.

13. Kelley and Lawyer, *How to Organize and Operate a Small Business,* pp. 491–521.

14. Raymond A. Marquardt and Anthony F. McGann, "Profit Analysis and the Firm's Credit Policy," *Business Ideas and Facts* 6 (Winter 1973): 12–18.

15. "A Sales Tool For All Seasons," *Sales Management* 113 (February 17, 1975): 1–48.

16. Ibid., pp. 12, 36.

17. Ibid., p. 12.

18. Gerald D. Grosner, *Turning Complaints into Profits* (Washington, D.C.: Small Business Administration, 1959), p. 58.

Case Study: Bill Jones, Appliance Salesperson

Bill Jones, age 46, was a career salesperson with Wells Appliances in Indianapolis, Ind. Bill had graduated from high school in 1954 and was immediately drafted into the Army. After he completed his obligation he returned to Indianapolis where he began to work for Mr. Wells as a warehouse/deliveryperson. He worked hard, didn't miss a day of work for eight years, and tried to save every dime he could to go to college. Even though the wages were good it was impossible to save enough to attend college full-time and somehow he had missed out on the G.I. Bill. He tried to go to night classes but they did not work out. In 1962 he met and married Bridget and now they have two children who are attending a local college and living at home.

During the intervening years Mr. Wells recognized Bill's diligence and promoted Bill to a floor sales position which he enjoyed. Eventually he became a store sales manager. Mr. Wells had retired three years ago and sold out to Acme, Inc., a holding company specializing in appliance stores. Acme retained the Wells name and two employees: Bill and Sally Olms, the bookkeeper/officeperson. Bill had been demoted to senior sales specialist supervising four parttime salespeople who were on straight commission. Bill was happy to have a job, but it was still a "downer" to return to the floor full-time. In addition, he was unhappy to return to a small base salary plus commission with a high quota instead of a good salary and a share of the profits which he had enjoyed in the last two years with Mr. Wells.

Bill's thoughts were interrupted by a woman's voice saying, "Could you help me please?" Bill turned around to see a middle-aged woman looking at refrigerators. "Oh, I'm sorry I didn't see you come in," Bill said apologetically. "How may I help you?" The woman replied angrily, "I'm looking for that special you had in the paper this morning, the 14-foot combination for $379. Here it is only 10:30 in the morning and I'll bet you don't have any!" "Unfortunately she's right," thought Bill.

Customer traffic in the store had been slow for the last six months. Customers were hostile and nasty. Every customer was looking for large price discounts but Acme refused to reduce a single price. Rather than lose sales and commissions Bill had sold his store's allocation of sale refrigerators before the ad had run. Acme had a firm policy against selling "advertised special merchandise" before the ad was run in the local newspaper. Jim, the North store manager and a good friend of Bill's, had offered to share his allocation with Bill so that the ad would be covered. Bill could have made arrangements to pick up two units on the way to work this morning but he was late, traffic was heavy, and he just plain forgot to get them.

Bill was brought back to the present when he heard, "Well do I have to go over to that phone and call the Better Business Bureau to complain that Wells is using false and misleading advertising or do I get to see that 'frig?'" she said, starting for the telephone on the sales desk.

Discussion Questions

1. What should Bill do in this situation?
2. How should a salesperson handle a "hostile" customer?
3. If Bill can't resolve the problem and she does call the BBB, what impact will this one incident have on Wells? On Bill? On Acme?
4. Suppose the woman had not been hostile. Should Bill try to "trade-her-up" into a current, bottom-of-the-line model? Should he attempt to "trade-her-up" into the top-of-the-line model which has the highest commission? Explain.

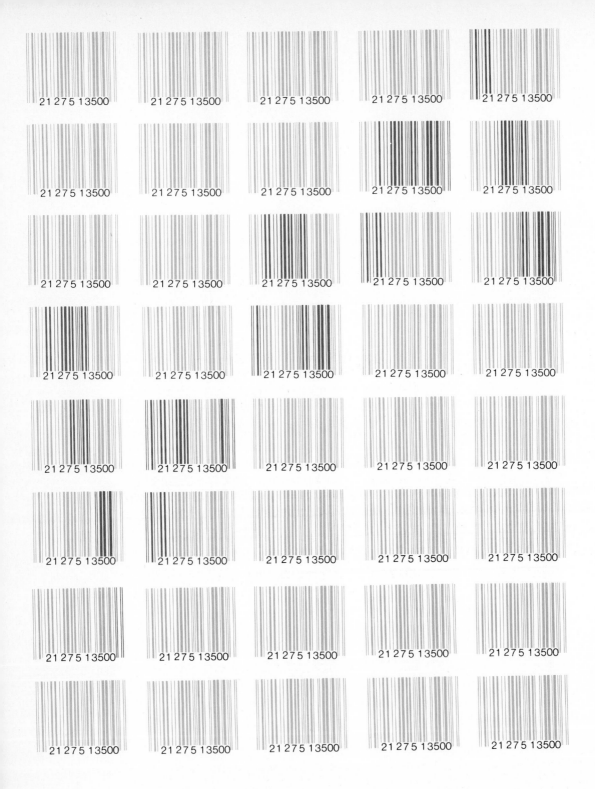

Part Three | Retail Operations Management

Comments from CEO

Helen Galland
President
Bonwit Teller

When Paul Bonwit and Edmund J. Teller opened their store, they could never have envisioned the metamorphosis that would take place over these 80 years. Some things, however, do not change. When the Bonwit Teller Emporium was established, the proprietors addressed themselves to a limited segment of the populace. They knew their customers' needs and catered to them. The formula was obviously successful, and in discussing Bonwit Teller today, a major point for consideration is our merchandising strategy and how it's arrived at.

The most important step in pinpointing a market is knowing your audience. Ours, at Bonwit Teller or *any* specialty shop, is obviously a smaller portion of available purchasing power. Lifestyles play an important role in buying habits. The time spent shopping, the kinds of merchandise bought, the price of airline tickets, the state of the stock market, and the second home syndrome, all help to determine marketing reactions. The tuned-in customer who is busy, fashion conscious, and aware of the material things life has to offer is where we focus our attention. Our consumer is the upper middle to very upper economic level. Our audience is limited, but meaningful. They want excitement through fashion and are willing to pay handsomely for it. If this need for goods fills a psychological abyss, we must take advantage of it.

Where the consumer is **geographically** is as important to us as **who** she or he is. Branch stores account for over sixty percent of business at Bonwit Teller, and reaching out to customers means research on a broader scale. The more we concentrate on the potential of branch stores, the healthier our business will be. While there is no question that we must present a uniform Bonwit Teller face wherever we are, the nuances of the merchandise mix can spell the difference between failure and success.

More and more our thinking must be tailored to the needs of the individual person or store. We aspire to the same purity of line, projection of good fashion, and the best quality at whatever price level we present. However, branch stores are often short changed. My feeling is that given equal opportunity, fair share of merchandise needs, autonomous and adequate advertising privileges, and the direct responsibility to go after sales at the local level, the results would justify the confidence in the branch stores. Communication must be constant; faster action and reaction on the part of the New York management team, a *genuine* concern for branch store needs and the ability at branch stores to express needs in a concise and specific manner, provide an easy route to greater sales and more profit.

No matter where the Bonwit Teller store is located, the service aspect of our business must be stressed. Aside from exclusive products and the fact that in some cases we might forecast trends better than others, we have no magic. We must be nicer to our customers because that is, indeed, more important than the merchandise we sell. The day that we relinquish personal contact with the customer and are not a pleasant place to shop, we have lost our reason for being.

Relationships with vendors are vital and they are two-way streets. We are prepared to work closely, give fashion direction where needed, and place dollars where our order pads are. In return, we must expect fine quality, respectable mark-ups, preference in delivery, cooperation in advertising, and ethical responsibility for our account. We want to be important to the manufacturer.

Basically, we are a buyer-oriented store, and we believe that we should stay that way. Selection of any given merchandise classification can rest with only one person. Guidelines and administrative direction must be offered, but we're kidding ourselves if we interject more than that. We do nothing more than add confusion. Creativity is an important characteristic for any buyer on the Bonwit Teller payroll, but good sound business sense is vital in today's marketplace—more so than ever before. This is the strong support management must be available for, even if the buyer can make it on his or her own.

There are major challenges ahead, but there are always survivors. The difficult economic environment drives us to sharper more creative merchandising and marketing techniques. An entrepreneurial merchant can always be assured of "making a living," but without optimism there is no reason for our being.

Chapter 16 | Managing and Designing the Retail Organization

Learning Goals

1. To understand the importance of human behavior and its impact on organization design and operation.
2. To learn the evolutionary steps involved in the growth and development of retail organizations.
3. To define different retailing organizational forms and when each is appropriate.
4. To discuss the changes taking place in retail organizations and the rationale for such changes.

Key Terms and Concepts

managerial functions
philosophy of human
  behavior
managerial style
job design
authority and responsibility
delegation process

span of management
functional specialization
product specialization
client specialization
geographic specialization
departmentation

Managerial Functions

Every retail manager must systematically combine money, merchandise, and human resources in an optimal location to provide the right goods and services at the right time, at the right place, and at the right price. In order to accomplish this challenging task each manager must plan, organize, staff, direct, and control. These fundamental managerial processes permit a group of people formed into an organization to accomplish goals and objectives far beyond their individual capacities.

Planning

The first chronological activity in the management process is planning, which determines where the firm currently stands in relation to its environment. Planning anticipates the future through application of forecasting techniques and decides in advance what, when, why, and how each member of the firm will accomplish the organization's objectives. (Previous chapters have discussed the merchandising plan. Chapter 17 will examine the challenges of properly staffing a retail store.) The planning process creates options before events occur. Hence planning gives the merchant a better opportunity to appropriately react as anticipated situations unfold.

Organizing

The second major management activity is organizing. This process involves assembling the necessary resources to accomplish the predetermined goals set forth in the planning process. Retail managers group common activities to form jobs which are then grouped in departments. In turn, the departments are assembled into divisions. As these resources are arranged they are assigned specific tasks to be performed at a certain level of efficiency within a given time frame. Buyers create complete seasonal buying plans by using the retail firm's dollars to purchase the needed merchandise to be delivered at a certain time and place to be sold by designated sales staff during appointed store hours. The results of these integrated planning efforts are recorded by the transaction centers and the funds are collected and recycled to be accumulated to implement the next seasonal plan.

Staffing

The third major managerial activity concerns staffing the newly created organization created in the second step. While this subject will be explored in depth in Chapter 17, one may briefly note that a manager must recruit, select, and place human resources in jobs which must be accomplished efficiently and effectively. Periodically individual employee performance must be compared with the assigned task or job description to evaluate performance. Any gaps between the present level of performance and the desired level stated in the job description become a subject for employee-management discussion. Additional training may be necessary if a lack of knowledge or skills is detected. Based on these periodic evaluations, employees are promoted, given merit raises, and generally rewarded for their performance.

Directing and Motivating

During performance of assigned tasks, employees must be directed and motivated to put forth their best effort so that the firm will prosper and they will continue to receive a paycheck. Actually, directing goes beyond seeking compliance behavior and attempts to channel employee energies into the most productive activities for both the firm and that individual. Each manager should attempt to tap the creative energies in all employees and encourage them to improve their own productivity and personal satisfaction from the job situation.

Controlling

Lastly, the manager must control the direction of the organization's daily activities and long-term growth and development. Each day's sales must be compared with the sales planned for the day as well as the figures from previous years. Regardless of whether the performance exceeded or failed to reach the desired goal, the manager should ask why any deviations occurred. Ideally, retailers would like performance to exceed planned levels; however, if excesses consistently occur the manager must question the appropriateness of the plan which generated the targets. Controlling involves constantly monitoring all phases of the retail activity to detect deviations and take corrective action if deemed appropriate.

Management as a Cycle of Events

From the previous discussion the impression may be gained that each managerial function occurs in a discrete, orderly fashion. Such is not the case. In fact, most managers rarely have the time to sit down and contemplate the future and plan for it. As a result they are constantly "putting out crisis fires," totally overcome by events and an organization which are out of control. Most authorities seem to agree that effective management begins when the manager gets control of his or her time and systematically plans the day's activities so that only 80 percent of the time becomes actually committed to managerial activities. The remaining 20 percent allows for unexpected interruptions and delays which are bound to creep into any schedule. Daily "to do" lists can be one method of systematically planning the most effective use of the manager's time, while organizing the activities and resources necessary to accomplish the important goals of efficiency and effectiveness.

Organizational Principles for Retailers

The basic ideas which make organizations effective are division of labor, specialization, and coordination. Organizations exist for one purpose: to accomplish goals which individuals acting alone cannot. Retail organizations are created to satisfy customer needs profitably. This end goal should be pursued systematically through the application of management principles in an organization setting.

Organization Philosophy, Structure and Policies

Every organization is founded on a set of implied or specific principles that reflect their philosophy of doing business. This **organizational philosophy** provides an overall perspective of why the firm was formed and how it plans to operate to reach its ultimate objectives: survival and growth. Such statements of philosophy are often incorporated into policy statements that serve as guides for the firm's personnel when making decisions, and they assist in informing the client system of customers, suppliers, government, and so forth, of the firm's predispositions toward them and their interface relations. Organizational philosophies are translated into organization structures that are designed to meet the firm's unique needs. For example, in 1980 Sears, Roebuck and Company adopted a new management philosophy which they referred to as the "Five Commitments" to guide the firm's decision making in the balance of the decade. These commitments were:

to strong, decentralized operating companies;

to a small and highly capable corporate staff;

to direct key resources—capital and people—most effectively;

to multiple career routes for key managers; and

to a strong leadership role for the corporate strategic planning committee.[1]

In order to implement this philosophy, the Sears organization had to be reshaped and transformed into a new entity. Under the new structural arrangements the chairpeople of Allstate, Merchandise, and Seraco groups, the chief financial officer, vice-chairman/corporate administrative officer, vice-president/corporate planning officer, vice-president/corporate general counsel, and vice-president/secretary all report to the chief executive officer. The main task of this group is to assist in setting goals, monitor performance, coordinate functions and report results.[2]

A new strategic planning committee was formed by bringing the chief executive officer, chief financial officer, corporate administrative officer, corporate planning officer, Merchandise group officer, Allstate group officer and Seraco group officer into one integrated team. In an attempt to explain the group's new challenge, the firm said, "While evolving from historical circumstances, the new organization recognizes that previously interrelated businesses have become more autonomous. In so doing, the structure provides for day-to-day running of each business by the chief executive of each group. The role of corporate staff is to define broader corporate goals and strategies, and to allocate resources to achieve those objectives."[3] In keeping with this charter the group adopted the major commitment of maximizing the short- and long-term rate of return.[4]

In order to achieve this goal the strategic planning committee set down performance criteria for each of the three major groups: Merchandise, Allstate, and Seraco. "The Merchandise Group, for example, is well represented geographically and is a mature business relative to the others. Within merchandising, investments will be geared to achieving productivity gains while accommodating selective expansion into growing market areas. Allstate's major growth opportunities center around its life insurance and commercial lines. Resources will be aimed at stimulating growth in these areas, while encouraging continued expansion of the other property and liability lines."[5]

After this statement was released the firm acquired a major stock brokerage firm and a national real estate organization to expand its financial efforts. Whether Sears succeeds in these ambitious endeavors remains to be seen, but one can observe that with the reorganization they appear to be on the right track.

The basic building block of the organization is the job. Managers must define the tasks to be accomplished if plans are to succeed. These activities are grouped into job clusters which one person can be expected to achieve efficiently. Such activities collectively form the job description. Common job titles found in retailing include sales associate, buyer, general merchandise manager, and vice-president for store operations. Each job must be related to another both vertically and horizontally so that the activities of all can be coordinated.

Delegation of Authority

Vertical relationships between jobs are formed when superiors delegate authority to subordinates to do their required tasks. In return the subordinates are charged with the accountability for using that authority in the most effective fashion. A buyer may have authority to sign a $10,000 order, but that same person is held accountable for the profitable timely sale of those goods.

In the previous example the job of buyer represented a division of labor and specialization of one person doing one vital part of the entire merchandising process. In order to achieve coordination and organizational synergy all jobs must be collectively grouped on some common basis such as by organizational function, product, client, or geographical location.

Functional Specialization

From an evolutionary perspective most retail firms begin as single-person proprietorships where the owner/manager makes all the decisions. Technical expertise beyond the owner's capability, such as accounting and legal advice, are purchased outside the firm in the form of consultation. As the firm survives and prospers the entrepreneur begins to assemble persons who are capable of providing daily technical or financial assistance to the firm such as bookkeeping or selling. Occasionally the founder of a firm is fortunate enough to find a skilled person who also wishes to "buy-into" the firm and become an active partner. If the two persons are compatible and have complementary interests such an arrangement permits the first degree of **functional specialization** while providing vitally needed working capital.

Product
Specialization

Once beyond this elemental level of functional specialization the retail firm usually develops **product specialization** which takes the form of departments. By using this form of retail structure persons can become specialists in certain product lines and their uses, and thus become better at meeting customer needs. For example, sporting goods stores have fishing tackle, golf, tennis, hunting, camping, and sports clothes departments. Those customers seeking the advice on which lure is used to catch small mouth bass will patronize the store which has the best assortment of tackle and the most knowledgeable fisherperson/ salesperson.

Client Specialization

When a retail store outgrows product departmentation the firm redesigns the structure around departments based on clients. Independent single unit department stores use women's, men's, children's, domestics and shoe departments as basic organizational divisions. Such organizational units provide a basis for collecting related products needed by the chosen target markets. This **client specialization** concept was captured by Paul Mazur in his classic rendering of the traditional department store organization sixty years ago (Figure 16.1). When the customer comes to purchase merchandise to meet a specific need the retail firm has an opportunity to provide other merchandise which may generate more sales as well as provide one-stop shopping convenience.

Lifestyle Grouping

Sometimes retail organizations will organize their jobs around specific client groups. Increasingly one finds boutiques and leisure shops in department stores which contain all those products and services to pursue a particular lifestyle. A men's leisure department might include sportswear, sporting goods, shoes, video tape recorders, stereos, and even fashion eyewear. The objective is to say to that prospective customer, "Come in and we'll tell you what you need to personify that lifestyle and be a member of the in-group." Such merchandising groupings were begun in department stores in the 1970s and now have been spun off into separate, independent stores such as the Limited.

Figure 16.1 Mazur Plan of Retail Organization

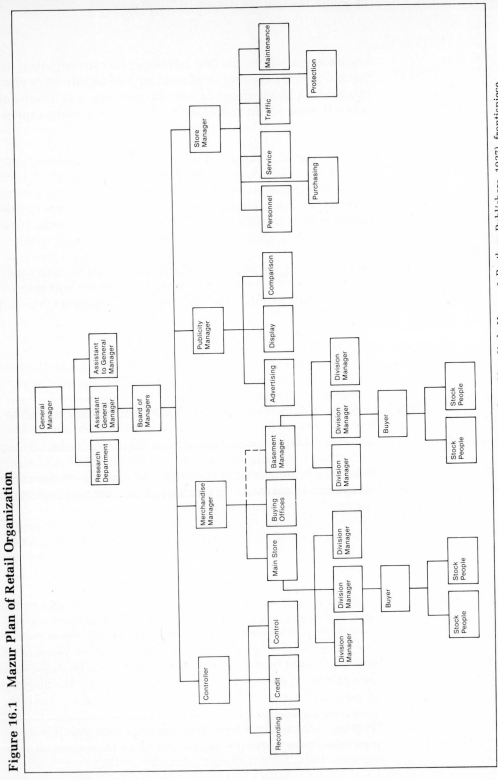

Source: Paul Mazur, *Principles of Organization Applied to Modern Retailing* (New York: Harper & Brothers Publishers, 1927), frontispiece.

Geographic
Specialization

Geographic specialization may occur at any time beyond the
functional organization stage. The owner/manager may develop a
particular product/service mix which is unique and decide to
franchise the retailing idea. Initially, similar units can be created
by franchisees, thus giving geographical dispersion to the retail
concept. Ultimately, the franchisor will be required to turn the
active management of the "mother" store over to hired management so that he or she may devote more time and energy to the
systematic expansion and operation of the franchising system.
This action leads to the creation of a new functional organization
based on geography.

Branch Stores

Alternately, independent department stores may choose to expand their operation and establish branches in new, developing
suburban areas or in nearby communities. Such action requires
the firm to use a combination of organizational forms. The branch
store is designed to reflect the same departmentation of the
originating store but downsized in both square footage and
product assortment. Department buyers in the main store assume
responsibility for merchandising their respective departments
and the store operations division takes care of store staffing,
building maintenance, and security. As branch stores are added,
most firms create a separate branch organizational unit within
the store operations department.

   Each time a retail firm chooses to redefine its target market
and segment it into smaller units the potential for structural reorganization is created. As management focuses its attention on
more narrow markets new departments are created, such as subdividing a children's department into boys' and girls' departments. When such action is taken another layer of organization
must be added to coordinate merchandising of the two new departments. The new coordinating position is usually called a *divisional merchandise manager/coordinator.*

Span of Control

Regardless of the departmental form chosen, each manager must
determine an optimal span of control. How many persons should
one person be expected to effectively direct and represent higher
management? The absolute number is dependent on the competencies of the manager and her or his subordinate associates,
the complexity of the tasks involved, the occurrence of activities,
the time constraints found in each job situation, and the degree
of physical separation among the subordinate associates. The
narrower the span of control the more levels of hierarchy will be
needed to coordinate the activities. Retail firms generally have
moderate span of control resulting in relatively flat organiza-

Figure 16.2   Famous–Barr Branch Store Organizational Structure

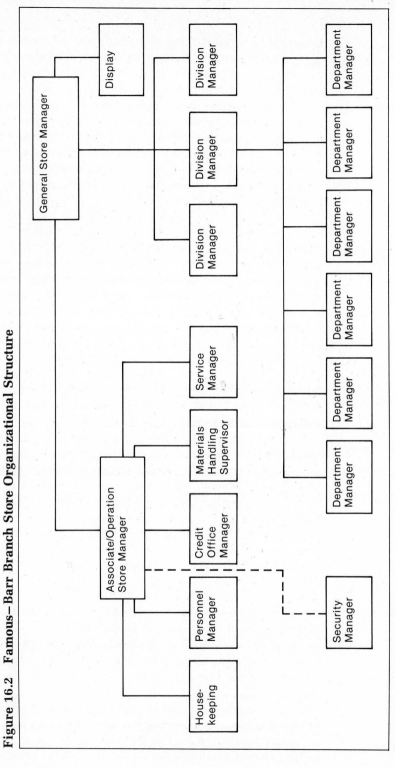

Source: Famous–Barr, Saint Louis, Mo. Reprinted by permission.

tions. No hard and fast rules can be laid down because each situation is different and requires unique consideration.

Unity of Command

Perhaps the most troublesome management principle in retailing today is the concept of "unity of command." While the concept is simple, its implementation is extremely difficult. The unity of command principle suggests that each subordinate should report to only one superior. When this principle is followed conflicting orders are reduced or eliminated so that the employee may concentrate his or her efforts on *the* superior's priority items. Unfortunately, many retail employees find themselves confronted with conflicting demands from department managers and competing buyers. Any action on the employee's part leads to potential conflict. As a result the employee often takes no action at all.

A recent situation brings the point into sharp perspective. A college graduate found herself in a large department store's management training program and was assigned as an assistant department manager in the domestics department of a suburban store. One morning the firm ran a newspaper advertisement featuring a price break on sheets and special purchase down comforters. When the trainee went to check stock levels and in-store signing before the store opened she found that the buyer had forgotten to order any in-store signs to cover the ad. The buyer told the trainee to use a "tear-sheet" copy for the ad and hand letter signs in black marker until she could get signs made and distributed. The store had a firm policy against such practices and the trainee knew that the assistant store manager would check her department for compliance. Both the buyer and the assistant store manager could directly affect the trainee's career with the firm.

Line-Staff Conflict

Conflicting request conditions often evolve out of classical line and staff organizations. A situation develops in which one person with the right to command (line) disagrees with an expert's (staff) view on what should be done to resolve the current problem. In the above situation the assistant store manager, in this case *line*, was enforcing company policy. The buyer, *staff*, knew that sales would be affected if the customers were unaware of the bedding promotion. Such line-staff conflicts occur daily in retail organizations everywhere and act as a debilitating force which reduces the organization's effectiveness.

Organizational Growth and Development

Assuming the organization continues to prosper and grow, departments are subsequently subdivided into smaller units and more

Figure 16.3 Famous–Barr Merchandising Division Buying Line

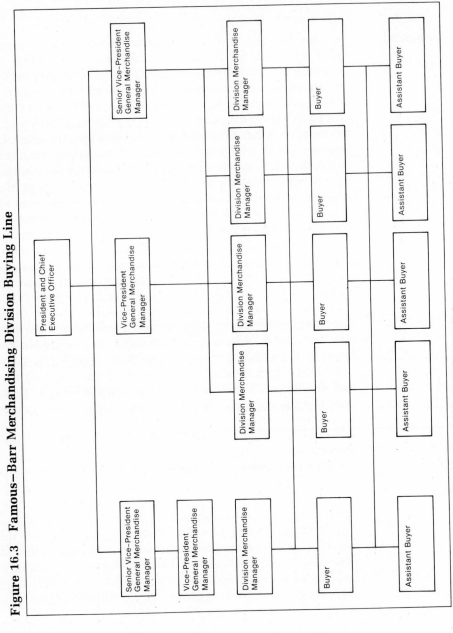

Source: Famous-Barr, Saint Louis, Mo. Reprinted by permission.

divisional managers are promoted or hired from outside the organization. As the number of divisional managers increase beyond the vice-president's ability to manage, new positions must be developed to coordinate the expanding divisional merchandise management group. This new level of authority and position is referred to as general merchandise managers.

Merchandising reorganization often is accompanied by staff departmentalization such as personnel, accounting, promotion/advertising, distribution, legal services, and real estate. As noted previously the accounting function usually emerges first, followed by personnel and promotion/advertising. They also may be subdivided at any time into functional, geographically specialized units, such as district personnel departments or regional promotional departments.

Growth through Merger

Retail chain stores may be formed by merging separate retail firms under one ownership group. This technique is quite common in the department store field. Often such ownership groups as Federated Department Stores, Allied Stores and Associated Dry Goods, Inc. have purchased local department stores yet let them maintain a certain degree of local autonomy and identity. Lord and Taylor, J. W. Robinsons, Goldwaters, and The Denver are all divisions of the Associated Dry Goods organization, as noted in Figure 16.4.

Each separate store is headed by a Chairman of the Board who holds a vice-president's position in the parent organization. Each store coordinates their long-range planning and financial requirements through and with the approval of the parent firm, but they are relatively free to develop and cultivate their own unique image and market in their separate locations.

Not all firms will evolve along the same path. Organizational research has demonstrated that all firms attempt to differentiate themselves from similar firms in the same industry. This

Figure 16.4   Retail Firm's Regional Organization

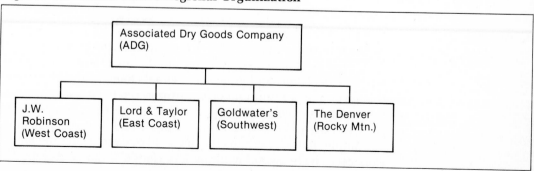

exclusivity results from management's decisions to do things more efficiently and effectively and also gives the firm its unique image. For example Emporium-Capwell, the San Francisco based department store chain, has changed their organizational chart to reflect the current interest in financial planning and control (Figure 16.5). The executive vice-president for finance and chief financial officer occupies the same level of authority as the executive vice-president for merchandising. By placing this activity high in the organization, the firm will be able to consider the impact of any policy decision which affects the firm's financial condition.

Dual Department Store Organization

Limited Merchandising Career, Opportunities

Department store executives faced with numerous sales staffing positions in branch stores have opted to organizationally separate buying and selling at the lowest level in the organization. Realistically not every retail management trainee can become a buyer-merchandiser, particularly as more and more firms centralize these activities in the main store or regional office. Therefore, new trainees can now opt for either merchandising or operations careers. In fact one study indicated that of the department stores responding, 78 percent wanted merchandise trainees to have four-year business degrees while those specializing in sales management needed only a two-year degree.[6] Unfortunately, pay scales for each career bear out this perceived difference.

Team Management at the Executive Level

A recent innovation in department store organization is the creation of **tandem management.**[7] Under this new arrangement the chief executive officer (CEO) and the president typically divide the executive management responsibilities, and each person is the final authority and decision maker in that area of the operation. Usually the CEO has come from a merchandising background so he or she assumes those duties while the president assumes the operational aspects of the firm (Figure 16.6).

Advantages

Generally exact placement of the retailing functions will depend on the interests and strengths of the tandem team members. Such sharing of responsibilities permits better attention to critical strategic decisions and allows personnel changes to take place at this level with a minimum of interruption to the organization, because both executives keep the other informed of critical issues, events, and the ultimate decisions which have been made and implemented. Perhaps the major advantage is that the top executives have a good working knowledge of day-to-day ac-

Figure 16.5 Emporium–Capwell

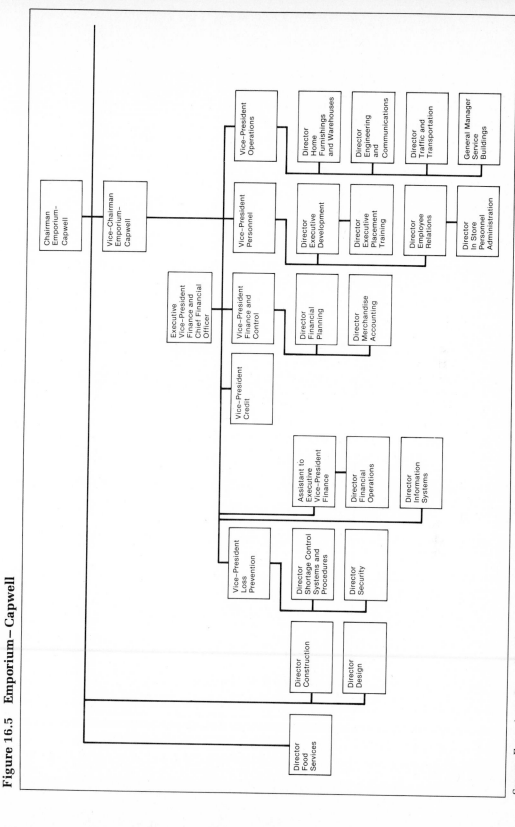

Source: Emporium–Capwell, San Francisco, California, a Division of Carter Hawley Hale Stores. Reprinted by permission.

Figure 16.5 Continued

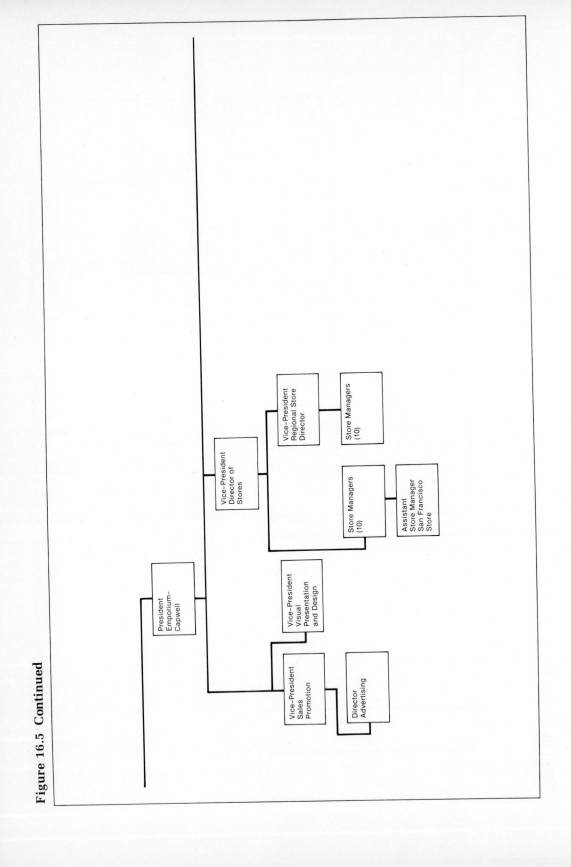

Figure 16.5 Continued

Figure 16.6   Tandem Organization for Team Management

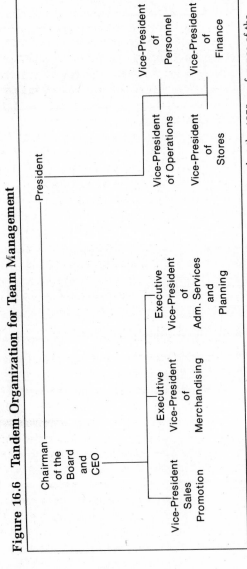

Source: John B. Gifford, "Tandem Management in Retailing," paper presented at the 1978 conference of the American Collegiate Retailing Association, New York, N.Y.

tivities and can take actions in the short run which are consistent with their long-range plans for growth and development.

Disadvantages

However with divided responsibilities the subordinates may encounter problems working for two bosses. While the separation of responsibilities appears clean and neat on paper, in practice most activities cut across functional lines and result in multiple supervision. This problem is best handled by frequent, in-depth discussions between the team-managers to maximize coordination and to minimize conflict.

Another disadvantage is that those who specialize in store operations have fewer opportunities to advance. Therefore one member of the team may be left behind to "break in" a new CEO merchandiser as each person ascends the career ladder. With fewer large stores being built most store operations specialists plateau at an earlier point than merchandisers, which can generate severe morale problems. One solution is to put upward mobile merchandisers in store operations for a limited period so they can cope with future presidential duties before being promoted to CEO positions.

Summary

The discussion has pointed out that there is a natural evolution of retail firm development which can be seen in the various organizational structures. Retail firms may grow vertically or horizontally depending on the competitive environment and the personal managerial style of the founder. Organizations are created by delegating authority and creating accountability. As the organizational hierarchy is formed its shape will be influenced by the span of control and the organization's management philosophy.

Department stores have unique organization arrangements usually based on the traditional Mazur plan. However, today major changes are taking place as departments are eliminated or leased to other firms. Tandem management at the executive level is injecting new vitality into an important segment of the retail system.

Retail chain stores growing out of the need to serve a different clientele, have evolved into centralized merchandising giants. Through central buying and distribution centers the chains have been able to concentrate their in-store activities on selling with the resulting change in organization. Local merchandising autonomy has been sacrificed for greater sales volume through greater standardization. Each chain organization is in a constant state of change as they attempt to better meet the changing needs of their target markets.

In the end, retail managers must remember that organization charts are just "x-ray" pictures of perceived relationships by one person at one point in time. Organization charts are useless without job description manuals so persons will know what they are expected to do. Retailing is a labor-intensive people business. No amount of automation will eliminate that vital human factor of one person relating to another in an attempt to better meet the customer needs. Retailing needs to re-examine its personnel policies and organization structures to more effectively attract and tap the creative energies of tomorrow's managers. Without good people an organization is nothing.

Questions

1. How does a retailer create an organization?

2. What factors should be considered when designing jobs? Explain.

3. When should a retail organization consider vertical growth and development? Horizontal growth and development?

4. How many subordinates can a store manager manage? Does this vary from person to person or from store to store? Why?

5. What are the four functions which form the core of specialization for the traditional department store under the Mazur plan? Is this the most effective organizational form for department stores today? Why or why not?

6. What is meant by tandem management? Why has it been proposed for retail executive organizational positions? Explain.

Footnotes

1. "Sears, Roebuck and Company: Annual Report 1980," Sears, Roebuck and Company, Chicago, Ill. (1981) p. 6.

2. Ibid.

3. Ibid.

4. Ibid.

5. Ibid.

6. Clarence E. Vincent and John S. Berens, "Changes in Department Store Organization: Implications for Curriculum Requirements for Management Trainees," *Journal of Marketing Education* 3 (Spring 1981): 22.

7. John B. Gifford, "Tandem Management in Retailing," paper presented at the 1978 Conference of the American Collegiate Retailing Association, New York, N.Y.

Case Study: Super-Sav Superfoods Market

Roger Kelly was justifiably proud of his independent Super-Sav Superfoods Market. Roger had bought a small local food store in 1955 and with hard work, long hours, and the help of his family he had built the store into a large supermarket which successfully competed with the big chain stores such as Safeway, Kroger, Alpha Beta and Ralph's.

Super-Sav had filled a unique niche in the local market. The firm concentrated on friendly, personal service with competitive prices. In the earlier years the store had offered 30-day charge accounts for a limited number of patrons, but five years ago Roger discontinued the practice and lowered prices instead. The store was known for the large stock of institutional sized cans of fruit and vegetables which appealed to large families because of lower per serving cost and convenience. The

Figure 16.7   Super-Sav Superfoods Market

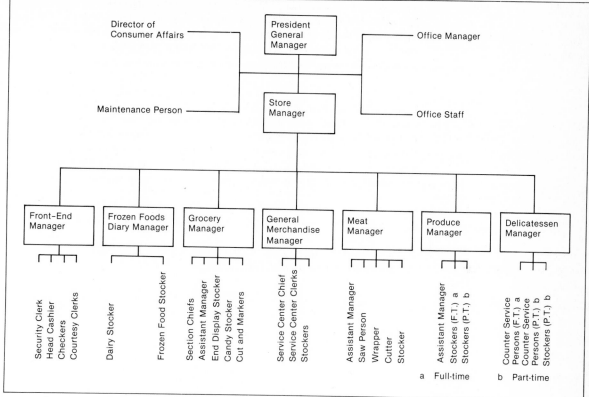

store also provided custom-cut meat service which was not readily available in the other stores. In summary, the store thrived on true customer service at competitive prices.

Over the years the store has been moved three times—each time into a larger remodeled facility. Finally, two years ago Roger saw his dream come true: he moved into a brand new building that had been custom designed for his operation. The store was free standing on the edge of a local shopping center which afforded ample parking space during peak business periods. With each move, the store organization had changed to reflect the growing and changing responsibilities resulting from adding or expanding various departments. Note the current organization chart.

Roger was not content to rest on his accomplishments. His new building was now paid for in full and the store's monthly receipts were up over 10 percent from the previous year. The new store design was paying off in significantly lower costs and it required less hourly staff. As the challenge of running the current store faded, Roger began to consider a new branch store in a new residential development. Market research indicated that the location is appropriate and that the planned space for a supermarket in the local shopping center has not yet been leased. The new store could be financed, at least in part, from the current "parent" store profits. Everything seemed perfect.

As Roger began to consider his new store, his thoughts turned to staffing the store. He was well aware that much of the store's past success was due to the "friendly" atmosphere which he fostered and nourished. He often was seen on the floor talking with customers and even carrying out sacks of groceries during peak periods. He knew that if he opened another store he couldn't always be there to monitor store personnel actions. Also, it would mean hiring and training new personnel in addition to transfering some of the current staff. Roger would be happy to see some of "his" people move up into positions of greater responsibility, yet he wasn't sure how to reorganize the firm's organization structure so that he could "oversee" both stores.

Discussion Questions

1. Design a new organization chart incorporating both the current and projected branch stores.
2. What different managerial problems might one anticipate in "overseeing" both stores? Explain.

Chapter 17 | Management of Human Resources

One of the least understood aspects of retail management is the effective utilization of the human resource. Without doubt, labor is the largest single contributor to a retailer's variable cost. A retailer can adhere rigidly to well-planned merchandise budgets, hold markdowns to a minimum, closely scrutinize transportation costs, and control shrinkage—and still suffer continuing poor performance due to inadequate human resource planning and utilization.

At the outset of this discussion it is critically important to realize that the total image and lasting perception of any retail establishment is strongly affected by the person-to-person relationship between the retail salesperson and the customer. This interaction should begin when the customer enters the store and usually terminates at the transaction center. Thus, the quality of this experience strongly affects the future customer's perception of the firm's mass media efforts as well as store patronage. Effective retailers know that the viability of the firm lies in relative satisfaction of customer needs at all levels in the firm, from the stockroom through the administrative offices to the salesfloor and occasionally to postpurchase adjustments. Every employee's best effort is required to provide customer satisfaction profitably.

Human Resource Role in Retailing

Today retail management is faced with unprecedented challenges in the effective utilization of the firm's human resources. The problems begin when one tries to establish appropriate organizational goals that reflect society's changed perception of what is demanded from the business community. Such goals as full employment; equal rights for minorities, women, and the handicapped; increased corporate taxation, consumerism, occupational health and safety standards; and labor reform all compete with the profit motive for priority consideration by management.

Individual employee considerations emerge as the firm begins designing jobs that provide entry-level challenge and motivation and lead to future career occupations that are stimulating and rewarding. Today's employees have been exposed to more education in the liberal tradition and expect considerable personal consideration and participation in the organization's decision-making process, which often requires job redesign.

Increased federal legislation, related court decisions, and resulting regulations have significantly increased the business community's level of responsibility in its dealings with employees. Personal equity, privacy, and compensation systems seem to be the main concerns of current employees.

The retailing industry is particularly affected because of its intense use of labor in the delivery of its product or service. Not surprisingly, research shows that retail managers spend approximately 80 percent of their time on people-related problems. Thus, the effective retail manager must be a human relations specialist as well as an excellent marketer.

Obviously, the text cannot provide a complete course in effective personnel management in one chapter, much less develop skill in interpersonal relations. The task is to highlight major areas of current concern and trust that the readers will be stimulated to take additional courses or expand their knowledge in this complex and dynamic field.

The Personnel Process

The personnel process involves the systematic linking of the personnel functions into an integrated system of policies, procedures, and rules that govern employee behavior while on the job.

Personnel functions include organizational planning and job design; employment planning; recruiting, selection, and placement; performance appraisal, training, and career development; compensation administration; and collective bargaining. All of these functions are implemented on a day-to-day basis through appropriate decision making and supervision.

Retail managers may experience a wide variety of personnel responsibilities, depending on the amount of functional specialization in their organizations. For example, a small entrepreneur-retailer may carry the entire responsibility for performance of personnel functions. On the other hand, a department manager in a large retail chain may be charged only with implementing personnel decisions made by a representative of a personnel department. In any case, the manager should be aware of the entire personnel process. Alernately, each supervisor serves as the immediate representative for the staff, and in that capacity serves as the one who relates its needs to higher management and, conversely, interprets company policy for employees. In this dual capacity the supervisor is the keystone of any effective personnel program.

Employment Planning

Employment planning attempts to determine systematically the future demand for human resources in the organization. The need for human resources is a derived demand; that is, employment is a function of the level of sales activity for the retail firm. The employment planning process is implemented by forecasting total aggregate demand, industry demand, and the retail firm's future demand for goods and services. Once the firm's sales forecast is determined, the number of employees needed can be derived along with a list of needed skills.

A firm's human resource needs are composed of those people to be hired for new positions and those to be replaced due to retirements, deaths, "quits," and firings. These latter elements comprise the replacement component that must be recruited, selected, and trained to fill job vacancies during the current planning period. Once these aggregate requirements have been estimated, the manager must identify specific persons who are ready for promotion and those who are promotable when given more time and appropriate training. Also, specific terminations must be determined and the timing of such managerial action must be established.

When these planned personnel changes have been identified and categorized, the manager must consider and plan for store

(margin note: Derived Demand)

(margin note: Human Resource Planning)

growth and/or decline and determine what effects such changes will have on the quality and quantity of the human resource required. All too often, overly optimistic managers anticipate constant store growth and are caught off-guard when temporary retrenchment is required. Accurate forecasting of the economic and competitive environment permits and encourages the manager to eliminate selectively the marginal producers in the departments rather than take the crisis action of indiscriminate layoffs. Through such judicious pruning the entire human resource can be adapted to changing situations.

Obviously, such a detailed analysis is not within the scope of small retail organizations but is a necessity in large organizations for continued personal and organizational growth.

Job Evaluation: What Constitutes a Job?

The second phase in human resource management begins with a successful attempt to achieve some degree of congruency between the skill needs of a job and a person's ability to perform those tasks. Thus, as technology and competitive conditions change, commensurate adjustments will have to be made in job clusters. Resulting task reassignments may require job alteration, and certain jobs may have to be eliminated. Constant vigilance in this area will result in more efficient operations.

Quantity of Activities

Quality of Performance

Two points must be emphasized concerning job formulation. First, the quantity of activities and the quality of performance involved in any job will significantly affect the later staffing and compensation processes. Specifically, the more activities that must be performed or the higher the quality of performance, the more one narrows the range of appropriate human resources. For example, an electronic repair shop in a small town ideally may require the services of an electronic technician to repair television sets, stereo equipment, video tape players, and pocket calculators. Unfortunately, servicing all these products probably requires an inventory of test equipment and spare parts as well as a level of skill that is beyond the resources of the shop. Therefore, the shop may limit its on-site repair service on television and stereos that the local repair person can handle and offer factory service for video disk players and calculators. Job formation should strike a balance between creating jobs that anyone can perform, and are more likely to be boring and dissatisfying, and jobs that are so unique that only one person in 10,000 could perform them adequately.

Job Design

Specific job tasks to be accomplished are found in the job descriptions, while the specific skill and related attributes of a successful job performer are found in the job specifications. Many small firms do not formalize each job in this manner because employees are in daily contact with each other and can make informal adjustments in the performance of assigned tasks to see that jobs get done. Also, the owner-manager is present to give instructions and supervise the individual, which allows greater individual flexibility in the order and method of accomplishing needed tasks.

Second, job formulation should include "elastic activities"; that is, the job should be expandable or contractable as a function of the person performing the assigned activities or it should be variable with the seasonality of sales volume. Admittedly, there are a certain minimum number of activities to be performed and a level of performance quality that any incumbent must meet, but as the job holder learns the job there should be opportunities for continuing challenge or job enlargement. It should be noted that not all individuals want to grow and develop in a job. They may simply want to perform the assigned activities at a minimum level of performance and seek their personal satisfaction elsewhere. There should be a place for both "upward mobiles" and "maintainers" in any retail organization.

Job Evaluation in an Ongoing Organization

Most retail students will not have the opportunity to form their own retail firms but rather will enter an organization with jobs already established. Job evaluation in this situation entails determining what activities each individual is performing and whether these tasks are appropriate for the current situation. Such investigations usually disclose needless duplication of effort, overlapping responsibilities, and a host of inefficiencies that creep into any system over time if constant vigilance is not maintained.

The process of job evaluation involves reporting all the activities performed by a person holding a job or position. Such data may be gathered by a self-report based on a diary of daily activities or by a trained observer recording both the activities performed and the amount of time spent in performance of each activity. Daily activity schedules are condensed after some appropriate period, such as a week's observations, and the recurring activities are filtered out. An intensive review of these activities should be made to identify appropriate and inappropriate activities and what changes in the job can be affected. Thus, the adjusted routine becomes the job description.

Job Description

The job description becomes a checklist of activities that must be performed by anyone occupying a particular position or job.

Job Content

More importantly, the job description serves as a guide for any new employee or promoted job holder by specifically detailing what he or she must do to meet the minimum performance levels of the job. It is important to stress that a job description should not be construed as a limiting classification; it is simply a compliance-level statement of minimum activity performance. While a job description may be biased by self-reporting in favor of the job holder, every effort must be made not to include personal biases in the job specifications.

Job Specifications

Job Qualifications

Job specifications state the specific personal attributes, abilities, knowledge, and skills necessary to perform a job satisfactorily. Under provisions of the Equal Rights Act of 1964 (amended in 1972), management may be called upon to prove that job specifications are based solely on ability to perform the assigned tasks and in no way are associated with the race, age, creed, color, sex, religion, or national origin of the job seeker. Many firms in the past have attempted to use minimum educational levels, such as a high school or college diploma, as a screening device to reduce their selection effort. Recently some firms have been called upon by the Equal Employment Opportunity Commission to defend such discriminating criteria and prove their relationship to successful performance of the associated jobs. Failure to establish such task performance-personal ability relationships may result in costly back pay to applicants who were unlawfully denied employment or advancement within the firm. Job descriptions must be based on demonstrated ability to perform the jobs successfully.

Recruitment

Sources of Potential Employees

"Where do you find good people?" This is the essence of the recruitment process. In the past, most organizations had three alternative strategies from which to choose: (1) actively go into the various labor markets and search for talent, (2) passively accept "walk ins" or those individuals who presented themselves for employment, or (3) combine the first two strategies.

Recently, due to the "new social awareness," large retail organizations have been encouraged to recruit potential employees throughout their metropolitan and local areas. Disadvantaged or underrepresented groups are being extended employment opportunities, special upgrading programs are being offered, and additional efforts are being made to bring all segments of the population into the employment mainstream of mass merchandising. "Can do" ability and associated self-confidence should be sought wherever it exists—ghetto, public employment agency, community college, or university.

Changing Personnel Mix

Unfortunately one must recognize that a three-level caste system prevails in large-scale retailing. Retail sales personnel and supportive stock room and janitorial staffs are found at the lowest level. The second level includes entry level managerial trainees and successful, upwardly mobile salespersons who have demonstrated personal initiative, self-confidence, and the ability to excel. The third level includes the store managers, corporate management, and professional staffs. Entry into the last category is usually accomplished through in-firm promotions with occasional importation of specialized talent to meet changing environmental needs. For example, when J. C. Penney decided to enter the tires, batteries, and accessories market they recruited top automotive merchandising talent from Montgomery Ward. Such actions are not too common but not unusual either.

Changing Skill Needs

Entry level positions into the managerial training programs, contrary to common belief, include a wide range of specializations. Besides the traditional career role models of store management and buyer, large retail firms are recruiting individuals with college degrees in civil engineering and physical distribution for jobs in materials management to design and manage warehouses and handle related traffic problems; persons majoring in accounting, computer science, and finance to staff the control function of the firms; and persons with degrees in human relations and personnel administration for managing the human resources of the organization. No longer is mass merchandising the sole province of merchandise graduates.

Career Tracks

The changing recruitment process represents a healthy realization on the part of retail employers that they should attempt to match potential personal abilities and levels of aspiration and achievement with realistic job and career tracks. Not every management trainee will become a store manager or a member of the executive staff. Selection procedures and self-awareness cannot assure such finite discriminatory decisions at this point in the development of testing and evaluative techniques. While some individual profile screening is possible at the present time, much more research and development is needed to refine the person-to-job matching process.

"Maintainers"

More importantly, the retail recruitment process should seek individuals who could be called "maintainers." They learn the merchandise, the needs of their customers, and the strengths and weaknesses of their staff, and then turn their attention to "playing the game" or "tuning the system" to find and provide better retail products and services for "their customers." Each day holds a series of new challenges, even though they repeatedly perform the same set of activities. Personal attributes for a successful career in this kind of retail activity are markedly different from those necessary for a career that revolves around a constantly changing job, job environment, or client system. Overt recognition of such retail career differences in searching for human resources makes the following selection process potentially more effective.

Selection

Discrimination

Selection is the most crucial phase of the personnel process. By definition, the selection process is the exercise of discriminating among potential employees. Discrimination is not inherently bad; it is a fact of life. The basis for choice, or discrimination, is the point at issue. By law, such choice must be made on ability and nothing else.

Aside from the legal issues, selection serves an important function for potential employees that is often overlooked. All firms have a responsibility to match the requirements of the job with the abilities of the applicant. Specific quantifiable skills such as elementary mathematical manipulations or manual dexterity can be easily assessed by valid reliable tests. However, when one attempts to measure a person's ability to interact with others or exercise personal judgment, the measurement task becomes much more complex. Additionally, personnel departments are increasingly being charged with assessing each potential employee's initial capacity for personal growth and development in a long-term career path with the organization. Through use of the latest bias-free psychological techniques, those persons can be identified who have a chance for a successful personally rewarding work experience in retailing. This assessment should not be considered a guarantee of success but rather an identification of personal potential for success.

Successive Hurdles

Applicants who have negotiated "successive hurdle" selective screenings, including interviewing and testing, are usually employed subject to any appropriate union agreement or state laws, such as basic health requirements for food retailers and the like.[1]

Multiple correlation

An alternate method of selection is "multiple correlation."[2] Instead of rejecting applicants at each evaluation point, the final hiring decision is reached after all the information—including the application form, interview results, and reference checks—is complete and any subsequent interviews or evaluation mechanisms have been executed. Some personnel specialists feel that this process is fairer to potential employees, even though such a process admittedly is more time consuming and costly. As penalties for improper selection systems become well known, more employers may begin to use the "whole person" selection process.

In many large retail firms the personnel specialists who are in charge of the selection process make the decision to hire an individual into the firm, but often the employee's specific placement is yet to be determined. Where does the person begin his or her employment, at what time, in what department, for whom? The placement or orientation process is the critical link in employee acculturation into the firm's environment and assimilation into the work group. The new employee, particularly in a large organization, must become acquainted with the firm's operating policies and procedures, be introduced to his or her superior and all members of the peer work group, and be apprised of the merchandise in the assigned area. It is a good practice to designate an experienced employee to show the new member the ropes, which will facilitate that person's acceptance by the work group as a member of the team.

Employee personal satisfaction and effective task performance will be highly affected by the initial acceptance or rejection by the relevant work group. Therefore the placement and orientation process deserves the same attention to detail as recruitment and selection procedures.

Direction and Supervision of Human Resources: Getting the Job Done Effectively

"Direction in the form of leading, motivating, teaching, guiding, developing, praising, and criticizing is the catalyst which really jells the enterprise."[3] The manager-supervisor is the vital link between that abstraction called "the company" and the staff. Each supervisor is the facilitator, supporter-critic, father confessor, representer-negotiator with the "higher powers" for all of the employees.

Effective supervision puts a heavy burden of responsibility on the manager to be "fair but firm" and "consistent but considerate." Supervision is much more than just giving orders and seeing that they are executed. Supervision is a dynamic, never-ending personal interaction between the supervisor and each worker-colleague, not only on a formal job basis but also on an informal human basis.

Many managers who have been exposed to "human relations" feel that the supervising pattern should be based on **sympathetic** understanding of individual needs and problems. Unfortunately, this position only breeds individual dependence and, ultimately, a hostile backlash of animosity from the affected employees.

Effective supervision is based on **empathetic,** problem-oriented, problem-solving behavior. Sympathy simply reinforces

Problem-solving

negative attitudes that perpetuate an individual's problem. It is the supervisor's responsibility to guide a person in the direction of improvement and development, but one cannot make an individual improve unless the rewards of change outweigh the benefits derived from the current behavior.

Effective supervision stresses positive motivation, enthusiasm for living, and a positive attitude bordering on optimism. "Can't do" has no place in effective supervision. The supervisor must change an ability that is based on a "can do" individual attitude to one of "will do." The appropriate catalyst is proper motivation and rewards.

Unfortunately, many department managers do not have the delegated power to vary rewards among individuals to encourage their personal growth and development. Rewards given by the personnel department are based on cost-of-living adjustments, longevity, or other nonproduction-related criteria. This limitation, combined with numerous other responsibilities, makes the department manager or assistant buyer's job of motivating the staff difficult.

Effective Supervision

Supervision and leadership are not necessarily the same phenomenon, although the terms have been frequently used synonymously. Ideally, one would like to have the leader also be the supervisor, but this is quite rare in practice. An effective supervisor is familiar with behavioral research and is aware of the problems associated with the position.

A supervisor-manager is an individual who has authority over organizational resources and some degree of responsibility for utilizing these resources for the profitable transfer of goods and services. Concurrent with these duties each supervisor is responsible for employee need satisfaction. A supervisor's authority comes from the stockholders (or owners) down through the managerial chain, and when an individual accepts employment in an organization each person implies consent to this authority. The

Hiring Contracts

employee and the employer form two contracts: a legal agreement to comply for a certain period in return for a package of compensation and a psychological contract that assumes equity and fairness to the employee and loyalty and best effort to the employer.[4] Thus, the supervisor is charged with more duties and responsibilities than just getting the job done or the task accomplished. The manager must realize that each individual is unique and varies in both ability and needs, yet all people have their own perception of what constitutes "fair and equitable" treat-

Fair and Equitable Treatment

ment for themselves and others. The astute supervisor soon learns that equitable treatment does not mean equal treatment for all. Each individual expects personal consideration of his or her own situation within some nebulous framework of fairness for others. The relevant "others" represent the individual's peer group as well as the informal groups always found in any organization. These informal groups form to meet the social and ego needs of the individual members. No matter how well the formal organization performs its duties, the informal organization will be present.

Informal Leader

At this point the potential for a supervisor-informal leader confrontation comes into play. As long as the supervisor-manager can provide the associates with personal need satisfaction, including higher-level need satisfaction, the leader and the informal group will be latent and inactive. However, if the supervisor, through ineptness or by higher managerial edict, is unable to fulfill employee expectations, an informal leader may come forth, galvanize the employees into social solidarity, and challenge the supervisor for effective control of the group.

Usually, this type of situation is found where subordinates have little job mobility or considerable tenure within an organization. In the retailing field, these individuals may be found in career or professional groups of sales personnel that represent the full-time corps of the sales organization. This problem may not be as potentially great in retailing as in manufacturing because of the former's high turnover in part-time employees. However, if the problem arises, it can be just as dysfunctional in retailing as elsewhere.

In summary, employee supervision is a complex task requiring genuine concern for the growth, development, and general well-being of all human resources. Leadership should precede supervision, relying on the latter only when all else fails. The effective supervisor, at all levels, translates abstract plans, policies, and procedures into reality through directing, coordinating, and supporting the "doers"—the goal-achieving, motivated employees.

People make things happen when the leader connects "can do" to "will do" and to "job well done."

Performance Appraisal

Performance appraisal is the process of comparing the current or recent performance of an individual with predetermined performance standards set forth in the job description. Conclusions drawn from this comparative process can be used in several fundamentally different ways, although the most common usage is for merit increases in wage and salary administration. Periodic performance appraisals can also identify individuals who are ready for promotion, or conversely, it can point out those individuals in need of further training or motivation in their current job.

Many attempts have been made to soften the image and impact of the evaluative process, but no matter how the activity is performed, the process is a potentially threatening situation for the employee. Managerial philosophy vis-à-vis its employees becomes extremely critical in determining how employees view and participate in the evaluative process. Most experts agree that performance appraisals should be made quarterly. The first and third evaluations should be directed primarily at identifying employee deficiencies and creating a systematic supportive program for improvement. These evaluations should review the behavior of the past six months in relation to mutually established quantifiable goals. Such programs are oriented toward developing the individual's potential and helping that individual meet some of the personal higher-order needs for achievement. These reviews should be mutual, collaborative sessions between the individual and the immediate superior.

The second and fourth evaluations should be conducted for compensation considerations by the superior, and the results should be conveyed to the employee with supporting rationale. Such evaluations should be based on some form of written record, such as production reports, a critical incidents diary, or other appropriate records of behavior.

Once factual data are collected, the comparison process can be undertaken. In each evaluative situation the supervisor's emphasis must be objectively focused on the person's performance of the assigned and understood tasks. The employee can be expected to perform only the tasks that are contained in the job description and mutually agreed upon. Thus, the importance of continually updating job descriptions to keep pace with the ever-changing job situation cannot be overemphasized.

A supplemental approach to performance appraisal has been developed and used more frequently in the last few years. In order to increase personal objectivity, peer ratings, subordinate ratings, group or committee ratings, and field-review methods have been selectively used.[5] Results of these evaluations can be compared with supervisory evaluations and any obvious discrepancies resolved.

Regardless of the combination of evaluative processes used, it is important to remember that the direct application of a generalized technique requires some specific modifications to deal with situations in a particular organization. In short, the appraisal system must be tested for validity and reliability. This is not only a good management practice but almost a necessity in future evaluations that may be subject to a court test by the

Equal Employment Opportunity Commission (brought by an aggrieved employee or by the commission itself). Again, discrimination must take place, but only on the basis of ability.

Appraisal Interview

Constructive
Communication

The appraisal process is not completed until the supervisor-manager discusses the results with the individual being evaluated, and they jointly plan for the individual's personal development. Although the concept of mutuality is critical to any behavioral change, it is important to note that not all appraisals result in negative or bad observations. For example, if the performance appraisal reveals that a department manager has met the quarterly sales goal, the person should be congratulated and encouraged to apply this winning game plan to the next period along with any needed modifications.

When communicating with the employee about the individual's appraisal results, it is very important for the supervisor-manager to concentrate on problem identification and generation of alternative solutions and to avoid any remarks that may be damaging to the employee's ego. Such supervisory thinking as "You're a lousy salesperson" has no place in constructive performance appraisal. If the employee is not measuring up to agreed-upon standards, what is the reason for this failure? Poor health, personal indifference due to lack of motivation, or inappropriate rewards—any of these could be a contributory cause.

Find the cause, devise a plan of action to remedy the situation, and set specific time/money milestones to check progress. Behavioral change occurs slowly, and an effective supervisor should channel job-related behavior for the mutual benefit of the individual and the organization.

Training and Development

Training and development programs vary widely in their scope and complexity. Some firms prefer to recruit trained, motivated employees to utilize premium compensation packages to retain such individuals, and to leave personal development to each person's initiative and mode of learning whether it be experience, night school, or other learning situations. On the other end of the spectrum, some organizations have in-house training and development programs specifically tailored for that retail firm and directed toward an individual's lifetime career development within the organization's many activities.

Regardless of the degree of a retailer's commitment to training and development programs, one fact is paramount: when such programs are properly designed, they will greatly facilitate a firm's adaptation to its environment. The benefits to the company are evident. Management must constantly recall that in order to change an organization one must first change the behavior of its people. People adapt, and organizations survive or perish on the basis of the appropriateness of their human adaptation.

Training

Many people in the retail industry tend to use the terms *training* and *development* interchangeably, which generates considerable confusion. **Training** and/or retraining refers to the acquisition of "basic skills and knowledge required in carrying out various specialized parts of the overall task of the enterprise."[6] Such skills as basic transaction center procedure, posting invoices, constructing advertising layouts, or operating a pin-ticket machine all constitute basic skills needed in the operation of some retail operations. Obviously, whenever a procedural change is introduced to increase efficiency or the amount of the average customer sale, the affected employees need to be informed and given an opportunity to practice the new selling technique. Experience has demonstrated that simply telling people about a new technique is not enough; they must practice it until they can demonstrate an acceptable performance level. For example, one may conduct a training session on suggestive selling that actually requires trainees to practice the art of selecting and selling related merchandise to fellow trainees. Such role-playing techniques and similar simulations have a demonstrated record of improving productivity.

OJT

Training methods vary from firm to firm, but the most common include on-the-job training (OJT), conferences or discussion, classroom training, programmed instruction, and education-employer cooperative programs. For example, the Emporium-Capwell division of Carter, Hawley, Hale Company runs four to five classes a year for persons who are new employees with undergraduate degrees and current employees who have been identified as "promotable to buyers." During the six-week on-the-job training experience each class of 25 to 30 trainees is given three days of orientation and systems training. This is followed by two and one-half weeks of a store assignment in which the trainee works with an experienced department sales manager to become familiar with this vital function. The trainee is exposed to seminars in such topics as security, sales staffing, supervision of sales performance, shortage control, floor merchandising discipline, visual presentation, transportation problems, retail math, functions of the buying office, trend and item merchandising, advertising and demographics, and concludes with a two and one-half hour test over the material presented.[7]

In the final three weeks of the training period individuals are assigned to an experienced buyer and assistant buyer. After successfully completing the initial six weeks of training the trainee begins interviewing for a department sales manager position in one of the firm's 20 stores (See Exhibit 17.1). The normal career path for the trainee would lead upward from department sales manager to assistant buyer to buyer within three to five years. Once promoted to a buyer position the individual is responsible for $1 to $9 million of sales for the firm.

Exhibit 17.1 Position Description

Position Title: Department Sales Manager
Major Function: To develop growth in sales through the proper management and merchandising of the department.

Specific Duties and Responsibilities

I. Merchandise Planning and Analysis
  1. To analyze department customers to influence the buying staff in planning assortments and stock depth which will develop the proper merchandise mix for the customer.
  2. To participate in the development of semiannual sales plans and goals.
  3. To analyze and interpret statistical reports and to take action where needed in order to achieve planned sales goals.
  4. To identify fast-selling merchandise and to communicate needs to the central buying organization; to follow through to ensure that the requests for stock replenishments are implemented.
  5. To identify slow-selling merchandise through analysis of reports, observation, and counts, and to suggest plans for disposition of this merchandise.
  6. To shop and analyze competition in the trade area to evaluate their assortments, prices, and merchandise presentation in order to be competitive in these areas.
  7. To review basic stock requirements to maintain the appropriate levels and to determine the needs for additions, deletions, and change of levels.
  8. To identify strengths and weaknesses of each department/classification and to develop a plan for increasing sales.
  9. To identify, track, and project key items.
  10. To make recommendations for needed physical changes and new fixtures in the department.

II. Advertising Responsibilities
  1. To insure that adequate stock is available for all advertised merchandise.
  2. To properly sign and display advertised merchandise.
  3. To communicate advertised merchandise to selling personnel.

III. Merchandise Presentation Responsibilities
  1. To present merchandise in a coordinated and exciting manner.
  2. To provide direction and merchandise information to display and sales staff.
  3. To allocate space according to profitability of merchandise, fashion versus basic merchandise, stock turn, volume, and timing.

Exhibit 17.1 Continued

IV. Operations and Customer Service Responsibilities
    1. To staff the department adequately with sales and stock help in order to achieve planned volume, sales production goals, and customer service standards.
    2. To handle customer adjustments courteously and promptly in compliance with the store's standards of customer service.
    3. To insure a standard of customer service that is both satisfactory and profitable through supervision and proper staffing.
    4. To maintain a clean, neat, and orderly appearance in all selling and stock areas.
V. Shortage Control Responsibilities
    1. To see that all paperwork (price changes, transfers, claims) is completed accurately and promptly.
    2. To check incoming merchandise for completeness and pricing.
    3. To prepare and take physical inventory.
    4. To comply with all store policies regarding shortage control.
    5. To insure that merchandise is sold in the correct department at the correct price.
    6. To alert sales personnel to problems of theft and shortage.
VI. Staff Development Responsibilities
    1. To set an example of selling standards for sales personnel.
    2. To develop staff in selling skills.
    3. To communicate special system procedures and changes to staff.
    4. To provide merchandise information to sales staff.
    5. To monitor progress through performance review in terms of productivity and customer service.
    6. To identify and develop staff members for additional responsibility.

Source: Emporium-Capwell, a Division of Carter Hawley Hale, Inc.

Individuals with a Master of Business Administration (M.B.A.) degree who gain employment with Emporium-Capwell are placed on a fast track and are expected to become buyers in one and one-half to two years (See Exhibit 17.2).

Continuing Training Programs

Most large retail firms have begun to appreciate the need for on-going training at all levels in the organization. Once aware of these needs the typical retailer soon realizes that the staff does not possess the resources or expertise to design and implement such an extensive training effort, so the firm turns to such outside training firms as Mohr or Dyna-Com.

Mohr's integrated approach is based on the concept of "train the trainer." Typically an account specialist develops a custom program of auditory, visual, and print materials for the client firm. Once these materials are produced, the trainer coaches twelve to twenty line managers to become master trainers using these customized materials. One such program was developed for Wanamakers of Philadelphia and initially involved six man-

Exhibit 17.2   Emporium-Capwell Executive Training Program for M.B.A.s

Content of Program

Emporium-Capwell's Executive Training Program for M.B.A. executives consists of eight weeks of on-the-job training and classroom instruction.

Training Assignments

1. *Branch Store*

   An M.B.A. trainee is placed in one of our larger stores for a total of six weeks under the supervision of the Merchandise Manager and the Store Manager. The six weeks is broken down as follows:

   two weeks—assistant to a department sales manager

   four weeks—assistant to merchandise manager

   While in a store, the M.B.A. trainee will first learn the fundamentals of the department sales manager position, including:

   a. Scheduling and supervising the staff

   b. Shifting floor presentation to create an exciting environment in which to shop.

   c. Learning all store procedures

   d. Organizing stock room by classification

   e. Analyzing floor layout

   As an assistant to the merchandise manager, the M.B.A. trainee will learn the fundamentals of store operation including:

   a. Handling customer service problems

   b. Analyzing sales of a department or complex

   c. Developing a plan of action to improve business

   Since the M.B.A. trainee by-passes the department sales manager position in his/her career development, the six weeks in a store is a very important segment of the training program.

2. *Buying Office*

   The final two-week training assignment will be in a buying office. Here the trainee will learn the basic buying procedures; how buys are negotiated; and how merchandise is shipped, moved and transferred. During this phase, the M.B.A. trainee will also have an opportunity to write purchase orders, visit resources, and handle receiving problems. This assignment will help prepare the M.B.A. for future interviews for the assistant buyer position.

Merchandise Seminars

M.B.A.'s along with our undergraduate trainees attend seminars on merchandising and management skills on a weekly, or biweekly basis. The sessions are taught by experts in our store—our divisional merchandise managers, buyers and store managers. The sessions include:

Merchandise Math	Labor Relations
Gross Margin Calculation	Shortage Control and Security/ Loss Prevention
Trend and Item Merchandising	
Merchandise Presentation	Merchandise Handling
Sales Staffing	Store Reports
	Supervisory Skills

A training manual, containing reference material for these seminars, is distributed to all executive trainees.

The first permanent placement for an M.B.A. is as an assistant buyer. Ideally, an M.B.A. will begin in a small to moderate size department and be moved to a larger, more complex area after several months. Two assistant buying positions will provide the trainees with a broader exposure to the business and thereby maximize an M.B.A.'s chances for success as a buyer.

Source: Emporium-Capwell, a Division of Carter Hawley Hale, Inc.

SSP

RSS

LCI
CBI

Macy's Training Program

agers in a four-day program entitled "Supervision of Sales Performance (SSP)." When the program was completed the six managers trained 15 training managers so they could train the firm's 5,000 regular salespersons in a program called "Retail Selling Skills (RSS)."[8] The effectiveness of the entire program is monitored by the six master trainers who, in turn, are given periodic refresher courses by Mohr's specialists.

Department stores are not limiting their training activities to just sales training. Two controversial buyer training methods, learner-controlled instruction (LCI) and competency-based instruction (CBI), are being adopted by firms who wish to improve employee productivity. The thrust of these techniques is to identify specific tasks and develop relevant competencies for day to day activities required by the job.

Not all retailers have been convinced that LCI or CBI programs are totally appropriate for their operations. Former May Department Stores' chief executive officer, David Babcock, has criticized the LCI approach as being, ". . . almost a mechanical, machine-type process." He continued, "In management training, you need to teach three skills: technical competence, managerial competence, and most of all, human relations competence."[9] Bird McCord, vice-president for personnel, National Retail Merchants Association, supports the same view by noting, "The retailing industry may be jeopardizing its ability to replenish its longer-term needs for executives who are capable of handling higher-level positions. People who are successful in running the retail organizational maze are those who have the capacity to mobilize human and nonhuman resources to get things done."[10]

One firm which is attempting to skillfully blend a wide range of training and development techniques into a well-balanced program is the R. H. Macy Company. Every year, about 1,000 new management and merchandising trainees are selected to join the R. H. Macy team. According to Mr. Paul Cholak, vice-president of corporate employee relations, before persons are chosen for these select teams, they undergo rigorous on-campus testing and then are required to go through the Macy's Assessment Center process.

When the candidate successfully overcomes these hurdles, he or she is offered employment as a trainee. If the individual accepts, the person will be assigned to a group of twenty to twenty-five trainees who are brought on board at frequent intervals throughout the year. Training experiences vary from division to division. If the trainee is assigned to the New York Division, that person can expect eleven weeks of formal training. The training will include lecture (15%), case study (40%), learner-controlled instruction (15%), group discussion (15%), and role playing (10%).

Formal training doesn't stop there but continues throughout each person's career and may take the form of vendor negotiations or employee relations. The importance of this training process is borne out by the fact that every person in the top 100 positions in the company came up through this system.

Advancement to Merchandise Manager

A few highly successful buyers may be promoted to the line position of merchandise managers. In this position a merchandise manager plans and coordinates the buying and selling activities for large stores. They allocate the various budget monies for buying, advertising, staffing and so forth to buyers to implement their merchandising decisions. They periodically review their merchandise plans to insure a balance in the emphasis and profitability of the store, particularly in establishing price lines.

In addition to their merchandising activities, most merchandise managers are responsible for final hiring decisions, sales promotion plans and their execution, and are usually responsible for creating and maintaining enthusiasm among the sales staff. Last, some merchandise managers actively participate in the actual negotiations with manufacturers' representatives while serving as the final arbiter of customer complaints.

Management Development

Management development, which has a broader scope than training, is directed toward the improvement of an individual's knowledge, skills, attitudes, perceptions, and personal characteristics in current and future managerial positions. Management development is increasingly extended not only to management trainees but to managers at all levels to improve their ability to cope with interpersonal relations. Interpersonal relations in retailing have become more important in recent years as more specialization has been required to keep pace with evolving markets. Cooperation and collaboration spell success, whereas individualism in large retail organizations is a relic of the past.

Management development may take the form of project or committee assignments, staff meetings, or simply coaching in an on-the-job assignment. Many professional associations and consulting firms offer management development courses both on and off the company's premises. Such development activities may take the form of in-basket exercises, management games, role-playing situations, sensitivity training, or professional reading. Regardless of the mode of instruction, the objective is the same: to increase the individual's ability to cope with a wide variety of situations by recognizing personal biases and to become better able to see the "real world" more objectively.

In summary, training and development are an expensive, never-ending price that an organization must pay as part of its costs of remaining competitive. Without some realistic program of constructive innovation, a retail firm's days on the economic scene are numbered.

Compensation in Retailing

The retail industry provides a wide range of compensation to those employed in its diverse institutions. A large portion of the industry's employees earn the minimum wage, while a select few earn salaries and bonuses in the hundreds of thousands of dollars. For years the retail industry has been viewed as "an employer of last resort" or a source of "temporary" employment by most of our nation's workers. Competitive pressures coupled with high turnover discouraged retailers from paying higher wages which would have attracted those persons interested in long-term employment.

Over the last ten years federally mandated programs have raised payroll costs significantly without any appreciable increases in employee productivity. In 1979–80, men's wear stores were spending about 18.6 percent of their total company sales in payroll costs, while mass merchandisers were paying just over 12 percent. These figures graphically illustrate the impact of automation and the extensive use of self-service which has resulted in a reduced need for labor in this labor intensive industry.

Many aspiring retailers consider careers in department stores as merchandisers. Initially few realize that there is a wide diversity in compensation among various firms for similarly titled jobs. In a survey taken in 1979 of merchandising personnel employed in department stores with an annual volume of $50 to $200 million, it was reported that the annual compensation for buyers ranged from $8,400 to over $37,500 with the average about $21,000. Divisional merchandise managers' rewards were between $26,000 and $60,000 with the average reported to be $41,000. At the top of the merchandising pyramid general merchandise managers' total compensation was between $50,000 and $117,500 while most averaged $75,500 per year.[11]

Today the actual hourly or monthly wage represents an increasingly smaller portion of the total compensation cost. In addition to the federal minimum wage, the union-negotiated wage, or salary determined in the labor market, the retail manager must consider the following fringe benefits:

1. Incentive sales programs
2. Federally required social security payments
3. Unemployment insurance and workmen's compensation payments
4. Fringe benefits of life, health, and accident insurance
5. Retirement plans
6. Supplemental unemployment benefits
7. Paid vacations, holidays, and sick leave
8. Time paid but not worked such as coffee breaks, lunch periods, time off for deaths in the family, and voting
9. Costs of maintaining employee records
10. Merchandise discounts to employees.

Many progressive firms are aware of the need to devote more resources to human resources in the firm but are precluded by depressed sales and rising costs. Perhaps Robert D. Kenzer summarized the industry's enlightened view when he noted, "If you want to make money, you've got to spend money and that means hiring the best available talent." He concludes, "The success of any retailing business ultimately depends on human resources. Location helps, merchandise helps; but people provide the real competitive edge."[12]

Viewing the compensation question from a broader perspective than day-to-day individual compensation issues, retail executives have come to the realization that they are well advised to compensate their human resources at a premium level and hence indirectly avoid the threat of unionization. As noted earlier, it has been shown that employees take collective action when they perceive that they are not being treated equitably. Consequently, if the employees are currently receiving total compensation benefits that are greater than a union can deliver through the process of collective bargaining, the employees are reluctant to join union activity. Thus, many managers see this alternative as beneficial to both employees and the firm over the long term. Whether this strategy will continue to be successful in the future remains to be seen.

Union-Management Relations

A complete discussion of industrial relations is beyond the scope of this text. It is important, however, to note some philosophical and legal aspects of union-management relations. From a philosophical point of view, a retail manager can view a union as a threat. In such a situation the union gains what management gives up or loses. The union movement is, from such a viewpoint, the adversary to be resisted by all legal means.

An alternative perspective is that a union can be a constructive partner in resolution of common or complementary interests.[13] Operating under this premise, one is not out to increase one's share of the economic rewards at the cost of the other party; rather, each partner is vitally interested in increasing the absolute amount of economic reward possible. History has emphasized the win-lose strategy, while the international economic scene suggests that national unions and retail management may find it more appropriate to act as partners to maintain or increase this nation's competitiveness in the world marketplace.

Contract Negotiation

A more particular concern to the retailer is the day-to-day relationship with the employees and the interpretation of a union contract. No matter how carefully the words of a labor agreement are chosen, no matter how well the negotiating representatives agree with each other on points in the contract, the provisions of the contract will be interpreted differently by both sides. If the supervisor and a union employee disagree, and that disagreement cannot be resolved by the union representative (the shop steward) and the supervisor's superior, the dispute becomes a formal grievance and must be settled by formal, agreed-upon procedures. Once grievance procedures are initiated, the supervisor-manager has lost control of the situation and must abide by the decision reached behind closed doors in a formal hearing. It becomes quite clear that when a retail firm becomes unionized the absolute formal authority of a supervisor-manager is markedly reduced, which means the superior cannot rely on an autocratic supervisory style to supervise the department effectively. Employee consultation and participation in decision making, in a limited sense, becomes a practical necessity if the supervisor is going to be successful.

Another important implication of unionization is that the supervisor-manager loses considerable discretion in the use of the firm's reward and punishment mechanisms. In order to encourage, motivate, and channel the subordinates' behavior, the supervisor must rely on informal methods of leadership such as persuasion, influence, and negotiation relationships. Often a supervisor's management style may be dictated by company policy toward union employees, such as "following the book," "dealing at arm's length," and so forth. In that case, if a supervisor assumes an independent supervisory style, he or she risks higher management's wrath. Increasingly, the first line supervisor is the person in the middle.

Some Observations on Current Sales Force Personnel Practices

Generalizations about situations are always dangerous because one tends to overlook specific examples. With this qualification in mind it should be noted that a large gulf exists between "what ought to be" and "what is" in the practice of personnel management in the retail industry.

Today retail management is faced with unprecedented challenges in the effective utilization of the firm's human resources. According to Stanley J. Winkelman, chairman of the board of Winkelman Stores, Detroit,

> "To meet the challenges posed by inflation and threatened, reduced energy supplies, we must improve productivity. We must relearn the art of selling and of managing the selling function in order to achieve increased space utilization and, consequently, speedup of inventory turnover. This means a different balance between merchandising functions. In other words, how can we get more out of less space, or much more out of more space."[14]

As noted earlier leaders in the retail trade view the decade of the 1980s as the era of productivity improvement. One might recall that the definition of productivity is the amount of output measured in increased economic value per worker hour. Historically, all industries have successfully boosted productivity by substituting capital for labor, and retailing is no exception. As noted in Chapter 11 the retail industry is investing millions of dollars to improve their communication, information processing, and distribution facilities. Further investments in these sectors, while contributing to productivity, will not give current returns to scale, and in fact, may even give decreasing returns to scale. Retail management is fully aware of this projection and is now turning to long neglected human resources for improvement.

Employee Absenteeism and Turnover

The greatest problem facing personnel managers in retailing today is the employee absenteeism/turnover crisis. According to one report the average retail store lost 6.7 percent of its monthly workdays in 1981 due to missing employees. This rate even exceeds the 5.15 percent rate for government employees.[15] A second report noted that retail employee turnover averaged 60 percent annually and cited this phenomenon as the major cause of declining salesfloor productivity.[16]

Many explanations can be cited for these intolerable situations. Writing in his book, *The Retail Revolution: Market Transformation, Investment, and Labor in the Modern Department Store*, Barry Bluestone notes:

"Few industries have employee-separation rates as high as department stores. Rather than a permanent occupation, today the retail trade provides most of its younger workers with a one-way station in their career. For some it is an introduction to the world of work; for other workers it is a supplement to the regular job. . . . The $90 billion industry is increasingly responsible for providing part-time jobs for those in school, similar to the sorts of 'pocket-money' job opportunities offered by grocery stores, restaurants, and other secondary employers. Moreover, for many women over the age of 25, the retail sector has become a place for periodic employment. For some men in this age group it provides temporary jobs when they are laid off from their normal employers, or when they or their families require a second source of earnings. . . . What is then overwhelmingly clear—for every age group and for both men and women—is the declining permanency within the industry. Fewer workers consider the department store sector to offer a satisfactory career—with the presumable exception of those who obtain choice managerial slots."[17]

Temporary Jobs

The retail industry must bear some responsibility for this situation. As the minimum wage began to climb the industry, according to Bluestone, sought out those seeking part-time work in order to give them scheduling flexibility and to reduce their dependency on higher cost labor.[18] This strategy seemed to work in the short-run, but now both the retail industry and its consumers are paying for less productivity.

Given this situation what is to be done? At the sales associate or clerk level, Mr. Charles Griffin, president of Sanger-Harris in Dallas, suggests, "We must staff our stores with informed, concerned, and interested salespeople. To do this, we must dignify the selling function by creating (1) compensation programs for sales achievement, (2) recognition programs for sales achievers, and (3) design sales-oriented career paths that retain top salespeople and give them incentive to grow and produce."[19] Large or innovative retail firms are beginning to implement sophisticated recruitment, training and development, compensation, and other retention-oriented programs for career retail management specialists. Top management is also giving belated recognition to the personnel department by elevating the top position to the rank of vice-president, on a par with the chief operating officer and the chief accounting officer, and giving the function much needed resources. With this new charge, personnel departments will be able to implement effective personnel programs which improve employee morale, comply with federal and state equal employment practice regulations, improve productivity and cus-

Recognize Sales Achievers

tomer satisfaction. Any significant decline in economic activity will show this reversal process, but eventually the decade of the 1980s should see a major improvement in retail personnel practices.

Retail Employment Opportunities: Future Trends and Challenges

Retailing employment during the 1980s is expected to rise at about the same rate as that of other occupations in our national economy. Such employment will be affected by both the consumers' desire to spend and their ability to fund buying activities. These propensities will be influenced by consumers' employment levels, the adequacy of that income, and their willingness to assume debt.

Outlook for Selected Retail Careers

Buyer

When referring to retail careers many people first think of buyers. Since the postwar years the general public has associated department store buyers with a rich, active, decisive, glamorous life built around the fashion industry. While it is true that a few buyers for large department stores do periodically travel abroad and partake of such a lifestyle, most of the 115,000 buyers and merchandise managers employed in 1978 lead a much more routine existence. All the nonfashion merchandise which consumers need, ranging from automobile tires to canned zucchini, must be selected and purchased in advance so that goods are in the right place, at the right time, in the right assortment, at the right price. Such responsibilities call for resourcefulness, good judgment, and self-confidence in one's ability to anticipate customer preferences. Mistakes are costly and may result in loss of employment for the unfortunate buyer or merchandise manager if they err too often.

Employment opportunities should fall below projected growth for the whole retail sector as increased use of computerized systems to maintain inventories and increase standardization of merchandise assortments reduce the need for buyers. Replacement needs will dictate job availability rather than expansion in the occupation. The highest paying buyer positions can be found with discount department stores and other mass merchandising firms. Merchandising positions, ranging from assistant buyers to general merchandise managers, enjoy compensation ranging from $10,000 to $200,000 but the most common compensation range runs from $25,000 to $35,000 per year, with performance bonuses for outstanding achievement.

Retail Foodstore

The retail foodstore sector offers employment to more than 2.3 million employees in supermarkets, small grocery stores, convenience stores, and specialty foodstores. Approximately 40 percent of these employees are either clerical or specialized department employees such as meat cutters and produce processors. About 25 percent of the workforce are laborers working as order fillers and stock and merchandise handlers. Managers and administrators, including buyers, account for another 20 percent. The remaining 15 percent is composed of a wide range of skilled professionals such as accountants, personnel professionals, and skilled craftspeople such as bakers and mechanics.

Those persons with bachelor's degrees in business administration, marketing, or graduates in food industry management will be in demand for managerial, sales, research, planning, and other professional positions. Starting salaries begin about $15,000 for management and sales trainees with experienced managers earning considerably more. With increased automation of the information systems in the 1980s, the retail food store may offer new exciting opportunities for innovative marketers.

Retail Finance

Retail finance, formerly dominated by commercial banking, is expected to provide more jobs than any other sector in the retail industry. While most job opportunities will be concentrated in the clerical levels, college graduates will find many professional opportunities such as officer and management trainees, accountants, auditors, statisticians, computer programmers, system analysts, and marketing specialists. As deregulation of this sector continues, traditional retail financing institutions will be joined by new institutional firms. Competition for the consumer's "banking business" is expected to generate a particular need for marketing-oriented personnel who will be capable of effectively merchandising a variety of financial services. If these forecasts and projections are realized, this sector may provide the most challenging and rewarding retailing careers during the 1980s.

This decade will experience major changes in the retailing industry. With consumer preferences shifting toward quality and value in purchases and an increased propensity to save rather than consume, retail employment will change significantly at all levels in the industry. Clerical-level employment will decline as stores introduce technology and older, less efficient units are closed. Middle-level managerial employment opportunities will decline as their job activities are performed by sophisticated computers which will be part of new integrated management information systems. Real challenges in the field will be associated with designing and implementing these new systems and with development of innovative modes of consumer communication in the home and in local shopping areas. Successful retail careers will be fewer in number but more rewarding for those willing to make the commitment and assume the risks.

Some other possible retail service industries include insurance, hotel management, food, personal finance, protective services, real estate, and financial securities. Each industry has its own unique characteristics and employment potential. Anyone interested in these specialized retail careers is advised to consult career counselors for further detailed information.

Summary

This discussion has attempted to give a general overview of the management of human resources in retailing. Organizational philosophy significantly influences the practice of personnel activities in every organization. The degree of delegation of authority strongly affects the design of jobs and shapes job specifications for positions at all levels in the organizational structure. Current government enforcement of employment legislation is strongly restricting the freedom of organizations in their selection and promotion of the firm's employees as well as structuring their conditions of employment.

In chronological order, personnel functions include recruitment, selection, placement, performance appraisal, training and development, wage and salary administration, fringe benefit management, attending to the general occupational health and safety of employees, and constant effort to maintain and improve the firm's personnel system. This order of presentation represents a normal employment sequence, but in the real world of retailing the process is not this orderly. A manager may be faced with a "no show" employee problem one minute and a "suggestive" selling problem the next. This acknowledgment of the behavior required of a manager in the competitive situation need not be considered a hindrance as long as the manager remains consistent in decisions on personnel matters. The need for consistency mandates that a manager formulate guiding personnel philosophies ahead of time, so that when crises arise adequate preparations have been made to cope with the situation.

Selected employment opportunities for retail buyers and managers look bright through the mid 1980s, subject to continued economic growth and development. The fast paced world of retailing will continue to provide an excellent arena for tackling the challenge and problems of human resource management.

Questions

1. Why should retail managers be concerned with human resource management when most stores are designed and merchandised for self-service operation?
2. What is the relationship between organization philosophies and goals and the way employees are managed? Explain.
3. How can job design improve productivity, morale, and profitability of retail employees?
4. Why should retail job descriptions have "elastic parameters"? Explain.

5. What responsibilities does Title VII of the Civil Rights Act of 1964 (amended in 1972) place on the personnel managers in retail firms employing fifteen or more persons? Explain.

6. If you want to become the president of a large retail chain, what educational requirements are necessary. What entry level position would you apply for?

7. What must a supervisor or department manager do to change the employees' attitudes toward the job from "can do" to "will do"? Explain.

8. What are the significant differences between employee training and development?

9. What personal characteristics or qualities tend to increase an individual's chances for success in retail buying? In store management?

10. What are the future employment prospects for retail bankers during the 1980s? What environmental variables might change the current predictions?

Footnotes

1. Herbert J. Chruden and Arthur W. Sherman, Jr., *Personnel Management,* 3d ed. (Cincinnati: South-Western Publishing Co., 1968), p. 161.

2. Ibid.

3. Arion Q. Sartain and Atlan W. Baker, *The Supervisor and His Job,* 2d ed. (New York: McGraw-Hill, 1972), p. 14.

4. Edgar H. Schein, *Organization Psychology* (Englewood Cliffs, N.J.: Prentice-Hall, 1965), p. 11.

5. Chruden and Sherman, *Personnel Management,* p. 277.

6. Wendell French, *The Personnel Management Process,* 2d ed. (Boston: Houghton Mifflin, 1970), p. 481.

7. Norine Holthe, *Executive Training Program Manual,* Emporium-Capwell, San Francisco. 1981.

8. Lewis A. Spalding, "People Business," *Stores* (March 1981): 42.

9. Lance Ringel, "Buyer Training," *Stores* (April 1981): 48.

10. Ibid.

11. "To Pay to Play Retailers," *Retail Week* (December 1, 1979): 47.

12. "Managing Prospective Managers," *Chain Store Age Executive* (May 1981): 80.

13. Richard E. Walton and Robert B. McKersie, *A Behavioral Theory of Labor Relations* (New York: McGraw-Hill, 1965), p. 4.

14. "The Big Drive for Efficiency in Retailing," *Chain Store Age Executive* (May 1980): 138.

15. William George Shuster, "Absenteeism: Retailers Are Hit Hardest," *Jewelers' Circular-Keystone* (November 1981): 46.

16. Lewis A. Spalding, "People Business," *Stores* (March 1981): 42.

17. Barry Bluestone et al. *The Retail Revolution: Market Transformation, Investment, and Labor in the Modern Department Store* (Boston: Auburn Publishing Company, 1981), p. 91.

18. Ibid., p. 95.

19. Spalding, "People Business," p. 43.

Case Study: Lane's Toyland

Lane's Toyland, located in San Jose, California was begun by Dale Lane in 1976 after he had completed his M.B.A. at Stanford. While he was attending the university he had become quite fascinated by the challenges presented by venture management. He really hadn't wanted to work for a large company. He liked the atmosphere in the lower Bay area and didn't want to move away after graduation. He began to plan his own business during his last quarter in a venture class, exploring several possible entrepreneurial opportunities. After due consideration, he decided the toy business represented the best opportunity in the San Jose area.

Just before graduation his parents were killed in a car crash and he inherited $100,000 after taxes. After a proper mourning period he dedicated all his energies to forming the new business and operating the store. It was an instant success. Literally overnight Dale had more business than he could handle, so he hired additional sales staff and a store manager so he could concentrate on merchandising and other operational details.

In the first four years, Lane's Toyland expanded into four different locations in the lower Bay area. Each new store met with great success and business continued to increase. The payroll grew to forty sales persons, five store managers, an advertising manager, office manager, accountant/computer specialist, three buyers, and a sales and merchandise manager. Sales began to plateau in late 1980, but all stores were making a 23–30 percent return on their investment. Then in January 1981 sales dropped off by 50 percent over previous years. February continued the trend with sales down 40 percent followed by March down 35 percent. April, May, and June followed the earlier pattern but recovered some, down to an average of 20 percent.

Alert to these signals in the first part of the year, Dale began to take action to contain the losses by cutting inventory, increasing store hours, closing two marginally profitable stores, and transferring the full-time sales staff to the remaining stores. Other cost cutting actions were taken with some effect.

The late summer months showed continued sales improvement with July, August, and September sales down about 10 percent from the previous year. Then in October, the "bottom fell out" of the toy business, sales decreased 90 percent, and Lane's Toyland suffered its first loss since the firm was formed. The poor year had depleted most of the working capital. For the first time in the firm's history, Dale had to borrow funds for operations because he had tied all his available funds up in inventory for the Christmas selling season. A trip to his local bank indicated that his credit was acceptable due to his inventory position and that the rate of interest would be 23 percent, renegotiable each month based on the current prime rate.

On November 2nd, Dale must set his staffing plan for the Christmas season. He has kept all forty full-time sales people in the remaining three stores. The stores are open from 10 a.m. to 8 p.m. Monday to Saturday and Sunday twelve to six. Each sales associate works a five-day, forty-hour per week schedule. Beginning November 27th through December 23rd the stores will be open Monday through Saturday 10 a.m. to 10 p.m. and Sunday, 12–10 p.m. Each sales associate receives a salary of $280 per week plus fringe benefits of FICA, unemployment compensation, fully paid medical and dental insurance, plus two weeks paid vacation after the first full year of satisfactory employment. Each of the three store managers earns $450 per week plus 8 percent of the annual net profits of their store. Administrative payroll costs include $2,000 per month for the sales and merchandise manager, $1,800 a month per buyer, $2,000 per month for the accountant / computer specialist, and $2,000 a month for the advertising manager. Office staff includes one receptionist/typist at $1,600 a month, and one clerk at $1,400 per month. The office manager quit last month when her request for a raise was not granted.

Discussion Questions   1. Determine staffing needs for the Christmas selling season.
                             2. Develop a weekly schedule for each store.

Chapter 18 | Obtaining and Conserving Money through Control

Learning Goals

1. To know the sources of funds for retailers.
2. To understand the basic accounting records that are used in retailing.
3. To be able to discuss how cash flow forecasting can meet the firm's need for funds.
4. To learn ways that financial and operating ratios can increase firm profitability.
5. To be aware of the need to protect the firm's assets by using insurance.

Key Terms and Concepts

short-term funds	income statement
floor-plan financing	cash flow forecast
factoring	operating ratios
intermediate term credit	financial ratios
long-term credit	current ratio
assets	quick ratio
liabilities	collection period
owner's equity	net-sales-to-inventory ratio
balance sheet	net-profits-on-net-sales ratio
current assets	net-profits-on-tangible-net-
first in-first out (FIFO)	worth-ratio
last in-first out (LIFO)	insurance
retail inventory method	return on assets chart

Adequate capital is a basic requirement for all retail operations. It is impossible to operate a retail outlet successfully unless sufficient funds are available, because the need for money is present in all phases of retailing. This chapter discusses sources of funds and the control concepts used in accounting, inventory evaluation, and finance. Retailing cash flow analysis and financial ratios also are presented.

The amount of capital required should be estimated before making a commitment to purchase, lease, or build. The estimate must include a reasonable safety margin that allows for unexpected demands for money not included in the original, carefully prepared estimate. The type and size of the retail outlet determine the capital requirement. It may require as little as a few thousand dollars to establish a small, limited-line outlet in leased facilities, while several million dollars may be needed to establish a large, fully stocked, wide-merchandise-line outlet in store-owned facilities. The purchaser of an established retail outlet can estimate the capital requirements by using company records. Purchase price for the outlet can be added to the estimated costs needed for remodeling, inventory changes, living expenses, additional working capital, and contingencies until the outlet is opened for business. Then a cash flow analysis can be performed to estimate ongoing capital requirements.

Estimating capital requirements for a new firm's outlet is considerably more difficult. Cost information may be obtained from comparable retail outlets in other communities. Trade associations, the Small Business Administration, university research bureaus, and other business organizations frequently prepare publications that contain cost estimates. Careful estimation procedures should also be used to ensure that inflation and unforeseen contingencies have been accounted for in the final estimation. Fixture and equipment costs should also be estimated, by obtaining bids from at least two different logical suppliers.

Sources and Applications of Funds

Sources from which capital may be obtained can be evaluated after the estimated capital requirement is determined. Generally, the retailer's own capital is the most important source of retail funds. Financing may be difficult to obtain unless the owner's investment funds account for about half of the required funds.

Three different types of retail financing are required to ensure that adequate funds are available. Short-term credit consists of funds that are used mainly as operating capital for periods of less than one year. Intermediate term credit consists of loans needed to finance fixed assets, such as machines, fixtures, equipment, etc. These loans vary in length from one to ten years and are generally paid on a monthly basis. Long-term financing involves loans made primarily to purchase buildings and land. They are generally made for more than ten years.

Sources of Short-term Funds

Several sources are available for obtaining the **short-term funds** (funds that are loaned for a period of no more than one year). As discussed in Chapter 10, operating (short-term) capital may be obtained from vendors, who may make an inventory available on a thirty-, sixty-, or ninety-day credit basis. These terms allow the retailers to turn inventories over once before the invoice is due. It must be recalled, however, that considerable cash discounts can be obtained by paying bills before they are due. Thus, firms may find it profitable not to use this source of funds unless it is a matter of financial necessity.

Commercial banks provide short-term loans that can be acquired for operating capital if the retailer can show (by a cash flow and/or net worth analysis) that the loan will be repaid within a specified period. Simple commercial loans, generally made for 30 to 120 days, are one of the most common methods of obtaining short-term financing. Commercial banks generally make these short-term loans for seasonal financing and/or building up of retail inventories. These loans may be secured by requiring the retailer to pledge some type of assets as collateral such as inventory, accounts receivable, or stock. If the bank believes it can rely upon the retailer's credit reputation, it can make an unsecured loan, which does not require a pledge based upon physical collateral but upon a signature for a specified credit purpose. Some of the information that banks need to evaluate a loan application is presented in Table 18.1.

Floor-plan financing is an example of bank financing that requires the retailer to use inventories as collateral. Floor-inventory financing is most common for retailers who do not have sufficient working capital to purchase an adequate inventory for their marketing needs. To be eligible for a loan in this case, the inventory must have unit value high enough to permit separate and positive identification by serial number.

Procedures for handling floor-plan financing begin when the supplier delivers the merchandise and prepares a draft on the retailer's bank for the full cost of the merchandise. The bank then contacts the retailer to determine if the merchandise is acceptable and if he/she wants to pay for the merchandise. If payment is to be made, the bank usually debits the retailer's account with 10 percent of the value of the merchandise plus freight costs. The remaining 90 percent of the cost is due in ninety days, but financing can be obtained up to three additional ninety-day periods, providing at least 10 percent of the balance is paid before each option is renewed. The bank sends the original payment made by the retailer, along with its check for the remaining 90 percent of the merchandise value, to the supplier. This payment is made as soon as the retailer indicates the merchandise has been accepted.

Banks that lend money under the floor-plan financing agreement usually inspect the inventory monthly on an unannounced basis. The retailers are also required to keep all merchandise insured. The interest rate charged on floor-plan financing is generally 1 to 2 percent above the prime interest rate.

Table 18.1 Information Needed by Banks to Analyze a Loan Application

Statement Item	Additional Information Needed	Why Information Is Needed
Cash	Where is it deposited? Is any of it restricted or pledged?	To establish total banking relationships.
Accounts Receivable	How many are current? Are they collectable? How many should be written off?	Frequently used as bank collateral. Banks need to determine a realistic current value.
Inventory	How is it valued? How marketable is it? Is it excessive or partly obsolete?	Frequently used as collateral. Bank needs to know its value in the event of liquidation.
Notes Receivable	Why do they exist? Are they collectable? Could they be assigned to the bank?	Only financial institutions should routinely have notes as assets.
Due from Officers and Employees	What circumstances caused these loans to be made? Are they collectable? When will they be paid?	In excess these assets reflect poorly on management.
Due from Affiliated or Related Business Investments	What are the circumstances? Are they collectable? When will they be paid? What are they? Why were they made? How are they valued? How liquid? Could they be assigned to the bank as collateral?	Indicate a need for consolidated and consolidating statements. It is hard to support the credit needs of a customer who uses working capital to make speculative investments.
Property and Equipment	How is it valued? Is it all supporting the needs of the business? Is it encumbered? If so, how much and with whom?	Bank may want to pay these and secure a first lien position in support of its loan.
Leases and Leasehold Improvements	What are they? What are the terms? Are they assignable? Any value in liquidation?	Frequent source of off balance sheet accounting.
Notes Payable	What are the terms, rates and maturities? Will loan be used to retire all or part of these notes?	Can the customer service these and the proposed loans?
Trade Accounts Payable	Are trade payables being kept current?	The trade can force the customer into liquidation.
Other Current Payables	Insurance current? FICA? Income taxes when due? Payroll?	All are sources of potential trouble.
Term Debt	What assets offset the term debt? What are the current maturities? Can they be serviced on schedule?	Usually a significant part of the demand on a customer's cash flow.
Contingent Liabilities	What liabilities (real or potential) are there that are not shown on the financial statements?	These can be a serious source of trouble to the customer and the bank.
Sales	How are sales recognized? Are sales made with recourse? Have the goods or services been delivered? How many returns are there?	To establish that sales are actual and not book entries.
Expenses	Are executive salaries adequate or excessive? Is depreciation in line with asset values? What are the trends in C & A expenses?	Executive salaries and unnecessary expense items can be major source of working capital drain.
Other Income	What is its source? Will it continue?	Can the bank rely on it as a source of repayment.
Other Expenses	Why do they exist? Will they continue in the future?	Can the customer meet these payments?
Income Taxes	Do these appear reasonable? When was the customer last audited by the IRS?	Always a source of potential trouble. The bank wants copies of recent tax returns.
Profits	What are the trends? How reliable? What margin is there? Sufficient to service all debt?	This is the bank's primary source of repayment on most loans.
Dividends or Withdrawals	What is the historical pattern? How much will probably be drawn this year?	The bank may want to control these by a loan agreement.

Source: First National Bank of Albuquerque. Table first appeared in Edmond E. Pace and Frank Collins, "Bankers-Accountants-Financial Statements: Their Relationship to Small Business Loan Decisions," *Journal of Small Business Management*, October 1976. Reprinted by permission.

Retailers can also sell their customers' notes (or installment promissory notes) to a commercial bank to obtain short-term funds. The bank then advances money to the retailer against the customer notes. Another alternative is to retain the retail customer notes and use them as collateral for obtaining short-term loans from other sources. The interest rate charged by banks will vary according to the going interest rate, the degree of risk associated with the retail firm involved, and the financial reputation of the borrower. The interest rate charged by commercial banks is usually lower than the savings the retail outlet could obtain by paying its bills promptly and getting a cash discount from its vendors. Not using vendor credit to the limit also provides a safety margin which could be used if unforeseen needs for funds occur.

Factoring offers yet another possibility for short-term financing. Factoring involves selling a retailer's accounts receivable to another party. The advantages of factoring are:

Improves cash flow. Daily advances can be made against new accounts receivable.

May improve return on investment.

Frees up dollars now tied up in low earning assets.

Provides source of short-term funds.

Financial tax flexibility may be provided by some companies that allow advances on receivables to be based on either a loan or purchase basis.

If the accounts receivable are sold "without recourse," the buyer (or factor) assumes the loss resulting from any uncollected accounts. This offers the advantage of eliminating losses due to bad accounts, but it can cause consumer relation problems if the factor is not public relations minded. The relatively high commission—usually 1 to 3 percent of the total amount—is one disadvantage of this method of financing.

Sources of Intermediate-term Funds

Intermediate term credit, used to finance fixed assets (such as equipment, machines, fixtures, etc.), is generally granted for one to ten years. Such capital is needed as a means for small retailers to finance fixed assets that will depreciate over time. The primary difference between an intermediate term loan and a short-term loan is that a formal loan agreement is always needed. Many banks extend a **line of credit** to borrowers of intermediate term loans. The line of credit is a fixed amount, say $50,000, that a retail borrower can have outstanding at any one time. The retailer can borrow continually up to that specified amount on a permanent basis.

Frequently, suppliers of capital equipment that is required in retailing will lease their products to retailers. Equipment leasing can reduce the fixed-capital investment needed so that the retailer's funds can be used in other, hopefully better-yielding activities. Other liberalized trade credit techniques—such as lease with option to buy, buying equipment on installment terms, and so forth—can also frequently provide a source of intermediate retail capital.

Sources of Long-term Funds	Long-term loans can be applied to construct a new building or to buy a store or warehouse. **Long-term credit** differs from intermediate credit in the type of security needed. The lender must have assurances that the retailer is stable and large enough to be in existence over a period of years. Mortgages make up the bulk of long-term debt owed by small retailers because they seldom have the resources for selling a bond issue. Small retailers frequently must invest their own savings in the firm to meet long-term credit needs.

Mortgage bankers and insurance companies may finance real estate or construction capital requirements. Generally, these financial firms are interested only in financing large projects and, hence, are more likely to finance large retail outlets or entire shopping centers. Local savings and loan associations are good sources for long-term loans for small retailers who have a good credit reputation.

Other Financial Sources	The Small Business Administration (SBA), an agency of the federal government, provides short, intermediate, and long-term retail capital to small retailers. In addition to making cooperative loans with private lending firms and making direct loans to small retailers, the SBA also provides financial and management assistance. If borrowing appears to be the answer to a retail firm's problem, the SBA will help the retailer obtain a bank loan or will furnish part of the required capital itself, providing the bank cannot lend all of the money and SBA funds are available.

If the local bank cannot lend any of the money, the SBA will consider lending the entire amount as a direct government loan. In loaning money to small retail firms, the SBA is not in competition with private sources. The SBA steps in only when private financing cannot meet the needs of the small businessperson. SBA loans vary in amount from $500 to $500,000.

In addition to its general loan program, the SBA offers a small loan program which is designed to meet the needs of the very small or newly established retailer. The limited-loan participation plan is designed to help worthy firms that have only limited tangible collateral. Under this plan, private banks and the SBA cooperate in extending financing to the small retailer.

Another source of capital is the Small Business Investment Corporation, which is licensed and regulated by the SBA. It is designed to be a profit-making company and may be either privately or publicly owned and operated. The SBIC is in business to furnish capital and consulting and advisory services to small businesses.

Numerous other federal loan sources are applicable to the small retailer in certain instances. A retailer who is a veteran could utilize the Veterans' Administration to acquire real estate, supplies, equipment, and working capital. Loans can also be obtained through the Bureau of Indian Affairs by Indians and Eskimos who have no other source of financing. Loans are also granted to citizens of other minority groups through the SBA.

A small retailer who has justifiable needs for additional capital and a financial structure strong enough to offer reasonable assurance of success and repayment should be able to obtain the necessary funds from one of the previously mentioned sources.

Accounting Systems

Sound recordkeeping and accounting practices are needed to conduct a successful retail business. The numbers and types of records needed depend upon management goals and needs. Small retailers may not require much detailed data on each merchandise line or department as large retailers require. The small retailer or the branch manager may be able to observe sales and inventories on each line and make decisions (based upon merchandise movement) before any of the financial records are available. It is nevertheless advisable to use accounting records to confirm the observation and to ensure that the firm's profitability corresonds to expectations.

A well-designed system of accounting should provide a record of all transactions that can be used to prepare periodic financial statements and reports. Properly prepared financial records can provide measurements of profitability and retail performance. An effective accounting system must also provide a basis for business planning. Only after a retailer can determine "where he/she has been" can "where he/she is going" be determined. Thus, complete and accurate financial records are needed and must be used to make retail decisions. Accounting records can also detect errors, theft, and fraud. Finally, retailers must have an accurate record of the availability and use of their assets because profits are maximized by making the most efficient use of these assets.

Several accounting terms and concepts make important contributions to the basic records used by retailers. An **asset** is anything of value owned by the retailer and a **liability** is anything owed by the retailer. **Retail assets** consist of land, buildings, equipment, furniture, fixtures, supplies, inventory, cash, and accounts receivable. **Retail liabilities** consist of accounts payable, notes payable, accrued wages, and accrued taxes.

The owner's investment or **equity** in the retail enterprise amounts to the difference between the total retail assets and total retail liabilities. All accounting systems are based on this concept—assets equal liabilities plus owner's equity.

Nearly all accounting records are based upon the double entry concept, which simply records the twofold effect every transaction has upon the equation, assets = liabilities + owner's equity. For example, assume that a retailer pays $1,000 in cash for merchandise that has just been delivered to his store. In this case the value of one asset (inventory) will be increased by $1,000, but the value of another asset (cash) is reduced by $1,000, the total asset value remains unchanged, and the equation remains in balance.

In accounting terminology, every transaction involves at least one debit entry in one or more accounts and at least one credit entry in other accounts, so that total debits always equal total credits.

Basic Retail Records   The financial record of a retail outlet begins when merchandise is purchased by the retailer and the information is recorded. Most retailers bring this information together by recording daily transactions in one or more journals, which provide a complete record of each transaction in chronological order. Many retailers transfer the journal information to ledger accounts, which are records of the increases and decreases of each type of income, expense, asset, liability, or capital. Retailers use as many ledger accounts as they believe are needed to classify their business activities.

Ledger accounts are employed to organize the data from the journals so that the business transactions can be grouped. This grouping provides the information needed to prepare the two basic financial statements: the balance sheet and the income statement. Information contained in either the balance sheet or the income statement can be used to make nearly every analysis needed to measure the financial performance of the retail enterprise.

Balance Sheet

The **balance sheet** shows the financial condition of the firm on a given date. This report is called the balance sheet because it represents the equation, assets = liabilities + owner's equity, and thus summarizes the various assets, liabilities, and owner's equity accounts. The balance sheet also contains information on the relationship between creditors' claims on the assets and the percentage of assets held in the form of owner's equity in the firm. Comparison of a current balance sheet with balance sheets for previous periods allows the proprietor conveniently to observe changes in the firm's financial condition. The balance sheet is a good summary report that eliminates the necessity of examining many detailed records.

Table 18.2 is a typical balance sheet, together with brief explanations of the terms contained in a balance sheet. Most of the terms are described in sufficient detail in the table so that they do not require further explanation. Those balance sheet concepts that require elaboration will now be discussed.

Table 18.2   Typical Retail Balance Sheet

Assets	December 31, 1982	
Current Assets		
Cash	$9,150	
Accounts Receivable	5,300	
Merchandise on Hand	12,750	
Total Current Assets		$27,200
Fixed Assets		
Building, Equipment and Fixtures		$41,500
Total Assets		$68,700
Liabilities and Owner's Equity		
Current Liabilities		
Accounts Payable	$3,170	
Current Maturity of Long-Term Debt	$1,000	
Total Current Liabilities		$ 4,170
Long-term Debt		
Notes Payable		$16,200
Total Liabilities		$20,370
A. Jones, Capital		$48,330
Total Liabilities and Owner's Equity		$68,700

Current assets (cash, accounts receivable, inventories, and government securities) may be turned into cash quickly. **Retail inventories** comprise finished merchandise that is displayed in the store. Inventory values change as prices fluctuate, so retail inventories are usually valued at cost or current market price, whichever is lower. This method avoids overstatement of earnings and assets as a result of wholesale price increases.

The LIFO and FIFO methods are used to establish inventory values when a physical count of items is feasible. The **first in-first out (FIFO)** method assumes that the oldest items are sold before later-purchased items are sold. This method allows "inventory profits" (caused by increased merchandise prices at the wholesale level) to be included as income. Such inventory profits are not realized profits if the rising wholesale prices are followed by a price decline.

Another method of determining inventory evaluation is the **last in-first out (LIFO)** method. This method is designed to cushion the impact of rapid price changes by matching current costs against current revenues. Sales are costed on the basis of inventory purchased most recently (last in), while first-in inventory is regarded as unsold merchandise. The LIFO method results in the application of a higher unit cost to items sold and a lower unit cost to inventory still unsold during a period of rising prices. Many retail firms have switched to the LIFO method recently as inflation has caused prices of merchandise to rise rapidly. When prices are rising, the LIFO method allows the firm to value the cost of merchandise sold higher than it can be valued under the FIFO method. This results in a lower profit on the firm's income statement, which allows the firm to pay less income taxes. (Table 18.3) Internal Revenue Service regulations do not allow a retailer to make frequent switches from one inventory valuation method to another. Thus, the most current regulations must be consulted before a firm changes its method of inventory evaluation.

The **retail inventory method** of estimating cost valuation of inventory is applied when a physical count is not feasible. This method is used in many chain stores to gain better control over store managers by charging goods to stores both at cost and retail prices. The retail method of inventory evaluation provides a procedure for determining the cost value of a closing inventory stated in retail price value. This method requires that both inventory and purchase figures be recorded and charged to each department in both retail prices and at cost. Complete records are maintained (in retail prices) on all additions to and reductions from stock. The markup percentage is determined, allowing one to calculate the cost percentage on the total merchandise handled. Closing retail book inventory (the retail value of the mer-

**Table 18.3   Effect of FIFO and LIFO Inventory Evaluation
Methods on Retailer's Cost of Merchandise**

Situation

Beginning inventory—10,000 units with a $1 per unit purchase cost
Purchases made during the year—10,000 units with a $1.20 per unit
purchase cost
Sales—15,000 units at $2 per unit

Calculation of Goods Sold Costs

A.   Using the first in-first out method of inventory evaluation:

10,000 units @ $1 (the per unit cost of the beginning inventory) plus	= $10,000
5,000 units @ $1.20 (the per unit cost of merchandise purchased during the year)	= $ 6,000
Equals the Total Cost of Goods Sold	= $16,000

B. Using the last in-first out method of inventory evaluation:

10,000 units @ $1.20 (the per unit cost of merchandise purchased during the year) plus	= $12,000
5,000 units @ $1 (the per unit cost of beginning inventory)	= $ 5,000
Equals the Total Cost of Goods Sold	= $17,000

---

chandise on hand in the closing inventory) is calculated from the
records. Cost percentage is then applied to the retail book inventory and an annual physical inventory is taken (in retail prices)
to check the accuracy of the method.

The closing physical inventory (in retail prices) can be converted to a cost valuation by using the following formula: cost
value of inventory = retail value of inventory × cost percentage.
An example of the retail method of valuing ending inventory is
given in Table 18.4. It should be noted that when a store using
the retail method makes additional markups and markdowns it
must keep a record of them. These data are then employed to calculate its cost ratio and to estimate its ending cost valuation of
inventory as shown in Table 18.4.

One should also note that markups enter into the calculation of
the cost percentage but markdowns do not. This results in an intentionally conservative figure for ending inventory.

**Reasons for Adopting
the Retail Method**

The retail inventory method is widely used in chain stores, department stores, departmentalized specialty stores, and in many
independent stores. Widespread adoption of this method is due
to several factors. First, the retail method enables the retailer to
determine the results of the operations at frequent intervals
without the cost of making a physical count of goods. This is essential under today's highly competitive conditions. Second, be-

cause of price lines, preretailing, and buying methods, retailers today are thinking more in terms of selling prices rather than cost prices. Third, the retail system of accounting provides an effective but simple method of controlling merchandise departmentally in terms of retail prices. Fourth, it allows one to take a physical inventory more quickly and less expensively than under the cost method because it is not necessary to assign cost to each item. Fifth, it enables the retailer to take the inventory on a staggered basis; inventories can be taken in different departments at different times, and the figures can be adjusted to the general closing of the books. Sixth, it furnishes information on shortages and thus directs attention to measures by which they may be reduced. Seventh, through the book inventory figure, it provides an equitable basis upon which to base insurance coverage and settle claims; and finally, it furnishes a sound, workable basis for the dollar control of merchandise.

Fixed assets, with the exception of land, have a limited useful life, so the process of depreciation assigns a portion of the assets' cost as expense for each accounting period. Depreciation is subtracted from fixed asset values so that the asset value is stated at the amount of unexpired cost. It is important to note that the depreciated amount is not a cash expenditure of money but merely a decrease in the value of company-owned assets.

Liabilities, which are on the other side of the assets-equal-liabilities-plus-owners'-equity equation, may be divided into two

Table 18.4 Retail Method of Determining Valuation of Inventory

Goods Available	At Cost	At Retail
Opening inventory	$20,000	$30,000
plus		
Net purchases	$35,000	$51,000
plus		
Additional markups		$ 2,100
equals	———	
Goods Available for Sale	$55,000	$83,100
Cost Percent (ratio of cost to retail)		
$55,000/$83,100 equals 66.2%		
Net Sales at retail		$59,900
plus		
Reductions (markdowns and cash discounts)		$ 3,500
equals		
Total Sales and Reductions		$63,400
Ending Inventory at Retail		$19,700
($83,100 minus $63,400)		
Ending Inventory at Cost		$13,041
($19,700 times 66.2%)		

classes of debt. Current liabilities are amounts due and payable within one year. Long-term debt does not have to be paid until at least one year has elapsed. Current liabilities include:

Accounts payable are money that is owed to vendors and other unpaid costs that are incurred in operating a retail business.

Accrued liabilities are items such as unpaid wages, salaries, and commissions that have accumulated but are not yet due for payment.

Current maturity of long-term debt is the amount of long-term debt due within the upcoming year.

Federal income and other taxes are all accrued taxes.

Dividends payable are dividends declared by the board of directors but not yet paid.

Company capital comprises *all* sums (including preferred stock, common stock, retained earnings) used in the business. The retail enterprise may have raised funds through the sale of long-term debt (mortgage bonds or debentures) or by selling ownership in the company by issuing common and/or preferred stock. The amount included in the long-term debt caption is the amount of the principal due at maturity less any amount that is payable in less than one year.

Income Statement

The **income statement** gives the retail manager a summary of income and expenses over a period of time. Income statements are usually prepared monthly, quarterly, semiannually, and annually. Comparison of a current income statement with the corresponding statement for the previous year allows the proprietor to observe trends in income, expenses, and profits. In most retail operations, sales records are generally broken down by major departments. Such divisions more accurately show the response of sales and profits to changes in the retail mix. These breakdowns also allow the manager to continually identify the performance of each department. Table 18.5 is a typical annual income statement.

Retailers need to observe more detailed monthly income statements to determine if any significant sales or cost changes are occurring. Table 18.6 is an example of a monthly income statement that allows one to make comparisons with the same month last year and with the year-to-date performance. The performance of the XYZ store in June of 1982 and for the first six months of 1982 appears to be an improvement over correspond-

Table 18.5   Retail Income Statement

Revenue		December 31, 1982
Gross Sales	$99,300	
Less: Sales returns and allowances	930	
Net Sales		$98,370
Cost of Goods Sold		
Merchandise inventory, January 1, 1982	$ 9,700	
Merchandise purchases	46,320	
Goods Available for Sale	$56,020	
Less: Merchandise inventory, December 31, 1982	10,050	
Cost Of Goods Sold		$45,970
Gross Profit (net sales—cost of goods sold)		$52,400
Operating Expenses		
Rent expenses	$ 4,800	
Advertising expenses	$ 1,650	
Salaries expense	$15,230	
Payroll tax expense	$ 1,060	
Utilities expense	$ 2,710	
Total Operating Expenses		$25,450
Net income (gross profit—total operating expense)		$26,950

ing periods in 1981. Not only have sales increased in 1982 but operating and net profits also have increased. The increase in net profits occurred despite a slight reduction in gross margin percentage. Better utilization of employees and the spreading of the fixed costs (such as rent, insurance, depreciation, taxes) over a larger sales volume allowed the store to reduce its total expenses on a percent-of-sales basis.

Other Retail Records

Retailers should also keep a detailed record of accounts receivable so customer billing can be handled accurately and good customer relations maintained. In addition, these records can provide the detailed information needed to evaluate the firm's credit and collection policy. For example, the number and names of customers who are slow payers can easily be identified by examining the accounts receivable records.

Detailed information on accounts payable can help protect the financial reputation of the retail firm. Organized accounts payable records allow retailers to identify due accounts as well as invoices that allow cash discounts if payment is made promptly.

Most retailers also maintain separate and more detailed inven-

Table 18.6 Income Statement for Month of June, 1981 and 1982, XYZ Store

| | This Month | | | | Year to Date | | | |
| | For This Year | | For Last Year | | For This Year | | For Last Year | |
Item	$	% of Sales $	$	% of Sales $	$	% of Sales $	$	% of Sales $
Net sales	102,900	100.0	90,300	100.0	610,800	100.0	570,000	100.0
Less cost of goods sold:								
Beginning inventory	70,000	68.0	60,000	66.4	70,000	11.5	60,000	10.5
Merchandise purchases	70,000	68.0	70,000	77.5	410,000	67.1	390,000	68.4
Merchandise available for sales	140,000	136.1	130,000	144.0	480,000	78.6	450,000	78.9
Less ending inventory	70,000	68.0	70,000	77.5	70,000	11.5	70,000	12.3
Cost of goods sold	70,000	68.0	60,000	66.4	410,000	67.1	380,000	66.7
Gross margin	32,900	32.0	30,300	33.6	200,800	32.9	190,000	33.3
Less expenses:								
Salaries, wages, commissions	10,290	10.0	9,560	10.6	60,800	10.0	59,600	10.5
Rent	3,087	3.0	3,000	3.3	18,522	3.0	18,000	3.2
Utilities	515	0.5	510	0.6	3,118	0.5	3,120	0.5
Repairs and maintenance	3,087	3.0	3,100	3.4	15,200	2.5	14,700	2.6
Delivery expense	515	0.5	450	0.5	3,200	0.5	2,700	0.5
Supplies	515	0.5	510	0.6	3,150	0.5	3,020	0.5
Advertising	2,058	2.0	2,100	2.3	12,210	2.0	12,080	2.1
Depreciation	2,675	2.6	2,675	3.0	16,050	2.6	16,050	2.8
Bad debts	410	0.4	500	0.6	2,530	0.4	2,410	0.4
Taxes and licenses	1,545	1.5	1,500	1.7	9,210	1.5	9,020	1.6
Insurance	1,030	1.0	1,010	1.1	6,180	1.0	6,060	1.1
Interest	1,030	1.0	950	1.1	6,210	1.0	5,940	1.0
Other expenses	3,084	3.0	3,060	3.4	18,010	2.9	18,080	3.2
Total expenses	29,841	29.0	28,925	32.0	174,390	28.6	170,780	30.0
Operating profit (loss)	3,059	3.0	1,375	1.6	26,410	4.3	19,220	3.3
Other income	2,058	2.0	2,015	2.2	10,100	1.7	9,700	1.7
Net profit (loss)	5,117	5.0	3,390	3.8	36,510	6.0	28,920	5.0

tory records which are essential to the control and security of retail stocks. Inventory records also provide the data needed for making buying decisions and for effective merchandise management.

Detailed sales records may be used to provide a basis for the compensation of retail sales personnel. These sales records may also provide information useful in marketing research activities such as determining trading areas, identifying market targets, and the like.

Finally, accurate and detailed tax records must be maintained. These records should contain all the information needed to fill out the various tax forms requested by all levels of government.

Separate departmental records may be maintained on a monthly basis to allow retail management to identify changes in operating performance in each area. A monthly departmental operating statement, similar to that for the total store in Table 18.6, can identify performance changes within each department. Expense records on such items as salaries, wages, and supplies can be maintained on a departmental basis. Other expenses must be allocated to the various departments on the basis of time, space, or capital requirements for each department. For example, total store rent could be allocated to each department on the basis of square footage occupied by that department. Cost accountants can provide valuable assistance in the allocation of these expenses to each department.

Operating a Retail Accounting System

Development and use of accounting records are essential because they allow retail managers to carry out more effective planning and control. Appropriate accounting records can reveal errors, employee fraud, and waste and can identify other sales and expense areas that may require changes if retail performance is to be improved.

Retail firms need a good accounting system to safeguard business assets and prevent errors. The accounting records must be accurately and honestly maintained for each of the many transactions that occur each day in a retail organization. A system of checks and balances should be used so no employee will have complete control of any business transaction. Cashiers or account collectors who handle cash should not maintain the accounting books. Where possible, record analyses and reports should be the responsibility of at least two people. Cash register tapes should be used to double check the amount of cash received by the cashier. Employee earnings and purchase expenditures should be computed by one person and then rechecked for accuracy and honesty by another individual.

The typical store manager is deeply involved in the operations of business. Frequently this person believes more would be accomplished by spending time doing tasks within the store instead of sitting at a desk analyzing accounting records. If this is the case, a manager should consider using part-time outside accountants and financial consultants who can help develop and operate an effective program.

Frequent meetings with outside accountants may involve a comparison of performance in the previous month with that of a year ago and then with the preceding month. Major performance deviations and current and future plans should be discussed. Regular discussions of this type allow many retailers to avoid making serious business errors.

A list of questions that small retailers should ask their accountants on an annual basis is presented in Table 18.7.

Table 18.7   Questions Small Retailers Should Ask Their Outside Accountants on an Annual Basis

1. Are the firm's cash assets being properly protected?
   Are receipts deposited in total daily?
   Should different people handle accounts receivable and accounts payable?
2. Are the firm's fixed assets being properly protected?
   What depreciation methods should be used to minimize taxes?
   Is the investment tax credit being used to reduce taxes?
3. Have the firm's payroll tax returns and deposits been made on time?
   Have the federal withholding funds been deposited in a federal depository bank on at least a monthly basis?
   Have state and federal quarterly information reports been filed?
4. Have the firm's estimated income tax deposits been made on time?
5. Are all the necessary records required by the various state, federal, and local authorities available?
   What is the statute of limitations for each type of record?
6. Have all required state annual reports been filed?
   If the firm is incorporated, has an annual corporate report been made to the state?
   Do other states in which the firm conducts business require an annual report?
7. Is the firm using the best legal form of organization?
   Can the business be divided into several separate taxable entities such as a corporation, a partnership, a sole proprietorship, or subchapter S corporation to reduce taxes?
   What will such a change cost in time and dollars?
   What new reports are required if the change is made?
8. Are present accounting systems appropriate for the current size of the firm?
   Can minicomputers, a UPC system, and time sharing computer systems be used to reduce costs and increase timeliness and accuracy of data?
   Are there any new accounting information systems available that would improve the firm's operating efficiency?

Large retail organizations are likely to maintain their own accounting department which performs nearly all of the firm's accounting services (except the independent audit). Functions of this internal accounting department are the same as those of an outside accounting service. The same honest, objective appraisals must be made to reduce errors, fraud, and waste.

Both internal and outside accounting systems are likely to make increased use of electronic data processing equipment. Such equipment speeds the processing of sales and expense data. Thus, information is available for managerial review faster than under the manual system. In addition, electronic systems are able to make detailed calculations on ratios and percentages that are essential for more effective retail management.

Financial Planning

Financial management in a retail firm involves two objectives. First, an adequate flow of cash must be provided to meet current liabilities as they come due. Second, the retail firm must operate as profitably as possible in the long run.

Cash Flow Forecast

Cash flow forecast may be used to develop a plan that will ensure that adequate cash is available to pay bills as they come due. Retail cash receipts and cash disbursements fluctuate independently of each other. Thus, during certain periods of the year, cash inflows (sales receipts) exceed cash outflows and a surplus is created in cash. During other seasons of the year, cash outflows exceed sales revenue. In this case additional cash is needed to prevent a deficit, unless a surplus has been accumulating in the cash account. The cash flow process is illustrated in Figure 18.1.

Effective cash flow management involves an analysis of the timing of cash receipts and disbursements to identify the periods when the working capital may be inadequate or excessive in terms of meeting current liabilities. Maintaining excessive amounts of surplus cash (as nonworking dollars) violates the profit objective. These excessive cash reserves involve an *opportunity cost* equal to the amount they would bring if they were used in some other way, either within the retail store (advertising, reducing the amount of a mortgage, fixture improvements, and so forth) or outside the retail store (investment in interest-bearing notes, and so forth).

An inadequate cash level is also detrimental to the profit maximizing objective. Inadequate working capital may result in insufficient advertising, inventories, and the like, resulting in

Figure 18.1   Cash Flow Process

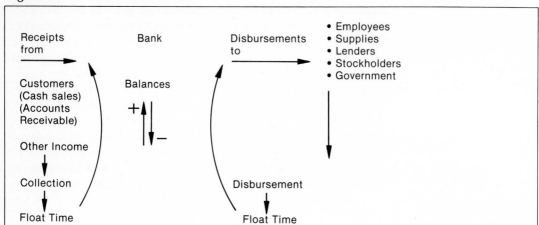

consumer dissatisfaction and a loss in retail sales. It may also force the retailer to pass up trade discounts or even cause a loss in the credit standing of the firm.

Cash flow analysis expresses future retail income and expenditures on a dollar basis, so it is simply a prediction of future cash flows based on an expected sales volume. Cash flow records movement of cash into retail inventories, receivables, and back into cash. This analysis reveals future needs for short-term funds by indicating when cash inflows will exceed outflows and vice versa. A cash flow analysis is vitally important to a retailer since it identifies what the firm can do to reach its objective of maintaining adequate (but not excessive) cash balances.

The first step in a cash flow forecast is to establish the period covered by the plan. The analysis may be prepared on a monthly (or even weekly) basis to project the cash condition for the next six months or next year of business. The procedure is simply to record expected cash inflows and outflows and add (or subtract) the expected amount of the net increase (or decrease) to (or from) the original cash balance to obtain the expected cash balance at the end of the period.

The second step is the estimation of sales. Sales forecasting techniques are described in Chapter 9; however, it is important to note that both internal factors (such as changes in promotion, price policy, and productive personnel) and external factors (such as changes in competition, economic conditions, seasonality patterns, and consumer preferences) affect a retailer's sales level. Thus, sales estimating procedures must use these variables to forecast sales volume accurately.

One cannot overemphasize the importance of sales forecasting. The accuracy of the entire cash flow analysis is highly dependent upon the accuracy of the sales forecast. Hence, every effort should be made to develop an accurate forecasting method. This usually requires a great deal of experience and good judgment. Historical data on past sales are usually analyzed to determine trends and seasonal sales patterns. Fortunately, it is usually easier to forecast sales for a store or group of stores than for an item or a specific merchandise line. Seasonal patterns on total store sales are not likely to change rapidly. Although the composition of the sales may change rapidly, the total volume is not likely to fluctuate widely unless the relative competitive position of the retail outlet(s) changes or unless the total industry sales are changing rapidly.

The third step entails anticipation of future cash inflows derived from the estimated sales level. The firm's credit policy will determine how closely cash inflows relate to sales, and this relationship should be identical if retail sales are made on a strictly cash basis. Of course, handling credit sales will also affect this cash-inflow-to-sales relationship. If most or all of the sales are made on a bank credit card basis such as Master Card, or VISA, the retailer will be reimbursed almost immediately after the handling charge (usually 2 to 6 percent of sales) has been deducted. Factoring of accounts receivable will accomplish the same result, namely, a close relationship of cash inflow to sales volume. Historical records, combined with an analysis of the firm's retail credit policy, can generally yield a highly reliable estimate of the relationship between sales volume and cash inflow.

The fourth step is an analysis of the expected cash outflow for the previously specified time period(s). Historical purchase and expenditure records, employee payroll data, contracts, negotiated purchase agreements, and other commitments can be analyzed to obtain an estimate of upcoming expenditures.

The fifth step involves comparison of estimated cash inflow against the estimated outflow to determine the net cash gain or loss for the period. This consists merely of subtracting the expected outflow (determined in step 4) from the expected inflow (determined in step 3) to obtain the net change in the cash balance.

Cash flow analysis also provides, in **the sixth step,** an estimated cash balance for the end of the specified period(s). The expected cash balance is obtained by adding the net gain (or subtracting the net loss) for the period—as calculated in step 5—to the cash balance at the beginning of the period.

These six steps, which constitute the cash flow forecast, provide all the information necessary to plan a retailer's needs for short-term capital. Table 18.8 is an example of a cash flow forecast for a retail firm. Additions to working capital are required when the expected cash balance reaches a prespecified minimum level. The additions to short-term funds may come from either internal or external sources.

The main internal sources of funds are the liquidation of inventories and short-term investments, cash sales, and a turnover of accounts receivable. Retail credit policies are not likely to be changed frequently simply to provide extra cash during a short-term period of cash deficiency. Consumers become committed to established retail credit policies and are likely to switch retailers if an outlet continually changes its credit rules. Promotions can be used to increase cash sales during periods when cash shortages are likely to exist; however, retail management must consider the overall effect such promotions may have upon future

Table 18.8   Cash Flow Forecast

	January Budget	February Budget	March Budget
Expected Cash Receipts			
Cash sales	$12,000	$13,000	$20,000
Collections on accounts receivable	10,000	10,000	10,000
Other income	300	300	300
Total cash receipts	$22,300	$23,300	$30,300
Expected Cash Payments			
Raw materials, merchandise, and supplies	14,000	16,000	20,000
Payroll	2,500	2,500	3,000
Other expenses (including maintenance)	500	500	600
Advertising	300	300	500
Selling expense	1,200	1,200	1,200
Administrative expense (including salary of owner-manager)	1,500	1,500	1,500
New store facilities and equipment	2,500	1,000	1,000
Other payments (taxes including estimated income tax, repayment of loans, interest, etc.)	300	300	500
Total cash payments	22,800	23,300	28,300
Expected cash balance at beginning of month	1,000	1,000	1,000
Cash increase or decrease	—500	0	2,000
Expected cash balance at end of month	500	1,000	3,000
Desired working cash balance	1,000	1,000	1,000
Loans Needed			
Total amount of cash borrowed[a]	500	500	0
Loan repayment due	0	0	0
Cash available for owners, dividends, etc.	0	0	1,500

[a] Assuming no debt on Jan. 1 and that surplus cash is used for loan repayment.

sales, store image, and so forth. Thus, the stimulation of cash sales is not likely to be a solution to a short-term deficit cash balance problem.

Liquidation of short-term investments is frequently made to generate needed cash. Indeed, some money is sometimes put into liquid short-term investments not only to obtain a return on the money but also to provide a safety margin in case cash is needed internally at a later date. External sources of funds (banks, trade credit, and so forth) are required if internal sources cannot provide sufficient cash.

Ratio Analysis

Retailers not only attempt to meet current liabilities as their bills come due but also attempt to operate as profitably as possible. Thus, retailers must have a way to measure profitability and operating efficiency of their enterprises. Examination of selected ratios and relationships derived from data in the firm's balance sheet and income statement can provide helpful appraisals of the current and past performance of that firm. External financial sources, moreover, frequently require these data before they will grant loans to a firm.

A number of different ratios and relationships can be applied by the retailer to measure the past and current performance of the firm. Ratios are generally compared both on a historical basis and against the industrial standards considered normal for that type of retailing. Several different standards are available from various trade sources and such sources as the Small Business Administration, the U.S. Department of Commerce, Dun & Bradstreet, National Cash Register, Robert Morris Associates, etc. The inexperienced retailer must rely heavily upon the standards developed by these sources. An experienced retailer is more likely to establish individualized standards and make historical comparisons on each ratio.

Operating Ratios

Retail **operating ratios** express relationships among the items in the income statement to provide an evaluation of the firm's operating performance. Operating ratios yield a detailed understanding of the retail expenses involved in generating sales. These ratios can be used as tools to lower costs and improve efficiency within the retail firm.

A detailed breakdown of expenses is usually required to calculate the important operating ratios for a retailer. The operating ratios are calculated by dividing each item in a detailed income statement by the retailer's net sales figure and multiplying the result by 100. This procedure allows the ratios to relate each ex-

Table 18.9   Operating Ratios Frequently Used to Measure Retailers' Operating Efficiency

Ratio	Characteristics
1. Gross sales as % of net sales	Measures percentage of shrinkage occurring from returns, allowances, cash discounts.
2. Cost of goods sold as % of net sales	Cost of goods sold may be defined to be beginning inventory valued at cost plus net purchases less ending inventory valued at cost to provide a ratio that measures the relative importance of inventory cost to net sales volume.
3. Gross profit as % of net sales	Gross profit may be defined to be the net sales minus cost of goods sold as defined in item 2; this ratio will measure the relative performance of the firm before selling, general, administrative and interest expenses are deducted.
4. Operating expenses as % of net sales	Ratios may be calculated for each of the expense accounts (wages, supplies, maintenance, advertising, administrative salaries, bad debts, utilities, insurance, rent taxes, depreciation) as well as an overall operating expense ratio. Expenses are often grouped into controllable or uncontrollable categories to provide a measure of the relative flexibility of the firm. Watch year-to-year changes.
5. Operating profit as % of net sales	Operating profit is gross profit minus total operating expenses (listed in item 4); so ratio is pretax profit margin as % of net sales.
6. Net income before income taxes as % of net sales	Net income is operating profit minus the amount needed to meet interest payment on debt.
7. Net income after income taxes as % of net sales	Measure of after-tax profitability of retail firm stated as % of net sales.

pense or income item to net sales by expressing each item on a percentage of net sales basis. These percentage figures are then studied to provide suggestions that will improve retail operating efficiency. Some retailers calculate and analyze some operating ratios each week on a department-by-department basis, which provides excellent control. Knowledge of current gross operating profit margins, inventory levels, and expense ratios can allow the retailer to spot a weakness before it becomes a serious problem. Up-to-date ratio analysis can also let the retailer quickly determine the effects of changes in the retailing mix.

Thus, a comparative analysis of operating ratio values over a period of time can be used to identify the cost of sales and expense trends. The year-to-year comparisons of expenses as a percentage of net sales provide an important measurement of a firm's performance. Relatively small changes in the value of an operating ratio should be brought to the attention of the firm's top management. Operating ratios that are normally used to measure a retailer's performance are listed and explained in Table 18.9. Of course, retailers like to observe declining values for the cost of goods sold and operating expense ratios described in the figure. On the other hand, they also like to observe increasing values for their net sales as a percentage of gross sales, gross profit, operating profit, and for both net income ratios.

Table 18.10 Men's Wear and Women's Wear Outlet Expenses (Percentages)

	Median of All Firms	Median of Firms Handling Men's Wear Only	Median of Firms Handling Women's Wear
Cost of Goods Sold (% of net sales, excluding leased departments, except as noted.)			
Ending inventory at cost	25.6	25.9	25.6
Gross cost of merchandise sold	57.2	57.2	57.0
Net workroom costs	2.2	2.2	2.0
a. Workroom payroll	2.4	2.4	2.6
b. All other expenses	0.3	0.3	0.2
Total cost of merchandise sold	59.1	59.0	59.1
Gross margin, excluding leased department income and sales	41.0	41.0	41.0
Income from leased departments	0.9	0.9	1.0
Gross margin, including income from leased departments, as a percent of total net sales	41.2	41.2	41.2
Payroll (total)	18.5	18.6	18.1
a. Payroll of owners and officers	6.4	6.6	5.6
b. Selling payroll	9.7	9.6	9.9
c. Non-selling payroll	2.5	2.4	2.6
Advertising	2.9	3.0	2.8
Taxes (total)	1.9	1.8	1.9
a. All state and local taxes with the exception of payroll taxes and Federal income taxes	0.5	0.5	0.6
b. Social security and unemployment taxes	1.3	1.3	1.3
Supplies	2.2	2.2	2.3
a. Wrapping and packing supplies	0.8	0.8	0.9
b. Other supplies (cleaning, stationery)	0.4	0.4	0.5
c. Heat, light	1.0	1.0	1.0
Services Purchased (total)	1.3	1.3	1.3
a. Data processing/service charges	0.6	0.6	0.6
b. Credit card service fees	0.3	0.3	0.3
c. Other outside service fees, delivery, alarm service, buying offices, etc.	0.4	0.4	0.5
Unclassified	0.5	0.5	0.4
Traveling	0.6	0.6	0.7
Communications	0.5	0.5	0.5
Pensions	0.9	1.0	0.9
Insurance (total)	1.5	1.7	1.4
a. Workmen's compensation insurance, sickness, accident, group medical, group hospital and life insurance premiums	0.9	0.9	0.8
b. All other insurance premiums	0.7	0.7	0.6
Depreciation (total)	0.9	0.9	1.0
Professional services	0.4	0.4	0.3
Donations	0.1	0.1	0.1
Bad debts	0.2	0.2	0.2
Equipment costs	0.4	0.4	0.4
Real property rentals	3.6	3.8	3.2
Total expenses	37.3	37.5	36.3
Net Gain (% of total net sales, except as noted.)			
Operating profit, including income from leased departments	3.8	3.6	3.9
a. Net other income	1.1	1.0	1.2
b. Net other expense	1.3	1.1	1.5
Net profit, before federal income taxes	3.9	3.8	4.2

Source: Menswear Retailers of America, "1979 Annual Business Survey Men's Store Operating Experiences."

New retailers can use average industry ratios to make an annual expense forecast. An example of the expenses encountered by men's and women's wear outlets is presented in Table 18.10. Similar expense estimates for other types of retailers are available from trade associations.

Financial Ratios

A **financial ratio** expresses the relationship between two items on the firm's balance sheet or between one item on the income statement and one item on the balance sheet. These ratios can be analyzed to provide a basis for making comparisons on the historical performance of the firm. Financial ratios can also be used to make comparisons with similar retail operations and can thereby identify areas of relative financial weakness and strength. Thus, financial ratio analysis provides guides for spotting trends toward better or poorer performance.

Average financial ratio values for numerous types of retail businesses are presented in Table 18.11. Several ratios are used to measure a firm's liquidity. The **current ratio** indicates the ability of the firm to meet its current obligations and still maintain a safety margin to allow for possible shrinkage in the value of its inventories and accounts receivable.[1] The current ratio (ratio 2 in Table 18.11) is expressed in mathematical terms as: current ratio = current assets ÷ current liabilities.

High-volume, high-turnover outlets that handle merchandise whose demand is relatively stable do not require as much safety margin as low-volume, slow-turnover outlets that handle merchandise whose demand fluctuates widely. Thus, chain grocery stores may have a current ratio of slightly less than 2:1 and still be very able to meet their current obligations. Less stable types of retail business generally attempt to maintain at least a 2:1 relationship, although an extremely high current ratio merely indicates that excess cash is lying idle or that excessive inventories are being maintained.

The **quick ratio,** or "acid test," is calculated as (cash + marketable securities + accounts receivable) / current liabilities. This ratio also measures a retail organization's ability to meet its current obligations, but it is a more severe test because it concentrates on strictly liquid assets whose value is not likely to change radically. Inventories are not included in the numerator of the equation, so the quick ratio really evaluates the chance that a firm could pay its current obligations with readily convertible funds on hand. A quick ratio of less than 1:1 is a warning signal that a retail business would have to sell from inventory to meet current liabilities if the firm were pressured into paying its bills and could not borrow additional funds.

Table 18.11 Median Values of Financial Ratios for Selected Retail Businesses

Line of Business (number reporting)	Quick ratio Times	Current ratio Times	Current liabilities to net worth Per cent	Current liabilities to inventory Per cent	Total liabilities to net worth Per cent	Fixed assets to net worth Per cent	Net sales to inventory Times	Total assets to net sales Per cent	Net sales to working capital Times	Accounts payable to net sales Per cent	Return on net sales Per cent	Return on total assets Per cent	Return on net worth Per cent
Auto and home supply stores	1.4	3.1	33.6	55.7	57.2	28.4	4.9	49.1	4.4	5.9	4.9	4.6	10.7
Clothing and furnishings men's and boys'	1.1	4.8	20.3	38.7	30.7	19.7	3.4	67.4	2.6	5.3	7.1	6.6	8.1
Department stores	1.0	3.1	45.0	60.3	61.5	20.6	4.7	44.4	4.6	4.3	2.6	5.9	11.2
Eating places	0.9	1.6	32.5	—	76.1	92.7	—	50.0	11.7	3.3	5.4	8.5	16.4
Family clothing stores	0.9	4.5	22.1	32.4	35.0	16.8	3.6	60.1	3.3	3.9	8.1	10.9	15.6
Furniture stores	1.4	3.3	34.1	56.9	46.6	22.3	4.6	65.5	2.7	4.8	4.0	5.7	10.0
Gasoline service stations	0.9	2.1	46.0	148.6	66.5	45.5	27.1	30.3	15.8	2.5	4.1	10.2	17.5
Gift, novelty and souvenir shops	1.0	3.9	14.8	42.6	35.2	45.3	3.7	67.7	3.3	4.1	7.2	8.7	14.6
Grocery stores	0.7	2.3	36.1	73.9	61.4	55.2	17.7	16.8	18.0	2.1	1.8	8.8	17.6
Hardware stores	1.4	5.1	20.5	30.6	38.0	16.6	4.0	54.0	3.2	4.8	4.2	7.5	12.0
Hobby, toy and game shops	0.5	2.8	40.7	56.5	59.6	22.9	3.9	43.1	4.9	6.7	4.1	9.7	15.1
Household appliance, radio and television stores	0.9	2.8	30.8	67.7	48.6	36.2	4.6	56.1	4.7	5.9	4.2	6.3	11.5
Jewelry stores	0.8	3.6	35.9	41.2	44.5	13.5	2.3	79.5	2.2	9.2	8.0	10.2	16.6
Lumber and other building materials dealers	1.3	2.8	36.5	73.3	54.3	17.6	6.2	42.9	4.7	4.9	2.9	8.9	13.6
Motor vehicle dealers (new and used)	0.3	1.5	175.4	86.5	182.9	20.1	6.1	27.0	14.2	0.9	1.0	3.6	10.8
Sewing, needlework, and piece goods stores	0.5	3.8	20.8	39.2	35.0	31.7	3.3	66.2	3.4	5.8	5.1	6.8	9.4
Shoe stores	0.6	3.2	31.4	45.8	45.4	19.4	3.2	55.0	3.1	6.1	4.7	6.5	10.8
Sporting goods stores and bicycle shops	0.5	3.4	26.8	48.0	44.4	19.0	3.3	59.7	3.6	5.4	4.7	8.7	15.6
Women's ready-to-wear stores	1.2	3.4	25.5	60.6	32.9	25.8	5.0	69.0	3.7	5.2	5.2	6.4	10.1

Definitions of Terms

Current Debt—Total of all liabilities due within one year from statement date including current payments on serial notes, mortgages, debentures or other funded debts. This item also includes current reserves, such as gross reserves for federal income and excess profit taxes, reserves for contingencies set up for specific purposes but does not include reserves for depreciation.

Fixed Assets—The sum of the cost value of land and the depreciated book values of buildings, leasehold improvements, fixtures, furniture, machinery, tools and equipment.

Inventory—The sum of raw material, material in process and finished merchandise. It does not include supplies.

Net Sales—The dollar volume of business transacted for 365 days net after deductions for returns, allowances and discounts from gross sales.

Net Working Capital—The excess of the current assets over the current debt.

Tangible Net Worth—The sum of all outstanding preferred or preference stocks (if any) and outstanding common stocks, surplus and undivided profits, less any intangible items in the assets, such as goodwill, trademarks, patents, copyrights, leaseholds, mailing list, treasury stock, organizational expenses, and underwriting discounts and expenses.

Reprinted with the special permission of Dun's Business Month, November 1981, Copyright 1981, Dun and Bradstreet Publications Corporation.

Several other ratios can be used to appraise the turnover relationships in retailing. The **collection period** (accounts receivable divided by average daily sales) is a rough measure of the overall quality of accounts receivable and of the credit policies used by the retailer. The collection period calculation can be compared to both the retailer's credit terms and to competitors' experience to determine if a collection problem exists.

A frequent rule of thumb states that "the collection period should be no more than one-third greater than the net selling terms."[2] According to this rule, the collection period should not exceed 40 days for a retailer with selling terms of a 2 percent discount in 10 days, net 30 days. For retailers selling on an installment basis, "the collection period of the installment accounts, based on net sales after deducting the aggregate down payments, should be no more than 1/3 greater than 1/2 the average selling terms. If the average selling terms are 18 equal monthly installments, for example, 1/2 those terms would be 9 months, and 1/3 increase would give a standard of 12 months."[3] These rules of thumb have been designed to allow flexibility for a normal volume of slow but generally good accounts.

The **net-sales-to-inventory ratio** in Table 18.11 expresses a rough measure of the frequency with which the average level of inventory investment was "turned over" on an annual basis. Inventory should be valued in retail dollars if net sales are figured. A higher turnover rate indicates that the business has managed to operate with a relatively small inventory investment, which indicates that the inventory is relatively current and contains little unusable stock. A high turnover ratio could also mean that inadequate inventories are being maintained. The latter could have a detrimental effect upon long-term profits if consumers are increasingly dissatisfied with out-of-stock conditions and if it is easy for them to buy these items at competing outlets.

Retail profitability may be examined in relation to sales volume or in relation to the investment required. There are several profit margin ratios that are used to describe the relationship of profits to sales volume. The **net-profits-on-net-sales ratio** merely expresses net retail dollar profits as a percentage of net retail sales dollars, or equals (net profit dollars / net sales dollars) × 100. This ratio is an indicator of the relative efficiency of the retail operation over time.

A more critical test of retail efficiency and profitability is provided by the **return-on-investment (or asset) ratio.** A high profit percentage on sales may be obtained on a relatively low sales volume. The result will be a low profit percentage on retail investment.

The **net-profits-on-tangible-net-worth ratio** is one measure of return on investment that expresses net profit dollars as a percentage of tangible net worth. This ratio measures the return to the owners of the business after all taxes and interest have been paid. Hence, it can be used to evaluate the earning power of the ownership investment in the retail enterprise.

The return-on-investment ratio can also describe profitability relative to investment in assets. This ratio is calculated as (net profit / total assets) × 100. This measure relates net profits to the firm's total assets (inventory, accounts receivable, cash, and fixed assets).

Return-on-Investment (Asset) Analysis

Return on Assets Chart

The return-on-assets analysis allows retail management to analyze most of the data in the previously discussed ratios in such a way that the firm's profitability can be determined. The return-on-assets chart in Figure 18.2 allows the retailer to establish goals in each segment in the chart. The top portion of the chart is used to determine net profit as a percentage of sales. The lower part is used to calculate asset turnover. The return-on-assets percentage is merely asset turnover times net profit percentage, so it equals the product of these two ratios. Since space has been provided for income taxes, the final return-on-assets percentage is an after-tax figure.

Retailers can improve their profitability by influencing the values of most of the factors in the return-on-assets chart. Cost of goods might be decreased by improved buying procedures. Expenses might be decreased by better sales training. Sales might be increased by better displays, improved promotion, and a better merchandise mix. Other income may be increased by taking advantages of cash discounts, placing excess cash in revenue-generating (but liquid) investments, and obtaining earnings from revolving credit programs. Managing these four factors properly can lead to an improvement in the profit-to-sales ratio.

The controllable factors in the bottom portion of the chart are inventory levels, accounts receivable levels, and other current assets. Inventory levels generally make up the largest portion of retail assets. Thus, every effort should be made to increase the net-sales-to-inventory ratio by eliminating nonessential stocks. If accounts receivable become too high, a retailer may want to reevaluate the credit policy to see if the finance charge could be raised or the due date shortened. Accounts receivable management was discussed earlier in this chapter, but it is im-

Figure 18.2   Return-on-Assets Chart

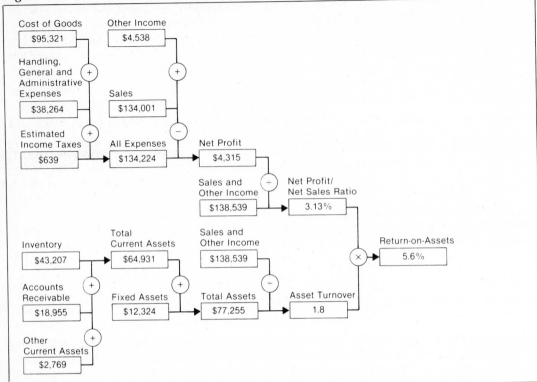

Source: Reprinted with special permission from the November 1970 issue of *Banking*. Journal of the American Bankers Association. Copyright © 1970 by the American Bankers Association.

portant to note the role it plays in determining return on retail assets. Other current assets consist mostly of cash, so placing excess funds in liquid investments improves the situation for both other income and other current assets categories.

The chief benefit of using the return-on-asset approach is that it demonstrates the interdependence of these controllable factors. Reducing inventory and accounts receivable levels will certainly improve the asset turnover, but if sales are decreased because of the reductions in these assets, then the profit-to-sales ratio is also reduced. The result might be a decline in the return on assets instead of the desired increase.

These interrelationships make it possible to design a system of management control that can monitor the effect of changes in a retail firm's performance as expressed in the various components of the ratios. Retail management can use the ratio dependencies shown in Figure 18.2 to provide a series of charts that reveal performance trends. The reader may trace the effect that a change in any of the components will have upon the firm's return-on-asset calculation.

For example, the retailer described in Figure 18.2 may increase promotion by $5,000 per year. Suppose management estimates that the cost of goods sold, sales volume, and taxes will all increase by 20 percent as a result of the increase in advertising. If no other changes are anticipated, then the firm's new return-on-assets chart reveals that its return on assets has increased from 5.6 percent to 9.0 percent (Figure 18.3).

Thus, retailers can estimate the effect that changes in their retailing mix will have on any of the factors contained in the return-on-assets chart and trace through the chart the effect those changes will have on their return-on-assets percentage. Use of the return-on-assets chart in this manner can provide guidelines for making major changes in retail policies. This is illustrated in

Figure 18.3 Changes in Return-on-Assets Chart When Firm Increases Sales, Cost of Goods, and Taxes by 20 Percent as a Result of a $5,000 Increase in Promotion

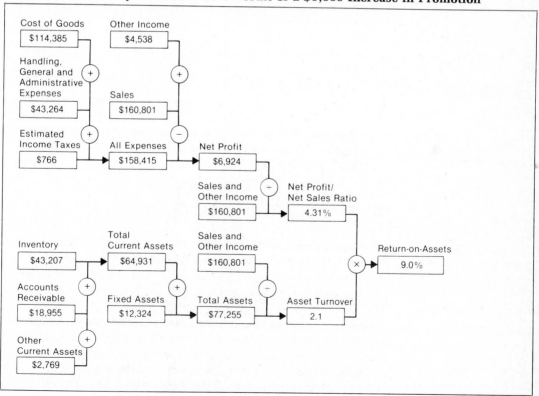

the previous example by the $5,000 increase in promotion, which led to a $2,609 increase in net profits although the action resulted in a $5,000 increase in the handling, general, and administrative expense category. The increase in net profits and increase in return on assets percentage indicate that this change should significantly benefit the firm.

Common Financial Mistakes

Retailers are involved in such a dynamic environment that they can easily get carried away with their emotions and concentrate nearly all of their effort on short-term problems. This leads to implementation of a philosophy of "let the accountant worry about the firm's financial condition." It is true that accountants are a vital source of information. However, the outside public accounting firms and accounting departments of large retail organizations are not responsible for the retailer's profit situation. They receive neither the rewards associated with a good profit nor the direct monetary loss suffered when a firm is not performing well.

Thus, retail management cannot rely entirely on accountants to place the firm in a sound financial condition. Hopefully, the procedures developed in this text will assist the retailer in developing good financial and merchandise planning and control policies.

There are some common types of mistakes that frequently cause retailers to suffer a decline in profits:

1. Lack of knowledge and use of proper accounting procedures.
2. Lack of knowledge and use of financial analysis.
3. Overly optimistic estimates of sales volume.
4. Lack of sufficient start-up capital.
5. Lack of working capital.
6. Overstating cash inflow.
7. Understating cash outflow.
8. Slow collection on accounts receivable.
9. Too many customer bad debts.
10. Improper inventory levels.
11. Inadequate productivity of retail space.

In very extreme cases these mistakes result in a failure for the firm that finds itself unable to meet its financial obligations. Most of these mistakes can be avoided with proper forewarning and the administration of a good merchandise budget and the financial analysis techniques discussed in this chapter. An overly optimistic estimate of sales volume is a major problem for new retail firms that do not have past sales records to guide them. These firms can use the techniques presented in Chapters 6 and 7 to guide their estimates, but they must be realistic in terms of making the evaluations. Perhaps the best preventative action that can be taken is a two-year apprenticeship. Such employment experience with the best retailer in the aspiring retailer's specialization is a virtual requirement to get the feel of the business.

A lack of both start-up capital and working capital (generally defined as current assets minus current liabilities) can also be improved by working for a salary during these apprenticeship years and saving a portion of the salary for start-up capital. The pay-back situation can be advanced by obtaining a high percentage of long-term financing (as opposed to short-term loans) when the firm is started. After the firm is established, it is wise for the growing firm to reinvest a large proportion of its profits back into the firm. Irresponsible or ill-timed withdrawals should be avoided because they can seriously weaken the financial structure of the firm.

Even experienced retail management can overestimate cash inflow and underestimate cash outflow. It is just human nature to remember all the good and forget some of the bad. Thus, consultation with last year's checkbook record of deposits and expenses can aid the memory process and provide a more realistic estimate of cash inflows and outflows.

Acceptance of bank credit cards such as Master Card and VISA can eliminate the problem of slow collection on accounts receivable. Bank credit cards cost the retailer a percentage of the gross sales dollar, but they can increase sales as well as provide a nearly instant source of cash. They can also eliminate losses due to customer bad debts, since the banks assume responsibility for collecting charge sales made on their cards.

Inventory levels are frequently too large to generate the profit level desired by retail management. In other cases the inventory level is so low it encourages customers to go to competitive outlets. Inventory planning requires careful thought on the effect different inventory levels will have upon sales and profit. The inventory planning methods presented in Chapter 10 and the return on asset model discussed in this chapter can assist the manager in making more intelligent decisions on inventory levels.

Inadequate productivity of the retailer's selling space can also cause the firm's profit to decline. Constant monitoring of factors such as sales, gross margin, and net profits on the basis of per square foot of building area can reveal whether the firm is encountering problems in the use of its physical space.

Risk and Insurance

Retail firms operate under risk of loss from many sources. Retail managers must learn how to use the various kinds of **insurance** (a means of providing protection against a risk) to reduce the effects of these risks, because unexpected losses can mean the difference between growth and failure. Insurance plays a vital role in forestalling damage that the unexpected can do to the retail firm. Remember, all of the work and money that is placed in a store can be destroyed in a matter of minutes by fire, lawsuit, flood, theft, and so forth.

Retail organizations lack funds for total coverage against all types of risks. The retail manager must develop a planned approach to risk management by identifying the most crucial areas that require coverage. Table 18.12 contains a list of the most common types of business risk and the types of insurance coverage available to retailers. Periodic reviews of the insurance program are needed to keep retail management abreast of changes in the type and size of risks that the firm faces. Replacement values of buildings, inventories, equipment, and so forth are increasing rapidly due to inflationary pressures. Thus, coverage should reflect these higher values.

Once the risks have been recognized, retail managers can investigate the methods of reducing costs of coverage. The following considerations are important.

1. Determine which risks to insure against by estimating the amount of loss each peril could cause the firm.
2. Cover the largest loss exposure first, after considering premium costs and the funds available for protection. Be certain that coverage on all property and equipment is adequate to reflect its true current value. Conducting periodic independent appraisals of property values can enhance the firm's ability to prove the amount of loss if a loss should occur.
3. Use as high a deductible coverage as the firm can afford to carry. This will result in a considerable decrease in premium cost.
4. Buy insurance in as large a unit as possible to reduce premium costs. "Package" policies are frequently very suitable for the coverage needed by retail organizations. It is best to conduct all of the firm's insurance with one good agent, because the account will then be large enough that the agent will be able to provide outstanding service. However, it is a good practice to have a competing agent examine the firm's insurance policies occasionally. Perhaps the competing agent will make

Table 18.12 Types of Business Risk and Insurance Protection Available

Type of Risk	Form of Protection
Loss of earning power	Business interruption insurance
	Profits insurance
	Rent insurance
	Life insurance on key personnel
Loss of property (destruction or damage)	Fire insurance
	Marine insurance
	Windstorm insurance
	Tornado insurance
	Explosion insurance
	Riot and insurrection insurance
	Automobile, fire, and collision insurance
	Aircraft insurance
	Property depreciation insurance
Theft or infidelity	Auto theft insurance
	Burlary, theft insurance
	Forgery insurance
	Fidelity insurance
Failure of others	Credit insurance
	Surety bonding
	Title insurance
Loss of property (legal liability)	Workmen's compensation insurance
	Employers' liability insurance
	Contractual liability
	Public liability insurance
	Advertiser's liability
	Automobile liability insurance
	Power plant insurance
	Elevator insurance
	Product liability insurance
	Sports liability insurance
	Physicians' insurance
	Aircraft insurance

Source: Reprinted from Harvey C. Krentzman, *Managing for Profits* (Washington, D.C.: Small Business Administration, 1968), p. 155.

suggestions that will provide better coverage and/or reduce the premium cost.

5. Be aware of the firm's previous experience. Such knowledge can be used to acquire lower insurance rates or as a basis for changing to another form of insurance. Doing everything possible to minimize losses is essential to accomplish a reduced loss experience.

6. Develop a plan to implement good risk and insurance management. First, a clear statement of insurance objectives is needed. Second, select an insurance agent who is aware (or can become aware) of the firm's exposure to loss. Third, establish insurance responsibility with one individual or group. Finally, keep complete records of all insurance policies, premiums paid, losses, and loss recoveries to get better coverage at lower costs in the future.

7. When a loss occurs, immediately notify your agent. This will reduce the period of time needed to recover the firm's monetary loss and establish the date on which the loss occurred.

Summary

The retailer's own capital is the most important source of funds for the firm. Large retailers issue stock that represents ownership in the company for the buyers of that stock. Independent retailers usually supply a portion of their own funds to the firm.

Outside sources of funds vary by the type of money that is required. The most common source of short-term funds is commercial banks. The Small Business Administration is a common source of long-term funds.

Retailers must maintain accounting records and control tools to evaluate their business activity. The balance sheet and income statement are the basic summary records that contain the data needed to chart the firm's financial performance.

Care must be taken in the interpretation of data obtained from these accounting records. For example, one must determine which method (LIFO, FIFO or the retail method) determines the cost of the merchandise inventory. Inflationary pressures are forcing more firms to switch to the LIFO method, because LIFO allows the retailer to value the cost of merchandise sold at a higher value than it can be valued under the FIFO method. This results in a lower profit figure on the firm's income statement but also allows the firm to pay less in income taxes.

Retail financial planning involves two objectives: providing an adequate flow of cash to meet current liabilities as they come due and operating as profitably as possible in the long run.

Cash flow forecasting is used to plan monetary inflows and outflows so that adequate cash is available to pay bills. It is very easy to forget past expenditures, so it is recommended that the preparer of a cash flow forecast consult last year's check stubs or income statement to improve forecast accuracy.

Trends in the value of the firm's financial ratios and operating ratios can help evaluate its profitability and the direction the firm's profits are headed. They can also be used when preparing next year's budget.

Return-on-assets analysis is a good method for tracing the interrelationships between the various financial ratios and for evaluating the desirability of making a change in the firm's retailing mix.

Questions

1. Referring to Figure 18.2 trace the effects that an increase in the cost of merchandise by 10 percent will have upon return-on-assets if the retail price cannot be increased.

2. A supplier of electronic data processing equipment has devised a system which he claims will allow the retailer described in Figure 18.2 to reduce the average inventory level by 15 percent without incurring any change in sales. This new system will result in an annual increase of $10,000 in the handling, general, and administration expenses category. Will the change be worthwhile? What would the retailer's new return-on-assets percentage be if the new system were implemented?

3. List the major financial statements and tools used by retailers and discuss the function of each.

4. Define and distinguish between periodic and perpetual methods of inventory control. Discuss the advantages and disadvantages of each.

5. Define and distinguish between LIFO and FIFO inventory valuation methods. Discuss the advantages and disadvantages of each and indicate which you would recommend during inflationary times.

6. Discuss the reasons some retailers use the retail method of inventory valuation.

7. What are the best sources of short-term funds for an established retailer?

8. What are the best sources of long-term funds for a beginning retailer?

9. What is a firm's collection period? How long should it be before a management becomes concerned?

10. Develop an insurance plan for a new sporting goods store that owns its own building and facilities.

11. Calculate the operating ratios for the firm described in Table 18.6. Assume that this firm is a men's wear store. Analyze its performance using information from the text and outside publications.

12. According to the return-on-assets model, what three items are included as a retailer's current assets?

Footnotes

1. Erich A. Helfert, *Techniques of Financial Analysis* (Homewood, Ill.: Richard D. Irwin, 1967), pp. 58–73.

2. *How to Control Accounts Receivable for Greater Profit* (New York: Dun & Bradstreet, 1966), p. 22.

3. Ibid.

Case Study: Big Valu Mass Merchandisers

Mark Gibson has recently been hired as a consultant to Big Valu Stores Inc. Big Valu has had a company philosophy of growing as fast as possible since 1978 when Mr. Jerry Wilbur became president of the company. Under Mr. Wilbur's guidance Big Valu sales have increased by 38 percent mainly in credit sales and by the introduction of private label merchandise.

Company performance is presented in Table 18.13. Mr. Wilbur is beginning to be concerned that the vendors are starting to press for quicker payment on their merchandise. He has been impressing upon

Table 18.13   Performance of Big Valu Stores, Inc.

	1978	1979	1980	1981	1982
Sales	$13,090,000	$14,100,000	$16,340,000	$18,210,000	$18,215,000
Gross margin (% of sales)	33.2	32.5	31.8	30.9	26.3
Selling, general and administrative expenses (% of sales including credit)	28.0	28.3	28.2	29.5	39.9
Inventory (% of sales)	20.8	21.7	24.3	24.4	23.1
Long-term debt/equity	0.1	0.4	0.4	0.7	1.9

each vendor the importance of a large account, such as Big Valu, to their sales and profits.

Mark Gibson has been hired to improve company relations and analyze the company's performance.

Discussion Questions

1. What outside sources might Mr. Gibson consult to guide him in his tasks?
2. Using the data presented in Table 18.13 and that obtained from the text and outside sources, analyze the performance of Big Valu and make recommendations about what they should do in the future.

Part Four | Retailing Services

Comments from the CEO

William V. Roberti,
Senior Vice-president
Maas Brothers

The 1980s will be prosperous for those retailers that can continue to stimulate the traditional customer and cultivate the updated customer. Each retailer must identify these customers and evaluate the markets they serve.

When I started my retail career in 1968, branch stores were being built at an accelerated rate. Today, we see department stores spreading across entire states and in many cases crossing state lines.

We have eight merchandising objectives at Maas Brothers to guide us into the 1980s:

1. **Assortment merchandising** is planning for each department by classification and price line. This plan must be flexible to follow business trends.
2. **Action items** includes selling activity of an item that indicates opportunity for immediate exploitation. Action items must be identified, reported, and acted upon by the buyer.
3. **Key item merchandising** involves items identified in advance of the season for volume exploitation. Special inventory investment, department location, and sales promotion are required.
4. **Never out basics** indicates a total commitment to being in stock on key merchandise items that should always be available to the customer every day in each unit store.
5. **One step up program** is an additional layer of fashion merchandise which may reflect increased pricepoints depending on the individual department. The result of this plan would raise the taste level and look of the department.
6. **Special value promotion** offers honest value to the customer or the promotion is not run. These promotions must develop from regular stock successful selling.
7. **Fashion right merchandising** is a total commitment to being first with fashion and ahead of competition.
8. **Advertised merchandise** must be planned with the view to maximize production from each exposure.

We feel if these eight simple objectives are followed that we will continue to expand our business far into the 1980s.

Earlier I mentioned the "one step up" program. This program is probably the single most important element of the eight steps to thrust us forward into the 1980s. It must not only be enforced in the Merchandise Division, but the Sales Promotion and Visual Merchandising Divisions as well. This one facet of the business will definitely set us apart from our competition, giving us the edge in visual presentation and sales.

Chapter 19 | Consumer Service Firms

Learning Goals

1. To be aware of the size and growth of consumer expenditures for services.
2. To discuss the different classifications of service firms.
3. To understand the pecularities encountered in marketing of services.

Key Terms and Concepts

service industry
rented goods service
owned goods service
nongoods service
repeat business
cost pricing
contingency payment
pricing
fixed pricing

value pricing
loss leader pricing
high price maintenance
discount pricing
flexible discriminatory
    pricing
price lining
critical path analysis

The field of retailing is much broader than simply selling goods to consumers; it includes the marketing of services as well. This might appear too broad a definition for retailing until one takes a closer look at the type of services offered today. A great number, if not the majority, of these services are in direct competition with traditional retailing. This chapter discusses the peculiarities encountered in the *service industry* (an industry concerned with any work that is not connected with the manufacture or processing of a product or commodity or the wholesaling or retailing of a good).

The owner of a diaper service faces competition not only from other diaper service firms but also from retailers who sell disposable and nondisposable diapers. Innovations in retailing and in such retail products as low-cost disposable diapers may affect his business far more than any competitive efforts by other firms that offer a similar service.

Many retailers have recognized the sales potential in the rental process and have added rental service to their line. It is common practice in many areas for paint stores to rent ladders, tarps, rollers, and other complementary equipment. Retailers with leisure-time products, such as motor bikes, canoes, and campers, have discovered substantial extra profits and sales potential in the rental business.

The service industry is not confined to a single market segment. It increasingly markets to all income and age groups and offers services from the day of birth through death. Weddings, bar mitzvahs, showers, and other special occasions are serviced by this industry, with goods and services ranging from rented chairs to thousand dollar ice carvings. Wheelchairs, crutches, special hospital beds, and oxygen respirators are some of the products offered for rent to serve people in sickness and injury.

The potential for the application of modern marketing and management techniques in the service industry is scarcely confined to running a better "mom and pop" type operation. This industry has formed huge national and multinational organizations.

Growth is apparent even in industries traditionally thought of as strictly the province for small independents. Service Corporation International of Houston during a four-year period acquired 101 funeral homes and 36 cemeteries in twelve states, Washington, D.C., and six Canadian provinces, making it the largest in the industry. Yet, impressive as this growth is, it represents less than 3 percent of total industry revenues in an industry composed of 20,000 U.S. funeral service firms and 10,000 nonprofit cemeteries reporting approximately $3.5 billion in gross receipts.[1]

Growth of the Service Industry

The term **service industry** can be highly misleading, depending upon how the statistics are compiled. It is abundantly clear that a tremendous growth in the service industry sector has occurred in the last few decades. The United States is now described as the first service economy the world has ever seen, with two out of every three workers in the private labor force involved in a service capacity. This figure has been estimated to reach 80 percent by 1990.

It is a complex task to separate all the functions that can logically be classified as service retailing to calculate a dollar and cents value for the service industry. The fact is that the service industry is very large and obviously growing. Consumer spending for services exceeded 47 percent of the typical American family's budget in 1980 (Figure 19.1). In the early fifties, services claimed about 35 percent of the consumer's expenditures. Although prices for services have risen faster than prices for goods, there has been a trend for consumers to buy more services from a wider assortment of service offerings.

Figure 19.1   Personal Consumption Expenditures for Durable Goods, Nondurable Goods, and Services in $ Billion, 1975–1981

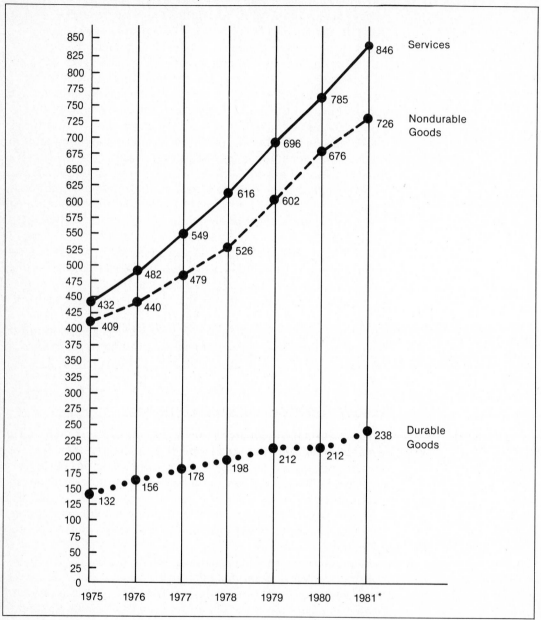

* First quarter only.

Source: *Survey of Current Business* (Washington, D.C.: Government Printing Office), February 1976, p. 8; January 1979, p. 14; and June, 1981, p. 11.

Classification of Consumer Service Firms

Although the service industry is highly fragmented, it can be grouped roughly into three main classifications.[2]

As the name implies, **rented goods service** means that these firms rent products—ranging from heavy-duty trucks to costumes for the Halloween dance. They may, however, engage in the sale of products at the same time.

Firms categorized as **owned goods services** repair products, sell value (added to a product through custom work), or otherwise improve existing products. Upholstery shops, gunsmiths, antique clock repair shops, ski repair shops, and many others are examples of such firms. In almost every case they also sell products at retail, such as gun oil, upholstery sprays and cleaners, keys to wind clocks, ski wax and bindings, and thousands of other products.

The primary product for **nongoods service** firms is not a product but a service. Beauty salons, funeral parlors, poodle barber shops, travel agencies, and insurance and financial institutions are a few examples.

The previous classification of retail services by rental goods, owned goods, and nongoods should not be interpreted as meaning that a retailer must be one or the other type. In practice, the retail mix of a firm (such as Sears) includes each of these areas, plus the regular merchandising services.

In recent years traditional retailers have expanded into a variety of services. Expansion has generally been accomplished in the following ways:

1. *Acquisition or establishment of service* Under this system the retailer acquires majority interest in the service company and then offers it as a part of the store's total merchandising mix. Insurance and finance companies have been among the major services established in this way.

2. *Leased department* Travel agencies, optical service, and shoe repair represent services that are commonly sold through an independent service retailer who simply leases space from another retailer. In addition to paying the lease, the lessee may agree to share a percentage of the gross.

3. *Tie-in agreement* In these cases the retailer may do no more than agree to provide a signed order to the vendor of services, who then reimburses the retailer with a commission. Banks and car dealers often have such arrangements for car loans. In other cases the retailer may sell the entire package of services under his or her name but, in actuality, perform nothing more than the selling and bill-collecting functions. The service vendor then performs the actual service.

The strength of tie-in agreements depends upon the amount of natural cohesion between the two parties. This is often referred to as reciprocity (you scratch my back—I'll scratch yours). To be successful, each party must feel it is gaining more than it could if it were to act independently.

Steps in Marketing Service

Retailers can benefit from service marketing by considering the following marketing activities.

Defining the Offering

An accurate generic definition of the service offering is required if a service firm is going to keep pace with or ahead of changes made by competitors and benefit from changes in consumer wants. Creative thinking can be rewarded with a tremendous growth in business volume. For example, some financial institutions are expanding their offering by providing one-stop services including real estate development, investment management, credit card services, leasing services, safety deposit facilities, insurance coverage, savings facilities, travel scheduling, accounting services, and other money-related activities.

Defining the Target Market

Segmenting the broad generic definition into similar subgroups of people who have common characteristics and then identifying and meeting the needs of the most attractive segments can be a very profitable strategy to follow. An accurate definition of market segment needs will allow the service firm to tailor its service offering and the marketing of that offering to best satisfy the segment consumers.[3] Categorization of the population into different segments can be based not only on traditional demographic factors but also upon consumer attitudes, activities, needs, and motivations. Indeed, in service marketing these four considerations may be the most profitable way to segment the market.

In addition to determining the market target groups, it is equally important for some service firms to determine which groups to avoid. Many professional service firms (such as market research firms, advertising agencies, lawyers, and so forth) are restrained from entering certain businesses because of possible conflicts of interests. For example, marketing research firms and advertising agencies usually refuse to handle two competing products simultaneously. In some cases it may be possible to set up separate task groups for each account and work on competitive accounts, but both competitors should be made aware of the situation and agree to it before the second competitive client is added to the list of clientele.

Planning Differentiated Service Offerings

Effectively selling to different market segments usually requires a different marketing approach. Each segment of a market for a given service will not respond to the same approach. Service presentation must be geared to the needs of the target market segments. Service firms can provide a differential advantage in their service offering if any part of that offering creates a special value in the minds of their customers.

For example, the manager of a suburban auto repair shop might cater to commuters who catch the train to work in the city. The auto service firm could drive customers to the station when they arrive in the morning and meet them at the evening train. Other extras, such as washing and cleaning the car at no extra charge, may be provided on repair jobs that cost over a certain amount.

Development of companion service offerings frequently is based upon the desire to use all of the firm's resources at near-capacity levels. Near-capacity utilization in retailing firms generally allows overhead costs to be spread over a larger number of sales units and therefore results in a per unit reduction in selling costs. Service firms have a more important advantage in operating at full capacity because their offerings are generally so perishable that they cannot be stored. There is no way to market the rental car that was not rented yesterday, or the unused time that an interior decorator or barber spent waiting for customers. Thus, it is important to develop a service offering that can reverse the underutilization of capacity and recapture labor and capital costs as regularly and as completely as possible.

Identifying and Evaluating New Service Offerings

New idea generation of service offerings is likely to originate with the consumer. Service firms benefit from a relatively short channel of communication that extends from the consumer through the service personnel (employees or agents of the service retailer) to the firm's management. Consumer problems can be translated into business opportunities if service personnel are impressed with the importance of reporting these consumer problems (as well as their recommendations for a solution) to the firm's management. A service firm's management can then screen out the better ideas, rank them in priority, and perform a business analysis of the best ideas. The business analysis would focus on sales projections, cost considerations, and evaluation of the company's resources (including managerial ability) to determine profitability and availability of compatible equipment and knowledge. The effect of current client satisfaction with the new offering is also important.

One difficulty associated with development of new service offerings is that they are seldom patentable and only a few are proprietary. Thus, timing and resourcefulness are major ways that service firms can stay ahead of competitors. The need to search continually for new ideas and methods of better serving consumer desires is implied by the lack of protection provided by legal means. Progressive service firms must conduct continued service development programs if they are to keep ahead of the competitor who is simply copying old service offerings. The consequences of this competition through imitative action are evident by the ease of entry into many service industries and by the existence of many small service outlets.

Under the Lanham Act of 1946 the service industry has acquired the legal protection of "service marks," which are supposed to be the legal counterpart of the trademark.[4] The Lanham Act also made provisions for legal use of the "certification mark" and "collective mark" as service marks for the promotion of services. However, relatively few service outlets have applied service marks to gain the advantages of market control, uniformity, and guarantee of quality that brand names appear to offer consumers. Perhaps future service marketing will make better use of the service mark to gain a competitive advantage over service-imitating competitors. A pizza parlor provides an example of a service firm that uses a service mark as identification on a carry-out package.

Service Warranties

The provision of service warranties is another area in which service retailers can create a differentiated offering. The increasing importance of consumerism and the passage of new legislation necessitates the service retailer to offer a good warranty policy to obtain consumer good will and resulting publicity by acting before competition or legal requirements preclude action.

By 1970 the Uniform Commercial Code had replaced the Uniform Sales Act in every state except Louisiana.[5] Under the Uniform Commercial Code, service warranties are included as "express warranties." An express warranty arises as part of the bargaining process between buyer and seller. Case law since 1960 shows that service retailers create express warranties by selling claims and by advertising. The growing number of warranty cases is influenced by class action possibilities against both the service firm and the manufacturer of the items.[6]

Thus, it is likely that warranties will become an important issue to service retailers, and courts are likely to see an increase in the number of cases involving service retailers. A service firm that recognizes this trend can take steps not only to avoid possible court action but to turn the warranty into a promotable item by including a unique and clear statement of warranty as part of its service offering.

Establishing higher warranty standards than those set by the industry can offset some problems. One illustration is a policy of guarantees on parts and labor by a repair shop. If sixty days is standard in the industry, the service firm could establish a *ninety*-day warranty policy. The extra thirty days provides an indication of the firm's good intentions and conveys to the customers an impression of high performance standards in the services performed. Making an exception for a good customer who experiences difficulties several days after the guarantee has expired can also generate consumer good will.

Guarantees of performance may be more difficult to substantiate for a service than for goods because for many services there is no acceptable method of measuring quality. The end result of service activity is frequently identifiable only in intangible terms. However, the performance of many services can be evaluated in tangible terms such as speed, accuracy, frequency of service, and so forth. If it is possible to substantiate claims, service firms benefit from these claims, because the buyer of services frequently may not feel comfortable assessing the worth of a complex of activities that comprise the service offering. That is, the consumer frequently feels helpless because his or her fate is in the hands of the service firm. Inclusion of a guarantee can reduce this feeling of uncertainty.

Many services (for example, medical, accounting, insurance, interior decorating, beauty shops) do not offer their skills and resources per se but really offer the consumer confidence, hope, or the reduction of uncertainty. In these cases the service firm promises more certainty in an area in which customers feel unsure.

Displaying an industry code of ethics is one way to remind consumers of the quality service they can expect to receive from a service firm. However, merely displaying the code does little good unless service personnel live up to that code.

Reducing Consumer Uncertainty

It follows that the service firm will want to design a service offering that will minimize consumer uncertainty. Creating consumer awareness of the need for a service must be an objective of the firm's promotional effort. Frequently, the consumer will be aware that there is (or is likely to be) a problem. However, in many cases (making a will, obtaining a medical checkup, obtaining insurance, and so on) consumers may not be aware of their need for this service. In these cases an awareness promotional campaign is essential for the industry or the individual firm.

Deciding what service is applicable for solving the consumer's problems is the next step. Successful service performance depends on a clear understanding of the customer's problems. Ideally, the potential service customer would approach the service firm with an objective description of the problem and request help in solving it. In reality, however, consumers infrequently take this approach. Thus, it is the job of the service firm to determine the consumer's problems through direct questioning. If subtle questioning results in an in-depth problem definition, the service offering can be tailored to meet the consumer's individual needs.

The consumer should be given an honest opinion backed up by facts on the worth of each purchase alternative. The objective is to gain customer confidence by giving an honest estimate; but even honest estimates are sometimes doubted by consumers, especially if the service outlet also sells new or replacement equipment. However, a consistent honest approach should win the trust of most consumers over the long run.

Selecting the employee who should render the service depends upon the person's demonstrable knowledge and skill in the claimed area of competence. Obviously demonstrable skill and knowledge will create consumer confidence. Many service retailers fail to recognize and acknowledge that they cannot do all things; that is, that there are limits to their skill and knowledge. In this case referrals to other people within the firm may be needed, or maybe it requires an honest admission that no one in the firm has the competence in that specialized area. Failure to admit incompetence in an area can cost a service firm longtime business if a customer loses confidence in the firm because of one bad experience. However, admission of incompetence, if repeated several times, can point out new areas of expertise that could be included in the service offering.

How the service is performed is also important in establishing consumer confidence, and respecting the customer's time can gain consumer respect. People become distrustful of a service firm that always breaks promised service schedules. Every effort should be made to keep on schedule and not overcommit service personnel. Some service delays are unavoidable. When this occurs the consumer should be informed that a repairperson is going to be delayed. This allows the consumer to adjust his or her schedule. In the repair business, providing a replacement for consumers to use while theirs is being repaired can lessen consumer aggravation when the service period is delayed.

Consumers also appreciate consideration and promptness in being informed when the estimated cost of service is changed because of unforeseen circumstances. In the repair business, the consumer may think that the revised cost is more than the item is worth and decide to purchase a new item. Additional reasons for consumer dissatisfaction with professional services are presented in Table 19.1.

Table 19.1 Major Reasons for Consumer Dissatisfaction with Professional Services*

Reasons	% Mentioned
The service was provided in a careless, unprofessional manner.	19.2
The service was not completed in the agreed time.	4.3
The service was not performed correctly the first time.	8.8
I was charged for services that were not performed.	3.5
I was charged for materials or medicines that were not furnished.	0.8
The fee was much higher than the amount agreed upon in advance.	3.7
The fee was much higher than an advertised price for the service received.	0.8
The quality of materials or medicines which were furnished was inferior.	1.8
Things were worse after the service than before.	6.8
The item was lost or broken.	1.8
A professional confidence was violated to my embarrassment or injury.	2.9
The professional advice I received was incorrect and caused me substantial losses.	3.7
Services were performed in an incompetent manner with very harmful results.	8.2
I was tricked by the person providing the service into buying services I didn't want.	2.2
Results fell far short of those claimed in ads.	2.3
I was harassed by bill collectors.	1.4
Credit terms were misrepresented to me.	0.6
The warranty (guarantee) did not cover everything that went wrong.	0.8
I feel I was treated with extreme rudeness.	5.9
I feel I was treated like an object rather than as an individual.	12.3
Other reasons not listed.	8.2

* Based on 194 highly dissatisfied respondents.
Source: John A. Quelch and Stephen B. Ash "Consumer Satisfaction with Professional Services," *Marketing of Services,* Proceedings Series edited by James H. Donnelly and William R. George, Chicago: American Marketing Association, 1981, p. 85. Reprinted with permission.

Location

Location is another factor used by service firm to establish a differentiated service mix. For example, studies of consumer preference for airline service have shown that the most important reasons a consumer selects one airline over another are that the airline is going to the desired location at the desired time. Other factors, such as meal service, in-flight movies, stewardesses, magazine selection, and so forth are much less important.

The same is true of other retail services. It is not likely that a consumer will travel across town to a muffler shop, brake repair garage, shoe repair store, or laundromat if there is a comparable shop in the neighborhood, even if the nearby shop is not the favorite one.

Large car-rental agencies have been faced with stiff price competition from industry newcomers in recent years. Even so, they have been able to maintain their basic price policies because of their favorable image and the widespread availability of their rental counters. It is easier for an air travel customer, particularly one on an expense account, to walk to the Hertz, Avis, or National counter than to call one of the competitive off-grounds firms and wait for a car to be delivered.

Studies have demonstrated the savings that can be realized by riding the bus rather than driving one's car to work. Yet, if an ample supply of gasoline is available, the real or imagined convenience of driving one's own car continues to win out over bus service in most American cities. Motels must be located near a highway so that they are easily accessible to motorists. Laundry and cleaning firms must be conveniently available to their customers, even if the firm has to create the convenience by offering pickup and delivery service in the case of a poorly located firm. The list could go on and on, but it is generally true that location is an important consideration for all service firms that are visited personally by their customers. Unless very skilled personal expertise is involved, consumers are likely to patronize the service firm that requires the least effort to reach.

Services involving a considerable amount of personal skill (such as those of the medical doctor, lawyer, music instructor) and those service firms that are never visited by the customer can utilize relatively inconvenient locations. Examples of firms that are seldom visited by customers are window washing and television and radio repair services. These service firms can pay the lower rents generally associated with an inconvenient location and still satisfy their consumers' needs. Facilities do not have to be as elaborate for seldom-visited service firms, since the telephone is their primary method of communication with consumers.

Service firms requiring customer visitation, on the other hand, depend upon a neat external appearance to draw the consumer inside. The interior must be neat, clean, comfortable, and pleasant, especially if consumers have to wait for service. The layout, equipment, and furniture should convey an appropriate impression, being both attractive and functional. The land, building layout, equipment, and furniture should generate the desired image for the firm—in the same manner that goods retailers use these factors to project a store image.

Planning the Promotional Mix

Aside from packaging, the communication channels available to service firms are identical to those available to merchandise retailers. Many promotional methods are rejected by service retailers as being too brash and costly without any real consideration given to their relationship to the firms' service offering and the habits of their target markets.

Some services can effectively use more promotional expenditures than others. Medical doctors, lawyers, and related professional service firms are restricted by their professional organizations in the type and amount of promotions. Besides advertising, personal selling, point-of-purchase promotions, and public relations, there are many other kinds of sales promotion that service firms can use in making consumers aware of their offering and instilling consumer confidence in the quality of service offered. The main difficulty is selecting techniques that project the appropriate image.

Advertising

Service advertising differs from product advertising because it is more difficult (and sometimes impossible) to illustrate the use or benefits of a service. Thus, service advertising is likely to depend more on image appeals. Differences in advertising media are strongly influenced by the size of the service firm and by accepted practice within each service industry. Small service firms may be content with a listing in the Yellow Pages, while large service firms (such as H & R Block) may rely heavily upon television advertising. Yellow Page advertising and select forms of specialty and direct-mail advertising for small service firms can mean the crucial difference between a sale or an empty cash drawer.

Sign Media

The mobility of many services, such as Greyhound or a U-Haul Trailer, gives certain service industries an extremely important advertising tool. In a period of twenty-four hours a jet may be seen by thousands of potential customers in a number of states and nations. Airlines and car rental industries also have learned that their personnel can serve as subtle public relations and advertising media. It is small wonder that such industries carefully regulate the social activities of uniformed employees.

Point-of-Purchase Promotion

Point-of-purchase advertising is critical to many service firms. Unlike products, the point of purchase may be in the customer's home or office rather than a store. Nevertheless, there is a point of sale for all services, just as for any product.

The often overlooked business card can be an effective medium at the point of purchase. Business cards are retained by people, particularly businesspeople. Since they are often held together with a rubber band or simply tossed into a desk drawer, it is important to give careful consideration to their design. Whenever possible, they should be distinctive and carry the service mark of the company.

It is equally important to plan carefully for the distribution of business cards and flyers in the service retail store. Service shops often fail to provide display racks or piles of cards and flyers for customers. Some service firms have found that a pleased customer will gladly distribute such items to friends. Unless the retailer of goods has particularly distinctive merchandise or prices, it is unlikely he can share in this willingness of customers to cooperate gladly in advertising.

Word of Mouth

Service retailer success is probably much more dependent upon word-of-mouth advertising than goods retailing. A high level of consumer satisfaction is the most crucial factor in obtaining good word-of-mouth advertising. Although much practical research is needed in this area, service retailers continually need to be aware of the "bad-mouth syndrome."[7] Unless consumers are satisfied all service firms are vulnerable to an infection of "bad mouthing" which sweeps through a population.

Bumper Stickers

Bumper stickers can be used effectively to promote services, particularly if the sticker is designed to capture the curiosity of the reader. Service retailers of glamorous or "in" places and events are able to capitalize on the use of bumper stickers in a method that most retailers would never dare attempt. It is difficult to imagine parking lot attendants at a Sears store suddenly descending upon all cars in the lot with bumper stickers advertising the store. Yet this is precisely what happens at a variety of recreational-service areas, ranging from Reptile Gardens to the newest 40-acre amusement park.

Perhaps a consumer's psychological need is met through bumper stickers, or else there would be far more objection to their use. Bumper stickers may meet many of the same needs as college and fraternity window stickers and the travel decals that were popular during the 1950s. They may say to others "I have visited unusual places" or "I am also a member of the group that enjoys 'in' things."

Other Specialty Advertising Forms	The service industry is particularly well suited to many forms of specialty advertising. A survey by the Specialty Advertising Association International showed that of the top ten groups of particular interest to specialty advertisers, seven were service-type industries.[8] Retail establishments such as camera and jewelry stores were given very low interest rankings by distributors of specialty advertising, while banks and savings and loan associations ranked high.

The type of specialty item selected by a service retailer is only as good as the thought behind it and the application it has to the target market. In far too many cases a specialty gimmick has been used simply because it seemed clever and inexpensive. On the other hand the success of Avis, with its "We Try Harder" buttons in a variety of foreign languages, is an example of the exposure that a good specialty item can give a service retailer.

Promotion by Telephone	To many retailers the telephone is more of a hindrance to doing business than an aid. Many managers of supermarkets, discount houses, and other mass merchandising outlets believe that the telephone simply interrupts or intrudes on management and personnel time without adding to sales. This is scarcely the case with most service retailers, yet many treat the telephone as if it were a nuisance.

Generally, when a person calls a service retail establishment, he or she is genuinely interested in learning more about the retailer's service and should be regarded as a potential customer. A call from a potential customer should be viewed as the near culmination of all the efforts a firm has expended in advertising, public relations, location selection, and total imagery. It is the firm's chance to invite the customer to use its services, and may also be the moment to close a sale.

Thus, the telephone should be considered the "hot line" and should not be left to indiscriminate answering by anyone who may or may not be handy. Programs should be established for the purpose of training personnel in the correct use of the phone.

Order blanks and writing material should be placed near the phone, and a follow-through system should be implemented. Airlines are leaders in this field and may be viewed as models. The Bell Telephone System should also be contacted for help, since it has trained experts to assist firms and provide free educational films.

Customer Contact and Personal Selling

A large portion, if not the majority, of service retailers are highly dependent upon direct consumer contact. This has been true even in the case of services originally based on the concept of self-service. In some areas, the increasing personal crime rate has created a need for attendants in, say, laundromats. Owners of these establishments have discovered that attendants can do more than just police; they can greet customers, instruct them in the use of machines, and provide additional revenue by ironing clothes.

To be successful, a service retailer must place primary emphasis on customer contact. This should begin before the business doors are even opened. In the case of service businesses that serve a local area, a key to success can be door-to-door calling on customers. The message is simple. After an introduction, the service retailer tells the consumer about the service and what it can do for him/her, asks for future business, and asks the consumer to tell his or her friends. An inexpensive specialty gift item, with the retailer's name, address, and phone number imprinted on it, should be left with the potential customer. Customer contact then continues every minute of the service retailer's day.

There can rarely be too much customer contact. This message must continually be transmitted to all personnel or it will soon be forgotten. The teller at a savings and loan firm who shows displeasure at opening piggy banks and counting loose change is a very weak link in the service chain. Unreturned phone calls from customers, an empty, dirty pot at the free coffee table, and halfhearted welcomes to customers who bring in two-for-one or other promotional coupons are examples of the negatives in customer contact. Correct customer contact must be a continuous philosophy that permeates all levels of a service retailer's organization.

Relatively less emphasis can be placed on personal selling by service firms that make most of their sales to customers who have already decided to buy when they make their initial contact with the service firm. Such a service firm can advertise to attract new customers and then concentrate on building repeat business by providing prompt, efficient service. For example, radio and television repair shops receive a telephone call requesting repair service. The customer does not need to be sold on the fact that he or she needs help. In this case the role of a service person may not include any selling, or it may be limited to a suggestion that the consumer upgrade the purchase by replacing more parts which will provide a longer, more productive life.

On the other hand, extensive use of personal selling may be required of service firms that contact customers who are not committed to buying at the time of the original contact with the firm. Good personal selling techniques are required in this case. These techniques begin with an understanding of the customer's problem and end with an explanation of how the firm's service offerings can satisfy those needs.

Personal selling plays a different role in the marketing of services than it does in the selling of products. Retailers of goods generally place more reliance on tangible product benefits to consumers in their advertising and selling. Service firms are, of necessity, likely to turn to images that communicate the benefits to the purchaser.

Repeat Business

The success of many service firms is dependent upon obtaining **repeat business,** in which consumers continually come back to the same facility to satisfy their needs. Repeat consumer business is based on satisfying the consumer with the service that was previously experienced. Satisfied consumers of services tend to show loyalty to the service firm and to return when they have a new problem that appears to fall within the area of the firm's expertise.

Established professional service firms such as doctors, lawyers, and accountants rely upon repeat business as the core, if not the entire source, of their business. In these cases, and in other service areas, additional business is fairly predictable and is forthcoming almost automatically, as long as a proper relationship is maintained with satisfied customers.[9]

Generating repeat sales from customers revolves mostly around the professional people who provide the services. Consumers become tied to personalities, particularly if they receive prompt, efficient service from the service person. The degree of loyalty may be affected by the amount of skill that the consumer perceives is required to solve problems. For example, a consumer is likely to be more loyal to a doctor than to a barber. However, some customers change barber shops every time their favorite barber changes employment. Although no one is indispensable, these strong personal preferences must be recognized by service firms' management.

The importance of the service professional affects the firm's selling activity considerably. Technical service people are not as likely to want to develop selling techniques to the degree that good salespeople may consider essential for their profession. As a result, the selling of former service customers is likely to be less organized and systematic than in product retail outlets. Instead, service selling is more centered on opportunity selling, which consists of the technical service person's sensing an opportunity for future service and then communicating the benefits of that service to the customer.

Undoubtedly, one of the best ways to build repeat business is to perform excellent service all of the time. A difficulty arises, however, because the customer is frequently unable to judge the quality of the service. Thus, excellent service alone is not sufficient. It must be accompanied by an informal and discreet method of letting the customer become aware of the excellent service received.

Some scheduling of periodic contact is required if repeat business is to be maintained. As time passes from the date that the original service was performed, the less likely it is that the customer will return to the same service firm for future work. Making periodic contact can remind the customer of the excellent service received, and can also remind him or her that time has passed and updated service may be beneficial. For example, dentists, and doctors use a good card-filing system to identify customers who are due for their periodic checkup.

Opportunities for suggesting the benefits of some further service should be advanced to build repeat business. An accountant who is making a regular audit might suggest a way of improving a firm's accounting practices or a way of making better managerial use of the data the firm already has. Many bowling firms help to build a permanent clientele by organizing and promoting bowling leagues, which use pressure from the team members to encourage each individual to be there at bowling time. Surely other service firms can use this competitive motivation to build repeat business.

Cooperative associations and chain organizations frequently build permanent patronage. For example, motels and restaurants benefit from association with one nationally advertised name. Generally the chain, franchise, or cooperative association establishes quality standards, inspects each establishment periodically, and extends the privilege of continued association only to those firms that meet the established standards. Their consumers, perceiving a more consistent type of service, tend to become loyal customers of the various associations' member firms. This consistent service concept is likely to grow in importance as people do more traveling and change their place of residence more frequently.

Customer relations—performing those activities that are designed to make the client personally attached to one of the firm's technical service people—is another method of stimulating repeat business. Providing special considerations, such as lunch, small gifts, and so forth are methods of building consumer loyalty.

Credit

Credit is also effective to generate business for service firms. Service firms have too long restricted the granting of credit because they sold intangible offerings that could not be repossessed if the consumer refused to pay any debt. The fact that unused capacity in service firms cannot be sold later makes the granting of credit attractive even if there are occasional losses due to bad debts. Compared to goods retailers, the service firm with excess capacity certainly has less to lose by granting credit and risking losses due to increases in accounts receivable.

Bank credit card plans have taken away most of the bad debt problem. These plans make it easier and more economical for a service firm to make credit sales on small purchases.

In addition, surprising market segments can sometimes be discovered through research no more involved than examining company records. Many airlines found that their credit policies for unmarried young women were unduly restrictive. A policy of extending credit to married women or those over twenty-five did not take into account the number of gainfully employed career women. The number of people in this market segment is large, is growing, and is fully able to assume credit responsibility.

Planning Pricing Strategy

Developing good pricing strategies for service firms is an important activity. Most service firms have relatively little capital, so pricing and time usage are the main factors in generating profits. In addition, because of imperfect consumer knowledge about the quality of service performed, many services are less subject to the pressures and controls of the marketplace than goods retailers. As a result, these service firms have greater flexibility in their pricing activities. Service firms can select many different pricing strategies, and the major alternatives will now be discussed.

Cost Pricing

Cost pricing is a method of obtaining prices by adding all of the chargeable costs. This method requires a reliable cost accounting system that identifies the costs and time for each phase of service. Allocatable costs are then assigned to each customer, and these costs are multiplied by a markup factor (2.5 is common for many professional service firms), which must cover profit, rent, utilities, insurance, taxes, and other nonallocatable fixed costs.

For example, a service firm performing a job that is estimated to cost $1,000 in wages and other allocatable costs would charge the customer $2,500 if the 2.5 markup factor is applied. Only the value of service people's time on this particular piece of work would be included in the $1,000 cost estimate. The time that these service people spend idle, in retraining, and so forth, would not be included in the allocatable costs, but would have to be recovered in the markup charge.

A major disadvantage of the cost pricing system is the difficulty of identifying and accurately allocating costs. For example, questions frequently arise on the ways to identify and allocate developmental costs, proposed costs, general administrative costs, and so forth. Good cost accounting systems can answer many of these questions, but all procedures are subject to the dedication of management and service people. Cost pricing will not work unless everyone keeps records that indicate how much time is devoted to each activity and each service job. Frequently, because it is difficult to convince professional service people of this fact, many service firms cannot calculate the profit and loss contribution of individual types of services, individual jobs, customers, and so forth. Instead, they wonder why the overall profitability of the enterprise is low relative to what they think it should be.

Another disadvantage of the cost pricing method is that if costs are used as the sole basis for the establishment of price, there may be no incentive for controlling costs. However, competitive markets usually provide an indication, via decreased business, of when this is occurring.

Contingency Payment Pricing

Contingency payment pricing is when the price for a service is quoted as contingent upon task accomplishment. It is similar to a commission fee for a salesperson, since no charge is made unless the task is performed. This method is used by real estate agencies, employment agencies, and similar organizations.

The contingency system offers a great deal of motivation to complete the work successfully. Difficulty arises in defining what constitutes successful performance of the task.

Fixed Pricing

A **fixed** or **uniform price** is achieved by a controlling body such as a professional organization, governmental regulation, or informed agreement. Actually, this is a result of a pricing decision and not a method used to reach a decision. The service firm must abide by it, however, so its pricing strategy is predetermined by the controlling body. Transportation companies engaged in interstate commerce (moving companies, trucking firms, railroads, airlines) and beauty shops and barber shops are examples.

Value Pricing

Value pricing is based on the belief that buyers will respond to price in relation to the value that they associate with the service. One should recall that customers of most services have difficulty appraising the technical worth of the service offering because it is generally so intangible. The purchasing decision is likely to be based on the consumer's perception of the value of the service offering. Frequently, when consumers have difficulty appraising the worth of an offering, an association of poor quality is attached to discount prices. Thus, value pricing may amount to a "what the market will bear" pricing policy, since the price is not based on cost but on the value the consumer attaches to the service.

Value pricing can be defended as fair despite the nonassociation of price with costs. Price, in this case, is associated with worth, so new ideas, new methods, and new knowledge that are valuable to the client are paid for in proportion to their value to the customer. Value pricing in small, local areas where there are no alternative sources of supply, or in cases of very essential services (such as brain surgery), may not be considered a just pricing policy by consumers.[10]

Planning Pricing Tactics

Service pricing strategy, no matter how it is determined, must guide shorter term (or tactical) decisions to establish the actual quoted price. The same tactical pricing techniques that are used to sell goods can be modified effectively to sell services. The application of some of the major pricing tactics to the service area will now be discussed.

Loss Leader Pricing

Loss leader pricing is a deliberate reduction in price to establish initial contact with a customer. It is frequently used by service firms such as auto service stations or dancing studios, which give price reductions as get-acquainted offers. One disadvantage of loss leader pricing is that a low price may tend to establish a price ceiling, above which the consumer may resist price increases if the customer knows the service is the same but the price is higher.

High Price
Maintenance

As the name implies, **high price maintenance** is the practice of
establishing a price that is higher than the price offered by competitors. Both experience and marketing studies have demonstrated that some consumers tend to associate the price of the
product or service with the quality.[11]

It is apparent that some service retailers follow this practice as
a price policy. These seem to be the larger, more secure firms that
have achieved a reputation and have carved out a particular
market segment. Evidence of this practice was demonstrated in a
study of the pest control industry on Long Island, New York.
This study found that a small segment of this service industry
was able to maintain higher prices. The study concluded that
"they seem to be the major participants in the industry, able to
hold out against the price threat of the low-price sellers."[12]

Discount Pricing

Discount pricing is a tactic that provides a price quotation that is
subject to a discount on some predetermined basis such as time
schedule, volume of purchases over a stated time period, extent
of commitment, and so forth. Discount pricing is widely used by
leasing firms and many other service agencies. It provides an
incentive for the consumer to remain loyal to the service firm because costs are reduced by purchasing all (or most) of the available services from one firm. Widespread discount pricing is
explained by the fact that service firms are faced with a continuing problem because they are unable to inventory their particular service. If the goods inventory of a retailer does not sell,
it can sometimes be returned to the vendor or stored or placed on
sale. This is not the case with a firm such as an airline or movie
theater. Once the plane has left the ground, the empty seats are
forever lost as revenue for that flight. As a result, service firms
with this problem often turn to the practice of charging different
customers different prices for only slightly different services.

Youth fares, tour packages, and Saturday afternoon matinees
are examples of this type of pricing. Only rarely are these firms
able to sell all their services without the aid of discount pricing.
As a result, the concept of market segmentation is of paramount
importance to firms in the service industry. It becomes a necessity to analyze market segments to determine new promotions
and prices that might appeal to them. In the case of regulated
and interstate firms, differentiated or discount pricing and
promotion are automatically open to official debate and legal
regulation.

Flexible Pricing

Flexible pricing is the practice of charging customers different
prices according to their perceived willingness to pay. This ap-

pears to be common practice in many sectors of the service industry, particularly in those where a custom price quote is needed for each job. For example, the study of the pest control industry on Long Island, New York demonstrates flexible pricing by that industry. It was found that 58 percent of the sample surveyed demonstrated that flexible pricing had been used. In other words, about 58 percent of the customers were charged different prices for the same work.[13]

The same study concluded that the best marketers in the pest control industry follow these practices:

1. Set annual total project and sales volume goals
2. Keep a definite profit margin in mind when quoting jobs
3. Have good knowledge of costs
4. Review price schedules regularly
5. Try to secure higher, rather than lower or average, prices
6. Tend to be flexible in pricing

An interesting conclusion of the pest control study was that ". . . The smallest firms appeared to be the poorest marketers and medium sized firms the best."

Price Lining

Price lining is a tactic whereby prices are not varied, but the quality or extent of the service provided is adjusted to reflect changes in costs. This removes price as a major negotiating point, but the consumer may be able to perceive the change in the service offering and associate it with an inferior image of the firm in general. Leasing firms frequently employ price lining when they make available, at different rental charges, different quality levels of the same item (garden rototillers with various size engines, for example).

The policy of price lining may sometimes be a questionable practice. A consumer may be quite willing to receive a lower horsepower rental tool but may expect a constant level of quality in regard to other services.

The repair sector of the service industry is an example. A study has shown that consumers are willing to pay disproportionately higher repair prices to have lower cost products repaired. In other words, they do not expect to receive lower quality repair service simply because the item, such as a toaster, costs less than a stove or refrigerator. They expect to have both repaired properly.[14] Appliance owners seem to recognize that there is a basic cost for servicing their equipment regardless of the value of the product.

Procurement and Inventory Control

Procurement in most service firms is generally limited to buying equipment and supplies. The inventory control problem, therefore, is not large unless the service handles physical items as part of its consumer service business. Control of the work in process can be very important for small repair shops, laundries, photography developers, and the like. Accurate control is mandatory in these firms if consumer satisfaction is to be obtained and a permanent clientele maintained. Inventory costs for these firms are not likely to be large, but they cannot risk the loss of business associated with a consumer whose possession has been lost.

There are a few service firms that encounter large inventory costs as part of doing business. Auto repair garages, radio and television repair shops, and so forth face the traditional retail problem of deciding how much inventory they can afford to keep on hand. In this case, the decision rules discussed in Chapter 9 can be applied to evaluate inventory levels.

Scheduling the Work Load

Work scheduling is of considerable importance in service firms because of the perishability of the unused labor and the consumer ill will generated by not meeting a deadline. Work-scheduling tasks, similar to those in manufacturing companies, are faced by most service firms. Labor costs comprise such a large percentage of total costs for most service firms that management must consider all possibilities to improve the work flow.

Such techniques as critical path analysis, control boards, and so forth can improve the overall labor performance by making better utilization of employee time. **Critical path analysis,** which is simply a planning tool, provides a diagram that shows which jobs must be completed before other jobs can be started. It also uses estimated time requirements needed to perform each job so that they can be scheduled in an order that will minimize the time needed to complete the total job. This tool can identify bottlenecks that limit the amount of work generated by a service firm.

Even small service firms can benefit from the type of thinking that critical path analysis requires. For example, parts can be ordered before they are needed so that they are available when needed by service people. Repair and maintenance work can be done during idle time, so that equipment is in top shape and ready to operate at full speed during peak service hours. The list could continue indefinitely, but suffice it to say that proper planning, scheduling, and control procedures can result in increased profits for most service firms.

Rewards for servicing consumers more efficiently can be substantial. For example, until recently anyone who lost an American Express card had to wait two or more weeks to obtain a replacement. A change in the processing operation has now resulted in consumers' cards being replaced in as little as two days. Faster replacement of lost cards has caused their consumer to be happier with American Express. It also provided the company with an extra $2.4 million in revenue, as it loses $2.70 in charge volume for every day that a user is without a card.[15]

Summary

Marketing of services differs from merchandise marketing in that:

1. Repeat customer business is absolutely required.
2. The firm's offering cannot be stored, so it is even more important to operate at near-capacity levels.
3. It is more difficult for the consumer to measure the quality or worth of services offered.
4. Service firms are particularly vulnerable to the "bad-mouth syndrome" because it is difficult for consumers to judge the value of a service.

Thus, most of a service firm's marketing effort can be aimed at reducing consumer uncertainty. A consumer's confidence can be gained by analyzing the problem and providing an honest opinion, backed up by facts based on the worth of each alternative solution from the consumer's viewpoint. Competent employees should render the service, as demonstrable skill and knowledge will create consumer confidence. Warranties should reinforce the quality image.

Respecting the customer's time can gain that person's respect, since people become distrustful of a service firm that always breaks its promised service schedules. Some service delays are unavoidable, but the consumer should be informed that there is going to be a delay. Consumers also appreciate promptness in being informed when cost estimates are changed because of unforeseen circumstances.

Repeat business can be built upon satisfying the consumer so he or she comes back to the service outlet. Consumers frequently become tied to personalities and develop a loyalty to the person who is believed to deliver excellent quality and prompt and efficient service. Periodic contact can be made with consumers to remind them of the excellent service the consumer received and of the passage of time, i.e., that it is time once again to schedule a periodic checkup, oil change, etc.

Pricing strategy for services is based upon a number of things: cost plus a markup factor; the value that consumers perceive to be associated with the service; and some relationship to competitors' price (such as a high price maintenance policy or a discount policy).

Questions

1. How can the manager of an auto repair service facility protect or increase the firm's market share?
2. How may the legal profession promote their business? Design a promotional package for a local legal firm.
3. Design a marketing mix for the following service firms:
   a. a local real estate agency
   b. a local air line
   c. a professional public accounting firm
   d. a local beauty shop
4. Discuss how consumer expenditures for: (a) durable goods, (b) nondurable goods, and (c) services have changed during the past eight years.
5. Give two examples of (a) a rented goods service firm, (b) an owned goods service firm, and (c) a nongoods service firm.
6. Discuss the ways that traditional retailers can expand into the marketing of services.
7. How can service firms reduce consumer uncertainty?
8. Develop a promotional plan using the telephone for:
   a. an interstate bus service
   b. a management consulting firm
   c. a local motel
   d. a local restaurant
9. Discuss the factors that should be considered in establishing the credit policy of (a) a beauty shop, (b) a local barber, and (c) a motel.

Footnotes

1. Sam Weiner, "Monumental Undertaking," *Financial Trend* 18 (January 28–February 3, 1973): 7, 10, 12, 15.

2. John M. Rathmell, "What Is Meant by Service?" *Journal of Marketing* 30 (October 1966): 32–36.

3. Richard P. Carr, Jr., "Developing a New Residential Market for Carpeting: Some Mistakes and Successes," *Journal of Marketing* 41 (July 1977): 101–102.

4. Robert C. Judd, "Similarities or Differences in Product and Service Retailing," *Journal of Retailing* 43 (Winter 1968): 3.

5. Commerce Clearing House, *Products Liability Reporter* (Chicago: Commerce Clearing House, 1970), paragraph 1010.

6. Heningsen v. Bloomfield Motors, 32 N.J. 358, 161 A. 2d 69 (1960).

7. Johan Arndt, "Word of Mouth Advertising and Informal Communications," in Donald F. Cox, ed., *Risk Taking and Information Handling in Consumer Behavior* (Boston: Harvard University Graduate School of Business Administration, 1967), pp. 188–239.

8. George Z. Herpel and Richard A. Collins, *Specialty Advertising in Marketing* (Homewood, Ill.: Richard D. Irwin, 1972), pp. 181–182.

9. Robert E. Sibson, *Managing Professional Service Enterprises* (New York: Pitman, 1971), p. 114.

10. See also R. E. Sibson, *"A Service,"* in E. Marting, ed., *Creative Pricing* (New York: American Management Association, 1968), pp. 146–155.

11. J. D. McConnell, "The Development of Brand Loyalty: An Experimental Study," *Journal of Marketing Research* 5 (February 1968): 13–19; J. D. McConnell, "The Price-Quality Relationship in an Experimental Setting,"

Journal of Marketing Research 5 (August 1968): 300–303; J. D. McConnell, "An Experimental Examination of the Price-Quality Relationship," *Journal of Business* 42 (October 1968): 331–334; and Martin L. Lansidsen, "The Relationship between Price and Perceived Quality: An Experimental Study," *Markeds Dommuniksjon* 2 (1973) Argang 10, 1–12.

12. Martin R. Scklissel, "Pricing in a Service Industry," *M.S.U. Business Topics* 25 (Spring 1977): 37–48.

13. Ibid.

14. Adler Lee and James D. Hlavacek, "The Relationship between Price and Repair Service for Consumer Durables," *Journal of Marketing* 90 (April 1976): 80–82.

15. "Boosting Productivity at American Express," *Business Week*, 5 (October 1981): 62.

Case Study: Barnes Auto Service

Ray Barnes has developed a plan to establish an aid service to stranded motorists by leasing vans in seven counties serving the Chicago area. Each van would be equipped with a stock of batteries. Consumers who have trouble starting their autos would be able to dial a toll-free 800 number and Barnes would then send a repair van to them within the hour. If the test showed the battery was faulty, the van driver would sell and install a replacement battery on the spot for between $40 and $70. If only a jump start is needed, the driver would charge a flat fee of $15.

Mr. Barnes has made arrangements to purchase the batteries from a leading supplier of private label batteries. Negotiations made with the battery manufacturer will allow Mr. Barnes to obtain a 50 percent markup based on retail price. He can usually buy a battery for about $25 and sell it for $50 and still offer a price that is comparable to those in shopping centers and auto service outlets.

The monthly cost to lease the 24 vans is about $7,000. This year Mr. Barnes plans to use a hefty promotion program which includes 260 prime-time radio spots, 105 thirty-second television ads and full-page ads in the two Chicago daily papers.

Discussion Questions

1. Develop a promotional plan and budget for Barnes Auto Service.
2. If Barnes could capture 5 percent of the replacement battery market would you recommend that he go ahead with his idea? Include data and your reasoning in your answer.
3. Who are the major competitors for Barnes?
4. What problems do you believe Barnes will encounter in this project? Should he go ahead with his idea? Why or why not?

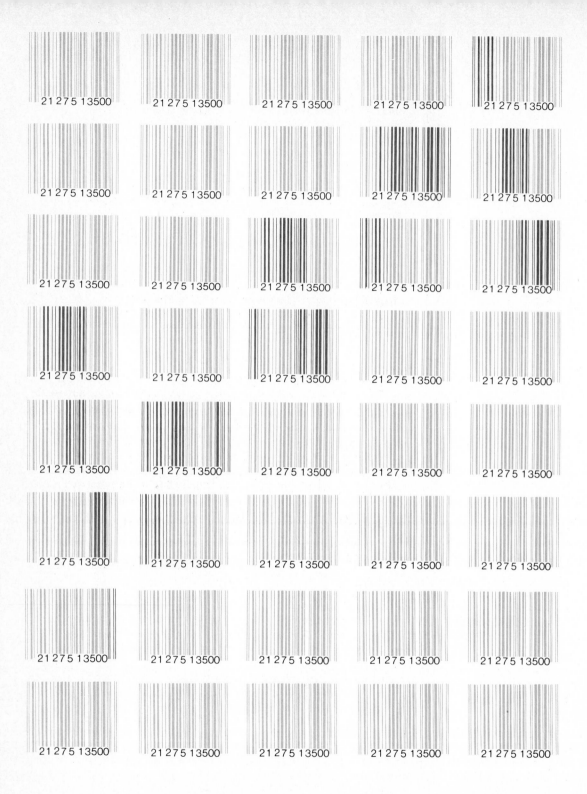

Comment from the CEO

Charles E. Griffin
President
Sanger-Harris

Department store retailing in the 1980s will continue to be pressured as in the 1950s, 1960s, and 1970s with alternate forms of consumer shopping. Proliferation of mass discounters, specialized discounters, manufacturers' outlets, catalog shopping, and unregulated cable television will create an unparalleled era of department store competition.

In my judgment, department stores have the competitive advantage, providing they market all the resources at their disposal.

Some of the major advantages accruing to department stores are the convenience of one-stop shopping (time being an increasingly important factor to working consumers); the excitement of shopping where special events, personalities, demonstrations, and even "how-to" classes are a continuum; the all important element of service to busy consumers (in the form of helpful salespeople, video film rental libraries, beauty salons, personal shoppers for the business person, credit services, and considerate return policies); and the location of modern contemporary stores in major regional malls.

These are just a few of an endless list of advantages that department stores have and can bring to the consumer of the 1980s.

Key points that follow are those areas of concentration that we feel will give our company, and other department stores that follow the same path, continued growth and a "reason for being" in the 1980s.

Merchandise—Our offerings must be aimed at multi-level consumers, and creating "merchandise difference" should be the consummate challenge. We must offer merchandise that makes the competition wither by comparison. The "merchandise difference" can be from branded resources, private labels, and imports. The challenges are to sell fashion, not utility; to be first with trends in our markets; and to always be cognizant of giving the consumer quality and good value. Protection of quality and value for our customer is endemic to survival of the department store franchise.

Service—Department stores have survived until now because they have been service-oriented. Erosion of this great strength in the 1970s must be reversed if we are to flourish in the 1980s. Selling service is our major challenge. We must staff our stores with informed, concerned, and interested salespeople. To do this, we must dignify the selling function by creating (1) compensation programs that reward sales achievement, (2) recognition programs for sales achievers, and (3) sales-oriented career paths that retain top salespeople and give them incentive to grow and produce. We must continue to look for new and different services to offer, as well as reexamining ongoing services. Exercise classes, backgammon classes, video film rentals, or redefinition of a credit program for student shoppers are all examples of services we offer in a department store. We must react to and anticipate consumer service needs in the 1980s if we are to flourish.

In fact, the 1980s are going to require the department store to market itself as a product. We must learn to compete in all media and vie for consumers' attention as if we were marketing a consumer packaged product. In our store, we intend to expand broadcast to more than sixty percent of our total publicity expenditure. In addition, we will expand our in-store display and special events to continue to accentuate differences between our store and our competition. The advent of cable TV can be a plus to a department store (perhaps a store owning its own cable outlet can function as a "catalog on the air").

In summary, department stores have a strong history of survival. If we are to grow in the 1980s, we must market our product, not just offer goods and services.

Chapter 20 | Using Management Information Systems and Marketing Research

Key Terms and Concepts

management information system
merchandise profitabilty analysis
vendor analysis
item analysis
price-line analysis
retail personnel reporting
retail market research

primary data
secondary data
observation
experimental research
survey
personal interview
telephone interview
mail questionnaire

No retail firm can be effectively managed without some type of information system. Progressive retail organizations are beginning to guide their decision making with an integrated information system. Computers are allowing retail management to bring together data and information from many different sources and integrate each piece of information into a company-wide decision support system.

Such a **management information system** should be consistent, credible, and able to produce useful, timely information. The system must be consistent in the sense that its output should agree with known information, or deviations must be explainable. Consistency leads to credibility, which assures the decision makers that (1) the information provided them represents the best estimate of the true state of their organization, and (2) the techniques used to gather and analyze the information are reliable. Retail decision makers may not be interested in details of specific procedures, but they are interested in data sources and in understanding the procedure for obtaining and analyzing information.

J. C. Penney Company provides an example of a retailer employing an integrated management system.[1] The company is divided into 28 merchandise profit centers. Each merchandise center consists of a business entity that is believed to behave homogeneously. These groups of similar merchandise are managed in the same manner. Examples of some of the groupings are: women's sportswear, jewelry, housewares, major appliances, and automotive. J. C. Penney Company has a five-year planning system for each merchandise grouping which produces a complete financial income statement for the current year, the following year, and the fifth year. The system is based upon different economic, competitive, and marketplace reaction assumptions. The result is a simulation of the real world environment that allows company management to assess the impact that different company marketing and management strategies have upon sales and profits. The Penney's information system is also capable of producing fast turnaround reports on special requests made by management.

Designing a Retail Management Information System

The key to effective dissemination of information lies in the company reporting system. It should be tailored to the particular organization so that a multilevel reporting structure exists. This structure categorizes the reporting so that the amount of detail in each report is determined by the information requirements for each level of management. An organizational chart indicates the responsibilities of each person. Thus, guidelines are provided for deciding who needs what kind of information.

In a large retail organization the chief executive officer must receive:

1. A summary report on each division in the company.
2. Information on which to evaluate operating expenses and performance, which results in a need for information on profitability by department and by store.
3. An analysis of the company's sales and financial condition relative to the rest of the industry and to the company's plan.

Because he or she performs a different set of duties, the vice-president of merchandising needs to receive a report that can evaluate performance, measure division profitability, assess return on investment, and identify trends in expenses and sales. Thus, the vice-president receives this and previous years' figures for the company and industry on: (1) profitability per square foot by store and department, (2) return on investment by store and department, and (3) operating costs and buyer expenses.

The number of levels in the management structure varies from company to company, but the degree of report detail is usually larger in the lower levels of management. The buyer, for example, is usually responsible for performance at the stockkeeping unit level and for planning purchases, transfers, markdowns, and returns to vendors. To make effective decisions, the buyer requires very detailed data on performances by department, inventory level, merchandise category, style and/or class, and price range. A buyer also needs very current and specific data on markdowns, gross margin, and open-to-buy. Thus, although the buyer and chief executive officer both evaluate performance, they use different scales to do so and thus require different kinds of information.

Gathering the Needed Information

After the degree of detail necessary for various management reports is determined, the specific data and information must be obtained. Profitability is the ultimate concern at every management level, so a **merchandise profitability analysis** must be performed in a manner appropriate for each management level. A list of the information needed to analyze profitability of each department in the firm includes:

Name and classification of department, number of square feet, and percentage of total square feet.

Sales (in total dollars, per square foot, and percentage of total dollars).

Gross profit (in total dollars and in percentage of contribution).

Inventory (in total dollars at the beginning and end of the month and per square foot).

Annual stock turnover (in number of inventory turnovers this year compared to last year).

Profitability (in dollars and dollars per square foot).

Return on investment (in dollars and dollars per square foot).

The information generated from these reports can be used to make forecasts, establish marketing plans, and plan future budgets.

Vendor analysis is another important input into the management information system of any retail firm. Retail firm profitability depends heavily upon the purchases that its buyers make. Vendors can be evaluated by information on their:

Total dollar amount of purchases

Timing of delivery on purchases

Total markdowns in dollars

Percentage of purchases resulting in markdowns

Gross margin in dollars derived through merchandise purchases

Gross margin percentage derived from merchandise purchases

This information is analyzed to make decisions regarding the desirability of continuing to employ each vendor.

Item analysis consists of a series of reports that are designed to assist management in determining which items should be given more or less (1) shelf space, (2) advertising, or (3) placement in the departmental budget. To perform an item analysis, each item is evaluated on:

Rate of sale

Inventory level

Dollar gross margin

Percentage gross margin

Gross margin per square foot of shelf or floor space

Price-line analysis can be performed by grouping the information obtained for an item analysis. Performance of different price lines not only influences buyers planning, but it also provides an indication of trends in consumer shopping patterns. For example, increases in sales of higher price-line merchandise indicate that the store's customers are trading up to higher quality merchandise than they have in the past. In contrast, increased sales of lower price-lines indicate that customers are becoming bargain hunters. This type of information should be included in the basic company planning process.

A **retail personnel reporting subsystem** involves retail employees inputting into the firm's management information system. It comprises more than just employee productivity analysis. Retail employees are the firm's "eyes and ears to the marketplace." They meet the consumer and usually the suppliers face-to-face, so they are in a good position to pick up significant information that would never appear in the usual summary statistics of the company. When such information is correlated in the total management information system, it frequently reveals changes in consumer buying habits or changes in the economic or competitive environment. The critical element for the success of this system is to establish employee motivation to seek and communicate information to their superiors. Their role as intelligence gatherers for the firm should be emphasized and facilitated by designing forms that are easy to complete. Establishment of a simple but fast routing system for this information is essential. This routing system must be designed by someone who knows who in the retail organization can use various types of information. Although most of the information obtained from the retail personnel reporting subsystem will not be received by the chief executive officer, the importance of receiving good information cannot be overemphasized. Retail buyers are particularly likely to reap the benefits of this information. Information needed as inputs into a retail personnel reporting subsystem includes:

Salesforce costs stated both in dollars and as a percentage of sales

Management and sales support wages stated in both dollars and as a percentage of sales

Out-of-stock merchandise

Merchandise requested by consumers but not handled by store

Consumer comments on competitor's marketing activities

Consumer comments on price, service, merchandise or promotional offerings of the firm

Final input into a retail management information system is marketing research (Figure 20.1). The remainder of the chapter focuses upon the use of marketing research in the retail firm. Before discussing this important input to the firm's management information system it is important to remember the sequence of the retail organization reporting scheme. Recall that people at different levels in a retail organization have different functions and thus need different information. Useful reporting systems focus each person's attention on the "need-to-know" information for that person. A list of factors that should be considered when determining the information need of each person includes:

Types of decisions regularly made by the individual

Types of information needed to make these decisions

Types of information currently received

Figure 20.1 Retail Firm Management Information System

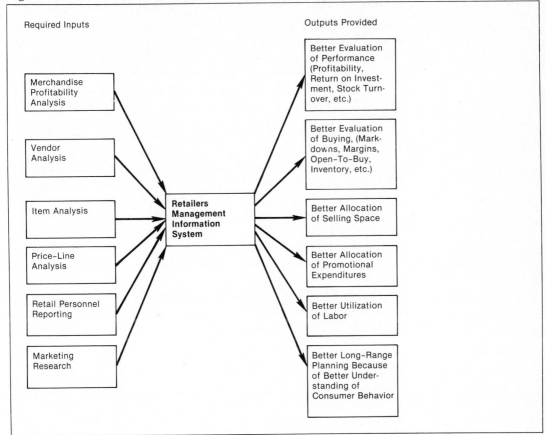

Types of information not now received

Schedule of information needed

List of specific topics' information needs

There is no reason to provide more detail than needed. Too much information not only increases cost but increases the likelihood that the report will not be used at all.

A final requirement of a good reporting system is *timeliness*. Besides being accurate, concise, and clear a good reporting system has to have speed. A good report delivered after a decision has been made has no value. In today's retailing environment speed is essential, as the early bird not only appears to get the worms but leaves none to satisfy the late arrivers.

Marketing Research in the Retail Firm

Retail market research is the process of systematically searching for, collecting, and analyzing information that can be used by the retailer in developing management strategies. The goal of retail research is to reduce the risks associated with the decision making process. Thus, it is similar to the concept of buying insurance. Retailers incur the cost of research because they want to minimize potential losses that can occur because they were not well informed when they made a major decision.

Although research is usually used to solve problems it can also be used to examine what is currently being done. New and better ways of operating can be developed as a result of such ongoing research involving establishment of guidelines that automatically warn the retailer of possible trouble areas.

Only in recent years have retailers begun to recognize the importance of marketing research.

A recent survey of 21 major retail organizations revealed that these firms engaged in marketing research by spending about 0.03 percent of their sales dollars on diverse marketing research activities.[2] The type of research being conducted by these retailers is presented in Table 20.1. Survey results revealed that a commitment to marketing research is significantly associated with a large retail organization's ability to generate sales and profits. Study findings showed that the more years that a large retail firm has been engaged in marketing research activities, the better are its values on the key operating ratios of net income to total assets, sales to square feet of store space, and sales to inventories. These findings appear to indicate that marketing research

Table 20.1 Research Conducted by 13 Major Retail Firms

Research Type	% of All Firms
Store location and trade area research	100
Consumer profile and attitude analysis	92
Promotion and advertising research	92
Personnel research	85
Business economics and corporate research	92
In-store traffic patterns	77
Product research	69

Source: Nancy J. Nighswonger and Claude R. Martin Jr., "A Study of Marketing Research Commitment by Major Retailers," Working Paper No. 207, Ann Arbor, Michigan, Graduate School of Business Administration, The University of Michigan, 1980, p. 5.

is an investment that should provide increasing benefits over time.

A recent article appearing in *Stores* magazine describes the wide variety of marketing research that Sears, Penneys, Federated, Bloomingdales and Robinsons use in their retail operations.[3] Increased marketing research by retailers is a result of these firms' adopting the marketing concept.

The marketing concept, which stresses the satisfaction of consumers at a profit, has increased the need for retailers to observe changing consumer demands. Marketing research can assist the retailer in observing consumers and making intelligent decisions. Retailers should have a basic understanding of research procedures so that they can contract for outside research studies, or conduct the studies themselves, and understand the results better. This chapter concentrates on marketing research in a retail environment.

Research can be beneficial to the retailer whenever a decision must be made. The question then becomes one of establishing priorities on the types of problems that are considered important enough to warrant marketing research. The level of expenditure on research should be related to the importance of the decision. Decisions involving significant costs or serious consequences for the retailer are likely to benefit considerably from the added information provided by research.

Decisions that do not involve much added cost or do not have serious implications for the retailer's present business may not require the use of much, if any, research. However, the expected payoff from new sales resulting from a change in the retailing mix must be considered as important as the added cost involved in making the change. This "opportunity cost" is frequently overlooked by retailers who view the importance of the decision only from the "What will it cost me?" approach. They do not consider the "What will it make for me if the idea works?" concept.

Small- and medium-sized independent outlets are especially prone to view research from the cost approach instead of looking at both the benefit and the cost approaches. As a result they give away a prime competitive advantage to the large chain retail organizations who employ well-qualified people to conduct their research activities.

The strategic areas of retailing such as location, merchandise policy, pricing policy, promotional allocations, and allocation or performance of sales personnel usually account for the most important decisions that a retailer makes. Consequently, they may account for most of the firm's research activity.

The retailer must start today to conceptualize the marketing plan philosophy as a way of running a business. The marketing plan concept should become a way of life for the retailer, enabling development of specific goals and objectives for guiding day-to-day operations. It matters little whether his is a multiple-store operation or a single-store outlet, the problems faced are basically the same: To attract more customers and to convince each customer to buy more of what the store has to sell.

In order to attract more customers and generate more sales, the retailer should begin his marketing planning activity by researching the following:

—What motivates present customers to buy at his store? What do they like or dislike about his store? How far do they drive to reach his store?

—Why do other consumers within his trading area not buy in his store? Are they aware of his store and the lines of merchandise he carries? What is his store's image in the minds of consumers?

—What are the strengths and weaknesses of his competition as identified by consumers in the market? How do consumers rate his store compared to his competition's, for quality of merchandise, selection, pricing, customer service, convenience, store operations, etc.?

—How well has he penetrated the market areas his store(s) serves? By what current definition? Pins in a map? Zip codes? Or, more specifically, census tracts?

Only after these questions have been answered through sound marketing research techniques can the retailer logically approach the marketing plan concept. The marketing plan which would then follow would include rational, attainable goals and the marketing strategies required to support the achievement of those goals.

Such marketing objectives can only be projected on the basis of a concise definition of current market positioning which properly identifies current problems and opportunities for the retailer. In today's challenging economic environment, the utilization of marketing research tools and sound marketing planning are critical. Now, more than ever![4]

Thus far we have seen that research is used to enable retail management to make informed decisions. This chapter will cover the steps in the research process itself.

Identifying the Central Problems and Opportunities

This phase consists of investigating the environment to determine just where the firm is going and how the competitive firms and consumer demands are changing. This type of research can reveal causes for changes that have occurred. Once these underlying causal factors are identified, they can reveal new opportunities for the firm. For example, some retailers noticed the trend toward increased suburban shopping patterns during the 1950s and 1960s and moved outlets to the suburbs. Other retailers were not aware of the shift to more suburban shopping and did not expand or relocate from their downtown sites. The result of their failure to recognize the change in the environment has been a significant loss in their share of the market, and in some cases they had to go out of business.

Determining Sources of Information

This step consists of a thorough search for all relevant information available from within the firm and from outside sources. If relatively little secondary information is available and little is known about the problem being investigated, then a special uniquely designed research project may be the only way to obtain data that can be used to solve the firm's problems.

Primary Data

Primary data are pieces of information that are collected by the firm or its representatives by actively observing, experimenting, or surveying people. These data are called primary because the retail firm must gather its own information or hire someone else to conduct a special study for that firm.

Secondary Data

Secondary data are the facts that currently exist within the firm or industry and existing facts collected from sources outside the firm or industry. Examples of secondary data are company data available from sales records, customer return forms, merchandise budgets, promotional plans, inventory control records, invoices, warranty records, credit card sales, customer checks, financial records, and so forth. Secondary data is available from many different outside sources, such as from industry trade associations. Trade associations can usually refer retailers to the major sources of information that have been collected for that type of business. Retail trade journals also provide current information on industry trends.

Figure 20.2 Where Chain Executives See Problems and Opportunities, and Possible Solutions

		% Conversion (From 5-point scale)
1	Intensify energy management solutions	83
2	Improve direct delivery systems and controls	75
3	Adopt better space management methods	75
4	Tighten standards on deal buying	75
5	Increase minimum movement required for existing items	65
6	Operate with lower total inventory[a]	65
7	Expand backhaul	63
8	Increase capital investment to reduce labor intensiveness	63
9	Stress private label	60
10	Stress/adopt generics	60
11	Delay new store construction	58
12	Accelerate installation of scanning systems	55
13	Increase ratio of part-time employees	55
14	Accept fewer new items	55
15	Reduce number of brands per category	45
16	Reduce number of items carried	40
17	Switch service departments to self-service to cut labor costs	40
18	Accelerate store closings	33
19	Add more non-food lines	33

1	Difficulty in maintaining the current net profit margin	79
2	Difficulty in generating sufficient capital internally to support growth	79
3	Operating problems due to high interest rates	78
4	Difficulty in obtaining capital from outside sources	76
5	Difficulty in achieving enough sales to offset inflation	74
6	Trading down by consumers	70
7	Increase in ratio of labor costs to sales	68
8	Generic or private label sales growth	57
9	Bankruptcies or Chapter XI proceedings	51
10	Difficulties in financing inventories	50
11	Store closings	49
12	Competition from drug stores, discounters and other retailers who are taking on food	41
13	Difficulty in settling with unions	35
14	Price wars	27
15	Consumer activist activities	27
16	Politically inspired attacks on the industry	27
17	Market share for "bare-bones" formats	23
18	Problems with suppliers	10

[a] Only those with warehouses.
Source: Reprinted with permission from *Progressive Grocer* (April 1981), p. 96.

An example of useful information published by trade publications is presented in Figure 20.2. These data were obtained from a *Progressive Grocer* survey of grocery store executives. The reader benefits from their thinking at a low monetary cost because *Progressive Grocer* spreads the survey and analysis cost over all of its readership through its regular subscription price.

Government sources are also important contributors of retail information. State sales tax records provide the most current and accurate estimate of sales for each retail category on a city or county basis. This can be used to calculate the individual firm's share of the market by simply dividing the individual firm's sales by the sales of all firms in the area. By observing the firm's share of the market on a quarterly basis, retail management can determine whether the firm is obtaining an increasing or decreasing share of the market. Such information allows management to evaluate the performance of the firm relative to competition. An increasing share indicates the firm is gaining on competition in the battle for consumer dollar expenditures. A decreasing share indicates that the firm is not keeping up with competition.

Other state offices, such as the State Examiner's Office, provide data on bank and savings and loan association deposits. Such data measures community attractiveness. A rapid increase in deposits indicates the community is prospering and healthy. The implication is that retailers who do a good job in satisfying consumer demands will share in this increasing prosperity. A slow growth in financial deposits indicates that consumers are not going to be able to increase their spending on retail items.

Local business firms are also good sources of retail information. A number of utility connections can provide an accurate and current estimate of town and country population. In some areas voter registration records can provide population estimates for small areas within a county, city, or town.

Determining the Method of Obtaining Primary Information	The three basic methods of gathering primary data should be studied to determine which is most appropriate for the particular problem being investigated.
Observation	**Personal observation** techniques involve watching consumer actions in an inconspicuous manner. Thus, retail personnel observe consumers' actions to draw conclusions from what they see. Small independent retailers especially employ this method to keep abreast of changes in consumer wants and to evaluate their merchandise offering and performance of their personnel.

Some retailers seek shopping services to evaluate their sales-people. The hired but unknown shopper comes into the store and pretends to be interested in some particular kind of merchandise. The hired shopper then asks questions about the goods and may even purchase them. The shopper, after leaving the store, evaluates the performance of the salesperson. Such an evaluation can be analyzed by the retailer to suggest improvements in the salesperson's presentation.

Other observation studies involve a traffic count. This technique consists of counting the numbers of passerby and noting certain characteristics of their behavior, for example whether they were on foot or in an auto, which direction they were going, whether they entered the store, or whether they noticed a specific window display.

An outside traffic count can be used to locate outlets that depend heavily upon foot or auto traffic. Sites with the heaviest pedestrian traffic are believed to be the best locations for stores selling convenience goods. Knowledge of the direction of the traffic flow outside the store can help determine the types of window displays and entrance facilities needed to provide maximum inducement for the passing person to enter the store.

Traffic counts and direction of traffic flow data inside the store can be used to maximize the exposure of departments that sell impulse goods and of all merchandise in general.

Experimentation

Experimental research is used when retailers want to study the cause and effect relationship between two or more elements in the retailing mix. For example, a retailer could change the number of shopping hours to see what effect it has upon sales and profits. Experimentation should be conducted under controlled conditions that hold the levels of all other factors constant and allow only the factor under investigation to be varied. This is a significant advantage of experimentation research over observation research, since observation does not involve controlled conditions. Thus, a retailer can observe consumer reactions to a change in store hours; but unless the other factors are held constant, the retailer will not be able to determine if the change in sales was due to the change in store hours or to changes in some other factors.

The chief disadvantages of experimental research are the difficulties encountered in attempting to hold the factors constant. It is difficult to prevent changes in activity for competitors, the government, the climate, economic conditions, and so forth from affecting the results of the experiment. Careful research designs can overcome these difficulties but they do require several months of time and the services of a well-qualified researcher.

Survey

Some information needed by retailers cannot be obtained by mere observation of consumer actions or by experimental techniques. The **survey** method is the other major technique used by retailers. The three kinds of surveys are by personal interview, telephone, and mail. The choice between these three methods is influenced by the type of information requested in the questionnaire, the type of respondents, and the cost of using each alternative.

Personal Interview Method The **personal interview** consists of the interviewer obtaining the information from respondents in face-to-face meetings. This type of interview allows the interviewer to obtain answers to a great number of questions. More detailed information can be obtained; why consumers believe or act as they said they do can be determined. Thus, it is used when open-ended projective techniques are needed to determine the consumer's attitudes.

Personal interviews generally result in a higher percentage of completed questionnaires than is the case for telephone interviewing or mail approach. This higher completion rate may cover a more representative group of respondents because many people will not respond to a mail survey and many people are not included in a sample from a telephone book.

On the other hand, more bias can creep into the interviewer's reporting of consumers' responses unless trained interviewers are used. Responses to personal questions may also be more biased if the personal interview is used, because the respondent may be more embarrassed.[5] The interviewer should be given a list of specific people or houses to contact; if not, a bias toward selecting the better-appearing houses can result. Also, interviewers can cheat by filling out a questionnaire without making an interview.

These disadvantages of the personal interview technique can be reduced considerably by thoroughly training interviewers to recheck 10 to 20 percent of the responses and by using other good research methods. But the major disadvantage— substantially greater expense per completed interview—cannot be reduced by any significant degree.

Telephone Interview Method **Telephone interviewing** is similar to personal interviewing except that communication occurs over the telephone instead of in person. The interviewer can still probe, check conflicting statements, and use unstructured questions, except, of course, those requiring responses to complex scaling techniques, drawings, or photographs. The major advantages of telephone interviewing are the short time required to obtain the data and a relatively low cost of data collection. The questionnaire, however, may have to be a little shorter in a telephone interview than in a personal interview, since it is easier for the respondent to hang up the phone than throw the interviewer out of the house. For personal questions, telephone interviewing may be better than personal interviewing because the respondent may talk more freely than in a face-to-face interview.

Telephone interviewing must be done when respondents will not be irritated by the call, but some evening recalling is required to reach no-answer numbers of families where husband and wife both work. The same procedure is required for the personal interview; so there is no relative disadvantage to telephone interviewing because of the not-at-home problem.

Interviewer bias and cheating can also arise in telephone interviewing. However, if all interviews are made from a central location, the interviewer's technique can be controlled and checked with minimum effort.

The major difficulty in telephone surveys is drawing a representative sample of the target population. Unlisted numbers, families with a new telephone that is not yet listed, and families that do not have a telephone are excluded from the selection list and therefore are not represented in the sample unless random digit dialing can be employed.

Mail Questionnaires

Mail Questionnaire Method **Mail questionnaires** are sent to the respondent through the mail, attached to products, placed in shopping bags, or placed in newspapers. Respondents generally return the questionnaire by mail.

Mail questionnaires must usually be relatively short or the consumers will not send them back. Fewer probing and in-depth questions can be asked in mail questionnaires than in the personal interview. In addition, respondents tend to give briefer answers to open-end questions in mail surveys than in personal or telephone interviews.

Mail questionnaires reach nearly everyone, so the not-at-home problem is reduced, and families where both husband and wife work are reached. In addition, the mail method can be economical in reaching a sample of people who are widely scattered over a geographic area. However, the cost per completed interview depends upon the return rate. Frequently only 10 to 20 percent of the people who receive questionnaires by mail return them.

Thus, a sample bias may occur as only the people who are interested in the topic respond; and undereducated consumers may hesitate to write responses to open-end questions or may not even return the questionnaire. Writing short, easy-to-answer questions on attractive questionnaire forms which are accompanied by a cover letter, an incentive premium, and a self-addressed, prestamped return envelope, will increase the return rate and reduce some of this sample bias.

The mail questionnaire approach has some disadvantages, however. First the response to a mail survey is subject to a sequence bias in the questions asked: respondents can change their answers to early questions after they read the later questions. In addition, it is never quite certain whose response one is getting in a mail survey. The respondent can get aid in completing the questionnaire or even have someone else fill it out.

Putting Information to Work (Analysis and Interpretation)	The information obtained from the research project must be organized, analyzed, and presented in a clear manner regardless of which techniques are used to gather data. Failure to summarize the findings properly and draw managerial conclusions from the project frequently leads to a waste of time and money. Remember, the purpose of research is to provide information that can better assist the retail manager in the decision-making process. Thus, data obtained from a research project must help management solve its problems. If not, it is worthless.
Getting More from Marketing Research	Although retailers are not expected to be experts in the field of research, it is wise to have a basic understanding of research procedures. This can prove to be very helpful when the retailer is contracting for research services or accepting the final results.

The costs of marketing research can be high. It is common for major studies to cost $10,000 or more. If a retailer were going to purchase $10,000 worth of merchandise from a vendor, he or she would automatically check the merchandise to see that it conformed with the purchase order. Unfortunately, such a basic step is too often overlooked by clients who purchase marketing research work.

There are several steps that a retailer can take to ensure the best purchase and application of research data.

1. Hire research employees who indicate a research orientation. In other words, hire professionals for your company's marketing research department—people who are truly interested in the field and have demonstrated their interest through their training, writing, and experience. In far too many cases the marketing research department is a short-run training ground for middle management. Personnel are moved there from a variety of areas regardless of training.

2. Know from whom you are buying research. The same

qualities that apply to a lawyer are equally valid for researchers: experience, education, general background, success with other clients, and the individual's specialty. It is well known that not all lawyers are qualified to do patent work, and the same thing is true with many areas of marketing research. It is essential to determine the individual's or the firm's areas of specialty; but all too often the answer from the researcher is, "We can do anything!" Seldom is this correct.

It is equally important to determine what other products or services the researcher is selling, such as advertising, public relations, or image work. It is questionable how objective such firms can be if the sale of other services rests upon the research results.

3. Who will do the actual research? Don't buy the old story, "We have qualified interviewers." In far too many cases these interviewers are part-time workers who may or may not have been given more than a five-minute set of instructions. All interviewers should be checked to be certain they are conducting the interviews completely and according to instructions.

4. Come to a firm price agreement. Research is not a blank-check operation and should not be treated as such.

5. Require a written proposal and record major design changes in writing. Don't even consider anything like this all-too-typical agreement: "Dear Bob, Thanks for lunch and the invitation to work with you in the study we discussed. We will proceed soon." In the first place, poor old Bob doesn't even know who should pay for the lunch, and in the second place he's buying trouble.

A good proposal should contain detailed statements on six major elements.

    a. *The problem* Often the researcher and the client do not agree on or understand the basic problem. Unless there is agreement here, there can be nothing but chaos.

    b. *Objectives* These should state, "To determine . . ."

    c. *Methodology* This statement does not have to be long and involved, but it should give the client a basic idea of the data collection method to be used, the sampling procedure, and the sample size.

    d. *Definition of terms* Terms such as "the Chicago market" should be clearly defined, since the client may be thinking of the Chicago phone district and the researcher may be thinking of the Loop.

    e. *Time schedule*

    f. *Cost*

6. Demand an interim report. This report doesn't have to be lengthy (it can be a letter), but it should give the client an idea of the progress to date and the expected time of completion, plus an indication of any unusual problems that have been discovered.

7.   Inspect the test market. Make sure the test market is set up well. The only way to do this is to visit the area in person. It is not unusual to find that test markets have been established for the wrong retail outlets or shelf space.

8.   Don't accept the word of experts as a substitute for objective research. This is especially true in international marketing research. Since income data and other statistics may be difficult to obtain in other countries, the researcher sometimes takes short cuts. Results from fifty government officials, ten bankers, and forty school teachers are not a substitute for a good sample of the potential users of a household product.

9.   Examine the sampling technique from a logical standpoint. Do not worry about the hieroglyphics of statistics. The major questions are:

   a. Is the size sufficient?
   b. Who will be included in this sample?
   c. Does the sample match the objectives?

10. Keep a diary of the outside environment. What important political, climatic, and social events took place during the time of the study that could easily affect the results?

11. Ask for a copy of the report before the presentation. Otherwise, the final presentation is simply a "dog and pony show." It is impossible for anyone to understand thoroughly the mass of results that will be thrown at one during a final, one-hour presentation. Come to that meeting prepared, by having read the report. The researcher will not like this and will do his or her best to avoid giving a prior copy of the report, but it is to your advantage to demand one.

12. Do not accept unfinished work. It is easy to give the client a huge bulk of data, but what do they mean? A retailer would not accept the work sheets of an accountant as the finished balance sheet, and the same is true for marketing research.

13. Make sure the report is readable; if it is not, reject it. The report must be written in a style that can be read by a layperson and that lends itself to decision making. If you cannot read it, chances are the president cannot either—and it will only gather dust and quickly grow useless.

14. Ask for clarification of details. The details of a research report are questioned as the details of a balance sheet are questioned.

15. Don't let statistics throw you. Keep asking the researcher, "What is the purpose of this test?" Ask until it is explained in a manner that an ordinary intelligent executive can understand. Basically, statistics serve these purposes:

      a. To determine sample size

      b. To test a hypothesis

      c. To forecast

16. If necessary, ask the consultant to come back to explain the data further. If this was not agreed to in the original contract, pay extra.

17. Have the report checked and analyzed by others. If in-house capability exists, use it! If not, pay a small consulting fee to an outsider to evaluate the report.

18. Realize that the best research by the most qualified individual in the world is not 100 percent perfect. Any report can be picked apart in some area (trial lawyers long ago learned this). The point is not to be ridiculous about the depth of criticism but, instead, to look for gross errors and misinterpretation of data.

19. Apply common sense. Do not completely disregard gut feeling or forget past experiences.

Marketing research is an excellent aid in retail decision making when it is done well and used with thought. However, decision making is far too complex ever to let a research report replace all other considerations. In the final analysis, there is no substitute for sound management decision making by seasoned and knowledgeable executives who know how to use research as a useful tool.

Using Electronic Scanner Systems in Research

Electronic scanner systems have made it possible for retailers to obtain research data within a time period that has never before been possible. For the first time, the retailer can quickly receive feedback on making a change in any element of the marketing mix and determine what strategies have or haven't worked. Actual sales data are available on an individual item basis on an extremely timely schedule. As the use of scanners linked to computers increases, retailers will utilize this extremely valuable information in many uniquely different wages.

Summary

The expansion of retail organizations beyond a single location has increased the need for conducting research before making huge investments in land, buildings, and fixtures. The resulting growth in location and trade area research has provided the operational base from which other research activities have expanded.

Today, retail researchers are developing programs based on the firm's objectives. These programs assist the retailer in making improvements in the functions that propel the firm beyond its current levels of performance.

Research can be beneficial to the retailer whenever an important decision must be made. Priorities must be established and the level of research expenditures related to the financial consequences of the decision.

Retailers should be aware of the basic research procedures discussed in this chapter so they can spend their research dollar more wisely. The following steps of the research process illustrate the sequence of a retailer's research efforts:

1. Identify the central problem and opportunities.
2. Determine the sources of information that are available from within the firm and from outside sources.
3. Determine which methods (observation, survey, or experimentation) will be used to obtain primary information.
4. Collect data by using an appropriate questionnaire or some other suitable recording device.
5. Analyze and interpret the data carefully so the project findings can be put to use in the firm.

The use of electronic scanning systems by retailers has provided research data that have many implications for marketing and merchandising. Shrinkage can be reduced, front-end productivity increased, pricing decisions evaluated, private label merchandise evaluated, in-store displays analyzed, advertising effectiveness determined, shelf allocations evaluated, labor scheduling improved, and inventory can be controlled in a much more efficient manner when the electronic system is used as a research tool.

Questions

1. Who needs to use marketing research more, the small independent retailer or the large chain retailer? Who does use marketing research more, the small retailer or the chain retailer? Discuss.
2. Develop a list of secondary sources that you would search if you were going to open a new women's apparel shop.
3. What are the advantages and disadvantages of retailers using secondary data to assist them in making managerial decisions?
4. What are the advantages and disadvantages of retailers using primary data to assist them in making managerial decisions?
5. Under what conditions should a retailer use the observation method of collecting primary data? What are the advantages of using this method? What are the disadvantages?
6. Under what conditions should a retailer use the experimental method of collecting primary data? What are the advantages and disadvantages of using this technique?
7. When should a retailer use the survey method of collecting primary data? What are the advantages and disadvantages of using this method?
8. Develop a complete research project that is designed to determine what people think of a local supermarket and determine why they do or do not shop at this market. Include (a) a listing of the secondary sources you would check before conducting any surveys, (b) a description of the

method you would use to collect primary data, (c) a description of who will collect the data, (d) a sampling plan, (e) a copy of any forms that will be used to collect the primary data, (f) a summary of how the data would be analyzed, (g) a description of how the data could be used by the supermarket to increase its sales and profits, and (g) an estimate of what it would cost to conduct the project.

9. Design a management information system for: (a) a large corporate retail chain such as Montgomery Ward, (b) a regional supermarket chain, and (c) a specialty women's wear outlet. Describe how these systems would differ for the three types of retailers.

Footnotes

1. Allen S. King, "Computer Decision Support Systems Must Be Credible, Consistent, and Provide Timely Data," *Marketing News,* Dec. 12, 1980, p. 11.
2. Nancy J. Nighswonger and Claude R. Martin Jr., "A Study of Marketing Research Commitment by Major Retailers," Working Paper No. 207, Ann Arbor, Michigan Graduate School of Business Administration, The University of Michigan, 1980, pp. 2–14.
3. Isadore Barmash, "Research," *Stores* (April 1981):19–24.
4. Walter G. Walker, "Marketing Research Is Important in Retailing, Now, More than Ever," *Marketing News,* 14 March 1975, p. 9
5. William F. O'Dell, "Personal Interviews or Mail Panels," *Journal of Marketing* 26 (October 1962):34–39.

Chapter 21 | Retail Audit

The retail audit involves more than a financial audit; the retail audit consists of a review of the major ingredients in the effective retail management process, while a financial audit discloses the retail performance of the firm in dollars. The **financial audit** is a formal examination of the results of past practices, but it does not reveal current management practices that may lead to financial difficulties. The **inventory audit** is another audit that is frequently used to verify that the firm possesses stock valued at a stated level of dollars. This audit is needed not only to prevent and detect employee theft but also to determine the extent of damage or out-of-date merchandise and record-keeping errors.

Nature of Retailing Audits

There is no universally established definition of the term *retail audit*. As used in this book, a **retail audit** consists of a broad analysis that includes a systematic evaluation of all retail procedures and practices. The primary purpose of the retail audit is to develop an independent judgment of the quality of the firm's effort to improve the future performance of its retail outlet(s). Retail management is always seeking improvements. Frequently retail managers are so involved in their day-to-day activities that they cannot determine if the activities are being performed in an optimum manner. The retail audit, with its fresh, overall independent evaluation of the effort, can stimulate a retailer to make needed changes before inefficient procedures are reflected in a poor financial performance.

There are two basic types of retail audit: systems-level and activity-level audits. A **systems-level audit** consists of an examination of all the elements that the retailer uses to market goods and/or services.[1] Particular emphasis is placed upon the relative importance of each of these elements. It is designed to develop a total evaluation of the retailer's marketing effort. Appraisal deals not so much with particular marketing activities as with their relationships with one another. Systems-level audits, however, do attempt to identify specific activities that appear to require closer investigation.[2]

The **activity-level audit** examines and evaluates in depth certain functional elements of the retail operation. It is a closer more detailed investigation into one or more of the specific retailing activities.

Establishment of a good management information system as outlined in Chapter 20 will make it much easier for a firm to conduct either a systems-level or an activity-level retail audit. Much of the information needed to conduct the in-depth study required in a retail audit is already available through an established management information system.

Systems-Level (Horizontal) Retail Auditing

A comprehensive systems-level audit involves a periodic evaluation of both the basic framework used to generate retail activities and the performance of retail actions. The systems-level audit is comprehensive because it is an appraisal of all of the elements in the retail effort, not merely an evaluation of the most problem-ridden activities. Confining retail audits to occasions of company difficulties is likely to result in missed sales and/or lost cost-reduction opportunities. Successful retail organizations can benefit from retail auditing procedures by maintaining an objective view of changes occurring in both the outside marketing environment and the internal company operations.

Retail audits should be scheduled annually so that the retail audit is a regular part of the periodic review of the long-range company plan. The retail audit comprises the first two steps in the business planning process, and the latter begins with the retailer's diagnosis of the market situation and the factors believed to be responsible for it.

Diagnosis

The **diagnosis** phase attempts to determine where the retail firm is situated now and why it is situated there. Careful analysis of recent trends in company sales and market shares by territory, merchandise line, and other breakdowns can be used to identify the firm's current retail position. Image studies might be conducted to determine what consumers think of the retailer as a source of goods and services.

A more complete listing of questions to be answered during the diagnosis phase of the retail audit is presented in Table 21.1.

Prognosis

A second step in the planning process, **prognosis** involves an estimate of where the retailer is likely to go if the present policies are continued in a marketplace that follows recent shopping trends. This step consists of determining where the retailer is headed; a prediction is made about the future. Naturally, all pre-

Table 21.1   Questions to Be Answered during Diagnosis Phase of the Retail Audit

---

A. Markets

1.   Who are the firm's major markets?
2.   What are the major market segments in each market?
3.   What are the present and expected future size and the characteristics of each market segment?

B. Customers

4.   How do the customers feel toward and perceive the firm?
5.   How do customers make their purchase or adoption decisions?
6.   What is the present and expected future state of customer needs and satisfaction?

C. Competitors

7.   Who are the firm's major competitors?
8.   What trends can be foreseen in competition?

D. Macroenvironment

9.   What are the main relevant developments with respect to demography, economy, technology, government, and culture that will affect the firm's situation?

Source: Philip Kotler, *Marketing for Nonprofit Organizations,* © 1975, p. 57. Adapted by permission of Prentice-Hall, Inc., Englewood Cliffs, N.J.

dictions will not be correct, but management that is aware of and incorporates recent trends in its forecasting is generally more accurate than management that does not believe in forecasting and hence assumes that nothing is going to change.

Systematic retail sales and profit prognosis consists of forecasting (1) industry sales, (2) company sales, (3) company revenues, costs, and profits, (4) investment required, and (5) rate of profit return on investment.[3]

Retail industry sales are usually forecast by calculating statistical demand analysis, which correlates sales of the particular category to related factors such as employment, consumer income, and so forth.[4] Recent trends of the retailer's market share of retail sales for the owner's merchandise category can be studied to determine expected company sales.

The predictions made for the third item—company revenues, costs, and profits—involve the same process discussed in Chapter 18 as cash flow analysis. Cost are forecast by using past cost-to-sales relationships, and expected profit is simply the result of subtracting costs from sales.

The volume of needed investment (item 4) is based on the level of expenditure believed to be needed to sustain the present retail activities.

The last item (calculating the return on investment) reveals how profitable the retail operation is likely to be if things continue as they appear to be heading.

Objectives

The retail audit then turns to an evaluation of the firm's marketing and profit objectives. The **objectives** step consists of a determination of where the company should be headed in the future. A clear statement of the retailer's profit objectives is needed. For example, such a statement may establish a goal of obtaining an annual return on investment of X percent. However, explicit marketing objectives must also be established to satisfy consumers' needs at a profit. If this is not done, retail outlets and organizations can become obsolete quite rapidly as shopping patterns and preferences change.

Continuous changes in the retailer's marketing environment necessitate a clear statement of the definition of the firm's business. Objectives must define which consumer needs are to be satisfied by the firm's retailing efforts. Objectives should identify those market segments that appear to offer the most long-range profit potential and those segments in which the retailer believes he or she has the competitive advantage. Marketing and competitive environment changes at an increasingly faster rate, so it is now easier to identify and enter a market niche by tuning in to these changes faster than competitors.

For example, a department store has used these concepts to clarify its marketing objectives. It recognized that the taste-making forces of American society have changed. The twenty-year-olds of the 1970s were the first generation reflecting the impact of growing up under the influence of a constant bombard-ment of television commercials and programs that emphasize that you should "live life with real gusto because you only have one chance." Thus, television's influence on the behavior of the young is probably more important than the traditional generators of values, namely, schools, churches, and parents. These factors, combined with the emphasis that all age groups placed on youth or on "looking young," were deemed to have an important im-pact upon the local clothing business.

The underlying desire in the United States is for consumers to buy goods and services that will make them appear to be at least ten years younger than they really are. The fashion-making forces have changed; no longer are fashions first adopted by upper-class Europeans and Americans, then "trickling down" to adoption by the U.S. middle-class consumers to adoption by the U.S. lower class. Instead, the young "street people" have begun to generate fashion. Everybody else has followed this lead be-cause of the basic desire to appear to be younger.

These rapid changes in the environment allowed the depart-ment store to enter a market niche that was not being captured by competitors who were still selling essentially the conservative style of clothing that did not reflect the fashion consciousness of a growing segment of the market. The market was segmented not only on the basis of demographic characteristics such as age, sex, social class, and so forth, but also on the basis of psychographics of lifestyle. The market segment that was fashion conscious was found to be growing and its preferences changing toward youth-generated styles. The department store adjusted its mer-chandise line to meet the needs of this market segment. It also promoted a whole new progressive retail image by generating a "making happiness happen" theme.

The image was carried over into nonclothing merchandise lines such as towels, bedding, and linens. In this case, the target customers were fashion-conscious people who were buying tow-els and bedding not merely for their functional uses but for their decorative purposes. Thus, the consumer was willing to pay much higher prices for goods that would match a color-decoration scheme. Additionally, the consumer was more likely to make more frequent repurchases of the item after growing tired of a particular decorative theme. Most of these goods would not wear out physically but they would be discarded early when they were no longer in style. Of course, more frequent consumer

Table 21.2   Retail Policy Rating Form

Outstanding Condition	Average Condition	Deficient Condition
1. Company policies and objectives clearly defined and understood by all.	1. Company general policies not clearly defined or understood.	1. No general policy except to carry on company tradition.
2. All current and potential economic factors recognized in overall company planning.	2. Sporadic consideration of potential economic factors in company planning.	2. Planning done under impulse.
3. Aggressive participation in trade and business associations.	3. Interest in trade and business associations limited.	3. Trade and business associations regarded as a necessary evil.
4. Company kept currently informed on federal, state, and local regulations.	4. Government relationships determined by legal counsel but not passed along to company executives.	4. No policy on governmental matters. Local governmental office called when in doubt or in trouble.

Source: This form is a revised version of forms presented in Howard Ellsworth Sommer, *How to Analyze Your Own Business*, Management Aids No. 46, (Washington, D.C.: Small Business Administration, 1971).

repurchases tend to generate additional sales and to build store loyalty if the consumer is satisfied with his or her purchase. The slowness of competitors to recognize these changes allowed the department store to establish itself as the leader in catering to this most profitable market segment.

Establishing retail objectives involves more than selection of generic marketing objectives (such as satisfying the clothing needs of a growing segment of fashion-conscious, local consumers, as illustrated in the above example). Retail objectives also involve the establishment of specific sales and profit target objectives. These targets should be set on a realistic basis that reflects an unbiased evaluation of the retail firm's capabilities.

Table 21.2 contains a form that auditors can use to analyze the present condition of stated company policy for any retail firm. The form contains a description of three classifications on each item—outstanding, average, deficient. The auditor can objectively select the category that most accurately describes the situation in that specific retail firm. The auditor will be able to identify the areas requiring the most attention by reviewing all the category ratings for each area.

Program

The efforts of retail auditors can then be focused upon the retailer's **program** that achieves the objectives that have been established. The retailer's program consists of the decisions and policies on the level, allocation, and mix of the total marketing effort.

Initially the auditor wants to examine the level of resources the retailer is using in the marketing effort, because this level must be adequate to meet the firm's stated objectives. This involves an objective look at the total sales-generating budget to determine if the budget is large enough to allow the firm to accomplish its objectives. The evaluation might consist of an analysis of the relationship of sales volume to the level of the market budget. This analysis can reveal if past additions to the marketing budget resulted in increased sales and profits.

The auditor can also appraise the desirability of changing the balance among the retailer's marketing activities. A retail firm's marketing allocations can become unduly influenced by particularly strong functional area executives. An independent, objective appraisal of the retailer's marketing allocations may reveal an excessive use of advertising, personal selling, merchandise styling, price reductions, and the like. The more effective retail sales-generating programs offer a balance among all the available alternatives. It is not easy to identify when to shift money from one functional area to another, but analysis of past retail sales and expenditure data can guide this appraisal. Industry data can also be used to identify the functional areas that might be emphasized by the retailer. Larger emphasis upon a particular area, such as advertising, does not, however, indicate that the firm uses too much advertising relative to its other marketing efforts. The sales response may increase faster than the increased advertising expenditure for this particular retailer because the outlet is situated in a below average location.

Finally, retail auditors also examine how the marketing expenditure is allocated to various target market segments. The appraisal would evaluate the retailer's efforts vis-à-vis geographical areas, merchandise lines, and consumer segments. The task is essentially that of determining whether the current allocation generates maximum sales and profits for the given budget level. This is not an easy task, but an analysis of customer trading areas, consumer image, and purchase patterns can provide the basis for recommending an increase or reduction in marketing effort toward each target market segment.

Table 21.3 contains three categories that describe a retail firm's efforts to evaluate its sales and merchandising activities.

Implementation (Tactics)

Retail management may have designed an excellent program, but the firm's performance will depend upon **implementation,** or the proper execution of that program. Thus, the retail auditor focuses on both the *tactical means* and the *procedures* used to accomplish the objectives. An examination of the alternatives available

Table 21.3 Retail Sales and Promotion Activities Evaluation Form

Outstanding Condition	Average Condition	Deficient Condition
1. Sound sales program based on known customer needs. Market research and analysis supported by good advertising and sales program.	1. Sales program based on past customer experience. Market potential not known. Advertising not selective.	1. Sales coverage incomplete. Knowledge of competition limited.
2. Sales budgets classified by products, customers, sales people, merchandise departments, geographic districts.	2. Sales total estimated but not budgeted by products to customers and geographic districts.	2. No sales budgets.
3. Sound pricing based on consumer demand and merchandise handling considerations.	3. Price structure rigid. Accurate product costs not used in setting sales prices.	3. Costs information not generally used in setting prices.
4. Profit or loss determined by sales people, customers' products, and geographic districts.	4. No attempt to analyze gross and net profit by sales people, products, customers.	4. No sales analyses.
5. Selective selling effort directed toward maximum profit possibilities.	5. Selling effort not directed toward best profit possibilities.	5. No selective selling program.
6. Trained sales people intelligently directed and compensated.	6. Sales people closely supervised but training program inadequate.	6. Sales people not well trained or supervised. Compensation not comparable to competitors'.
7. All sales records maintained currently.	7. Sales records not always maintained on a current basis.	7. No sales records beyond orders booked and sales billed.

Source: Form is revised version of forms in Howard Ellsworth Sommer, *How to Analyze Your Own Business.* Management Aids No. 46 (Washington, D.C.: Small Business Administration, 1971).

for each *tactical decision* can reveal if the reasoning behind each decision was logical. The auditor has an advantage in examining these decisions after they have been made, since it is then possible to observe the consequences of each decision. (Hindsight is much better than foresight.) If such a historical examination is not periodically made by an auditor, it is not likely to be made at all. Regular retail management can (and usually does) become so occupied with the day-to-day operating procedures that it does not have time for periodic analyses of this type.

Tactical retail decisions are needed in many areas, including the following:

Selecting criteria used in hiring personnel.

Selecting sales personnel compensation procedures.

Selecting among different choices of vendors.

Selecting among different modes of transportation to the warehouse and store.

Selecting among different merchandise assortments.

Selecting among different advertising media.

Selecting among different promotional themes.

Selecting among different amounts and kinds of price discounts.

Selecting among different consumer credit plans.

Selecting among different consumer services.[5]

Retail auditors also want to examine the more important *procedures* used by the retailer to determine if improvements can be made. Procedures describe the way actions occur in the retail organization. Every retailer has numerous procedures regulating the flow of supplies, equipment, inventory, information, and personnel. Procedures, then, essentially identify who does what, when the action is performed, and how the action is performed. Special efforts must be made to determine if the most practical and most productive procedures are being used. The auditor must evaluate each procedure to determine if new technological advances (such as new computer capabilities or new management techniques) could increase retail efficiency.

Procedures that influence the retail performance include:

Developing current sales and cost information.

Sales forecasting techniques.

Determining current status of retail inventory.

Routing of consumer product requests through the retail organization.

Handling and expediting of customer orders.

Handling and acting on new product and sales ideas.

Training new salespeople.

Preparation of marketing and promotional programs.

Gathering information on competitors.

Consumer checkout procedures.

Consumer charging and billing procedures.

Gathering information on attractiveness of current and proposed store locations.

Developing control procedures to establish retail standards.[6]

Tables 21.4 and 21.5 contain three category descriptions of both tactical means and procedures that a retailer can adopt to assess personnel relations and merchandise assortment.

Organization

The **organization audit** consists of an evaluation of the adequacy of retail management personnel both as a group and on an individual basis. An assessment of the way the retail organization functions is also needed to identify possible weaknesses in such areas as the lines of authority and responsibility and the communication channels that relay consumer desires to the appropriate retail decision maker.

A major factor contributing to business failure is a lack of experience on the part of key retail personnel. A successful retail firm must use the talent of people who have a knowledge of (1) buying, (2) products in demand by consumers, (3) how to attract customers, and (4) handling finances.

The amount of experience required is dependent upon the size and type of the retail operation. A complex retail organization, formal management practices, and established formal communications channels are required as different merchandise lines are offered and more outlets are opened. Single-unit operators especially should note the increased managerial effort required to open the second outlet. The business frequently runs smoothly until the new outlet is established; then the operator discovers that he can't communicate with the store employees unless he is continually present in the store.

The retail auditor cannot neglect any areas of the systems-level retail audit because all aspects affect retail performance. However, major emphasis must be placed upon the evaluation of retail objectives and programs. Establishment of effective retail objectives and programs provides the foundation for retail success. Poor store locations, merchandise lines, and store images cannot be overcome by making sudden changes in tactical or procedural areas. In other words, a retailer's strategy as reflected by objectives and programs is a long-run concept that cannot be changed in a short period of time. It takes time to locate and establish outlets on good retail sites or to establish the desired retail image in the minds of potential customers. Thus, undetected errors made

Table 21.4   Retail Personnel Policy Evaluation Form

Outstanding Condition	Average Condition	Deficient Condition
1. An executive vested with adequate authority formulates sound industrial relations policies and represents the company in labor negotiations.	1. Value of industrial relations realized, but authority and responsibility not clearly defined.	1. Industrial relations function is one of employment only, also coupled with other unrelated functions.
2. An industrial relations program minimizes labor turnover, builds employee morale and efficiency.	2. Industrial relations program not planned ahead, but ably administered; employee morale and efficiency average.	2. Little consideration given to industrial relations—employee turnover high.
3. Program for effective selecting, testing, placing, and training of all personnel.	3. Employee selection not developed beyond separate formulas used by office manager for clerical help and by employment manager for all other help.	3. No uniform procedure for applicant screening, placement, and training. Original interviewing left to each department head.
4. Salary and wage rates equitable and fair for each job classification from common labor to top management established by sound job evaluation methods.	4. No job evaluation program. Wage rates increased under pressure. Top management and supervisory positions awarded largely on the basis of seniority.	4. Job rates fixed by personal opinion.
5. Incentive plans for all levels of employees based on an equitable measurement of performance.	5. Incentive plans for some employees only.	5. No incentive plan.
6. Individual history and progress records for each employee kept up to date as an inventory of qualifications.	6. Some records, but they are incomplete.	6. No records kept on individual employees beyond payroll requirements.

Source: Form is revised version of forms in Howard Ellsworth Sommer, *How to Analyze Your Own Business.* Management Aids No. 46 (Washington, D.C.: Small Business Administration, 1971).

in establishing retailing strategy will have a severe effect on future performance for many years.

Consequences of poor tactical decisions and/or procedures will also adversely affect retail performance. However, they can usually be changed within a year after the mistake is recognized. The tendency for most people in retail management to spend most of their time dealing with problems of a tactical or procedural nature usually leads to identifying these problems more quickly than more strategical problems.

Control

Retail objectives, programs, tactics, procedures, and organizations are all based upon assumptions and expectations made by retail management. Rapid changes in the competitive environment and in customer preferences frequently go against management's assumptions and expectations. Thus, a control section must be incorporated into the retailer's audit. Retail **control** consists of monitoring the effectiveness of the retail plan and preparing several contingency plans that will shorten the retailer's reaction time to these kinds of changes.

The control section should establish performance standards that will be checked periodically to determine if the retailer's plan is leading to the achievement of its stated objectives. Tables 21.6 and 21.7 contain descriptions of control areas that are frequently used by retailers. First, good accounting procedures must be established to provide necessary data. Then standard costs and budgets can be established to indicate areas where the objectives are not being met. Finally, the financial condition of the firm must be analyzed periodically to detect any shortage of funds.

A listing of the major marketing questions that must be answered in the objectives, programs, implementation, and organization phases of the systems-level retail audit is presented in Table 21.8.

Table 21.5 Retail Merchandise Assortment Evaluation Form

Outstanding Condition	Average Condition	Deficient Condition
1. Continuous search for improved products and for the development of new products and markets.	1. Search effort spasmodic; objectives not definite.	1. No search for new products or markets.
2. Merchandise and service offerings thoroughly planned and highly organized under expert supervision with qualified personnel.	2. Merchandise search activities not well organized.	2. No personnel qualified to conduct merchandise search activities.
3. Close cooperation with merchandising and sales personnel to insure market acceptance.	3. The company has a program for merchandise search, but these activities are not carried out in cooperation with other retail divisions.	3. Need for merchandise search ignored. No desire to add new products to assortment.

Source: Form is revised version of forms in Howard Ellsworth Sommer, *How to Analyze Your Own Business.* Management Aids No. 46 (Washington, D.C.: Small Business Administration, 1971).

Table 21.6   Retail Accounting Procedures Evaluation Form

Outstanding Condition	Average Condition	Deficient Condition
1. Procedures, record forms, reports designed to produce required information at lowest cost.	1. Accounting fairly comprehensive, accurate, prompt and well managed— some written procedures.	1. Accounting accurate from bookkeeping standpoint, but generally "old-fashioned" and incomplete.
2. Accounting data supplied promptly in a form best adapted to its use by management.	2. Accounting data not adequate in comparison with most modern control standards.	2. Accounting not highly regarded as a tool of management.
3. Modern accounting equipment used effectively in preparation of necessary information and reports.	3. Accounting machines used but not adaptable to modern methods.	3. Accounting equipment antiquated, cumbersome, and wasteful.
4. Cost system designed to reflect all variances between standard and actual costs.	4. Cost accounting fairly accurate, but not organized to provide standard cost information.	4. No standard costs. Job costs inaccurate and uncontrolled.
5. Variances from standard performances supplied currently to management for corrective action.	5. Records and reports not best suited to control costs and expenses.	5. Cost information mostly estimated. Monthly profit and loss statements inaccurate.
6. Unnecessary accounting records eliminated— management control reports furnished as needed.	6. Many records, reports, and statistics maintained that are not useful as a tool of management.	6. Some records and reports prepared; have no practical advantage.
7. All control records and costs integrated with standard costs.	7. Records unrelated to control; therefore, of little assistance.	7. Production records required for suitable cost control not maintained.
8. All estimates for product pricing based on standard costs; loss of volume or profit is indicated.	8. Estimates not checked against actual cost.	8. Estimates determined by past performance and competition.
9. The effect that sales mixture and product selling prices have on the total company profits is known at all times.	9. No knowledge of the effect on total business profits of individual product or order pricing.	9. Profit or loss estimated monthly; verified and adjusted annually to inventory; no profit or loss known by product breakdown.

Source: Form is revised version of forms in Howard Ellsworth Sommer, *How to Analyze Your Own Business.*
Management Aids No. 46 (Washington, D.C.: Small Business Administration, 1971).

Table 21.7   Retail Financial and Budgetary Control Procedures Evaluation Form

Outstanding Condition	Average Condition	Deficient Condition
Budgetary Control		
1. Budgetary control of all expenditures based on flexible performance standards equitably established by operating levels.	1. Budget structure rigid; ratios of expense to sales based on past performance, not on predetermined, flexible performance standards.	1. No attempt made to budget or forecast performance.
2. Sales budget by merchandise line, salesmen, customers and territories—based on market analyses.	2. Sales budget by merchandise line, salesmen, customers and territories—based on past sales performance only.	2. No sales budget. No quotas for salesmen. No program.
3. Knowledge and control of the effect of all selling price changes on budgeted amount of total net profits.	3. No centralized control of selling prices within limits of predetermined profit requirements.	3. No established pricing policy. Cost estimates ignored where considerable volume is involved. Effect of cutting prices to meet competition not projected in terms of lost profits.
4. Daily, weekly, or monthly reports on the performance of all departments controlled through: (a) standard or budgeted performance; and (b) variance form standard performance.	4. Divisional accounting reports periodically exhibited: (a) comparison of current with past periods; (b) no standards; therefore no comparison of actual results with what should have been accomplished.	4. No budgets; no broad long-term planning. Policies vacillating because not founded on complete comparative information and thorough analysis.
Finance		
1. Forecast of working capital and cash requirements for planned business volume and profit level.	1. No forecast of working capital or cash requirements. Funds not always obtained or employed.	1. Working capital and cash inadequate; credit policy lax. No forward planning.
2. Adequate reserves for replacement of obsolescent and depreciating assets—represented by earmarked liquid funds to the extent required.	2. Depreciation reserves conditioned on allowable deductions for tax purposes only; not properly planned from a capital asset replacement point of view.	2. Nominal reserves without due regard to actual value of assets; frequently used for purposes other than originally intended.
3. Dividend policy consistent with sound, long-term financial program.	3. No definite financial or dividend policy.	3. Financing dictated by immediate need for cash to meet pressing obligations.

Source: Form is revised version of forms in Howard Ellsworth Sommer, *How to Analyze Your Own Business.* Management Aids No. 46 (Washington, D.C.: Small Business Administration, 1971).

Table 21.8   Major Marketing Questions to Be Answered during the Objectives, Program, Implementation, and Organization Phases of the Systems-Level Retail Audit

A. Objectives

1. What are the firm's long-run and short-run overall objectives and marketing objectives?
2. Are the objectives stated in a clear rank order and in a form that permits planning and measurement of achievement?
3. Are the marketing objectives reasonable for the firm, given its competitive position, resources, and opportunities?

B. Program

1. What is the firm's core strategy for achieving its objectives, and is it likely to succeed?
2. Is the firm allocating enough resources (or too many) to accomplish the marketing tasks?
3. Are the marketing resources allocated optimally to the various markets, territories, stores, departments, and products of the firm?
4. Are the marketing resources allocated optimally to the major elements of the marketing mix; that is product quality, personal contact, promotion, and distribution?

C. Implementation

1. Does the firm develop an annual marketing plan? Is the planning procedure effective?
2. Does the firm implement control procedures (monthly, quarterly, and so forth) to insure that its annual plan objectives are being achieved?
3. Does the firm carry out periodic studies to determine the contribution and effectiveness of various marketing activities?
4. Does the firm have an adequate marketing information system to service the needs of managers for planning and controlling operations in various markets?

D. Organization

1. Does the firm have a high-level marketing officer to analyze, plan, and implement the marketing work of the firm?
2. Are the other persons directly involved in marketing activity able people? Is there a need for more training, incentives, supervision, or evaluation?
3. Are the marketing responsibilities optimally structured to serve the needs of different marketing activities, products, markets, and territories?
4. Do the firm's personnel understand and practice the marketing concept?

Source: Questions are adapted from Philip Kotler, *Marketing for Nonprofit Organization* (Englewood Cliffs, New Jersey: Prentice-Hall Inc., 1975), p. 69. Reprinted by permission of Prentice-Hall, Inc. Englewood Cliffs, New Jersey.

Activity-Level (Vertical) Retail Auditing

The framework to conduct the system-level audit is also useful for auditing any specific activity. The coverage under an activity audit then consists of:

1. Determining and appraising retail management's *objectives* for that specific activity. The appraisal determines if the activity objectives are appropriate in terms of the firm's market targets, opportunities, and resources.

2. Determining if a satisfactory *program* is being used to achieve the activity's objectives. This consists of an evaluation of the level of the activity's total budget and the allocation of the money spent from the activity budget.

3. Determining the firm's *implementation* of the program in terms of making tactical decisions and using suitable retail procedures.

4. An appraisal of the departmental *organization* in terms of the distribution of authority and responsibility, the performance of the people who occupy the positions, and the intra- and interdepartmental communication process.

The activity-level audits are usually conducted when a problem appears to exist in any activity area. The problem may be uncovered by the systems-level audit or by management simply believing that something seems to be going wrong in a particular activity. A brief discussion of some of the points that may be analyzed in specific activity audits is now in order.

Customer Analysis

Identifying the retailer's most profitable customers is one of the most important things to determine in a retail market analysis. Not all customers generate profits for the store they patronize, and retailers can use their resources in an inefficient way by catering to customers who buy only low-margin items on an infrequent basis but demand extra services. No retail outlet can be all things to all people, so the retail effort must be oriented to serve and satisfy profitable customers. Customers who do not pay their bills on time or who habitually return purchases add to the cost of conducting business. The low profit margins generally obtained in retailing may not be large enough to allow that kind of customer to be serviced at a profit. One way to determine if customers are paying their way is to estimate what it costs to serve different kinds of consumers and to sell different-size orders. Retailers must be cautious in the way they identify unprofitable customers and in the way they treat them after they have been identified. Unprofitable consumers communicate with many potentially profitable customers. Bad word-of-mouth advertising can, of course, affect the purchase patterns of the profitable consumers.

No stores can serve everyone. The retail audit must determine if management has adequately defined the group(s) of customers (market targets) that the store is going to serve. The audit should reflect the fact that small stores are more effective in catering to distinct groups, such as customers who have special tastes or interests, local residents, business people working nearby, and so forth. Larger retail organizations may cater to several different market targets by using boutiques, subdividing large departments, establishing bargain basements, and so on.

Customer Relations

Customer relations revolve around the type of store image that management seeks to implant in the minds of customers. The retail audit must determine if a clear definition of the desired store image has been made. First, is store management aware of the store's special features—the special kinds of merchandise and services it offers? Are these special features communicated to both present and potential customers?

Many outlets suffer because store personnel fumble their roles after the customer has been attracted to the store. Stores that cannot match the merchandise assortments and low prices offered by mass merchandising competitors must gain their strength from special services. Is quick delivery service, personal customer attention, and the ability to help solve specific customer problems, such as garden care, interior decorating, clothing selection, being used to attract and retain customers? If not, why not?

The retail audit should also determine if salespeople are treating each customer as an individual rather than as one of the crowd. Do they greet customers by name? Are salespeople helping consumers by listening to their problems and offering solutions? Have campaigns been conducted to encourage employees to be considerate of customers' viewpoints? As a competitive advantage, courtesy, especially at the cash register or checkout counter, is a powerful attraction. The customer gets the last impression of the store in the checkout process, and a friendly and interested employee can make certain that it is a good impression.

Is service being provided on the merchandise after it has been sold? In some cases this consists of merely returning goods to the factory for repair. In other cases it involves on-the-spot maintenance. In either case, the service should be provided quickly and courteously.

Is retailing management aware of the customer's need for convenience and shopping ease? A comfortable customer lounge can serve as both a meeting and a resting place. A "free" cup of coffee and other small extras can make a store a more enjoyable place to shop. Consumer convenience may also be provided by posting and maintaining regular store hours. This allows the consumer to depend on the store's being open and to adjust purchasing and consumption patterns to the store hours. The small cost involved in providing such services frequently yields large returns in repeat business.

Location

A good location is essential for the successful operation of any retail firm. One of the most frequent mistakes is made by retailers who want to minimize the monthly rental payment needed to obtain a good location. These retailers suffer because they will not pay enough rent to secure a good location that could generate volume sales. As a result, they have to spend more money to promote the store and still may not be able to attract convenience-oriented consumers.

The retail audit should determine if new outlets would increase the retailer's profits. If new outlets are being considered, is the firm's selection procedure an objective evaluation? The selection of a city or town that will contain the new outlet should be based upon characteristics such as population, area growth potential, consumer income and purchasing power, the purchasing habits of potential consumers, legislative restrictions, and competition. The index of retail saturation discussed in Chapter 7 may be used to measure the relative retail potential of an area.

Local trading area analysis of the most promising cities or towns can indicate if the firm's existing outlets are covering the market area that can be serviced profitably by the organization. New outlets may be required to serve areas in which few customers reside. This usually will be the case when each outlet's trading area is small, and when per outlet retailing costs do not decline rapidly as sales volume increases. Naturally, the firm should examine the characteristics of potential consumers residing in an area not currently being reached by the firm's existing retail outlets. A new outlet will not be warranted automatically unless the demographics and life styles of people residing in this untapped area are similar to those of the target market customers of the existing outlets. In untapped areas where residents' characteristics differ from those of current outlets, the firm could open a new outlet under a new name. Management may want to create a different store image that could better serve the needs of consumers in areas of sufficient size that will justify this additional expense. The location audit should include evaluations of the outlet's accessibility to residents of the trading area and its compatibility with nearby businesses.

Outlet Layout

The retail audit should determine if the layout of the selling floor is planned for the convenience of the customer. This may be accomplished by providing a clear indication of the location of the different types of merchandise and by displaying related merchandise close together. Merchandise should be attractively displayed where customers can handle it (instead of having to ask a sales person to show it) so as to enhance sales and reduce clerical cost. Goods that the customer may not be specifically looking for, but is likely to buy if reminded of them by their visibility, should be displayed prominently. Impulse goods are usually displayed on sales counters near the store entrances and at other heavy traffic points. Interspersing impulse goods with demand items can also increase the chance that the consumer will see the impulse merchandise.

The audit should also evaluate the image that the layout projects to the store's customers. Is it consistent with the expectations of the outlet's target market?

Promotion

The retail audit may initially focus on the firm's promotional strategy. General objectives of the retail promotion efforts are to:

1. Increase the competitive position of the outlet by obtaining a larger share of the retail business in the trade area.
2. Encourage consumers residing outside the trade area to shop at the firm's retail outlet.
3. Stimulate consumers to increase the level of retail purchases.
4. Create and maintain a favorable store image consistent with the quality of merchandise offered, the service provided, and the convenience of the location.

Thus, the audit must determine how successful the retailer has been in accomplishing these objectives.

Has the retailer determined what "message" should be communicated to the consumers? The message should be selected to accomplish objective 4 for the target market customers.

Other considerations that should be investigated in the retail audit of the promotion activity include an evaluation of the consistency of the promotional activity. Small amounts of advertising on a frequent basis are generally more effective in creating the desired image than large amounts of advertising on an infrequent basis. Constant reminders that the store carries certain merchandise lines, that new products are now available, that expert service and advice is available at the store, and that the store offers specific advantages in specific areas are required to reinforce the consumer's image of the store. Stores that rely upon strictly "sale-price reduction" advertising do little to attain a favorable quality and service image. The level of expenditure for promotional activities should be related to the expected sales level for the store. Promotional activity should be increased before the sales peak is expected to occur. Large advertising expenditures just prior to payday or normal shopping days are more likely to stimulate sales because consumers will have the ability to respond to the message.

Tactical considerations can also be made during an audit. For example, advertisement can be improved by retaining copies of the advertisements previously used and evaluating their effectiveness. Successful advertisements frequently contain products and/or appeals that can be featured again to repeat the former success. Cost of the advertisement, media usage, weather conditions, and unusual competitors' activities should be recorded and analyzed in the process of identifying the effective advertisements.

Pricing

The retail audit should determine if prices are established to provide as much markup as possible without losing substantial sales volume. Have price levels been raised and lowered on different items over a period of time? This will allow the retailer to identify those items whose demand is highly dependent upon price. Setting a lower markup on those items responsive to price changes can bring enough added sales to yield a larger total profit. Price reduction on these key items, however, may disturb the public image of the store. Maintaining or raising prices on items whose sales do not respond to price changes can result in higher profits, provided this action does not damage the store image projected to consumers. Higher markups should be obtained on items whose risk and handling costs are high and/or whose turnover rate is relatively low. These higher markups will offset the lower markups that are taken on competitive merchandise.

Has the outlet established price lines that provide good merchandise assortments at the price levels demanded by its target market consumers? This practice can be a profitable pricing strategy.

Temporary price markdowns can cater to customer groups that do not respond to regular prices. This can result in increased sales and may result in increased dollar margin.

However, the promotion must be truthful. Prices quoted in advertisements should reflect the store's intent to sell the merchandise at the stated price. Misleading promotions result in possible legal action and consumer ill will that, in the long run, far outweigh the temporary increase in store profits generated by the misleading promotions.

Buying

The retail audit may include an analysis to determine if the selection of merchandise assortments is meeting the needs of the retailer's target market consumers. Adequate stocking and quick reordering of new items that have been showing volume sales potential must be done to complement the buyer's original subjective judgment of consumers' needs. Can the firm that is being audited receive additional merchandise quickly? Why not? What can be done to improve speed of delivery?

Retail buyers should also be comparing new item offerings with the present merchandise assortment. Shelf space is not utilized efficiently if the new items are so similar that they merely represent a duplication of the current product offering.

Is central group buying being used advantageously on some items where individual store buyers cannot obtain style and price preferences? A central buying office may be able to act more quickly on new market offerings and developments, since it has a broader picture of lines that are coming in and going out of style.

Is a written buying plan being used to guide the selections of the retail buyer who attends a particular market or trade show? The buying plan should be based upon such factors as price line, type, material, size, and color, and should not be left to chance. It does not normally specify style numbers but may include the number of different styles that the retailer wants to carry.

The audit should also contain an evaluation of the way the retailer increases profits by taking advantage of available trade, quantity, seasonal, and cash discounts. Careful planning and proper timing of orders can result in substantial discounts not otherwise available. Transportation charges also can be reduced by proper planning. Placing orders too late for slower but cheaper delivery methods, ordering in uneconomical quantities (for example, ordering fifty-pound lots when the minimum charge is for one hundred pounds), permitting unnecessarily heavy packing materials, and so forth result in excessive transportation costs. Procedures should confirm that the order always specifies the method of transportation and the consolidator of the shipments.

Merchandise and Inventory Control

Merchandise control begins by checking the description and number of units of merchandise received against the description of the goods ordered. All orders must be followed to see that goods are shipped and received on time. Late delivery of ordered goods can result in consumer ill will and lost sales which may necessitate price markdowns to eventually move the merchandise.

Organizing the store by departments allows retail management to determine the profitability of each merchandise group and the performance of employees. Department records should include information on gross sales, physical inventories, value of purchases, markdowns, direct department expenses, cash discounts, and other data needed to construct departmental operating statements. Sales, inventory, and purchase records must be kept by merchandise groups for each department if retailers want to balance inventories and purchases with sales. These records can be used to develop a model stock plan that can maintain a balance between breadth and depth of merchandise assortments. A unit plan can be developed to indicate the number of different items that should be carried in stock and the number of each variety that should be stocked to avoid out-of-stock conditions. The model variety can be broken down by price lines, types, materials, colors, and sizes.

A constant supply of staple and reorder items is essential if a retailer is going to maintain a steady stream of customers. Retailers should prepare a list of selected items that are deemed important enough to warrant particular efforts to almost never be out of stock. The item's rate of sale, its delivery period, the planned frequency of reorder, and the desired amount of safety stock can be considered to minimize the level of stock-outs on these key items.

A unit control system should be developed for nonstaple merchandise lines. This system may consist of a daily or weekly analysis of sales on nonstaple items, or it may involve keeping daily inventory records by computer hookup to the store's cash registers. These unit control records allow retail management to identify fast- and slow-selling items quickly. This quick identification allows the retailers to reorder the best-selling items promptly and in sufficient volume to minimize out-of-stock conditions. Slow-selling items are identified faster, so they may be promoted and sold at reduced prices, thereby reducing the inventory investment and shelf space allocated to slow-moving merchandise.

Additional planning is required on goods that have a short selling season. The introduction of short-lived seasonal or fad goods is likely to result in a loss unless careful preplanning is done in determining:

1. When the first orders are to be placed.
2. When retail stocks are to be complete.
3. The expected duration of the peak selling period.
4. The start of the merchandise clearance sales.
5. The date that the remainder of the merchandise should be completely sold out.

Adequate safeguards must be adopted to minimize the theft, breakage, soiling, spoiling, and fading of merchandise if the retail firm is to operate profitably. Pilferage is rapidly becoming one of the greatest retailing problems. Detection and control systems must be established and implemented, or the level of stock shortage is likely to exceed the net profit level.

Periodic checks should be made to ensure that a sufficient level of insurance is carried to cover changes in the value of merchandise, real estate, buildings, and equipment. The coverage on public liability insurance should be evaluated at the same time. Inflation and greater awards on liability suits have caused many retailers to be underinsured when tragedy strikes.

A retail audit should contain an evaluation of the performance on these basic merchandise and inventory control factors.

Budgetary Control

Retail plans must be expressed in terms of a budget that establishes goals for sales, stocks, markups, and expenses. The audit should investigate the budgetary process used by the retailer. The budgetary period takes the form of both short-run and annual planning. The short-term budget must be prepared weekly or monthly to assure adequate control of current operations. The annual budget contains the expected cash flow for the upcoming year. It should include expected changes in costs and revenues resulting from implementing the retail plan.

Both kinds of budgets are more effective when the employees responsible for achieving the stated objectives have a chance to participate in the formulation of the goals. Previous company experience and published data on other firms engaged in a similar business provide a basis of comparison for determining the budget. The control process should also involve a comparison of actual company results against previous budget projections. Merchandising, promotion, and expense plans can then be adjusted as indicated by the deviation from the projections. Open-to-buy and open-to-spend controls are needed to keep purchases consistent with previous plans. These plans must be revised as changes in the competition and environment occur if the retailer is to remain responsive to changes in consumer purchasing patterns.

Retail Organization and Personnel Management

Retail firms should be organized so that each employee takes orders from and is under the direct supervision of only one person. This type of organization can avoid the conflicts of divided responsibility. The retail audit should determine if the functions and lines of authority have been established in writing, preferably on organization charts. This will assist all employees to understand their areas of responsibility and the relationship of their work to that of others in the retailing organization.

Written job specifications are essential in selecting, training, and evaluating personnel. The "management objective" approach can be effective in insisting that employees set specific objectives for themselves. These objectives will guide their own activities and performance for the stated period of time. If the personal objectives that an employee first suggests seem inadequate, they may be upgraded by mutual consent. Once agreed upon, these objectives become the immediate supervisor's basis of evaluation.

The audit might also determine if top-level retail management is delegating as much authority as possible to those employees immediately responsible to it. Delegation of authority can free top management from spending most of its time on unnecessary operating details. Top retail management and department managers can usually improve retail performance by allocating more of their time to planning, organization, coordination, supervision, and control activities.

Regular and consistent supervision of employees is more effective than sporadic criticism of poor performance. A retail audit will show whether this is being done.

Another factor that should be included in the activity audit is the retailer's compensation policy. Wages and other forms of compensation must be competitive with wages paid by other firms. Wages must also be adjusted to the difficulties and responsibilities of each job. Most of the retail salesperson's earnings generally come from a base salary which is supplemented with a commission on sales. The more reliance that is placed on commission, the more incentive the salespeople have to make sales. Other incentive plans give consideration to employees' needs for recognition, security, reasonable hours, congenial working conditions, and opportunities for advancement. Commission and quota bonus plans usually provide incentives for salespeople, while seasonal bonus plans may provide more incentives for supervisors. Whatever pay plan is used, the pay policy (including overtime policy) should be clear to all employees.

Credit

A retail credit policy should be based on the costs of granting credit against the benefits obtained by granting credit. Bank credit card plans have advantages in that the store's cash is not tied up in accounts receivable. In addition, there are fewer problems in opening accounts and collecting overdue bills. Bank credit card plans, however, may weaken customer loyalty to the firm's outlets. The retailer's own credit card plan may encourage store loyalty because the card cannot be used in competing stores. If the retail firm uses its own credit plan, it must establish definite credit limits, explain the rules carefully to all applicants, and follow up promptly when customers do not make payments as agreed.

Periodic reviews should be made of the accounts receivable and revolving credit accounts to determine the collection period, the percentage of accounts that are current, overdue, and so forth. These regular reviews will be helpful when management sets up bad-debt reserves and establishes credit and collection policies. The firm's performance on bad debts, collection period, and so on can be compared with data for similar stores. An audit of a retailer's credit policy should reflect these considerations.

Taxes and Legal Obligations

Important changes in tax and legal regulations occur frequently. The retail audit should determine if one specific individual or group is responsible for submitting the required taxes and various legal reports. Maintaining a calendar that shows when the various taxes and reports are due is a must as requirements and regulations become more numerous and more complex. Specialists in tax and other legal matters are required in order to keep up to date on the latest rulings. Laws on advertising, labeling, selling, and guarantee practices are changing rapidly, so periodic checks must be made to determine if the current practices satisfy the current laws and regulations. Wise retailers recognize legitimate consumer complaints. Through group action these retailers try to pass legislation that serves the consumer but does not add significant costs to the retailing effort.

Implementing a Retail Audit

Success of the retail audit depends upon who conducts the audit and when it is scheduled. The retail audit can be conducted either internally, by an individual or group of individuals who are permanent members of the retail organization, or externally by outside consultants. The **internal audit** has the advantage that the auditors are intimately familiar with the operation and, as a result, the cost is reduced considerably. However, an objective unbiased audit is not likely from an internal audit. Each member of the retail organization is likely to suppress any shortcomings in his or her operation. Even those internal auditors who try to remain objective may take a more narrow view of the firm's opportunities and shortcomings than will outside or external auditors.

Advantages of the **external audit** are derived from the consultants' broad experience in many different areas. Retailers are able to benefit from the experience of others by not duplicating their mistakes. The external auditors are also likely to be more objective, since they have no self-interest to preserve. Finally, external auditors are more likely to concentrate on the execution of the audit, since internal auditors can concentrate on the audit only if they are not concerned with time-consuming, day-to-day operating details.

The major disadvantage of using an external auditor is that the consultant must spend a lot of time becoming familiar with the internal aspects of the firm before making an appraisal. This disadvantage is not great when the company enters a long-term relationship with a consulting organization, under which the consultants become familiar with the retailer's operations as they audit first one and then another of the company's operations on a fairly continuous basis. Their contribution can be enhanced even more if they work with an internal task force that provides information, studies the auditor's reports, and implements the important recommendations in the consultant's reports.

Annual systems-level audits should be scheduled so that they can provide input into the retailer's annual planning efforts. Activity-level audits should be scheduled as determined in the systems-level audit. An activity-level audit should be scheduled whenever the annual systems-level audit or retail performance reveals that an activity is in great need of reform or supervision.

Interpretation of the Retail Audit

It should not be concluded that positive findings in most of the areas covered by the systems-level and activity-level audits will assure the retail firm of a profitable future or that no further investigation is warranted. Even if the results of the audit seem to indicate that everything is well, it does not mean that management can afford to stop creating new approaches to reach the current or expanded target markets. The retail audit is only a tool that seeks to indicate information about the effectiveness of the organization. It can point out some crucial areas that warrant management's attention. When these weaknesses are revealed, the retail organization can rectify the situation sooner and more easily than if no systematic review process were used.

Financial audits and market research projects must be used in the retail audit to provide a truly creative approach to long-range retail planning. Creative changes should be made in an orderly manner by making only one change at a time so that its effectiveness can be measured. Continual changing of the entire program will generally allow management to evaluate only the success of the entire program, not each of the retail activities. When a reasonably successful plan has been developed, it is usually better to maintain it first and make only one major change at a time. All changes should be measured on a cost-versus-results basis. The evaluation then centers around the question, "Were the results worth the amount of time, talent, and money used to accomplish them?"

Summary

Periodic systems-level and necessary activity-level auditing keep management's efforts concentrated on identifying trends, establishing objectives and policies, and acquiring and analyzing the data needed for objective decision making. It causes management to become more alert to needed changes caused by shifts in consumer shopping patterns and shifts in the competitive or legal environment.

The systems-level retail audit begins with the retailer's *diagnosis* of the market situation and the factors believed to be responsible for it. This phase of the audit determines where the firm is situated now and why it is now in the situation. The second stage of the systems-level audit is the *prognosis* step, which involves an estimate of where the retailer is likely to go if present policies are continued. In step three, the systems-level audit then turns to an *evaluation* of the firm's marketing and profit objectives to determine where the firm should be headed in the future. The fourth step of a systems-level retail audit is the establishment of a *program* that is to be used to achieve the objectives that have been established in step three. The fifth step of a systems-level audit is the *implementation* of the program. Attention is focused upon both the tactical means and procedures that need to be used to properly execute the program. *Organization* matters are then evaluated in step six, in which the audit evaluates the adequacy of retail management personnel to identify possible weaknesses in such areas as the lines of authority and the communication channels used to relay consumers' desires to the decision maker. The final step of a systems-level audit is the establishment of *control* procedures, which involve the establishment of performance standards that are checked periodically to determine if the retailer's plan is leading to its stated objectives.

This same audit framework can be used to audit any specific activity. The activity-level audits are usually conducted when a problem appears to exist in any activity area such as consumer relations, location, layout, promotion, pricing, buying, merchandise management, inventory control, budgetary control, organizational structure, personnel management, credit, taxes, and legal areas.

Retail audits can be conducted internally by permanent members of the firm or externally by outside consultants. Permanent employees are likely to be more familiar with the business than are outside consultants. However, employees are also likely to be more biased and protective of their position than are outside consultants.

Questions

1.   Today the "geriatric set" is larger in numbers than ever before in history and it shows no signs of becoming smaller. Yet, we see a continued emphasis on "young living" in all forms of merchandising.

Discuss the marketing and especially the retailing implications of this situation.

2. How does a retail audit differ from an accounting audit? Do you think the average CPA would make a good retail auditor?

3. How can a small retailer best identify the firm's target segment? Why is it necessary to do so?

4. Should location audits be part of every retail audit? Why or why not?

5. Would you expect a layout audit to be more useful in a variety store or in an appliance store? Why?

6. Constant price manipulations can be detrimental to customer relations, but these manipulations can provide data for calculating demand elasticities. How would you "balance" this situation?

7. How can a retailer decide when to start using private labels? How can he decide what volume of selling space to allocate to private label goods?

8. What is the use of spending time and money on inventory control? Why not just order large quantities of everything and use your time and money in the sales effort?

9. Retail managers often provide many benefits for their employees, and sometimes approach or even exceed unions' benefits. Union organizers accuse management of doing this just to prevent collective bargaining, and they refer to the practice as "paternalism." Do you think the union accusation is justified? Identify any possible ulterior motives on both sides. Is unionization in the best interest of the employees?

10. Distinguish between an internal and external retail audit. Discuss the advantages and disadvantages of each.

11. How should a retailer decide how often a retail audit should be performed? Be specific with regard to internal and external audits and what factors determine their frequency.

Footnotes

1. Richard D. Crips, "Auditing the Functional Elements of a Marketing Operation," *Analyzing and Improving Marketing Performance*, Report No. 32 (New York: American Management Association, 1959), pp. 16–17.

2. Philip Kotler, *Marketing Management, Analysis, Planning, and Control* (Englewood Cliffs, N.J.: Prentice-Hall, 1967), p. 595.

3. Ibid., pp. 155–162.

4. Ibid., pp. 114–120.

5. Ibid., p. 601.

6. Ibid., p. 161.

Glossary*

A

absenteeism and turnover
Absenteeism refers to the collective effect of employees not reporting for work as assigned. Turnover refers to the process of replacing employees who quit or are terminated.

accessory items Merchandise that is coordinated with other larger items.

accordion theory A theory describing the tendency for the retail business to follow an alternating pattern in which general-line, wide assortment retailers are followed by specialized, narrow-line retailers.

accounting The method of recording all the transactions affecting the financial condition of a given business.

accounts payable A current **liability** that represents the amount owed to a creditor for merchandise or services purchased on an open account or short-term credit.

accounts receivable Money owed a business enterprise for merchandise bought without giving a note or other evidence of debt.

accrual system A method of apportioning expense and income for the period in which each is incurred, regardless of the date of payment or collection.

accrued interest payable Interest accumulated on an indebtedness that is not yet paid.

acid test ratio A ratio that indicates the ability of a business enterprise to meet its current obligations. The formula used to determine the ratio is as follows:

$$\frac{\text{Cash plus Receivables plus Marketable Securities}}{\text{Current Liabilities}}$$

Frequently, a 1:1 ratio is considered satisfactory.

activity-level audit An evaluation of a specific activity in the retail effort. The activity may have been identified as a problem area during a **systems level retail audit.**

additional markup An increase in price above the original retail price. Thus, if one hundred articles, originally retailed at $1 each, are marked up to $1.09, the additional markup is $9 for the lot.

advance dating An arrangement in which the seller sets some specific future date when the terms become applicable. This date, which is some time after actual shipment, gives additional time for payment and to have the **cash discount** deducted, since the time for payment of the **invoice** is computed from the advance dating rather than from the invoice date. Example: For an order placed on April 10 and shipped on April 25, 1/10, n/30 as of June 1, the payment dates in full or less discount are calculated from June 1.

advance orders Orders placed with vendors before both the normal buying season and the immediate needs of the retailer are established.

* Note: Terms within the definitions that are printed in bold-face type are themselves defined in the glossary.

advertising A paid form of nonpersonal presentation of goods, services, or ideas to consumers made by an identified sponsor.

advertising agency An organization that prepares **copy** and **layout,** selects media, works on advertising strategy, and produces the advertisement.

advertising allowance A discount retailers earn by advertising the supplier's products in the local media.

advertising medium The vehicle by which the advertiser's message is carried to its audience. Advertising media are often classified as (1) print media and (2) broadcast media.

affiliated buying A retail buying practice wherein several independent retailers consolidate their orders to gain economies of scale in buying.

AIDCA process An acronym describing what an advertisement should accomplish: attract *attention,* stimulate *interest,* create *desire, convince* the consumer, and suggest that the individual take *action.*

allocated expenses Nondirect expenses for which good and appropriate bases of expense distribution exist, so that the assignment of expense represents a reasonable estimate of the true expense incurred by each department in a retailing organization.

allowances from vendors Rebates and credits granted by manufacturers and wholesalers on purchases made by the retailer.

anchor A large retail store located at one end of a shopping center which is used to attract customers to the center. Department stores typically anchor regional shopping centers; branch department stores and discount stores anchor community shopping centers; and a supermarket is an anchor for a neighborhood shopping center.

annual sales forecast Estimated level of retail sales for the year.

anticipation An extra discount (usually 6 percent per year) allowed by vendors when a bill is paid before the expiration of the **cash discount** period.

asset Anything owned by an individual or a business that has commercial or exchange value. Assets may consist of specific property or claims against others.

assortment The number of different product items that a retailer stocks within a particular product line.

atmospherics The overall sensory (i.e., sight, sound, smell, and touch) impressions that a store's physical facilities and merchandising activities create.

augmented product The tangible items combined with the whole set of services that accompany the product when it is sold to the consumer.

authority The assigned right to command others or commit firm resources.

automatic reorder Reordering of **staple merchandise** on the basis of a predetermined minimum quantity. When this minimum quantity is reached, a new order is automatically made.

B

back orders An order a buyer has not received on time from a seller.

backup stock Additional merchandise that is available in a warehouse or in a stock room. Backup stock is particularly important for runners or best-selling staples.

bad check A check that is not honored for payment when it is presented to the designated financial institution.

bad debts Amounts due on open accounts that have proved to be uncollectable.

bait-leader pricing Advertising a product at an extremely low price, then refusing to sell it when a customer wants to buy the item and using persuasive power to switch the customer to another, higher-priced item. Sometimes called bait-and-switch tactics.

balance sheet An itemized statement that lists the total assets and total liabilities of a given business to portray its net worth at a given moment in time.

balanced stock A balanced assortment that makes the items customers want available throughout all price ranges in proportion to consumer demand.

bank credit card A bank card that entitles the holder to purchase merchandise or services at any place of business where the card is honored. The card-holder receives one monthly statement from the bank. Usually no service charge is assessed on merchandise purchases paid for within twenty-five days of the statement rendering date. The bank immediately reimburses the merchant accepting the card and charges a monthly fee based on dollar volume.

bank credit plans Commercial bank consumer credit agreements which permit the user to use a bank credit card to make purchases and defer payment until billed or pay the balance over a protracted time period.

bargain basement The downstairs division of a department store that emphasizes special values.

bargain store A store that stocks everything that can be sold in quantity at a below-market price. Distress merchandise and seconds are often stocked in huge quantities, but little attempt is made to maintain a **balanced stock** assortment.

base-point pricing The price to the buyer is the price of the product plus freight from a specified point, regardless of the buyer's or the seller's location.

basic assortment The smallest number of pieces within a merchandise group that will provide sufficient sizes, colors, style numbers, and so forth to satisfy customer demand.

basic stock The assortment plan of products to be kept continuously on hand for a defined period, usually at least one year. It includes a list of staple items to be carried in stock, reorder points, and reorder quantities. Nonstaple items can become basic when, for fashion or fad reasons, they enjoy intensified customer demand.

basic stock method A method of planning inventory levels by ordering enough stock to begin the sales period with an inventory that exceeds the estimated period sales by some basic inventory level.

big ticket item A high-priced merchandise item.

billed cost Invoice cost of purchases less **trade** and **quantity discounts.**

bill of lading A receipt issued by a carrier for merchandise to be delivered to a person at some distant point.

bill of sale A formal legal document that conveys title to specific property from the seller to the buyer.

blanket orders Orders a retailer places with suppliers for merchandise for all or part of a season.

book inventory A statement of the amount of retail stock on hand according to a **perpetual inventory system.**

boutique A small shop selling fashions or fad items. It may be independent or located in a special area within a larger store.

boutique layout A store layout in which the sales floor is arranged into individual areas that are built around a particular shopping theme.

branch store An outlet of a central store extended into another geographic area of the market.

brand A word, mark, symbol, or a combination of these that identifies the product or service offered by a seller.

break even point A retail sales volume that will provide just enough revenue to cover the direct expenses most likely to be incurred. It is the sales volume at which the stores expected to receive neither a profit nor a loss.

broadcast media Radio and television.

broker A limited-function agent wholesaler whose primary service is to bring buyers and sellers together in order to complete a business transaction.

brown goods A category of durable goods which has traditionally been dominated by the color brown *e.g.*, radios, stereos, and television sets.

bulk marking A marking procedure in which the retailer places similar merchandise with the same price on one display and attaches one price card to the entire display.

business associated site A retail location that is situated near other retail firms.

buying committee A committee which makes collective decisions on what merchandise is to be added or dropped from the store's product offering.

buying group (buying office, resident buying office) An organization representing a group of noncompeting stores formed primarily for buying merchandise.

buying power index (BPI) A relative measure of the effective buying power of a segment of the market, published annually by *Sales and Marketing Management's Survey of Buying Power.* It is an estimated value of the ability of an area to purchase consumer goods, especially mass merchandised products sold at popular prices. For example, if area A has a BPI of 0.06, its market potential is double that of area B, which has a BPI of 0.03.

buying process The search, evaluation, selection, and review activities that are carried out by the buyers for a retail firm.

C

capital investments The dollar amounts invested in capital or fixed assets or in long-term securities as contrasted with those funds invested in current assets or short-term securities.

capital management The process of planning and controlling the retailer's equity capital and borrowed capital.

capital turnover The ratio between **net sales** and the average inventory valued at cost. It is calculated as: net sales ÷ average inventory at cost.

careers in retailing The various fields of retailing that offer opportunities for lifetime employment.

carriage trade A wealthy class of customers.

carrier Any commercial railroad, trucking firm, airline, express company, bus line, steamship line, or river barge company that transports merchandise from a vendor to a purchaser.

carry outs Merchandise carried from the store by the customer.

cash discount A discount allowed by a vendor for paying the invoice within an agreed time. Example: 2/10 means that a 2 percent discount is allowed if the bill is paid within ten days of the date of the invoice.

cash flow forecast A projection of cash inflows and outflows. It is used to insure the expected cash balance at the end of a specified time period.

cash on delivery The buyer must make payment when the goods are delivered.

cash receipts report A form used by salespeople to list cash received from sale of merchandise at the end of each day's business.

catalog wholesaler A limited-function middleperson who solicits retail orders through the mail using catalogs.

CATV See **Community Antenna Television System.**

central business district The downtown area, which is composed of convenience stores that serve the downtown employees and **shopping goods** stores and specialty shops that attract consumers to the area.

centralized buying All buying done by a central merchandise staff, which may be located in corporate headquarters.

chain stores Two or more stores carrying similar merchandise that are owned by one company.

charge-a-plate The copyrighted name of the small identification plate that shows that a customer has a charge account with a specific firm.

Clayton Act An act that outlaws discrimination in prices, exclusive and tying contracts, intercorporate stockholdings, and interlocking directorates, whenever their effect "may be to substantially lessen competition or tend to create a monopoly."

clearance sale A promotional event designed to sell outdated merchandise in order to make room for new merchandise.

client specialization The separation of organizational activities on the basis of the unique requirements of specific customer groups.

closed stock Merchandise sets sold to the customer with the understanding that the store does not promise to keep individual items of the set in stock in the future.

closeout sale A promotional sales event on a merchandise line for which the retailer plans to discontinue the line.

cold-canvass method A selling method in which salespeople solicit sales door-to-door without an advanced selection of homes or giving prior notice to potential consumers.

C.O.D. See **cash on delivery.**

cognition The consumer's total belief system which consists of the individual's values, ideas, and attitudes.

collection period A ratio that indicates the size of a firm's **accounts receivables** stated in the number of days it takes to obtain that volume of sales.

Community Antenna Television System (CATV) A method whereby the signal received by an antenna can relay programs to subscribers through a cable.

community shopping center A planned shopping area consisting of twenty to forty stores, including at least one department store, and 75,000 to 300,000 square feet in store area that serves 20,000 to 100,000 people.

compatibility of nearby businesses The relationship that exists when two retailers, because of their proximity to each other,

have a larger sales volume together than they would have if they were located in separate areas.

compatibility of product lines The degree to which merchandise lines are related to each other as opposed to unrelated (scrambled) merchandise.

compensating salespeople The package of commission, salary, bonus, and fringe benefits paid to salespeople.

compensation components The elements contained in an employee's total compensation package.

compensation levels The amount of compensation paid to employees performing similar tasks.

competitive parity approach A method of determining the level of a firm's advertising budget by matching competitors' outlays for **promotion.**

complementary items Goods or services that are companions and/or are consumed jointly, for example, shirts and ties, ham and eggs.

consignee The ultimate receiver of goods.

consignment purchases Goods owned by a **vendor** that are received by a retailer under an arrangement whereby the store has the right to return to the vendor any portion of the lot unsold within a specified period.

consignor The originator of a shipment.

consistent merchandise assortment Merchandise that is closely related in terms of consumer end use.

consolidated delivery Delivery service performed by an independent organization that accumulates and delivers packages from various stores.

conspicuous consumption The use of goods or services by a consumer for the purpose of creating a display that will impress others.

consumerism The activities that consumers use to exert their influence upon government, retailers, wholesalers, and producers.

Consumer Product Warranty and Guaranty Act of 1970 Legislation passed to protect the consumer against product defects and malfunctions.

contingency payment pricing A price quoted for a service that is contingent upon the accomplishment of the task.

control The final step in a retail audit, which consists of monitoring the effectiveness of the retail plan and preparing contingency plans to be used if acceptable progress is not being made.

controllable expenses Retail expenses directly controlled and adjusted by the retailer as warranted by operating conditions.

convenience goods Goods that the consumer desires to purchase with a minimum of effort. Purchase is usually made at the most convenient and accessible place.

cooperative advertising A way of advertising whereby the manufacturer or wholesaler offers to pay some portion (most commonly 50 percent) of the cost that the retailer incurs in advertising the vendor's items in a local medium.

cooperative group A contractual business organization formed by several independent retailers.

copy The verbal and visual elements that constitute a finished advertisement.

corporation A legal business entity which is authorized by state law to operate as a single person even though it may consist of many persons.

cost The price at which goods are purchased in the wholesale market, including the billed cost and transportation cost. The billed cost is the amount charged by the seller before deducting **cash discounts.** Transportation cost is the amount charged the store for delivery of the goods.

cost (or market method) of inventory valuation Valuing an inventory at the cost price of the items involved or at their current market value, whichever is lower.

cost of merchandise sold The store's cost on merchandise that has been sold during a specific period.

cost per thousand potential customers The cost needed to reach one thousand potential customers who would be receiving a specific form of advertising. It is used in comparing the costs of alternative advertising vehicles.

cost pricing A method of obtaining price by adding all of the chargeable costs together.

coupons Small cards or cutouts found in magazines, newspapers, direct-mail envelopes, and retail outlets that customers can use to receive discounts or free merchandise.

credit record analysis An analysis of addresses from a firm's credit records to determine a store's **trading area.**

critical path analysis A planning tool that shows which jobs must be completed before other jobs can be started. It also analyzes time requirements needed to perform each job so that appropriate scheduling can minimize the time needed to complete the total job.

cues Stimuli within the individual and/or in the environment that influence the consumer's response. Cues are weaker than **drives.**

cumulative markon dollars The difference between the delivered cost of merchandise, including transportation costs, and the cumulative selling prices as originally set.

current ratio The ratio obtained by dividing current **assets** by current debt. A value greater than 2 : 1 indicates the ability of the firm to meet its current obligations and still maintain a safety margin.

customer interview A method of surveying customers to discover their attitudes and shopping habits.

customer service policies The strategy of retail outlets with regard to customer services such as credit, delivery, gift wrapping, coffee lounge, and so forth.

cut-case display Use of original shipping cartons for displaying merchandise in a retail outlet.

cycle billing Correlating alphabetical breakdowns to specific days of the month when billing customers' accounts so that billing for each consumer group occurs on the same day each month.

D

dating terms The amount of time the retailer has to obtain a cash discount or to pay the net invoice in full.

debit A debit entry in accounting records will increase the balance of an asset or expense account and decrease the balance of a liability account. All asset and expense accounts normally have debit balances and all liability, capital, and income accounts normally have credit balances.

deferred payment plans Permit customers to make purchases of large ticket items, such as refrigerators, and pay for them over a specific defined period at a certain rate which includes total interest charges. Usually requires a separate chattel mortgage be executed at the time of purchase.

delegation process Assigning authority and creating responsibility to act in behalf of a superior of the firm.

delivery period The expected period of time occurring between ordering the merchandise and receiving it into stock.

delivery service A customer service offered by a retail outlet through which purchased items are handled and delivered to the place demanded by the consumer.

demand curve A schedule that indicates the quantity of an item that can be sold during a specified period at many different price levels.

demographic characteristics Distinguishing characteristics of a given population such as age, sex, income, educational background, occupation, etc.

departmentalizing Organizing related merchandise into a group and identifying the collection as a department.

department store A retail outlet that offers a large variety of goods under one roof. It has at least twenty-five employees and its merchandise includes apparel, appliances, home furnishings, and dry goods.

depreciation Loss in value of an asset as a result of the passage of time or use.

depth of merchandise assortment The number of items offered within each merchandise line. In a deep assortment many different items within the line are stocked.

diagnosis An investigation in a retail audit that attempts to determine what the firm's present position is and why it holds that position.

direction Supervisory activity that includes leading, motivating, teaching, guiding, developing, praising, and criticizing employees.

direct expenses Expenses incurred separately for the benefit of a specific department within a store. Direct expenses common to most departmentalized stores are selling payroll, salaries of buyer and assistants, promotional costs, and delivery charges. These four classes of direct expense usually total about 40 percent of the store's total expenses.

direct mail advertising Advertising that asks for and delivers the order by mail.

discount pricing A reduced pricing strategy used by retail outlets.

discount store A store that operates on a lower margin than conventional stores that sell the same type of merchandise

discounts to employees and customers Retail reductions offered as a matter of policy to give a preferential price to certain favored groups.

discretionary expenditures Those purchases in which the consumer is not motivated by a compelling need and is not generally governed by habit and which entail some deliberation prior to purchase.

discretionary income The part of the consumer's income that involves a choice of spending or saving. Thus, it is considered to be that portion of income above an amount that is required to buy essential items.

display stock In-store merchandise which is placed in

various display fixtures where customers can directly examine it.

diversionary pricing The practice of setting a low price on selected goods or services to develop a low price image for the entire offering of the firm.

dollar control The analysis and planning of sales and stocks in terms of dollar value.

drives Strong internal physiological or social stimuli that impel an individual to action.

drop ship A shipping method in which merchandise is shipped directly to a specific **branch store.** This procedure saves the time and expense of a vendor shipping to a central warehouse then having merchandise reshipped to the branch, but it is more expensive in terms of freight cost.

durable goods Products which last a long time and which survive many uses, i.e., furniture, appliances, and automobiles.

E

economic order quantity That quantity of merchandise that achieves a balance between average order costs and inventory costs.

economic value of a retail facility The value of a retail project based upon its estimated future earning potential.

EDP See **Electronic Data Processing.**

elasticity of demand The ratio of the percentage change in quantity sold to the percentage change in price.

Electronic Data Processing (EDP) The science of converting data by electronic means to any desired form.

end-of-aisle Spaces fronting on the main traffic aisles. These locations are particularly important for displaying **impulse items.**

end-of-month (E.O.M.) dating Dating that requires the retailer to pay within a certain number of days from the end of the month during which the goods were shipped. When a bill is dated the twenty-sixth of the month or later, E.O.M. dating begins from the end of the following month. Example: 2/10 E.O.M. dating, when the invoice date is April 10, indicates required payment on May 10 (ten days from the end of April).

esteem needs Human needs for reputation, self-respect, prestige, success, and achievement.

exclusive territory An agreement whereby supplier grants a retailer exclusive rights to sell their products within a defined geographic area. In return, the retailer agrees not to sell the product anywhere except within the agreed-upon area.

expenditures Outlays made during an accounting period.

expense budget A retailer plan to control operating expenses. It is a forecast of the money needed during a given accounting period to operate business.

expense center A functional center within the store's operation which incurs operating expenses.

expense center accounting An expense classification system in which retail operating expenses are classified into functional classes (i.e., management, direct selling, customer services).

expense classification The grouping of expense accounts according to a standard plan.

expenses Costs of operating a business, other than the costs of merchandise, that are properly chargeable to a specified accounting period.

experimental approach The practice of holding other variables as constant as possible in order to determine the response that the firm gets by changing one element (advertising, price, and so forth) in its **reailing mix.**

expressed warranties Written and oral statements which the retailer makes to consumers about a product and its performance and which the retailer is legally obligated to fulfill.

external audit A retail audit conducted by people outside the firm.

extra dating The granting of a specified number of days in addition to the ordinary dating terms. Example: 2/10−30 extra means 2 percent may be deducted if the bill is paid in forty days from invoice date.

eye level merchandising The concept that merchandise displayed at eye level sells better than merchandise placed either higher or lower.

F

facing A shelf stock that is one unit wide extending to the top and back of the shelf in a display case.

factor A financing organization that specializes in lending money using **accounts receivable** or inventory as a pledge.

factoring The practice whereby a business sells the firm's **accounts receivable** to another party.

fair trade laws Laws that permit a manufacturer to establish, under certain conditions, a minimum resale price for his products.

family life cycle A concept that divides the population into different age groups, with each group representing a different stage in life.

fashion cycle A term describing the sales curve of fashion goods. A fashion cycle follows the same stages as the **product life cycle,** but the growth stage is very rapid and the decline stage is very sudden and severe.

fashion goods Items whose major appeal is a frequent change in design.

FIFO See **first in-first out method of inventory valuation.**

fifty percent—thirty-three percent—seventeen percent A concept that gives one an indication of the value of the retail selling space in a retail outlet.

financial audit An investigation that discloses the performance of a firm in dollars.

financial ratios A series of ratios that express the relationship between items on the firm's **balance sheet** or between item(s) on the **income statement** and item(s) on the balance sheet. These ratios are examined for trends and compared against industry averages to identify areas of financial strength and weakness.

financial statements The **income statement** and **balance sheet** are the firm's major financial statements.

first in-first out method of inventory valuation (FIFO) A method of determining the value of an inventory, when costs of individual items in the inventory are not identified, that assumes that goods sell in the same order in which they were received into stock. The goods in the inventory are assumed to be the newest goods purchased and are assigned the cost value of the newest goods.

fixed assets Those assets of a permanent nature required for the normal conduct of a business. Example: furniture and fixtures, land, buildings, and so forth.

fixed costs Those costs that the firm incurs whether it is open or closed for business.

fixed pricing A method of obtaining a price for an item by adding all of the chargeable costs together.

flexible discriminatory pricing The practice of charging customers different prices according to their perceived willingness to pay.

floor plan financing A type of financing that supplies the capital to permit a retailer to acquire samples of the product or products to display for sale and that is liquidated when the sale is consummated.

forward stock In-store stock which serves as backup stock and which is temporarily stored on the sales floor near its selling department.

franchising An agreement whereby an organization that has developed a successful retail product or service extends to others, for a fee, the right to engage in the business if they agree to follow the franchisor's established pattern of operations.

free-flow layout pattern A store layout that uses a series of circular or U-shaped patterns, which results in irregular, curving aisles and much open space.

free on board (F.O.B.) A shipping term that signifies that the vendor or shipper retains title and pays all charges to F.O.B. point.

free-standing site A retail site that is not adjacent to other retailing businesses.

full line Stock of a given classification of goods that includes every variety of style, in every color, in every size, and in every material that a customer can reasonably expect to obtain at a given price.

functional discount A discount granted to buyers based upon the marketing activities performed by that buyer. A type of trade discount.

functional middleperson An independent business that assists in transferring title to goods without taking title to the goods in the process.

functional needs Those consumer needs that are linked to the practical uses of an item or service.

functional specialization The separation of organizational activities needed to buy, transport, sort, store, promote and sell goods and services.

future dating The practice of allowing the retailer additional time to take advantage of a cash discount and/or to pay the net amount of the invoice. The most frequently used future dating term is 2/10, n30: a 2 percent cash discount if paid within ten days of the invoice date—if not, the net invoice amount is due within thirty days of the invoice date.

G

general ledger The summary of all operating and control accounts in which the income and financial status of a business are reflected.

general merchandise stores Retail stores that handle a large number of lines of merchandise.

general trading area The entire city or county where a retail outlet may be located.

generative business Those sales a retail outlet makes because of efforts of the store to attract consumers.

generic product Identifying the essential benefit that the buyer expects to get from a product or service; also a nonbranded item sold at lower cost because of lower advertising and packaging costs.

geographical specialization The separation of organizational activities on the basis of unique geographical entities such as the Rocky Mountain area or suburban verses urban areas which have identifiable boundaries.

gift certificate A certificate, suitably engraved, that can be used for the indicated cash value in a designated store.

grading Comparing goods with a previously established criterion as to the acceptability of certain aspects of the goods.

gravity The concept that the drawing power of each store is directly related to the type and/or size of the retailer's operation and inversely related to the distance between the consumer and the store.

grid layout pattern A store **layout** where fixtures and aisles are arranged in a rectangular pattern.

gross cost of merchandise handled The sum of **opening inventory** plus purchases and additions billed at cost.

gross cost of merchandise sold The cost of merchandise sold without adjustments for alteration costs and **cash discounts** earned on purchases. It equals the closing inventory at cost subtracted from the total merchandise handled at cost.

gross margin The difference between net sales and the total cost of merchandise sold.

gross margin return on inventory (GMROI) A merchandise management tool that measures the predictability associated with merchandise by multiplying the gross margin percent times stock turnover.

gross purchases (cost) The billed cost of merchandise purchased for resale during a given period, including special charges made by the sellers.

gross sales The sum of all prices charged customers during a given period for goods purchased by them, before subtracting deductions for returns from and allowances to customers. Gross sales include cash sales, open account credit sales, revolving credit sales, and installment sales.

group buying The action of individual stores consolidating their buying requirements into one group activity to gain bargaining power.

guarantee (guaranty) A statement by which the seller promises to do certain things should the item or service bought not perform as specified or prove to be defective in some way within a certain time after being put into use.

H

handling process Activities involved in moving goods from the vendor through the retail outlet.

hand-to-mouth buying The buying practice wherein the retailer buys only the product type and quantity when it is absolutely needed.

hard goods A category of major appliances, including refrigerators, ranges, washing machines, dryers, hot water heaters, air conditioners, and so forth.

high price maintenance The practice of establishing a price that is higher than the price offered by competitors.

hold slip A form used to identify merchandise that a customer desires to purchase at a later time.

honor system A system in which employees record their own working time on time sheets.

horizontal integration The acquisition by one company of another company in the same or related lines of business and on

the same level in the channel of distribution (the consumer being considered as the base).

house organ A publication for a store's employees.

housekeeping The action of presenting merchandise in a neat, attractive, and orderly manner. Includes physical maintenance (cleanliness) of the entire store.

human resource planning Systematic planning for acquiring the persons needed to fill job vacancies.

hypermarket A combination warehouse, **discount store**, and supermarket that sells merchandise at below normal retail prices and stacks the goods up to twelve feet high.

I

implementation The fifth step in a retail audit, which focuses upon the tactical means and procedures used to accomplish the firm's **objectives.**

implied warranty Implicit assurance that the retailer and/or manufacturer will be responsible and accountable for the performance of an item or service sold to consumers.

impulse items Goods or services that are purchased on the spur of the moment and without prior planning.

income elasticity of demand The change in quantity demanded that may be expected to result from a one percent change in income, other factors remaining constant.

income statement The financial statement that contains the operating results during a specified period of time. The main elements of the income statement are the **net sales** revenue from which the **cost of goods sold** is deducted to give **gross margin,** which must cover operating expenses and net income to the firm.

inconsistent merchandise assortment A grouping of merchandise lines that are not related to one another in terms of consumer usage.

index of retail saturation A method for retailers to choose among alternatives for the location of a new outlet by determining to what degree the number of stores in an area meet consumer demand.

indirect expenses Expenses which cannot be directly attributed to the operations of a particular department.

individual markup Markup calculated on a single merchandise item.

inelastic demand A demand condition in which consumers are *insensitive* to changes in prices, so a large change in price produces only a small change in demand.

inflation A situation in which prices are increasing throughout the economy.

initial markup percentage The difference between the total merchandise handled at retail and the total merchandise handled at cost, expressed as a percentage of the retail. Synonyms are cumulative initial markup percentage, cumulative markon percentage and cumulative initial markon percentage.

installment account A system of buying whereby the consumer makes a down payment and pays a specified amount, including a service charge, per month.

institutional advertising Advertising designed to build long-term good will for the advertiser rather than to stimulate immediate purchase of a product or service.

in-store traffic pattern The pattern of consumer movements within a store. Analysis of traffic patterns provides information helpful in planning store layout and making merchandise arrangement decisions.

insurance A means of providing protection against a risk.

integrated marketing Using the firm's entire effort in a coordinated manner to build a desirable and consistent image in the minds of consumers.

integrated retailing A retail organization that also conducts business in some other level of the distribution channel such as warehousing, trucking, or manufacturing.

intensive distribution Distribution that gives maximum exposure of goods to buyers in the market since it uses as many different types of retailers and retail locations as possible.

interest The price paid for the use of borrowed money.

intermediate terms credit Borrowed funds that must be paid back during a one- to ten-year period.

internal audit A retail audit conducted by full-time employees of the firm.

in transit Merchandise that has been shipped from the vendor but has not been received by the retailer.

inventory audit Counting stock to verify that the firm possesses stock valued at a stated level of dollars.

inventory overage The value by which **physical inventory** exceeds **perpetual** (or book) **inventory.**

inventory shortage The value by which **perpetual** (or book) **inventory** exceeds **physical inventory.**

inventory valuation A determination of the proper value

of the inventory. The usual rule is "cost or market, whichever is lower." So, if an article in the inventory cost the store $100 but is now replaceable for $90, it is valued at $90. If it is replaceable for $110, however, it is valued at $100.

invoice A bill prepared by a seller of goods or services given to the buyer. The invoice usually itemizes all articles included in the bill.

invoice cut-off Setting a specific time after which invoices received will not be included in the calculation of the inventory on hand. After this time, the merchandise corresponding to these invoices will not be included in the **physical inventory** count.

irregulars Merchandise items that were produced with some type of a flaw and which are typically offered to the retailer and the final consumer at substantially reduced prices.

item analysis An input into a management information system which contains information on shelf space, advertising, sales, inventory level and gross margin for the major items sold by a retailer.

J

jobber A wholesaler who buys from manufacturers and importers and sells the merchandise to retailers.

job design The mode in which tasks are assembled to form a job cluster.

job description A statement of the duties, requirements and other features of the job. It is used for purposes of determining the rate of pay and advertising the position when it is vacant.

job evaluation A determination of the relative worth and importance of each position in a firm. A job

evaluation program may be used to establish wages, determine promotion requirements, establish incentives, and so forth.

job specifications A statement that includes a description of the necessary skills, abilities, and education that are needed to perform the job.

journal A book of original entry for a specialized type of entry such as cash disbursements, cash receipts, purchases, sales, and so forth.

K

key item A best seller that is in great demand and is placed on the "never-out" stock list to ensure adequate selection.

keystoning policy The doubling of wholesale cost to arrive at a retail price for all items.

kickback A part of a fee, commission, or wage that is turned back to an individual in appreciation of the patronage or service rendered. It is an unethical practice because the funds are not paid back to the vending company but to the individual.

L

last in-first out method of inventory control (LIFO) A method of inventory evaluation used when physical counts can be obtained. It means that the price shown on the last incoming shipment of the particular item is the one that will be used for current valuations and cost. With fast moving items this should be close to market value.

law of retail gravitation A formula for determining the interchange of retail trade between cities. It was formulated in 1931 by William J. Reilly and purports to tell at what distance between two cities a consumer would be indifferent to going to either city.

layaway A deferred payment purchase agreement in which merchandise is held by the store for the customer until it is completely paid for.

layout (1) A working drawing showing how an advertisement or publication is to look. (2) The arrangement of fixtures or departments in a store. (3) The arrangement of units in an office.

lead tenants The major attractions, such as department stores, that draw consumers to a shopping center.

lead time The time expected to elapse between the day of placing an order and the day of arrival of the goods.

learning The change in an individual's response tendencies as a result of the effects of his or her insights and experiences.

leased department A department (usually in specialized lines of merchandise) within either a conventional department, discount, or specialty store which is managed by an outside party under a contractual arrangement with the store.

ledger A record of final entry in bookkeeping that contains all debits and credits from the journal. It refers both to individual records and to the whole group of ledger accounts.

leverage (1) The degree to which changes in sales volume affect profits as a result of **fixed costs.** For example, a relatively small increase in sales normally causes a relatively large increase in profits since many costs are fixed regardless of business volume. (2) The degree to which a retail firm uses debt instead of equity in its financing.

liability Money owed by a retailer to another person or firm.

license plate analysis Recording customers' license numbers and

obtaining their addresses from county registration files (or from a published book) to determine a store's trading area.

life style The characteristic mode of living for a segment of or the whole of a society. It is concerned with those unique qualities that distinguish one group or culture from others.

LIFO See **last in—first out method of inventory valuation.**

life style merchandising Marketing strategies based on the mode of living of a particular market segment.

line of credit An agreement between a bank and a retailer whereby the bank agrees, over a future period, to lend the retailer funds up to an agreed maximum amount.

liquidity A term used to describe the solvency of a business. It has special reference to how readily assets can be converted into cash without loss.

liquidity ratio The ratio obtained by adding cash to marketable securities and accounts receivable and then dividing the sum by current **liabilities.** A value of less than 1 : 1 indicates the firm will have to sell some of its inventory to meet current liabilities.

list price The gross billed price, which is subject to a trade discount. In some cases, the list price is the retail price suggested by a manufacturer or vendor.

logotype A store's identifying symbol which appears in all of the store's advertisements.

long-term funds Borrowed funds for which the repayment term for the entire principle is ten years or more.

loss-leader pricing Advertising and selling merchandise at or

below cost to bring customers into the store.

low-price leaders Items that are priced at reduced markup percentage to attract customers.

M

mail questionnaire A means of obtaining information from consumers via the mails.

maintained markup The difference between **net sales** and the **gross cost of merchandise sold.** It is the margin on sales before making adjustments for **cash discounts** earned and alteration costs.

man hours The summation of all the productive hours worked by all employees in a work center during a given period.

management by objective (MBO) A program that uses professional management techniques, merchandise, and economic trend indicators to keep ahead of competition. For example, these may be aimed at the goal of increasing sales per square foot—one of the key factors that measures earnings in retail business.

management information system (MIS) A data processing system that is designed to furnish management and supervisory personnel with current information using computers or other organized data collection techniques.

managerial functions The activities of planning, organizing, directing and controlling the resources in an organization so that the end product is greater than the sum of the individual contributions.

managerial style A personal mode of behavior in a managerial role which balances the concern of employees with the needs of the firm, all expressed as a form of specialized leadership.

manifest A shipping form used by carriers for consolidation purposes. It lists all pertinent information (consignor, consignee, commodity classification, number and weight of packages, and sometimes cost) used by carriers within a store and by stores in transfer operations from central warehouse to branches.

mannequin A clothing model representing the human form used in display windows and on ready-to-wear selling floors to display apparel.

manpower development A program directed toward the improvement of an individual's knowledge, skills, attitudes, perceptions, and personal characteristics in current and future management positions.

manufacturers' agent A middleman who sells a part of the output of client manufacturers in a specified territory.

manufacturer sponsored franchise systems A franchise system in which the franchisor is a manufacturer. In most cases, manufacturers who market their products through franchise do not charge a franchising fee, however they do expect a franchisee to live up to their operating guidelines and carry their merchandise lines. In some cases distributors will carry only the franchisor's merchandise line while in others the agreement allows for the distributors to handle several lines. Examples are auto dealers, oil companies, Schwinn Bicycle, dealerships, and some tire outlets.

manufacturer's representative A selling agent capable of giving informative talks to selling personnel.

marginal analysis A method of planning inventory levels, promotional expenditures, or changes in price by analyzing what effect the last unit that has been added has upon the firm's profits.

marginal cost The addition to total cost represented by the sale of one additional unit of product or service.

marginal return to space The addition to gross margin caused by the addition of one unit of shelf **facing** for a good. Profit maximization for the retailer occurs when marginal returns to space are the same for all items.

marginal revenue The addition to total revenue resulting from the sale of one additional unit of a good or service.

markdown A retail price reduction caused by a reduction in the value of the goods. Thus, if one hundred articles retailing at $1 each become slow-selling, and are reduced to 89 cents, the markdown is $11 for the lot.

markdown percentage The percentage that a reduction in price is of the reduced price.

market segmentation A process of identifying and categorizing consumers into mutually exclusive groups (segments) that have relatively homogeneous responses to controllable marketing variables.

market share One firm's proportion of the industry's total actual volume.

market share to selling space share ratio The ratio between an individual store's share of the market in an area and its share of total store selling space is calculated for present stores and is used to forecast sales for a new retail outlet.

marketing Those business associated activities that direct the flow of goods or services from the producer to the consumer.

marketing channel A team of marketing institutions which directs a flow of goods and services from producers to consumers.

marketing concept Focusing all company activity on what will best serve the consumer at a profit to the firm.

marketing functions Those activities that are performed to place goods and services in consumers' hands at the time, at the place, and in the form demanded by consumers.

marketing middleperson services The services provided by vendors.

marketing mix The total complex of the firm's marketing effort. It includes pricing, promotion, product, and location. The central problem in planning the mix is to find that combination that will produce the maximum net income.

marketing research The systematic gathering, recording, and analyzing of information about problems relating to the marketing of goods and services.

marketing specialists Those people who perform marketing functions for manufacturers, wholesalers, or retailers.

marketing strategy A plan for marketing a product over a long period of time.

marking Placing the correct price tag on new merchandise.

markon The difference between cost price as billed (before deductions for **cash discount**) and retail price at which merchandise is originally offered.

markup The difference between the cost and the retail price of merchandise. In equation form: Markup = Retail − Cost. If an article is offered for sale at $100 and costs $65, the markup is $35. When the term *markup* is used in this book, it is (unless otherwise specified) the initial markup, which is the difference between the original retail price placed on purchases and the cost.

markup percentage The mark-up divided by the retail. In equation form it is mark up ÷ retail. If retail is $100, costs $65, and mark-up is $35, the mark-up percent is $35 ÷ $100 = 35%. The term percent of retail means the same as percent on retail and is called mark-up percentage in this book.

markup percent of cost The markup divided by the cost. In equation form, it is markup ÷ cost. If retail is $100, cost $65, and markup $35, the markup percent is $35 ÷ $65 = 53.8%. Markup percent on cost is higher than markup percent on retail. The generally accepted plan is to express markup on retail. Note: In all problems in this book, markup is expressed as a percentage of retail, unless it is specifically stated to be a percentage of cost.

markup percent on retail. The markup divided by the retail. In equation form, it is markup ÷ retail. If retail is $100, cost $65, and markup $35, the markup percent is $35 ÷ $100 = 35%. The term percent of retail means the same as percent on retail.

marquee An exterior store-front canopy which usually displays the store's name and logo.

mass merchandising The self-service store displaying and selling all kinds of merchandise. Displays tend to be massive; customers usually push wire carts to collect and carry their own selection of merchandise to cashier checkout counters.

maximizing space productivity Arrangement of selling fixtures and display of merchandise to produce increased sales volume per square foot of selling space.

maximum stock The amount of stock that should be on hand and on order just after a reorder is placed. As a formula:

Maximum = delivery period + safety factor + reorder period.

These may be expressed in terms of **weeks' supply** or in terms of units of goods. Since the *minimum* equals the *delivery period* plus the *safety factor*, the *maximum* (in weeks' supply) may also be expressed as the *minimum* plus the *reorder period*.

mazur plan A retail organizational plan which divides the retail organization into the four functional divisions of finance, merchandising, promotion, and operations.

media mix The planning, use, and coordination of advertising and promotional media, including: interior and exterior display, newspaper, direct mail, radio, TV, magazine, transit, and outdoor advertising.

media representatives The sales and/or service representatives from newspapers, radio, television, and other forms of advertising.

memorandum and consignment selling A marketing arrangement in which a vendor agrees to take back goods if they are not sold during a specific period of time.

merchandise assortment A selection composed of a series of demand related merchandise items that is unique and distinguishable as a separate entity. Examples include such wide product combinations as furniture, appliances, home furnishings, wearing apparel, sporting goods, etc.

merchandise budget A statement prepared by management containing planned commitments for all the components of the merchandise mix (sales, reductions, stocks, margins, and purchases) for a planning period (usually a season).

merchandise charge Extraneous costs, such as shipping charges, insurance, demurrage, and so forth, applied to cost of merchandise prior to markon.

merchandise classification A type of classification applied to a merchandise group within a department and controlled by dollar volume rather than by units.

merchandise control Maintaining accurate figures on purchases and sales of merchandise, either by dollar or by units, in such a way that the movement is monitored.

merchandise costs The billed cost of merchandise less any applicable trade or quantity discounts, plus inbound transportation costs if paid by the store.

merchandise line A specific product or service within a merchandise class, for example, sport and dress shirts within men's wearing apparel.

merchandise manager The executive (sometimes called merchandising manager) in charge of a merchandising division of a store.

merchandise marts The buildings that house showrooms for manufacturers and importers where store buyers and merchandise managers can inspect many lines in a minimal amount of time.

merchandising The planning involved in marketing the right merchandise, at the right place, at the right time, in the right quantities, and at the right price.

merchandising division The division of the store that is responsible for planning stock assortments, for buying, and for **merchandise control.** It shares with the other divisions the responsibility for balancing the growth and profit factors.

merchandise profitability analysis An input into a management information system which contains an analysis of: space turnover, sales, gross profit, inventory, stock turnover, net profit and return on investment by department.

middle management. The secondary layer of divisional managers, that is, assistants.

middlepeople Individuals, firms, or corporations that function between producers and ultimate consumers, assuming title to merchandise or assisting directly in its transfer.

minimum stock The amount of stock that a store plans to have on hand at the moment a reorder is placed. The minimum level should cover probable sales during the **delivery period** and allow for a safety factor.

MIS See **Management Information System.**

model stock A planned assortment of units of merchandise balanced to anticipate customer demand and resulting in the planned stock-turn.

multiple-unit pricing Pricing a number of like products together as a unit of one.

multiunit establishment One of two or more establishments in the same general kind of business that are operated by the same firm.

monthly sales index An index figure that is calculated in such a way that an average month's sales is 100. The percentage that a monthly sales index deviates from 100 is the percentage deviation of that month's sales from an average month. For example, an index of 120 for June indicates that June sales are 20 percent higher than an average month's sales.

mortgage An instrument of conveyance (generally of real estate) from a borrower, called the mortgagor, to the lender, called the mortgagee.

motivation The driving force behind consumer behavior and desires that initiates behavior.

N

national brand A brand name owned by a manufacturer.

natural division of expenses An expense classification system in which the retailer classifies expenses based on each kind of expense, without regard for which store functions incurred the expense or where (store or department) the expense was incurred.

negotiation process The final stage of the buying process during which price, terms, delivery dates, and so forth are determined.

neighborhood cluster A group of several stores in a residential district of a city composed mainly of **convenience goods** stores such a groceries, drugstores, and bakery goods stores, and service establishments such as dry cleaners and barber shops. Most patronage comes from residents of the area immediately surrounding the location.

neighborhood shopping center A group of ten to fifteen food, drug, sundry, and personal service stores situated on about six acres and serving about 10,000 people from under 75,000 square feet of selling space.

net alteration costs The difference between the cost the store incurs in performing the alterations and the amounts, if any, paid by the customers for this service. It is treated as an addition to the gross cost of merchandise sold.

net credit period The length of time for which mercantile credit is extended. For example, 2/10, net 30, provides a net credit period of thirty days.

net invoice price The net value of the invoice which is the total invoice price minus trade, quantity, and seasonal discounts.

net operating income (profit) Net sales less net cost of goods sold less operating expenses.

net profits on net sales ratio A ratio that expresses a firm's net dollar profits as a percentage of its net retail sales dollar volume.

net profit on tangible net worth ratio A ratio that measures the firm's **return on investment.**

net profit plan An expense allocation method in which all *direct* expenses are allocated to the particular departments that incurred them. *Indirect* expenses are allocated to particular departments based on a prejudged set of criteria.

net purchases The cost of purchases plus freight in, less purchase returns, allowances, and **cash discounts** taken.

net sales The difference between the **gross sales** and **returns and allowances to customers** during a specified period.

net sales to net inventory ratio A measure of the firm's **turnover** of inventory.

net space yield concept A way of determining how retail selling space can be used in the most productive way with respect to handling costs, space costs, and margins.

net terms A condition of sale calling for the payment of the billed amount of the invoice at a specified date with no **cash discount** deduction. If the date is not specified, payment in thirty days from the date of invoice is generally considered acceptable.

net worth The **owner's equity** in the store computed as the difference between assets and liabilities.

never-out merchandise The key items listed separately from a **model stock** plan or **basic stock** list, or especially identified on the basic stock list by colored stars or other suitable means that are always in stock.

newspaper A print medium issued frequently (daily or weekly) and devoted mainly to reports of latest developments. It is a timely advertising medium for which audiences may be selected on a sharply geographic base or on the basis of demographics.

nondiscretionary expenditures Consumer spending that represents contractual, necessary, and habitual expenditures.

nongoods service The renting of goods as opposed to selling them.

nonprice competition Any competitive activity, such as promotion, that does not involve price manipulation.

nonfunctional needs Those consumer needs that are not linked to the practical use of an item or service but that are associated with the image of the item or service.

nonselling area Floor space other than the selling area used to conduct business in a retail outlet. It may include entrances, show windows, vertical transportation facilities, offices, boiler and engine rooms, alteration rooms and workrooms, repair shops, receiving and marking rooms, and stockrooms.

nonsigner clause A provision of the fair trade laws whereby all retailers had to agree to the terms of a resale price maintenance agreement if it was assigned by a single retailer in a state operating under this provision.

nonstore retailing A form of retailing such as telephone shopping, door-to-door selling, and catalog buying, in which a consumer contact occurs outside the confines of the retail store.

notes payable The name of a **ledger** account or **balance sheet** item showing the liabilities to banks, trade, and other creditors evidenced by promissory notes.

notions department The department in department stores, drug stores, variety stores, and discount stores that carries small sundries that are usually considered small-ticket necessities, such as ribbons and needles.

number of stock turns Stock **turnover** is calculated by dividing average inventory at retail into the **net sales** for the year. Average inventory is the sum of the retail inventories at the end of each month added to the initial **opening inventory** and divided by thirteen, the number of inventories used.

O

objectives The third step in a **retail audit,** which consists of a determination of where the firm should be headed in the future.

objective and task approach A method of determining the level of a firm's advertising budget by defining the promotional objectives as specifically as possible and then determining the costs associated with accomplishing each goal.

observation A way of obtaining information by watching consumers' actions.

occupancy expense An expense related to the use of property such as rent, heat, light, depreciation, upkeep, and general care of premises.

odd lot Broken lots or unbalanced assortments reduced in price for quick turnover.

odd pricing The use of uneven prices such as $9.95 rather than $10.00.

off retail percentage The **markdown** is calculated as a percentage of the original price. For example, an item originally retails for $100 and is marked down to $60; the off-retail percentage is 40 percent.

off-season pricing A form of **markdown** given during an otherwise low sales period.

one-cent sale Selling two articles of a certain class at one cent more than the price of one.

100 percent location The retail site that has the greatest exposure to a retail store's **target market** customers.

on order Merchandise purchased but not yet received.

one-price policy A policy in which at a given time all customers pay the same price for any given item of merchandise.

open code dating The date marked on perishable products to indicate the last day that the food can be sold in the store and stated in a code that can be understood by the customer.

open order An order placed without a price or delivery stipulation. It is sent to a market representative in a **resident buying office** without specifying a vendor.

open stock Additional and/or replacement pieces of merchandise, for example, china dinnerware, that are carried in bulk and kept in stock for several years.

opening inventory The value of the inventory on hand at the beginning of an accounting period.

open-to-buy The amount of merchandise that may be ordered for delivery during a control period. It is the difference between the planned purchases and the commitments already made for the period.

operating expenses Amounts disbursed or incurred in order to operate the business as distinct from outlays to finance the business.

operating franchise Normally a single unit located on a specific site. Examples are a Dairy Queen unit or a McDonald's restaurant.

operating ratios A series of ratios that express relationships among the various items in the firm's **income statement.** These ratios are used to observe relative costs and improve the profitability of the firm.

operating statement A financial statement indicating the operating results for a given period. The format is to deduct the cost of sales from sales revenue, resulting in gross margin, which covers expenses and profit for the firm. See **income statement.**

ordinary dating The usual method of dating, as illustrated by such terms as 2/10, net 30. The two specified elements are the **cash discount** and the **net credit period.** The cash discount may be deducted if the bill is paid within the discount period (ten days); otherwise, the full amount is due at the end of the credit period (thirty days in the example given). Both the cash discount and the net credit periods are usually counted from the date of the invoice, which is usually also the date of shipment.

organization audit The sixth step of a **retail audit,** which evaluates the adequacy of retail management personnel.

organizational philosophy The set of principles upon which a firm is founded.

other income Income from sources other than the sale of merchandise. Such sources include, among others, **interest** and dividends received, carrying charges collected on **installment accounts,** and profits from the redeeming of securities.

outdoor advertising An **advertising medium** in which the message is not delivered to the audience, but rather, the units are placed in strategic locations where they can be seen by an audience on the move.

out of stock A lack of merchandise in a store.

overage The amount by which a **physical inventory** exceeds the figure generated by the **perpetual inventory system.**

overbought A condition in which a store buyer has become committed to purchases in excess of the planned purchase allotment for a merchandising period.

overhead A synonym for fixed expenses.

overstored The condition that exists when an area has more stores than are needed to satisfy consumer demand.

owned goods service Service performed on existing products.

owner's equity The amount of money the owners of a business have invested in that firm.

P

partnership A relationship based upon an agreement between two or more persons who combine their resources and activities in a joint enterprise and share by specified agreement in the management and in the profits or losses.

payback period The estimated period of time in which a project will generate enough cash to equal its cost.

payroll expense percent The total payroll for the work center expressed as a percent of the total sales. When the work center services the store, the sales are the store sales, but where the selling department is regarded as a work center, the sales are the department sales.

per capita method A method of forecasting annual retail sales in which the annual dollar per capita expenditure in a specified merchandise category is multiplied by the number of people residing in the trade area.

percentage deviation method A method of planning inventory levels that involves ordering stocks so that the beginning inventory fluctuates from the planned average stock by 50 percent of the sales fluctuations from the average period sales.

percentage of income method A method of forecasting annual retail sales in which the total annual dollar personal income in an area is multiplied by the percentage of annual personal income spent in the specified merchandise category.

percentage of retail sales method A method of forecasting annual retail sales in which the total annual dollar retail sales in an area is multiplied by the percentage of annual retail sales obtained by the specified merchandise category.

percentage of sales approach A method of determining the level of a firm's advertising budget by establishing promotional expenditures at a prespecified percentage of the estimated sales volume.

perception What the consumer "sees" as influenced by past experience, present attitudes, and inclinations.

performance appraisal The process of comparing the current performance of an individual with predetermined performance standards set forth in the **job description.**

periodic inventory method of classification control The determination of sales data within each merchandise classification from periodic counts of the inventory on hand.

perpetual inventory method of classification control The determination of sales data within each merchandise classification from periodic counts of the inventory on hand.

perpetual inventory system A method of keeping track of the inventory of a firm by continuous recording of the movement of items into and out of the firm.

personal interview A survey method in which the interviewer obtains information from respondents in face-to-face meetings.

personal selling Any activity that involves an oral presentation for the purpose of making a sale.

personnel process The process involving the systematic linking of the personnel functions into an integrated system of policies, procedures, and rules that govern employee behavior while on the job.

philosophy of human behavior A systematic, personal understanding of why humans behave the way they do and a basis on which to predict human behavior.

physical inventory The quantity or the value of merchandise on hand at a given time as determined by an actual count.

physical inventory at cost The value of an inventory at aggregate **cost** prices.

physical inventory at retail The value of an inventory at aggregate retail prices.

physical inventory system of unit control A system of stock control whereby the stock is counted at periodic intervals and the unit sales are derived from the inventory and purchase data.

physiological needs The most basic type of human needs such as hunger, thirst, and sex.

pilferage Stealing in small quantities.

planned obsolescence Making changes in merchandise features for the sake of increasing consumption, as in the practice of frequent model changes.

planned shopping center A concentration of a number of stores of different types developed as a unit.

point-of-purchase promotions Signs and displays at the final point of sale. These items are flexible as to permanence, format, position, and location.

position media Advertising media that include all types of signs, posters, programs, menus, directories, sky writing, and transportation advertising.

possession utility The characteristics of a good that make it possible to satisfy the human desire to have the right to use the item as needed.

preauthorizing The practice of obtaining credit authorization for charge-send transactions before allowing the package or merchandise to leave the department.

prebuying process The planning activities that precede the actual buying of goods by a buyer for a retail outlet.

predatory pricing A pricing tactic whereby the retailer charges different prices on the same merchandise in different markets to eliminate competition in one or more of those markets.

premarking or preticketing The price marking of merchandise by the manufacturer.

prepackaging Merchandise packaging provided by the vendor for convenient display and for the take-with customer or for delivery by store.

prepay Payment of all shipping charges for merchandise by the vendor, who rebills these charges to the purchaser on an invoice for the merchandise.

prepayment dating An immediate dating term that requires the retailer to make payment when the order is placed and stipulates that the order will not be processed until the supplier receives full payment.

preretailing A retail marking system in which the selling price of merchandise is determined before it is purchased and recorded on the store's copy of the purchase order so that the store's markers can put the selling price on the merchandise as soon as it is received.

preticketing The marking of the price on the merchandise by the manufacturers in an attempt to influence retailers' price.

price elasticity of demand coefficient The change in quantity demanded that may be expected to result from a 1 percent change in price, other factors remaining constant.

price leadership A method of retail price determination in which retailers set their prices according to the prices announced by a leading retailer.

price-line analysis An input into a management information system which contains information on sales, inventory level, gross margin, and consumer buying habits for merchandise in different price lines.

price lining Buying goods to sell at a limited number of predetermined selling prices.

price strategy The development of a long-range plan to use price as a form of market cultivation.

primary data Data collected by the firm or its representatives by actively observing, experimenting, or surveying people.

print media Any media printed on paper and distributed to consumers.

private brand A brand name owned by a middleperson.

private label pricing The pricing of private label merchandise which is those items that are promoted under a retailer's own brand name, for example, Safeway's Townhouse, Sears' Kenmore, JC Penney's Towncraft, Ward's Signature. Such private label items are usually priced to sell lower than national brand items of comparable size, but still generate a higher markup than obtained from national brand merchandise.

probability sample A sampling technique in which each individual in the total population has an equal chance of being selected.

procurement Activities within a firm devoted to the buying function.

producers' cooperative marketing Type of cooperative marketing that primarily involves the sale of products of the membership.

product In a narrow sense, the physical thing marketed. In a broad sense, it consists of the satisfactions that may be derived from its use or consumption, including values added by **middlemen.**

product differentiation The situation in which two products of similar characteristics and end use are manufactured by different producers and acquire divergent images in the minds of consumer segments. This usually comes about through promotional activities.

product image How the consumer perceives the characteristics of a product.

productivity The output of work on a per hour basis. It is found by dividing the work load by the number of hours required to handle the load.

product life cycle The stages through which products move while on the market—introduction, growth, maturity, and decline.

product line Any grouping of related products which is satisfying a particular consumer need, used together, or purchased or used by a similar customer group.

product specialization The separation of organizational activities needed to procure and sell a specific product or product line.

prognosis The second step in a **retail audit,** which is an estimate of where the retailer is likely to go if present policies are used in a marketplace that follows current trends.

program The four step in a **retail audit,** which focuses upon the means of obtaining the firm's objectives.

promotion Any means used to stimulate sales or generate a favorable image in the minds of consumers.

promotional allowances An amount granted to the store by the seller of merchandise to cover all or part of the store's cost of advertising or otherwise promoting the sale of the merchandise to the consumer.

promotional calendar A calendar that contains the firm's promotional plans.

promotional mix The combination of all means used for promoting sales.

prorated expenses Joint expenses that cannot be charged directly to selling departments nor allocated

to them on a basis that measures the service each has received. They are assigned to selling departments pro rata to dollar sales volume.

psychographics A concept that describes the lifestyle characteristics of consumers.

public market A wholesale or retail market supervised or administered by a municipality which rents space or stalls to dealers; also municipal market, community market.

public relations A planned program of policies and conduct designed to build confidence and increase understanding on the part of customers, suppliers, competitors, employees, stockholders, creditors, the local community, and the government.

public warehouse A storage facility that does not take title to the goods it handles. It may issue receipts, which can be used as security for loans.

publicity Public exposure, either favorable or unfavorable, for which a firm has not paid.

purchase order The written document issued by the purchasing department of a firm to a vendor to procure goods to fill a requirement.

purchasing agent The person authorized to acquire materials needed for operation and maintenance of a retail outlet.

purchasing manual A policy manual containing broad policy statements affecting the purchasing aspects of the entire firm. It may also be a procedures manual detailing how each activity is to be handled.

push money (PM) A bonus that salespeople receive on each sale made of specially designated merchandise.

Q

quantity discount A discount allowed when a given quantity is purchased. It is an inducement to buy a larger than average amount and may be deducted regardless of when the bill is paid.

quick assets Those assets that, in the ordinary course of business, will be converted into cash within a reasonably short period of time, usually one year.

quota A goal figure that salespeople are expected to achieve. If they sell more than their quota they may be paid a bonus.

R

rack jobber A limited-function wholesaler who receives payment only for actual goods sold.

radio An audio broadcast advertising medium whose coverage is geographic, with some stations appealing to specific ethnic or age groups. It provides reasonable flexibility to the advertiser but has two limitations: no possibility of later reference by the audience and no graphic portrayals.

raincheck A deferred purchase agreement which allows a consumer to purchase an out-of-stock advertised special at a future date at the current reduced price, regardless of the future retail price.

random sampling A form of probability sampling in which each unit in the universe has an equal chance of being chosen.

rebate A refund given to consumers for purchasing a product under prescribed circumstances and used by manufacturers to stimulate the sale of a particular product, brand, style, or model.

receipt of goods dating (R.O.G.) Dating is computed, not from the date of the bill, but rather from the day the goods are received by the store.

receivables The **accounts receivable** owned by a business.

receiving The process of accepting new merchandise at a store.

receiving apron A form attached to a store's **purchase order** that contains information concerning the status of a vendor's shipment.

reference group Any group of people that is capable of influencing the behavior of an individual.

regional shopping center The largest type of shopping center, with several **department stores** providing the main drawing power for more than 300,000 square feet of selling space.

reinforcement The power of a favorable experience to generate a stronger motivation to repeat the action.

rented goods service The renting of goods as opposed to selling them.

reorder period The frequency planned for reordering a specific item.

repeat business Business generated by a consumer's returning to the same firm to purchase goods or services.

resident buying office An office established by a retailer or group of retailers to serve only that group by supplying them with information and buying assistance.

response The individual's reaction to all of the **cues.**

responsibility The accountability for actions taken by a manager in behalf of a firm while utilizing authority.

retail The price at which goods are offered for sale.

retail audit A self-analysis of a firm, conducted periodically to determine the strengths and weaknesses of the firm in reaching its **target market** at a profit to the firm.

retail classification systems Methods of classifying retail firms from the viewpoint of: (1) merchandise offered, (2) number of outlets owned, (3) relative emphasis on price, and (4) number of surrounding stores.

retail deductions The retail value that is subtracted from total merchandise handled at retail during a given period. It consists of **net sales** plus retail reductions.

retail inventory method A method of determining the cost or market value of an inventory by listing and totaling the goods on hand at current retail prices and translating this retail value into cost.

retail life cycle A description of a retail firm's life from beginning to end. It is the same as the **product life cycle,** applied to a firm.

retail market research The process of systematically searching for, collecting, and analyzing information that can be used in developing retail strategies.

retail organizational mission the reason for a retailers' existence.

retail personnel reporting An input into a management information system which contains information on: cost of salesforce, cost of management, out-of-stock merchandise, merchandise requested by consumers but not carried by the retailer, consumer comments on competitor's marketing activities and on the firm's own marketing efforts.

retail reductions The difference between the aggregate original retail value of merchandise disposed of during a period and **net sales.** It is the sum of **markdowns,** merchandise **shortages,** and **discounts to employees and customers.**

retail store cooperative A store owned and managed by a number of consumers. Patronage refunds are frequently determined by the proportion of business each participant buys of the total sales made by the store.

retailing The business activity that is concerned with selling goods to ultimate consumers.

retailing mix The variables (including product, price, promotion, place, operating policy, buying, and human resource considerations) that a retail store can combine in alternative ways to obtain a strategy for attracting its customers.

retained earnings The portion of a retailer's capital that is derived from earnings and has not been paid out in the form of dividends.

return on investment approach to advertising A method of determining the level of a firm's advertising budget obtained by viewing promotion as a capital investment rather than a current expense.

return on investment (ROI) or return on assets ratio A concept used as a tool for deciding among alternative promotional plans.

return per square foot The amount of dollar contribution that is obtained from a square foot of selling space.

returns and allowances to customers The dollar total of goods returned to the store and of reductions in the price given to customers. It is deducted from **gross sales** to get **net sales.**

returns and allowances to vendor The dollar sum of purchased goods that are returned to the supplier and unplanned reductions in purchase price.

revolving credit A consumer credit plan that is commonly used for purchase of merchandise on a nonsecured basis.

revolving credit plan Permits a customer to charge purchases and pay for the purchases and interest charges in equal monthly payments based on the outstanding balance at the time of billing or highest previous balance.

R.O.G. dating See **receipt of goods dating.**

run-of-paper (ROP) A term indicating that the position of an advertisement will be at the publisher's discretion.

run of schedule time (ROS) Time is allocated for an advertisement wherever in the schedule the radio or television station sees fit.

S

safety needs Consumer needs based on the desire for security, protection, and order.

safety stock A reserve for contingencies, especially for unforeseen increases in rate of sale. It may be expressed in terms of **weeks' supply** or as a specific quantity in units.

sales The dollar amounts received by the store in exchange for merchandise sold to customers during an accounting period.

sales clerk A person in a retail store who records the customers' purchases, is responsible for maintaining stock, and assists the customer in making a selection.

sales forecast An estimate of sales, in dollars or physical units, for a specified future period under a proposed marketing

program and an assumed set of economic forces.

sales slip A slip of paper generated by a cash register showing the dollar and cents amount of purchase.

sales promotion Those marketing activities (besides **advertising, personal selling,** and **publicity**) that stimulate sales. These activities include displays, shows, and demonstrations.

scanning The process wherein the input into a checkout terminal is accomplished by passing a coded ticket over a "reader" or by having a "wand" pass over the ticket. Scanning may be done by a non-human-readable bar code called the **universal product code (UPC),** or by human readable optical recognition characters.

scrambled merchandising A condition in retailing in which a store takes on merchandise to sell that is unrelated to the regular lines carried by the store.

SCSA Standard consolidated statistical area is composed of two standard metropolitan statistical areas (SMSA).

seasonal dating A form of **advance dating** that is allowed on merchandise of a seasonal nature. It is granted by a manufacturer to induce early buying of seasonal goods so as to keep the plant occupied during slack seasons.

seasonal sales forecast The estimated level of retail sales for a specific period of the year.

secondary data Data that are gathered by others, rather than by the retailer himself.

secondary shopping district A well-developed cluster of stores outside the central business district, and generally found in larger cities. The sale of **convenience goods** predominates, but **shopping** and **specialty goods** are of considerable significance.

selective distribution The practice of limiting the outlets for one's product to those that will contribute most to profits and prestige.

self-actualization needs The final goal on Maslow's hierarchy of motives list. It consists of developing one's self to the fullest.

self-service A type of retail operation where the customer is exposed to merchandise that may be examined without sales assistance.

selling area That part of the sales floor devoted exclusively to selling.

selling process A procedure consisting of creating awareness of a need, developing customer comprehension of the firm's offering, providing the basis for customer conviction that the offer is a good offer, and encouraging customers to make a purchase.

service area That part of the sales floor that is devoted to servicing the selling area.

service industry The industry which contains: (1) rented goods service, (2) owned goods service, and (3) nongoods service.

service mark A mark used in the sale or advertising of **services** to identify those of a given firm and to distinguish them from those of others.

services Any work that is not connected with the manufacture, production, or processing of a product or commodity or the wholesaling or retailing of a good.

service sponsored franchise system The service industry franchisees are somewhat different from manufacturer and wholesaler sponsored franchisees in that the primary goal of manufacturers and wholesalers is to sell merchandise, so they generally don't charge a franchise

fee. In the service industry the main product is often the good will of the franchisor, so they normally do charge a franchising fee. Examples of the service industry franchise systems are McDonald's, Burger King, Wendy's, Pizza Hut, Kentucky Fried Chicken, Taco Bell, Pamida's, Holiday Inn, H & R Block, convenience food stores such as 7-Eleven, etc.

shared business That part of a retail outlet's sales that is obtained because of the generative pulling power of nearby retailers.

shoplifting The stealing of a store's merchandise by customers.

shopping goods The type of item that the consumer usually wishes to purchase only after comparing quality, price, and style in a number of sources.

shopping the competition The practice of having store employees make price and product comparisons in competitive outlets.

short-term funds Borrowed funds that must be paid back in one year or less.

shortage The loss caused by **pilferage, shoplifting,** and damaged merchandise.

shrinkage The difference between actual stock on hand and the **book inventory.**

SMSA Standard metropolitan statistical area is an economic and social unit composed of one city unit containing at least 50,000 persons.

social class A group of people who are about equal to one another in prestige and community status. People within a social class regularly interact among members of their group and share the same general goals and philosophy of life.

social needs The consumer's needs for affection and belonging.

soft goods Merchandise made of a textile base.

source marking The **preticketing** of merchandise by a source before shipment. It is very important in expediting the arrival of merchandise on a selling floor because the merchandise is not held up in receiving for price ticketing by store.

span of management The number of persons or functions one manager can manage.

specialty advertising Advertising in which consumers are given an object (calendar, ball-point pen, key ring, ashtray, ruler, and so forth) with the firm name and possibly with other information printed on the item.

specialty goods The type of item that has such an attraction for a consumer that the consumer will go considerably out of the way to purchase it.

specialty stores Stores concentrating on a specific classification of merchandise, for example, jewelry, books, or men's clothing.

standard industrial classification system A classification system in which each industrial market segment is identified with a number for which statistics are collected by the government, thereby providing a great deal of information for the marketer.

standing order An arrangement with a vendor to make shipments periodically in specified quantities for a set period.

staple merchandise Goods that have a fairly active demand that continues over a period of years, and which the retailer finds it necessary to carry in stock continuously.

stock alterations The cost of altering and renovating goods in stock as distinct from goods ordered by customers.

stock book A record, usually maintained by the buyer, of purchases (made from orders) and of sales (obtained from stubs of price tickets).

stock control A broad term for various systems and methods used to control stock.

stock shortage All unexplained or unrecorded shrinkages in the value of merchandise available for sale.

stock-sales ratio The ratio between the retail stock at the first of the month and sales for that month.

stock to sales method A method of planning inventory levels that involves multiplying the estimated sales volume for a period by the planned beginning-of-the-month stock-sales ratio to obtain the desired beginning of the period inventory.

stock turnover The ratio between sales and average inventory. It is calculated in any one of the following ways: (1) Net sales ÷ average inventory at retail (2) Gross cost of goods sold ÷ average inventory at cost (3) Number of units sold ÷ average unit inventory.

stock turn rate The number of stock-turns for a period of one year.

store coupons A print medium sponsored by the store itself and indicating a "cents-off" or "free" deal by the store.

store image The overall personality of a store as viewed by consumers.

store layout The interior retail store arrangement of departments or groupings of merchandise.

store services Any service that is not directly related to the actual sale of specific product within the store, such as **layaway,** gift wrapping, credit, delivery.

storing land The purchase of vacant land located in the development path of a city for possible future use.

straight commission Compensation based solely on applying an agreed upon percentage of the selling price of goods and services sales made by the employee.

straight salary compensation plan A compensation plan in which the retail employee is paid a set salary that does not vary with sales productivity.

strategic fundamentalism The philosophy of providing only those products and services which the customers view as providing utility and which they will be willing to support with their purchases.

strategic growth strategies A specific set of plans which chart a future course of action which results in orderly, controlled growth in a retail firm.

strategic planning process The assessment of a current situation, the forecasting of the future as it affects the current situation and the design of a plan of action to accomplish a set of desired objectives.

strategic positioning The creation of a unique image in the minds of the target market based on assembling a specific collection of goods and services which are currently appealing to this chosen group and which will continue to be attractive to them in the future.

stub The second part of the price ticket, which is removed by the salesperson at time of sale for unit merchandise control.

stub control A **perpetual inventory system** of **unit control** in which sales information is obtained from stubs of price tickets rather than from sales checks.

substitute items Goods or services that consumers perceive as being fairly similar.

supervision The act of overseeing and being responsible for employee performance.

survey Using personal interviews, the telephone, or direct mail to obtain consumer opinion.

suscipient business That part of a retail outlet's sales that is obtained from people whose principal purpose for being near the retail outlet is not because the store or its neighbors attracted them.

systems-level audit A periodic evaluation of all the elements used in the retail effort.

systems selling The idea of selling the **total product concept.**

T

tangible assets Those **assets** that are of a physical and material nature such as cash, land, buildings, and so forth.

target market The particular segment of a total population that a particular retail store focuses all its merchandising expertise on to accomplish the profit objectives of the store.

telephone interview A survey technique in which the interviewer obtains information from respondents over the telephone.

television A broadcast medium that provides visual, aural, and motion communication possibilities.

tenant mix The variety of stores offered within a shopping center. To have an ideal draw a shopping center should offer several department stores and many specialty stores offering diverse kinds of merchandise and services.

terms of sale The terms agreed upon governing payment, invoice dating, and discounts.

territorial franchise A territorial franchise is granted by the parent franchisor on sales by other franchise units in the territory. The territorial franchisor usually establishes and trains sub-franchisees. An example is a branded oil company jobber who owns his own service station and leases it out.

testimonial An opinion given by the endorser of a product for the purpose of persuading others to use the product.

thirty-day open account plan Permits purchasers to charge merchandise and pay the full amount within thirty days of the billing date.

total cost of merchandise sold The **cost of merchandise sold** after adjustment for **net alteration costs** and **cash discounts** earned, when they exist

total merchandise handled The sum of the beginning inventory plus purchases. It must be calculated at cost and, if the **retail inventory method** is used, at retail also.

total product concept The tangible item combined with the whole set of services that accompany it when it is sold to the consumer.

tracer A person in the receiving and marking area and traffic department who traces delayed or lost shipments of incoming merchandise and lost deliveries to customers.

trade discount A discount allowed only to certain classes of buyers, such as jobbers or other middlemen, and in some cases to retailers. Such discounts are deductible, no matter when the invoice is paid. It is synonymous with **functional discount.**

trademark Any word, name, symbol, device, or any combination of these adopted and used by a manufacturer or merchant to identify goods and distinguish them from those manufactured or sold by others. It is, thus, a **brand** name used on goods moving in the channels of trade.

trade show An exhibition where manufacturers meet to show their merchandise.

trading area The surrounding area from which most of the store's trade is drawn.

trading area overlay A transparent plastic sheet on which a store's trading area is plotted. This sheet is then placed over a map to spot the geographical area for that store.

trading up A legitimate business activity in which a salesperson attempts to interest prospects or customers in goods of higher price that the salesperson feels can be shown to provide superior benefits.

traffic The number of persons who enter or pass by a store or a department within a store.

training The acquisition of basic skills and knowledge required in performing one's job.

training and development Providing initial and continuing education for employees so that they may perform their present duties more effectively and provide opportunities for individual growth and advancement in the firm.

transactions per square foot A figure obtained by dividing the number of gross transactions of sales checks for a department by the average number of square feet of selling space the department occupies.

transfer in A purchase from another department or another unit of a chain or branch store system rather than from an outside vendor.

transfer out Value of merchandise conveyed to another department or unit of a **chain** or **branch store** system. It is not a sale in that it is not a source of profit.

transit advertising An advertising medium designed primarily to present the advertiser's message to an audience using public transportation or exposed to vehicles carrying passengers from one point to another.

turnover The total number of times, within a given period, that a stock of goods is sold and replaced.

tying contracts A conditional selling arrangement between retailers and suppliers in which a supplier agrees to sell a retailer a highly sought after line of products if the retailer will agree to return to buy additional product lines from the same supplier.

U

understored The condition that exists when an area has too few stores to meet the needs of the consumer community.

unfair practices acts Laws that establish a floor below which the retail prices of goods may not legally be set. The floor is usually either invoice cost or invoice cost plus a certain modest percentage.

unit billing A single statement of the total price, with the list of articles purchased posted on a detachable strip, which the store retains for adjustment purposes.

unit control The analysis and planning of sales and stocks in terms of pieces of merchandise.

unit pricing (1) The practice of pricing all items on a per unit basis. (2) The practice of pricing each item so that the price tag shows the price per unit of weight or volume in the package.

universal product code (UPC) A national, coordinated system of product identification by which a ten-digit number is assigned to every grocery product sold through retail grocery channels in the United States. The UPC is designed so that at the checkout counter an electronic scanner will read the symbol on the product and automatically transmit the information to a computer, which controls the cash register.

upgrading Increasing price lines by offering better quality and assortments in a specific classification of products.

V

value pricing The practice of pricing goods and services according to the value that consumers perceive to be attached to the item or service.

variable costs Operating expenses affected by changes in sales volume, increasing as sales increase and decreasing as sales decrease.

variety store A retail store offering a wide assortment and variety of articles that are mainly relatively low priced.

vendor The party who sells, or agrees to sell, an item or property to which he has title.

vendor analysis An input into a management information system which contains data on performance by merchandise and services purchased from all suppliers.

vertical integration The acquisition of a company operating at a different level in the channel distribution than the acquiring company (the consumer being considered as the base). It is backward if the acquired company is farther away from the consumer, forward if nearer to the consumer.

visual front An open storefront design that has no vision barrier between the interior and the exterior of the store.

visual merchandising Presenting merchandise to its best selling advantage and for maximum traffic exposure.

voluntary chain A group of stores organized by a wholesaler around a common interest in the goods or services the wholesaler can provide.

W

want-slip system The organized recording by sales clerks of merchandise asked for by customers but not in stock.

warehouse receipt A receipt given by a warehouse firm to the owner of goods that are deposited in the warehouse. These goods may not be withdrawn without surrendering the receipt, so this document can be used as collateral for obtaining loans from financial institutions.

warranty A synonym for **guarantee.**

weeks' supply method A method of planning inventory levels based on using a predetermined number of weeks' supply to achieve a desired stock turnover.

wheel of retailing An explanation of the evolution of retail institutions that is based on the premise that new types of retail firms first appear as low-margin, low-price establishments. They upgrade their facilities and services as time passes and thus require higher margins. Eventually they become high-cost, high-price retailers and are vulnerable to the next low-margin innovator.

white space Space not occupied by print or art in an advertisement.

wholesaler A business concerned with selling to those who buy for resale or industrial use.

wholesale sponsored franchise systems A franchise system whereby the franchisor is a wholesaler. Examples of wholesaler sponsored systems are in the grocery, drug, hardware, and automobile supply industries where large wholesaler sponsored franchises are quite common, and the dealers are normally assembled as voluntary chains working with the wholesaler. Examples are Western Auto, ACE Hardware, NAPA.

width of merchandise offering The assortment factors necessary to meet the demands of the market and to meet competition.

will call Another name applied to **layaway.**

window displays A display in a store window that reflects what the store carries.

work the line To systematically review past sales records and current stock positions, and to project sales estimates for the next sales period in order to determine the amount **open-to-buy** for each merchandise line stated in units and purchase dollars. Then, in consultation with the sales representative, the buyer reviews the current merchandise offerings. Past poor performers and discontinued items are deleted; new, interest generating goods are added and the staple line is reordered. The end product is an order stating the specific quantities being ordered by lot number and size, the price, all **terms** and conditions **of sale,** and specific shipping instructions.

working capital The excess of current assets over current liabilities. It represents the capital immediately available for the continued operation of the business.

X, Y, Z

Yellow Pages The classified listing and advertising of business firms contained in a telephone book, a print advertising medium.

youth market Everyone under twenty-five years of age.

zone pricing The delivered cost based on factory price plus averaged freight rate for a section or territory to which goods are shipped. This yields the same delivered cost to all retailers located in the zone.

Index